Collected Poems

Collected Poems

Conrad Aiken

CONRAD AIKEN

Collected Poems

SECOND EDITION

New York
OXFORD UNIVERSITY PRESS
1970

1750

pl

Preface to the First Edition

*

WITH ONLY one important exception, the poems in this collection
are printed in chronological order, the order in which they were
written. The exception is 'Changing Mind,' which, although writ-
ten in 1925, is here printed in *The Divine Pilgrim,* with the
group of earlier 'symphonies'—from 'The Charnel Rose' to 'The
Pilgrimage of Festus'—for which it serves as a *coda.* As in *Se-
lected Poems,* 1929, nothing is here reprinted from my first book,
Earth Triumphant, as nothing was there considered to be even
remotely salvageable. From my second book, *Turns and Movies,*
the title poem, omitted from *Selected Poems,* is here retained,
for in a later view it seems to me, although immature and un-
even, to have at least a crude vitality. From the third book, too,
Nocturne of Remembered Spring, it was difficult to find any-
thing worth keeping: the one specimen here exhibited will serve
as a sufficient example of the lengths to which an obsession with
the 'musical' analogies of poetry could be carried. Thereafter,
with a few minor exceptions, the successive volumes are given in
their entirety, and in the order in which the poems were written,
which was not invariably the order in which they were published.
'John Deth,' for example, although published in 1930, was actu-
ally written in 1922, three years before the 'Borborigmi'' poems
which came out in the 1925 edition of *Priapus and the Pool.*
Similarly, 'Blues for Ruby Matrix' and 'The Poet in Granada'—
poems which were roughly contemporary with the *Preludes* and
Landscape West of Eden, but had to wait for a later occasion—
are here put back in their proper context.

C. A.

Brewster, Massachusetts
June 1953

Contents

✳

THE MORNING SONG OF LORD ZERO

THE TINSEL CIRCUIT

Collected Poems

Collected Poems

TURNS AND MOVIES

*

I. ROSE AND MURRAY

After the movie, when the lights come up,
He takes her powdered hand behind the wings;
She, all in yellow, like a buttercup,
Lifts her white face, yearns up to him, and clings;
And with a silent, gliding step they move
Over the footlights, in familiar glare,
Panther-like in the Tango whirl of love,
He fawning close on her with idiot stare.
Swiftly they cross the stage. O lyric ease!
The drunken music follows the sure feet,
The swaying elbows, intergliding knees,
Moving with slow precision on the beat.
She was a waitress in a restaurant,
He picked her up and taught her how to dance.
Love-phrases that he whispered her still haunt.
She feels his arms, lifts an appealing glance,
But knows he spent last evening with Zudora;
And knows that certain changes are before her.

The brilliant spotlight circles them around,
Flashing the spangles on her weighted dress.
He mimics wooing her, without a sound,
Flatters her with a smoothly smiled caress.
He fears that she will some day queer his act;
Feeling her anger. He will quit her soon.
He nods for faster music. He will contract
Another partner, under another moon.
Meanwhile, 'smooth stuff.' He lets his dry eyes flit

Over the yellow faces there below;
Maybe he'll cut down on his drinks a bit,
Not to annoy her, and to spoil the show. . .
Zudora, waiting for her turn to come,
Watches them from the wings, and fatly leers
At the girl's younger face, so white and dumb,
And the fixed, anguished eyes, ready for tears.

She lies beside him, with a false wedding-ring,
In a cheap room, with moonlight on the floor;
The moonlit curtains remind her much of spring,
Of a spring evening on the Coney shore.
And while he sleeps, knowing she ought to hate,
She still clings to the lover that she knew, —
The one that, with a pencil, on a plate,
Drew a heart and wrote, 'I'd die for you.'

II. THE APOLLO TRIO

From acting profile parts in the 'legit,'
He came to this; and he is sick of it.
The singing part is easy. What he hates
Is traveling with these damned degenerates,
Tight-trousered, scented, both with women's hips,
With penciled eyes, and lean vermilioned lips.
Loving each other so, they pick on him, —
Horse him, off stage and on. He smiles, is grim,
Plays up the part, saving his final card
Till Jones should dare to slap his face too hard.
But what's 'too hard'? — Meanwhile, four times a day
He drinks, to make things pleasanter; while they
(Those damned degenerates) eat up cocaine.
The call-boy calls him on. And once again
With a crushed hat, long hair, and powdered face,
Dressed as the villain, in black, he booms deep bass,
Asks the fool question, takes the slap, and sings
As if he did for the first time all those things.

My God, how tired he is of hearing Jones,
Simpering sweetly in falsetto tones,
'Chase me, boys, I issue trading-stamps':
Tired of grease-paint, dirty clothes, and lamps.
At ease on sawdust floors, he leans and drinks,
Swapping old stories with the crowd; or thinks,
Roving a blear green eye about the bar,
Of the girl he loved, or the one time he was star.

III. TWO MCNEILS

He skips out lithe and tense into the light,
Throws off his gown, and smiling, lifts his hands
With a theatric gesture, opening fingers,
Like a vain child. And having rippled slowly
Under the smooth white tights the gleaming muscles,
Smiling again, he turns; and lifts black weights, —
Staggering, flushing deep his face and neck, —
To drop them with a crash. She, sweet and blonde,
Stands by (in white tights too), smiles at the people,
Catching the handkerchief he tosses to her
When he has wiped his hands; and at the end,
Feigning timidity, sits in a chair
Which he heaves up to balance in his teeth.
But as she sits there, waving frantic hands,
And sees his coarse red fist gesticulating,
She looks down on him with a look of hatred,
And wishes he would only burst a vein.

'Where did you get that ring?' he said to her,
While they were waiting turn. She looked at it,
Twisting her head to this side and to that
To see it sparkle. 'What is that to you?'
'That drummer gave it to you. I've seen him watch you.'
'What if he does?' 'You cut it out, that's all!
Don't you forget that time that I half-killed Schmidt.'
She smiled at him. 'Why drag that up again?'

Then, they went on, — he quivering, she cool. . .
And as she caught his handkerchief, she turned
Disgusted from him, thinking of her lover;
And how he said in his delicious voice,
'I'll meet you Thursday night at half-past ten.'

IV. DUVAL'S BIRDS

The parrot, screeching, flew out into the darkness,
Circled three times above the upturned faces
With a great whir of brilliant outspread wings,
And then returned to stagger on her finger.
She bowed and smiled, eliciting applause. . .
The property man hated her dirty birds.
But it had taken years — yes, years — to train them,
To shoulder flags, strike bells by tweaking strings,
Or climb sedately little flights of stairs.
When they were stubborn, she tapped them with a wand,
And her eyes glittered a little under the eyebrows.
The red one flapped and flapped on a swinging wire;
The little white ones winked round yellow eyes.

V. GABRIEL DE FORD

He slips in through the stage-door, always singing;
Still singing, he slips out, without a word
To stage-door man, or any of the others.
All through his act, wagging upon each hand
A grotesque manikin, he laughs and sings,
Sings with a far-off ventriloquial voice
Through fixed and smiling lips. Sometimes, not often,
He barely moves his mouth, for a ghostly word.
You see his throat fill, or his nostrils quiver.
But then, staring ahead with stretched white eyes,
And never stirring, he throws his voice way off,
Faintly under the stage, or in the wings,
Creeping nearer, or fading to a whisper.
And since he always sings and never talks,

And flits by nervously, swinging his cane,
Rumors are thick about him through the circuit.
Some say he hates the women, and loves men:
That once, out West, he tried to kiss a man,
Was badly hurt, then almost killed himself.
Others maintain a woman jilted him.
But the one story they tell everywhere
Is how, at his father's funeral, he threw his voice
Suddenly into the coffin; and all the mourners
Jumped from their seats and ran, and women fainted,
And the preacher stopped the service, white as wax.

Zudora said a friend of hers had seen him
Mooning alone at 'Carmen.' And at the end
He cried like a baby: what do you think of that.

VI. VIOLET MOORE AND BERT MOORE

He thinks her little feet should pass
Where dandelions star thickly grass;
Her hands should lift in sunlit air,
Sea-wind should tangle up her hair.
Green leaves, he says, have never heard
A sweeter ragtime mockingbird,
Nor has the moon-man ever seen,
Or man in the spotlight, leering green,
Such a beguiling, smiling queen.

Her eyes, he says, are stars at dusk,
Her mouth as sweet as red-rose-musk;
And when she dances his young heart swells
With flutes and viols and silver bells;
His brain is dizzy, his senses swim,
When she slants her ragtime eyes at him. . .

Moonlight shadows, he bids her see,
Move no more silently than she.

It was this way, he says, she came,
Into his cold heart, bearing flame.
And now that his heart is all on fire
Will she refuse his heart's desire? —
And O! has the Moon Man ever seen
(Or the spotlight devil, leering green)
A sweeter shadow upon a screen?

VII. ZUDORA

Here on the pale beach, in the darkness;
With the full moon just to rise;
They sit alone, and look over the sea,
Or into each other's eyes. . .

She pokes her parasol into the sleepy sand,
Or sifts the lazy whiteness through her hand.

'A lovely night,' he says. 'The moon,
Comes up for you and me.
Just like a blind old spotlight there,
Fizzing across the sea!'

She pays no heed, nor even turns her head:
He slides his arm around her waist instead.

'Why don't we do a sketch together? —
Those songs you sing are swell.
Where did you get them, anyway?
They suit you awfully well.'

She will not turn to him — will not resist.
Impassive, she submits to being kissed.

'My husband wrote all four of them.
You know, — my husband drowned.
He was always sickly, soon depressed. . .
But still she hears the sound

Of a stateroom door shut hard, and footsteps going
Swiftly and steadily; and the dark sea flowing.

She hears the cold sea flowing, and sees his eyes
Hollow with disenchantment, sick surprise, —

And hate of her whom he had loved too well. . .
She lowers her eyes, demurely prods a shell.

'Yes. We might do an act together.
That would be very nice.'
He kisses her passionately, and thinks
She's carnal, but cold as ice.

VIII. AMOROSA AND COMPANY

Well, there was still a sure hand, anyway,
When she stood up alone, in a casket of light,
In the jet velvet blackness; and round her neck,
And along her outstretched naked gleaming arms,
Felt the cool python slowly coil and coil. .
But that was for the snake, more than for her.
And when that Russian upstart ran out dancing,
Flinging her little knees up, so affected,
And throwing her arms about so foolishly,
The audience went half-crazy with applause!
Pretty? Well, if you call it pretty, to have
That listless scanty flaxen hair, and eyes
So sentimentally blue. When she was hired,
She was half-starved, poor thing, and cried and cried, —
And, really, it was half in pity she took her.
And now to have her getting all the notice,
With those ridiculous dances! Hopping about,
Frisking her hands up, perking her rat's head sideways,
Smiling, or looking sad, running and jumping,
Or toddling on her toes — it was disgusting.
And as if that weren't enough, to have her men

All whining round this girl like a lot of tom-cats,
Even her husband! — (not that *she* wanted him).
And then, to have that cornet player get up
And give her a box of roses, on top of all! . . .
She wondered if her strength would fail her, sometimes;
And if, instead of smiling, when the girl
Was given an encore (taking her hand to share it),
She'd suddenly burst out laughing and slap her face:
The wretched thin little measly skin-and-bones!

— She paused, fatigued with combing out her hair,
Sick of trying to get those scraps of tinsel,
And stared at red mirrored eyes. She was getting old.

IX. BAIN'S CATS AND RATS

Quiet, and almost bashful, and seldom looking
Into the rows of eyes below and above,
He went about his work as if alone;
His cats, upon their table, sat and yawned:
Or, paws curled under, blinked their sleepy eyes.
And one by one, with deft pale hand, he lifted
Rats from a lidded box, and set each one
On a little pedestal. And then a cat,
Black, with green insolent eyes, gravely and sleekly
Stepped over them, and sniffed, and waved his tail,
And glared at the spotlight with his ears laid back,
And leapt back to the table. . . The audience laughed. . .
Later, when one cat balked, he gave up weakly,
And let the curtain fall, with scant applause.

Ten years before this he had lost his wife.
He was a trapeze artist: in his act,
While hanging from the trapeze by his legs,
Lifted the girl up in a jeweled girdle
Clenched in his teeth, and twirled her with his hands,
In darkness, with the spotlight blazing on them.

It was a love-match. — Many had envied them.
But he was always queer, a moody man,
And things got quickly on his nerves. The girl,
Perhaps, had been too young . . . But anyway,
One night before his act they heard him scolding —
'For Christ's sake, put less powder on your arms!
Look at my clothes — look here!' — And that same night
He let her fall — or anyway, she fell,
And died without a word. Soon after that
He quit the trapeze work, and got these rats. . .

Sometimes there on the stage, he heard himself
Saying, until the words grew meaningless,
Multiplying themselves in tireless rhythms,
'I'm sick of her. But how get rid of her?
Why don't I let her fall? — She's killing me!'
And then he'd glance, half-scared, into the wings.

X. THE CORNET

When she came out, that white little Russian dancer,
With her bright hair, and her eyes so young, so young,
He suddenly lost his leader, and all the players,
And only heard an immortal music sung, —

Of dryads flashing in the green woods of April,
On cobwebs trembling over the deep wet grass:
Fleeing their shadows with laughter, with hands uplifted,
Through the whirled sinister sun he saw them pass, —

Lovely immortals gone, yet existing somewhere,
Still somewhere laughing in woods of immortal green,
Youth he had lived among fires, or dreamed of living,
Lovers in youth once seen, or dreamed he had seen. . .

And watching her knees flash up, and her young hands beckon,
And the hair that streamed behind, and the taunting eyes.

He felt this place dissolving in living darkness,
And through the darkness he felt his childhood rise,

Soft, and shining, and sweet, hands filled with petals. . .
And watching her dance, he was grateful to forget
These fiddlers, leaning and drawing their bows together,
And the tired fingers on the stops of his cornet.

XI.

Sitting in a café, and watching her reflection
Smoke a cigarette, or drinking coffee,
She laughed hard-heartedly at his dejection. . .
He laid his cigarette down in his saucer,
And stolid with despair
Put his elbows on the table, ran his fingers through his hair.

Watching how her lips primmed, dusty in the mirror,
To meet the gilded tip between her fingers,
As the cigarette approached them in her hand:
She told him he was seriously in error. . .
And noticing how her lips moved, in reflection,
She thought it queer, she said,
That in spite of all her warnings he should go and lose his head.

Just as she was smiling, the noisy music started;
She tapped upon the tablecloth in rhythm. . .
Were those blue eyes of hers so icy-hearted?
How was it, otherwise, she could not like him?
Women were different, then,
From these strangely childlike passionate selfish men. . .

She rose and took his arm; they slowly walked together
Out through the maze of tables, people drinking,
Into the windy void of rainy weather. . .
And in the taxi, sitting dark beside him,

She moved, and touched his knee,
And when he kissed her, hated him, but kissed him, passionately.

XII. AERIAL DODDS

Ingratitude — the damned ingratitude!
After these years, and all he'd done for him,
To run away like this without a word!
Without so much as thanks, — and still a boy, —
Though he had taken him as a child and trained him!
This moment, he could kill him with his hands,
Wring his young neck. . . And worst of all, to think,
After he'd poured out love on him so long,
That he should run off with that rotten girl,
That whore, who couldn't dance, and couldn't sing,
Who only kept her job because, being shameless,
She splashed about in the spotlight like a mermaid!
My God; he'd kill him if he ever found him.
Had he been cruel to him? No, not cruel.
Sure, he had whipped him sometimes, — once in a while, —
Partly for discipline, of course. . . But never
More than to make him shrink, or his lips tremble,
His cheeks a little white. Not more than that.
And then, he had loved him so! And given him things,
All the money he needed, and all the clothes. . .
— And the boy had been a foundling to begin with!

He got up from his chair, groped in the darkness,
And struck a match under the mantelpiece, —
Watching it spurt from blue to yellow flame,
Startling the room with agitated shadows.
And one by one he lifted from the trunk
The clothes the boy had worn: the soft-soled shoes;
The white ones with the sockets in the heels,
For whirling in the swing; the satin tights,
And the broad golden girdle, crystal starred.

He had looked lovely in this sleek white satin —
And he remembered now the day they bought it;
And how he stood up, smiling, by the mirror,
With big blue fearless eyes, and curly hair,
Just as he looked, sitting in his trapeze,
Wiping his hands so calm, and gazing down.
His throat was just like ivory, in this lace. . .
And he had looked so slim, so like a child,
So white and fragile!
                                    And now, my God, he'd gone.
And he would never touch again that skin,
So young and soft; or have against his mouth
Those curls . . . or feel the long-tongued venomous whip
Curl round those knees, and see the young mouth tremble.

                                    XIII.

How is it that I am now so softly awakened,
My leaves shaken down with music? —
Darling, I love you.

It is not your mouth, for I have known mouths before, —
Though your mouth is more alive than roses,
Roses singing softly
To green leaves after rain.

It is not your eyes, for I have dived often in eyes, —
Though your eyes, even in the yellow glare of footlights,
Are windows into eternal dusk.

Nor is it the live white flashing of your feet,
Nor your gay hands, catching at motes in the spotlight;
Nor the abrupt thick music of your laughter,
When, against the hideous backdrop,
With all its crudities brilliantly lighted,
Suddenly you catch sight of your alarming shadow,
Whirling and contracting.

How is it, then, that I am now so keenly aware,
So sensitive to the surges of the wind, or the light,
Heaving silently under blue seas of air? —
Darling, I love you, I am immersed in you.

It is not the unraveled night-time of your hair, —
Though I grow drunk when you press it upon my face:
And though when you gloss its length with a golden brush
I am strings that tremble under a bow.

It was that night I saw you dancing,
The whirl and impalpable float of your garment,
Your throat lifted, your face aglow
(Like waterlilies in moonlight were your knees).

It was that night I heard you singing
In the green-room after your dance was over,
Faint and uneven through the thickness of walls.

(How shall I come to you through the dullness of walls,
Thrusting aside the hands of bitter opinion?)

It was that afternoon, early in June,
When, tired with a sleepless night, and my act performed,
Feeling as stale as streets,
We met under dropping boughs, and you smiled to me:
And we sat by a watery surface of clouds and sky.

I hear only the susurration of intimate leaves;
The stealthy gliding of branches upon slow air.

I see only the point of your chin in sunlight;
And the sinister blue of sunlight on your hair.

The sunlight settles downward upon us in silence.

Now we thrust up through grass-blades and encounter,
Pushing white hands amid the green.
Your face flowers whitely among cold leaves.

Soil clings to you, bark falls from you,
You rouse and stretch upward, exhaling earth, inhaling sky,
I touch you, and we drift off together like moons.
Earth dips from under.

We are alone in an immensity of sunlight,
Specks in an infinite golden radiance,
Whirled and tossed upon cataracts and silent torrents.
Give me your hands, darling! We float downward.

XIV. BOARDMAN AND COFFIN

I told him straight, if he touched me, just once more, —
That way, you know, — I'd kill him. And I did.
Why shouldn't I? I told him straight I would.
And here I am! — And I hope to God I die.
You wouldn't think this hand could hit so hard, —
Look, there's still powder on it, and rouge on the nails!
Maybe it's blood. — I told him, if he touched me! —
And he'd come grinning up, and think, because
The house was watching everything we did,
That he could touch me, while he danced with me, —
That way, you know, — and get away with it. . .
Well, you can't say I didn't give him warning.
My God, I hated him! The things he did!
You wouldn't believe them if I told them to you,
They were so nasty. They almost killed me, — killed me, —
Night after night! — Well, anyway, he's dead,
Dead as a stick, or a stone, or an old cigar-butt.
You wouldn't think I would do a thing like that, —
I don't look strong, do I? — But when you're dancing,
You've got to keep in shape. And then, my God! —
When he came leering downward with those eyes,
Those red-brown eyes, like fire, like a vampire's eyes,
I thought I'd scream, go mad, or fling myself
Over the footlights, into the orchestra, —
Anywhere, anywhere, — only to get away!

They were like wheels of fire, those eyes of his, —
Whirling and whirling, and always getting bigger;
Like terrible doors, with fires roaring inside them,
Roaring and roaring, and always coming nearer, —
And sort of sucking at me, and pulling my dress,
And pressing hot cruel fingers against my breasts,
And blowing my hair up, and pushing against my knees, —
And all the while laughing and laughing at me!
O, it was terrible, terrible, — like a nightmare,
Slowly leaning downward upon you and crushing,
And your heart stops beating, and you can't move a finger,
But lie there sweating! —

I had to kill him, — that's all, — I had to kill him.
I told him straight, if he touched me just once more, —
That way, you know, — I'd kill him. And I did.
Those fire-wheel eyes! Do you know what I thought I was doing?
Well, when they came down, bigger and bigger, and whirling,
Whirling so fast, with fire all round the rims,
And the spokes all going so quick you couldn't see them,
Only a sort of blur, — I thought I'd stop them,
By suddenly sticking a knife in through the spokes!
And I did. And all of a sudden the music stopped —
Just like grand opera! And he was kneeling there,
Putting his hands down, sort of groping, and nodding,
As if he were looking for something. Ha! A joke.
And seeing that he was done for, I stabbed myself:
A Jap I knew once showed me how to do it.
And I heard great bells go roaring down the darkness;
And a wind rushed after them. And that was all.

XV. DANCING ADAIRS

Behold me, in my chiffon, gauze, and tinsel,
Flitting out of the shadow into the spotlight,
And into the shadow again, without a whisper! —
Firefly's my name. I am evanescent.

Firefly's your name. You are evanescent.
But I follow you as remorselessly as darkness,
And shut you in and enclose you, at last, and always,
Till you are lost, — as a voice is lost in silence.

Till I am lost, as a voice is lost in silence. . .
Are you the one who would close so cool about me?
My fire sheds into and through you and beyond you:
How can your fingers hold me? I am elusive.

How can my fingers hold you? You are elusive?
Yes, you are flame; but I surround and love you,
Always extend beyond you, cool, eternal,
To take you into my heart's great void of silence.

You shut me into your heart's great void of silence. . .
O sweet and soothing end for a life of whirling!
Now I am still, whose life was mazed with motion.
Now I sink into you, for love of sleep.

Discordants

I

Music I heard with you was more than music,
And bread I broke with you was more than bread;
Now that I am without you, all is desolate;
All that was once so beautiful is dead.

Your hands once touched this table and this silver,
And I have seen your fingers hold this glass.
These things do not remember you, belovèd, —
And yet your touch upon them will not pass.

For it was in my heart you moved among them,
And blessed them with your hands and with your eyes;

And in my heart they will remember always, —
They knew you once, O beautiful and wise.

II

My heart has become as hard as a city street,
The horses trample upon it, it sings like iron,
All day long and all night long they beat,
They ring like the hooves of time.

My heart has become as drab as a city park,
The grass is worn with the feet of shameless lovers,
A match is struck, there is kissing in the dark,
The moon comes, pale with sleep.

My heart is torn with the sound of raucous voices,
They shout from the slums, from the streets, from the crowded
        places,
And tunes from a hurdy-gurdy that coldly rejoices
Shoot arrows into my heart.

III

Dead Cleopatra lies in a crystal casket,
Wrapped and spiced by the cunningest of hands.
Around her neck they have put a golden necklace,
Her tatbebs, it is said, are worn with sands.

Dead Cleopatra was once revered in Egypt,
Warm-eyed she was, this princess of the South.
Now she is very old and dry and faded,
With black bitumen they have sealed up her mouth.

O sweet clean earth, from whom the green blade cometh!
When we are dead, my best belovèd and I,
Close well above us, that we may rest forever,
Sending up grass and blossoms to the sky.

IV

In the noisy street,
Where the sifted sunlight yellows the pallid faces,
Sudden I close my eyes, and on my eyelids
Feel from the far-off sea a cool faint spray, —

A breath on my cheek,
From the tumbling breakers and foam, the hard sand shattered,
Gulls in the high wind whistling, flashing waters,
Smoke from the flashing waters blown on rocks;

— And I know once more,
O dearly belovèd! — that all these seas are between us,
Tumult and madness, desolate save for the sea-gulls,
You on the farther shore, and I in this street.

All Lovely Things

All lovely things will have an ending,
All lovely things will fade and die,
And youth, that's now so bravely spending,
Will beg a penny by and by.

Fine ladies all are soon forgotten,
And goldenrod is dust when dead,
The sweetest flesh and flowers are rotten
And cobwebs tent the brightest head.

Come back, true love! Sweet youth, return! —
But time goes on, and will, unheeding,
Though hands will reach, and eyes will yearn,
And the wild days set true hearts bleeding.

Come back, true love! Sweet youth, remain! —
But goldenrod and daisies wither,

And over them blows autumn rain,
They pass, they pass, and know not whither.

Episode in Grey

I

So, to begin with, dust blows down the street,
In lazy clouds and swirls, and after that
Tatters of paper and straws, and waves of heat,
And leaves plague-bitten; under a tree a cat
Sprawls in the sapless grass, and shuts his eye.
And sitting behind closed shutters you hear a beat
Of melancholy steps go slowly by,
See crooked rays of shadows reeling,
Fantastic fever shapes, across your ceiling;
And in the enormous silence that ensues
You think how dusty and limp the green leaves hang,
Or hear a bell shake out its hourly news
In clang on languid clang.
And time and sky, those items of our lives,
Seem but as windlestraws
In the gigantic vortex of our hearts:
We move, we change, we hesitate, we pause,
In tune with vast self-generating laws;
The hour predestined comes; predestined it departs.

II

And after days of dust have swirled and gone,
And sparrows arch their wings in the meagre shade,
When the late tulips have wilted on their stems,
And even by the pool's rim the grasses fade,
Then, after all, but now perhaps too late,
The long-expected clouds mount up again . . .
Yes, we have had too long to wait:

There is no assuagement in the sound of rain.
We hear its pleasure among the leaves,
We hear its liquid parting from the eaves,
We look, and in each other's eyes
See lost illusions and answerless questions rise.
You light the lamp, and with your nerveless hands
Thrust your gleaming needle and draw your strands
Of lilac through pale silk . . . You lower your head,
And you are silent, and for all I know
You wish this time had never come, that somehow it might go,
Or even — as I wish too — that we were dead.
We are agreed. And though we say no word,
We read each other's veins, profoundly know
The tedium of a tune too often heard,
Too much rehearsed . . . We heard it come and go,
We played our parts with such pathetic care,
I the accompaniment and you the air,
Reversed our roles, with chord and discord chiming,
Suspension slowly to resolution climbing, —
Yet somehow, through no fault of you or me,
Drew out the affair too long, only to learn
Our sweet musicianship could only earn
A tardy kindness, sad futility.
Did you delay too long your acquiescence,
Surrendering only when desire was dead?
Did I persuade too long, command too seldom?
No answer shall be said,
There is no need for answer, for we know
When we first drew together, with slow steps,
Assaying and presaging with sure eyes,
It was predestined so.

III

And now, you say, we cannot move apart . . .
The minutes, the hours, the days we wove together
In a mesh of pain have bound us, heart to heart:

We strain in a tender hatred, wondering whether
The hurt we do will hurt the other more,
Or more ourselves . . . We move in a close-linked pain,
And stretch, and feel soft anguish at the core,
And praise each other the while our eyes complain.
We should have seen the coming of this day.
We should have known that two such lives as ours,
Such lives of ruined cities, crumbled houses,
Perspectives of black ruins fouled with flowers,
Could not be brought together without probings . . .
We should have known the day must come at last
When we should see the alluring present crumble
Among the horrible slag-heaps of the past.
Too old we were at heart, and too accomplished
In pause and counter-pause, and feigned confusion;
Too skilfully we played, too well responded,
Too calmly saw and weighed the veiled allusion:
And yet, for all our wisdom, could not see
Where all was certainty no love could be.
We have deceived ourselves, but not each other:
Pretending love for what we could not love,
Now in a love of ghosts we are bound together
And struggle and cry and rage, and cannot move.

IV

Shall we be honest then, and tear apart? . . .
Your hands lie limp, you hear rebukes and pleadings,
And a soft fiery tearing in your heart
Presages sleepless nights, imagined bleedings . . .
No, we have grown together: every motion,
In laugh, and look, and question and reply,
Since first we met and joined in this deception,
More subtly fused our brains, till 'you' and 'I'
Are mere abstractions, interchangeable,
And death to one is death to both.
We hate each other tenderly and well,

We think of partings and are nothing loth,
Our kissings are a fanged and poisonous thing;
And we should strike more bitterly, did we know
The pain would not return; and so we cling
In desperate heartlessness, and cannot go . . .
Two perfect lovers snared in a single snare! —
Snared in a love of making love too well.
Our music sweeps us on, we know not where,
We are sliced with violin, and stabbed with bell,
And cannot end what we ourselves have started;
Mad with desire we seize and crush and tear,
Only to find it is ourselves we torture,
Playing a dissonance which we cannot bear.
You are not she I passionately made love to,
Nor am I he you cunningly adored.
The overtones we thought we heard were echoes,
The lily we thrust our hands to is a sword.

v

After long days of dust we lie and listen
To the silverly woven harmonies of rain,
Your eyes look past me, dark with pain,
You think how the thin leaves thrill and drip and glisten,
And touch my hair with your hand . . . We should be wise, —
The tremor of your body seems to say, —
If like these leaves we forgot the dusty day;
And closed our eyes,
And took what passion gives, without complaining
That love is not our lot.
Steadily falls the rain, all night it will be raining,
And we shall sleep, and know it not.
This hand that touches me is not the hand
Of the silver queen I dreamed of, nor these lips
The red lips of the cool white-hearted nereid . . .
Passion comes over us with its dark eclipse.

VI

And so, to end with — who shall say the end?
Who first will break this compact — you or I?
This much we know — it must be done abruptly,
No soft preludic speech, no sudden cry,
No murderously indifferent glance of eye . . .
But some day one of us, grown half possessed
With pain unbearable, will walk away
Into the emptiness of time he came from,
Saying no word, since there's no word to say.

THE DIVINE PILGRIM

I

The Charnel Rose

A SYMPHONY

*

PART I

1

She rose in moonlight, and stood, confronting sea,
With her bare arms uplifted,
And lifted her voice in the silence foolishly:
And her face was small, and her voice was small.
'O moon!' she cried, 'I think how you must tire
Forever circling earth, so silently;
Earth, who is dark and makes you no reply.'
But the moon said nothing, no word at all,
She only heard the little waves rush and fall;
And saw the moon go quietly down the sky.

Like a white figurehead in the seafaring wind,
She stood in the moonlight,
And heard her voice cry, ghostly and thinned,
Over the seethe of foam,
Saying 'O numberless waters, I think it strange
How you can always shadow her face, and change
And yet never weary of her, having no ease.'
But the sea said nothing, no word at all:
Unquietly, as in sleep, she saw it rise and fall;
And the moon spread a net of silver over the foam.

She lifted her hands and let them fall again,
Impatient of the silence. And in despair,
Hopeless of final answer against her pain,
She said, to the stealthy air,
'O air, far traveller, who from the stars are blown,
Float pollen of suns, you are an unseen sea
Lifting and bearing the worlds, eternally.
O air, do you not weary of your task?'
— She stood in the silence, frightened and alone,
And heard her syllables ask and ask.

And then, as she walked in moonlight, so alone,
Lost and small in a soulless sea,
Hearing no voice make answer to her own,
From that infinity, —
Suddenly she was aware of a low whisper,
A dreadful heartless sound; and she stood still, —
There in the beach grass, on a sandy hill, —
And heard the stars, making a ghostly whisper;
And the soulless whisper of sun and moon and tree;
And the sea, rising and falling with a blind moan.

And as she faded into the night,
A glimmer of white,
With her arms uplifted and her face bowed down;
Sinking, again, into the sleep of the sands,
The sea-sands white and brown;
Or among the sea-grass rustling as one more blade,
Pushing before her face her cinquefoil hands;
Or sliding, stealthy as foam, into the sea,
With a slow seethe and whisper:

Too late to find her, yet not too late to see,
Came he, who sought forever unsatisfied,
And saw her enter and shut the darkness,
Desired and swift,
And caught at the rays of the moon, yet found but darkness,

Caught at the flash of her feet, to fill his hands
With the sleepy pour of sands.

'O moon!' he said: 'was it you I followed?
You, who put silver madness into my eyes? — '
But he only heard, in the dark, a stifled laughter,
And the rattle of dead leaves blowing.
'O wind! — ' he said — 'was it you I followed?
Your hand I felt against my face? — '
But he only heard, in the dark, a stifled laughter,
And shadows crept past him, with furtive pace,
Breathing night upon him; and one by one
The ghosts of leaves flew past him, seeking the sun.

And a silent star slipped golden down the darkness,
Down the great wall, leaving no trace in sky,
And years went with it, and worlds. And he dreamed still
Of a fleeter shadow among the shadows running,
Foam into foam, without a gesture or cry,
Leaving him there, alone, on a lonely hill.

2

Evening: in the twilight town
One by one the stars stepped down,
Each to assume his destined place:
And there he saw the destined face.

Her eyes were void, her eyes were deep:
She came like one who moved in sleep:
And when she looked across the night
Beneath, among, those points of light,
Into his heart she shot a pang,
As if a voice within him sang,
Sang and was silent. Down the street,
And lost in darkness, fled the feet;
Ambiguous, the street-lamp's gleam
Mocked at her eyes: and then the dream

From shuttered window, shadowed hall,
Chuckled beyond a lampless wall.

Among the crowding lights he went,
Where faces massed like lilies blent,
And this time plucked and made his own
Above snarled music's undertone:
Breathing the perfume of her hair,
He touched her arm: but suddenly there
As in a dance of shadows fleeing
(His eyes were shut for fear of seeing)
He watched red roses drop apart
Each to disclose a charnel heart.

Ghostly with powder in the night,
Her hand upon his arm was white:
Her gown was white, and lightly blew,
A gauze of flame it burned him through.
Under the singing lamp she stood,
And smiled in subtly fugitive mood,
From depth to depth of wingless skies
Withdrawing batlike down her eyes:
And in his heart an echo came
Of quick dust quaking under flame.

Pale walls enclosed them. One light shed
A yellow flicker across the bed.
Loud steps rang through the street, and then
The hush of night grew deep again.
Two shadows on the wall made one —
What human walls were here flung down,
The light extinguished as in pain,
The weak light dying in the brain?
Green leaves pushed up through yielding air
Greedy for life: she loosed her hair
With conscious and indifferent hands.
. . . High on his cliff, above hard sands,

He saw the moonlit ocean come
In ever-inward rings of foam,
Heard them break to shoot and seethe
Ever inward far beneath:
The ringed horizon rhythmic coming
And in the moonlight silent foaming:
But the dream changed: thick minutes dripped:
Between his fingers a fleet light slipped:
      Was gone, was lost:
And on the sand, or in his brain,
He saw red roses fall again:
Rose-wreathed skeletons advanced
And clumsily lifted foot and danced:
And he saw the roses drop apart
Each to disclose a charnel heart.

Whose were these loathed and empty eyes?
Who, falling, in these wingless skies?
This was not she: he rose, withdrew:
One shadow on the wall made two,
The human walls stood up again:
Far in the night, or in his brain,
He heard her whisper, felt her pass,
Shadow of spirit over glass.

3

And a silent star slipped golden down the darkness,
Taking his life with it, like a little cloud
Consumed in fire and speed, diffused in darkness:
Tangled and caught together, the days, the years,
His voice, his lifted hands,
Were ravelled and sped; where, by the sea, he bowed
And dreamed of the foam that crept back into the sea,
And the wandering leaves that soared back into the tree.

4

Roses, he thought, were kin to her,
Pure text of dust; and learning these
He might more surely win to her,
Speak her own tongue to pledge and please.
What vernal kinship, then, was this
That spoke and perished in a breath?
In leaves, she was near enough to kiss,
And yet, impalpable as death.
Spading dark earth, he tore apart
Exquisite roots: she fled from him.
Her stigma, in the crocus heart,
Probed for delicately, would swim
Lazily faint away on air,
Not to be caught or held: she fled
Before him, wavering, everywhere,
A summer's secret behind her shed.
Music? He found it under earth,
Quick veins of fire: he heard her sing.
Upward it broke, a springing mirth,
A fugitive and amazing thing,
It flashed before his crazy feet,
He danced upon it, it would not stay,
His hands against its brightness beat,
But still it broke in light away.
O bird — he cried — if bird you are,
Keep still those frantic wings a while! . . .
Thus dancing for the evening star,
In hope to capture it by guile.

5

The moon rose, and the moon set;
And the stars rushed up and whirled and set;
And again they swarmed, after a shaft of sunlight;
And the blue dusk closed above him, like an ocean of regret.

White trident fires were lit on the tops of towers;
Monstrous and black the towers broke the sky.
The ghostly fountain shot and tumbled in showers;
Gaunt leaves leaned down above it, thirstily.
The gold fish, and the fish with fins of silver,
Quivered in lamplight, rose with sinister eye,
And darted into the darkness, silently.

The faces that looked at him were his own faces,
They streamed along the streets, they licked like fire,
Flowed with undulant paces,
Reflected in the darkness stared at him,
Contemplative, despairing,
Swept silently aside, becoming dim,
With a vague impotent gesture at the sky,
Uncontrolled and little caring;
And he watched them with an introspective eye.

To shape this world of leaderless ghostly passions —
Or else be mobbed by it — there was the question:
Green leaves above him whispered the slow question,
Black ripples on the pool chuckled of passions.
And between the uneasy shoulders of two trees,
Huge, against impalpable gust of blue,
A golden star slid down to leafy seas,
A star he somehow knew.

Youths tripped after him, laughing, but he fled them:
He heard them mock him, in affected tones.
Their lamia mouths, so smiling, bade him fear them.
His own face leered at him, with timid lust,
Was overwhelmed in night.
He turned aside, and walked in graveyard dust, —
In the dew-dabbled, clinging dust, —
And terror seized him, seeing the stones so white;
And the wet grass, frozen and motionless in moonlight;
And the green-tongued moonlight, crawling in thick dust.

Was it murky vapor, here, that dulled the stars? —
Or his own guilty breath that clouded heaven? —
Pale hands struck down with spades.
And it was he, with dew upon his face,
Who dug the foul earth in that dripping place,
Turning his back on heaven.
And it was he who found the desired dead;
And kissed the languid head;
While shadows frisked about him in moonlight,
Whirled and capered and leapt,
Caught each other and mimicked lust in the moonlight,
In the dew-wet dust, above the dead who slept.

But this — was it this he rose from and desired?
Black mould of leaves clung wetly about his feet.
He was lost, and alone, and tired,
A mist curled round him coldly, touched his face,
Shadows with eyes were gathering in that place;
And he dreamed of a lamplit street.
But roses fell through the darkness,
They writhed before him out of the mould,
Opened their hearts to pour out darkness,
Darkness of flesh, of lust grown old.
He struggled against them, beat,
Broke them with hands to feel the blood flow warm,
Reeled, when they opened their hearts,
Feeling them with their eyes closed push and swarm,
Thronging about his throat, pressing his mouth,
Beating his temples, choking his breath . . .
Help, you stars! — wet darkness showered upon him.
He was dissolved in a deep cold dream of death.

White fires were lit upon the tops of towers,
The towers shouldered the sky:
The ghostly fountain shot and tumbled in showers,
Gaunt leaves leaned down above it, thirstily.
And he looked with laughter upon the lamplit ripples

Each with its little image of the light,
And thought the minds of men were like black ripples,
Ripples of darkness, darkly huddled in night,
Each of them with its image of lamp or star,
Thinking itself the star.

And it seemed to him, as he looked upon them, laughing,
That he was the star they all in fright reflected.
He was the god who had been rejected,
Stoned and trampled upon in a filthy street,
Hung up in lamplight for young men to beat,
Cursed and spat upon; and all for saying
There was no life save life of fast and praying.
Or had he been a beggar, with bare feet?
Or a cruel ascetic, trampling roses down? . . .
Roses are death! he cried. He turned in hatred,
And saw red fires burst up above the town;
And a swarm of faces rising, green with hatred.

And silence descended, on dripping trees:
And dew-spats slowly spat from leaves to stones.
He had walked these gardens, he thought, before.
The fountain chuckled;
The leaves rustled, in whispers, along a shore.
And the moon rose, and the moon set;
And the stars rushed up and swarmed and set;
And again they swarmed, after a shaft of sunlight;
And the blue dusk closed above him, like an ocean of regret.

PART II

1

And at times it seemed,
Walking with her of whom he subtly dreamed,

That her young body was ringed with flame,
Hover of fire,
And that she went and came,
Impalpable fiery blossom of desire,
Into his heart and out of his heart again,
With every breath; and every breath was pain.
And if he touched her hand, she drew away,
Becoming someone vast; and stretched her hair
Suddenly, like black rain, across the sun.
Till he grew fearful, seeing her there,
To think that he loved such a one,
Who rose against the sky to shut out day.

But at times it seemed,
Walking with her of whom he subtly dreamed,
(Music beneath the sea)
That she was texture of earth no less than he;
Among the leaves her face
Gleamed with familiar grace;
And walking slowly through old gardens,
Among the cool blue cedars,
Spreading her hands in the silent dazzle of sunlight,
Her voice and the air were sweetly married;
Her laughter trembled like music out of the earth;
Her body was like the cool blue cedars,
Fragrant in sunlight.
And he quivered, to think that he was the blade, in sunlight,
To flash, and strip these boughs, and spill their fragrance.

Wind hurried the last year's leaves, their shadows hurried,
And clouds blew down the sky.
Where would they be with a year gone by?
Let us be quick: there is time to overcome:
The earth grows old, the moon is already dead,
But you are young, you tremble because you love me,
It is all we have. Let nothing more be said.

What do we care for a star that floats down heaven,
That fiery tear of time?
It spoke to us once, it will not speak again,
It will be no more remembered than last year's rain;
There will be other dusks for us to walk through,
And other stars will float down heaven.
Time is undone: between our hands it slips,
Goes out between us, the breath upon our lips.

Do not look over your shoulder to see it falling!
Shadows gather and brood, under the trees.
The world grows silent, it listens to hear us walking;
Let the star perish: we wander as we please.
Or is the earth beneath us an old star falling,
Falling through twilight to leafy seas?
The night grows damp: I will take your arm.
Follow the lanterns, lest we come to harm.

2

Green-fingered dryad, break from your oak-tree!
Flash from your pool, blue nymph!
Leaves have whispered your secret, the sands have betrayed you,
Water-lilies have told of your hearts.
Cold and gold and green-gleamed white,
Deep-petalled, and pollened, as they:
These are your hearts. Come out, green-fingered!
Rise from your pool, blue nymph.

She that I knew by the sphinx
Imperceptibly shrinks in your eyes:
The lotus uncloses and glistens,
I drink your mouth in the dark.

Now you no longer escape me — I have you!
This is you, this light in my fingers;

This air in my palm!
These grains of sand are worlds of sunlight;
These grains of dust are worlds of moonlight;
I give them to you that you may love them,
Tawny nasturtium.

Rain slowly falls in the sleepy garden;
It patters and purrs and seethes.
How the young grass rejoices in cool bubbles!
It drinks cold silver.
The slow drops that fall from the eaves
Dig little pits among pebbles:
Or patter and glance from laurel leaves
In tiny shatters of fire.

It rains, and the streets are dark;
The leaves make a mournful sound in the hidden garden.
It rains and the streets are cold . . .
But you, who walked alone beside that sea,
Or flashed your hands into sunlight out of foam, —
You that I never thought to capture, —
Hearing the rain, you cling to me all night long;
Hearing the rain sing a mournful song,
You hold my head on your breast and cling to me.

Green hills, with sunlight flecked, and azure shadows;
Dun hills and blue, run down beneath my feet:
The sea mourns, and the sheep are scattered.
Tired of the shrill flute, I cry through the evening,
The stars are rising and I desire you,
We will desert our gods and meet.

Do we brush the dust from the petal with too much kissing?
Is the clear dew gone from the grass?
I am consumed with grief
For the dark wet bruise on the leaf.
But the seconds drip like raindrops,

I fear at the end of night our hearts must pass,
Let us drink this night while we have it, let us drink it all.

If I should destroy you! But could I destroy by loving?
O my beloved, I dread some death in this,
Something there is that perishes with the kiss,
I hear in your heart the grief of autumnal rains;
The pouring of merciless sea-waves along your veins.
Is it you, I hold? Is it you? Or the earth, or the sea?
Answer me with your mouth and cling to me.

Rain slowly falls in the bitter garden;
It rains: the streets grow dark.
The leaves make a sorrowful sound in the hidden garden;
It rains, and the streets grow cold.
These are my hands, that tremble upon your face, —
Trembling lest love depart from our shadowy place;
Lest suddenly in my arms you become a sea
Laughing, with numberless waves, to murder me.

3

White fires were lit on the mountain-tops of towers,
Monstrous and black the towers carved the sky.
The ghostly fountain shot and tumbled in wavering showers,
Gaunt leaves leaned down above it thirstily.
The gold fish, and the fish with fins of copper,
Quivered in lamplight, rose with motionless eye,
And darted into the darkness, silently.

To shape this chaos of leaderless ghostly passions —
Or else be mobbed by it — there was the question.
Dry leaves above him whispered the slow question,
Black ripples on the pool chuckled of passion.
And through the shadows drifted his own white face,
With ashes in his eyes, where before was fire;

And he sorrowed for himself in that strange place,
And for a once more unfulfilled desire.

Were the hands of lust red with the murder of love?
And must desire forever defeat its end?
He was tired: he longed for death.
He turned, but met himself again in darkness,
Pacing noiselessly, like a ghost, through darkness;
And upon his face came softly his own breath.

Cold wind dissolved him: white foam seethed above him:
Green darkness drank him down.
Here was a cold full music like an ocean
Wherein to sink from death to death and drown.
Fishes gaped at him, with eyes like lanterns.
The sea-floor spread to take him, smooth and brown.
Under this ocean, were there no desires? —
The sands bubbled, and roses shot soft fires.
And skeletons whizzed before him, and whistled behind him,
And heavily danced wherever the shadows hid them,
And stormed dead roses about his feet;
Flash, bright scythe of death! They danced forever.
He heard their drunken footsteps beat and beat.

And the music he had heard so long ago,
Now failing fainter, seemed ever to grow
Deeper and more desirable. He heard
The bells of surf on rocks; and shattering water stirred
Memory of a woman once seen there,
Lifting in moonlight a golden weight of hair:

A woman who fled before him, looking backward
To laugh in the moonlight, always, before she vanished: . . .
A woman of fire, a woman of earth,
Dreamed of in every birth.
O laughter, heard so little, lost so soon!
Come back! — Thus moans the sea to the failing moon.

And the moon rose; the moon set;
The stars rushed up, and whirled, and set;
And again they thronged, after a shaft of sunlight;
And the blue dusk closed above him, like an ocean of regret.

PART III

1

Bright hair, turning in sunlight, and turning feet,
Brown hands turning in air, —
They are gone forever; they are no longer fleet.

She, whose mouth I was once so crazed with kissing,
Whose eyes were like deep fires, —
The grass that puffs in the fields is far more lovely.

Now let the shadows lengthen before me,
And old men die in the street:
Let the sun pass: we seek fantastic darkness.

Light now the lanterns, and let us see your faces,
New friends of goblin birth! —
Ah, but the heart sinks, leaving thus that sunlight.

He turned, and saw the world go down behind him,
Into the sounding darkness;
Voices out of tumult cried to remind him,
Wailed, and were lost in wind;
Desolate darkness, darkness of sad adventure,
Peril with watchful eyes,
Shut closely about him. Night blew out the lanterns.
Rapt clouds devoured the skies.

2

Red is the color of blood, and I will seek it:
I have sought it in the grass,
It is the color of steep sun seen through eyelids.

It is hidden under the suave flesh of women, —
Flows there, quietly flows.
It mounts from the heart to the temples, the singing mouth —
As cold sap climbs the rose.

I am confused in webs and knots of scarlet
Spun from the darkness;
Or shuttled from the mouths of thirsty spiders.

Madness for red! I devour the leaves of autumn.
I tire of the green of the world.
I am myself a mouth for blood.

Here, in the golden haze of the late slant sun,
Let us walk, with the light in our eyes,
To a single bench, from the outset predetermined.
Look: there are sea gulls in these city skies,
Kindled against the blue!
But I do not think of the sea gulls, I think of you.

Your eyes, with the late sun in them,
Are like blue pools dazzled with yellow petals.
This pale green suits them well.
Here is your finger, with an emerald on it:
The one I gave you. I say these things politely —
But what I think beneath them, who can tell?

November sun is sunlight poured through honey:
Old things, in such a light, grow subtle and fine.
Bare oaks are like still fire.
Talk to me: now we drink the evening's wine.

Look, how our shadows creep along the gravel! —
And this way, how the gravel begins to shine!

This is the time of day for recollections?
For sentimental regrets, oblique allusions?
Rose-leaves, shrivelled in a musty jar.
Scatter them to the wind! There are tempests coming.
It is dark, with a malign star.

If human mouths were really roses, my dear, —
(Why must we link things so? —)
I would tear yours petal from petal with slow murder.
I would pluck the stamens, the pistils,
The gold and the green, —
Spreading the subtle sweetness that was your breath
On a cold wave of death.

Now let us walk back, slowly, as we came.
We will light the room with candles; they may shine
Like rows of yellow eyes.
Your hair is like spun fire, by candle-flame.
You smile at me — say nothing. You are wise.
For I think of you, flung down brutal darkness;
Crushed and red, with pale face.
I think of you, with your hair disordered and dripping,
And myself rising red from that embrace.

3

Music, withdrawing to a point of silence,
Took his heart down over the edge of the world:
Cliffs, and the sea, and stars.
Sleep might be merciful, if it were dreamless;
But sleep was a rage of winds.

Dusk, withdrawing to a single lamplight
At the end of an infinite street —

He saw his ghost walk down that street forever,
And heard the eternal rhythm of his feet.
And if he should reach at last that final gutter,
Today, or tomorrow,
Or, maybe, after the death of himself and time;
And stand at the ultimate curbstone by the stars:
Would the secret of his desire
Blossom out of the dark with a burst of fire?
Or would he hear the eternal arc-lamp sputter,
Only that; and see lewd shadows crawl;
And find the stars were street-lamps after all?
Music, quivering to a point of silence,
Drew his heart down over the edge of the world.

Dancers arose; he had not seen them;
Hissing cymbals clashed;
Scarlet and green together writhed in darkness,
Billows of saffron rolled against the darkness,
White arms shot up, eyes flashed,
The grass rose vivid green against the black . . .
But this was idle. His youth could not come back.

And the music whispered down to a breath of silence,
Sighing his heart down over the edge of the world.

4

He reeled in a poppy field, and dreamed:
Live scarlet crackled and crawled and gleamed;
And before him, over red fields, ran
A shape half woman and half man.
Cold cypresses, in formal row,
Marched to a blue hill, bald with snow;
Cold flutes on shivering air were blown,
Thin and faint in sober tone,
And he went forward, guessing there
New incense on the haunted air.

Under that azure cypress grove
He saw white feet like silver move,
And white hands deftly lifted up
For dusky gleam of golden cup;
A voice in ritual speech he heard,
Measuring death in every word.
Through the veins of men like these
Flowed warm blood, — or froth of seas?
Reedy were these hands: and chill.
His heart, beneath such eyes, lay still.

Roses out of the cool earth bloom,
To flourish on a rain-dark tomb;
And music just as sweetly springs
From rain-cold silver strings.
Feeding on pale mouths, he learned
That they, no less than scarlet, burned;
Touching hands as cold as sea,
Foam in fire they seemed to be.

Here was no day, but always night;
The leaves on all the trees blew white;
And yet, within them, he was told,
The sap flowed reddish, and not cold.
Pale hands, — drop my heart! he cried.
They pressed around him to deride.
With delicate claws they plucked at him,
With delicate mouths they leered at him.
He was not one of them, said they, —
Only the dull and brutish clay.
He heard them mimic, one by one,
Out of his blood. He saw the sun.

And cymbals clashed: he thought their sound was scarlet.
And he was shouting between them, a thing of red.

5

The sun's blood turns to orange, and round the sky,
Flows in a broad low band.
The street lamp winks in the twilight a dismal eye.
The eternal mistress lifts her hand
To rearrange for the thousandth time her hair,
With amber things out of an ancient tomb,
For the deathless lover who climbs and climbs the stair.
The stars above us, — they are pale streaming bubbles
Seen by a sea-shape in translucent noon.
Globed and green, bursting to disappear.
Listen; and through the immortal hush you'll hear
Persistent, those eternal footsteps climb,
Up creaking gas-lit stairs in perfect time.

What does it matter? there are white sands here:
Rippled with the secular musings of the sea.
We have seen her comb her hair,
With her elbows shining bare;
And seen her turn the small brown sensuous head.
We have seen old roses opening by a mirror,
And darkness filled with rain,
And the hot unsteady lamplight on a bed.
But here, in the sifted dusk,
Where only a pure light settles out of the world,
We meet in eternal quiet, — talk musingly, —
On a white sand, silvered with spectral shells,
Rippled with the green musings of the sea.

Something there is in roses — you remember —
That's poisonous and red, torrid, malignant.
There was a savage music in them
That filled the innocent blood with swarm of petals.
But beloved, now we are free:
Now we are set in a love of deathless shape,
Immutable, brooded on by the sea.

Yet, it is strange — behind that altar,
Carved with cold foam of time,
Skeletons lay: I saw them in the dusk.
Shells winked between the ribs, and over the hands
Rippled the obedient sands.

6

The sun's blood turns to orange, and round the sky
Flows in a broad low band.
The eternal mistress lifts her hand,
To rearrange her hair,
For the deathless lover who climbs and climbs the stair.

Have we not seen him climb, — or climbed, ourselves, —
Up the eternal azure of those stairs?
Ridiculous, to those who stay behind,
Or chuckle, meditating, from afar:
The small pathetic back, in silhouette,
Dwindling against a star.

Why do we think these things in retrospect?
Must we, being cold,
Reach out to sunset fires to warm our hands?
It is as if we were growing old;
And sought, in disillusionment, to cling
To something loved in youth, some daybreak thing.

Something about you fades . . . you are not he
Whom I saw first:
Your garments, once so subtle,
Dull to the insistent stare; and now your mind
Is a garden whose pools and paths I know too well.

Here's change, in changelessness: and we go down
Once more to the old chaos.

Lost hands repel and cling, the last waves break,
Once more we are forgotten, and forsake.

The sun's blood fades to orange; now the sky
Shrinks to a faint green bubble above our hands.
The gliding street lamp winks a sinister eye,
Around it swirl grey skeletons on the sands.

I will seek the eternal secret in this darkness:
The little seed that opens to gulf the world.

PART IV

1

Through the deep night, the night of forgetfulness,
Men ran with streaming torches,
Pale mouths shouted,
Bright fires were bristling backward on the wind;
And he heard fanatic feet
Ring echoing into darkness down the street.
Into the night they sank. Bubbles of sound,
Dilating greenly upward through the darkness,
Showed him where men had drowned.

What towers above him trembled? Up them swarmed
Thick smoke of leaves, a fire of bursting roses,
Licking the sky.
The towers were smothered; they crumbled in roar of flame;
They crashed and spouted. And when they showered before him,
Strange things rushed out of them; and whistled by.
These men with bristling torches,
Filling the darkness with cries and fire,
Falling and turning and sinking into the night, —
These were himself, rising in rage against him;
The sky hung red and bright;

And above the crash of walls he heard a cry,
'The hour has come! Now let the tyrant die!'

To shape this world of leaderless ghostly passions, —
Or else be mobbed by it — there was the riddle.
Gaunt leaves above him whispered the slow question;
Black ripples on the pool chuckled of passions.
And between the uneasy shoulders of two trees,
Huge, against impalpable breath of blue,
A golden star slipped down to leafy seas,
A star he somehow knew.

Now came the final hour:
Clear music, silver horns and muted strings,
Seduced from temporal air his willing feet.
Below him sang in vain that scarlet darkness.
Now should the infinite soul be made complete.

2

I bring seven candles of scented wax,
Seven candles of peacock flame:
Black webs of smoke above them weave:
And I, I shake with shame.

For though your face, in the altar-light,
Is a vision I should not see,
I would have you leave your jewelled frame
And break your heart for me.

No priest forbids — step down, I pray!
Now darkness floods the air,
And I have taken your ringless hand,
And loosed your seven-starred hair:

And then unclasp the supple clasp
To let your mantle fall

That night may know your naked side
And love consume you all.

God-haunted eyes and holy mouth!
No wings now fold you in:
The mystic marriage is blessed with feast,
The sacrament with sin:

Invisible veins of lightning run
Like hot gold through the night,
The sacred kiss beneath my kiss
Is open to my delight.

Seven eyes of peacock flame I bring,
Seven candles of scented flame:
Black webs of smoke above them tremble:
I tremble, too, with shame.

3

Rain seethed upon him, — with black streaks through the day,
With white streaks through the night.
Around a lantern undulant through the darkness
He saw old pale leaves fall.
Silent, he saw them swarming over the light.
Deep darkness drowned them all.

Some edge there is in love — at the beginning, —
That flashes and dims. And so with all things sought.
If rain dropped upward through the grass, he thought, —
And fell to the clouds — and beyond the clouds to sun . . .
Might love find consummation?

Let us invert the world:
Let us delude ourselves that dust may rise,
That earth relents at last.
Red lilies, rapidly growing, bloom in darkness.
A pebble, dropped, is flung down soundless skies.

4

He turned in the dusk, and saw none coming behind him;
He listened, and heard no sound.
'I am Christ!' he cried. His words were lost in the silence.
Three scarlet leaves of a maple fell to the ground.
But he felt beneath his sandals the pushing of roses,
And did not dare to move.

He turned in the night, and saw no shadow behind him;
He listened, and heard no voice.
'I am Christ!' he cried. A whisper of leaves denied him.
'And while I live, no more shall man rejoice.'
The moon rose, huge and cold, behind a hill:
The trees shook silver; the night grew chill.

Why was the world so mute, the world his body?
He smiled, to think it slept.
The leaves above him quivered along black branches;
Dew dropped beneath white stars.
'It is the third day. I have risen,' he said.
Among the dead leaves, whispers crept.

'How did I know it was time? Perhaps I dreamed.
The dusk of the third day came.
I lay upon stones. A shaft of the low sun gleamed
Through a single crack, and a cobweb sang like flame.
Petals of blood had purpled those grey sands.
But the great rock was as nothing before my hands.

'But all this happened before, somewhere' he said —
'In this same twilight I strove from this same tomb:
Lifting with dusty hands a great white rock.
My eyes were dazzled with sun. They were used to gloom.
I saw that hill, black, on a sky bright red.
But where, then, are my disciples?' He looked behind him;
And the blue night lay still.

'I saw black bats, as I had seen them before, —
In the sharp twilight. They twittered against the sky.
But it seemed to me that I stood on a pathless shore
Invisible waves before me surged to die . . .
To die? There is no death. No death!' he said.
A thick bough guarded the moonlight from his head.

Disembodied, he flowed with the flow of night;
Caught up with stars and wind.
The moon with an army of red clouds hurried before him,
In silent tremendous haste.
Seas clashed together beneath him; they roared and showered;
Earth shook beneath his feet.
And he stood at the end of an infinite lamplit street.

He rang a bell in the street; lifting his voice,
Beneath the lamp at every corner he cried
'I am Christ returned, from the dead!
It was I you wounded, I that you crucified,
It was I who wept and bled.
Did I not prophesy, three days ago?
You sealed a great white rock above my head.
And I come to tell you the things you do not know.'

Laughter rushed round him; they spat upon his face;
They struck him and beat him down.
Thinking him dead, they left him in that place:
Lying against an old wall, crushed and bleeding,
With lamplight on his face.

And children mocked at him; and he could not answer;
For how could the dead explain
That all was predetermined, all immortal?
How could he make it clear,
To children, who came to kick him, and to jeer,
(With the blood so slowly struggling through his brain,)
That man's salvation rose through pain?

Remote this was, and strange. A lamp grew dim,
Drawn to a thin swift streak along the sky.
A sinister planet poised to revolve on him.
He was a soundless motion. He could not cry.
And dark things whistled beneath him. And a cold shade,
Bottomless, gulfed him down. And he was afraid.

And he tossed in the darkness, as one who in fever dreams
Of bathing at last in the fullness of cold streams,
Bright, beneath leaves, by sand.
Roses, cover my body! I am tired of struggle.
Old twilight, take my hand!

He saw a green hill, clear, in the evening sky.
Night came. Three crosses fell.

5

To muse in the afternoon by a convent wall, —
Here, at the bottom of a vast blue well of sun;
To watch the lizard breathe and crawl,
And know yourself the world and lizard in one:
Let us lose ourselves, and all we meditate,
To melt, through dream, in the timeless dream of fate.

The infinite mind uncloses like a lotus, —
And we are the heart of it. Come, — take my hand!
And drift with the drift of wind.
You a note, and I a note,
In a sea of music we tremble and fall and float.
That spinning world is an old, old recollection:
It dissolves in darkness. But the mind is not dismayed.
We were confused, a while, in loves and hatreds, —
We fought for light or shade.
Now all is changed: we climb the solid air;
This azure light is a pinnacled carven stair.

Now what you muse already is on my tongue:
You smile, and utter the secrets of my heart.
Somewhere, long since, there was a pebble flung:
From that drowned cry we start.
Somewhere I blossom. Somewhere my brown leaves fall.
Somewhere I cry, somewhere I sing.
Yet, we are musing by a convent wall.
In a depth of sun . . . on an afternoon in spring.

We must escape this temporal flesh and place, —
Step freely away in dream . . . though lizards creep,
Rustling the vines, and a cool air chills the face,
A pulse of menace trembling beneath our sleep . . .
There is no vine, no lizard! We draw no breath.
We are the soundless ecstasy of death.

I have seen bees, poised in the quiet sun,
Winnowing, with rapid invisible wings,
Judas petals, littered upon a path.
I must forget them. I must forget them all.
I must forget this sun, — myself, — this wall.

Here, then, at last, grown weary of long pursuing,
We find the perfect darkness!
The infinite spreads before us, and shrinks to nothing.
Or must we remember, always, that sound of voices,
Our little cave of dusk?

Dancers arose: he had not seen them:
Hissing cymbals clashed.
The great rose blossomed with a clang of light
And withered in silent fire.
He was a part of the maniac laughter of chaos;
Rebellious chaos of unfulfilled desire.

6

Twilight: a cold green sky.
Low massed clouds, with dazzling sinister edges,
And a sea gull, falling in high pale sunlight.

Dusk, — the encroachment of poisonous shadows,
The leisurely lighting of lamps;
And a gradual silence of restless trees.

Mist of twilight in my heart:
I who was always catching at fire.
Mould of black leaves under my feet;
I, whose star was desire.

Earth spins in her shadow. Let us turn and go back
To the first of our loves —
The one who was moonlight and the fall of white roses!

We are struck down. We hear no music.
The moisture of night is in our hands.
Time takes us. We are eternal.

II

The Jig of Forslin

*

PART I

1

In the clear evening, as the lamps were lighted,
Forslin, sitting alone in his strange world,
Meditated; yet through his musings heard
The dying footfalls of the tired day

Monotonously ebb and ebb away
Into the smouldering west;
And heard the dark world slowly come to rest.
Now, as the real world dwindled and grew dim,
His dreams came back to him . . .
Now, as one who stands
In the aquarium's gloom, by ghostly sands,
Watching the glide of fish beneath pale bubbles, —
The bubbles quietly streaming
Cool and white and green . . . poured in silver . . .
He did not know if this were wake or dreaming;
But thought to lean, reach out his hands, and swim.
Some things there were, that, being remembered clearly,
Pierced with a troubling gleam
His lucid dream:
As, — that he had stepped in from a blare of sunlight
Over the watery threshold to this gloom;
Sharp red roofs; blue sky; rich autumn trees
Shaking their gold out on the breeze;
And then, after eternities had vanished,
That he was oldish, and that his name was Forslin,
And that he sat in a small bare gaslit room.

In the mute evening, as the music sounded,
Each voice of it, weaving gold or silver,
Seemed to open a separate door for him . . .
Suave horns eluded him down corridors;
Persuasive violins
Sang of nocturnal sins;
And ever and again came the hoarse clash
Of cymbals; as a voice that swore of murder.
Which way to choose, in all this labyrinth?
Did all lead in to the selfsame chamber?
No matter: he would go . . .
In the evening, as the music sounded;
Streaming swift and thin, or huddled slow . . .

Coffee-cups and artificial palm-trees;
Cigarette-tips glowing in the shadows;
And the mellow gleams in polished marble floors.
The ceaseless footsteps clashed on the cold marble,
The sinister footman turned the revolving doors.
And there was he, sitting alone in silence,
Hearing his heart tick out the hours;
The futile watcher, chronicle of dead days;
While the dancers whirled and danced,
And the murderers chose their knives,
And the lovers leaned, to kiss, through laurel flowers.

The palm-trees trembled faintly on the music —
Stirred by an undertone.
Or rose this music only in his brain?
The eyes of women, the fans, the jewelled fingers,
The soon-checked smiles, the swift words lost in laughter,
Coffee and cigarettes . . . He sat alone.
The sea of twilight swept his heart again.

And now as one who stands
In the aquarium's green, by cloudy sands,
Watching the glide of fish beneath soft bubbles, —
The bubbles briefly streaming,
Cold and white . . . poured in silver . . .
He did not know if this were wake or dreaming:
But thought to lean, reach out his hands, and swim.

2

Let us drown, then, if to drown is but to change:
Drown in the days of those whose days are strange;
Close our eyes, and drown;
Wearily, without effort, at our leisure,
In some strange sea-pool, lit with sun and treasure,
Sink slowly down
From the bright waves above our phantom hands
To vales of twilight sands.

Grown weary of ourselves, these tedious hours,
Our voices, our eternal pulses drumming,
Our doubts, our hesitations, our regrets,
And the shrinking self that sits within and cowers,
Let us descend in some strange sea-pool;
Creep through the caves to hear the great tide coming;
Forget our souls that murmur of unpaid debts.

I heard a story, once, of one who murdered,
For what, I cannot remember; but he murdered.
With a knife's greedy edge, or with white hands —
What does it matter? The swift deed was done . . .
That was a sombre sea-pool to explore —
Strange things are on that floor.

And once, the music I was listening to
Suddenly opened, like a luminous book,
To one bright page that told of a strange thing:
A man stepped out in the purple of an arc-light,
A man I knew — I knew him well —
And because the harlot he loved had jilted him,
He held his breath, and died.

Was I that man? How should I know?
Yet, when I die, that man will die with me.
Deep music now, with lap and flow,
Green music streaked with gleams and bubbles of light,
Bears me softly away. Come down with me! . . .
We will live strange lives before this night.

3

The corners of the ceiling are blown like mist,
Are gathered in lazy swirls and blown away.
My eyes are fixed upon a single picture:
This, only, seems to stay.
An old man lurching slowly out of darkness,

A bag upon his shoulders growing monstrous . . .
Now he is gone, before I see his face.
I am spread upon a fog, and know no place.

The yellow footlights blazing before my feet;
The same familiar curving wall of fire.
Soft music trembles sweet . . .
Below me and above me turn the faces,
Rows on rows of luminous living faces,
And the furtive watchful eyes;
I stand before them, somehow grown eternal;
They smile upon me from their eternal places;
And now, at the chosen moment, the music dies.

You see me: I am plain: and growing baldish.
The clothes I wear are old, but carefully kept.
You do not know — indeed, how should you know? —
That for years I have hardly eaten, hardly slept, —
To learn this thing. That does not matter, to you.
You yawn, and wait to see what I can do.

When I was young, juggling was all I did:
I was the best of them;
But growing older, I wanted something better.
To do the impossible! That was the question.
And so I left the stage, and after months,
I thought of this — lying in bed one night —
It seemed ridiculous, too, it was so simple.
To balance one ball on another ball —
Tossing the upper one, to catch it, falling,
In easy balance again — that was the thing!
I started in next day.

Well, sir, you wouldn't believe how hard it was.
Mind you, I wasn't a greenhorn, but an expert —
Made balls, or cards, or hoops, or wooden bottles,

Do anything but talk. But this, by heaven,
This was a man's job! And it took me years.

Practice, practice, practice! That's all it was.
Three times a year I took the stage again
To earn the money to keep alive with:
Used the old tricks, of course, though getting rusty.
Then I'd get off once more, and find a room
With a high ceiling, for plenty of space,
And go to work again. It was three years
Before I got that balancing down cold —
The balancing, not the tossing: just to balance
The one ball on the other, and keep it there . . .
Then came the tossing. That was harder.
Sometimes, by God, I thought I was going crazy!
My brain was full of crashing marble balls.
I'd reach out every direction and try to catch them —
I couldn't, of course, — they'd all crash to the floor,
And keep on banging till my heart fell dead.
It seemed as if my mind was a dark room,
With a ceiling much too low; and every time
I flung a ball up, a million hit that ceiling.
They hit the gas jet. They broke the foolish lamp shades.
I was always getting ousted for breaking things,
Denting the ceiling, cracking the plaster and walls.

The lady who lived above me complained of the noise:
So did the man who lived below me.
For five years more I seemed to be always moving —
Always cramming my collars into a bag,
And searching the columns of furnished rooms.

In ten years, though, I had the thing down perfect.
Ten years! I was over forty, and growing grey.
I hadn't married because I hadn't dared to —
No money for it. It was taking chances.
Though as for that, I suppose I might have married,

A girl I met down south, doing a sketch —
I liked her — she was willing, more than willing;
But I had this thing so on my mind, you see,
I couldn't be bothered, somehow, and let it go.

I took my trick to the agents — and they went crazy.
They said they'd never seen a trick to touch it:
O, nothing to it! It was easy getting it on.
One man only — by George, I laughed at him! —
Said the thing looked too easy, and wouldn't take.
But they gave me a little advance for a suit of clothes —
I needed it — and, finally, set the night.

All this, you see, is what is standing before you —
Only, that you don't know it, and I can't tell you.
You see me: I am plain: and growing baldish.
For me, you are rows of faces, lazy eyes.
What does it matter, to you, *who* entertains you? . . .

Now, at the chosen moment, the music dies . . .

I balance the one ball on the other —
It seems so simple — and toss it up, and catch it
In easy balance . . . (My God!)

I'll do it again — for Christ's sake watch me this time!
I balance the one ball on the other . . .
Dip it, and toss it up, and softly catch it
In easy balance again . . . I toss it and catch it . . .
I walk around and keep it balancing there . . .
I toss it and catch it . . . And all the hands are silent!

What is it I am trying to balance — brains?
Or a foolish human life?
There's the curtain falling — and I am over.
I will breathe gas tonight in a locked room,
And forget those faces . . .
Get out of my way! I'm going home.

4

That window, in which you saw the light winked out
Behind the yellow shades — was that his room?
Tomorrow, we'll search the papers . . . Tonight blows cold . . .
Where shall we turn, among bright cobblestones?
This white carnation I wear is growing old.

I have spent years at something; and I am tired.
Let us lounge in a bright café, and listen to music —
Music, threading the smoke of cigarettes . . .
Vermouth, then coffee . . . How much shall we tip the waiter?
Here the fatigued mind wanders and forgets.

I walked by the river, once, and heard the waves
Slapping the sunlit stones . . . But was that I?
Or was it I who saw a pigeon falling
Down a sheer tower wall against the sky?
Or was it I who heard one night the rain
Weaving in silver an intricate pattern of pain?

These things are idle — they do not matter.
If I was born at midnight or high noon, —
Then, or now, or tomorrow, and to whom —
Is this so relevant? Or is it chatter?
My friends, believe me — it is more worth while
To lean for the moment into dream, and smile.

5

Yes; this is manifest: a suicide;
The gas still hissing. Open the windows wide . . .

He closed the door and locked it; and he heard,
In a sudden backward yearning of his mind,
His own slow steps knock wearily up the stairs.
Should he light the gas, then turn it out again?
Survey once more the bed, the floor, the chairs?

He saw himself limp down the windy street,
Bending his face against the relentless cold.
The sharp wind made him cry.
Seen through his tears, bright lamps were rayed and daggered.
Grey ghostly clouds streamed over a starry sky.

He had not dined tonight, nor would he dine —
What, among graveyard friends, was bread or wine?
He closed the stage-door, stumbled in the street.
They said, you turned deep blue: your tongue lolled out . . .
The cobblestones went dizzy beneath his feet.

And now, in a backward yearning of his mind,
He heard his own harsh steps rasp up the stairs,
Thrust the remorseless key in, lit the gas,
Regarded, motionless, the floor, the chairs . . .

A small room: small and dull: yet large enough.
Space for the living: and more than space for the dead.
The ceiling cracked — no matter. It was old.
There was the window, with the shade drawn down.
There were his hat and coat, laid on the bed.

And now, with thumb and finger he turned twice
The foolish valve that brought a double darkness — ;
And would he wait, in comfort, in a chair?
Or, running the yellow shade up, through the window
Watch cold stars play tragedy out there?

A cab went by, and rumbled into distance;
The hollow ringing hooves echoed and echoed,
In perfect rhythm, always, growing faint.
So went his pulse-beats down remote dark alleys,
With a far rhythmic echo, like complaint.

He listened for them . . . they beat, they beat . . . and beat;
A little curl of dust, a golden vapor,

Idly floating upward from every one.
Upon what streaming road, what cloudy river,
Did those wild horses run?

Someone, once, tried to juggle with stars,
Tried to balance a sun upon a moon,
But found, at last, the sun was much too big . . .
Or was it that the moon was much too small?
There would be flaming death if it should fall.
It fell. And a billion devils danced a jig.

No: it was someone learning to swallow fire —
Strangling to death.
Someone trying, in a great gust of flame,
To draw one deep cool breath . . .
No use, of course. If fire once got within,
It would consume him all.
But this was peace, this darkness! — like old music,
Music heard in a dream; or hid in a wall;
Like a slow music, moving under a sea,
A waveless music, seethed and frothed with starlight,
Desireless; cold; and dead.

His hands were tightly clasped beneath his head.

6

Death, among violins and paper roses,
Leering upon a waltz, in evening dress,
Taking his lady's arm with bow and smile —
This is unreal. Let us pull off our gloves:
Open the doors, and take the air a while.

Death would be sweet, if one might poison music —
Feel a rich rhythm, with its freight of languor,
Feeding under the heart with every beat:
Faint with a waltz in the blood,

Laugh and topple and fall,
Feel the cold marble flush beneath soft feet.

Frivolous death! He plays at cards, drinks coffee,
Sips a cordial, or asks his partner the time.
He straightens his cuffs, flicks off an ash, is silent,
Lowers his eyes, and muses on a crime.

Well, no matter. We deal in juxtapositions.
We cry and love, we laugh and hate.
I think of a shrewd blade hidden inside my brain;
And crumple a roseleaf while I meditate.

And while, in the warm dark seats, we watch the spotlight
Dazzle upon the singer's hair and eyes,
The pink tongue, and the diamonds on her fingers, —
Out in the hall, an epileptic lies
On the white stone. The usher lifts his head:
The young man laughs at the crowd and falls back dead.

                                7

Things mused upon are, in the mind, like music,
They flow, they have a rhythm, they close and open,
And sweetly return upon themselves in rhyme.
Against the darkness they are woven,
They are lost for a little, and laugh again,
They fall or climb.

Here, it rains. The small clear bubbles
Pelt and scatter along the shimmering flagstones,
Leap and sing.
Streaks of silver slant from the eaves,
The sparrow puffs his feathers beneath broad leaves
And preens a darkened wing.

Yet round a windy corner of the mind,
A block away, or at the selfsame place, —

We meet you, face to face!
You cough with the dust, we hear you say once more,
There in the shadow of a deserted door,
You are cold, you have no money, and you are hungry.
You open your purse to show us that it is empty.
You are crying; and that is strange, for you are a whore.

. . . Bubbles of soft rain scurrying over a pavement, —
Slanting from dark eaves —
Where did I see a sparrow beneath broad leaves? . . .
Well, take us home with you; and when we have loved you,
(Stroked your drowsy hair, your subtle flesh,
And held your golden throat in the palms of hands)
When we have loved you, and rise
Once more into mortal evening out of your eyes,
We will both give you money; and you may go
To order peacocks' tongues, or a little snow.

. . . There is a seethe of foam far over our hands
On the pale surface . . .
We glide above our shadows along the sands . . .

If you are really so tired, take my arm.
Is this your door? . . . Give me the key.
Why don't you sell these hangings if you are poor?
You deserve to be.

. . . Something about your skin is like soft rain —
Cool and clear . . . it reminds me of many things.
Your eyes, they are like blue wells of pain —
I remember a sparrow, preening his wet wings.
He sat under broad leaves, puffing his feathers and winking.
What are you thinking?

Now that you're here — there's no use in your going . . .
Wait till the morning. When we have loved we'll sleep.
Sleep is better than wine; and hunger will keep.

. . . Rain, rain, rain. All night the rain.
The roofs are wet, the eaves drip.
The pelted leaves bend down and rise again.
The bubbles chirp and skip.

This is spring. The snowdrops start to grow,
The rain will wash them clean.
This is spring, the warm drops wound the snow,
The black earth aches with green . . .

And now that it is morning, we will go.
What do we care for you — you, only a whore?
Starve if you like! You'll have to end it sometime.
There will be plenty more.
Sell your hangings, pawn your dress, your ear-rings.
What do we care? You knew we wouldn't pay.
That's right, cry! It'll make you feel much better, —
Meanwhile, we go our way . . .

The lamps are turned out on the music racks,
The concert ends, the people rise,
The applause behind us roars like rain on a roof,
The great doors close. We shrink beneath blue skies.
Was this a music? Or did I hear a story?
Yet I remember well that hair, those eyes . . .

And much besides, that, nimble even as music,
Sings, flashes, is gone . . .
For a million years the gods have been telling me secrets.
I do not remember one.

PART II

1

Let us succumb to this soft blue wave of music:
Endure its pressure, let it explore our souls,

Inquisitive, cold, and strange.
We will pay no heed to a plaintive bell that tolls
Far over our heads, in sunlight . . . forever restless . . .
But yield our depths to the silent flow of change.

Here all is dark, all leans upon the stream.
Here we may flow from opiate sound to sound,
Embodied in music. Here we may live our dream.
Here is no striving, no choosing. We do not know
Whither we drift, but shut our eyes and go.

I have surrendered my heart to chords of sound,
Sweet successions of falling sound;
A star is snared in sinister boughs of twilight
Against a pale green sky.
I have surrendered my soul to a pleading music;
I drink a poison of melody and I die.

Here are hands I reached from the dust to touch,
Eyes I loved in the darkness and left behind,
Here, unforgotten mouths I never kissed.
I tried with hands to brush aside a mist . . .
Come, let us flow with the music, and seek, and find.

Once I loved; and once I died; and once
I murdered my lover, my lover who had betrayed me.
Once I stepped from the threshold, and saw my body
Huddled in purple snow.
Once I escaped my flesh and rose on starlight.
The theme returns. We bow our hearts and go.

One night, I swam with pilgrims by the moon,
Swam by moonlight in a wide blue river;
A field of flax in flower.
I drowned among the stalks, the tossing stars.
I breathed green foam. I was covered with seethe of leaves.

But who was he I left behind me, waiting
There on the platform, reading an evening paper?
He looked up once, to see if it would rain.
Great leaves are turned between us. Moons are scattered.
The theme recurs . . . And we drift on again.

2

If we should rise from whirl to silver whirl,
Through yellowing light to a faintly chiming surface,
And shatter the film . . . what discords should we hear?
Monstrous shadows blot and disintegrate;
The stars above our earth are cold and clear;

And we walk, as we have walked a thousand times,
Past trees and curbs and gutters,
Mark how the arc-lamp dims and starts and sputters,
Muse bewitching scandals, ponder crimes,
Laugh with a friend, concealing what we think,
Or sit, to chat and drink.

Someone has been to have his fortune told —
With Tarot cards. The pentacles and wands
Tell him he hates the women, and is cold.
He laughs, we laugh, — we wonder if he lies,
Watching a wizened question in his eyes.

And if he lies, and if last night he slept
With some flushed harlot, or his latest lover,
We muse upon him, and marvel what it is
That yields his banal soul these ecstasies:
Is it his voice that sets a woman trembling,
The hesitant speech, the sidelong trick of eyes,
The heavy brow, the dead white skin?
Or is he all the while dissembling, —
Like us, though starved, incapable of sin?

We chronicle his speech, and afterwards
Confer upon him . . . We ravel out his brain.
We have remembered certain curious words
He uttered once when drinking: these explain . . .
Priests of dissection are we: we dissect him.
It is ourselves have pain, but pleasant pain.

And so, good-night. The white clouds gulf the stars,
Dust blows down the street,
Through divers moonlit canyons glide our feet.

3

Before us ghostly paths flow into the darkness,
Slant upon windy darkness, weave and gleam.
Or are they climbs of music, half-remembered?
Or do we gaze at some unsteady dream?

This is the night for murder: Get us knives:
We have long sought for this.
What queen, tonight, is murdered with a kiss?
What kings tonight shall forfeit their rash lives?
Rosamund, with a red skull in her hands;
Helen in starlight, watching beacons flare;
Or Cleopatra, combing her blue-black hair . . .

She lies before me, smiling. She has betrayed me . . .
Her flesh was sweeter to me than orange-blossoms,
Her hair more marvellous to me than night.
Her voice was a breaking of golden ripples,
I stood in her eyes as in a sea of light.
I loved her for all these things . . . But she has betrayed me.
Tell them to play loud music in the hall —
Blow horns, beat drums, and strike on brass . . .
No one shall hear us now. We are hidden in tumult.

I would remind you of our wedding-night,
Of the sweet music we listened to through love . . .
But you demur, just as I hoped: you say
'Why talk of that?' — pretending modesty;
And sigh, and drop your eyes . . . Yes, you remember
My mouth upon your eyelids, and it disgusts you.
For now you have found a mouth you desire much more.

This purple silk that suits your throat so well —
(How I have loved that throat! It dazzles me.)
And these jade scarabs trembling from your ears:
Do you remember when I gave them to you?
And how you clung to me?
And do you remember dropping from your hair
White hyacinth flowers? . . .

No, you are musing — you stare, but do not see:
Your eyes are fixed upon the foolish fountain;
You seem to listen: hearing whose voice, I wonder?

I would remind you of the day we walked
Beside the river, twisting each other's hands —
Queer, what a pang can be in the flesh of hands! —
And saw white pigeons flying across the water,
And golden flakes of light dancing in azure,
And broad pale streams of sun poured down the west.
We were both young. The world lay luminous:
Every petal and cobweb trembled music . . .
Do you remember — or is this commonplace?
And do I — perhaps — touch things you would forget?

You guess I am angry — I have betrayed myself.
You open your eyes, startled, a little wider —
Things are unfolding here you did not dream of.
Do you divine the virgin knife, perhaps . . . ?
What was I going to say . . . O yes, the time
I saw you first . . . so many years ago . . .

My God, how innocent your eyes looked, too! —
All in white, by the palace door, you stood,
Talking with some young thing,
Until you saw me come, and turned your head
In an absent way to dart my eyes with yours . . .
There was your whole soul in that little trick —
I could not see it, then . . . I see it now.

Why has the music stopped? I gave no order.
Let it continue. Not the strings,
But horns and drums. And gnashing of brass . . .

They say young what's-his-name — you know, the captain —
Has come to town again. O, don't you know him?
I thought you did. But then, it's no great matter.
His quarters are not so spacious as they were,
And somewhat dark . . . And yet he was reputed
A man of fabulous wealth! And many ladies,
(Or so they say,)
Wear costly favors from him — rings and bracelets —
Why do you hide your hand? — and such-like trifles.

You are pale. I have mentioned something that concerns you.
Was it this captain? . . . I hope you notice
I use the past tense, now, in speaking of him.
Yes, it's a pity — he was full of promise —
Quick of eye, though somewhat tardy of arm . . .
And think of all the ladies with broken hearts!

Sit still, my dear. It's no use running now.
You guess my purpose: and, surely, you give me credit
For planning all details with scrupulous care!
The doors are locked — the curtains drawn across them —
No one would hear you if you beat upon them.
And even if you could scream, in so great terror,
Could you scream louder than horns and cymbals and gongs?

You should have been a player, and played to music.
How well you mimic horror! Your stretched eyes
Almost persuade me that you understand me.
Now, will you take death quietly, — or with struggle?
Take my advice: let it be soft and certain —
Surrender to it, make it a suicide —
A slow thin push at the heart, and then, red darkness.

This is a pity: I loved you. I will not blame you,
Now that it's all too late.
This little knife, for the moment, is my tongue.
But we were happy, in our season, —
And it is you who shaped this end.

Here's my knife — between my fingers I press it,
And into the panic heart . . .
Do you still hear the music? Do you still see me?
Do wide lights swim and dazzle before your eyes?

Make haste, great queen! The darkness opens for you . . .
Now they can stop their music. I am tired.
Shall I withdraw the knife, — or leave it there?

4

We move in the music, and are one with it.
You close your eyes, your fan against my arm.
Sometimes, I have thought this tongue of yours had wit.

But are you real, in spite of lips and eyes,
And the webbed hair translucent against the light —
You, who upon this music fall and rise?

What would you say if as we smoothly turn
To the slow waltz that beats these walls, this floor;
Or as we wave past palm-trees through the door;
If I should mildly observe, as commonplace,

'Yes, I murdered my wife this afternoon' . . .
Would you think me out of tune?

My hands are red with murder, if you could see them —
Or were they certain hands inside my brain?
It is difficult to explain . . .
Two lovers, once, went walking beside a river:
There was a white cloak and a wet red stain . . .

And a blade comes gliding in along the music,
Between the pulses. — What becomes of it?
Does it only cut the page, — or pierce a heart? . . .
The hypocritical music sighs and turns.
It murmurs of palms, of artificial ferns.

And now there are horns and drums, they strike on silver,
Cymbals are smitten, great gongs clang:
It is as if they did it to drown a murder.
They deafen the air with clamor, they hide a scream . . .
Do I dance or murder now? Or do I dream?

No, this was real, this murder — she is there,
Lying among her roses where I left her,
With her eyes closed and a pale rose in her hair . . .
And you, with whom I dance, — or think I dance, —
Thin out and vanish like sound upon still air.

5

This dust I softly blow across my hand,
Fibreless now, was the soft woven fragrance
She threw about her throat as evening came.
Here are the rings. Here is a comb of amber.
Here, the small silver plate that tells her name.
There is no trace of blood, here in the dust —
No trace of violence. Dust is most discreet.
All that is hinted is sedate and sweet.

A goblin-ring of junipers marks the place —
Half way up the hillside. I remember
How white, beside the juniper, was her face . . .
There is a graveyard look to juniper —
Furtive and sinister.
It sidles out of the graves to keep an eye
On the black crows that caw beneath this sky.

There is no need that murder should be known.
Murderers are foolish. In their panic,
They leave a scarf, a handkerchief, a knife,
The newly purchased pistol, on the floor —
And leaving this, of course, they leave much more.

Once, I killed a priest, before his altar,
With his own crucifix —
Smashed through a stained glass window, in the moonlight,
To steal the silver chalice, the candlesticks . . .
They tracked my footsteps through the snow,
I heard them coming, and hid in a door —
And I struck one down with the heavy candlestick,
But what was one to four? . . .
The rest is vague. I saw it long ago.

And once I murdered, by the waterfront:
A drunken sailor, in a peg-house brawl.
We were all drinking, and laughing, and having a love-feast,
And somehow got to quarreling after a while.
Maybe it was jealousy — I don't know.
But all of a sudden this boy went red with rum,
I saw his little eyes shut up and burn,
'By God,' he says, 'I'll fix you!' — He pulls a knife
And runs for me, with his slavering mouth wide open.

All the rest were lying around the floor
Half soused, and naked, and all too scared to help.
In the smoky light I jumped across pale bodies,

Stepped on somebody's hand and heard him yell,
Tripped over somebody's leg, went sprawling headlong,
But somehow managed to get behind a table
Just before he reached me. I grabbed the lamp,
One of those heavy glass ones, and let him have it
Smash in the forehead. And he dropped without a whimper.
It crushed his brain in, oh it was something awful! . . .
No one, not even his mother, would have known him.
So we just slipped him quietly off the wharf
Into the river, and that was the end of it.

And then, before I came to peg-house pimping, —
Or was it after? Time is confusing me,
Time is a circle, a snake that devours itself . . .
For a moment I peer up closely into starlight,
For a moment I walk once more a lamplit street,
See all things clearly out of time and space.
I smoke, and narrow my eyes to meditate,
Hear music swell and die, see coffins pass,
Watch the blown daisies bend upon the grass,
Glide through revolving doors to walk on marble,
To listen amused to the swift uneven footfalls,
Or the complaints of violins hidden in walls;
To climb at last to a little dingy room,
Three flights up or more,
And listen, through the loneliness and gloom,
To the drowsy footfalls of the tired day
Monotonously ebb and ebb away
Into the smouldering west;
And hear the dark world slowly come to rest . . .

And then, before I came to peg-house pimping,
Or maybe afterwards — what does it matter?
This happened; well, it must have been before . . .
I smell the circus smell — the stale rank sawdust,
Hear elephants snorting dust and straws;
I see once more the chariots rumbling round,

The red-mouthed clown, the enormous crowd applauding,
Trumpets blowing, greyhounds leaping through hoops;
And I see my wife, in spangles, with a whip in her hand,
Chivvying sullen leopards to their cages.

She left me, because she liked the red-mouthed clown.
Both of them quit the circus; and for years
I hunted for them, swearing I'd kill them both.
I went on day by day, doing my stunt, —
The dive of death, — as if it hadn't happened:
Twice a day I took the Dive of Death,
Falling a hundred feet to a little net.
And all the while I nursed my grievance, and waited.

At last I found them: they were still living together,
Drinking and starving there, with a boy and a girl.
On a bright Sunday noon I went and found them.
I knocked on the door. 'Come in!' she said . . .
And there she was, feeding bread to a parrot,
Thin, but looking the same; and there was he
Rocking his head on a scarlet table-cloth,
Silly with beer. 'Well, here I am, Marie!' —
She screamed, and half got up. The boy and girl
Came running in, they grabbed me round the legs.
'Harry!' she gasped, the tears rolled down her cheeks,
Her face grew redder and redder, she began to gurgle;
But I locked my hands around her dirty throat,
And though they bit me, I choked her till she was dead.

Her man looked up, and waved a hand toward me,
And fell asleep again. I took the children
And flung them down from the balcony to the courtyard:
I suppose I shouldn't have done it. Then I climbed
Up on the railing, and folded my arms, all ready
For one last Dive of Death. And there they got me . . .
Those damned fool neighbors heard the children screaming,
And spoiled the climax. And so they marched me off

Through Sunday streets, with people coming from church,
And bells tolling, and the May sun shining;
For the last time I walked under elm-trees and oak-trees,
And saw the grass, and the shadows of pebbles, and people.
But I had paid her out, as I said I would . . .
So what did I care? My hands were satisfied . . .

6

Wind blows: the dying music recedes from me;
The shadows of trees revolve and melt in the wind;
And papers skip and pirouette over the grass.
The lamps are lighted, the sea-gulls drift to sea,
Night falls with a shrill of horns; or is it daybreak?
Realities fade; dreams come; and dreams pass.

No matter how swift I run, the stars run with me . . .
Let us lounge in a bright café and listen to music,
Music, treading the smoke of cigarettes.
For years I have borne in my heart a burden of hatred . . .
Vermouth, then coffee . . . how much should we tip the waiter?
Here the fatigued mind wanders and forgets.

PART III

1

Now that the sun flows over the edge of the hills,
Over blue peaks of dream,
And brightly again down into the frosted meadows,
We hear young maidens singing, and silently watch them
Dance in the sharp light, wheeling their long blue shadows . . .

This is as if in the drowse of noon,
White petals trembled down from the boughs of heaven.
We stretch our hands, we close our eyes, we lift our faces;
The fall of the sun is a poured music.

This is as if, in the going of twilight,
When skies are pale and stars are cold,
Dew should rise from the grass in little bubbles,
And tinkle in music among green leaves.

Something immortal lives in such an air —
We breathe, we change.
Our bodies become as cold and bright as starlight,
Our hearts grow young and strange.

Let us extend ourselves as evening shadows
And learn the nocturnal secrets of these meadows.

2

Some have wedded sea-girls and lived in the sea,
Hearing the whisper of surf far over their hands,
And tuned their loving
To green and purple twilight, lazily moving
On the cold sway of tides;
Watching the little fish blow bubbles and sands;
And the ships passing, like dark clouds, silently.

And I was one of these, but wearied of it,
Of the faint laughter, and the ghostly speech,
And so in the moonlight I climbed the pebbled hill,
And stood up, startled, on a sunlit beach . . .
I remember her glaucous eyes, her long cool fingers,
And the pale mouth, and the sad white face —
And her voice, thinly singing, an elfin music
Heard in an elfin place . . .
But that was long ago. I do not remember
What was her name, or why it was that I loved her.

Some are moonstruck, and love a demon woman;
And wander the world forever after
Hearing an echo of marvelous laughter:

These are pale, as who have seen holy things,
They stumble on stones,
Their eyes are forever startled by knowledge of wings . . .
My blood was tranced at night by the palest woman,
But when I kissed her the blood in my veins went cold,
Her mouth was as cold as the sea.
Among the leaves she rose like fire;
Her eyes were phosphor: her cold hands burned.
But when the red sun clanged she fell from me,
She fell from my lips with an anguished cry,
And a jewelled snake I saw her lie
Wreathing her sluggish ashes in green grass beaded with dew,
Her little eyes red in the sun.
My heart lay dead when I saw the thing I had done,
And I struck at the wind, I ran in the dark,
I kissed the huge hands of time, I laughed at rain;
For I who had loved a lamia, well I knew
I should never again love a mortal, or see her again . . .

Grey ghosts move in the lamplight: these are dreams.
Turn back the page, strike a profounder chord,
We will resolve these phantoms in clear fire.
Our spirits have ridden abroad.
Far off, we hear the gallop of demon desire.

3

As one who dreams, in a light sleep, may hear
Sounds through his dream, — bells, or passing steps
On the floor above him, or in the street below, —
Rhythmic, precise and clear:
Or voices muttering in an adjacent room,
Lifting a moment, to die again; —
Yet all the while he will pursue his dream,
Guessing a sinister purport in well-known sounds,
And still in his own deep silent world remain:
So now I guess the world from which I came,

In flares of light, ghosts of remembered sound,
Which haunt me here . . . A voice, a street, a bell . . .
Whence do I come, and why? And what's my name?

And you, who cut an orange upon a plate,
With a small silver knife, and lean, and smile, —
You whose mouth is a sly carnivorous flower,
Whose flesh is softer and cooler than rainy wind, —
I gaze upon you, and muse strange aberrations,
I hear unearthly music, ghostly flutes;
I dance in a black eclipse, and through my veins
Is a cold froth of sea; and you are forgotten . . .

And you, who when your act is over peer
Witchlike between the curtains, above the footlights,
Holding the curtains with jewelled hands, to smile
A slow and mordant smile from cavernous eyes —
What hideous things amuse you secretly?
What have you drunk to make your lips so red?
And when the moon creeps up, and stars dance coldly,
And crickets cry in the dew, and dead leaves fall,
Do you spread bat-wings from a starlit wall? . . .

Music dissolves and dies, — and sings again,
Changing its mood; the lights wink out in darkness,
A shrill wind crosses us, we are blown and stagger.
Our footsteps ring intense. The lights return.
And we have silently changed . . . To what, to whom?

4

Midnight it was, or just before;
And as I dipt for the hundredth time
The small white quill to add a rhyme
To the cold page, in candlelight,
Whereon my treatise slowly grew, —

Someone harshly knocked at the door;
And marvelling I became aware
That with that knock the entire night
Went mad; a sudden tempest blew;
And shrieking goblins rode the air.

Alarmed, not knowing why, I rose
And dropt my quill across the page.
What demon now, what archimage,
So roiled the dark? And my blood froze
When through the keyhole, with the wind,
A freezing whisper, strangely thinned,
Called my name out, called it twice . . .
My heart lay still, lay black as ice.
The candle trembled in my hands;
Between my fingers the dim light went;
Shadows hurried and shrank and blent,
Huddled, grotesque, in sarabands,
Amazed my eyes, till dumb I stood,
And seemed to see upon that air
Goblins with serpents in their hair,
Mouths contorted for soundless cries,
And hands like claws, and wounded throats,
And winking embers instead of eyes.
The blood went backward to my heart.
Thrice in the night a horn was blown.
And then it seemed that I had known,
For ages, even before my birth,
When I was out with wind and fire,
And had not bargained yet with earth,
That this same night the horn would blow
To call me forth. And I would go.
And so, as haunted dead might do,
I drew the bolt and dropped the chain,
And stood in dream, and only knew
The door had opened and closed again:

Until between my eyelids came
A woman's face, a sheath of flame,
The wink of opals in dusky hair,
A golden throat, a smile like fire,
And eyes that seemed to burn the air
So luminous were they with desire.
She laid one hand upon my arm
And straight a blaze was in my veins,
It pierced me so I feared a charm,
And shrank; whereat, pale, hurriedly,
She whispered 'Quickly! Come with me!
All shall be clear! But now make haste —
Four hours till dawn, no time to waste!' —
The amazing whiteness of her skin
Had snared my eyes, and now her voice
Seethed in my ears, and a ghost of sin
Died, and above it I heard rejoice
Loud violins, in chords ascending,
And laughter of virgins; I blew the light,
And followed her, heedless of the ending,
Into the carnival of that night.

(Make haste, beloved! the night passes,
The day breaks, the cock crows,
Mist slinks away in the sunlight,
And the thin blood drips from the rose.)

Black stallions rushed us through the air,
Their hooves upon the wind struck fire;
Rivers, and hills, and a moonlit spire
Glided beneath us, and then a flare
Of gusty torches beckoned us down
To a palace-gate in a darkened town.
She took my hand and led me in
Through walls of basalt and walls of jade,
And I wondered, to hear a violin

Sweetly within that marble played.
I heard it sing, a wandering tone,
Imprisoned forever in that deep stone.

And then upon a couch we lay,
And heard invisible spirits play
A ghostly music; the candles muttered,
Rose-leaves trembled upon the floor,
Lay still, or rose on the air and fluttered;
And while the moon went dwindling down
Poisoning with black web the skies,
She narrowed her eyelids, and fixed her eyes,
Fiercely upon me; and searched me so
With speeding fire in every shred
That I, consumed with a witching glow,
Knew scarcely if I were alive or dead:
But lay upon her breast, and kissed
The deep red mouth, and drank the breath,
And heard it gasping, how it hissed
To mimic the ecstasy of death.
Above us in a censer burning
Was dust of lotos-flowers, and there
Ghosts of smoke were ever turning,
And gliding along the sleepy air,
And reaching hands, and showing faces,
Or coiling slowly like blue snakes,
To charm us moveless in our places . . .
But then she softly raised her head
And smiled through brooding eyes, and said
'O lover, I have seen you twice.
You changed my veins to veins of ice.
The first time, it was Easter Eve, —
By the church door you stood alone;
You listened to the priests intone
In pallid voices, mournfully;
The second time you passed by me

In the dusk, but did not see . . .'
Her whisper hissed through every vein
And flowered coldly in my brain . . .

I slept, how long I do not know;
But in my sleep saw huge lights flare,
And felt a rushing of wild air,
And heard great walls rock to and fro . . .
Make haste, beloved! The cock crows,
And the cold blood drips from the rose . . .

. . . And then I woke in my own room,
And saw the first pale creep of sun
Drip through the dewed shutters, and run
Across the floor, and in that gloom
Marvelled to find that I had slept
In robe and sandals, and had kept
One bruised white rose-leaf in my hand —
From whom? — and could not understand.

For seven days my quill I dipt
To wreathe my filigrees of script:
For seven nights, when midnight came,
I swooned, I swept away on flame,
Flew on the stallions of the air,
Heard goblins laugh, saw torches flare,
And all night long, while music mourned,
Hidden under the vibrant floor,
I heard the insidious voice implore,
As one who speaks from under the earth,
Imploring music, imploring mirth,
Before the allotted time was done
And cock crew up the sullen sun.
Day by day my face grew pale,
Hollowed and purple were my eyes,
I blinked beneath too brilliant skies:
And sometimes my weak hand would fail,

Blotting the page whereon I wrought . . .
This woman is a witch! I thought . . .
And I resolved that night to find
If this were real, or in my mind.

Viol and flute and violin
Remote through labyrinths complained.
Her hand was foam upon my skin.
And then I closed my eyes and feigned
A sudden sleep; whereat her eyes
Peered, and darkened, and opened wide,
Her white brow flushed, and by my side
Laughing, with little ecstatic cries,
She kissed my mouth, she stroked my hair
And fed upon me with fevered stare.
'One little drop!' she murmured then —
'One little bubble from this red vein,
And safe I await the sun again — '

I heard my heart hiss loud and slow;
A gust of wind through the curtains came;
It flapped the upright candle-flame.
Her famishing eyes began to glow,
She bared my arm; with a golden pin,
Leaned, and tenderly pricked the skin.
And as the small red bubble rose,
Her eyes grew bright with an evil light,
She fawned upon me; and my heart froze
Seeing her teeth so sharp and white.

Vampire! I cried. The flame puffed out.
Two blazing eyes withdrew from me.
The music tore discordantly.
The darkness swarmed with a goblin rout.
Great horns shattered, and walls were falling,
Green eyes glowed, voices were calling;
Stars above me paled in the sky,

Far off I heard one mournful cry —
Or under the earth — and then I found
I lay alone on leafy ground.
And when stars died, and the cock crowed,
The first pale gleam of sunlight showed
That it was on a grave I lay,
A new-made grave of sodden clay.

That night I took a priest with me;
And sharp at midnight, secretly,
By lantern-light, with spade and pick,
Striking on stones with metal click,
We laid a golden coffin bare,
And sprinkled the holy water there.
And straight we heard a sorrowful cry;
Something upon the air went by;
Far off, slowly, pealed a bell,
A voice sobbed, and silence fell.
And I grew sad, to think that I
Should make that marvelous spirit die.
Make haste, beloved! The night passes,
The day creeps, the cock crows,
Mist slinks away in the pale sun,
And the opened grave must close.

5

Vampires, they say, blow an unearthly beauty,
Their bodies are all suffused with a soft witch-fire,
Their flesh like opal . . . their hair like the float of night.
Why do we muse upon them, what secret's in them?
Is it because, at last, we love the darkness,
Love all things in it, tired of too much light?

Here on the lamplit pavement, in the city,
Where the high stars are lost in the city's glow,

The eyes of harlots go always to and fro —
They rise from a dark world we know nothing of,
Their faces are white, with a strange love —
And are they vampires, or do I only dream? . . .
Lamps on the long bare asphalt coldly gleam.

And hearing the ragtime from a cabaret,
And catching a glimpse, through turning doors,
Of a spangled dancer swaying with drunken eyes,
Applauded and stared at by pimps and whores —
What decadent dreams before us rise? . . .

The pulse of the music thickens, it grows macabre,
The horns are a stertorous breath,
Someone is dying, someone is raging at death . . .
Around a coffin they dance, they pelt dead roses,
They stand the coffin on end, a loud spring clangs,
And suddenly like a door the coffin uncloses:

And a skeleton leers upon us in evening dress, —
There in the coffin he stands,
With his hat in his white-gloved hands,
And bows, and smiles, and puffs at a cigarette.
Harlots blow kisses to him, and fall, forgotten,
The great clock strikes; soft petals drift to the floor;
One by one the dancers float through the door,
Hair is dust, flesh is rotten,
The coffin goes down into darkness, and we forget. . .

Who told us this? Was it a music we heard,
A picture we saw, a dream we dreamed? . . .
I am pale, I am strangely tired.
A warm dream lay upon me, its red eyes gleamed,
It sucked my breath . . . It sighed . . . It afflicted me . . .
But was that dream desired, or undesired?

We must seek other tunes, another fragrance:
This slows the blood in our hearts, and cloys our veins.
Open the windows. Show us the stars. We drowse.

Part IV

1

Twilight is spacious, near things in it seem far,
And distant things seem near.
Now in the green west hangs a yellow star.
And now across old waters you may hear
The profound gloom of bells among still trees,
Like a rolling of huge boulders beneath seas.

Silent as thought in evening contemplation
Weaves the bat under the gathering stars.
Silent as dew we seek new incarnation,
Meditate new avatars.
In a clear dusk like this
Mary climbed up the hill to seek her son,
To lower him down from the cross, and kiss
The pale wounds, every one.

Men with wings
In the dusk walked softly after her.
She did not see them, but may have felt
The winnowed air around her stir,
She did not see them, but may have known
Why her son's body was light as a little stone.
She may have guessed that other hands were there
Moving the watchful air.

Now, unless persuaded by searching music,
Which suddenly opens the portals of the mind,
We guess no angels,

And are contented to be blind.
Let us blow silver horns in the twilight,
And lift our hearts to the yellow star in the green,
To find perhaps, if, while the dew is rising,
Clear things may not be seen.

2

Under a tree I sit, and cross my knees,
And smoke a cigarette.
You nod to me: you think perhaps you know me.
But I escape you, I am none of these;
I leave my name behind me, I forget.

I hear a fountain shattering into a pool;
I see the goldfish slanting under the cool;
And suddenly all is frozen into silence.
And among the firs, or over desert grass,
Or out of a cloud of dust, or out of darkness,
Or on the first slow patter of sultry rain,
I hear a voice cry 'Marvels have come to pass, —
The like of which shall not be seen again!'

And behold, across a sea one came to us,
Treading the wave's edge with his naked feet,
Gently, as one might walk in a ploughed field.
We stand where the soft waves on the shingle beat,
In a blowing mist, and press together in terror,
And marvel that all our eyes might share one error.

For if the fisher's fine-spun net must sink,
Or pebbles flung by a boy, or the thin sand,
How shall we understand
That flesh and blood might tread on the sea-water
And foam not wet the ankles? We must think
That all we know is lost, or only a dream,
That dreams are real, and real things only dream.

And if a man may walk to us like this
On the unstable sea, as on a beach,
With his head bowed in thought —
Then we have been deceived in what men teach,
And all our knowledge has come to nought;
And a lit flame should seek the earth,
And leaves, falling, should seek the sky,
And surely we should enter the womb for birth,
And sing from the ashes when we die.

Or was the man a god, perhaps, or devil?
They say he healed the sick by stroke of hands;
And gave the sights of the earth to the blind.
And I have heard that he could touch a fig-tree,
And say to it, 'Be withered!' and it would shrink
Like a cursed thing, and writhe its leaves, and die.
How shall we understand such things, I wonder,
Unless there are things invisible to the eye?

And there was Lazarus, raised from the dead:
To whom he spoke quietly, in the dusk, —
Lazarus, three days dead, and mortified;
And the pale body trembled; as from a swoon,
Sweating, the sleeper woke, and raised his head;
And turned his puzzled eyes from side to side.

Should we not, then, hear voices in a stone,
Talking of heaven and hell?
Or if one walked beside a sea, alone,
Hear broodings of a bell? —
Or on a green hill in the evening's fire,
If we should stand and listen to poplar trees,
Should we not hear the lit leaves suddenly choir
A jargon of silver music against the sky? —
Or the dew sing, or dust profoundly cry? —

If this is possible, then all things are:
And I may leave my body crumpled there
Like an old garment on the floor;
To walk abroad on the unbetraying air;
To pass through every door,
And see the hills of the earth, or climb a star.

Wound me with spears, you only stab the wind;
You nail my cloak against a bitter tree;
You do not injure me.
I pass through the crowd, the dark crowd busy with murder,
Through the linked arms I pass;
And slowly descend the hill, through dew-wet grass.

3

They tell me John, at Herod's court, is dead:
John, with whom I talked beneath a plane-tree:
John, whose holy touch is on my head.

Herod, mark my words, you shall pay for this!
You shall forever yield to the dance of demons;
And see your grizzled head in a bowl of fire.

They say his loud voice crying from the cistern,
Calling the curse of God upon Herodias,
Troubled her night and day.
She heard his restless chain clank in the cistern.
In the night-time she heard him cry 'Adulteress!' —
And Herod heard him, and laughed; and the Roman captains;
And now he is dead, they say.

For in the banquet-room
The lovely Jewess crept and danced,
While he was drinking wine she came and danced.
Dance, Jewess! For much depends upon you:

And you shall be rewarded with something precious.
Behind the curtains Herodias quivers,
Her cruel eyes are narrowed upon you;
And Herod follows you through a cloud of wine.

There is no music in the banquet-room,
But the snores of sodden guests.
Dance, Jewess! Dance, Salome!
Beautiful are your hands, beautiful are your breasts.
You are young and lovely, your body is slender,
You waver like a running fire,
Herodias hates you, behind the tall curtain,
And Herod beams upon you through a cloud of desire.

She dances through the old heart of Herod,
Causing him great pain and sadness;
She draws the sap of longing into his veins;
She smiles, and he smiles too.
He trembles, watching the languor of her body,
Her cool deliberate feet.
And John is quiet, in the dark cistern,
Hearing above his head a rhythmic beat.

And now they have rewarded her with a precious thing —
She laughs, and carries it high upon her hands,
She dances with it, she weeps upon it —
She kisses the bloody hair.
She bears it before her on a bright salver,
She is pale with love, she dances slowly;
And Herod cries into his shaken wine-cup,
Cries, for giving the harlot a thing that is holy.

Dance, Jewess! Dance, white-kneed Salome!
Laugh or cry, what does it matter?
Your little mouth is red with the blood of a prophet;
The cry in the wilderness is on your platter.
Dust, too, arises over the desert and dances,

And sleeps again under a winter moon.
Salome, Herod, Herodias — you shall all perish,
You shall all be dust soon . . .

Sometime, I should like to see this Jewess, Salome —
She is fair, they say, and young.
Through her, things come to pass as prophesied:
God speaks with a strange tongue.

And so at the court of Herod, he is dead.
John, with whom I talked by an old plane-tree.
John, whose fiery hands are on my head.

4

You smoke with me: you do not think
That I have stood by Jordan's brink:
You talk with me, and do not guess
That I have power to curse or bless.
You think you know me, know my name,
Can tell me how and whence I came —
Is knowing to be so simple, then?
And am I one, or a million, men?

Brother Peter walked up and down
The cloister shade in a corded gown.
The fountain splashed by the blue yew trees,
And the sun was shot with glistening bees.
From hill to hill sang bell to bell,
The May sky dreamed; and softly fell,
Some in shadow, and some in sun,
Small Judas petals, one by one.

Brother Peter was sick with care,
His pulse rehearsed slow tunes of prayer.
His heart was like a yellowing leaf,
From bell to bell he turned his grief.

He did not see the bright drops spatter,
Nor Judas blossoms blow and scatter,
He did not see the bees weave by,
Nor sombre yews in the soft May sky —
But up and down his sandalled feet
Soft on the dustless flagstones beat.
And up and down his musings went
Weaving a pattern of discontent.

At Fiesole, betwixt bell and bell,
It was there the hideous thing befell;
Working there with Brother Paul
Pruning the vine-leaves on a wall.
Among the ghostly olive-trees
That shook like silver in the breeze,
A peasant girl came singing by,
Golden of skin and quick of eye,
She turned her cheek and glanced at him,
And straight he forgot his seraphim.
Fior di Ginestra — so she sang,
And yellow bloom in his grey heart sprang, —
Yellow blossoms were on his tongue
And this was May, and he was young.

He looked aside, but Brother Paul
Worked at the far end of the wall.
He looked again, and she had turned,
And smiled, and all his body burned.
And — Holy Mary! who taught him this?
Sudden he blew the girl a kiss.
Her brown feet flashed above the grass,
And through the gate he saw them pass —
She waved a hand, the gate went clang,
And *Fior di Ginestra* — so she sang.

He counted beads, he begged of Heaven
That so great sin might be forgiven;

But all, that seemed so simple there,
Turned, in the cloister, to despair.
He lit two candles of pointed flame
And sought to forget in work his shame:
Opened the marvellous manuscript,
Embossed with azure and gold, and dipt
His brush in gummy cups of paint
For the wings and aureole of a saint.
The bright hues swam beneath his eyes;
He shrank with horror to see arise
Her clear face there, her singing smile.
He dropped his brushes. This was vile.

He prayed and fasted. All night long
He knelt and prayed; until the song
Of birds in the cloister pierced his cell
With drowsy beams; and the matin bell.
All day he fasted, all day prayed.
Up and down, in the cloister's shade,
Slowly he paced, and did not see
How late sun sprinkled the blue yew tree.

Moonlight through the cell door came
And quivered its edges with pale blue flame.
But since the Christ had been betrayed
Was it enough that he fasted, prayed?
He took the thongs down from the shelf
And silent, in moonlight, scourged himself.

Said Brother Paul, 'Now what can ail
Our Brother Peter, who looks so pale?'
Slant eyes peered askance at him;
And sudden the columns reeled to swim —
They tilted and ran before his eyes
Low and brown along blue skies,
A flash of green, a gleam of white,
Paths and fountain. . . Then came night.

They laid his body beside the pool,
Where the yew tree shade spread blue and cool;
Into the spring they dipped their hands
Above the wavering pebbles and sands,
Lifted their eyes for Heaven's grace,
And bathed with silver the sleeping face.
They spoke in whispers, round him kneeling.
Lay brothers, through the garden stealing,
Dropping spade or pruning-hook,
Came to the fountain-side, to look.

An hour passed. And in the shade
Still he dreamed, while the Abbot prayed.
Bees in the Judas-blossoms clinging
Shook down petals, larks rose singing,
The noon was filled with bubbles of sound,
The pure sky dreamed, serene, profound.
And then at last his thin hands stirred, —
He raised his head, and spoke no word,
Looked round him with unknowing eyes,
And shrank, beneath too brilliant skies.
'Shall I be pardoned, Christ, for this?
I have betrayed you with a kiss.

'I alone of the chosen few
Was not of Galilee, they knew.
And so they came at dusk to me, —
In the garden, by a purple tree.
Thirty pieces of silver there,
Thirty glints in the twilight air —
Thirty silver whispers spoken, —
Master, forgive! my vows were broken.
I did not clearly know, I swear,
What thing it was I was doing there;
Nor did I guess from such soft breath,
That men like these could purpose death.

'O Master! When we supped that night
On the bare board by candle-light,
I knew your great heart had divined
The venomous secret in my mind.
For when you drank, and broke the bread,
It was to me you turned your head
Saying, with grave eyes, quietly,
"When you do this, remember me."
I was confused; I knew my sin;
The Pharisees and Sanhedrin
Cried in my veins. And so I rose,
Too weak to tell you all, I chose
To do the thing I was bought to do;
I brought them, led them in to you,
I marked you with the unholy kiss.
And I was paid with coins for this.

'Staves shall blossom in scarlet flowers,
And all dumb mouths have singing powers;
There shall be wedding of dust and sea
Before my soul is given me . . .
They come in the night with staff and sword,
They have wried his hands with hempen cord;
Through filthy streets they jostle him;
And all grows faint, and all grows dim.

'On Olivet we shrink. We see
The black procession to Calvary.
The soldiers sway with ripple of spears,
The trumpets cry, the rabble jeers.
Jesus is whipped for being slow,
The great cross pains his shoulder so.
Once he falls, though we hear no sound,
And lies unmoving on the ground;
And as he falls my soul falls too:
I am dazed, I know not what I do . . .

The little whip-lash flickers in sun,
My body feels the cool blood run,
The red welts ridge and sear my skin,
My eyes are blind with the blood of sin.
But a girl has lifted him a cup
He drinks, and again he staggers up.
I am spent with watching. I have no breath.
My body is stretched to verge of death.

'They have climbed the hill they call the Skull.
The crowd packs close . . . Hollow and dull,
The ominous mallet-strokes resound.
He is stretched out silent on the ground.
Far off, we hear the brass nails driven;
The sullen echoes knock at heaven.
Far off, three crosses toss and rise
Black and little against the skies.
One faint voice wails agony —
It was a thief, it was not He.

'He writhes his head from side to side.
O holy Christ I have crucified! —
I twist there on the cross with you;
And what you suffer I suffer too.

'Ravens gather: they blot the sun:
Out of the sky the light has run.
The orchards dim, the hill grows stark,
The earth rocks thrice in clamorous dark.
Great wheels rumble, and horses neigh;
Like mist the darkness rolls away.
The sun breaks forth. The birds again
Sing, as after a shower of rain.

'Blue in the gulf the clear stream flows
Through humid gardens of lily and rose.
Above the gardens, in terraces,

Are almond-trees, then olive-trees;
Above them all one tree, alone,
Stands in the sky. The blossom blown
Purples the ground, and purples the bough.
And there Death sings in the blossoms now.
I seek this blossoming leafless tree.
It shall forever be named for me.'

5

Twilight is spacious, near things in it seem far,
And distant things seem near.
Now in the green west hangs a yellow star;
And now across old waters you may hear
The profound gloom of bells among still trees,
Like a rolling of huge boulders beneath seas.

Peter said that Christ, though crucified,
Had not died;
But that escaping from his cerements,
In human flesh, with mortal sense,
Amazed at such an ending,
He fled alone, and hid in Galilee,
And lived in secret, spending
His days and nights, perplexed, in contemplation:
And did not know if this were surely he.

Did Peter tell me this? Or was I Peter?
Or did I listen to a tavern-story?
Green leaves thrust out and fall. It was long ago.
Dust has been heaped upon us . . . We have perished.
We clamor again. And again we are dust and blow.

Well, let us take the music, and drift with it
Into the darkness . . . It is exquisite.

PART V

1

As sometimes, in the playhouse,
While *pizzicati* shimmer, and lights are low,
And the hero pleads his love in the crude moonlight,
Or the villain staggers to shadows after a blow:
Suddenly through the quiet, from dark streets,
Through walls and doors a sound from the world is heard,
A shout, a piercing whistle, sharp and clear,
Or a horn, blown and echoing, or a loud cry, —
And the lovers and the blue moonlight seem absurd;
And the slow music, and the well-ordered words,
The flute-players with white hands, and the footlights, seem
Unreal and soundless as a dream:
So, as I follow silently through my mind
The devious paths that wind
Among old forests lamia-haunted,
Through silences enchanted,
Or into the glare and sound and vibrant dust
Of labyrinthine cities, among pale faces,
Among the glidings of uncounted eyes,
Wearing the fire of love, the tinsel of lust,
Singing in music, or uttering cries;
Dying in garrets to the dull tick of clocks;
Swinging in gaslit cellars from knotted ropes;
Catching with claws at illusory hopes;
Lying with perfumed harlots or picking locks; —
Measuring out the intolerable hours
In the strange secret hearts of those unknown,
To dive to slimy pavements from high towers,
Or walk abroad in the light of the stars, alone, —

So, in an instant, through this silent dream,
Sounds from the real world break, —

Suddenly I awake,
And hear familiar voices, just as though
I had dozed a second and missed a word or two.
I see the familiar street-lamps gleam,
Or find myself sitting, as long ago,
In the same café among the people I knew, —
With the same coffee before me, and between my fingers
The same slow cigarette consuming in smoke:
And in my ears an echo of music lingers,
And the sound of a dying sentence that someone spoke.

And I am amazed, I do not know
If this is I, who drink vermouth,
Or whether that was I who rode the air.
I fell to an outspread net; I stabbed my lover;
I kissed a vampire's hair . . .

Dreams, in the mind, move silently to and fro
As winds through the clear sky blow, —
I do not guess
Whence they come or whither they go.
A soft air, like a music, divides the smoke, —
The lazily shifting smoke of the cigarettes, —
We follow upon it; and the tired heart forgets . . .

Once I must have loved, for I remember
Seeing her white face, and the clear green eyes . . .
I followed her through the slanting silver of rain;
I followed the sound of her breathing through the darkness;
Till at last, and suddenly, she dissolved in the sunlight,
I was engulfed in a dazzle of silent skies.

Once, I stood by a curbstone in the moonlight,
A carriage stopped, a face leaned out;
The carriage was silvered and ghostly in the moonlight.
We sat together talking in intimate darkness,
The wheels murmured, the hooves beat;

Together we echoed alone down an infinite street.
And as the street-lamps slanted across her eyes,
And swam into darkness again through spear-like shadows,
She was shy, she laughed . . . But that was long ago.
And when I left her, or why, or who she was,
I never shall know.

I have climbed stairs with a candle between my palms
To seek the eternal secret behind a door.
I have struck matches and seen serene white faces.
Once in the darkness I heard her singing,
And followed the music into her heart;
Sometimes, I have found delight in secret places . . .
But ever I turn and turn, with my turning shadow,
Ever like smoke I am blown and spread and die,
Dissolved in the speckless brilliance of a sky . . .

Well, no matter; I die, but all dies with me;
The world reels out into silence;
The darkness of death comes suddenly over the sun.

2

Rhythms there are that take the blood with magic,
Smoothing it out in silver;
Rhythms there are that die in the brain's dark chambers
Like a blowing fragrance.
Yet through these rhythms laughter is always breaking,
We dream our dreams, but dream forever waking,
The elfin horns are silenced, the mouths we kissed
Are blown aside like mist.

Isolda, leaning among her coffee-cups,
Smiles at me.
Helen of Sparta, bearing a silver tray,
Laughs at me.

Isolda, I will meet you to-night in moonlight,
And praise your golden hair.
Helen, I will walk with you by the sea-waves
And kiss you there.

One leaned down from a balcony sweet with jasmine
To blow her kiss to me.
One over cobwebs danced in the cold of the moon.
One came late by the dark of a city wall.
By the dust of a new-made grave, one came too soon.

Fall, rhythms! Die, music! My lovers betray me —
They kiss me, and sing, but their brothers are creeping to slay me.
A darkness is in their eyes, foreboding death.
They have conspired with silence to suck my breath.
One ran into the pinewood, calling me after
With a wave of her hand:
One, with a soft hypocritical laughter,
Slid through the lips of the sand.
One ran lightly up silver ladders of rain;
I never saw her again.

Fall, rhythms! Die, music! For always, in moonlight,
Soon as I start to praise, and she to love,
The moonlight is shattered, the petals are blown away.
Darkness whistles between us, the music shudders,
The enchantment passes, the audience rises,
The curtain falls, the musicians cease to play.

And once more I must go,
As I have gone before a thousand times,
To a little dingy room: and light the gas
And read the evening paper; or at the window,
Observe the old moon, shining upon the rooftops;
Or watch, in the street, the lonely harlots pass.

3

The astrologer's red face slowly turned towards me
Against a blackboard figured with horoscopes;
An old man nodded; a woman sighed.
'Now here's a little blue-eyed girl in Virgo,
Loved by a syphilitic, twice her age . . .'
Among the ghostly stars a whisper died.
And as one walking down a corridor
Towards a lamplit mirror
Sees his own body, remote and small and dim,
Insubstantial and vague, come slowly nearer,
With equal steps, and fixed eyes always clearer,
Until at last it sharply faces him, —
So, in the darkness of that air,
He slowly became aware
That it was he who lay upon the bed
With a pillow beneath his head:
He suddenly faced his own identity,
He knew himself, grown old and tired and ill,
And saw the white spread flowing away in darkness,
Or into infinity.

He was tired: he wished to die.
If one could only, by an act of will,
Stop the sick heart forever! If one could only
Shake off this hideous sickness, like a dream! —
He was exhausted by thick vertigo:
Weary in every nerve, in every vein,
Of slow, exact, mechanical, measured steps.
The heights of curbstones stretched his chin to heaven.
The widths of puddles wedged his brain apart.
And he was compelled, even with eyes wide open,
To fight his way through jeering darkness,
To calculate on suddenly spreading oceans,
Scale monstrous cliffs of curbstone with one step:

And always, at the moment of his achievement,
Unwarily, he raised his eyes, —
Raised them, one second, from the relentless ground, —
And, suddenly, he went crashing down in chaos.

It was a pity if one who, like himself,
Clung with his naked nerves to the edge of the gulf,
Could not so rest his eyes on a little flower!
It was a pity if a black wind must come
And blow it away from him.
It was a pity, if, by some harsh enchantment,
Like some rank fog from the envious heart of the world,
A ladderless wall should silently rise between them.
It was true she was young, it was true he was twice her age,
It was true she was pretty, and not yet disillusioned,
That he was sick and old and might soon die, —
But because in his youth the fire of life had seared him, —
Was that a reason that all should be denied him?
Was that a reason the gods thought adequate?
No, not for this! —
She came, then, through the corridors of his brain,
Walking into a chamber cool and fair;
Her feet made music over the floors of his brain,
She exhaled a fragrance there;
She walked forever through the chambers of his brain,
With young blue eyes, white face, and yellow hair.

Why had the harlot been so importunate?
Why, against his will,
Had he so weakly consented to go with her?
He must have been tired, that night, he must have been lonely,
He must have been lonely and tired, or he'd never have done it . . .
She was lean and ugly, and vulgar in every fibre,
Her eyes were shallow and hard, her face was powdered,
She spat between kisses . . . And soon as their love was over
She left him to walk the streets.

And now the whole sick world in the nauseous darkness
Sprawled like a harlot's body, diseased and old;
And the darkness in which he struggled,
Seemed like the harlot's hair.
And as he tossed and turned and closed his eyes
He saw her horrible face before him rise,
Her lean red mouth, her pale consumptive cheeks:
He saw her lips just opening for a smile,
Malicious and slow and vile . . .
Wherever he turned, her face was there,
She smiled, and raised blue elbows to comb her hair.
And all this torture for that ambiguous pleasure!
And to be told he must not slake his fever
In the cool stream that sang before his feet!
That he must reel forever and grasp at nothing,
Dragged to a vortex on waves of oily heat!

Beyond this darkness, beyond this yellow darkness,
No doubt there was a world in which men laughed,
In which the grass was dusted blue with dew-fall.
No doubt there was a world in which girls sang,
And waited for their lovers to come by moonlight . . .
But was it not for him?

She came, then, through the corridors of his brain,
Walking into a chamber cool and fair:
Her feet made music over the floors of his brain;
She exhaled a fragrance there:
She walked forever through the chambers of his brain;
With young blue eyes, pale face, and yellow hair.
And he remembered, with peace, that she had said
She loved him. . . But would she love him when he was dead?

The astrologer's red face slowly turned towards me
Against a blackboard scrolled with horoscopes,
An old man nodded, a woman sighed.
'Now here's a little blue-eyed girl in Virgo . . .

Loved by a syphilitic. . .' A ghostly whisper
Floated among his deathless stars, and died.

4

You say, before the music starts, while still
Cacophonies of tuning drawl and mutter, —
Snarls of horns and cries of violins, —
That so-and-so has just divorced his wife,
That Paul is dead, leaving his work unfinished, —
And what's-her-name was hurried, secretly,
To an asylum. . . What says the music, then?. . .

Winds pour from the chattering south,
Warm foam crumbles along lava beaches,
Parrots are screeching green
In a sky of smouldering blue.
Dull broad leaves struggle against the sun.
And I am there, and you. . . .

You say, the time has come to make decisions, —
Question and vacillation must be ended:
Life is too short, and one must choose his way.
Laura was right in breaking her engagement.
They were all foolish to gossip as they did. . .
And wasn't it strange. . .

Shell-roads glare and shimmer,
Heat is trembling on scarlet rooftops,
Bland leaves stealthily creep and stare.
Let us go up among the pinewoods,
Let us go up the wind, it is cooler there;
Let us go slowly along hot yellow beaches
To where blue pinewoods lead us upward. . .

No, it was not good taste, to say the least. . .
So soon! With spring grass not yet sharp above him! —
And Helen said. . . And Beatrice said. . .

Sunlight tempers how subtly into moonlight!
Gold to silver, an alchemy of sound;
Rose to silence. . . And here we dream.
Green clouds slowly sway and revolve above us,
Blue clouds dilate and suddenly vanish,
Gold stars are swallowed or gleam.
Under these moving arches like ghosts we seem!
Are we real, or must we perish? —
We blow in the air, like leaves our words are blown. . .
Did you hear what I said? . . .
I said that I loved you, that we are alone. . .
A rushing of green clouds scatters the stars overhead,
A roar of waves has scattered my words.
I am running, silent, through nets of shadows,
I am caught in the shadows of branches.
I follow your face, but now it has paled and gone,
Like a ghostly reflection of the running moon. . .

As for friendship, you say, — can women know it?
No! it is always love, with women, or nothing. . .
There, you can see her now — she's turned her head:
And that's the latest way to arrange your hair.

Moonlight spreads how gorgeously into sunlight!
Blue rocks bask in the sun,
Dragon flies weave shuttles of blue through gold,
Up the green hill we run,
And lie in the dazzle, and watch the clouds
Swim in intense deep blue,
Dissolving, streaming, amassing coldly. . .
Golden is noon; golden are you;
Black bees cling and balance in goldenrod;
You laugh in the low-voiced grass,
Watching with lazy sun-filled eyes
Silent eternity streamed in the blue above you. . .
And you do not hear the blood in my brain that cries,
'I love you, I love you, I love you! . . .'

You say, that cello-player, with the black eyes,
Wrote music once, conducted symphonies,
Had great ambitions. . . He drank himself to this.
Poor fellow! Is that true? — And so good-looking!

5

Music from concertinas in an alley,
Tinkle of glasses through a swinging door,
And cats with cold green eyes:
I have seen it all a thousand times before.
A thousand nights have died as this night dies. . .
Take my arm, and come along with me.
We'll spend this night contentedly.
When the book is opened just put down —
Oh, any names, it doesn't matter! . . .
They ask no questions there; they know me there;
And follow me up the stair. . .

Take my arm! You aren't afraid of me? . . .
You wouldn't want to leave me, — would you dear?
Isn't it sweet, this warm June evening air!
This is the place, right here. . .

Turn the lights out. . . No? You want to see me?
Well, all right. Aren't you funny, though!
My hair is short because I've had a fever, —
It's just begun to grow.
That's a hair-net — haven't you ever seen one?
Haven't you ever loved a girl before?
Lovely! I never thought my breasts were lovely! —
This is a ring my father wore.

Most men — they're so indifferent; but you, —
You like me, don't you. You're so nice to me.
You look at me, somehow, as if you loved me. . .
Dear, take me with you somewhere by the sea.

We'll go in swimming and lie on the beach together,
And love each other all night through.
All I need is a pair of gloves, — and a feather
To trim my hat with, green or blue.

Your hands, touching my face, stroking my forehead, —
What is it they remind me of?
All sorts of things when I was young and little;
And the first time I fell in love. . .
Kiss me, dear. You kiss me as if you meant it.
Keep the ring — it's brass — to remember me by.
Don't forget to write me. Turn the lights out.
Soon as you've left, I'm going to sleep, — or try. . .

Now you've gone. And I'm alone once more,
Staring against the darkness;
As I have stared a thousand times before.
You walk through lonely streets in quiet moonlight.
You'll throw away the worthless ring I wore.
Where are you going? What will you see to-morrow?
Who will your lovers be?
How long, — I wonder, — will you remember me? . . .

6

Music from concertinas in an alley,
And cats with slow green eyes, —
A thousand nights have died as this night dies.
The stars dance out, the air blows warm to-night,
The girls are all in white.
Bargains are struck, they laugh, they glide away,
Some to love and some to lust.
In smoky lounges tired musicians play.
The harlot's slippers are grey with dust. . .

And now we turn towards a depth of sleep,
Tired of music, of lamps and cigarettes,
Tired of fevered faces.

Now let us seek a solitude, and rest
In dark and quiet places.

Let us go in through labyrinthine darkness
Seeking the strange cool secret of ourselves,
To stretch ourselves in soundless shadow, and sleep.
Let us go in through labyrinthine darkness.
Wind whistles. We are falling. The night is deep.

Who am I? Am I he that loved and murdered?
Who walked in sunlight, heard a music playing?
Or saw a pigeon tumbling down a wall?
Someone drowned in the cold floods of my heart.
Someone fell to a net — I saw him fall.

I have run in through earth and out again,
I have been under seas, among hot stars;
My eyes are dazzled; my feet are tired.
Someone hated me, and pursued, and killed me.
For a million years my body has been desired.

Tired of change, I seek the unmoving centre —
But is it moveless, — or are all things turning?
Great wheels revolve. I fall among them and die.
My veins are streets. Millions of men rush through them.
Which, in this terrible multitude, is I?

I hurry to him, I plunge through jostling darkness,
I think I see his face —
He's gone. And a sinister stranger leers at me.
Countless eyes of strangers are turned toward me.
Who's this that all our eyes are turned to see?

We look at him, but suddenly he has vanished,
We turn in the darkness, we murmur at one another,
We snarl with hatred, we strike, we kill, we run.
We whirl in the silence, become a soundless vortex.

We lift our idiot faces to the sun.
We flow together; we rage, we shout, we sing;
Pour and engulf; recoil, disgorge, and spring.

7

The walls of the city are rolled away;
And suddenly all the lighted rooms are bare,
Numberless gas-jets flare,
Thousands of secret lives, with unconcern,
Yawn and turn.
Men in their shirtsleeves reading papers,
Women by mirrors combing out their hair,
Children sleeping, old men dying,
The furtive lover half way up the stair;
And in tumultuous cabarets
And music-filled cafés,
Dancers among white tables slowly turning,
Face fixed on face with passionate yearning,
Following ever the interwreathing beat
With spellbound feet.
The old violinist, with white hair,
Leaves his music, tosses his arms in the air,
Snaps his fingers and sings;
Maenad maidens in bacchanalian dance
Follow as in a trance
With heads thrown back, shut eyes, and yearning throats
The menacing mournful notes.
The young man drinks and leans across the table,
Through clamor of music and hurrying feet
Desperate to repeat
What she, who lowers her eyes, has heard before;
And across his shoulder, while he has turned away,
She smiles to her lover who smiles beside the door. . .

Darkness descends, more walls are rolled away. . .
Sudden, they lower the curtain on the play. . .

A chorus-girl has fainted before the footlights;
She is hurried off, her child is born and dies,
In a hotel bedroom white and weak she lies,
While chorus-girls about her giggle and joke,
And the young men smoke,
And all are asking, 'Who was the father, dear?
No one will hear!' —

The sky above grows suddenly coppery red,
Sparks and smoke go up across the stars,
Wheels rumble, the men rush out of bars
To see great horses pass.
Thick flames burst from the windows and spout up walls,
The firemen's faces are white in the ghastly light,
A ladder is raised, up it a fireman crawls;
And suddenly with a roar the ladder falls
With the falling housefront into a storm of fire,
And the crowd shrieks, and presses back from the heat,
And the twisted flame spouts higher. . .
A woman had started to carry her child downstairs,
She was driven back by a gust of flame in her face,
They lay on the scorching floor to escape the smoke,
The child at last ceased crying,
She knew that her child was dead, that she herself was dying. . .
Peal, bells! Crash, walls! . . .
Into the quiet darkness at last it falls. . .
Policemen loiter along their beats
Through deserted streets.
And now, while the houses sleep,
The burglars scale the moonlit walls, or creep
Up cobbled alleys; doors are quietly forced,
Panes are cut and tapped, to fall with a chime,
Fitfully flits and falls
The nervous arc of light on floors and walls.
Safes are drilled, silver turns and glistens,
A whistle is blown, the night falls suddenly still,
Sweating the marauder listens,

Glides to the window-sill,
And under the watchful stars, at last, is gone.
And then over glimmering walls and waking streets,
Among grey ash-cans, creeping to numberless rooms,
Comes the cold soulless dawn.

8

Time. . . Time. . . Time. . .
And through the immortal silence we may hear
The choral stars like great clocks tick and chime.
Destiny, with inquisitorial eye,
Regards the jewelled movement of the sky.
And there alone, in a little lamplit room,
Immortal, changeless, in a changeless dream,
Forslin sits and meditates; and hears
The hurrying days go down to join the years.
In the evening, as the lamps are lighted,
Sitting alone in his deep world,
He meditates; and through his musing hears
The tired footfalls of the dying day
Monotonously ebb and ebb away
Into the smouldering west;
And hears the dark world slowly come to rest.
Now, as the real world dwindles and grows dim,
His dreams come back to him:
Now, as one who stands
In the aquarium's gloom, by creeping sands,
Watching the glide of fish beneath pale bubbles,
The bubbles briefly streaming,
Cold and white and green, poured in silver, —
He does not know if this is wake or dreaming;
But thinks to lean, reach out his hands, and swim. . .

The music weaves about him, gold and silver;
The music chatters, the music sings,
The music sinks and dies.

Who dies, who lives? What leaves remain forever?
Who knows the secret of the immortal springs?
Who laughs, who kills, who cries?

We hold them all, they walk our dreams forever,
Nothing perishes in that haunted air,
Nothing but is immortal there.
And we ourselves, dying with all our worlds,
Will only pass the ghostly portal
Into another's dream; and so live on
Through dream to dream, immortal.

III

The House of Dust

*

PART I

1

The sun goes down in a cold pale flare of light.
The trees grow dark: the shadows lean to the east:
And lights wink out through the windows, one by one.
A clamor of frosty sirens mourns at the night.
Pale slate-grey clouds whirl up from the sunken sun.

And the wandering one, the inquisitive dreamer of dreams,
The eternal asker of answers, stands in the street,
And lifts his palms for the first cold ghost of rain.
The purple lights leap down the hill before him.
The gorgeous night has begun again.

'I will ask them all, I will ask them all their dreams,
I will hold my light above them and seek their faces.
I will hear them whisper, invisible in their veins . . .'

The eternal asker of answers becomes as darkness,
Or as a wind blown over a forest,
Or as the numberless voices of autumn rains.

We hear him and take him among us, like a gust of music,
Like the ghost of a music we have somewhere heard;
We crowd through the streets in a dazzle of broken lamplight,
We pour in a sinister wave, ascend a stair,
With laughter and cry, word upon murmured word;
We flow, we descend, we turn . . . and the eternal dreamer
Moves among us like light, like evening air.

Good-night! Good-night! Good-night! We go our ways,
The rain runs over the pavement before our feet,
The cold rain falls, the rain sings.
We walk, we run, we ride. We turn our faces
To what the eternal evening brings.

Our hands are hot and raw with the stones we have laid,
We have built a tower of stone high into the sky,
We have built a city of towers.
Our hands are light, they are singing with emptiness.
Our souls are light; they have shaken a burden of hours.
What did we build it for? Was it all a dream?
Ghostly above us in lamplight the towers gleam.
And after a while they will fall to dust and rain;
Or else we will tear them down with impatient hands;
And hew rock out of the earth, and build them again.

2

One, from his high bright window in a tower,
Leans out, as evening falls,
And sees the advancing curtain of the shower
Splashing its silver on roofs and walls:
Sees how, swift as a shadow, it crosses the city,
And murmurs beyond far walls to the sea,

Leaving a glimmer of water in the dark canyons,
And silver falling from eave and tree.

One, from his high bright window, looking down,
Gazes over the rain-bright town,
And thinks its towers are like a dream.
The western windows flame in the sun's last flare,
Pale roofs begin to gleam.

Looking down from a window high in a wall
He sees us all;
Lifting our pallid faces towards the rain,
Searching the sky, and going our ways again,
Standing in doorways, waiting under the trees.
There, in the high bright window he dreams, and sees
What we are blind to, — we who mass and crowd
From wall to wall in the darkening of a cloud.
The gulls drift slowly above the city of towers,
Over the roofs to the darkening sea they fly;
Night falls swiftly on an evening of rain.
The yellow lamps wink one by one again.
The towers reach higher and blacker against the sky.

3

One, where the pale sea foamed at the yellow sand,
With wave upon slowly shattering wave,
Turned to the city of towers as evening fell;
And slowly walked by the darkening road toward it;
And saw how the towers darkened against the sky;
And across the distance heard the toll of a bell.

Along the darkening road he hurried alone
With his eyes cast down,
And thought how the streets were hoarse with a tide of people,
With clamor of voices, and numberless faces.
And it seemed to him, of a sudden, that he would drown

Here in the quiet of evening air,
These empty and voiceless places.
And he hurried towards the city, to enter there.

Along the darkening road, between tall trees
That made a sinister whisper, loudly he walked.
Behind him, sea-gulls dipped over long grey seas.
Before him, numberless lovers smiled and talked.
And death was observed with sudden cries,
And birth with laughter and pain.
And the trees grew taller and blacker against the skies
And night came down again.

4

Up high black walls, up sombre terraces,
Clinging like luminous birds to the sides of cliffs,
The yellow lights went climbing towards the sky.
From high black walls, gleaming vaguely with rain,
Each yellow light looked down like a golden eye.

They trembled from coign to coign, and tower to tower,
Along high terraces quicker than dream they flew.
And some of them steadily glowed, and some soon vanished,
And some strange shadows threw.

And behind them all the ghosts of thoughts went moving,
Restlessly moving in each lamplit room,
From chair to mirror, from mirror to fire;
From some, the light was scarcely more than a gloom:
From some, a dazzling desire.

And there was one, beneath black eaves, who thought,
Combing with lifted arms her golden hair,
Of the lover who hurried towards her through the night;
And there was one who dreamed of a sudden death
As she blew out her light.

And there was one who turned from clamoring streets,
And walked in lamplit gardens among black trees,
And looked at the windy sky,
And thought with terror how stones and roots would freeze
And birds in the dead boughs cry.

And she hurried back, as snow fell, mixed with rain,
To mingle among the crowds again,
To jostle beneath blue lamps along the street;
And lost herself in the warm bright coiling dream,
With a sound of murmuring voices and shuffling feet.

And one, from his high bright window looking down
On luminous chasms that cleft the basalt town,
Hearing a sea-like murmur rise,
Desired to leave his dream, descend from the tower,
And drown in waves of shouts and laughter and cries.

5

The snow floats down upon us, mingled with rain.
It eddies around pale lilac lamps, and falls
Down golden-windowed walls.
We were all born of flesh, in a flare of pain,
We do not remember the red roots whence we rose,
But we know that we rose and walked, that after a while
We shall lie down again.

The snow floats down upon us, we turn, we turn,
Through gorges filled with light we sound and flow.
One is struck down and hurt, we crowd about him,
We bear him away, gaze after his listless body;
But whether he lives or dies we do not know.

One of us sings in the street, and we listen to him;
The words ring over us like vague bells of sorrow.
He sings of a house he lived in long ago.

It is strange; this house of dust was the house I lived in;
The house you lived in, the house that all of us know.
And coiling slowly about him, and laughing at him,
And throwing him pennies, we bear away
A mournful echo of other times and places,
And follow a dream . . . a dream that will not stay.

Down long broad flights of lamplit stairs we flow;
Noisy, in scattered waves, crowding and shouting;
In broken slow cascades.
The gardens extend before us . . . We spread out swiftly;
Trees are above us, and darkness. The canyon fades.

And we recall, with a gleaming stab of sadness,
Vaguely and incoherently, some dream
Of a world we came from, a world of sun-blue hills.
A black wood whispers around us, green eyes gleam;
Someone cries in the forest, and someone kills.
We flow to the east, to the white-lined shivering sea;
We reach to the west, where the whirling sun went down;
We close our eyes to music in bright cafés.
We diverge from clamorous streets to streets that are silent.
We loaf where the wind-spilled fountain plays.

And, growing tired, we turn aside at last,
Remember our secret selves, seek out our towers,
Lay weary hands on the banisters, and climb;
Climbing, each, to his little four-square dream
Of love or lust or beauty or death or crime.

6

Over the darkened city, the city of towers,
The city of a thousand gates,
Over the gleaming terraced roofs, the huddled towers,
Over a somnolent whisper of loves and hates,

The slow wind flows, drearily streams and falls,
With a mournful sound down rain-dark walls.
On one side purples the lustrous dusk of the sea,
And dreams in white at the city's feet;
On one side sleep the plains, with heaped-up hills.
Oaks and beeches whisper in rings about it.
Above the trees are towers where dread bells beat.
The fisherman draws his streaming net from the sea
And sails toward the far-off city, that seems
Like one vague tower.
The dark bow plunges to foam on blue-black waves,
And shrill rain seethes like a ghostly music about him
In a quiet shower.

Rain with a shrill seethe sings on the lapsing waves;
Rain thrills over the roofs again;
Like a shadow of shifting silver it crosses the city;
The lamps in the streets are streamed with rain;
And sparrows complain beneath deep eaves,
And among torn leaves
The sea-gulls, blowing from tower to lower tower,
From wall to remoter wall,
Skim with the driven rain to the rising sea-sound
And close grey wings and fall.

. . . Hearing great rain above me, I now remember
A girl who stood by the door and shut her eyes:
Her pale cheeks glistened with rain, she stood and shivered.
Into a forest of silver she vanished slowly . . .
Voices about me rise:
Voices clear and silvery, voices of raindrops, —
'We struck with silver claws, we struck her down.
We are the ghosts of the singing furies . . .'
A chorus of elfin voices blowing about me
Weaves to a babel of sound. Each cries a secret.
I run among them, reach out vain hands, and drown.

'I am the one who stood beside you and smiled,
Thinking your face so strangely young . . .'
'I am the one who loved you but did not dare.'
'I am the one you followed through crowded streets,
The one who escaped you, the one with red-gleamed hair.'

'I am the one you saw to-day, who fell
Senseless before you, hearing a certain bell:
A bell that broke dark memories in my brain.'
'I am the one who passed unnoticed before you,
Invisible, in a cloud of secret pain.'

'I am the one who suddenly cried, beholding
The face of a certain man on the dazzling screen.
They wrote me that he was dead. It was long ago.
I walked in the streets for a long while, hearing nothing,
And returned to see it again. And it was so.'

Weave, weave, weave, you streaks of rain!
I am dissolved and woven again.
Thousands of faces rise and vanish before me.
Thousands of voices weave in the rain.

'I am the one who rode beside you, blinking
At a dazzle of golden lights.
Tempests of music swept me: I was thinking
Of the gorgeous promise of certain nights:
Of the woman who suddenly smiled at me this day,
Smiled in a certain delicious sidelong way,
And turned, as she reached the door,
To smile once more.
Her hands are whiter than snow on midnight water.
Her throat is golden and full of golden laughter,
Her eyes are strange as the stealth of the moon
On a night in June.
She runs among whistling leaves; I hurry after;
She dances over white-waved water;

Her body is white and fragrant and cool,
Magnolia petals that float on a white-starred pool.
I have dreamed of her, dreaming for many nights
Of a broken music and golden lights,
Of broken webs of silver, heavily falling
Between my hands and their white desire:
And dark-leaved boughs, edged with a golden radiance,
Dipping to screen a fire.
I dream that I walk with her beneath high trees,
But as I lean to kiss her face,
She is blown aloft on wind, I catch at leaves,
And run in a moonless place;
And I hear a crashing of terrible rocks flung down,
And shattering trees and cracking walls,
And a net of intense white flame roars over the town,
And someone cries; and darkness falls.
But now she has leaned and smiled at me,
My veins are afire with music,
Her eyes have kissed me, my body is turned to light;
I shall dream to her secret heart tonight . . . '
He rises and moves away, he says no word,
He folds his evening paper and turns away;
I rush through the dark with rows of lamplit faces;
Fire bells peal, and some of us turn to listen,
And some sit motionless in their accustomed places.

Cold rain lashes the car-roof, scurries in gusts,
Streams down the windows in waves and ripples of lustre;
The lamps in the streets are distorted and strange.
Someone takes his watch from his pocket and yawns.
One peers out in the night for the place to change.

Rain . . . rain . . . rain. . . we are buried in rain,
It will rain forever, the swift wheels hiss through water,
Pale sheets of water gleam in the windy street.
The pealing of bells is lost in a drive of rain-drops.
Remote and hurried the great bells beat.

'I am the one whom life so shrewdly betrayed,
Misfortune dogs me, it always hunted me down.
And to-day the woman I love lies dead.
I gave her roses, a ring with opals;
These hands have touched her head.

'I bound her to me in all soft ways,
I bound her to me in a net of days,
Yet now she has gone in silence and said no word.
How can we face these dazzling things, I ask you?
There is no use: we cry: and are not heard.

'They cover a body with roses . . . I shall not see it. . .
Must one return to the lifeless walls of a city
Whose soul is charred by fire? . . . '
His eyes are closed, his lips press tightly together.
Wheels hiss beneath us. He yields us our desire.

'No, do not stare so — he is weak with grief,
He cannot face you, he turns his eyes aside;
He is confused with pain.
I suffered this. I know. It was long ago.
He closes his eyes and drowns in death again.'

The wind hurls blows at the rain-starred glistening windows,
The wind shrills down from the half-seen walls.
We flow on the mournful wind in a dream of dying;
And at last a silence falls.

7

Midnight; bells toll, and along the cloud-high towers
The golden lights go out.
The yellow windows darken, the shades are drawn,
In thousands of rooms we sleep, we await the dawn,
We lie face down, we dream,
We cry aloud with terror, half rise, or seem

To stare at the ceiling or walls.
Midnight . . . the last of shattering bell-notes falls.
A rush of silence whirls over cloud-high towers,
A vortex of soundless hours.

'The bells have just struck twelve: I should be sleeping.
But I cannot delay any longer to write and tell you.
The woman is dead.
She died — you know the way. Just as we planned.
Smiling, with open sunlit eyes.
Smiling upon the outstretched fatal hand. . .'

He folds his letter, steps softly down the stairs.
The doors are closed and silent. A gas-jet flares.
His shadow disturbs a shadow of balustrades.
The door swings shut behind. Night roars above him.
Into the night he fades.

Wind; wind; wind; carving the walls;
Blowing the water that gleams in the street;
Blowing the rain, the sleet.
In the dark alley, an old tree cracks and falls,
Oak-boughs moan in the haunted air;
Lamps blow down with a crash and tinkle of glass.
Darkness whistles. Wild hours pass.

And those whom sleep eludes lie wide-eyed, hearing
Above their heads a goblin night go by;
Children are waked, and cry,
The young girl hears the roar in her sleep, and dreams
That her lover is caught in a burning tower,
She clutches the pillow, she gasps for breath, she screams . . .
And then by degrees her breath grows quiet and slow,
She dreams of an evening, long ago:
Of colored lanterns balancing under trees,
Some of them softly catching afire;
And beneath the lanterns a motionless face she sees,

Golden with lamplight, smiling, serene.
The leaves are a pale and glittering green,
The sound of horns blows over the trampled grass,
Shadows of dancers pass.
The face smiles closer to hers, she tries to lean
Backward, away, the eyes burn close and strange,
The face is beginning to change, —
It is her lover, she no longer desires to resist,
She is held and kissed.

Wind, wind, wind. . . Wind in an enormous brain
Blowing dark thoughts like fallen leaves.
It dashes the leaves on walls, it whirls then again;
And the enormous sleeper vaguely and stupidly dreams
And desires to stir, to resist a ghost of pain.

One, whom the city imprisoned because of his cunning,
Who dreamed for years in a tower,
Seizes this hour
Of tumult and wind. He files through the rusted bar,
Leans his face to the rain, laughs up at the night,
Slides down the knotted sheet, swings over the wall,
To fall to the street with a cat-like fall,
Slinks round a quavering rim of windy light,
And at last is gone,
Leaving his empty cell for the pallor of dawn.

The mother whose child was buried to-day
Turns her face to the window; her face is grey;
And all her body is cold with the coldness of rain.
He would have grown as easily as a tree,
He would have spread a pleasure of shade above her,
He would have been his father again.
His growth was ended by a freezing invisible shadow.
She lies, and does not move, and is stabbed by the rain.

Wind, wind, wind; we toss and dream;
We dream we are clouds and stars, blown in a stream:
Windows rattle above our beds;
We reach vague-gesturing hands, we lift our heads,
Hear sounds far off, — and dream, with quivering breath,
Our curious separate ways through life and death.

8

The white fog creeps from the cold sea over the city,
Over the pale grey tumbled towers, —
And settles among the roofs, the pale grey walls.
Along damp sinuous streets it crawls,
Curls like a dream among the motionless trees
And seems to freeze.

The fog slips ghostlike into a thousand rooms,
Whirls over sleeping faces,
Spins in an atomy dance round misty street lamps;
And blows in cloudy waves over open spaces.

And one from his high bright window, looking down,
Peers at the cloud-white town,
And thinks its island towers are like a dream.
It seems an enormous sleeper, within whose brain
Laborious shadows revolve and break and gleam.

PART II

1

The round red sun heaves darkly out of the sea.
The walls and towers are warmed and gleam.
Sounds go drowsily up from streets and wharves.
The city stirs like one in a dream.

And the mist ascends by dazzling walls and windows,
Where one by one we wake and rise.
We gaze at the pale grey lustrous sea a moment,
We rub the darkness from our eyes,

And face our thousand devious secret mornings.
And do not see how the pale mist, slowly ascending,
Shaped by the sun, shines like a white-robed prophet
Compassionate over our towers bending.

We descend our separate stairs toward the day,
Merge in the somnolent mass that fills the street,
Lift our eyes to the soft blue space of sky,
And walk by the well-known walls with accustomed feet.

2

More towers must yet be built — more towers destroyed —
Great rocks hoisted in air;
And he must seek his bread in high pale sunlight
With gulls about him, and clouds just over his eyes . . .
And so he did not mention his dream of falling
But drank his coffee in silence, and heard in his ears
That horrible whistle of wind, and felt his breath
Sucked out of him, and saw the tower flash by
And the small tree swell beneath him. . .
He patted his boy on the head, and kissed his wife,
Looked quickly around the room, to remember it, —
And so went out . . . For once, he forgot his pail.

Something had changed — but it was not the street —
The street was just the same — it was himself.
Puddles flashed in the sun. In the pawn-shop door
The same old black cat winked green amber eyes;
The butcher stood by his window tying his apron;
The same men walked beside him, smoking pipes,
Reading the morning paper. . .

He would not yield, he thought, and walk more slowly,
As if he knew for certain he walked to death:
But with his usual pace, — deliberate, firm,
Looking about him calmly, watching the world,
Taking his ease. . . Yet, when he thought again
Of the same dream, now dreamed three separate times,
Always the same, and heard that whistling wind,
And saw the windows flashing upward past him, —
He slowed his pace a little, and thought with horror
How monstrously that small tree thrust to meet him! . . .
He slowed his pace a little and remembered his wife.

Was forty, then, too old for work like this?
Why should it be? He'd never been afraid —
His eye was sure, his hand was steady. . .
But dreams had meanings.
He walked more slowly, and looked along the roofs,
All built by men, and saw the pale blue sky;
And suddenly he was dizzy with looking at it,
It seemed to whirl and swim,
It seemed the color of terror, of speed, of death. . .
He lowered his eyes to the stones, he walked more slowly;
His thoughts were blown and scattered like leaves;
He thought of the pail . . . Why, then, was it forgotten?
Because he would not need it?

Then, just as he was grouping his thoughts again
About that drug-store corner, under an arc-lamp,
Where first he met the girl whom he would marry, —
That blue-eyed innocent girl, in a soft blouse, —
He waved his hand for signal, and up he went
In the dusty chute that hugged the wall;
Above the tree; from girdered floor to floor;
Above the flattening roofs, until the sea
Lay wide and waved before him . . . And then he stepped
Giddily out, from that security,
To the red rib of iron against the sky,

And walked along it, feeling it sing and tremble;
And looking down one instant, saw the tree
Just as he dreamed it was; and looked away,
And up again, feeling his blood go wild.

He gave the signal; the long girder swung
Closer upon him, dropped clanging into place,
Almost pushing him off. Pneumatic hammers
Began their madhouse clatter, the white-hot rivets
Were tossed from below and deftly caught in pails;
He signalled again, and wiped his mouth, and thought
A place so high in the air should be more quiet.
The tree, far down below, teased at his eyes,
Teased at the corners of them, until he looked,
And felt his body go suddenly small and light;
Felt his brain float off like a dwindling vapor;
And heard a whistle of wind, and saw a tree
Come plunging up to him, and thought to himself,
'By God — I'm done for now, the dream was right. . .

3

The warm sun dreams in the dust, the warm sun falls
On bright red roofs and walls;
The trees in the park exhale a ghost of rain;
We go from door to door in the streets again,
Talking, laughing, dreaming, turning our faces,
Recalling other times and places.
We crowd, not knowing why, around a gate,
We crowd together and wait,
A stretcher is carried out, voices are stilled,
The ambulance drives away.
We watch its roof flash by, hear someone say
'A man fell off the building and was killed —
Fell right into a barrel. . .' We turn again
Among the frightened eyes of white-faced men,
And go our separate ways, each bearing with him

A thing he tries, but vainly, to forget, —
A sickened crowd, a stretcher red and wet.

A hurdy-gurdy sings in the crowded street,
The golden notes skip over the sunlit stones,
Wings are upon our feet.
The sun seems warmer, the winding street more bright,
Sparrows come whirring down in a cloud of light.
We bear our dreams among us, bear them all,
Like hurdy-gurdy music they rise and fall,
Climb to beauty and die.
The wandering lover dreams of his lover's mouth,
And smiles at the hostile sky.
The broker smokes his pipe, and sees a fortune.
The murderer hears a cry.

4

'Draw three cards, and I will tell your future.
Draw three cards, and lay them down,
Rest your palms upon them, stare at the crystal,
And think of time . . . My father was a clown,

My mother was a gypsy out of Egypt;
And she was gotten with child in a strange way;
And I was born in a cold eclipse of the moon,
With the future in my eyes as clear as day.'

I sit before the gold-embroidered curtain
And think her face is like a wrinkled desert.
The crystal burns in lamplight beneath my eyes.
A dragon slowly coils on the scaly curtain.
Upon a scarlet cloth a white skull lies.

'Your hand is on the hand that holds three lilies.
You will live long, love many times.

I see a dark girl here who once betrayed you.
I see a shadow of secret crimes.

'There was a man who came intent to kill you,
And hid behind a door and waited for you;
There was a woman who smiled at you and lied.
There was a golden girl who loved you, begged you.
Crawled after you, and died.

'There is a ghost of murder in your blood —
Coming or past, I know not which.
And here is danger — a woman with sea-green eyes,
And white-skinned as a witch. . .'

The words hiss into me, like raindrops falling
On sleepy fire. She smiles a meaning smile.
Suspicion eats my brain; I ask a question;
Something is creeping at me, something vile;

And suddenly on the wall behind her head
I see a monstrous shadow strike and spread,
The lamp puffs out, a great blow crashes down.
I plunge through the curtain, run through dark to the street,
And hear swift steps retreat.

The shades are drawn, the door is locked behind me.
Behind the door I hear a hammer sounding.
I walk in a cloud of wonder; I am glad.
I mingle among the crowds; my heart is pounding;
You do not guess the adventure I have had!

Yet you, too, all have had your dark adventures,
Your sudden adventures, or strange, or sweet.
My peril goes out from me, is blown among you.
We loiter, dreaming together, along the street.

5

Round white clouds roll slowly above the housetops,
Over the clear red roofs they flow and pass.
A flock of pigeons rises, blue wings flashing,
Rises with whistle of wings, hovers an instant,
And settles again on tarnished grass.
And one old man looks down from a dusty window
And sees the pigeons circling about the fountain
And desires once more to walk among those trees.
Lovers walk in the noontime by that fountain.
Pigeons dip their beaks to drink from the water.
And soon the pond must freeze.

The light wind blows to his ears a sound of laughter,
Young men shuffle their feet, loaf in the sunlight;
A girl's laugh rings like a bell.
But clearer than all these sounds is a sound he hears
More in his secret heart than in his ears, —
A hammer's steady crescendo, like a knell.
He hears the snarl of pineboards under the plane,
The rhythmic saw, and then the hammer again, —
Playing with delicate strokes that sombre scale.
And the fountain dwindles, the sunlight seems to pale.

Time is a dream, he thinks, a destroying dream;
It lays great cities in dust, it fills the seas;
It covers the face of beauty, and tumbles walls.
Where was the woman he loved? Where was his youth?
Where was the dream that burned his brain like fire?
Even a dream grows grey at last and falls.
He opened his book once more, beside the window,
And read the printed words upon that page.
The sunlight touched his hand; his eyes moved slowly,
The quiet words enchanted time and age.

'Death is never an ending, death is a change;
Death is beautiful, for death is strange;
Death is one dream out of another flowing;
Death is a chorded music, softly going
By sweet transition from key to richer key.
Death is a meeting place of sea and sea.'

6

She turned her head on the pillow, and cried once more.
And drawing a shaken breath, and closing her eyes,
To shut out, if she could, this dingy room,
The wigs and costumes scattered around the floor, —
Yellows and greens in the dark, — she walked again
Those nightmare streets which she had walked so often.
Here, at a certain corner, under an arc-lamp,
Blown by a bitter wind, she stopped and looked
In through the brilliant windows of a drug-store,
And wondered if she dared to ask for poison:
But it was late, few customers were there,
The eyes of all the clerks would freeze upon her,
And she would wilt, and cry. . . Here, by the river,
She listened to the water slapping the wall,
And felt queer fascination in its blackness:
But it was cold, the little waves looked cruel,
The stars were keen, and a dash of spray
Struck her cheek, and withered her veins. And so
She dragged herself once more to home, and bed.

Paul hadn't guessed it yet — though twice, already,
She'd fainted — once, the first time, on the stage.
So she must tell him soon — or else — get out.
How could she say it? That was the hideous thing.
She'd rather die than say it! and all the trouble,
Months when she couldn't earn a cent, and then,
If he refused to marry her . . . well, what?
She saw him laughing, making a foolish joke,

His grey eyes turning quickly; and the words
Fled from her tongue. She saw him sitting silent,
Brooding over his morning coffee, maybe,
And tried again . . . she bit her lips, and trembled,
And looked away, and said . . . 'Say Paul, boy, — listen —
There's something I must tell you . . .' There she stopped,
Wondering what he'd say. What would he say?
'Spring it, kid! Don't look so serious!'
'But what I've got to say — *is* — serious!'
Then she could see how, suddenly, he would sober,
His eyes would darken, he'd look so terrifying —
He always did — and what could she do but cry?

If it were Felix! If it were only Felix! —
She wouldn't mind so much. But as it was,
Bitterness choked her, she had half a mind
To pay out Felix for never having liked her,
By making people think that it was him.
She'd write a letter to someone, before she died, —
Just saying 'Felix did it — and wouldn't marry.'
And then she'd die. But that was hard on Paul.
Paul would never forgive her — he'd never forgive her!
Sometimes she almost thought Paul really loved her.
She saw him look reproachfully at her coffin.

And then she closed her eyes and walked again
Those nightmare streets that she had walked so often:
Under an arc-lamp swinging in the wind
She stood, and stared in through a drug-store window,
Watching a clerk wrap up a little pill-box.
But it was late. No customers were there, —
Pitiless eyes would freeze her secret in her.
And then — what poison would she dare to ask for?
And if they asked her why, what would she say?

7

Two lovers, here at the corner, by the steeple,
Two lovers blow together like music blowing:
And the crowd dissolves about them like a sea.
Recurring waves of sound break vaguely about them,
They drift from wall to wall, from tree to tree.
'Well, am I late?' Upward they look and laugh,
They look at the great clock's golden hands,
They laugh and talk, not knowing what they say:
Only, their words like music seem to play;
And seeming to walk, they tread strange sarabands.

'I brought you this . . .' the soft words float like stars
Down the smooth heaven of her memory.
She stands again by a garden wall,
The peach tree is in bloom, pink blossoms fall,
Water sings from an opened tap, the bees
Glisten and murmur among the trees.
Someone calls from the house. She does not answer.
Backward she leans her head,
And dreamily smiles at the peach-tree leaves, wherethrough
She sees an infinite May sky spread
A vault profoundly blue.
The voice from the house fades far away,
The glistening leaves more vaguely ripple and sway.
The tap is closed, the water ceases to hiss.
Silence . . . blue sky . . . and then, 'I brought you this . . .'
She turns again, and smiles. He does not know
She smiles from long ago.

She turns to him and smiles . . . Sunlight above him
Roars like a vast invisible sea,
Gold is beaten before him, shrill bells of silver;
He is released of weight, his body is free,
He lifts his arms to swim,
Dark years like sinister tides coil under him.

The lazy sea-waves crumble along the beach
With a whirring sound like wind in bells,
He lies outstretched on the yellow wind-worn sands
Reaching his lazy hands
Among the golden grains and sea-white shells.
'One white rose . . . or is it pink, to-day?'
They pause and smile, not caring what they say,
If only they may talk.
The crowd flows past them like dividing waters.
Dreaming they stand, dreaming they walk.

'Pink, — to-day!' — Face turns to dream-bright face,
Green leaves rise round them, sunshine settles upon them,
Water, in drops of silver, falls from the rose.
She smiles at a face that smiles through leaves from the mirror.
She breathes the fragrance; her dark eyes close.

Time is dissolved, it blows like a little dust:
Time, like a flurry of rain,
Patters and passes, starring the window-pane.
Once, long ago, one night,
She saw the lightning, with long blue quiver of light,
Ripping the darkness . . . and as she turned in terror
A soft face leaned above her, leaned softly down,
Softly around her a breath of roses was blown,
She sank in waves of quiet, she seemed to float
In a sea of silence . . . and soft steps grew remote.

'Well, let us walk in the park . . . The sun is warm,
We'll sit on a bench and talk . . . ' They turn and glide,
The crowd of faces wavers and breaks and flows.
'Look how the oak-tops turn to gold in the sunlight!
Look how the tower is changed and glows!'
Two lovers move in the crowd like a link of music,
We press upon them, we hold them, and let them pass;
A chord of music strikes us and straight we tremble;
We tremble like wind-blown grass.

What was this dream we had, a dream of music,
Music that rose from the opening earth like magic
And shook its beauty upon us and died away?
The long cold streets extend once more before us.
The red sun drops, the walls grow grey.

8

Well, — it was two days after my husband died —
Two days! And the earth still raw above him.
And I was sweeping the carpet in their hall.
In number four — the room with the red wall-paper —
Some chorus girls and men were singing that song
'They'll soon be lighting candles
Round a box with silver handles' — and hearing them sing it
I started to cry. Just then he came along
And stopped on the stairs and turned and looked at me,
And took the cigar from his mouth, and sort of smiled,
And said, 'Say, what's the matter?' and then came down
Where I was leaning against the wall,
And touched my shoulder, and put his arm around me.
And I was so sad, thinking about it, —
Thinking that it was raining, and a cold night,
With Jim so unaccustomed to being dead, —
That I was happy to have him sympathize,
To feel his arm, and leaned against him and cried.
And before I knew it, he got me into a room
Where a table was set, and no one there,
And sat me down on a sofa, and held me close,
And talked to me, telling me not to cry,
That it was all right, he'd look after me, —
But not to cry, my eyes were getting red,
Which didn't make me pretty. And he was so nice,
That when he turned my face between his hands,
And looked at me, with those blue eyes of his,
And smiled, and leaned, and kissed me —
Somehow I couldn't tell him not to do it,

Somehow I didn't mind, I let him kiss me,
And closed my eyes. Well, that was how it started.
For when my heart was eased with crying, and grief
Had passed and left me quiet, somehow it seemed
As if it wasn't honest to change my mind,
To send him away, or say I hadn't meant it —
And, anyway, it seemed so hard to explain.
And so we sat and talked, not talking much,
But meaning as much in silence as in words,
There in that empty room with palms about us,
That private dining-room . . . And as we sat there
I felt my future changing, day by day,
With unknown streets opening left and right,
New streets with farther lights, new taller houses,
Doors swinging into hallways filled with light,
Half-opened luminous windows, with white curtains
Streaming out in the night, and sudden music, —
And thinking of this, and through it half remembering
A quick and horrible death, my husband's eyes,
The broken-plastered walls, my boy asleep, —
It seemed as if my brain would break in two.
My voice began to tremble . . . and when I stood,
And told him I must go, and said good-night —
I couldn't see the end. How would it end?
Would he come back tomorrow? Or would he not?
And did I want him to — or would I rather
Look for another job? — He took my shoulders
Between his hands, and looked down at me,
And smiled, and said good-night. If he had kissed me,
That would have — well, I don't know; but he didn't.
And so I went downstairs, then, half elated,
Hoping to close the door before the party
In number four should sing that song again —
'They'll soon be lighting candles round a box with silver
     handles' —
And sure enough, I did.
And my eyes were filled with tears. And I was happy.

9

Noon. We sit at tables and sip our coffee,
We read the papers for tales of lust or crime.
The door swings shut behind the latest comer.
We set our watches, regard the time.

My eyes are worn with measuring cloths of purple,
And golden cloths, and wavering cloths, and pale.
I dream of a crowd of faces, white with menace.
Hands reach up to tear me. My brain will fail.

Here, where the walls go down beneath our picks,
These walls whose windows gape against the sky,
Atom by atom of flesh and brain and marble
Will build a glittering tower before we die.

The young boy whistles, hurrying down the street,
The young girl hums beneath her breath.
One goes out to vision, and does not know it.
And one goes down to death.

10

'Number four — the girl who died on the table —
The girl with golden hair — '
The purpling body lies on the polished marble.
We open the throat, and lay the thyroid bare.

One, who held the ether-cone, remembers
Her dark blue frightened eyes.
He heard the sharp breath quiver, and saw her breast
More hurriedly fall and rise.
Her hands made futile gestures, she turned her head
Fighting for breath; her cheeks were flushed to scarlet, —
And, suddenly, she was dead.

And all the wishes that hurried along her veins
Came to the darkness of a sudden wall.
Confusion ran among them, they whirled and clamored,
They fell, they rose, they struck, they shouted,
Till at last a pallor of silence hushed them all.

What was her name? Where had she walked that morning?
Through what dark forest came her feet?
Along what sunlit walls, what peopled street?

Backward he dreamed along a chain of days,
He saw her go her strange and secret ways,
Waking and sleeping, noon and night.
She sat by a mirror, braiding her golden hair.
She read a story by candlelight.

Her shadow ran before her along the street,
She walked with rhythmic feet,
Turned a corner, descended a stair.
She bought a paper, held it to scan the headlines,
Smiled for a moment at sea-gulls high in sunlight,
And drew deep breaths of air.

Days passed, bright clouds of days. Nights passed. And music
Murmured within the walls of lighted windows.
She lifted her face to the light and danced.
The dancers wreathed and grouped in moving patterns,
Clustered, receded, streamed, advanced.

Her dress was purple, her slippers were golden,
Her eyes were blue; and a purple orchid
Opened its golden heart on her breast.
She leaned to the surly languor of lazy music,
Leaned on her partner's arm to rest.

The violins were weaving a weft of silver,
The horns were weaving a lustrous brede of gold,

And time was caught in a glistening pattern,
Time, too elusive to hold.

Shadows of leaves fell over her face, — and sunlight:
She turned her face away.
Nearer she moved to a crouching darkness
With every step and day.

Death, who at first had thought of her only an instant,
At a great distance, across the night,
Smiled from a window upon her, and followed her slowly
From purple light to light.

Once, in her sleep, he spoke out clearly, crying,
'I am the murderer, death.
I am the lover who keeps his appointment
At the doors of breath!'

She rose and stared at her own reflection,
Half dreading there to find
The dark-eyed ghost, waiting beside her,
Or reaching from behind
To lay pale hands upon her shoulders.
Or was this in her mind?

She combed her hair. The sunlight glimmered
Along the tossing strands.
Was there a stillness in this hair, —
A quiet in these hands?

Death was a dream. It could not change these eyes,
Blow out their light, or turn this mouth to dust.
She combed her hair and sang. She would live forever:
Leaves flew past her window along a gust.

11

Snow falls. The sky is grey, and sullenly glares
With purple lights in the canyoned street.
The fiery sign on the dark tower wreathes and flares.
The trodden grass in the park is covered with white,
The streets grow silent beneath our feet.
The city dreams, it forgets its past to-night.

And one, from his high bright window looking down
Over the enchanted whiteness of the town,
Seeing through whirls of white the vague grey towers,
Desires like this to forget what will not pass,
The littered papers, the dust, the tarnished grass.
Deep in his heart old bells are beaten again,
Slurred bells of grief and pain,
Dull echoes of hideous times and poisonous places.
He desires to drown in a cold white peace of snow.
He desires to forget a million faces.

In one room breathes a woman who dies of hunger.
The clock ticks slowly and stops. And no one winds it.
In one room fade grey violets in a vase.
Snowflakes faintly hiss and melt on the window.
In one room, minute by minute, the flutist plays
The lamplit page of music, the tireless scales.
His hands are trembling, his short breath fails.

In one room, silently, lover looks upon lover,
And thinks the air is fire.
The drunkard swears and touches the harlot's heartstrings
With the sudden hand of desire.

And one goes late in the streets, and thinks of murder;
And one lies staring, and thinks of death.
And one, who has suffered, clenches her hands despairing,
And holds her breath.

And the new are born who desire to destroy the old;
And fires are kindled and quenched; and walls flung down.
The slow night whirls in snow over towers of slumbering vision,
And whiteness hushes the town.

PART III

1

You read — what is it, then that you are reading?
What pattern moves so silently in your mind?
Your bright hand turns the page.
I watch you from my window, unsuspected:
You move in an alien land, a silent age.

. . . The poet — what was his name — ? Tokkei — Tokkei —
The poet walked alone in a cold late rain,
And thought his grief was like the crying of sea-birds;
For his lover was dead, he never would love again.

Rain in the dreams of the mind — rain forever —
Rain in the sky of the heart — rain in the willows —
But then he saw this face, this face like flame,
This quiet lady, this portrait by Hiroshige;
And took it home with him; and with it came

What unexpected changes, subtle as weather!
The dark room, cold as rain,
Grew faintly fragrant, stirred with a stir of April,
Warmed its corners with light again,

And smoke of incense curled about this portrait,
And the quiet lady there,
So young, so quietly smiling, with calm hands,
Seemed ready to loose her hair,

And smile, and lean from the picture, or say one word,
The word already clear,
Which seemed to rise like light between her eyelids.
He held his breath to hear,

And smiled for shame, and drank a cup of wine,
And held a candle, and searched her face
Through all the little shadows, to see what secret
Might give so warm a grace.

Was it the quiet mouth, restrained a little?
The eyes, half-turned aside?
The jade ring on her wrist, still almost swinging?
The secret was denied,

He chose his favorite brush and drew three verses,
And slept; and as he slept
A dream came into his heart, his lover entered,
And chided him, and wept.

And in the morning, waking, he remembered,
And thought the dream was strange.
Why did his darkened lover rise from the garden?
He turned, and felt a change,

As if a someone hidden smiled and watched him . . .
Yet there was only sunlight there.
Until he saw those young eyes, quietly smiling,
And held his breath to stare,

And could have sworn her cheek had turned — a little . . .
Had slightly turned away . . .
Sunlight dozed on the floor. He sat and wondered,
Nor left his room that day.

And that day, and for many days thereafter,
He sat alone, and thought

No lady had ever lived so beautiful
As this that Hiroshige wrought.

Or if she lived, no matter in what country,
By what far river or hill or lonely sea,
He would look in every face until he found her.
There was no other as fair as she.

And before her quiet face he burned soft incense,
And brought her every day
Boughs of the peach, or almond, or snow-white cherry,
And somehow, she seemed to say,

This silent lady, young, and quietly smiling,
That she was happy there;
And sometimes, seeing this, he started to tremble,
And desired to touch her hair,

To lay his palm along her hand, touch faintly
With delicate finger-tips
The ghostly smile that seemed to hover and vanish
Upon her lips.

Until he knew he loved this quiet lady;
And night by night a dread
Leered at his dreams, for he knew that Hiroshige
Was many centuries dead, —

And the lady, too, was dead, and all who knew her,
Dead, and long turned to dust.
The thin moon waxed and waned, and left him paler,
The peach leaves flew in a gust,

And he would surely have died; but there one day
A wise man, white with age,
Stared at the portrait, and said, 'This Hiroshige
Knew more than archimage, —

'Cunningly drew the body, and called the spirit,
Till partly it entered there.
Sometimes, at death, it entered the portrait wholly.
Do all I say with care,

'And she you love may come to you when you call her.'
So then this ghost, Tokkei,
Ran in the sun, bought wine of a hundred merchants,
And alone at the end of day

Entered the darkening room, and faced the portrait,
And saw the quiet eyes
Gleaming and young in the dusk, and held the wine cup,
And knelt, and did not rise,

And said, aloud, 'Lo-san, will you drink this wine?'
Said it three times aloud.
And at the third the faint blue smoke of incense
Rose to the walls in a cloud,

And the lips moved faintly, and the eyes, and the calm hands
    stirred;
And suddenly, with a sigh,
The quiet lady came slowly down from the portrait,
And stood, while worlds went by,

And lifted her young white hands and took the wine cup;
And the poet trembled, and said,
'Lo-san, will you stay forever?' — 'Yes, I will stay.' —
'But what when I am dead?'

'When you are dead your spirit will find my spirit,
And then we shall die no more.'
Music came down upon them, and spring returning,
They remembered worlds before,

And years went over the earth, and over the sea,
And lovers were born and spoke and died,

But forever in sunlight went these two immortal,
Tokkei and the quiet bride.

2

The lamplit page is turned, the dream forgotten;
The music changes key, you wake, remember
Deep worlds you lived before, — deep worlds hereafter
Of leaf on falling leaf, shadow on sandgrain,
Rain and sorrow, and dust and laughter.

Helen was late, and Miriam came too soon.
Joseph was dead, his wife and children starving.
Elaine was married and soon to have a child.
You dreamed last night of fiddler-crabs with fiddles;
They played a buzzing melody, and you smiled.

To-morrow — what? And what of yesterday?
Through soundless labyrinths of wish you pass,
Through many doors to the one door of all.
Soon as it's opened we shall hear a music:
Or see a skeleton fall.

We walk with you. Where is it that you lead us?
We climb the muffled stairs beneath high lanterns.
We descend again. We grope through darkened cells.
You say: this darkness, here, will slowly kill me.
It creeps and weighs upon me. Is full of bells.

This is the thing remembered I would forget —
No matter where I go, how soft I tread,
This ghostly gesture menaces me with death.
Fatigue! it says, and points its finger at me;
Touches my throat and stops my breath.

My fans — my jewels — the portrait of my husband —
The torn certificate for my daughter's grave —

These are but mortal seconds in immortal time.
They brush me, fall away: like drops of water.
They signify no crime.

Let us retrace our steps: I have deceived you:
Nothing is here I could not frankly tell you:
No hint of guilt, or faithlessness, or threat.
Dreams — they are madness. Staring eyes — illusion.
Let us return, hear music, and forget.

3

Of what she said to me that night — no matter:
The strange thing came next day.
My brain was full of music — something she played me — ;
I couldn't remember it all, but phrases of it
Wreathed and wreathed among faint memories,
Seeking for something, trying to tell me something,
Urging to restlessness: verging on grief.
I tried to play the tune, from memory, —
But memory failed: the chords and discords climbed
And found no resolution — only hung there,
And left me morbid . . . Where, then, had I heard it?
What secret dusty chamber was it hinting?
'Dust,' it said, 'dust . . . and dust . . . and sunlight . . .
A cold clear April evening . . . snow, bedraggled,
Rain-worn snow, dappling the hideous grass.
And someone walking alone; and someone saying
That all must end, for the time had come to go . . .'
These were the phrases . . . but behind, beneath them
A greater shadow moved: and in this shadow
I stood and guessed . . . Was it the blue-eyed lady?
The one who always danced in golden slippers —
And had I danced with her, — upon this music?
Or was it further back — the unplumbed twilight
Of childhood? — No — much recenter than that.

You know, without my telling you, how sometimes
A word or name eludes you, and you seek it
Through running ghosts of shadow, — leaping at it,
Lying in wait for it to spring upon it,
Spreading faint snares for it of sense or sound:
Until, of a sudden, as if in a phantom forest,
You hear it, see it flash among the branches,
And scarcely knowing how, suddenly have it —
Well, it was so I followed down this music,
Glimpsing a face in darkness, hearing a cry,
Remembering days forgotten, moods exhausted,
Corners in sunlight, puddles reflecting stars — ;
Until, of a sudden, and least of all suspected,
The thing resolved itself: and I remembered
An April afternoon, eight years ago —
Or was it nine? — no matter — call it nine —
A room in which the last of sunlight faded;
A vase of violets, fragrance in tall curtains;
And, she who played the same thing later, playing.

She played this tune. And in the middle of it
Abruptly broke it off, letting her hands
Fall in her lap. She sat there so a moment,
With shoulders drooped, then lifted up a rose,
One great white rose, wide opened like a lotos,
And pressed it to her cheek, and closed her eyes.
'You know — we've got to end this — Miriam loves you.
If she should ever know, or even guess it, —
What would she do? — Listen! — I'm not absurd.
I'm sure of it. If you had eyes, for women —
To understand them — which you've never had —
You'd know it too . . .' So went this colloquy,
Half humorous, with undertones of pathos,
Half grave, half flippant . . . while her fingers, softly,
Felt for this tune, played it and let it fall,
Now note by plaintive note, now chord by chord,
Repeating phrases with a kind of pleasure.

Was it symbolic of the woman's weakness
That she could neither break it — nor conclude?
It paused . . . and wandered . . . paused again; while she,
Perplexed and tired, half told me I must go, —
Half asked me if I thought I ought to go.

Well, April passed with many other evenings,
Evenings like this, with later suns and warmer,
With violets always there, and fragrant curtains.
And she was right: and Miriam found it out.
And after that, when eight deep years had passed —
Or nine — we met once more, — by accident.
But was it just by accident, I wonder,
She played this tune? — Or what, then, was intended?

4

The cigarette-smoke loops and slides above us,
Dipping and swirling as the waiter passes;
You strike a match and stare upon the flame.
The tiny fire leaps in your eyes a moment,
And dwindles away as silently as it came.

This melody, you say, has certain voices —
They rise like nereids from a river, singing,
Lift white faces, and dive to darkness again.
Wherever you go you bear this river with you:
A leaf falls, — and it flows, and you have pain.

So says the tune to you — but what to me?
What to the waiter, as he pours your coffee,
The violinist who suavely draws his bow?
That man, who folds his paper, overhears it.
A thousand themes revolve and fall and flow.

Some one there is who sees a virgin stepping
Down marble stairs to a deep tomb of roses:

At the last moment she lifts remembering eyes.
Green leaves blow down. The place is checked with shadows.
A long-drawn murmur of rain goes down the skies.
And oaks are stripped and bare, and smoke with lightning:
And clouds are blown and torn upon high forests,
And the great sea shakes its walls.
And then falls silence . . . And through long silence falls
This melody once more:
'Down endless stairs she goes, as once before.'

So says the tune to him — but what to me?
What are the worlds I see?
What shapes fantastic, terrible dreams?
I go my secret way, down secret alleys;
My errand is not so simple as it seems.

5

This is the house. On one side there is darkness,
On one side there is light.
Into the darkness you may lift your lanterns —
O, any number — it will still be night.
And here are echoing stairs to lead you downward
To long sonorous halls.
And here is spring forever at these windows,
With roses on the walls.

This is her room. On one side there is singing —
On one side not a sound.
At one step she could move from love to silence,
Feel myriad darkness coiling round.
And here the balcony from which she heard you,
Your steady footsteps on the stair.
And here the glass in which she saw your shadow
As she unbound her hair.

Here is the room — with ghostly walls dissolving —
The twilight room in which she called you 'lover';
And the floorless room in which she called you 'friend.'
So many times, in doubt, she ran between them! —
Through draughty corridors of darkening end.

Here she could stand with one dim light above her
And hear far echos, like a sea in caverns,
Murmur away at hollowed walls of stone.
And here, in a roofless room where it was raining,
She bore the patient sorrow of rain alone.

Your words were walls which suddenly froze around her.
Your words were windows, — large enough for moonlight,
Too small to let her through.
Your letters — spacious cloisters faint with music.
The music that assuaged her there was you.

How many times she heard your step ascending
Yet never saw your face!
She heard them turn again, ring slowly fainter,
Till silence swept the place.
Why had you gone? . . . The door, perhaps, mistaken . . .
You would go elsewhere. The deep walls were shaken.

A certain rose-leaf — sent without intention —
Became, with time, a woven web of fire —
She wore it, and was warm.
A certain hurried glance, let fall at parting,
Became, with time, the flashings of a storm.

Yet, there was nothing asked, no hint to tell you
Of secret symbols carved in secret chambers
From all you did and said.
Nothing was done, until at last she knew you.
Nothing was known, till, somehow, she was dead.

How did she die? — You say, she died of poison.
Simple and swift. And much to be regretted.
You did not see her pass
So many thousand times from light to darkness,
Pausing so many times before her glass;

You did not see how many times she hurried
To lean from certain windows, vainly hoping,
Passionate still for beauty, remembered spring.
You did not know how long she clung to twilight,
You did not hear her sing.

Did she, then, make the choice, and step out bravely
From sound to silence — close, herself, those windows?
Or was it true, instead,
That darkness moved, — for once, — and so possessed her? . . .
We'll never know, you say, for she is dead.

6

You see that porcelain ranged there in the window —
Platters and soup-plates done with pale pink rosebuds,
And tiny violets, and wreaths of ivy?
See how the pattern clings to the gleaming edges!
They're works of art — minutely seen and felt,
Each petal done devoutly. Is it failure
To spend your blood like this?

Study them . . . you will see there, in the porcelain,
If you stare hard enough, a sort of swimming
Of lights and shadows, ghosts within a crystal —
My brain unfolding! There you'll see me sitting
Day after day, close to a certain window,
Looking down, sometimes, to see the people.
Sometimes my wife comes there to speak to me.
Sometimes the grey cat waves his tail around me.
Goldfish swim in a bowl, glisten in sunlight,

Dilate to a gorgeous size, blow delicate bubbles,
Drowse among dark green weeds. On rainy days,
You'll see a gas-light shedding light behind me —
An eye-shade round my forehead. There I sit,
Twirling the tiny brushes in my paint-cups,
Painting the pale pink rosebuds, minute violets,
Exquisite wreaths of dark green ivy leaves.
On this leaf, goes a dream I dreamed last night
Of two soft-patterned toads — I thought them stones,
Until they hopped! And then a great black spider, —
Tarantula, perhaps, a hideous thing, —
It crossed the room in one tremendous leap.
Here, — as I coil the stems between two leaves, —
It is as if, dwindling to atomy size,
I cried the secret between two universes.
A friend of mine took hasheesh once, and said
Just as he fell asleep he had a dream, —
Though with his eyes wide open, —
And felt, or saw, or knew himself a part
Of marvelous slowly-wreathing intricate patterns,
Plane upon plane, depth upon depth,
Amazing leaves, folding one on another,
Voluted grasses, twists and curves and spirals —
All of it darkly moving . . . as for me,
I need no hasheesh for it — it's too easy!
Soon as I shut my eyes I set out walking
In a monstrous jungle of monstrous pale pink roseleaves,
Violets purple as death, dripping with water,
And ivy-leaves as big as clouds above me.

Here, in a simple pattern of separate violets —
With scalloped edges gilded — here you have me
Thinking of something else. My wife, you know, —
There's something lacking — force, or will, or passion,
I don't know what it is — and so, sometimes,
When I am tired, or haven't slept three nights,
Or it is cloudy, with a threat of rain,

I get uneasy — just like poplar trees
Ruffling their leaves — and I begin to think
Of poor Pauline, so many years ago,
And that delicious night. Where is she now?
I meant to write — but she has moved, by this time,
And then, besides, she might find out I'm married.
Well, there is more — I'm getting old and timid —
The years have gnawed my will. I've lost my nerve!
I never strike out boldly as I used to —
But sit here, painting violets, and remember
That thrilling night. Photographers, she said,
Asked her to pose for them; her eyes and forehead, —
Dark brown eyes, and a smooth and pallid forehead, —
Were thought so beautiful. — And so they were.
Pauline . . . These violets are like words remembered.
Darling! she whispered . . . Darling! . . . Darling! . . . Darling!
Well, I suppose such days can come but once.
Lord, how happy we were!

Here, if you only knew it, is a story —
Here, in these leaves. I stopped my work to tell it,
And then, when I had finished, went on thinking:
A man I saw on a train — I was still a boy —
Who killed himself by diving against a wall.
Here is a recollection of my wife,
When she was still my sweetheart, years ago.
It's funny how things change, — just change, by growing,
Without an effort . . . And here are trivial things, —
A chill, an errand forgotten, a cut while shaving;
A friend of mine who tells me he is married.
Or is that last so trivial? Well, no matter!

This is the sort of thing you'll see of me,
If you look hard enough. This, in its way,
Is a kind of fame. My life arranged before you
In scrolls of leaves, rosebuds, violets, ivy,
Clustered or wreathed on plate and cup and platter.

Sometimes, I say, I'm just like John the Baptist —
You have my head before you . . . on a platter.

7

Wind blows. Snow falls. The great clock in its tower
Ticks with reverberant coil and tolls the hour:
At the deep sudden stroke the pigeons fly.
The fine snow flutes the cracks between the flagstones.
We close our coats, and hurry, and search the sky.

One mounts up to beauty, serenely singing,
Forgetful of the steps that cry behind him;
One drifts slowly down from a waking dream.
One, foreseeing, lingers forever unmoving.
Upward and downward, past him there, we stream.

One has death in his eyes: and walks more slowly.
Death, among jonquils, told him a freezing secret.
A cloud blows over his eyes, he ponders earth.
He sees in the world a forest of sunlit jonquils:
A slow black poison huddles beneath that mirth.

Death, from street to alley, from door to window,
Cries out his news, — of unplumbed worlds approaching,
Of a cloud of darkness soon to destroy the tower.
But why comes death, — he asks, — in a world so perfect?
Or why the minute's grey in the golden hour?
Sunlight, a sudden glissando, sinister, troubled,
A drift of wind-torn petals, before him passes
Down jangled streets, and dies.
The bodies of old and young, of maimed and lovely,
Are slowly borne to earth, with a dirge of cries.

Down cobbled streets they come; down huddled stairways;
Through silent halls; through carven golden doorways;
From freezing rooms as bare as rock.

The curtains are closed across deserted windows.
Earth streams out of the shovel; the pebbles knock.

Mary, whose hands rejoiced to move in shadow;
Silent Elaine; grave Anne, who sang so clearly;
Fugitive Helen, who loved and walked alone;
Miriam too soon dead, darkly remembered;
Childless Ruth, who sorrowed, but could not atone;

Jean, whose laughter flashed over depths of terror,
And Eloise, who desired to love but dared not;
Doris, who turned alone to the dark and cried, —
They are blown away like windflung chords of music,
They drift away; the sudden music has died.

And one, with death in his eyes, comes walking slowly
And sees the shadow of death in many faces,
And thinks the world is strange.
He desires immortal youth and spring forever,
And belief that knows no change.

8

We sit together and talk, or smoke in silence.
You say (but use no words) 'this night is passing
As other nights when we are dead will pass.'
Perhaps I misconstrue you: you mean only,
'How deathly pale my face looks in that glass.'

You say: 'We sit and talk, of things important.
How many others like ourselves, this instant,
Mark the pendulum swinging against the wall?
How many others, laughing, sip their coffee —
Or stare at mirrors, and do not talk at all?

'This is the moment' (so you would say, in silence)
'When suddenly we have had too much of laughter:

And a freezing stillness falls, no word to say.
Our mouths feel foolish . . . For all the days hereafter
What have we saved — what news, what tune, what play?

'We see each other as vain and futile tricksters, —
Posturing like bald apes before a mirror;
No pity dims our eyes.
How many others, like ourselves, this instant,
See how the great world wizens, and are wise?'

Well, you are right. No doubt, they fall, these seconds.
When suddenly all's distempered, vacuous, ugly,
And even those most like angels creep for schemes.
The one you love leans forward, smiles, deceives you,
Opens a door through which you see dark dreams.

But this is momentary . . . or else, enduring,
Leads you with devious eyes through mists and poisons
To horrible chaos, or suicide, or crime.
And all these others who at your conjuration
Grow pale, feeling the skeleton touch of time, —

Or, laughing sadly, talk of things important,
Or stare at mirrors, startled to see their faces,
Or drown in the waveless vacuum of their days, —
Suddenly, as from sleep, awake, forgetting
This nauseous dream; take up their accustomed ways,

Exhume the ghost of a joke, renew loud laughter,
Forget the moles above their sweethearts' eyebrows,
Lean to the music, rise,
And dance once more in a rose-festooned illusion
With kindness in their eyes.

They say (as we ourselves have said, remember)
'What wizardry this slow waltz works upon us!
And how it brings to mind forgotten things!'

They say 'How strange it is that one such evening
Can wake vague memories of so many springs!'

And so they go . . . In a thousand crowded places,
They sit to smile and talk, or rise to ragtime,
And, for their pleasures, agree or disagree.
With secret symbols they play on secret passions.
With cunning eyes they see

The innocent word that sets remembrance trembling,
The dubious word that sets the scared heart beating.
The pendulum on the wall
Shakes down seconds . . . They laugh at time, dissembling;
Or coil for a victim and do not talk at all.

9

From time to time, lifting his eyes, he sees
The soft blue starlight through the one small window,
The moon above black trees, and clouds, and Venus, —
And turns to write . . . The clock, behind ticks softly.

It is so long, indeed, since I have written, —
Two years, almost, your last is turning yellow, —
That these first words I write seem cold and strange.
Are you the man I knew, or have you altered?
Altered, of course — just as I too have altered —
And whether towards each other, or more apart,
We cannot say . . . I've just re-read your letter —
Not through forgetfulness, but more for pleasure —
Pondering much on all you say in it
Of mystic consciousness — divine conversion —
The sense of oneness with the infinite, —
Faith in the world, its beauty, and its purpose.
Well, you believe one must have faith, in some sort,
If one's to walk through this dark world contented.
But is the world so dark? Or is it rather

Our own brute minds, — in which we hurry, trembling,
Through streets as yet unlighted? This, I think.

You have been always, let me say, 'romantic,' —
Eager for color, for beauty, soon discontented
With a world of dust and stones and flesh too ailing:
Even before the question grew to problem
And drove you bickering into metaphysics,
You met on lower planes the same great dragon,
Seeking release, some fleeting satisfaction,
In strange aesthetics . . . You tried, as I remember,
One after one, strange cults, and some, too, morbid,
The cruder first, more violent sensations,
Gorgeously carnal things, conceived and acted
With splendid animal thirst . . . Then, by degrees, —
Savoring all more delicate gradations
In all that hue and tone may play on flesh,
Or thought on brain, — you passed, if I may say so,
From red and scarlet through morbid greens to mauve.
Let us regard ourselves, you used to say,
As instruments of music, whereon our lives
Will play as we desire: and let us yield
These subtle bodies and subtler brains and nerves
To all experience plays . . . And so you went
From subtle theme to subtler, each heard once,
Twice or thrice at the most, tiring of each;
And closing one by one your doors, drew in
Slowly, through darkening labyrinths of feeling,
Towards the central chamber . . . Which now you've reached.

What, then's, the secret of this ultimate chamber —
Or innermost, rather? If I see it clearly
It is the last, and cunningest, resort
Of one who has found this world of dust and flesh, —
This world of lamentations, death, injustice,
Sickness, humiliation, slow defeat,
Bareness, and ugliness, and iteration, —

Too meaningless; or, if it has a meaning,
Too tiresomely insistent on one meaning:
Futility . . . This world, I hear you saying, —
With lifted chin, and arm in outflung gesture,
Coldly imperious, — this transient world,
What has it then to give, if not containing
Deep hints of nobler worlds? We know its beauties, —
Momentary and trivial for the most part,
Perceived through flesh, passing like flesh away, —
And know how much outweighed they are by darkness.
We are like searchers in a house of darkness,
A house of dust; we creep with little lanterns,
Throwing our tremulous arcs of light at random,
Now here, now there, seeing a plane, an angle,
An edge, a curve, a wall, a broken stairway
Leading to who knows what; but never seeing
The whole at once . . . We grope our way a little,
And then grow tired. No matter what we touch,
Dust is the answer — dust: dust everywhere.
If this were all — what were the use, you ask?
But this is not: for why should we be seeking,
Why should we bring this need to seek for beauty,
To lift our minds, if there were only dust?
This is the central chamber you have come to:
Turning your back to the world, until you came
To this deep room, and looked through rose-stained windows,
And saw the hues of the world so sweetly changed.

Well, in a measure, so only do we all.
I am not sure that you can be refuted.
At the very last we all put faith in something, —
You in this ghost that animates your world,
This ethical ghost, — and I, you'll say, in reason, —
Or sensuous beauty, — or in my secret self . . .
Though as for that you put your faith in these,
As much as I do — and then, forsaking reason, —
Ascending, you would say, to intuition, —

You predicate this ghost of yours, as well.
Of course, you might have argued, — and you should have, —
That no such deep appearance of design
Could shape our world without entailing purpose:
For can design exist without a purpose?
Without conceiving mind? . . . We are like children
Who find, upon the sand, beside a sea,
Strange patterns drawn, — circles, arcs, ellipses,
Graven in sand . . . Who drew them there, we wonder?
Or was it just the sea? — We pore upon them,
But find no answer — only suppositions.
And if these perfect shapes are evidence
Of immanent mind, it is but circumstantial:
We never come upon him at his work,
He never troubles us. He stands aloof —
Well, if he stands at all: is not concerned
With what we are or do. You, if you like,
May think he broods upon us, loves us, hates us,
Conceives some purpose of us. In so doing
You see, without much reason, will in law.
I am content to say, 'this world is ordered,
Happily so for us, by accident:
We go our ways untroubled save by laws
Of natural things.' Who makes the more assumption?
If we were wise — which God knows we are not —
(Notice I call on God!) we'd plumb this riddle
Not in the world we see, but in ourselves.
These brains of ours — these delicate spinal clusters —
Have limits: why not learn them, learn their cravings?
Which of the two minds, yours or mine, is sound?
Yours, which scorned the world that gave it freedom,
Until you managed to see that world as omen, —
Or mine, which likes the world, takes all for granted,
Sorrow as much as joy, and death as life? —
You lean on myth, and take more credit for it.
I stand alone . . . Well, I take credit, too.
You find your pleasure in 'being at one with all things' —

Fusing in lambent dream, rising and falling
As all things rise and fall . . . I do that too —
With reservations. I find more varied pleasure
In understanding: and so find beauty even
In this strange dream of yours you call the truth.

Well, I have bored you. And it's growing late.
For household news — what have you heard, I wonder?
You must have heard that Paul was dead, by this time —
Of spinal cancer. Nothing could be done —
We found it out too late. His death has changed me,
Deflected much of me that lived as he lived,
Saddened me, slowed me down. Such things will happen,
Life is composed of them; and it seems wisdom
To see them clearly, meditate upon them,
And understand what things flow out of them.
Otherwise, all goes on here much as always.
Why won't you come and see us, in the spring,
And bring old times with you? — If you could see me
Sitting here by the window, watching Venus
Go down behind my neighbor's poplar branches, —
Just where you used to sit, — I'm sure you'd come.
This year, they say, the springtime will be early.

10

What shall we talk of? Li Po? Hokusai?
You narrow your long dark eyes to fascinate me;
You smile a little . . . Outside, the night goes by.
I walk alone in a forest of ghostly trees . . .
Your pale hands rest palm downwards on your knees.

'These lines — converging, they suggest such distance!
The soul is drawn away, beyond horizons.
Lured out to what? One dares not think.
Sometimes, I glimpse these infinite perspectives
In intimate talk (with such as you) and shrink.

'One feels so petty! — One feels such — emptiness! — '
You mimic horror, let fall your lifted hand,
And smile at me; with brooding tenderness.
Alone on darkened waters I fall and rise;
Slow waves above me break, faint waves of cries.

'And then these colors . . . but who would dare describe them?
This faint rose-coral pink . . . this green — pistachio? —
So insubstantial! Like the dim ghostly things
Two lovers find in love's still-twilight chambers.
Old peacock-fans, and fragrant silks, and rings.

'Rings, let us say, drawn from the skeleton finger
Of some great lady, many centuries nameless, —
Or is that too sepulchral? — dulled with dust;
And necklaces that crumble if you touch them;
And gold brocades that, breathed on, fall to rust.

'No — I am wrong . . . it is not these I sought for — !
Why did they come to mind? You understand me — ?
You know these strange vagaries of the brain! — '
— I walk alone in a forest of ghostly trees;
Your pale hands rest palm downwards on your knees;
These strange vagaries of yours are all too plain.

'But why perplex ourselves with tedious problems
Of art or . . . such things? . . . while we sit here, living,
With all that's in our secret hearts to say! — '
Hearts? — Your pale hand softly strokes the satin.
You play deep music — know well what you play.
You stroke the satin with thrilling of finger-tips,
You smile, with faintly perfumed lips,
You loose your thoughts like birds.
We know your words are foolish, yet here we stay,
I to be played on, you to play;
We know our words are foolish, yet sit here bound
In a web of sound.

'How beautiful is intimate talk like this! —
It is as if we dissolved grey walls between us,
Stepped through the solid portals, become but shadows,
To hear a hidden secret . . . Our own vast shadows
Lean to a giant size on windy walls,
Or dwindle away; we hear our soft footfalls
Echo behind us, ghostly clear,
Music sings far off, flows suddenly near,
And dies away like rain.
We walk through subterranean caves again, —
Vaguely above us feeling
A shadowy weight of frescos on the ceiling,
Strange half-lit things,
Soundless grotesques with writhing claws and wings:
And here a beautiful face looks down upon us;
And someone hurries before, unseen, and sings.
Have we seen all, I wonder, in these chambers —
Or is there yet some gorgeous vault, arched low,
Where sleeps an amazing beauty we do not know?'

The question falls: we walk in silence together,
Thinking of that deep vault and of its secret.
This lamp, these books, this fire
Are suddenly blown away in a whistling darkness.
Deep walls crash down in the whirlwind of desire.

11

Now, when the moon slid under the cloud
And the cold clear dark of starlight fell,
He heard in his blood the well-known bell
Tolling slowly in heaves of sound,
Slowly beating, slowly beating,
Shaking its pulse on the stagnant air:
Sometimes it swung completely round,
Horribly gasping as if for breath;
Falling down with an anguished cry.

Now the red bat, he mused, will fly;
Something is marked, this night, for death.
And while he mused, along his blood
Flew ghostly voices, remote and thin,
They rose in the cavern of his brain,
Like ghosts they died away again;
And hands upon his heart were laid,
And music upon his flesh was played,
Until, as he was bidden to do,
He walked the wood he so well knew.
Through the cold dew he moved his feet,
And heard far off, as under the earth,
Discordant music in shuddering tones,
Screams of laughter, horrible mirth,
Clapping of hands, and thudding of drums,
And the long-drawn wail of one in pain.
To-night, he thought, I shall die again,
We shall die again in the red-eyed fire
To meet on the edge of the wood beyond
With the placid gaze of fed desire . . .
He walked; and behind the whisper of trees,
In and out, one walked with him:
She parted the branches and peered at him,
Through lowered lids her two eyes burned,
He heard her breath, he saw her hand,
Wherever he turned his way, she turned:
Kept pace with him, now fast, now slow;
Moving her white knees as he moved.
This is the one I have always loved;
This is the one whose bat-soul comes
To dance with me, flesh to flesh,
In the starlight dance of horns and drums.

The walls and roofs, the scarlet towers,
Sank down behind a rushing sky.
He heard a sweet song just begun
Abruptly shatter in tones and die.

It whirled away. Cold silence fell.
And again came tollings of a bell.

This air is alive with witches: the white witch rides
Swifter than smoke on the starlit wind.
In the clear darkness, while the moon hides,
They come like dreams, like something remembered.
Let us hurry! beloved; take my hand,
Forget these things that trouble your eyes,
Forget, forget! Our flesh is changed,
Lighter than smoke we wreathe and rise.

The cold air hisses between us . . . Beloved, beloved,
What was the word you said?
Something about clear music that sang through water.
I cannot remember. The storm-drops break on the leaves.
Something was lost in the darkness. Someone is dead.
Someone lies in the garden and grieves.
Look how the branches are tossed in this air,
Flinging their green to the earth!
Black clouds rush to devour the stars in the sky,
The moon stares down like a half-closed eye.
The leaves are scattered, the birds are blown,
Oaks crash down in the darkness,
We run from our windblown shadows; we are running alone.

The moon was darkened: across it flew
The swift grey tenebrous shape he knew,
Like a thing of smoke it crossed the sky,
The witch! he said. And he heard a cry,
And another came, and another came,
And one, grown duskily red with blood,
Floated an instant across the moon,
Hung like a dull fantastic flame.
The earth has veins: they throb to-night,
The earth swells warm beneath my feet,
The tips of the trees grow red and bright,

The leaves are swollen, I feel them beat,
They press together, they push and sigh,
They listen to hear the great bat cry,
The great red bat with the woman's face.
Hurry! he said. And pace for pace
That other, who trod the dark with him,
Crushed the live leaves, reached out white hands
And closed her eyes, the better to see
The priests with claws, the lovers with hooves,
The fire-lit rock, the sarabands.
I am here! she said. The bough he broke —
Was it the snapping bough that spoke?
I am here! she said. The white thigh gleamed
Cold in starlight among dark leaves,
The head thrown backward as he had dreamed,
The shadowy red deep jasper mouth;
And the lifted hands, and the virgin breasts,
Passed beside him, and vanished away.
I am here! she cried. He answered 'Stay!'
And laughter arose, and near and far
Answering laughter rose and died.
Who is there? in the dark? he cried.
He stood in terror, and heard a sound
Of terrible hooves on the hollow ground;
They rushed, were still; a silence fell;
And he heard deep tollings of a bell.

Look beloved! Why do you hide your face?
Look, in the centre there, above the fire,
They are bearing the boy who blasphemed love!
They are playing a piercing music upon him
With a bow of living wire!
The virgin harlot sings,
She leans above the beautiful anguished body,
And draws slow music from those strings.
They dance around him, they fling red roses upon him,
They trample him with their naked feet,

His cries are lost in laughter,
Their feet grow dark with his blood, they beat and beat,
They dance upon him, until he cries no more.
Have we not heard that cry before?
Somewhere, somewhere,
Beside a sea, in the green evening,
Beneath green clouds, in a copper sky . . .
Was it you? was it I?
They have quenched the fires, they dance in the darkness,
The satyrs have run among them to seize and tear,
Look! he has caught one by the hair,
She screams and falls, he bears her away with him,
And the night grows full of whistling wings.
Far off, one voice, serene and sweet,
Rises and sings.

'By the clear waters where once I died,
In the calm evening bright with stars. . .'
Where have I heard these words? Was it you who sang them?
It was long ago.
Let us hurry, beloved! the hard hooves trample;
The treetops tremble and glow.

In the clear dark, on silent wings,
The red bat hovers beneath her moon;
She drops through the fragrant night, and clings
Fast in the shadow, with hands like claws,
With soft eyes closed and mouth that feeds,
To the young white flesh that warmly bleeds.
The maidens circle in dance, and raise
From lifting throats a soft-sung praise;
Their knees and breasts are white and bare,
They have hung pale roses in their hair,
Each of them as she dances by
Peers at the blood with a narrowed eye.
See how the red wing wraps him round,

See how the white youth struggles in vain!
The weak arms writhe in a soundless pain;
He writhes in the soft red veiny wings,
But still she whispers upon him and clings.
This is the secret feast of love,
Look well, look well, before it dies,
See how the red one trembles above,
See how quiet the white one lies!

Wind through the trees . . . and a voice is heard
Singing far off. The dead leaves fall.
'By the clear waters where once I died,
In the calm evening bright with stars,
One among numberless avatars,
I wedded a mortal, a mortal bride,
And lay on the stones and gave my flesh,
And entered the hunger of him I loved.
How shall I ever escape this mesh
Or be from my lover's body removed?'
Dead leaves stream through the hurrying air
And the maenads dance with flying hair.

The priests with hooves, the lovers with horns,
Rise in the starlight, one by one,
They draw their knives on the spurting throats,
They smear the column with blood of goats,
They dabble the blood on hair and lips
And wait like stones for the moon's eclipse.
They stand like stones and stare at the sky
Where the moon leers down like a half-closed eye.
In the green moonlight still they stand
While wind flows over the darkened sand
And brood on the soft forgotten things
That filled their shadowy yesterdays.
Where are the breasts, the scarlet wings?
They gaze at each other with troubled gaze.

And then, as the shadow closes the moon,
Shout, and strike with their hooves the ground,
And rush through the dark, and fill the night
With a slowly dying clamor of sound.

There, where the great walls crowd the stars,
There, by the black wind-riven walls,
In a grove of twisted leafless trees,
Who are these pilgrims, who are these,
These three, the one of whom stands upright,
While one lies weeping and one of them crawls?
The face that he turned was a wounded face,
I heard the dripping of blood on stones.
Hooves had trampled and torn this place,
And the leaves were strewn with blood and bones.
Sometimes, I think, beneath my feet,
The warm earth stretches herself and sighs.
Listen! I heard the slow heart beat.
I will lie on this grass as a lover lies
And reach to the north and reach to the south
And seek in the darkness for her mouth.

Beloved, beloved, where the slow waves of the wind
Shatter pale foam among great trees,
Under the hurrying stars, under the heaving arches,
Like one whirled down under shadowy seas,
I run to find you, I run and cry,
Where are you? Where are you? It is I. It is I.
It is your eyes I seek, it is your hair,
Your starlight body that breathes in the darkness there.
Under the darkness I feel you stirring.
Is this you? Is this you?
Bats in this air go whirring.
And this soft mouth that darkly meets my mouth,
Is this the soft mouth I knew?
Darkness, and wind in the tortured trees;
And the patter of dew.

Dance! Dance! Dance! Dance!
Dance till the brain is red with speed!
Dance till you fall! Lift your torches!
Kiss your lovers until they bleed!
Backward I draw your anguished hair
Until your eyes are stretched with pain;
Backward I press you until you cry,
Your lips grow white, I kiss you again,
I will take a torch and set you afire,
I will break your body and fling it away.
Look, you are trembling . . . Lie still, beloved!
Lock your hands in my hair, and say
Darling! darling! darling! darling!
All night long till the break of day.

Is it your heart I hear beneath me,
Or the far tolling of that tower?
The voices are still that cried around us.
The woods grow still for the sacred hour.
Rise, white lover! the day draws near.
The grey trees lean to the east in fear.
'By the clear waters where once I died . . .'
Beloved, whose voice was this that cried?
'By the clear waters that reach the sun
By the clear waves that starward run,
I found love's body and lost his soul,
And crumbled in flame that should have annealed.
How shall I ever again be whole,
By what dark waters shall I be healed?'

Silence . . . the red leaves, one by one,
Fall. Far off, the maenads run.
Silence. Beneath my naked feet
The veins of the red earth swell and beat.
The dead leaves sigh on the troubled air,
Far off the maenads bind their hair.

Hurry, beloved! the day comes soon.
The fire is drawn from the heart of the moon.

The great bell cracks and falls at last.
The moon whirls out. The sky grows still.
Look, how the white cloud crosses the stars
And suddenly drops behind the hill!
Your eyes are placid, you smile at me,
We sit in the room by candle-light.
We peer in each other's veins and see
No sign of the horror we saw this night.
Only, a song is in your ears,
A song you have heard, you think, in dream:
The song which only the demon hears,
In the dark forest where maenads scream.

'By the clear waters where once I died,
In the calm evening bright with stars . . .'
What do the strange words mean? you say, —
And touch my hand, and turn away.

12

The half-shut doors through which we heard those discords
Are softly closed. Horns mutter down to silence.
The stars whirl out, the night grows deep.
Darkness settles upon us. A vague refrain
Drowsily teases at the drowsy brain.
In numberless rooms we stretch ourselves and sleep.

Where have we been? What savage orgy of chaos
Whirls in our dreams? — We suddenly wake in darkness,
Open our eyes, cry out, and sleep once more.
We dream we are numberless sea-waves languidly foaming
A warm white moonlit shore;
Or clouds blown over a sky at midnight,

Or a sound of rain.
We open our eyes and stare at the coiling darkness,
And enter our dreams again.

PART IV

1

'This envelope you say has something in it
Which once belonged to your dead son — or something
He knew, was fond of? Something he remembers? —
The soul flies far, and we can only call it
By things like these . . . a photograph, a letter,
Ribbon, or charm, or watch . . .'

. . . Wind flows softly, the long slow even wind,
Over the low roofs white with snow;
Wind blows, bearing cold clouds over the ocean,
One by one they melt and flow, —

Streaming one by one over trees and towers,
Coiling and gleaming in shafts of sun;
Wind flows, bearing clouds; the hurrying shadows
Flow under them one by one . . .

'. . . A spirit darkens before me . . . it is the spirit
Which in the flesh you called your son . . . A spirit
Young and strong and beautiful . . .

'He says that he is happy, is much honored;
Forgives and is forgiven . . . rain and wind
Do not perplex him . . . storm and dust forgotten . . .
The glittering wheels in wheels of time are broken
And laid aside . . .'

'Ask him why he did the thing he did!'

'He is unhappy. This thing, he says, transcends you:
Dust cannot hold what shines beyond the dust.
What seems calamity is less than a sigh;
What seems disgrace is nothing.'

'Ask him if the one he hurt is there,
And if she loves him still!'

'He tells you she is there, and loves him still, —
Not as she did, but as all spirits love . . .
A cloud of spirits has gathered about him.
They praise him and call him, they do him honor;
He is more beautiful, he shines upon them.'

. . . Wind flows softly, the long deep tremulous wind,
Over the low roofs white with snow.
Wind flows, bearing dreams; they gather and vanish,
One by one they sing and flow;

Over the outstretched lands of days remembered,
Over remembered tower and wall,
One by one they gather and talk in the darkness,
Rise and glimmer and fall . . .

'Ask him why he did the thing he did!
He knows I will understand!'

                              'It is too late:
He will not hear me: I have lost my power.'

'Three times I've asked him! He will never tell me.
God have mercy upon him. I will ask no more.'

2

The door is shut. She leaves the curtained office,
And down the grey-walled stairs comes trembling slowly

Towards the dazzling street.
Her withered hand clings tightly to the railing.
The long stairs rise and fall beneath her feet.

Here in the brilliant sun we jostle, waiting
To tear her secret out . . . We laugh, we hurry,
We go our way, revolving, sinister, slow.
She blinks in the sun, and then steps faintly downward.
We whirl her away, we shout, we spin, we flow.

Where have you been, old lady? We know your secret! —
Voices jangle about her, jeers, and laughter.
She trembles, tries to hurry, averts her eyes.
Tell us the truth, old lady! where have you been?
She turns and turns, her brain grows dark with cries.

Look at the old fool tremble! She's been paying, —
Paying good money, too, — to talk to spirits.
She thinks she's heard a message from one dead!
What did he tell you? Is he well and happy?
Don't lie to us — we all know what he said.

He said the one he murdered once still loves him;
He said the wheels in wheels of time are broken;
And dust and storm forgotten; and all forgiven. . .
But what you asked he wouldn't tell you, though, —
Ha ha! there's one thing you will never know!
That's what you get for meddling so with heaven!

Where have you been, old lady? Where are you going?
We know, we know! She's been to gab with spirits.
Look at the old fool! getting ready to cry!
What have you got in an envelope, old lady?
A lock of hair? An eyelash from his eye?

How do you know the medium didn't fool you?
Perhaps he had no spirit — perhaps he killed it.

Here she comes! the old fool's lost her son.
What did he have — blue eyes and golden hair?
We know your secret! what's done is done.

Look out, you'll fall — and fall, if you're not careful,
Right into an open grave . . . but what's the hurry?
You don't think you will find him when you're dead?
Cry! Cry! Look at her mouth all twisted, —
Look at her eyes all red!

We know you — know your name and all about you,
All you remember and think, and all you scheme for.
We tear your secret out, we leave you, go
Laughing down the street . . . Die, if you want to!
Die, then, if you're in such a hurry to know! —

. . . She falls. We lift her head. The wasted body
Weighs nothing in our hands. Does no one know her?
Was no one with her when she fell? . . .
We eddy about her, move away in silence.
We hear slow tollings of a bell.

3

Well, as you say, we live for small horizons:
We move in crowds, we flow and talk together,
Seeing so many eyes and hands and faces,
So many mouths, and all with secret meanings, —
Yet know so little of them; only seeing
The small bright circle of our consciousness,
Beyond which lies the dark. Some few we know —
Or think we know. Once, on a sun-bright morning,
I walked in a certain hallway, trying to find
A certain door: I found one, tried it, opened,
And there in a spacious chamber, brightly lighted,
A hundred men played music, loudly, swiftly,
While one tall woman sent her voice above them

In powerful incantation. . . Closing then the door
I heard it die behind me, fade to whisper, —
And walked in a quiet hallway as before.
Just such a glimpse, as through that opened door,
Is all we know of those we call our friends.
We hear a sudden music, see a playing
Of ordered thoughts — and all again is silence.
The music, we suppose (as in ourselves)
Goes on forever there, behind shut doors, —
As it continues after our departure,
So, we divine, it played before we came.
What do you know of me, or I of you?
Little enough . . . We set these doors ajar
Only for chosen movements of the music:
This passage (so I think — yet this is guesswork)
Will please him, — it is in a strain he fancies, —
More brilliant, though, than his; and while he likes it
He will be piqued . . . He looks at me bewildered
And thinks (to judge from self — this too is guesswork)
The music strangely subtle, deep in meaning,
Perplexed with implications; he suspects me
Of hidden riches, unexpected wisdom.
Or else I let him hear a lyric passage, —
Simple and clear; and all the while he listens
I make pretence to think my doors are closed.
This too bewilders him. He eyes me sidelong
Wondering 'Is he such a fool as this?
Or only mocking?' — There I let it end.
Sometimes, of course, and when we least suspect it —
When we pursue our thoughts with too much passion,
Talking with too great zeal — our doors fly open
Without intention; and the hungry watcher
Stares at the feast, carries away our secrets,
And laughs . . . but this, for many counts, is seldom.
And for the most part we vouchsafe our friends,
Our lovers too, only such few clear notes
As we shall deem them likely to admire:

'Praise me for this' we say, or 'laugh at this,'
Or 'marvel at my candor' . . . all the while
Withholding what's most precious to ourselves, —
Some sinister depth of lust or fear or hatred,
The sombre note that gives the chord its power;
Or a white loveliness — if such we know —
Too much like fire to speak of without shame.

Well, this being so, and we who know it being
So curious about those well-locked houses,
The minds of those we know, — to enter softly,
And steal from floor to floor up shadowy stairways,
From room to quiet room, from wall to wall,
Breathing deliberately the very air,
Pressing our hands and nerves against warm darkness
To learn what ghosts are there, —
Suppose for once I set my doors wide open
And bid you in . . . Suppose I try to tell you
The secrets of this house, and how I live here;
Suppose I tell you who I am, in fact.
Deceiving you — as far as I may know it —
Only so much as I deceive myself.

If you are clever you already see me
As one who moves forever in a cloud
Of warm bright vanity: a luminous cloud
Which falls on all things with a quivering magic,
Changing such outlines as a light may change,
Brightening what lies dark to me, concealing
Those things that will not change . . . I walk sustained
In a world of things that flatter me: a sky
Just as I would have had it; trees and grass
Just as I would have shaped and colored them;
Pigeons and clouds and sun and whirling shadows,
And stars that brightening climb through mist at nightfall, —
In some deep way I am aware these praise me:
Where they are beautiful, or hint of beauty,

They point, somehow, to me. This water says, —
Shimmering at the sky, or undulating
In broken gleaming parodies of clouds,
Rippled in blue, or sending from cool depths
To meet the falling leaf the leaf's clear image, —
This water says, there is some secret in you
Akin to my clear beauty, beauty swaying
To mirror beauty, silently responsive
To all that circles you. This bare tree says, —
Austere and stark and leafless, split with frost,
Resonant in the wind, with rigid branches
Flung out against the sky, — this tall tree says,
There is some cold austerity in you,
A frozen strength, with long roots gnarled on rocks,
Fertile and deep; you bide your time, are patient,
Serene in silence, bare to outward seeming,
Concealing what reserves of power and beauty!
What teeming Aprils! — chorus of leaves on leaves!
These houses say, such walls in walls as ours,
Such streets of walls, solid and smooth of surface,
Such hills and cities of walls, walls upon walls;
Motionless in the sun, or dark with rain;
Walls pierced with windows, where the light may enter;
Walls windowless where darkness is desired;
Towers and labyrinths and domes and chambers, —
Amazing deep recesses, dark on dark, —
All these are like the walls which shape your spirit:
You move, are warm, within them, laugh within them,
Proud of their depth and strength; or sally from them,
To blow your Roland's horn against the world.
This deep cool room, with shadowed walls and ceiling,
Tranquil and cloistral, fragrant of my mind,
This cool room says, — just such a room have you,
It waits you always at the tops of stairways,
Withdrawn, remote, familiar to your uses,
Where you may cease pretence and be yourself.
And this embroidery, hanging on this wall,

Hung there forever, — these so soundless glidings
Of dragons golden-scaled, sheer birds of azure,
Coilings of leaves in pale vermilion, griffins
Drawing their rainbow wings through involutions
Of mauve chrysanthemums and lotus flowers, —
This goblin wood where someone cries enchantment, —
This says, just such an involuted beauty
Of thought and coiling thought, dream linked with dream,
Image to image gliding, wreathing lights,
Soundlessly cries enchantment in your mind:
You need but sit and close your eyes a moment
To see these rich designs unfold themselves.

And so, all things discern me, name me, praise me —
I walk in a world of silent voices, praising;
And in this world you see me like a wraith
Blown softly here and there, on silent winds.
'Praise me' — I say; and look, not in a glass,
But in your eyes, to see my image there —
Or in your mind; you smile, I am contented;
You look at me, with interest unfeigned,
And listen — I am pleased; or else, alone,
I watch thin bubbles veering brightly upward
From unknown depths, — my silver thoughts ascending;
Saying now this, now that, hinting of all things, —
Dreams, and desires, half-wishes, half-regrets,
Faint ghosts of memory, strange recognitions, —
But all with one deep meaning: this is I,
This is the glistening secret holy I,
This silver-wingèd wonder, insubstantial,
This singing ghost . . . And hearing, I am warmed.

You see me moving, then, as one who moves
Forever at the centre of his circle:
A circle filled with light. And into it
Come bulging shapes from darkness, loom gigantic,
Or huddle in dark again. A clock ticks clearly,

A gas-jet steadily whirs, light streams across me;
Two church bells, with alternate beat, strike nine;
And through these things my pencil pushes softly
To weave grey webs of lines on this clear page.
Snow falls and melts; the eaves make liquid music;
Black wheel-tracks line the snow-touched street; I turn
And look one instant at the half-dark gardens,
Where skeleton elm-trees reach with frozen gesture
Above unsteady lamps, — the black boughs lifted
Against a luminous snow-filled grey-gold sky.
'Beauty!' I cry. My feet move on, and take me
Between dark walls, with orange squares for windows.
Beauty; beheld like someone half-forgotten,
Remembered, with slow pang, as one neglected.
Well, I am frustrate; life has beaten me,
The thing I strongly seized has turned to darkness,
And darkness takes my heart. . . These skeleton elm-trees —
Leaning against that grey-gold snow-filled sky —
Beauty! they say, and at the edge of darkness
Extend vain arms in a frozen gesture of protest.
Voices are raised, a door is slammed. The lovers,
Murmuring in an adjacent room, grow silent,
The eaves make liquid music. Hours have passed,
And nothing changes, and everything is changed.
Exultation is dead, Beauty is harlot, —
And walks the streets: the thing I strongly seized,
Has turned to darkness, and darkness takes my heart.

If you could solve this darkness you would have me.
This causeless melancholy that comes with rain,
Or on such days as this, when large wet snowflakes
Drop heavily, with rain . . . whence rises this?
Well, so-and-so, this morning when I saw him,
Seemed much preoccupied, and would not smile;
And you, I saw too much; and you, too little;
And the word I chose for you, the golden word,
The word that should have struck so deep in purpose,

And set so many doors of wish wide open,
You let it fall, and would not stoop for it,
And smiled at me, and would not let me guess
Whether you saw it fall. . . These things, together,
With other things, still slighter, wove to magic,
And this in turn drew up dark memories;
And there I stand. This magic breaks and bleeds me,
Turning all frustrate dreams to chords and discords, —
Faces, and griefs, and words, and sunlit evenings,
And chains, self-forged, that will not break nor lengthen,
And cries that none can answer, few will hear.
Have these words meaning? Or would you see more clearly
If I should say 'My second wife grows tedious,
Or, like gay tulip, keeps no perfumed secret'?
Or 'one day dies eventless as another,
Leaving the seeker still unsatisfied,
And more convinced life yields no satisfaction'?
Or 'seek too hard, the eyes at length grow sightless,
And beauty shines in vain'? —

                                        These things you ask for,
These you shall have. . . So, talking with my first wife,
At the dark end of evening, when she leaned
And smiled at me, her blue eyes weaving webs
Of finest fire, revolving me in scarlet, —
Calling to mind remote and small successions
Of countless other evenings ending so, —
I smiled, and met her kiss, and wished her dead;
Dead of a sudden sickness, or by my hands
Savagely killed; I saw her in her coffin,
I saw the coffin borne downstairs with trouble,
I saw myself alone there, palely watching,
Wearing a masque of grief so deeply acted
That grief itself possessed me. Time would pass,
And I would meet this girl, — my second wife —
And drop the masque of grief for one of passion.
Forward we move to meet, half hesitating,

We drown in each other's eyes, we laugh, we talk,
Looking now here, now there, and both pretending
We do not hear the powerful prelude begin
To throb beneath our words . . . The time approaches.
We lean unbalanced. The mute last glance between us,
Profoundly searching, opening, asking, yielding,
Is steadily met: our two lives draw together . . .
. . . 'What are you thinking of?' . . . My first wife's voice
Scattered these ghosts. 'Oh nothing — nothing much —
Just wondering where we'd be two years from now,
And what we might be doing . . .' And then remorse
Turned sharply in my mind to sudden pity,
And pity to acted passion. And one more evening
Drew to the usual end of sleep and silence.

And, as it is with this, so too with all things.
The pages of our lives are blurred palimpsest:
New lines are wreathed on old lines half-erased,
And those on older still; and so forever.
The old shines through the new, and colors it.
What's new? What's old? All things have double meanings, —
All things recur. I write a line, delighted,
(Or touch a woman's hand, or plumb a doctrine)
Only to find the same thing, known before, —
Only to find the same thing comes to-morrow.
This curious riddled dream I dreamed last night, —
Six years ago I dreamed it just as now;
The same man stooped to me; we rose from bondage,
And broke the accustomed order of our days,
And struck for the morning world, and light, and freedom.
What does it mean? Why is this hint repeated?
What anguish does it spring from, seek to end?

You see me, then, pass up and down these stairways,
Now through a beam of light, and now through shadow, —
Pursuing silent aims. No rest there is, —
No more for me than you. I move here always,

From quiet room to room, from wall to wall,
Searching and plotting, weaving a web of will.
This is my house, and now, perhaps, you know me.
Yet I confess, for all my best intentions,
Once more I have deceived you. . . I withhold
The one thing precious, the one dark wound that guides me;
And I have spread two snares for you, of lies.

4

He, in the room above, grown old and tired,
She, in the room below — his floor her ceiling —
Pursue their separate aims. He turns his light,
And throws himself on the bed, face down, in laughter.
She, by the window, smiles at a starlight night,

His watch — the same he has heard these cycles of ages —
Wearily chimes at seconds beneath his pillow.
The clock, upon her mantelpiece, strikes nine.
Strikes nine: And then she hears dull steps above her.
Strikes nine: And the new stars come up to shine.

His youth — far off — he sees it brightly walking
In a golden cloud. . . Wings flashing about it. . . Darkness
Walls it around with dripping enormous walls.
Old age — far off — her death — what do they matter?
Down the smooth purple night a streaked star falls.

She hears slow steps in the street — they chime like bells;
They climb to her heart, they break and flower in crimson,
Along her veins they ring and burn.
He hears his own slow steps tread down to silence.
Far off they pass. He knows they will never return.

Far off — on a smooth dark road — he hears them faintly.
The road, like a sombre river, quietly flowing,
Moves among murmurous walls. A deeper breath

Swells them to sound: he hears his steps more clearly.
And death seems nearer to him: or he to death.

What's death? — She smiles. The cool stone hurts her elbows.
The last of the rain-drops gather and fall from elm-boughs,
She sees them glisten and break. The arc-lamp sings,
The new leaves dip in the warm wet air and fragrance,
A sparrow whirs to the eaves, and shakes his wings.

And death seems far away, a door of roses,
A golden portal, where golden music closes,
Death seems far away:
And spring returns, the countless singing of lovers,
And spring returns to stay.

He, in the room above, grown old and tired,
Flings himself on the bed, face down, in laughter,
And clenches his hands, and remembers, and desires to die.
And she, by the window, smiles at a night of starlight.
. . . The indifferent clouds go slowly across the sky.

5

No, I shall not say why it is that I love you —
Why do you ask me, save for vanity?
Surely you would not have me, like a mirror,
Say 'yes, — your hair curls darkly back from the temples,
Your eyes are April grey . . . with jonquils in them'?
No, if I tell at all, I shall tell in silence.
I'll say — my childhood broke through chords of music
— Or were they chords of sun? — wherein fell shadows,
Or silences; I rose through waves of sunlight;
Or sometimes found an angel stooped above me
With wings of death, and a brow of cold clear beauty.
I lay in the warm sweet grass on a blue May morning,
My chin in a dandelion, my hands in clover,
And drowsed there like a bee. Blue days behind me

Reached like a chain of deep blue pools of magic,
Enchanted, silent, timeless. Days before me
Murmured of blue-sea mornings, noons of gold,
Green evenings streaked with lilac, bee-starred nights.
Confused soft clouds of foresight fled above.me.
Sharp shafts of insight dazzled my eyes and pierced me.
I ran and turned and spun and danced in the sunlight,
Shrank, sometimes, from the freezing silence of Number,
Or crept once more to the warm white cave of sleep.

No, I shall not say '*this* is why I praise you —
Because you say such wise things, or such foolish!'
You would not have me plead what you know better?
Let me instead be silent, only thinking — :
My childhood lives in me — or half-lives, rather —
And, if I close my eyes cool chords of logic
Flow up to me, long chords of wind and sunlight,
Shadows of intricate vines on sunlit walls,
Deep bells beating, with aeons of blue between them,
Grass blades leagues apart with worlds between them,
Walls thrust up to heaven with stars upon them.
I lay in my bed, and through the tall night window
Saw the green lightning lancing among the clouds,
And heard the harsh rain claw at the panes and roof.
How should I know — how should I now remember —
What half-dreamed God's wing curved above me?
What wings like swords? What eyes with the dread night in them?

This I shall say. — I lay by the hot white sand-dunes.
Small yellow flowers, sapless and squat and spiny,
Stared at the sky. And silently there above me,
Day after day, beyond all dreams or knowledge,
Presences swept, and over me streamed their shadows,
Swift and blue, or dark. What did they mean?
What sinister threat of power? What hint of weakness?
Prelude to what gigantic music, or subtle?
Only, I know, these shapes leaned over me,

Brooded upon me, paused, went flowing softly,
Glided and passed. I loved, I desired, I hated,
I struggled, I yielded and loved, was warmed to blossom.
You, when your eyes have evening sunlight in them,
Set these dunes before me, these salt bright flowers,
These presences. I drowse, they stream above me,
I struggle, I yield and love, I become that child.
You are the window (if I could tell I'd tell you)
Through which I see a clear far world of sunlight.
You are the silence (if you could hear you'd hear me)
In which I remember a thin still whisper of singing.
It is not you I laugh for, you I touch!
My hands, that touch you, suddenly touch a cobweb,
Coldly silvered, heavily silvered with dewdrops,
And clover, heavy with rain, in cold green grass.

6

As evening falls,
The walls grow luminous and warm, the walls
Tremble and glow with the lives within them moving.
How shall we live to-night, where shall we turn?
To what new light or darkness yearn?
A thousand winding stairs lead down before us;
And one by one, anonymous, we descend
By lamplit flowered walls, long balustrades,
Through half-lit halls which reach no end.

Take my arm, then, you or you or you,
And let us walk abroad on the solid air:
Look how the organist's head, in silhouette,
Leans to the lamplit music's orange square! . . .
The dim-globed lamps illumine rows of faces,
Rows of hands and arms and hungry eyes,
They have hurried down from numberless secret places,
From windy chambers next to the skies.
The music comes upon us . . . it shakes the darkness,

It shakes the darkness in our minds.
And brilliant figures suddenly throng the darkness,
Down the white shaft of light they run through darkness,
And in our hearts a dazzling dream unwinds.

Take my hand, then, walk with me
By the slow soundless crashings of a sea
Down miles on miles of glistening mirrorlike sand, —
Take my hand
And walk with me once more by crumbling walls;
Up mouldering stairs where grey-stemmed ivy clings,
To hear forgotten bells, as evening falls,
Rippling above us invisibly their slowly widening rings.
Did you once love me? Did you bear a name?
Did you once stand before me without shame?
Take my hand: your face is one I know,
I loved you, long ago:
You are like spring returned through snow.
Once, I know, I walked with you in starlight,
And many nights I slept and dreamed of you;
Come, let us climb once more these stairs of starlight,
This midnight stream of cloud-flung blue!
Music murmurs beneath us like a sea,
And faints to a ghostly whisper. Come with me!

Are you still doubtful of me — hesitant still,
Fearful, perhaps, that I may yet remember
What you would gladly, if you could, forget?
You were unfaithful once, you met your lover;
Still in your shame you bear that red-eyed ember;
And I was silent, — you remember my silence yet.
You knew, as well as I, I could not kill him,
Nor touch him with hot hands, nor yet with hate.
No, and it was not you I saw with anger.
Instead, I rose and beat at steel-walled fate,
Cried till I lay exhausted, sick, unfriended,
That life, so seeming sure, and love, so certain,

Should loose such evil, be so abruptly ended,
Ring down so suddenly an unlooked-for curtain.

Take my hand, then, come with me
By the white shadowy crashings of a sea.
Look how the long volutes of foam unfold
To spread their mottled shimmer along the sand!
Take my hand,
Do not remember how these depths are cold,
Nor how, when you are dead,
Green leagues of sea will glimmer above your head.
You lean your face upon your hands and cry,
The blown sand whispers about your feet,
Terrible seems it now to die, —
Terrible now, with life so incomplete,
To turn away from the balconies and the music,
The sunlit afternoons,
To hear behind you there a far-off laughter
Lost in a stirring of sand among dry dunes.
Die not sadly, you whom life has beaten!
Lift your face up, laughing, die like a queen!
Take cold flowers of foam in your warm white fingers!
Death's but a change of sky from blue to green.

As evening falls,
The walls grow luminous and warm, the walls
Tremble and glow . . . the music breathes upon us,
The rayed white shaft plays over our heads like magic,
And to and fro we move and lean and change.
You, in a world grown strange,
Laugh at a darkness, clench your hands despairing,
Smash your glass on the floor, no longer caring,
Sink suddenly down and cry.
You hear the applause that greets your latest rival,
You are forgotten: your rival — who knows? — is I.
I laugh in the warm bright light of answering laughter,
I am inspired and young . . . and though I see

You sitting alone there, dark, with shut eyes crying,
I bask in the light, and in your hate of me.
Failure? . . . well, the time comes soon or later.
The night must come. And I'll be one who clings,
Desperately, to hold the applause, one instant, —
To keep some youngster waiting in the wings.

The music changes tone . . . a room is darkened,
Someone is moving . . . the crack of white light widens,
And all is dark again; till suddenly falls
A wandering disk of light on floor and walls,
Winks out, returns again, climbs and descends,
Gleams on a clock, a glass, shrinks back to darkness;
And then at last, in the chaos of that place,
Dazzles like frozen fire on your clear face.
Well, I have found you. We have met at last.
Now you shall not escape me: in your eyes
I see the horrible huddlings of your past, —
All you remember blackens, utters cries,
Reaches far hands and faint. I hold the light
Close to your cheek, watch the pained pupils shrink, —
Watch the vile ghosts of all you vilely think.
Now all the hatreds of my life have met:
My fingers find the well-loved throat they seek,
And press, and fling you down . . . and then forget.
Who plays for me? What sudden drums keep time
To the ecstatic rhythm of my crime?
What flute shrills out as moonlight strikes the floor?
What violin so faintly cries
Seeing how strangely in the moon he lies?
The room grows dark once more,
The crack of white light narrows around the door,
And all is silent, except a slow complaining
Of flutes and violins, a music waning.

Take my hand, then, walk with me
By the slow soundless crashings of a sea.

Look, how white these shells are, on this sand!
Take my hand,
And watch the waves run inward from the sky
Line upon foaming line to plunge and die.
The dry grass creaks in the wind, the blown sand whispers,
The soft sand seethes on the dunes, the clear grains glisten,
Once they were rock . . . a chaos of golden boulders . . .
Now they are blown by the wind . . . we stand and listen
To the sliding of grain upon timeless grain
And feel our lives go past like a whisper of pain.
Have I not seen you, have we not met before
Here on this sun-and-sea-wrecked shore?
You shade your sea-grey eyes with a sunlit hand
And peer at me . . . far sea-gulls, in your eyes,
Flash in the sun, go down. I hear slow sand,
And shrink to nothing beneath blue brilliant skies.

The music ends. The screen grows dark. We hurry
To go our devious secret ways, forgetting
Those many lives. We loved, we laughed, we killed,
We danced in fire, we drowned in a whirl of sea-waves.
The flutes are stilled, and a thousand dreams are stilled.

Whose body have I found beside dark waters,
The cold white body garlanded with sea-weed?
Staring with wide eyes at the sky?
I bent my head above it, and cried in silence.
Only the things I dreamed of heard my cry.

Once I loved, and she I loved was murdered.
Again I loved, and love itself was murdered.
Vainly we follow the circle of mythic days.
The screen at last grows dark, the flutes are silent.
The doors are closed. We go our separate ways.

7

The sun goes down in a cold pale flare of light.
The trees grow dark: the shadows lean to the east:
And lights wink out through the windows, one by one.
A clamor of frosty sirens mourns at the night.
Pale slate-grey clouds whirl up from the sunken sun.

And the wandering one, the inquisitive dreamer of dreams,
The eternal asker of answers, stands in the street,
And lifts his palms for the first cold ghost of rain.
The purple lights leap down the hill before him.
The gorgeous night has begun again.

'I will ask them all, I will ask them all their dreams,
I will hold my light above them and seek their faces,
I will hear them whisper, invisible in their veins. . .'
The eternal asker of answers becomes as darkness,
Or as a wind blown over a forest,
Or as the numberless voices of autumn rains.

We hear him and take him among us like a gust of music,
Like the ghost of a music we have somewhere heard;
We crowd through the streets in a dazzle of broken lamplight,
We pour in a sinister mass, ascend a stair,
With laughter and cry, word upon murmured word,
We flow, we descend, we turn . . . and the eternal dreamer
Moves on among us like light, like evening air.

Good night! good night! good night! we go our ways,
The rain runs over the pavement before our feet,
The cold rain falls, the rain sings.
We walk, we run, we ride. We turn our faces
To what the eternal evening brings.

Our hands are hot and raw with the stones we have laid,
We have built a tower of stone high into the sky.

We have built a city of towers.
Our hands are light, they are singing with emptiness.
Our souls are light. They have shaken a burden of hours.
What did we build it for? Was it all a dream? . . .
Ghostly above us in lamplight the towers gleam . . .
And after a while they will fall to dust and rain;
Or else we will tear them down with impatient hands;
And hew rock out of the earth, and build them again.

IV

Senlin: A Biography

*

I. HIS DARK ORIGINS

1

Senlin sits before us, and we see him.
He smokes his pipe before us, and we hear him.
Is he small, with reddish hair,
Does he light his pipe with a meditative stare,
And a pointed flame reflected in both eyes?
Is he sad and happy and foolish and wise?
Did no one see him enter the doors of the city,
Looking about him at roofs and trees and skies?
'I stepped from a cloud,' he says, 'as evening fell;
I walked on the sound of a bell;
I ran with winged heels along a gust;
Or is it true that I laughed and sprang from dust? . . .
Has no one, in a great autumnal forest,
When the wind bares the trees,
Heard the sad horn of Senlin slowly blown?
Has no one, on a mountain in the spring,
Heard Senlin sing?
Perhaps I came alone on a snow-white horse, —

Riding alone from the deep-starred night.
Perhaps I came on a ship whose sails were music, —
Sailing from moon or sun on a river of light.'

He lights his pipe with a pointed flame.
'Yet, there were many autumns before I came,
And many springs. And more will come, long after
There is no horn from me, or song, or laughter.'

The city dissolves about us, and its walls
Become an ancient forest. There is no sound
Except where an old twig tires and falls;
Or a lizard among the dead leaves crawls;
Or a flutter is heard in darkness along the ground.

Has Senlin become a forest? Do we walk in Senlin?
Is Senlin the wood we walk in, — ourselves, — the world?
Senlin! we cry . . . Senlin! again . . . No answer,
Only soft broken echoes backward whirled. . .

Yet we would say: this is no wood at all,
But a small white room with a lamp upon the wall;
And Senlin, before us, pale, with reddish hair,
Lights his pipe with a meditative stare.

2

Senlin, walking beside us, swings his arms
And turns his head to look at walls and trees.
The wind comes whistling from shrill stars of winter,
The lights are jewels, black roots freeze.
'Did I, then, stretch from the bitter earth like these,
Reaching upward with slow and rigid pain
To seek, in another air, myself again?'

(Immense and solitary in a desert of rocks
Behold a bewildered oak

With white clouds screaming through its leafy brain.)
'Or was I the single ant, or tinier thing,
That crept from the rocks of buried time
And dedicated its holy life to climb
From atom to beetling atom, jagged grain to grain,
Patiently out of the darkness we call sleep
Into the hollow gigantic world of light
Thinking the sky to be its destined shell,
Hoping to fit it well! — '

The city dissolves about us; and its walls
Are mountains of rock cruelly carved by wind.
Sand streams down their wasting sides, sand
Mounts upward slowly about them: foot and hand
We crawl and bleed among them. Is this Senlin?
In the desert of Senlin must we live and die?
We hear the decay of rocks, the crash of boulders,
Snarling of sand on sand. 'Senlin!' we cry.
'Senlin!' again . . . Our shadows revolve in silence
Under the soulless brilliance of blue sky.

Yet we would say: these are no rocks at all,
Nor desert of sand . . . here by a city wall
White lights jewel the evening, black roots freeze,
And Senlin turns his head to look at trees.

3

It is evening, Senlin says, and in the evening,
By a silent shore, by a far distant sea,
White unicorns come gravely down to the water.
In the lilac dusk they come, they are white and stately,
Stars hang over the purple waveless sea;
A sea on which no sail was ever lifted,
Where a human voice was never heard.
The shadows of vague hills are dark on the water,
The silent stars seem silently to sing.

And gravely come white unicorns down to the water,
One by one they come and drink their fill;
And daisies burn like stars on the darkened hill.

It is evening Senlin says, and in the evening
The leaves on the trees, abandoned by the light,
Look to the earth, and whisper, and are still.
The bat with horned wings, tumbling through the darkness,
Breaks the web, and the spider falls to the ground.
The starry dewdrop gathers upon the oakleaf,
Clings to the edge, and falls without a sound.
Do maidens spread their white palms to the starlight
And walk three steps to the east and clearly sing?
Do dewdrops fall like a shower of stars from willows?
Has the small moon a ghostly ring? . . .
White skeletons dance on the moonlit grass,
Singing maidens are buried in deep graves,
The stars hang over a sea like polished glass . . .
And solemnly one by one in the darkness there
Neighing far off on the haunted air
White unicorns come gravely down to the water.

No silver bells are heard. The westering moon
Lights the pale floors of caverns by the sea.
Wet weed hangs on the rock. In shimmering pools
Left on the rocks by the receding sea
Starfish slowly turn their white and brown
Or writhe on the naked rocks and drown.
Do sea-girls haunt these caves — do we hear faint singing?
Do we hear from under the sea a thin bell ringing?
Was that a white hand lifted among the bubbles
And fallen softly back?
No, these shores and caverns all are silent,
Dead in the moonlight; only, far above,
On the smooth contours of these headlands,
White amid the eternal black,
One by one in the moonlight there

Neighing far off on the haunted air
The unicorns come down to the sea.

4

Senlin, walking before us in the sunlight,
Bending his long legs in a peculiar way,
Goes to his work with thoughts of the universe.
His hands are in his pockets, he smokes his pipe,
He is happily conscious of roofs and skies;
And, without turning his head, he turns his eyes
To regard white horses drawing a small white hearse.
The sky is brilliant between the roofs,
The windows flash in the yellow sun,
On the hard pavement ring the hoofs,
The light wheels softly run.
Bright particles of sunlight fall,
Quiver and flash, gyrate and burn,
Honey-like heat flows down the wall,
The white spokes dazzle and turn.

Senlin, walking before us in the sunlight,
Regards the hearse with an introspective eye.
'Is it my childhood there,' he asks,
'Sealed in a hearse and hurrying by?'
He taps his trowel against a stone;
The trowel sings with a silver tone.

'Nevertheless, I know this well.
Bury it deep and toll a bell,
Bury it under land or sea,
You cannot bury it save in me.'

It is as if his soul had become a city,
With noisily peopled streets, and through these streets
Senlin himself comes driving a small white hearse . . .
'Senlin!' we cry. He does not turn his head.

But is that Senlin? — or is this city Senlin, —
Quietly watching the burial of its dead?
Dumbly observing the cortège of its dead?
Yet we would say that all this is but madness:
Around a distant corner trots the hearse.
And Senlin walks before us in the sunlight
Happily conscious of his universe.

                                    5

In the hot noon, in an old and savage garden,
The peach-tree grows. Its ugly cruel roots
Rend and rifle the silent earth for moisture.
Above, in the blue, hang warm and golden fruits.
Look, how the cancerous roots crack mould and stone!
Earth, if she had a voice, would wail her pain.
Is she the victim? Or is the tree the victim?
Delicate blossoms opened in the rain,
Black bees flew among them in the sunlight,
And sacked them ruthlessly; and now a bird
Hangs, sharp-eyed, in the leaves, and pecks the fruit;
And the peach-tree dreams, and does not say a word.
. . . Senlin, tapping his trowel against a stone,
Observes this tree he planted: it is his own.

'You will think it strange,' says Senlin, 'but this tree
Utters profound things in this garden;
And in its silence speaks to me.
I have sensations, when I stand beneath it,
As if its leaves looked at me, and could see;
And these thin leaves, even in windless air,
Seem to be whispering me a choral music,
Insubstantial but debonair.

"Regard," they seem to say,
"Our idiot root, which going its brutal way
Has cracked your garden wall!

Ugly, is it not?
A desecration of this place . . .
And yet, without it, could we exist at all?"
Thus, rustling with importance, they seem to me
To make their apology;
Yet, while they apologize,
Ask me a wary question with their eyes.
Yes, it is true their origin is low —
Brutish and dull and cruel . . . and it is true
Their roots have cracked the wall. But do we know
The leaves less cruel — the root less beautiful?
Sometimes it seems as if there grew
In the dull garden of my mind
A tree like this, which, singing with delicate leaves,
Yet cracks the walls with cruel roots and blind.
Sometimes, indeed, it appears to me
That I myself am such a tree . . .'

. . . And as we hear from Senlin these strange words
So, slowly, in the sunlight, he becomes this tree:
And among the pleasant leaves hang sharp-eyed birds
While cruel roots dig downward secretly.

6

Rustling among his odds and ends of knowledge
Suddenly, to his wonder, Senlin finds
How Cleopatra and Senebtisi
Were dug by many hands from ancient tombs.
Cloth after scented cloth the sage unwinds:
Delicious, to see our futile modern sunlight
Dance like a harlot among these Dogs and Dooms!

First, the huge pyramid, with rock on rock
Bloodily piled to heaven; and under this
A gilded cavern, bat-festooned;
And here in rows on rows, with gods about them,

Cloudily lustrous, dim, the sacred coffins,
Silver-starred and crimson-mooned.

What holy secret shall we now uncover?
Inside the outer coffin is a second;
Inside the second, smaller, lies a third.
This one is carved, and like a human body;
And painted over with fish and bull and bird.
Here are men walking stiffly in procession,
Blowing horns or lifting spears.
Where do they march to? Where do they come from?
Soft whine of horns is in our ears.

Inside the third, a fourth . . . and this the artist, —
A priest, perhaps? — did most to make resemble
The flesh of her who lies within.
The brown eyes widely stare at the bat-hung ceiling.
The hair is black, the mouth is thin.

Princess! Secret of life! We come to praise you!
The torch is lowered, this coffin too we open,
And the dark air is drunk with musk and myrrh.
Here are the thousand white and scented wrappings,
The gilded mask, and jewelled eyes, of her.

And now the body itself, brown, gaunt, and ugly,
And the hollow skull, in which the brains are withered,
Lie bare before us. Princess, is this all?
Something there was we asked that is not answered.
Soft bats, in rows, hang on the lustred wall.

And all we hear is a whisper sound of music,
Of brass horns dustily raised and briefly blown,
And a cry of grief; and men in a stiff procession
Marching away and softly gone.

7

'And am I then, a pyramid?' says Senlin,
'In which are caves and coffins, where lies hidden
Some old and mocking hieroglyph of flesh?
Or am I rather the moonlight, spreading subtly
Above those stones and times?
Or the green blade of grass that bravely grows
Between two massive boulders of black basalt
Year after year, and fades and blows?'

Senlin, sitting before us in the lamplight,
Laughs, and lights his pipe. The yellow flame
Minutely flares in his eyes, minutely dwindles.
Does a blade of grass have Senlin for a name?
Yet we would say that we have seen him somewhere,
A tiny spear of green beneath the blue,
Playing his destiny in a sun-warmed crevice
With the gigantic fates of frost and dew.

Does a spider come and spin his gossamer ladder
Rung by silver rung
Chaining it fast to Senlin? Its faint shadow
Flung, waveringly, where his is flung?
Does a raindrop dazzle starlike down his length
Trying his futile strength?
A snowflake startle him? The stars defeat him?
Through aeons of dusk have birds above him sung?
Time is a wind, says Senlin; time, like music,
Blows over us its mournful beauty, passes,
And leaves behind a shadowy recollection, —
A helpless gesture of mist above the grasses.

8

In cold blue lucid dusk before the sunrise,
One yellow star sings over a peak of snow,

And melts and vanishes in a light like roses.
Through slanting mist, black rocks appear and glow.

The clouds flow downward, slowly as grey glaciers,
Or up to pale rose-azure pass.
Blue streams tinkle down from snow to boulders,
From boulders to white grass.

Icicles on the pine tree melt
And softly flash in the sun:
In long straight lines the star-drops fall
One by one.

Is a voice heard while the shadows still are long,
Borne slowly down on the sparkled air?
Is a thin bell heard from the peak of silence?
Is someone among the high snows there?

Where the blue stream flows coldly among the meadows
And mist still clings to rock and tree
Senlin walks alone; and from that twilight
Looks darkly up, to see

The calm unmoving peak of snow-white silence,
The rocks aflame with ice, the rose-blue sky . . .
Ghost-like, a cloud descends from twinkling ledges,
To nod before the dwindling sun and die.

'Something there is,' says Senlin, 'in that mountain,
Something forgotten now, that once I knew . . .'
We walk before a sun-tipped peak in silence,
Our shadows descend before us, long and blue.

II. HIS FUTILE PREOCCUPATIONS

1

I am a house, says Senlin, locked and darkened,
Sealed from the sun with wall and door and blind.

Summon me loudly, and you'll hear slow footsteps
Ring far and faint in the galleries of my mind.
You'll hear soft steps on an old and dusty stairway;
Peer darkly through some corner of a pane,
You'll see me with a faint light coming slowly,
Pausing above some balcony of the brain . . .

I am a city . . . In the blue light of evening
Wind wanders among my streets and makes them fair;
I am a room of rock . . . a maiden dances
Lifting her hands, tossing her golden hair.
She combs her hair, the room of rock is darkened,
She extends herself in me, and I am sleep.
It is my pride that starlight is above me;
I dream amid waves of air, my walls are deep.

I am a door . . . before me roils the darkness,
Behind me ring clear waves of sound and light.
Stand in the shadowy street outside, and listen —
The crying of violins assails the night . . .
My walls are deep, but the cries of music pierce them;
They shake with the sound of drums . . . yet it is strange
That I should know so little what means this music,
Hearing it always within me change and change.

Knock on the door, — and you shall have an answer.
Open the heavy walls to set me free,
And blow a horn to call me into the sunlight, —
And startled, then, what a strange thing you shall see!
Nuns, murderers, and drunkards, saints and sinners,
Lover and dancing girl and sage and clown
Will laugh upon you, and you will find me nowhere.
I am a room, a house, a street, a town.

2

It is morning, Senlin says, and in the morning
When the light drips through the shutters like the dew,

I arise, I face the sunrise,
And do the things my fathers learned to do.
Stars in the purple dusk above the rooftops
Pale in a saffron mist and seem to die,
And I myself on a swiftly tilting planet
Stand before a glass and tie my tie.

Vine leaves tap my window,
Dew-drops sing to the garden stones,
The robin chirps in the chinaberry tree
Repeating three clear tones.

It is morning. I stand by the mirror
And tie my tie once more.
While waves far off in a pale rose twilight
Crash on a coral shore.
I stand by a mirror and comb my hair:
How small and white my face! —
The green earth tilts through a sphere of air
And bathes in a flame of space.

There are houses hanging above the stars
And stars hung under a sea.
And a sun far off in a shell of silence
Dapples my walls for me.

It is morning, Senlin says, and in the morning
Should I not pause in the light to remember god?
Upright and firm I stand on a star unstable,
He is immense and lonely as a cloud.
I will dedicate this moment before my mirror
To him alone, for him I will comb my hair.
Accept these humble offerings, cloud of silence!
I will think of you as I descend the stair.

Vine leaves tap my window,
The snail-track shines on the stones,

Dew-drops flash from the chinaberry tree
Repeating two clear tones.

It is morning, I awake from a bed of silence,
Shining I rise from the starless waters of sleep.
The walls are about me still as in the evening,
I am the same, and the same name still I keep.
The earth revolves with me, yet makes no motion,
The stars pale silently in a coral sky.
In a whistling void I stand before my mirror,
Unconcerned, and tie my tie.

There are horses neighing on far-off hills
Tossing their long white manes,
And mountains flash in the rose-white dusk,
Their shoulders black with rains.
It is morning. I stand by the mirror
And surprise my soul once more;
The blue air rushes above my ceiling,
There are suns beneath my floor.

. . . It is morning, Senlin says, I ascend from darkness
And depart on the winds of space for I know not where,
My watch is wound, a key is in my pocket,
And the sky is darkened as I descend the stair.
There are shadows across the windows, clouds in heaven,
And a god among the stars; and I will go
Thinking of him as I might think of daybreak
And humming a tune I know.

Vine leaves tap at the window,
Dew-drops sing to the garden stones,
The robin chirps in the chinaberry tree
Repeating three clear tones.

3

I walk to my work, says Senlin, along a street
Superbly hung in space.
I lift these mortal stones, and with my trowel
I tap them into place.
But is god, perhaps, a giant who ties his tie
Grimacing before a colossal glass of sky?

These stones are heavy, these stones decay,
These stones are wet with rain,
I build them into a wall today,
Tomorrow they fall again.

Does god arise from a chaos of starless sleep,
Rise from the dark and stretch his arms and yawn;
And drowsily look from the window at his garden;
And rejoice at the dewdrop sparkling on his lawn?
Does he remember, suddenly, with amazement,
The yesterday he left in sleep, — his name, —
Or the glittering street superbly hung in wind
Along which, in the dusk, he slowly came?

I devise new patterns for laying stones
And build a stronger wall.
One drop of rain astonishes me
And I let my trowel fall.

The flashing of leaves delights my eyes,
Blue air delights my face;
I will dedicate this stone to god
As I tap it into its place.

4

That woman — did she try to attract my attention?
Is it true I saw her smile and nod?
She turned her head and smiled . . . was it for me?

It is better to think of work or god.
The clouds pile coldly above the houses
Slow wind revolves the leaves:
It begins to rain, and the first long drops
Are slantingly blown from eaves.

But it is true she tried to attract my attention!
She pressed a rose to her chin and smiled.
Her hand was white by the richness of her hair,
Her eyes were those of a child.
It is true she looked at me as if she liked me,
And turned away, afraid to look too long!
She watched me out of the corners of her eyes;
And, tapping time with fingers, hummed a song.

. . . Nevertheless, I will think of work,
With a trowel in my hands;
Or the vague god who blows like clouds
Above these dripping lands . . .

But . . . is it sure she tried to attract my attention?
She leaned her elbow in a peculiar way
There in the crowded room . . . she touched my hand . . .
She must have known, and yet, — she let it stay.
Music of flesh! Music of root and sod!
Leaf touching leaf in the rain!
Impalpable clouds of red ascend,
Red clouds blow over my brain.

Did she await from me some sign of acceptance?
I smoothed my hair with a faltering hand.
I started a feeble smile, but the smile was frozen:
Perhaps, I thought, I misunderstand.
Is it to be conceived that I could attract her —
This dull and futile flesh attract such fire?
I, — with a trowel's dulness in hand and brain! —
Take on some godlike aspect, rouse desire?

Incredible! . . . delicious! . . . I will wear
A brighter color of tie, arranged with care;
I will delight in god as I comb my hair.

And the conquests of my bolder past return
Like strains of music, some lost tune
Recalled from youth and a happier time.
I take my sweetheart's arm in the dusk once more;
Once more we climb

Up the forbidden stairway,
Under the flickering light, along the railing:
I catch her hand in the dark, we laugh once more,
I hear the rustle of silk, and follow swiftly,
And softly at last we close the door.

Yes, it is true that woman tried to attract me:
It is true she came out of time for me,
Came from the swirling and savage forest of earth,
The cruel eternity of the sea.
She parted the leaves of waves and rose from silence
Shining with secrets she did not know.
Music of dust! Music of web and web!
And I, bewildered, let her go.

I light my pipe. The flame is yellow,
Edged underneath with blue.
These thoughts are truer of god, perhaps,
Than thoughts of god are true.

5

It is noontime, Senlin says, and a street piano
Strikes sharply against the sunshine a harsh chord,
And the universe is suddenly agitated,
And pain to my heart goes glittering like a sword.
Do I imagine it? The dust is shaken,

The sunlight quivers, the brittle oak-leaves tremble.
The world, disturbed, conceals its agitation;
And I, too, will dissemble.

Yet it is sorrow has found my heart,
Sorrow for beauty, sorrow for death;
And pain twirls slowly among the trees.

The street-piano revolves its glittering music,
The sharp notes flash and dazzle and turn,
Memory's knives are in this sunlit silence,
They ripple and lazily burn.
The star on which my shadow falls is frightened, —
It does not move; my trowel taps a stone,
The sweet note wavers amid derisive music;
And I, in a horror of sunlight, stand alone.

Do not recall my weakness, savage music!
Let the knives rest!
Impersonal, harsh, the music revolves and glitters,
And the notes like poniards pierce my breast.
And I remember the shadows of webs on stones,
And the sound of rain on withered grass,
And a sorrowful face that looked without illusions
At its image in the glass.

Do not recall my childhood, pitiless music!
The green blades flicker and gleam,
The red bee bends the clover, deeply humming;
In the blue sea above me lazily stream
Cloud upon thin-blown cloud, revolving, scattering;
The mulberry tree rakes heaven and drops its fruit;
Amazing sunlight sings in the opened vault
On dust and bones; and I am mute.

It is noon; the bells let fall soft flowers of sound.
They turn on the air, they shrink in the flare of noon.

It is night; and I lie alone, and watch through the window
The terrible ice-white emptiness of the moon.
Small bells, far off, spill jewels of sound like rain,
A long wind hurries them whirled and far,
A cloud creeps over the moon, my bed is darkened,
I hold my breath and watch a star.

Do not disturb my memories, heartless music!
I stand once more by a vine-dark moonlit wall,
The sound of my footsteps dies in a void of moonlight,
And I watch white jasmine fall.
Is it my heart that falls? Does earth itself
Drift, a white petal, down the sky?
One bell-note goes to the stars in the blue-white silence,
Solitary and mournful, a somnolent cry.

6

Death himself in the rain . . . death himself . . .
Death in the savage sunlight . . . skeletal death . . .
I hear the clack of his feet,
Clearly on stones, softly in dust;
He hurries among the trees
Whirling the leaves, tossing his hands from waves.
Listen! the immortal footsteps beat!

Death himself in the grass, death himself,
Gyrating invisibly in the sun,
Scatters the grass-blades, whips the wind,
Tears at boughs with malignant laughter:
On the long echoing air I hear him run.

Death himself in the dusk, gathering lilacs,
Breaking a white-fleshed bough,
Strewing purple on a cobwebbed lawn,
Dancing, dancing,
The long red sun-rays glancing

On flailing arms, skipping with hideous knees,
Cavorting grotesque ecstasies:
I do not see him, but I see the lilacs fall,
I hear the scrape of knuckles against the wall,
The leaves are tossed and tremble where he plunges among them,
And I hear the sound of his breath,
Sharp and whistling, the rhythm of death.

It is evening: the lights on a long street balance and sway.
In the purple ether they swing and silently sing,
The street is a gossamer swung in space,
And death himself in the wind comes dancing along it,
And the lights, like raindrops, tremble and swing.
Hurry, spider, and spread your glistening web,
For death approaches!
Hurry, rose, and open your heart to the bee,
For death approaches!
Maiden, let down your hair for the hands of your lover,
Comb it with moonlight and wreathe it with leaves,
For death approaches!

Death, huge in the star; small in the sand-grain;
Death himself in the rain,
Drawing the rain about him like a garment of jewels:
I hear the sound of his feet
On the stairs of the wind, in the sun,
In the forests of the sea . . .
Listen! the immortal footsteps beat!

7

It is noontime, Senlin says. The sky is brilliant
Above a green and dreaming hill.
I lay my trowel down. The pool is cloudless,
The grass, the wall, the peach-tree, all are still.
It appears to me that I am one with these:
A hill, upon whose back are a wall and trees.

It is noontime: all seems still
Upon this green and flowering hill.

Yet suddenly, out of nowhere in the sky,
A cloud comes whirling, and flings
A lazily coiling vortex of shade on the hill.
It crosses the hill, and a bird in the peach-tree sings.
Amazing! Is there a change?
The hill seems somehow strange.
It is noontime. And in the tree
The leaves are delicately disturbed
Where the bird descends invisibly.
It is noontime. And in the pool
The sky is blue and cool.

Yet suddenly, out of nowhere,
Something flings itself at the hill,
Tears with claws at the earth,
Lunges and hisses and softly recoils,
Crashing against the green.
The peach-tree braces itself, the pool is frightened,
The grass blades quiver, the bird is still;
The wall silently struggles against the sunlight;
A terror stiffens the hill.
The trees turn rigidly, to face
Something that circles with slow pace:
The blue pool seems to shrink
From something that slides above its brink.
What struggle is this, ferocious and still —
What war in sunlight on this hill?
What is it creeping to dart
Like a knife-blade at my heart?

It is noontime, Senlin says, and all is tranquil:
The brilliant sky burns over a greenbright earth.
The peach-tree dreams in the sun, the wall is contented.
A bird in the peach-leaves, moving from sun to shadow,

Phrases again his unremembering mirth,
His lazily beautiful, foolish, mechanical mirth.

8

The pale blue gloom of evening comes
Among the phantom forests and walls
With a mournful and rhythmic sound of drums.
My heart is disturbed with a sound of myriad throbbing,
Persuasive and sinister, near and far:
In the blue evening of my heart
I hear the thrum of the evening star.

My work is uncompleted; and yet I hurry, —
Hearing the whispered pulsing of those drums, —
To enter the luminous walls and woods of night.
It is the eternal mistress of the world
Who shakes these drums for my delight.
Listen! the drums of the leaves, the drums of the dust,
The delicious quivering of this air!

I will leave my work unfinished, and I will go
With ringing and certain step through the laughter of chaos
To the one small room in the void I know.
Yesterday it was there, —
Will I find it tonight once more when I climb the stair?

The drums of the street beat swift and soft:
In the blue evening of my heart
I hear the throb of the bridal star.
It weaves deliciously in my brain
A tyrannous melody of her:
Hands in sunlight, threads of rain
Against a weeping face that fades,
Snow on a blackened window-pane;
Fire, in a dusk of hair entangled;
Flesh, more delicate than fruit;

And a voice that searches quivering nerves
For a string to mute.

My life is uncompleted: and yet I hurry
Among the tinkling forests and walls of evening
To a certain fragrant room.
Who is it that dances there, to a beating of drums,
While stars on a grey sea bud and bloom?
She stands at the top of the stair,
With the lamplight on her hair.
I will walk through the snarling of streams of space
And climb the long steps carved from wind
And rise once more towards her face.
Listen! the drums of the drowsy trees
Beating our nuptial ecstasies!

Music spins from the heart of silence
And twirls me softly upon the air:
It takes my hand and whispers to me:
It draws the web of the moonlight down.
There are hands, it says, as cool as snow,
The hands of the Venus of the sea;
There are waves of sound in a mermaid-cave; —
Come — then — come with me!
The flesh of the sea-rose new and cool,
The wavering image of her who comes
At dusk by a blue sea-pool.

Whispers upon the haunted air —
Whisper of foam-white arm and thigh;
And a shower of delicate lights blown down
From the laughing sky! . . .
Music spins from a far-off room.
Do you remember, — it seems to say, —
The mouth that smiled, beneath your mouth,
And kissed you . . . yesterday?

It is your own flesh waits for you.
Come! you are incomplete! . . .
The drums of the universe once more
Morosely beat.
It is the harlot of the world
Who clashes the leaves like ghostly drums
And disturbs the solitude of my heart
As evening comes!

I leave my work once more, and walk
Along a street that sways in the wind.
I leave these stones, and walk once more
Along infinity's shore.
I climb the golden-laddered stair;
Among the stars in the void I climb:
I ascend the golden-laddered hair
Of the harlot-queen of time:
She laughs from a window in the sky,
Her white arms downward reach to me!
We are the universe that spins
In a dim ethereal sea.

9

It is evening, Senlin says, and in the evening
The throbbing of drums has languidly died away.
Forest and sea are still. We breathe in silence
And strive to say the things flesh cannot say.
The soulless wind falls slowly about the earth
And finds no rest.
The lover stares at the setting star, — the wakeful lover
Who finds no peace on his lover's breast.
The snare of desire that bound us in is broken;
Softly, in sorrow, we draw apart, and see,
Far off, the beauty we thought our flesh had captured, —
The star we longed to be but could not be.

Come back! We will laugh once more at the words we said!
We say them slowly again, but the words are dead.
Come back, beloved! . . . The blue void falls between,
We cry to each other: alone; unknown; unseen.

We are the grains of sand that run and rustle
In the dry wind,
We are the grains of sand who thought ourselves
Immortal.
You touch my hand, time bears you away, —
An alien star for whom I have no word.
What are the meaningless things you say?
I answer you, but am not heard.

It is evening, Senlin says;
And a dream in ruin falls.
Once more we turn in pain, bewildered,
Among our finite walls:
The walls we built ourselves with patient hands;
For the god who sealed a question in our flesh.

10

It is moonlight. Alone, in silence,
I ascend my stairs once more,
While waves, remote in a pale blue starlight,
Crash on a coral shore.
It is moonlight. The garden is silent.
I stand in my room alone.
Across my wall, from the far-off moon,
A spear of fire is thrown.

There are houses hanging above the stars,
And stars hung under a sea;
And a wind from the long blue vault of time
Waves my curtains for me.

I wait in the dark once more,
Hung between space and space;
Before the mirror I lift my hands
And face my remembered face.

Is it I who stand in a question here,
Asking to know my name?
It is I; yet I know not whither I go;
Nor why; nor whence I came.

It is I, who awoke at dawn
And arose and descended the stair;
Conceiving a god in the eye of the sun, —
In a woman's hands and hair.
It is I, whose flesh is grey with the stones
I builded into a wall:
With a mournful melody in my brain
Of a tune I cannot recall.

There are roses to break: and mouths to kiss;
And the phantom king of death.
I remember a rain-drop on a stone;
An eye in the hawthorn breath . . .
And the star I laugh on tilts through heaven;
And the heavens are black and steep.
I will forget these things once more
In the silence of sleep.

III. HIS CLOUDY DESTINY

1

Senlin sat before us and we heard him.
He smoked his pipe before us and we saw him.
Was he small, with reddish hair,
Did he light his pipe with a meditative stare

And a twinkling flame reflected in blue eyes?
'I am alone': said Senlin; 'in a forest of leaves
The single leaf that creeps and falls.
The single blade of grass in a desert of grass
That none foresaw and none recalls.
The single shell that a green wave shatters
In tiny specks of whiteness on brown sands . . .
How shall you understand me with your hearts,
Who cannot reach me with your hands? . . .'

The city dissolves about us, and its walls
Are the sands beside a sea.
We plunge in a chaos of dunes, white waves before us
Crash on kelp tumultuously,
Gulls wheel over the foam, the clouds blow tattered,
The sun is swallowed . . . Has Senlin become a shore?
Is Senlin a grain of sand beneath our footsteps,
A speck of shell upon which waves will roar? . . .
Senlin! we cry . . . Senlin! again . . . no answer,
Only the crash of sea on a shell-white shore.

Yet, we would say, this is no shore at all,
But a small bright room with lamplight on the wall;
And the familiar chair
Where Senlin sat, with lamplight on his hair.

2

Senlin, alone before us, played a music.
Was it himself he played? . . . We sat and listened,
Perplexed and pleased and tired.
'Listen!' he said, 'and you will learn a secret —
Though it is not the secret you desired.
I have not found a meaning that will praise you!
Out of the heart of silence comes this music,
Quietly speaks and dies.
Look! there is one white star above black houses!

And a tiny man who climbs towards the skies!
Where does he walk to? What does he leave behind him?
What was his foolish name?
What did he stop to say, before he left you
As simply as he came?
"Death?" did it sound like, "love, and god, and laughter,
Sunlight, and work, and pain . . . ?"
No — it appears to me that these were symbols
Of simple truths he found no way to explain.
He spoke, but found you could not understand him —
You were alone, and he was alone.

'He sought to touch you, and found he could not reach you, —
He sought to understand you, and could not hear you.
And so this music, which I play before you, —
Does it mean only what it seems to mean?
Or is it a dance of foolish waves in sunlight
Above a desperate depth of things unseen?
Listen! Do you not hear the singing voices
Out of the darkness of this sea?
But no: you cannot hear them; for if you heard them
You would have heard and captured me.
Yet I am here, talking of laughter,
Laughter and love and work and god;
As I shall talk of these same things hereafter
In wave and sod.
Walk on a hill and call me: "Senlin! . . . Senlin! . . ."
Will I not answer you as clearly as now?
Listen to rain, and you will hear me speaking.
Look for my heart in the breaking of a bough . . .'

3

Senlin stood before us in the sunlight,
And laughed, and walked away.
Did no one see him leaving the doors of the city,
Looking behind him as if he wished to stay?

Has no one, in the forests of the evening,
Heard the sad horn of Senlin slowly blown?
For somewhere, in the worlds-in-worlds about us,
He changes still, unfriended and alone.
Is he the star on which we walk at daybreak,
The light that blinds our eyes?
'Senlin!' we cry. 'Senlin!' again . . . no answer:
Only the soulless brilliance of blue skies.

Yet we would say, this was no man at all,
But a dream we dreamed, and vividly recall;
And we are mad to walk in wind and rain
Hoping to find, somewhere, that dream again.

V

The Pilgrimage of Festus

*

I. HE PLANTS HIS BEANS IN THE EARLY MORNING

1

And at last, having sacked in imagination many cities
And seen the smoke of them spread fantastically along the sky,
Having set foot upon so many walls, fallen and blackened,
And heard the harsh lamentations of women,
And watched without pity the old men, betraying their vileness,
Tear at their beards, and curse, and die,
Festus, coming alone to an eastern place
Of brown savannahs and wind-gnawed trees,
Climbed a rock that faced alone to the northward
And sat, and clasped his knees.

There was before him the confluence of three rivers:
One from the north, one from the east, one from the west.

The one from the east was blue, the one from the west was green,
Black was the one from the north, and snow was on its breast.
The sound of their roaring came up in waves on the wind,
Into the tumultuous darkness of the south they went,
And Festus sat for a day and a night and watched them
And wondered what they meant.

'Look, Festus, how without regard for you and all your sorrow
The huge sun rises and crosses the sky
And your ridiculous shadow circles about you
Shortening and lengthening silently!
What does it matter to the sun that your robe is scarlet?
That the sword at your hand is old and green!
Already the winds gnaw at you, as they have gnawed at these trees
Careless of the many things you have done and seen.'

The day ended, and the slow-wheeling magnificent constellations
Glided like lights of ships down the river of space,
And Festus was disturbed once more, and wished to speak,
And heavily raised his head at last in sorrow,
And turned towards the stars his face,
And said: 'Look, Festus, how yet once more the immortals
Kindle their delicate lanterns and walk in the sky
While you on a lonely hill sit alone in sadness
And remember that you must die!
Look at the stars, Festus, treader of kingdoms,
You who carried the world like a bird in a cage,
You whose heart is a desert, gaunt with winter,
You whose sword in youth was a sevenfold lightning
Now worn and green with age!
Look! the immortals once more in the sky of your heart
The immortals you scorned and forgot
Walk in the dim blue gardens softly apart
To a music you taught them not! . . .'

Festus in starlight watched how the three great rivers,
Bearing perpetual stars on their breasts, roared down

To gorges and chasms and desolate plains
And jungles of death, and labyrinthine cities
Swept to pale harmonies by suns and rains;
And thought of the thousands of nights and days like music
Woven by him, and the roses of love and death
Fallen in petals in the darkness of his heart;
And he sent among them a breath
And set them blowing and trembling again, on graves,
On the stones of streets, by door and path and wall,
Whirled in the air from the boughs of swinging trees
To stream like stars on the wind and slowly fall
For the hands of children, the hair of women, the hearts of lovers,
The coffins waiting beneath the swinging trees,
And the myriad eyes that in his veins went to and fro
Seeking a dream forever and finding no ease.

'Listen, Festus! How the multitudes within you
Make a slow misty music of their own!
See how the walls of cities grow young again
With the spring upon them blown!
And you too, Festus! Treader in blood of kingdoms!
You walk in a moonlit wind of dream
And you and the worlds about you are young once more
And blossom and tinkle and sing and gleam!'

Then Festus laughed, for he looked in his heart and saw
His worlds made young again
And heard the sound of a many-peopled music
And joyously into the world of himself set forward
Forgetting the long black aftermath of pain.

2

'Listen, Festus! The music, as you lie sleeping,
Builds a world of hills and stars about you,
Cities of silver in forests of blue!
Bells are jingling, birds are saluting the daybreak,

The horns are spreading a meadow of gold for you.
Walls of stone and jewels rise in the music
Like exhalations laced with fire,
Children are playing and laughing beneath them,
The dew flashes on every spire! . . .'

. . . Festus lies alone, and watches across the ceiling
Vague spokes of shadows wheeling
Ghostly fantasias from the crowded world:
A woman passes in a vortex of light, a child passes,
Echoes and shadows and perfumes are faintly whirled . . .

'Listen, Festus! The music is making trees,
The music is making rivers and towers! . . .
Music flows over the pools of sky in clouds
And scatters a tinkle of showers! . . .
Far off there, on a balcony of the wind,
The scarf of a maiden gleams,
In a rose-gold shaft of sun her soft hair glistens,
The clouds open, the tower is kindled and beams!
The waves of the river in blue and pearl-strewn green
Flash down over rocks to the sea,
Walls of marble waver upon them and shatter,
And the mist of the willow-tree!'

. . . Festus stands in the sunlight at the window
And cruelly looks at roofs and rivers and skies,
And the trees tossing their never-escaping waves
Of swirling leaves, and laughs, and shuts his eyes.
'How many times this music has deceived me!
How many times I stoop and cup my hand
Thinking to capture in it the sparkle of water, —
And quench, once more, my thirst with sand!'

But as he closes his eyes, the music, circling,
Comes laughing about him and softly sings,
The trees whisper, the meadows tremble, and it seems to him

The music touches him with soft hands, the music, dancing about
    him,
Is a dance of immortal maidens in flaming eternal rings.

3

Festus, planting beans in the early morning,
Far in his heart, in a solitary plain,
Has a vision: the sun, like a golden monster
Heaving his crimson flanks from the streaming darkness,
No sooner seeks to rise than he is slain:
Out of a vast sarcophagus of cloud
Pours the black death of rain.

. . . Festus, holding beans in the palm of his hand,
Stands astonished . . . But this is least of all.
For as the rain comes wavering over the fields
Threshing the earth with silver in its fall,
Gathering into its numberless shafts of silver
What light there is, and leaving the sky a pall,

He sees, in the arrowy darkness,
In a flashing garment of rain
A grey man like a pilgrim
Come slowly over the plain.
On his shoulder is a phantom burden —
He stoops, his white beard glistens,
For an instant he pauses, solitary in the rain,
And stands and listens.

And his eyes, for a moment, rest on those of Festus,
And Festus, troubled, lets fall the beans from his hand . . .
'It is hard, Festus, that in this soul of yours,
This so colossal world of hills and oceans,
Forests and cities of men,
You keep us here forever in outer darkness,
Wretched, in wind and rain.

Shall we do nothing but feel upon our backs
The eternal lash of rain?
Shall we do nothing, day after day forever,
But plant these beans again?'

Festus guiltily looks at his beans a moment,
Lying white and rain-washed at his feet:
It appears to him that the rain is a gorgeous music,
Sorrowful, and slow, and sweet;
Telling of hills that lie beyond the plain
And beyond the hills a sea;
With beautiful women going and coming forever
Through stone-bright streets, by walls and domes of silver,
In a sound of music to towers of filigree. . .

'. . . It is hard, Festus, that in this soul of yours,
This world of clanging star and sun
With the horns of glory blowing from space to space
And the paean of daybreak just begun,
You keep us here alone in a wind-worn plain
Stooping to plant these beans in the dark and the rain . . .'

Then Festus, lifting his eyes,
Watches the old man pass
Slowly among the shafts of the rain
Across the wind-lashed grass,
On his shoulder a phantom burden,
Till somehow he is gone:
Leaving a thinning ghost of rain
And Festus standing alone.

And Festus, resting his hands upon his hoe,
Watches the ranks of the purple rain ascending
To the cloud sarcophagus from which they came.
And the sun once more swims up like a golden monster, —
Heaving out of the streaming dark his hissing flanks of flame.

4

Festus, lighting his pipe against the sun,
Smokes in the furrows, regarding tenderly
His beans which, one by one,
Now shoulder through the dark earth sturdily.
This clear green neck, so exquisitely bent —
See how it struggles till the stone relent! . . .
A long warm wind flows by
Under a clanging sky;
Poplars, a myriad shape,
Incline and shiver, whirl and escape;
The clods grow dry;
And one by one, in delicate russets and greens,
Festus observes his beans
Exult from the humid earth, intently spring
Into the sunlight. . . And it seems to him
That, if he listens, he will hear them sing. . .
'Ah, Festus! Look how we,
Who in our caverns could not see,
But only over the blind walls blindly grope
With sensitive hands . . . having no hearts to hope,
Scarcely a dream to guide us, —
Look now how we
Press from the black soil arrogantly,
As with loud drums and trumpets bravely blown,
And a shrill laugh for him who dares deride us! . . .
Have you no cave, no sunlight, of your own? . . .'

. . . Festus, blowing the blue smoke from his pipe
Pauses a moment in his morning walk,
Patient and patronizing, like a father
Who laughs in secret, hearing his children talk. . .

'Superbly moral beans! Self-righteous ones!
One might suppose you were not beans, but suns!
Wet from the earth, two minutes old, and we

Presume to talk philosophy! . . .
Yet, none the less, — naïvely upright beans, —
I stand abashed before you! . . .
Is it with your own voices that you speak? . . .
It is strangely like a music I have heard —
Not, as one would expect of you, a squeak
Fainter than gossamer or cry of mote,
But the original, vast, reverberant Word!
Crashing of stars to dust, the crack of moons,
Combustion of suns . . . is it not these I hear? . . .
Or is it only the delicate slipping of sand-grains
From the grotesque hands you rear? . . .'

Festus, blowing a cloud of smoke before him,
Has a vision: the beans no longer seem
Pale pygmies at his feet, but, dark and monstrous,
Green titans labouring in a colossal dream
With worlds upon their backs! Slowly they move,
The firmament strains and groans, a mountain falls,
They shake in ruins their everlasting walls . . .
Out of the dark they came,
To loosen torrents of water and rock and flame . . .

'But am I then,' says Festus, 'in a cavern
From which I dare not grow —
Into the universe which is myself? . . .'
. . . The poplar whirls in the wind; the beans, before him,
Climb the colossal and savage stairs of the sunlight, —
Heartless and dreamless, cruel, superbly slow.

5

'The world grows dark,' says Festus: 'evening falls,
And it is like the rising of grey walls.
Down the cold battlements of the west, the sun
Dolorously descends.
The wind mourns over the stark and shattered trees.
The deep day ends.

'How like the sorrowing of my heart is this,
This soft ascension of despair!
The warm red memories of my heart go down
In waves of mist . . . Let the stars find the air!

'Here by the gateway let me lean and dream
Of the world that waits for me:
Through the pierced battlements of the grey clouds gleam
Delicate lights; the stars come out: I see
Beyond the plain, beyond the hills, a golden city
Dizzy with shaken light, and through the streets
Petals are flung, and a festival roars and passes . . .
Steeples rock with bells, a dull drum beats:
And now to a delicate music the dancers come
Hurling up to the night a fountain of roses,
Whirling and laughing and burying under their petals
The mournfully throbbing and stubborn drum . . .
O dancers! dancers of silver! dancers of rose! . . .
Twinkling dancers who starlike tread that air! . . .
Lighter than waves you laugh against those walls;
How like the secret dreams of my heart you are
That dance once more as the cold of evening falls.

'. . . And now an emperor comes! and now an empress!
In a golden chariot drawn by five white stallions . . .
And now the steel-blue spears wave thick as rain
Of battalions and battalions!
. . . Am I an emperor? Is my word the law? . . .
And now the gods of brass and silver pass
Swaying and flashing, shaking their chaplets of roses,
Cruel, gigantic! And an elephant with torches,
Bearing an Egyptian god in a case of glass! . . .

'Listen: a horn! . . . a violin! . . .
Weaving together an air so golden thin
It cuts the heart in two.
A girl leans out in the roar above the torches,

Her hair is dark, she flings a camellia flower:
Strange girl, I cry to you! . . .

'Softer the horn sounds, fainter the violin,
The street is quiet. She draws the shutters in,
Her shadow silently whirls away.
Now that the streets grow dark and cold and empty
Who will stay, — who will stay
To watch the grey soft-footed priests go by
Lifting their white thin faces to the sky? . . .
Or who will stay to watch one coffin pass,
Under few stars, amid stale litter of petals,
While one man rides behind it on an ass, —
Looking neither to left nor right
But staring before him into the eternal night? . . .'

The city dwindles . . . the clouds go crumbling down . . .
The wind throbs harplike through old trees,
Dark is the plain, and ancient; and to Festus,
Leaning upon the ramparts of his world,
The thought comes that tonight the world will freeze.

6

And observing from old ramparts cold with time
How the hunted stars together choiring climb
From cloud to cloud, like pilgrims,
Dreamily, slowly ascending the long blue stairs of fate, —
Patient and pale, like those who, unresisting,
Go forth to death and close their eyes and wait, —

Festus dreams; he sees himself alone
Immense and dark on a pinnacle of the world,
Lying in starlight, hugely carved in stone.
Carved of rock is the pillow beneath his head,
Hewed in the black star-granite is his bed,
Solitary and vast his upturned face

Stares at the cloudless horror of space;
While sorrowfully about the bases of his mountain,
The pine-shagged headlands, vapour-furled,
He hears the desolate waves of death and time
Sadly withdrawn and once more sadly hurled.

'. . . Ah! Festus, is this you —
This ancient crumbling basalt that in the moonlight
Feebly glistens with dew?
Is this indeed you, Festus, —
This unresisting stone
On which old leaves are blown? . . .'

Yet not alone is Festus: in the blue vagueness there,
Close to the cold dew-drenched sarcophagus,
Crouched on the topmost stair,
A flute-player pale in the starlight blows his quavering flute
While Festus dreams above him, and is mute.
Sharp and quick are the notes, brief and piercing,
They whirl and fly in the dark like birds,
Discordant and strange they rise in the eternal silence
Like a madman's dishevelled laughter and words.
Over the black sarcophagus they are blown —
'Ah, Festus, do they not trouble your ears of stone?
Through starlit granite do they not dart
To pierce your stone-cold heart?
Do they disturb the rest
Of the stone hands on your breast? . . .'

But Festus does not stir
In the darkness of his sepulchre, —
A dream possesses him.
He hears, far down, the struggling crash of waves
By the bases of the mountain, glutting the muffled caves;
He hears the boulders falling to the grey torrents of the sea;
Wind flows over him mournfully,

Mists of the waves about him rise, the vermilion stars grow
    dim . . .
And lightly between the hands of the flute-player
Whirl forth shy birds of dream,
They twinkle above the sepulchre,
Their wings in the starlight gleam . . .
And now soft fire descends from their wings,
And Festus' dream glares red:
Cloud-palaces and kingdoms dark
And multitudinous cities of rose
Within his dream are spread . . .
'The spears of your armies, Festus, on this plain,
Are as the glimmering darkness of the rain! . . .
Listen! They call you emperor! . . .
And a crown is on your head!'

Festus, never stirring at all,
Lying forever aloft and alone in the starlight,
Sadly replies from the carven stone at last:
'Who are you, now, you strange flute-player,
Who, blowing your birds above me here in the silence,
Dare to disturb my rest? . . .
Do you think, with dreams like these,
To tempt me down, or drown me in those seas?
Ah! it is the sevenfold lightning alone
Will wake this heart of stone . . .'

Then, in the shadow of the sepulchre,
The flute-player, growing old,
Blows one weak note from the broken flute;
And the lightning, sevenfold,
Smoking clangs from a star, and splits
The eternal rock apart:
And into the sea the mountain falls,
The great waves laugh, and among them falls
Hissing and faint, far down, soon lost,
The ember of a heart. . .

. . . And Festus, leaning gravely above the ramparts,
Watching a blood-red star go down the sky,
Stands astonished. Was this indeed a dream?
Summits of snow await him far in the starlight:
Cities, beyond the snow-peaks, stir and gleam.

II. HE CLIMBS THE COLOSSAL AND SAVAGE STAIRS OF THE SUNLIGHT

1

'Beautiful darkener of hearts, weaver of silence,
Woman of the bitter desert and the bronze mountains,
Grim Sphinx brooding over the wind-flung dunes of time, —
Is it not enough that Festus brings you a kingdom?
Woman of the pale and sinister secret,
You who flash forth already laughing
From the tumultuous and cruel glare of jungles,
The black chasms of the sea, —
Will you demand yet more of me?
Desolate and heartless woman!
You who arise like a dry and savage wind
Withering the flesh, consuming cities:
You who above me in the night time
Tower, cold and blue as a caryatid,
Stone-like among the stars, —
Are the jewels and spoils of an empire not sufficient?
Are the notes of my flute not sweet to you?
Are my hands not yet dark enough with blood?

'Implacable sorceress,
Dancer among the black tombs of the Pharaohs!
Dancer among bats and serpents,
Whose cool shoulders are soft with cobwebs,
Whose eyes glow in the dusk like sepulchral jewels,
Whose hands are cruel;
You who glide like a priestess
Among the moist columns of moonlit roofless temples

On an errand of horror and secrecy;
Stealthy dancer amid leaves and green starlight,
Haunter of dead vineyards and houses defiled,
Laugher amid the grey wastes and waters of kingdoms, —
Is the anguish of my heart not enough for you?
Is the sorrow of my flesh not sufficient?
Must I destroy yet more for you, —
Even, at last, myself?

'Beautiful and pale-lipped visionary,
Votaress in the clear depths of whose dark eyes
Are the infinite silences of the skies
And the bursting and paling of stars;
You in whose smile are the flamings and fadings of suns,
In whose laughter are hidden the secrets of the past,
In whose "yes" are the blue corridors of eternity
In whose "no" flash the scarlet lightnings of death;
Look! my sword is red for you,
I have blown over empires the horns of desolation for you;
Towers have crashed into dust for you;
Men and women for you lie dead.

'Inscrutable enchantress,
Spinner of the everlasting blue-and-gold
Which takes captive the simplicities of the flesh;
You whose hand falls heavily on my heart,
You under whose smile I tremble and grow mighty,
You out of whose world-darkening shadow
I am weak and cannot rise to depart —
Tell me, since these offerings are insufficient,
These kingdoms not enough,
What more must I fling down the abysm of your hatred?
To what darkness and terror take my way?

'Listen! A sound of misery reaches your ears,
The lamentations of the dying,
The sound of the myriad homeless, wailing and crying

By glowing walls
In the smoky obscurity of the moon.
Listen again! The sound of singing,
And iron footsteps rhythmically ringing
In mountainous tread
Down the dark streets of the dying and the dead!
Drums beat, walls quiver,
My armies flow forever past me in the darkness,
Darkly glinting like a river;
They lap and curl in the torchlight by old walls;
Now here, now there, into the black swirling torrent
A loosened fragment falls.
And they bring home for you solemnly from strange lands
Vessels of gold and silver, coffers of brass,
Gods of vermilion and ivory encased in glass,
Birds in filigree cages,
Pale slave-women drooping in chains,
Prophets and priests and dancers and frightened sages,
Jewels that flash about you like tropic rains!
Musicians throb their strings for you
A singer from a far blue island sings for you;
Have I not yet brought you enough?

'Beautiful woman! golden woman whose heart is silence!
Azure pool of the eternal in which my soul bathes timidly!
Pity me, smile upon me, tell me the way
To the holy treasure which will unlock your love for me.'

2

'It is night-time,' Festus says, 'and in the night-time
All my dark dreams return, sadly reproach me
With unfulfilments. . . Why is it, old man of the rain,
That here, — as I toss and cannot sleep in the darkness
Under this lofty canopy of dusky azure
Which I have caused to be illuminated with silver planets, —
You return to me again?

Truly we have come far, no longer in outer darkness
Do we stoop and plant our beans in the wind and the rain!'

. . . Fragrance of lotus-flowers and sandalwood
Wavers and faints in the coolness of the room,
The great fountain, outside, crashes on a pavement of gold,
Trees plunge heavily in the thin starlight
Shaking slow cries from somnolent nightingales,
Wind hums over the palace walls,
The fountain perpetually falls . . .
And the eyes of the old man rest on those of Festus, —
Or is it a dream? — and Festus sharply recalls

The ancient furrows of earth, gleaming with rain,
Grey clouds sweeping the trees, the rain-dark plain,
Rain-drops rushing amid the grass,
And the coldness and the loneliness of clouds and winds; —
And he sees once more the old man pass
Troubled and grey into the greyness and the pain
Of the harsh-arrowed rain.

'. . . Ah, Festus, do not forget
It is but a little way we have travelled yet
From the wretched darkness of that time!
Shall we take forever our ease amid silks and music
Or, — up this colossal stairway, — shall we climb? . . .'

The words are softly murmured, the words die,
They are lost in the perpetual crash of the great fountain
On its pavement of gold,
The stars seem to be tossed on the leaves of trees.
And in the returning silence it seems to Festus
This ancient figure is but himself grown old, —
Grown old in misery and futility and loneliness,
Grown old in darkness and wretchedness,
Solitary and far in a wind-worn plain,
Planting his beans forever in the wind and the rain.

3

'. . . Now that the kings are conquered, west and east,'
Says Festus, 'let the dark world learn my name:
Carve it on walls! cut deeply every stone
With "Festus!" . . . till the stones beneath men's feet,
No matter where they go, to what dark borders,
Shrill "Festus! Festus! Festus!" I would have
The leaves of trees cry "Festus" in the wind,
The tongues of birds be slit that they may sing it,
The grass itself be rooted up and burned
If it be foolish and not learn to spell!
Let cities bear my name. In every province,
See that the capital be named for Festus:
The swordsman of the stars, enslaver of kings.
Do men have gods? . . . In the dark corners yet
Do men raise images of stone or brass,
Beat drums before them, weep in the dust before them,
Shed blood of goats? . . . Shatter these gods with hammers!
Slay those who worship them! For there shall be
But one god henceforth, and his name is Festus.
Set images of Festus in all shrines.
Hang lamps before them; and burn frankincense
For fragrance. Let the priests, if they desire it,
Make living sacrifices, — men and maidens,
Should they be beautiful, — for festivals . . .
It will be laughable in the streets to hear
The priests go singing "Festus!" . . .

                                              'There have been,
You tell me, kings before me who were great.
This one, you say, had men remove a mountain,
And where the mountain was he built a palace . . .
But this was nothing. Look! my slaves, like ants,
Assembling each his atomy grain from nowhere,
Swarm and disperse, and swarm again, and slowly,
Bleeding and dying (in thousands — and for me!)

Raise the dead mountain once more to the sky.
And look! how now a palace, all of glass,
Glistens upon it! Within it move musicians,
You see far off their rose and purple garments,
Their silver instruments; from room to room,
You see them gliding among walls of glass
Like blue and scarlet fish. How sweet their music!
Tinkling and waved, like music from the sea . . .
All music, truly, — now that we talk of music, —
Seems to be but a kind of praise of Festus.
. . . And this king, too (my noble predecessor! —),
Watched gladiators fight with nets and swords;
Laughed when he saw faint virgins flung to lions;
Taking a sort of pleasure, as you'll say,
In seeing the claws rip down the flower-like breasts,
Streak the poor flanks with red. . . But bloodshed bores me . . .
Let the gross mind love elephants in torchlight
Trampling the plashy flesh, or tossing entrails
Under the moon! For me, more subtle pleasures. . .
Here for example on a marble table
You have a princess from an eastern province,
Most delicately reared; and here are surgeons.
We bind her down with silken thongs, well-coloured,
Lest, moved too much by the flattery of the knives,
Too modest under the shrewdness of such tongues,
She'll writhe and spoil our play. . . For what's our purpose
But to explore this passion men call life
To the red and smoky end? to tear aside
Curtain on steamy curtain of red fibre
In hot pursuit of — what but life or death?

'Well — then — the first incision. . . Have it slow . . .
We sit in a ring about her, robed in white.
Hangings of gold and purple wave on the air
Along the walls: in golden bowls float roses,
Flowering vines blow in through the open window,
And there, outside, by the wall beneath the window,

We have musicians, young men, six or seven,
Strumming a silver accompaniment of strings.
Sweet is the morning! Sweet, too, is the season!
Judas blossoms melt in a sky of azure,
Float on an azure pool with scarce a ripple,
Or, fallen in dust, are fanned by wings of bees. . .
Princess, is there a lover awaits you somewhere, —
Comes in the moonlight, putting up his hands
Against a small-leaved bough to press it backward
Or break its fragrance? Stands in the blue-dark shadow
Close to a fountain, watching how it huddles
Its amethysts in the moonlight on wet marble, —
Repeating to himself in a foolish wonder
Your trifling vast eternal world-swung name?
You've heard him praise you, maybe, heard the music
Incredible with which his voice embalms you,
Saying his rituals of eyes and eyebrows,
Lips, hair, and tortured hands, the throat like honey,
The voice like — what? . . . But where's his praise to ours, —
His love to our love? Pale and faint externals!
While we, with steel-blue tongues, in sweet persistence
Press in from outwards, make our slow incision,
Dissect, as it were, the cry of pain itself . . .
We have our rituals no less than he.
Is this the golden eyebrow we have loved?
Let us discover if its roots are gold,
That they be also praised; and this sweet pulse
Shaking its music through its world of flesh,
The whole white tingling length, in bells of crimson, —
Making the small soft wrist so sweetly tremble,
Carrying into the brain's enchanted forest
Its elfin far-off murmur of horns and cymbals,
Sweet hint, amid that jungle dark and savage,
Of laughing girls and youths forever singing, —
Shall we explore it to its secret source,
To some black smoking pool? . . . The surgeons bend

Intently to their work, shadows of clouds
Darken the room, darken the leaning faces,
The rose-bowl's butterfly of reflected brilliance
Pales on the ceiling, and you, too, gentle princess,
Grow pale, grow paler still, but in the shadow
Of clouds how more gigantic! Your white mouth
No longer utters cries, your golden head
No longer turns from side to side, your eyes,
Immense and dark with pain, amazed and silent,
No longer search our faces for an answer
To riddles black as these! You only hear
A great wind roaring among stars and ruins,
Walls falling, planets blowing, the eternal wind
Of death and change poured harshly through this chaos,
Stifling our little lamps. . . Ah, princess, princess,
Dancer, laugher, singer, daughter of kings,
Inheritor of the earth! what now avail you
The beauty of flesh that shook our hearts, the dream
Which, dreamed in secret, seemed to you to change
This now too human flesh of yours to fire
Of self-consuming star in ether kindled! . . .
Where are the mirrors gone that sang your praise!
Where are the human hearts that danced like motes
In the sunshafts of your brilliance! Where the jewels
That worn by you burned down to a little dust!
Did we that loved you love but blood and sinew,
This flesh from bleeding flesh uprisen, this mortal
And so ephemeral jot in immortal time?
Look! your hands, which lovers desired to kiss,
Are bone and flesh, your eyes are jewels of water,
Your crimson pulse lies waste. . . The steel-blue tongues
Babble in blood, cry out in a chaos of silence,
Call you in vain! . . . Our love, then, — is it wasted?
Do we like darkling troubadours come too late
And foolishly sing in the moonlight under a window
Whence she we praise is gone? . . .

'We have no answer.
The thing we seek escapes us, as forever.
Let the musicians take their music elsewhere,
Play to the poor, the sick, — not to ourselves
Who find our power futile, and make of it
A cruelty. . . I am well named indeed.'

4

Festus, in a balcony lined with silk,
Whose colours flutter and flash in the noonday sun,
Watches his crowds flow past him in the street . . .
The awning above him casts a rose-tinged shade
On the veined marble of the balustrade:
He shuts his eyes, and the rhythms of the feet
Countless, incessant, conflicting and interwreathing,
Pound at the sky, are silent, beat and beat . . .
Look how these atoms swarm beneath blue skies!
The stones wear down beneath his very eyes . . .
The walls are slowly and softly abraded,
The colours are faded,
The city sinks smoothly away
To dust and clay. . .

Festus, chin upon palm, observes these faces
That swarm in the glare of noon from secret places.
Quickly they come and greedily go
To the dark-doored corners of the world they know.
Sorrow has carved them all:
They dare not lift their eyes from street or wall.

'You, now,' says Festus, 'you, whose eyes are young
And blue as the skies in which small clouds dissolve, —
You, barefooted, who run with an armful of flowers,
Morning-glory and trumpet-vine, —
What would you say to a life like mine? . . .
Music to send you to sleep, music to wake you,

Music by day and by night to chime your hours,
Dancers to dance for you, and a chariot to take you
To gather your flowers! . . .

'Walls and roofs of crystal wherethrough in the night
You watch the moon and stars dance slowly by, —
Lying alone in an ocean of starry light
Under the sky!
What should your couch be, truly, but chryselephantine?
And a purple-beaked parrot to perch on your hand:
And, — in the noon, — a gorgeous palanquin
To await your command.

'Where shall it be? To the blue Moon Gardens — ?
To hear in the fragrance of shade
A chorus of nightingales sing, in a darkness of vines,
Of a moon-silenced glade? . . .
Kings shall go with you, and roses fall whitely about you,
Queens from the east spill you salvers of fruit,
Horns flare before you; and the loveliest prince of them all,
With a ghost of a lute,

'Sing you how exquisite now are your lips and your eyebrows,
Your hands, the strange depths of your hair, —
You, whose terrible beauty, like a plague, like a curse,
A violence of air,
Blows out, — ah, poor little candles! — our empires and kingdoms,
Sends walls roaring down,
And leaves the huge world in a clamour of horrible darkness,
King babbling with clown! . . .

'Ah — you are frightened! You ask for no chariot of silver, —
No mantles embroidered with moons;
There are tears in your eyes! I will give you a penny — instead! —
Keep your mornings, your noons,
Wild grass for your feet, blue heavens as young as your eyes,
Your arms full of flowers!

You have your glories. And as for ourselves — well, who knows?
Perhaps we have ours.'

5

Festus, under a sun that burns like brass,
Leans from the wall to watch a coffin pass.
Was it preceded by a human cry, —
By one cracked trumpet-note? . . .
A sound of grief shakes faintly against the sky, —
Seems, even yet, like a ghost, to float
In the glare of the sun. . . And Festus is vaguely afraid,
And sets his goblet down on the balustrade.
Stirring upon it, the silver shapes grow dim,
Dilate and wreathe and swim.

. . . Yet there is nothing here that strains belief . . .
'Is it so strange,' — says Festus, — 'in the sunlight,
To see a coffin, — to hear a cry of grief? . . .'
The coffin sways and passes
Shaking slow waves of brilliance from polished glasses.
The sound of the hooves is scarcely heard.
How is it? — The street grows suddenly empty,
Across it whirls the shadow of a flying bird.
Festus leans in the sunlight from his wall:
The coffin is gone. No footstep comes at all.

And Festus smiles and lifts his goblet up
Under the profound blue silence of the sky
And he observes the sun, which in his cup
Swims like a small red eye,
And tilts it toward his lips, secretly laughing
To see that he should be quaffing
The sun in a cup of wine. . . But the sun escapes,
And faintly again — between the walls of the houses —
Ascends a human cry,
And a cracked trumpet-note, brief and shrill:

And the same coffin — or is it another? — passes again,
And again the street is still.

Yet there is nothing here that strains belief. . .
Is it so odd
To see a coffin — to hear a cry of grief? . . .
The coffin sways and passes,
Shaking slow waves of brilliance from polished glasses. . .
And Festus, setting his goblet wearily down
Amid the sunlit walls of the silent town,
Perceives, as in a dream,
How, one by one, the unmoving houses seem,
Under the profound blue silence of the sky,
Divulging silently,
Each, through soundless doors, its coffined dead . . .
The coffins pass, the trumpets crack and cry,
Black birds darken the sky;
The coffins wait beneath the swinging trees,
Graves are opened, the leaves fall:
And Festus, leaning heavily from his wall,
Goblet in hand, with the scarlet sun overhead,
Observes with horror, observes with astonishment,
That this dark world he rules is a world of coffins;
The city he rules is a city of the listless dead. . .

And sharply and sorrowfully he turns away
From the sound of hooves and wheels,
The crying of trumpets, the failing of voices;
But the last coffin approaches; the last cry of grief,
Shaken and brief,
Wavers amid grey walls; and the city is darkened;
And Festus watches the last slow coffin pass
While one man rides behind it on an ass —
Looking neither to left nor right,
Staring before him into the infinite.
Is it the old man of the rain?
Festus cries to him: but his cry descends

Into the silence as a stone falls into the sea,
And the coffin is gone, and the vision ends . . .
And Festus, wondering, lifts his goblet again,

And perceives in the streets the people coming and going,
The flashing of eyes and hands, the hurry of feet,
The laughter of living voices. . . And over it all
The sun whirls down its brazen clangour of heat;
The cymbals of heat clang down on roof and wall.

III. HE ENTERS THE FOREST OF DEPARTED GODS

1

'In this forest,' says Festus, 'this old and savage forest,
Among these trees
Which have performed, one knows, such cruelties, —
Where cruelties are even now performed — ;
In the silence of this forest, which conceals
Temples and tombs; among these gleams and glooms;
Where, amid the windy shiftings of these trees,
One sees in the dark for a moment a temple glisten;
Where, if one will listen
To the wind's long leafy swell
One hears the rustled stirring of a bell:
A small bell faintly clinked,
Sleepy and indistinct:
Or a deep bell which the winds forlornly toll;
Is it as some say true — Old man of the rain! —
That here the gods still dwell, —
That here in the shadowy noons they walk again,
That here the body may meet an unbodied soul? . . .'

(. . . The trees are still, the trees make hardly a sound,
The trees let fall old leaves in silence,
The old leaves touch, with a sigh, the ground.)

'In this forest,' says Festus, 'this forest of eternal life and death,
This forest in which the pools are fertile,
This forest of blind old roots and furtive breath —
Is it as some say true
That if I touch with my hands an oak or yew,
Or break a willow bough,
Among these leaves Confucius will come forward
In a robe of saffron silk, and stand
With one uplifted hand,
And say to me, "Be tranquil, stare at death,
Live as the grass lives, uncomplaining,
Be grateful for the sun." . . . Or among these trees
Shall I indeed hear the clear voice of the Buddha,
And see him, smiling, sit with folded knees
On the great lotus: and hear him say:
"Look through the little whirlings of night and day,
The dark brief flight of clouds and rain,
The red transparencies of pleasure and pain, —
To the white perfection of the infinite . . ."
Or find that other, Jesus of Nazareth,
Under a pear-tree, eating of the fruit,
And hear him say, "Heed not the absolute,
Love what is little, turn not your thoughts above
So much as here and round you, — mostly, love!" . . . ?'

(. . . The many trees, on the unseen waves of the air,
Rise slowly, turn, or slowly come to pause.
The leaves are laced together and parted again,
The small bell tinkles, the deep bell tolls,
A flurry of rain on the leaves makes a sound of applause . . .)
'And what shall I say to — Jesus of Nazareth?
Or, to Confucius, what shall I reply, —
Or what to Buddha? . . . Shall I indeed say, "It is I,
I, who carry the world like a bird in a cage,
I, for whom the world sings morning and evening?"
Shall I say: "How then shall I think you god or sage —

You who would have me live as the grass; or love it;
Or you who would have me lift clear eyes above it
To the silent ecstasy of life in death?" '

(. . . The trees of the forest are calm and stolid about him:
It is as if they eyed this man askance.
They stir a little, suspicious, not knowing his purpose;
And the irresponsible and capricious leaves
Catch at the ghost of an air and flash and dance.)

2

In the midst of a pool of sunlight, in the silence of the forest,
Festus sits on a stone:
The silence breaks in slow green waves about him.
He is alone.

'Look now, Confucius! . . . Jesus of Nazareth! . . .
Buddha, whose heart is an eternally opening flower — ! . . .
Look at the world of men I have left behind me
To seek you amid the mysteries of this forest. . .
What will you give me in place of this — what power,
What majesty, what secret dark dominion,
What lucid understanding of life and death?
What knowledges — Confucius, Jesus, Buddha —
What knowledges of grain and star have you?
Can you at will wear divers shapes and bodies:
Do I in error imagine you as trees
Opening rosy blossoms, or letting fall
Your glossy petals on a wall;
Can you at will let fall your hearts as dew
Among these leaves for the delight of a bee or a bird;
Can you indeed be silence, only; or in the twilight,
When the forest closes on its memories,
Let yourselves be heard
As whisper, only, or rustle, or creak, or sigh,
The shrinking of a leaf that is old and dry,

The snap of a dark root, underground, —
Can you, indeed, embody your souls as sound? . . .'

(A parrot swings on the bough of a mulberry tree,
Regarding Festus listlessly.
A mulberry leaf detaches itself, and falls,
Silently pirouetting through a pool of sunlight;
And the quiet above him builds itself green walls.)

'This silence now — this bird with crimson feathers —
Is it with these you speak to me?
Confucius, are you indeed this mulberry tree
Extending cold and green in a void of silence,
Bearing a crimson bird, or slowly and softly
Letting a single leaf fall, carefully?
Or if indeed these leaves were once your flesh;
Or if from among these leaves at a certain moment
In the eternal and golden recurrence of time
With a leafy rustle and chime
You step once more, having no other speech
Than sings from a choir of leaves in wind or rain, —
What, in the silence then, shall I hear you teach?
What syllables will fall, as this leaf falls,
Which shall remove forever death and pain?'

The mulberry tree makes no reply;
Placid and solitary beneath the sky,
Seeming to dream no dream of leaf or bird,
It sways in the pool of sunlight; and beneath it
The words of Festus fall and are not heard.

3

'Nevertheless,' says Festus, 'I await you:
In this silence I will wait . . .
In the darkness, in the greenly filtered starlight,
I will seek among white-blossomed boughs a gate,

I will find your old and secret ruin of temple,
With its bell that makes no sound:
I will touch it with cool hands, and tear away
The jasmine flowers that wrap it round.
Will it not ring? . . . Will it not cry aloud
From the immortal hearts of three great gods
To star and moon and the passing cloud? . . .
Will you not then come forward, like three children,
Performing miracles? Will you not say:
"This is he who gave his world away
For the knowledges that make a man immortal —
Let us light for him the portal
That will lead him out of time and space forever . . ." ?
Will you not touch my eyes with hands like silver,
Spread a net of music round me,
Pierce me, break me, and confound me
In a dazzling light of sound, in a tumult as of light?
Shall I pass beyond the walls of day and night? . . .

'Yet it is strange you say no word, nor manifest
Your hiding-places.
No wind there is, yet the treetops do not rest.
From gloom to gloom I seek your faces,
Bringing my world to give you like a jewel. . .
Ah, Jesus, Buddha, grey Confucius,
Is it as some say true
That I shall have no comfort out of you?
And is this forest but illusion
In which old ghosts of sound make soft confusion?'

4

The evening darkens: how insubstantial now
Whirls the black forest of departed gods!
Less than the glimmering blossom on this bough
Which the dead moon so wanly kindles;
Fallen with less sound than a cup of petals

On cobweb rent with dew;
Less real than these,
So now, so now, this old illusion dwindles;
I am alone, then, in this forest:
I walk alone amid these trees.
Confucius has not strength to lift a pebble,
Buddha, who is but vapour, casts no shadow,
Jesus is silent, under a stone. . .
Revere the moon, then, Festus, who, though dead,
Reveals this emptiness! Revere the moon.

Cool is the evening, cooler in the mind,
Where the dew falls among more phantom forests
On flowers ghostly and on hands unreal.
This is the forest where abide the gods,
This is the emptiness your moons reveal.
Be silent, Festus, here amid these trees
Which are yourself: be silent, dream among them,
Become a ghost yourself, in a world of ghosts;
Give yourself gods! Or if the gods obey not —

The gods obey not. And among these trees
I will discourse with Mephistopheles. . .

. . . Come with a clap of thunder! Shed bright fire
On oak and smoking maple! Split a rock
Or draw a molten cedar round about you!
Be horned with gold, wear diamonds on your brow,
Tailed like a serpent, star-tipped at the point:
Let every footstep be a tuft of smoke
In the anguished grass! . . . Or else, have none of these.
Be, as your master is, most sorrowful,
Count beads, say prayers, shed tears.

Look, where his ghost shines pale among the trees!
I will discourse with Mephistopheles. . .
Be not so fugitive! disclose your powers,

Show me what evil, in this world of evil,
Turns to a profit with a wave of the wand!
Tear open, with your silver-taloned hand,
The hearts of women; feed me on slow laughter,
Pluck richest music from poor strings of flesh!
Show yourself nimble — come and go like an actor
In garbs fantastic, wear a woman's body,
To dance before me naked and cold in sunlight:
Bring moonlight, teach me to love in such a fashion
I shall not surfeit of you, nor, being refused,
Beat out my love in sorrow! . . . But can this be
That Mephistopheles whom I have honoured?
Singular, he should look so like to me!

(. . . It is a woman's body shines before me:
It is a flake of the moon:
It is the intensity of my desire! . . .)

How lightly the wind blows you through this darkness!
How smoothly wrought, how curious is your body!
How colder than a sea-shell is your flesh!
And look: there are silver cobwebs woven about you,
Webs to be brushed away, to be breathed upon and broken,
Fine webs about your breast, cool webs about your heart!
You are among these trees which are myself;
You move beneath my thousand branches;
Pass slowly, meditate, retrace your steps,
Yet not too slowly pass,
Nor yet with too few footsteps touch this grass! . . .
I am about you as the darkness is:
Softly within me, ghost of light,
Turn and turn, amaze me with your beauty;
Be in me as the firefly in the night!

(. . . It is a woman's body shines before me:
Not an illusion, not Mephistopheles,

Not the intensity of my desire!
It is not the light of my heart among these trees, —
The light I cast before me and foolishly follow:
It is a woman's body . . . but what if, none of these,
It is not flesh, or beauty in flesh, or the desire for gods,
But the god himself, an ancient satyr,
Burning his heart in a tissue of sorceries? . . .)

Who was it gave you eyes so unlike mine?
Who was it took the huge sky filled with stars,
Twilight of time, twilight of infinity
Delicately conscious of the finite beauty of stars,
And gave it to you for darkness in your eyes?
See how the mandolin tinkle of my praise
Wavers and is extinguished, goes but so little, faintly,
Amid such midnight silence! Is it indeed
You, who move like a wandering lantern, going
In the conscious all-enfolding night of me —
Deeply within me glimmering, faintly revolving;
Or is it rather myself who drop old praises
Into an emptiness and darkness so profound?
Touch me, talk to me, cleave to me, turn about me,
Show me in all ways the amazement of your beauty,
Gleam, burn, pale before me, laughingly afflict me,
Tear with your hands at the honey that's hid in my heart!
I will submit to you, if you wish submission,
Or tower above you like terror, if terror you wish;
Be as the grass before you, or the forest above you. . .
We are together and the great world is our shadow.
Who brought us here? Who found your heart in fire? . . .

(Clouds flow up to the zenith, glide under the stars,
Seem curling coldly about them, are lit by the moon, —
Twice, thrice, — then shred on the air and die.
These are the centuries: I am old as granite:
I have been standing beneath these stars forever,
Forest grown upon forest, hill huddled on hill.

Star-dust has darkened my heart . . . snow-song . . . bird
    song . . .
How many aeons returning have whispered and thrilled me!
Rocks, how many, have crashed into dust beneath me!
Lovers, how many, have loved me and blown on the wind!)

You are the full cold cloud-dividing beauty
Of the August moon:
The moon in the warm blue-violet depths
Between snow cliffs of cloud:
The death-wind that shakes down a shower of stars
From the green tree of heaven.
I am the clouds that endeavour to close about you;
The stars that cling to the tree of heaven,
And, falling through you, are blest. . .
What is your name? Why have I sought you
As Jesus, Confucius, Buddha?
Or why, — among the memories of these trees, —
Did I perceive you as Mephistopheles? . . .
How simple and terrible are the words you use!
Your 'yes' what is it but 'forever,' —
The white tide of suns roaring down space on space
Through the everlasting sonorous blue canyon of time?
Your 'no' what is it but 'death,'
The sky of black basalt that crushes one soul?
Your 'beauty' — what tempests of music assail me!
What silence — stars in the spring! . . .
. . . I walk by a violet river paved with stars,
The music of earth about me moving softly
From stone to dust, from dust to tree.
I stand on a purple mountain at the daybreak
And watch a cloud procession, far below me,
Leisurely crossing a twilight sea.
Forests ascend about me and are fallen,
Stars are quenched in the rains of time:
Slowly the gods, in azure mantles of dream,
Leave behind them the hills that immortally gleam,

Descend with sorrowful footsteps. Slowly climb
The younger gods with sadness in their eyes
To hills less noble and to darker skies. . .
I walk by a purple river brimmed with stars,
Sad with the sadness of incomprehensible beauty,
Hearing in turn the voices of all things, lifting
Their patient questions. . . Valleys, how lovely are they,
One slope green with meadows, sun-enkindled,
One slope black with shadow, stark with boulders,
Tawny with sands, twinkling with streams! . . .
Sorrowful is my heart when I remember beauty,
It is with sorrow that I hear you dancing, —
Beautiful dancer on air and fire! —
In the old grey house of my heart:
I am the dust on which a rose has fallen,
The stone on which vain starlight falls;
How sadly unworthy of you are these grey cloisters,
These cobwebbed walls! . . .

(It is not a woman's body shining before me —
Not a flake of the moon —
Not the intensity of my desire! . . .

The darkness seems to freeze
In the immobile shapes of trees . . .

It is not Buddha, it is not Confucius,
Jesus, or Mephistopheles;
Not a dream, less than the dream of a dream . . .
It is myself alone, —
Touching with hands a world of ancient stone;
Summoning gods from it, — how fugitive and vain! —
Summoning gods to walk on the delicate shine of air,
Weaving out of the rock a gossamer
Vast as the world is, that therein might fall
A dew of stars! . . . Ah, Festus, Festus, Festus,

How always about you, greater than the world you dream of,
Rises immortally beyond you your own self's wall!)

5

Solitary, before daybreak, in a garden
Dark amid the unchanging snow,
Watching the last star fading in a fountain
Whence melodies of eternal water flow,

Festus, seeing the sky-line burn and brighten
Coldly, far above the hidden sun;
Seeing the golden thread of glory unravelled
Along the wall of mountains run,

Hears in his heart a cry of bewilderment;
And turning, now here, now there, —
Like one who pauses a moment before departure, —
Partakes of the grace of earth and air,

Drinks of the vast blue splendour of the sky,
The mile on mile of dew-blanched grass,
The cloud-swept trees, the stones, bare cliffs of bronze;
And in the pool, as in a glass,

Ringed round with nodding asters, frosted leaf-tips,
Stoops to see his image . . . and behold,
How faded is the scarlet of his mantle!
His face, how changed and old! . . .

          .   .   .   .

Sing now the birds: on every bough a bird sings;
Slowly at first, then fast and faster,
Till the walled garden thrills and shrills with music:
The cricket beneath the violet aster

Cries his joy to heaven as the first beam strikes him —
The foxgloves bend beneath a weight of bees;

Praise! praise! praise! the chorus rises;
Drowsily, happily, dumbly, sway the trees.

Fades the star in the fountain: and the sun comes.
How motionless stands Festus there!
A red leaf, falling slowly to meet a red leaf
That rises out of the infinite to the air,

Floats, is turned by the wind about his image . . .
Ah, Festus, is this you,
This ruin of man about whom leaves fall coldly
And asters nod their dew? . . .

Pale, phantasmal, swirls the forest of birches,
It is a dance of witch-girls white and slim;
Delicately flash their slender hands in the sunlight!
Cymbals hiss, their eyes are dim

Under the mist of hair they toss above them . . .
But Festus, turning never,
Heeding them not, nor the birds, nor the cricket shrilling,
Stares at the pool forever,

Seeking in vain to find, — somewhere, somewhere! —
In the pool, himself, the sky? —
The slight clear beautiful secret of these marvels,
Of birch, birds, cricket's cry,

Blue sky, blue pool, the red leaf falling and floating,
The wall of mountains, the garden, the snow,
And one old man — how sinister and bedraggled! —
Cawing there like a crow. . .

Instant the miracle is! He leans bewildered
Over the infinite, to search it through. . .
Loud sing the birds! on every bough a bird sings,
The cricket shrills, the day is blue.

IV. HE STRUGGLES IN THE NET OF HIMSELF

1

The silver flails of the rain
Thresh heavily, heavily on the floor of my heart;
The silver flails of the rain
Waver and crash over the desolate floor,
Coldly in the morning, in the evening slowly,
Separating sorrow for me from the miserable grain.
Is it kingdoms I lift up in my hands,
The purple cities of twilight, jewels of many lands,
Domes, courts, palaces, walls inlaid with gold?
Dust they are, as dust I let them fall,
Dust on the grass-blade are they all.
And you, Old Man of the Rain —
You whom at last I know
Are but myself grown old,
Old without glory or triumph or understanding —
Old without love, old without pity, —
Come! come upward out of the shadows of my heart,
You who have been my guardian angel,
Point before me once more to some new city,
Some yet more gorgeous kingdom of the east
For me to feed my heart on like a beast!
Point before me once more to some new god
The pathway to whose temple is not trod
Daily by blood-stained millions! Some new god
Who moves not merely to a sound of bells,
The sound of the pulse itself, the murmur of flesh
Heard in the strain of silence. . . Some new god
Who cries not captive in the glittering mesh
Woven out of the senses by the brain
Which beats against its world of flesh-in-pain!
I will not have a god who is myself! . . .
Yet it is not a new god I desire —
It is an old god, old as water and fire;

The ancient god whose secret is creation;
Or wisdom or an infinite contemplation. . .

But you are silent, bringing only to my mind
Visions of the bright-dark sorrowful world I find
Unrolled before me, — sky beyond wave of sky;
Suns, stars, moons, swung on their chains of fire;
Light-bearing winds, spaces prepared for darkness,
The horror and crash and chaos, the gorgeous planets
Burned down like candles; and the infinitesimal earth,
Falling to dust with its little crying of kings;
And the little minds of men that dream these things . . .
See how the cities flame in the abyss of night,
With shouts, with cymbals, with a corybantic delight,
Flinging their roses against the moon!
See Rome — that was the carnival of the world —
Melting away like a desert snow!
Let walls be hammered of brass, yet wind will blow.
And over all these things I have passed my hands,
Brooding upon them: I have lifted men and kingdoms,
And let them fall. . . Dreams, gods, visions, demons,
The strange dark music of the heart and brain
To which man marches, on his road to pain, —
All these I have sifted, I have sifted them like sands,
I have searched in vain for the secret of them all
And sadly I let them fall.

And you — Old Man of the Rain!
You, my deceiver, my ineludible daemon!
Haunter of shadows, whom always in the silence
Of the vacant world I hear
Blowing your feeble tunes on a rusted flute —
Blow one more melody, before you at last grow mute —
The one sharp lyric thing, —
Three notes or four, —
The arrow of music with the flame-like wing, —
Which will at last make nothing of earth and sky,

Swerve to the heart of things, that there in the darkness
The eternal god will wake from his sleep with a cry.

2

I will not have a god who is myself! . . .
But the million voices of the grass
Cry out upon me as I pass . . .
I will not have a god who is myself!
But the blue dome of basalt, ice-embossed,
Carved with hieroglyphs of frost,
Accuses me.
The clouds whip downward, the sudden rain
Beating against me with ghostly hands,
Shrills a chorus of hate for me.
Green hills, the far blue wavering plain,
Close in upon me, menace me,
The brown brook shatters against my brain . . .
Frightened, I ask the white birch tree
That shakes its cymbals in the sun,
'Is it true that an old god walks in me?' . . .
And the birch, not pausing in its race
With sun and cloud and river of fire,
Tosses backward a golden tress
From the half-seen hurrying witch-like face —
And answers — 'Yes!'

Terror! I rise, I hurry away
And about me wheels the encircling day.
A shadow pursues me, long and thin,
The low grass weeps and clings to me,
The birch-trees whirl with a cymbal din,
The juniper holds my knee.
The pebble I lift in the palm of my hand
Laments, 'Lo, you are the one who planned
This world of horror, this world of grief!
Of frost and screaming leaf!'

Silent, upon a hill I lie
And take to my heart the horror of sky.
And about me shout ten million voices:
'Lo! how the obscene god rejoices
There, alone, in his infamy!
And ah, how thrice accursed is he
Who drew us into this web of pain;
And ah, how thrice-blest would he be
Should he destroy again!
Let rocks curl upward in a slow vapour
And trees, like mist, dislimn in air,
Into the dark brain of the shaper
Let clouds like wandering dreams repair,
And seas, — become oh less than a sparkling
Drift or spray, — coil inward darkling,
And streams turn backward from the plain
Into the nothing of his brain . . .
Birds, from the tyranny of song
O be released, at last be still!
Rise like a spindrift, ancient hill,
And sands that have wept so long!'

Alone on an angry hill I lie
And take to my heart the horror of sky —
And the tortured world, in mutiny,
Curses me for my infamy.
The cloud strikes at me with its shadow,
Beats my face with its ragged wings:
A snare of darkness is in the meadow:
The wind coils round my thigh, and stings.
Trees, with javelins of leaf,
Strike me out of their wrath and grief.
Darkly, between them, sky and hill
Struggle to crush me out and kill.

I will not have a god in me!
I flee in panic, I dart to escape

This world of horror that flees with me —
This world that takes its horror of shape
From my own brain's poor cruelty.
I flee in terror — : O Festus, find
Some doorway out of the mind!

3

Yet, birch-tree, dancing in the sun,
I am the grass you dance upon!
I am the wind that calls you out,
O swift of foot, with a cymbal-shout:
O hate not me! I give to you
Meadows of daisies dim with dew,
Birds to people your cloud of dream
With daybreak songs that drowse and gleam,
Blue cowls of night, and the star-peaked air
To hood the enchantment of your hair:
I am your lover — oh hate not me,
Beautiful witch-like dancing tree!

And you, old basalt, hoar with rime,
Dogged brooder on doom and time
And the stars that clock your firmament —
Less than the spider who wheels his tent
For one June day in the powdery crack
That winters have riven across your back —
Tinier, weaker, less than he,
Am I, who adore you: hate not me!

Look — I will dream the world anew
A world more beautifully wrought for you!
White birch-trees on the clouds shall grow
And over the earth on the four winds blow, —
Nod to the stars; rustle at the sun;

Shine like candles, when the day is done,
Before the immortal altar of sky
And the sun's broad blazing half-closed eye.
Festus — look! — on a hilltop stands
How small! how hidden! and lifts weak hands
To the holy birches, like candles seven,
That burn on the crystalline wall of heaven . . .
Seven white birch-trees all on fire,
And birds in the flame-boughs twitter and choir!
Stars in the branches, the birds sing loud,
Roots like lightning shot through a cloud,
And the cloud on a twilight sea, cold green,
Sailing like the ship of a phantom queen.
Shafts of the mild light everywhere
Oar through the ocean of twilight air;
And now in the dusk falls a ghostly jingling
Of delicate bells on the birch-trees tingling,
And oh how sweetly is the fine air shaken!
The sleeping bells on the earth awaken,
There's a cry from a tower, a trill from a steeple,
A boom from a dome, the air begins to people
With a hurrying, shimmering, flashing of wings, —
Angels and demons: the whole sky sings.

Festus dreams: and the dead worlds change,
They glow, they shiver, they are glittering and strange.
Look, how a vine, all of silver interwoven,
Falls from the moon! the silver moon is cloven,
A ladder-way of roses shines down the sky,
The moon and the earth are bound to it and cry.
The sun turns a rose: its petals are the light:
Shadow is a short chord: melody is night:
Twilight is the mind of god: the spire sings seven,
And maidens, with slow steps, climb the air to heaven.
And Festus — Festus — dreaming on a stone,
Dreaming in a silence, a wilderness, alone,

Widens through the universe the rings of his dream
In waves going faintlier, till all things seem
Beautiful as music is, falling but to rise,
The wise man foolish, and the thistledown wise.
All things are music, and beautiful they are, —
Time is a raindrop, laughter is a star;
And the old man, climbing to a little hill of grass,
Laughs with astonishment to see the rocks are glass, —
Subtler than glass is! lucent as the air!
Windows through the earth! and he stands in a stare,
With a blue sky above him, and a bluer sky below,
And himself on the cloud where the seven birches grow.

. . . O birch-tree! . . . basalt! . . . open heart and sing
A song of praise for Festus! crown Festus king.
Statelier than God made, he makes the world anew, —
A world more beautifully dedicate for you.

4

Twilight, in the old grey house of Festus, —
The heart of Festus; and Festus there
Sorrowfully, amid the webs of centuries,
Breaking the bitter bread of despair.
Twilight, the melancholy slow wave of azure,
Putting out the lamps of dream.
Dust, from the stars of dust, quietly sifting,
And webs on the heart that used to gleam.

Time — the falling of old bells into the sea
Whence nothing returns again;
Life, the lifting of hands to the sunlight
Whose edge is pain.
O small weak foolish brain that dared, that dared
To dream it could ever shape
A world more singing out of this dust, ourselves!
To dream it could ever escape

The slow dull speech of dust, the gesture of dust,
The corruption of dust, and death.
'What but a spider am I among these webs
That shake against my breath?'
Light your candle, — you see one web the more,
The web whereto in pain you are bound.
Cry, sing, pray — and silence is a vaster silence.
We are but dust, and of dust the sound.

V. HE IS A MIRROR AND PERCEIVES HIS VACUITY

1

Old Man

Of the gods, Festus, truly there is no knowing:
A sorrowful lot are the gods, indifferent they are.
Better to snare with a net the blue wind's blowing,
Or scoop from the pool, with the palm of your hand, a star.

Festus

The worlds revolve, Old Man, the worlds revolve:
And miserably through the darkness we take our way.

Old Man

Give yourself gods, if you wish, with beautiful names,
Cry to them, morning and evening; on the steps of temples
Let silver trumpets with cloths of scarlet be blown
Shattering sunlight and driving poor birds to the clouds:
Fall by the altar of him, your favourite god,
Pale let your face be, famished your body, lie prone
Implore him, adore him; and visions, perhaps, like a fume
Will glisten and coil in the dusk of your brain's little room.
Yet god, though no smaller he be than the shell of the world
No greater is, truly, than the green blade of grass.

Festus

Miserably through the darkness we take our way . . .

Alas, that into this darkness which is ourselves
The light of ourselves sends forward so feeble a ray!

Old Man

And why should we trouble ourselves with a god whom we know
    not —
A god whom, god willing, we never shall know?
The world is the mirror of god; and we are but fragments.
And how shall a mirror look into its own depths, Festus?
And say that it did — what truly, save mirror, would show?

Festus

The light of ourselves, the small pointed light that so wavers
Amid this forest, ourselves, this forest of shadows —
Ah, in that place, how the weak voice is frightened and quavers!

Old Man

We cannot know god. Whence came we, or whither we go —
Trifles! Ignore them. Mere knowledge is nothing.
We come from the shadow, into shadow we blow,
Shadow we are, shadows only we know.

Festus

And yet, Old Man, it is something, amid these shadows, —
Out of such weakness, amid such pain, —
To have conceived a god! . . .
Greater, more nobly dark, is the vault of the brain
Which has conceived a god!

Old Man

Ah, Festus, think how foolish would be that mirror
Which, gazing into itself, — if it could do so, —
And seeing a cloud, and blue sky, imaged there,
Cried out: 'Behold how nobler than other mirrors
Am I, who have here conceived a sky, a cloud,
And small birds flying in a blue depth of air!'
The mirror reflects all things that pass before it.

The mind conceives those things that made and move it.
Ah, Festus, there is conceiving
Even in disbelieving! —

Festus

When we adore, it is the ancient god
Aroused in us, by his delight in light,
To praise himself with a sudden cry.
When we lament, it is his burden of sorrow,
The sorrowful knowledge of his imperfection,
Rising into the infinite like a sigh.
Wretched is he! . . . how far more wretched we,
Who have no selves, who are but lyre and flute
Broken by him, or blown upon, or mute!
Only in silence, only in nothingness,
We have our being. . . Let silence be our god!
Sleep be our beauty, darkness our abode.

Old Man

Sleep be our beauty, darkness our abode.
White be our sleep, in a vast blue tent of starlight!
Yet let us dream. . . Ah, though our selves be nothing,
Less than a shadow of clouds on a great water,
Less than a vapour of dew in the morning ascending,
Yes, though the dream be god's and not our own,
And the delight of the dream be also his, —
Still, let us dream. . . Delight and dream are his,
Yet, dreaming and delighting, we are god;
Dream and delight are ours.

Festus

How deep this forest of ourselves-in-god!
How pale the little lanterns of our faces!

Old Man

Beautiful are these boughs in the lamp-light seen . . .
Upward they soar and bear the stars for fruits.

And the clouds of leaves — are they watery blue? or green? —
Like clouds of moonlight blowing in darkness above us;
And downward, below this shell of the earth that trembles,
Reaching to stars still farther, go the roots.
How the world sings and shudders and swings about us!
Nothing is stable. We move, and the vast web trembles.
One false step and we fall . . . we fall . . .

Festus

How far, Old Man? — Only from the hand to the heart;
Only from god-in-ourselves to god-in-god.
Let the world shake to the sound of our foolish feet!
Across and across it, weave the skein of our footsteps.
Loud be our speech, for the echo is sweet.

Old Man

The worlds revolve, Festus, — the worlds revolve
In fiery rings down a blue airy vortex;
And the sound of enormous suns that clang together
Comes gently, after the centuries, to god, —
— A pleasant blur of cymbals.
Yet you and I, who walk here in this forest
Of arches under the stars, this goblin forest
We call our minds — how are we not astonished
That all this whirling lays not hold of us
And flings us out and down like fiery dust-motes
Into the vortex, — trees, rocks, dreams and all? . . .
Truly, my knees grow weak at the thought of it . . .
Yet I can laugh at the vision of you, Festus,
Shooting head-foremost upward like a comet!
Amazed and open-mouthed, your words of wisdom
Sucked out of you by the wind!

Festus

. . . Sea-pools, amid salt sea-rocks, in the evening,
Take the pale light of the sky, and lying still
Catch the first star . . . The great pale joyless sea,

Reaching forever restlessly,
Poor vacant slave to every whim of the air,
Cries there, beyond the rocks, wails at the sands,
Unconscious of the stars. . . In the blue evening
After the sunset, when the bastions of gold and vermilion,
The walls of violet, the pinnacles of opal and chrysolite,
Have crumbled fierily into the sea,
When the sea-birds are no longer rose-enkindled,
And one long cloud in the west lies smooth as stone:
Sea-pools, amid salt sea-rocks, lying still,
Take the pale light of the sky, and without effort
Catch the first star. . . Profound, profound and silent,
Thus comes the miracle: it is the secret of azure.
The brown sea-snails in the pool are undisturbed.

Old Man

Ah miserable destiny, Festus, miserable destiny,
To be, in the blue universe of the sea-pool,
A crab! . . . a crab for the most part silent,
That, softly sidling from coign of rock to coign,
Delicately touching, under the limpid water,
The hard edges of rocks with the tips of his claws,
Yet, shakes the pool, or pierces with his back
The azure . . . and routs the star.

Festus

Or sadder still
To be a pool inhabited by a crab;
And nightly to lose the image of one's desire
In one's own agitation, like the sea.

Old Man

You be the pool, Festus, and I the crab,
And in the blue twilight let us enact our drama . . .
It is the twilight hour of pilgrimage,
The infinite moment in the finite day.
On the blue arch we stand, the void beneath us,

A world at either end . . . How slowly, slowly,
The sea-gull settles in the pale air of heaven!
Like a rose-petal is he, he falls more softly.

Festus

It is the twilight hour of pilgrimage . . .
The forest to which we descend with curious footsteps,
The forest of ourselves, begins to darken . . .
Was that a footstep? and were those voices? — indistinct . . .

Old Man

It was perhaps the murmur of the blood
In our poor ears, so weary of long silence.

Festus

It is a music — it begins to rise
How delicately! like the breathing forth of leaves
In the slow forest of decay and birth!
It is as if the earth itself should sigh
Through the points of grass . . .

Old Man

Let us approach it: it is a solemn sound,
A shade too serious — but let us approach it.

Festus

The sounds of silver rise — it is as if
A tree grew fragrantly out of a well of light:
The tree itself, and all its boughs, of light,
And the leaves exhaled on the air as faint as sound . . .
Do you not feel, Old Man, as if this tree
Grew over you, and had its roots in you?

Old Man

We are the earth: this music is our tree . . .
And yet what misery it wakes in me!

Festus

Thus do we learn the unhappiness of god
When the mood takes him to create a world.
The boughs, like melancholy aspirations,
Turn in the fire of his heart, the fine leaves glisten,
They sing in the air . . . O bitter it is to love,
To shape with the hands of desire, to draw from darkness
The sleeping sorrowful dream . . . My eyes grow heavy,
My heart grows old, and aches with a too-great burden;
How sweet, now, would be sleep.

Old Man

Is it a music? . . . Just now it had a sound
Of human voices . . . voices of animals . . .
Discordant and melancholy . . . harsh . . .

Festus

It is a music dark and many-voiced
Perplexed and sorrowful . . .
How like the voices of the memory
It rises among the leaves! . . .
Moonlight, moonlight and rain — the sound of the leaves
When the cloud comes between them and the moon —
The secret of rain in the seclusion of night —
And the lover and his beloved in the darkness
Listening to the sound of rain, the sound of hearts,
The moving of hands unseen . . .

Old Man

Memory . . . a flight of wind through the forest of the mind,
Prolonged, prolonged and strange.
Whence comes it? . . . the boughs are in confusion,
Leaves fall, clouds gallop over the breathless moon,
Ghosts are blown from tombs . . . O singular miracle
To see our universe so blow and change
Obedient to this foolish wind from Nowhere!

Festus

The azure pool, the pool about the fountain,
Is perpetually astonished and replenished
By the flowing of the source that made and keeps it:
'Whence comes this water? It rises through myself,
Shoots upward, falls upon me, making rings
Of vanishing foam, filling the air with rainbows,
Drawing about me the happy chatter of birds. . .'
Thus rises memory; and thus this music
Rises out of the secrecy of ourselves
To fall upon us in rings of agitation.
To you, Old Man, what can it say to you
Save colour of sun, of light, sweet shapes of stones,
The delicate feel of dust? . . . But ah, to me
How richly it brings the darkness of great love!

Old Man

Is it a music? Again it had a sound
Of anguished voices — voices of animals —
Animals being murdered. . .

Festus

Sorrowful darkness in which we lose ourselves
To find the infinite . . . Hear how the beloved's heart
Beats in the darkness and becomes the world!
Dreamless and thoughtless we lie together in darkness
My hand is over her heart to hold its beating,
My mouth is over her mouth . . . ah divine murmur
Of mingled breath! . . . the world that sharply flowers,
The world in happiness!

Old Man

Alas, poor flesh! . . . You are a lover, Festus:
You have permitted this poor dull body of yours
To sing your wits away. So now this music
Falls over you like the voice of your beloved.

Resist it! Be not moved. It is a music
Of mortal origin and fleshly texture.
Who knows if to god's ears it may be only
A scream of pain?

Festus

It is a beauty of sound past all enduring;
The cry of the finite for the infinite;
The song of the infinite rising out of the darkness
Of the finite wall. It takes my soul from me.
Go nearer: part the boughs: say what you see!

Old Man

It is a music. . . Festus, I see them playing:
Among the trees: grotesque their faces are:
They sit in the moonlight, drawing their bows together . . .
It is the orchestra of butchers, Festus!
Gathered for holiday. . . They wear white aprons,
Green do they look in the moonlight, like green aprons
Darkly spotted. . . How sweet their music is! . . .
The hands that held the cleaver draw the bow.

Festus

Thus ends our pilgrimage! We come at last,
Here, in the twilight forests of our minds,
To this black dream. . . Better it would have been
To have remained forever there in the rain,
Planting our beans together in the wind-worn plain! . . .
Let us return. . . Are you content? . . . Let us return! . . .
Where are you? I am alone . . . I am alone.

2

And at last, having sacked in imagination many cities
And seen the smoke of them spread fantastically along the sky,
Having set foot upon so many walls, fallen and blackened,
And heard the harsh lamentations of women,

And watched without pity the old men, betraying their vileness,
Tear at their beards, and curse, and die,
Festus, coming alone to an eastern place
Of brown savannahs and wind-gnawed trees,
Climbed a rock that faced alone to the northward
And sat, and clasped his knees.

There was before him the confluence of three rivers:
One from the north, one from the east, one from the west.
The one from the east was blue, the one from the west was green,
Black was the one from the north, and snow was on its breast.
The sound of their roaring came up in waves on the wind,
Into the tumultuous darkness of the south they went,
And Festus sat for a day and a night and watched them
And wondered what they meant.

'Look, Festus, how without regard for you and all your sorrow
The huge sun rises and crosses the sky
And your ridiculous shadow circles about you
Shortening and lengthening silently!
What does it matter to the sun that your robe is scarlet?
That the sword at your hand is old and green!
Already the winds gnaw at you, as they have gnawed at these trees,
Careless of the many things you have done and seen.'

The day ended, and the slow-wheeling magnificent constellations
Glided like lights of ships down the river of space,
And Festus was disturbed once more, and wished to speak,
And heavily raised his head at last in sorrow,
And turned towards the stars his face,
And said: 'Look, Festus, how yet once more the immortals
Kindle their delicate lanterns and walk in the sky
While you on a lonely hill sit alone in sadness
And remember that you must die!
Look at the stars, Festus, treader of kingdoms,
You who carried the world like a bird in a cage,
You whose heart is a desert, gaunt with winter,

You whose sword in youth was a sevenfold lightning
Now worn and green with age!
Look! the immortals once more in the sky of your heart
The immortals you scorned and forgot
Walk in the dim blue gardens softly apart
To a music you taught them not! . . .'

Festus in starlight watched how the three great rivers,
Bearing perpetual stars on their breasts, roared down
To gorges and chasms and desolate plains
And jungles of death and labyrinthine cities
Swept to pale harmonies by suns and rains;

And thought of the thousands of nights and days like music
Woven by him, and the roses of love and death
Fallen in petals in the darkness of his heart,
And he sent among them a breath
And set them blowing and trembling again, on graves,
On the stones of streets, by door and path and wall,
Whirled in the air from the boughs of swinging trees
To stream like stars on the wind and slowly fall
For the hands of children, the hair of women, the hearts of lovers,
Whirled in the air from the boughs of swinging trees
And the myriad eyes that in his veins went to and fro
Seeking a dream forever and finding no ease.
'Listen, Festus! How the multitudes within you
Make a slow misty music of their own!
See how the walls of cities grow young again,
With the spring upon them blown!
And you too, Festus! Treader in blood of kingdoms!
You walk in a moonlit world of dream
And you and the worlds about you are young once more
And blossom and tinkle and sing and gleam!'

Then Festus laughed, for he looked in his heart and saw
His worlds made young again,
And heard the sound of a many-peopled music,

And joyously into the world of himself set forward
Forgetting the long black aftermath of pain.

VI

Changing Mind

1

The room filled with the sound of voices,
The voices weaving like vines or voices of viols,
And the voices mixed, filling the warm room
From wall to vibrant wall. It was then I saw
The talk itself, the fourfold torrent of talk
(Below the candles and above the fire)
Moving like golden water!

                              'Come under!' he said,
'Come down under the talk! Stoop your shoulders
And enter the darkness!'

                              Who could this be
Who spoke to me in secret, while those others
Wove with their spider-mouths the moving water?
It was not the small man, not the tall man,
And not the woman whose long hair of burnt gold
Fell on the talk and was woven into it;
Nor was it that other woman, who blew smoke
Over the golden hair and golden water.

                              'Come under!' he said;
And as he spoke I saw him! His white face
Came up laughing, with bright hair! He showed
(Turning upon his axis, a strong swimmer

Making himself a ball) how he could scoop
A hollow in bright air, turning within it;
His white arms, curving like a swimmer's, shaped
The dark sphere out of brightness. There he curled,
In that cold chrysalis, secret under the talk,
Carved in the light.

'You! Narcissus!' I said!
And softly, under the four-voiced dialogue,
In the bright ether, in the golden river
Of cabbalistic sound, I plunged, I found
The silver rind of peace, the hollow round
Carved out of nothing; curled there like a god.

The blue-eyed woman, leaning above the water,
Shook her scarab ear-rings, while her voice
Entered the stream. 'Nevertheless' — she said —
Leaning toward the golden foam her head —
'Nevertheless I am not dead;
Let him forget me at his peril!' — this she said,
Smiling, and showing the three rings on her finger,
The fourth of her left hand. Her arm was naked,
The low green bodice showed her bosom rising,
Rising more quickly, as with agitation.
'I can entice him still, my eye is quick
As a lizard's eye, my tongue is quick — '

' — as quick
As an aspic's!' — this the tall man rang, and laughed.
The small man also laughed, and the bright stream
Rose deeper; and I felt myself submerged,
Submerged deliciously.

The small man whistled:
After the four dull boulders of their laugh
Had sunk beside me, sending up four spouts
Of golden water. The long whistle

Ran like a nerve. It was blue, and reached
At the near end a gong, and at the far
A copper spring. This all four pressed at once,
And the long screaming nerve wound through the water,
While they above it leaned. Ah, did they see
How the blue nerve was grounded twice in me?
'Laugh if you like,' she said, whose golden hair
Fell round me fine as water-sifted sunlight,
'Whistle derision from Rome to Jericho;
Sell him to Doctor Wundt the psycho-analyst
Whose sex-ray eyes will separate him out
Into a handful of blank syllables, —
Like a grammarian, whose beak can parse
A sentence till its gaudy words mean nothing;
Yet if I smile above him, ah, you'll see!
Each idiot syllable of what was once
The multitudinous meaning of that brain
Will beat devotion and speak its love again!'

(Alas, it is true I am dispersed thus,
Dissected out on the glass-topped table,
The tweezers picking up syllables and putting them down,
Particles so small they have no colour;
I am dispersed, and yet I know
That sovereign eye, if once it glare its love,
Will reassemble me.)

                                  The other woman,
Blowing her smoke above the outspread hair
And woven water and hair, and the dying nerve
Of sibilation, spoke at last, and while she spoke
I saw the four walls leaning inward above the stream,
And her with the rings upon her fingers, leaning,
And the two men smiling above me.
Venus too was there, and the evening star,
And the inverted trees, and the terror-coloured sky.
Sky, trees, walls, gods, birds.

'Let him forget you at his peril, this you say?
O Alba, what a bloody jest is here!
If he remember you, the peril is yours.
You, then, are only you? this gold-ring-fingered,
Green-bodiced leman? No, no, be not deceived!
You are not only you, this one great golden
Goddess above the stream with sovereign eye!
You are not only the sea-cold marble, interfused
With sanguine warmth, yet pure as the sea-coral!
You are not only the one white god of forked
Flesh, bewildering ever, never sating!
How could this be?'

                  She blew a round blue cloud
Of smoke across the golden moving water,
  (Whereunder in my hollow I sat sleeping)
And smiled.

               'How could this be? You are but one
Of all our host; and us too he has seen.
Us he remembers when he remembers you:
The livid; the sore; the old; the worn; the wounded:
Hating the smell of us, you too he'll hate.
Ah, Alba, what a cruel jest is here!
For if you wake him, with that sovereign eye,
Teasing his flesh with the three-gold-ringed finger
Until, assembled, he again swims up:
Will it not be to me — to me also — he comes?
Me, the dead cormorant whom he so loathed
And buried by the sea?'

              She leaned, and then
I saw her weeping. Intolerable pity
Broke in my heart when thus I saw her weeping.
Her in blue muslin, tall and meagre, her
The starved blue cormorant whom I betrayed.

Then Doctor Wundt, the tall man, walked beside
The sparkling stream. His face was like a star.
Between the leaves, inexorable, he shone,
While the brown thrush, sequestered, hushed the wood
With meditative song. Anon the youths
Came from the wood and laughed with Socrates:
They saw him drink the hemlock, heard him say
Alpha and Omega. Thence up the hill
To Golgotha they jeered, and with them took
The sponge, the spear, the flask of vinegar,
And that poor king, whose madness, on a Friday,
Burned to a beauty like the evening star.
Hegel, too, came shoreward in that evening,
Leaning above me, leaning above the stream,
Whose motion (so he sighed at length) was only
Manifestation of the dialectic.
And others, too; some singly, some in groups,
Talking a little, or silent. There at last
My father also came. The dead leaf's step
Was his, rapid and light; and his young face
Shone like the evening star, inexorable.

And he and Doctor Wundt together spoke,
Flinging one image on the moving water,
With one voice spoke, wherewith the bird's voice chimed;
But what it was they said I could not hear.
Only, I heard the bird-voice tinkling 'peace'
Among the lapping leaves, and sound of weeping
Where the tall woman, the blue-muslined, leaned
Above the river; while the sovereign eye
Glared on the water to assemble me.
'Inheritor!' — this word my father said,
And Doctor Wundt said also. The word hung
Smokelike above the stream.

2

O Alba! Look! While thus Narcissus sleeps
Under the river, and beside him keeps
Conscious and yet unconscious my bright soul!
Look, how the dawn, the giant swimmer, comes
Over the sky, head downward, swimming slowly,
With powerful bright arms! Out of the east
The blue god looms, and with him come new worlds.
Those bubbles — look — that from his silver heel
Sparkle and burst, and those that from his mouth
Spiral, and those that bead his sides with light,
And those that globe his fingers — those are worlds,
That bursting seem to escape the godlike tether,
And yet do not escape. Is it from me they come —
From me to me? And is that sky myself?

It was the southeast wind, changing softly,
Who thus, eyes downward, swam upon my sky,
Bringing news of the southeast. The weather-vanes —
Golden cocks, ships, and a hundred arrows, —
All creaked at once, changed on a mile of steeples,
All changed at once, as thus the swimmer passed.
And all those bubbles
Whirling about him, voluting sleekly, bursting
With altered shape enlarged, these were the news
Of another country! These were the fields of corn!
These were the salt marshes, steaming in sunlight, where
The herons rise with trailed legs
And the wild horses stamp!
There, in long brightness, breaks the world-long sea!

                        The small man brooded
Darkly above me, darkly glowing,
Mephistopheles, holding in his wide hand
All these shapes. 'It is the kite country,'
He laughed, 'it is the land of kites; and there he walks.'

. . . And as he glowed above me, Chinese lantern
Burning with grinning mouth beneath the leaves,
And the pierced eyes cruel as the eyes of the kite-flyers,
Those others laughed: the tall man first, and then
More musically, melodious derision,
She who had wept, the cormorant, and she
Who threatened, glaring, to assemble me.
Ha, ha, they laughed, descending scale of scorn.
Three towers leaned above me, beating bells,
So that the air was beaten and confused.
Through this (harsh sabbath) mocked the pursuing voice:

'Childe Roland, leaving behind him the dark tower,
Came in the evening to the land of kites.
Peril was past. The skull of the dead horse
His foot broke; and the desert, where wild dogs
Bay up the moon from tall grass, this he crossed
In the long light. And in the kite country —'
(Ha, ha, they laughed, merry descending scale) —
'He saw the diamond kites all rise at once
From the flat land. And on each kite was bound
A weeping woman, the arms outstretched, the feet
Nailed at the foot!'

                               (Alas, how hard it is,
I helpless, bound thus, in my cave, asleep,
Bound in the stinging nerves of sound, these voices!)

'Under the sky of kites he steps, hearing
The sad singing and whimpering of the kites,
Seeing also the blood that drips from hands
Nailed to the Crosspiece, high in air. He climbs
Slowly in twilight to the weeping-cross . . .
Alas, good woman, you no sooner lust
Together concupiscent, your four arms
Enwreathed, your faces fused in one, your eyes

Sightless with foresight of the two-backed beast,
Than with derisive cries and cruel eyes
The kiteflyers come! Your outstretched hands they nail
Against the Crosspiece! Then down the hill they run
Drawing the kitecord with them, so that, weeping,
He hears you, weeping, blown aloft in air!'

Thus the small man, amid derisive laughter!
But it was not of the kites, nor the kite country,
The giant swimmer sang, who brought me news,
News of the southeast! O believe, believe!
Believe, grim four, believe me or I die!
It is from you this vision comes; while I
Dreamed that I swam, and with that swimmer came
Into the southeast of forgotten name.

3

The seven-man orchestra tuned up bubbling and squeaking.
Harry Frank, the conductor, stuffed a dirty handkerchief inside
his collar, turning goggle eyes to see if his friend Anne was in the
audience; and Tom, the drummer, with his prizefighter's mug,
was chatting with a couple of skirts in the front row. Lights!
Lights! O'Dwyer, his bloodshot eyes, looked round the cherubimed
corner of the proscenium arch to see what they were waiting for.
What were they waiting for? 'Hearts and Flowers.' Harry rapped
his frayed bow on the lamplit tripod, turned his smug Jewish
profile from Tom to O'Dwyer, sleekly smiling. He began briskly.
The theatre was full. Three thousand faces. Faces in rows like
flowers in beds.

And all this, mind you, was myself! myself still asleep under the
four-voiced dialogue! the fourfold river of talk! Here the three
thousand faces leaned down upon me, stamens and pistils! and
here I was the orchestra, a submarine orchestra, a telephone ex-
change of blue nerves, and a bare stage on which something was
about to happen! Here I was Luvic, warbling, her white arms fat
at the shoulders, like hams powdered, her green-ringed fingers

making in a fold of her dress that pill-rolling motion which is a
symptom of paralysis agitans, bugling

> Falling life and fading tree,
> Lines of white in a sullen sea,
> Shadows rising on you and me —

her pale mouth opening and shutting, flexing and reflexing, in
perfect time! Here I was Glozo, the card-eater, the ventriloquist,
who took goldfish out of his gold-toothed mouth, and Mrs. Glozo,
his plump-rumped assistant. Here I was Tozo, the Jap, and his
family of little Tozos, all exactly alike in pink fleshings, all short-
legged and bowlegged, lying on their long backs and twirling pur-
ple barrels (gold-star-emblazoned) on their pat-slapping soft feet,
tossing the purple barrels from one simian sole to another. Here I
was Nozo, the hobo, the awkward inflamed nose with a diamond
sparkling on its horn. I was each of these in turn, and then also I
was Bozo, the muscular trapeze artist, and all the while I was Harry
cocking his left eye over his fiddle, and Tom rubbing sandpaper
together (wisha wisha) while Mrs. Bishop put her perfumed hand
in his pocket, and three thousand yellow faces perched in rows like
birds, and a humming marble foyer with gilt mirrors, and O'Dwyer
crowding into the same telephone booth with Mrs. Harry Frank
(naughty-naughty) and the electric sign in Bosworth Place —

All this I was, and also the amphitheatre itself,
All this, but also a small room, a forest,
Trees full of birds walking down to the water's edge,
Socrates in a basket hanging beside the full moon, eating a
    partridge,
The young men pushing, hubbub on Golgotha,
The mad king among them, terrified, smelling the sweat of the
    crowd,
Hegel arriving on a sea-scallop accompanied by Venus, —
All this I was, but also those four strangers
Leaning above me, leaning above the stream,
The tall man, the small man, and the blue-eyed woman,
And that other woman, whose beauty, on a kite,

Rose to a beauty like the evening star.
Golgotha, the skull, was the amphitheatre,
The skull was my skull, and within it played
The seven-man orchestra, while Luvic sang —

Lights! Lights! O'Dwyer hoarsely cried,
His bloodshot eyes peeped round the gilded smooth
Belly of a cherub, who supported
Chryselephantine pillar of fruits and lutes and leaves.
The lights changed, the walls
Came closer, the crowd was blue, obscure, the forest
Nodded, the blue smoke rolled among the leaves
And nests of birds. The orchestra sat playing

Typewriters, telephones and telegraphs
Under the calcium light
And on the stage red ropes had squared a ring.
Out of the forest flew the songs of birds,
While hid in leaves the saxophone made moan.
Bang! said the gong, and the red giant from his corner
Sprang to the ring, shaking the boards. The other
Rose terrified, submissive, his thin hands
Ungloved, his chin defenceless, and his heart
Visibly beating.

    'You! Narcissus!' I said!
And as I rose the giant's hard glove crashed
Black on the visible heart, and the sick man
Shot through the ropes and fell against the arch
Under the cherub at O'Dwyer's feet.

ONE TWO THREE FOUR FIVE
SIX SEVEN EIGHT NINE —

        the red hand
Counted, jerking. At the fatal nine
The sick man rose, crawled through the ropes, his face
White as a dead man's in the calcium light,

His dark eyes burning with fever, his weak hands
Uplifted, trembling.

                    'You! Narcissus!' I said!
And saw again the hard black piston crash
Against the visible heart, and the sick man
Falling backward, on his back, in the dark corner,
Unconscious, motionless, his dark eyes
Wide open! Then the applause, roaring like rain!
The giant's bloody glove upheld! The gong clattering!
Bozo, Nozo, Glozo, the Tozos, cheering!
While from the forest blew a blast of sound,
Flutebirds and bubblebeaks, Harry and Tom,
The seven-man orchestra, the saxophone
Bubbling the *Himmelfahrt,* the Lo! the hero
Conquering comes!

                    Lights! O'Dwyer rubbed
A bright alpaca sleeve across the cherub,
The forest darkened, the nodding lilies
Darkened also, the bare stage diminished,
Bozo, Nozo, Glozo, the Tozos, all were gone,
Only the half-dead man, who lay alone,
His white dead face propped up against the backdrop,
Staring, with dying eyes. To him I knelt,
While Doctor Wundt, above me, in a box,
Leaned down among the leaves
Pleasantly laughing, and that other man,
My father, chill from the grave, leaned down and smiled.
And it was then the blue-eyed woman triumphed
And glared with sovereign eye above the stream:
'What thinks he now? What peril seeks he now?
Digs now what magic?'

                    'Digs in his heart a grave!'
Laughed Doctor Wundt. 'It is the half-dead man,
Himself, who longs to die; for him he digs.'

(It is true I ran to the dead man
And raised his head. Alas, what horror,
When I saw the chest-wall rotted, the heart
Hanging like a cluster of grapes,
Beating weakly, uncovered and sick.
Alas, too, what horror when he said:
Daily I fight here,
Daily I die for the world's delight
By the giant blow on my visible heart!)

Then from the wood arose a sigh of sound
Where lapped in leaves the seven-man orchestra,
Flutebird and bubblebeak, Harry and Tom,
Blew blue nostalgia out of 'Hearts and Flowers';
While Doctor Wundt, grown taller, and my father,
Flinging one haloed image on the stream,
Sang, with one voice, a mournful requiem.
'Inheritor!' This was the word they said,
But also sang, 'Alas, Narcissus dead,
Narcissus daily dead, that we may live!'

4

My father which art in earth
From whom I got my birth,
What is it that I inherit?
From the bones fallen apart
And the deciphered heart,
Body and spirit.

My mother which art in tomb
Who carriedst me in thy womb,
What is it that I inherit?
From the thought come to dust
And the remembered lust,
Body and spirit.

Father and mother, who gave
Life, love, and now the grave,
What is it that I can be?
Nothing but what lies here,
The hand still, the brain sere,
Naught lives in thee

Nor ever will live, save
It have within this grave
Roots in the mingled heart,
In the damp ashes wound
Where the past, underground,
Falls, falls apart.

1925

Improvisations: Lights and Snow

I

The girl in the room beneath
Before going to bed
Strums on a mandolin
The three simple tunes she knows.
How inadequate they are to tell what her heart feels!
When she has finished them several times
She thrums the strings aimlessly with her finger-nails
And smiles, and thinks happily of many things.

II

I stood for a long while before the shop-window
Looking at the blue butterflies embroidered on tawny silk.
The building was a tower before me,
Time was loud behind me,

Sun went over the housetops and dusty trees;
And there they were, glistening, brilliant, motionless,
Stitched in a golden sky
By yellow patient fingers long since turned to dust.

III

The first bell is silver,
And breathing darkness I think only of the long scythe of time.
The second bell is crimson,
And I think of a holiday night, with rockets
Furrowing the sky with red, and a soft shatter of stars.
The third bell is saffron and slow,
And I behold a long sunset over the sea
With wall on wall of castled cloud and glittering balustrades.
The fourth bell is colour of bronze,
I walk by a frozen lake in the dun light of dusk:
Muffled crackings run in the ice,
Trees creak, birds fly.
The fifth bell is cold clear azure,
Delicately tinged with green:
One golden star hangs melting in it,
And towards this, sleepily, I go.
The sixth bell is as if a pebble
Had been dropped into a deep sea far above me . . .
Rings of sound ebb slowly into the silence.

IV

On the day when my uncle and I drove to the cemetery,
Rain rattled on the roof of the carriage;
And talking constrainedly of this and that
We refrained from looking at the child's coffin on the seat before
    us.
When we reached the cemetery
We found that the thin snow on the grass

Was already darkly transparent with rain;
And boards had been laid upon it
That we might walk without wetting our feet.

V

When I was a boy, and saw bright rows of icicles
In many lengths along a wall
I was disappointed to find
That I could not play music upon them:
I ran my hand lightly across them
And they fell, tinkling.
I tell you this, young man, so that your expectations of life
Will not be too great.

VI

It is now two hours since I left you,
And the perfume of your hands is still on my hands.
And though since then
I have looked at the stars, walked in the cold blue streets,
And heard the dead leaves blowing over the ground
Under the trees,
I still remember the sound of your laughter.
How will it be, lady, when there is none to remember you
Even as long as this?
Will the dust braid your hair?

VII

The day opens with the brown light of snowfall
And past the window snowflakes fall and fall.
I sit in my chair all day and work and work
Measuring words against each other.
I open the piano and play a tune
But find it does not say what I feel,
I grow tired of measuring words against each other,

I grow tired of these four walls,
And I think of you, who write me that you have just had a
    daughter
And named her after your first sweetheart,
And you, who break your heart, far away,
In the confusion and savagery of a long war,
And you who, worn by the bitterness of winter,
Will soon go south.
The snowflakes fall almost straight in the brown light
Past my window,
And a sparrow finds refuge on my window-ledge.
This alone comes to me out of the world outside
As I measure word with word.

VIII

Many things perplex me and leave me troubled,
Many things are locked away in the white book of stars
Never to be opened by me.
The starred leaves are silently turned,
And the mooned leaves;
And as they are turned, fall the shadows of life and death.
Perplexed and troubled,
I light a small light in a small room,
The lighted walls come closer to me,
The familiar pictures are clear.
I sit in my favourite chair and turn in my mind
The tiny pages of my own life, whereon so little is written,
And hear at the eastern window the pressure of a long wind,
    coming
From I know not where.

How many times have I sat here,
How many times will I sit here again,
Thinking these same things over and over in solitude
As a child says over and over
The first word he has learned to say.

IX

This girl gave her heart to me,
And this, and this.
This one looked at me as if she loved me,
And silently walked away.
This one I saw once and loved, and saw her never again.

Shall I count them for you upon my fingers?
Or like a priest solemnly sliding beads?
Or pretend they are roses, pale pink, yellow, and white,
And arrange them for you in a wide bowl
To be set in sunlight?
See how nicely it sounds as I count them for you —
'This girl gave her heart to me
And this, and this' . . . !
And nevertheless my heart breaks when I think of them,
When I think their names,
And how, like leaves, they have changed and blown
And will lie at last, forgotten,
Under the snow.

X

It is night-time, and cold, and snow is falling,
And no wind grieves the walls.
In the small world of light around the arc-lamp
A swarm of snowflakes falls and falls.
The street grows silent. The last stranger passes.
The sound of his feet, in the snow, is indistinct.

What forgotten sadness is it, on a night like this,
Takes possession of my heart?
Why do I think of a camellia tree in a southern garden,
With pink blossoms among dark leaves,
Standing, surprised, in the snow?
Why do I think of spring?

The snowflakes, helplessly veering,
Fall silently past my window;
They come from darkness and enter darkness.
What is it in my heart is surprised and bewildered
Like that camellia tree,
Beautiful still in its glittering anguish?
And spring so far away!

XI

As I walked through the lamplit gardens,
On the thin white crust of snow,
So intensely was I thinking of my misfortune,
So clearly were my eyes fixed
On the face of this grief which has come to me,
That I did not notice the beautiful pale colouring
Of lamplight on the snow;
Nor the interlaced long blue shadows of trees;

And yet these things were there,
And the white lamps and orange lamps, and lamps of lilac were
     there,
As I have seen them so often before;
As they will be so often again
Long after my grief is forgotten.

And still, though I know this, and say this, it cannot console me.

XII

How many times have we been interrupted
Just as I was about to make up a story for you!
One time it was because we suddenly saw a firefly
Lighting his green lantern among the boughs of a fir-tree.
Marvellous! Marvellous! He is making for himself
A little tent of light in the darkness!
And one time it was because we saw a lilac lightning flash

Run wrinkling into the blue top of the mountain, —
We heard boulders of thunder rolling down upon us
And the plat-plat of drops on the window,
And we ran to watch the rain
Charging in wavering white clouds across the long grass of the
field!
Or at other times it was because we saw a star
Slipping easily out of the sky and falling, far off,
Among pine-dark hills;
Or because we found a crimson eft
Darting in the cold grass!

These things interrupted us and left us wondering;
And the stories, whatever they might have been,
Were never told.
A fairy, binding a daisy down and laughing?
A golden-haired princess caught in a cobweb?
A love-story of long ago?
Some day, just as we are beginning again,
Just as we blow the first sweet note,
Death itself will interrupt us.

XIII

My heart is an old house, and in that forlorn old house,
In the very centre, dark and forgotten,
Is a locked room where an enchanted princess
Lies sleeping.
But sometimes, in that dark house,
As if almost from the stars, far away,
Sounds whisper in that secret room —
Faint voices, music, a dying trill of laughter?
And suddenly, from her long sleep,
The beautiful princess awakes and dances.

Who is she? I do not know.
Why does she dance? Do not ask me! —

Yet to-day, when I saw you,
When I saw your eyes troubled with the trouble of happiness,
And your mouth trembling into a smile,
And your fingers put shyly forward, —
Softly, in that room,
The little princess arose
And danced;
And as she danced the old house gravely trembled
With its vague and delicious secret.

XIV

Like an old tree uprooted by the wind
And flung down cruelly
With roots bared to the sun and stars
And limp leaves brought to earth —
Torn from its house —
So do I seem to myself
When you have left me.

XV

The music of the morning is red and warm;
Snow lies against the walls;
And on the sloping roof in the yellow sunlight
Pigeons huddle against the wind.
The music of the evening is attenuated and thin —
The moon seen through a wave by a mermaid;
The crying of a violin.
Far down there, far down where the river turns to the west,
The delicate lights begin to twinkle
On the dusky arches of the bridge:
In the green sky a long cloud,
A smouldering wave of smoky crimson,
Breaks in the freezing wind: and above it, unabashed,
Remote, untouched, fierily palpitant,
Sings the first star.

Tetélestai

How shall we praise the magnificence of the dead,
The great man humbled, the haughty brought to dust?
Is there a horn we should not blow as proudly
For the meanest of us all, who creeps his days,
Guarding his heart from blows, to die obscurely?
I am no king, have laid no kingdoms waste,
Taken no princes captive, led no triumphs
Of weeping women through long walls of trumpets;
Say rather, I am no one, or an atom;
Say rather, two great gods, in a vault of starlight,
Play ponderingly at chess, and at the game's end
One of the pieces, shaken, falls to the floor
And runs to the darkest corner; and that piece
Forgotten there, left motionless, is I . . .
Say that I have no name, no gifts, no power,
Am only one of millions, mostly silent;
One who came with eyes and hands and a heart,
Looked on beauty, and loved it, and then left it.
Say that the fates of time and space obscured me,
Led me a thousand ways to pain, bemused me,
Wrapped me in ugliness; and like great spiders
Dispatched me at their leisure. . . Well, what then?
Should I not hear, as I lie down in dust,
The horns of glory blowing above my burial?

Morning and evening opened and closed above me:
Houses were built above me; trees let fall
Yellowing leaves upon me, hands of ghosts;
Rain has showered its arrows of silver upon me
Seeking my heart; winds have roared and tossed me;

Music in long blue waves of sound has borne me
A helpless weed to shores of unthought silence;
Time, above me, within me, crashed its gongs
Of terrible warning, sifting the dust of death;
And here I lie. Blow now your horns of glory
Harshly over my flesh, you trees, you waters!
You stars and suns, Canopus, Deneb, Rigel,
Let me, as I lie down, here in this dust,
Hear, far off, your whispered salutation!
Roar now above my decaying flesh, you winds,
Whirl out your earth-scents over this body, tell me
Of ferns and stagnant pools, wild roses, hillsides!
Anoint me, rain, let crash your silver arrows
On this hard flesh! I am the one who named you,
I lived in you, and now I die in you.
I your son, your daughter, treader of music,
Lie broken, conquered . . . Let me not fall in silence.

III

I, the restless one; the circler of circles;
Herdsman and roper of stars, who could not capture
The secret of self; I who was tyrant to weaklings,
Striker of children; destroyer of women; corrupter
Of innocent dreamers, and laugher at beauty; I,
Too easily brought to tears and weakness by music,
Baffled and broken by love, the helpless beholder
Of the war in my heart of desire with desire, the struggle
Of hatred with love, terror with hunger; I
Who laughed without knowing the cause of my laughter, who
    grew
Without wishing to grow, a servant to my own body;
Loved without reason the laughter and flesh of a woman,
Enduring such torments to find her! I who at last
Grow weaker, struggle more feebly, relent in my purpose,
Choose for my triumph an easier end, look backward
At earlier conquests; or, caught in the web, cry out

In a sudden and empty despair, 'Tetélestai!'
Pity me, now! I, who was arrogant, beg you!
Tell me, as I lie down, that I was courageous.
Blow horns of victory now, as I reel and am vanquished.
Shatter the sky with trumpets above my grave.

IV

. . . Look! this flesh how it crumbles to dust and is blown!
These bones, how they grind in the granite of frost and are noth-
    ing!
This skull, how it yawns for a flicker of time in the darkness,
Yet laughs not and sees not! It is crushed by a hammer of sun-
    light,
And the hands are destroyed. . . Press down through the leaves
    of the jasmine,
Dig through the interlaced roots -- nevermore will you find me;
I was no better than dust, yet you cannot replace me. . .
Take the soft dust in your hand — does it stir: does it sing?
Has it lips and a heart? Does it open its eyes to the sun?
Does it run, does it dream, does it burn with a secret, or tremble
In terror of death? Or ache with tremendous decisions? . . .
Listen! . . . It says: 'I lean by the river. The willows
Are yellowed with bud. White clouds roar up from the south
And darken the ripples; but they cannot darken my heart,
Nor the face like a star in my heart! . . . Rain falls on the water
And pelts it, and rings it with silver. The willow trees glisten,
The sparrows chirp under the eaves; but the face in my heart
Is a secret of music. . . I wait in the rain and am silent.'
Listen again! . . . It says: 'I have worked, I am tired,
The pencil dulls in my hand: I see through the window
Walls upon walls of windows with faces behind them,
Smoke floating up to the sky, an ascension of sea-gulls.
I am tired. I have struggled in vain, my decision was fruitless,
Why then do I wait? with darkness, so easy, at hand! . . .
But tomorrow, perhaps . . . I will wait and endure till tomor-
    row!' . . .

Or again: 'It is dark. The decision is made. I am vanquished
By terror of life. The walls mount slowly about me
In coldness. I had not the courage. I was forsaken.
I cried out, was answered by silence . . . Tetélestai! . . .'

V

Hear how it babbles! — Blow the dust out of your hand,
With its voices and visions, tread on it, forget it, turn homeward
With dreams in your brain. . . This, then, is the humble, the
      nameless, —
The lover, the husband and father, the struggler with shadows,
The one who went down under shoutings of chaos, the weakling
Who cried his 'forsaken!' like Christ on the darkening hill-
      top! . . .
This, then, is the one who implores, as he dwindles to silence,
A fanfare of glory. . . And which of us dares to deny him?

PUNCH: THE IMMORTAL LIAR

DOCUMENTS IN HIS HISTORY

*

PART I

Punch: The Immortal Liar

TWO OLD MEN WHO REMEMBERED PUNCH

I

Do I remember Punch? — Listen — I'll tell you.
I am an old man now, but I remember,
I saw him in the flesh. My, my, what flesh! . . .
I can still see him shut his eyes to sing, —
As he did always when he'd drunk too much! . . .
He was the splendidest fool I ever knew.

His great red nose was bent down like an ogre's,
His mouth was wide, he was half-bald, half-grey,
His legs were bandy. . . Every woman in town
Had slapped his face, — although, to hear him talk,
You'd think he'd kissed them all! He was a coward,
We kicked him, spat upon him, whipped him, cursed him,
And threw him out of doors. . . And yet, we liked him.

What lies he told! He had a genius for it.
He killed his wife, hopped upon Sheba's knee,
Walked and talked with devils, raped and murdered . . .
Why did we listen to him? . . . Why did we like him? . . .
Well, I don't know. Say rather that we loved him —
There was a something noble about the man.
Somehow, though small, he cast an enormous shadow.

The night before he died, we carried him home.
He stopped to lean on the churchyard wall a moment,
And stared at the tower clock. 'Listen!' he said.
'This heart that beats here, — underneath my hand, —
All of the clocks in the world keep time with it!
Even the stars in the sky, the sun and planets,
Measure their time by me! — I am the centre!'
We thrust him into his house. . . He fell down laughing . . .

Yes, there was something noble about the man.
He was half mad, no doubt, a sneak, a villain:
And yet, somehow, the world seemed greater for him;
And smaller when he died.

2

So that's your story, is it? — Well, here's mine!
Draw close your coats about you, cross yourselves —
And shut the door! There's a queer wind tonight
Howling as if some ghost were riding on it —
Whose ghost, God knows! And what I've got to tell you
Might crack the earth, and set the devil talking.
See the blue lightning twinkle on that window!
Look at the ashes dancing on that hearth!
Old Nick is riding trees, and at this instant —
Don't look! — may have his red eye at the keyhole.
You say: this Punch had something noble in him.
Noble! Good God! Are words to have no meanings?
Christ was a scoundrel then, and thieves are angels!
Noble! There's rain on the window for your answer,
Old Nick's tattoo of talons. Look outside,
You'll see him spurt off like a ball of fire,
You'll hear a peal of laughter, a clap of thunder,
And smoke will sting your eyes. If there was ever
A viler villain walked this fatal earth
Tell me his name! Mischief he was in flesh,
Mischief he left behind him in his seed,

And ruins rotting where he found his pleasure.
You say he lied. You say his crimes were fables.
But were they? Where is Judy? Dead and festering,
With a gravestone fallen down above her carrion.
Tell me, — what woman was there in this village
He didn't try to kiss? Not one, you know it;
And if he failed, that wasn't his fault, surely.
Who'll put his beer down, now, and swear on the Bible
He ever knew a good deed done by Punch? . . .
Ah! there's rain on the window for your answer.

Now, then, — you'll say, perhaps, I'm superstitious.
But am I? . . . Have I ever looked for signs? . . .
You knów me; and you know I'm no old woman
Who squints in a cup of tea-leaves for a portent.
But this I swear, and this I'll swear till doomsday, —
More things go on about us on this earth
Than flesh can know of. Trees have devils in them,
Ghosts go walking out on the waves of the air
And sing in the belfry when the bells are tolling.
What else are owls and bats but evil spirits —
Why do they haunt the churchyard if they're not?
No, I'm not superstitious, more than any
Who use their senses; but I'll tell you this;
The man we knew as Punch was no mere mortal.

Who was he? . . . Wait. I'll tell you. But before,
I've got three questions for you you can't answer!
Who saw Punch come to town? Who was his father?
Where did he come from? . . . Ah! You see; he's human,
(Or so you'd say,) yet no one ever knew
Just who he was, or what his business was.
Presto! and here he stood with a purse of money,
Out of a cloud, you might say, — dropped from heaven.
Again I say, — who saw Punch come to town? . . .
One man! One man alone of all this village
Saw how he came. Or did he? That's the question.

Old Crabbe it was — dead now these fifteen years —
And he it was who told me. . . It was spring,
And Crabbe, who was still a boy, was in the orchard
Beyond the churchyard — Gardy Gleason's orchard.
He climbed the wall that joins the churchyard wall
And skirts the road, and sat there, legs a-dangling,
To peel a stick. Now then, you know that wall —
You've climbed it after Gardy Gleason's apples;
And you, as well as I, know how the road
Dips down without a curve along the valley
A mile and more. . . Well, Crabbe was whittling there,
And looking down the road. And not a soul
Was in it: he was sure, for he was watching
To see his father's horse come round the turn.
Bare as your hand! A warm spring day, no clouds,
Bees in the apple-blossoms over his head,
And the sun behind his back. He saw his shadow
Slanting across the road, and almost reaching
The other wall; a thin high-shouldered shadow —
And started, as boys will, to fling his arms,
To see the shadow wave. . . And then, of a sudden,
Without a squeak or sound, another shadow
Slanted across the road and fell on the wall
Beyond his own, — and staid there. . . Arms in the air,
Young Crabbe went stiff with fright; he turned his head
And saw in the road, alone before him, — Punch!
Punch, with a bag and stick across one shoulder —
And a red grin on his face! . . .

                       Well — that was queer:
And young Crabbe felt his entrails coiling coldly.
Where had he come from — slid down out of the air? . . .
Popped from the ground? . . . But just as he was thinking
That after all the fellow might have found
The time to steal upon him, — while he waved
His arms and shadows there, — just then he noticed
A thing that made his hair stand up and creep:

The road, of course, was dusty at that season, —
And Punch's boots showed not a speck of dust . . .
This was enough! He slid back over the wall
And took the short-cut home.
                              So that's the first count.
The fellow suddenly comes to us from nowhere:
Breaks from the air as a fish might breach the sea.
Does flesh do things like that? Not human flesh!
Only the flesh of angels or of devils,
Which, having a look of flesh, yet, lighter than air,
Burns at the touch and blows in a wind like fire;
Or, seen at dusk, takes on a glow like phosphor . . .
He comes to us from nowhere; and he tells us
Of inquisitions, demons, saints, and hangmen.
Who ever heard — in our time — of such things?
Where was this village that he boasted of —
Who ever heard him name it? — And these people;
These constables and Ketches that he murdered
So humorously, to make so sweet a story; —
Where are they buried? . . . Ah, — you say, — he lied.
And so he did. He lied, — when he was drunk, —
Even of Polly Prim, whom we all knew . . .
But what does that prove? Nothing — no, sir, nothing!
For was he always lying? — That's the question! . . .

Consider, then. . . A mystery comes among us,
Ugly and vile beyond all human knowledge,
A walking vice; he lies, seduces, steals,
Gets roaring drunk, and leads our youth to mischief.
The village reeks with him. Corruption rules us.
Lechery shakes our walls, the women snicker,
The young men brawl. . . What's this — a sort of angel? . . .
And here are portents, too! . . . A rain like blood, —
And the laundry reddens where it dries on the walls;
Voices are heard; a curious sound of singing
Thrills from the church at night; and in the morning

A pig is dead on the altar with its throat cut.
The same night Janet Crowe has had a vision:
The door breaks in, the Devil comes in roaring
With a huge knife in his hands, seizes her hair,
And drags her screaming. . . When she wakes she's lying
Naked upon the floor; the door's wide open;
Her right hand's paralysed for three days after . . .
Next Judy's dead, and no one knows just how.
Punch finds her on the kitchen floor, he says, —
Her hair spread out, and poison on her lips.
Well, did she kill herself, — or was she murdered?
Polly, we know, maintains she killed herself —
And Punch says she was murdered. Who was right?
This much we know: we couldn't prove him guilty,
Nor, for that matter, find a trace of poison;
A darkness fell about her; and a silence
Which only owl's or devil's eyes could see through . . .
'Devils!' — Think hard about that word a minute;
Conjure these mysteries and freaks before you,
And then recall how strangely and how often
It sounded from a drunken tongue we knew.
Who was it, in the grass on Mory's hill,
Saw Satan walking there with his tail about him
And Faustus at his side? . . . Who was it told us
How he had stoned this devil and his clerk
And sent them capering mistily in the sunlight
Through buttercup and dogrose? . . . Last, — who was it
Mounted the wind and stepped through time and space
To talk with Sheba, Solomon, even Judas,
And all in fact — remark this well — save Christ?
Ah! Now we're coming to it. You begin
To see the dark conclusion I've been hinting!
And now I'll tell you what at last convinced me.
Draw close your coats about you! Cross yourselves!
Outside the window, there, in the rain and lightning,
Hangs some one else who listens to this story.

I had a dream: I dreamed it three times over.
The first time was the night that Punch lay dying;
The second time, the day we found him dead
With his feet against his door, and buried him;
The third time when a year had passed. I dreamed
A devil stood in the pulpit of our church
With a bible in his hands; his face was red,
His horns were glittering gold, his tail, like a serpent,
Was mooned and striped with colours that waned and waxed,
His teeth were sharp as jewels. There he laughed,
As the bible, fluttering open in his hands,
Turned to an infant's head, which down he dashed . . .
Or was it a rose, which turned on the floor to blood? . . .
We leapt in horror, and ran towards him shouting,
We chased him over the pews and down the stairs,
And into the vault; and there, in the darkest corner
We beat him down with sticks, we stoned and kicked him
And trampled on him, until at last, as snakes do,
He quivered, — only a little, — in seeming death.
We thrust his body, then, with the plashy tail
Wound twice about his belly, into a coffin,
And carried it to the graveyard; it was raining;
And some one cried aloud to us in the darkness
'Bury him now in holy ground; for then
His soul will wither and have no power to harm!'
And this we did. We dug a grave in haste
And tumbled the coffin in, and heaped it over
With mud and stones. The rain lashed down upon us;
And some one cried aloud to us in the darkness
'Drive now a cross of wood in the earth above him
And blast his soul.' And so we made a cross
And hammered it into the loosened earth with shovels.
But at the third stroke suddenly came a cry,
The wet earth flashed and opened, the coffin burst,
The devil leapt before us, thumbed his nose,
And laughing, with a low sound like boulders falling
Or far-off thunder, vanished into the rain.

We looked at the grave, and saw the earth heal over
Before our very eyes . . . roots, grass, and all. . .

Three times I dreamed this dream; — and from the third,
Waking in terror, on such a night as this
With large rain plashing on the walls and windows
And the chimney gulping wind, I suddenly saw
The meaning of my dream; I pulled my clothes on
And took my spade and lantern and went out
Into the darkness. Rain and clouds like smoke
Flew past the lantern; dark were all the houses;
The broken weather-vane on the church was clinking,
The churchyard gate groaned loudly as it opened,
And the oak-tree buzzed in the wind. I raised the lantern,
And saw the tall white pyramid of marble
That's next to Punch's grave. By this I set
The lantern down on the grass; and took my spade
And dug. The wet earth cut like cheese. In no time
I'd gone six feet. I held the lantern up
And looked down into the hole — and there was nothing.
Well, then — I thought perhaps I'd been mistaken — :
Dug to one side. I took the spade again
And dug two feet to the right, two feet to the left, —
Then lengthened it. And what I found was — nothing!
No trace! — no trace of coffin or of bones!
Only the rainy roots . . . I filled the grave
And went back home: and lay awake all night
Thinking about it. When the morning came, —
I don't know what it was got into my head, —
I sneaked back into the churchyard just for luck —
To see if I'd got the sods on straight, and rake
The dirt away. And what do you think I saw?
That grave was just as if I'd never dug there!
Healed over — like the grave I saw in the dream! . . .

Now then, you, over there! you say this Punch
Had something noble in him; tell me, will you —

What kind of a man is this, who comes from nowhere,
Runs through the town like fire, and when he's buried
Skips from the grave, and takes his coffin with him!
Angel or devil, maybe, but no mortal —
Nor angel, either! And I make no riddles.
Believe or not, that's what I saw. You've only
To take a spade, and dig, to prove me wrong. . .

And it's no sacrilege to dig for devils.

WHAT PUNCH TOLD THEM

Punch in a beer-house, drinking beer,
Booms with his voice so that all may hear,
Bangs on the table with a red-haired fist,
Writhes in his chair with a hump-backed twist,
Leers at his huge nose, in the glass,
And then proclaims, in a voice of brass:
Let all who would prosper and be free
Mark my words and listen to me!
Call me a hunchback? call me a clown?
I turned the universe upside down!
And where is the law or love or chain
That can't be broken by nerve or brain?

Of all my troubles my wife was first!
If once I loved her, at last I cursed!
I stole her out of her father's house,
Kissed her, made her my lawful spouse, —
And loved her, too, for a certain season . . .
And where's the woman who loves in reason?
She dogged me up; she dogged me down;
She tracked my footsteps through the town;
Kissed me, clung to me; asked for more;
'Punch, do you love me?' — till I swore
I'd break her neck! I'd fling her away!
Or sail to a foreign land and stay . . .

You've all got wives — now listen to me,
Learn how a man can go scot free!
Did I slit her gorge with a carving-knife —
Offer the hangman's noose my life?
Not Punch! — There are ways and ways to kill, —
Some take courage and some take skill . . .
Poor Judy's dead — and the constables think
She fell downstairs — but here, I wink!
Yes, sirs, there's ways and ways of dying,
Some with wailing and some with crying;
But some of us die in the dead of night
With never a sound in the candlelight.
They stretched her out in a coffin small,
They hid the coffin under a pall,
And the mourners came all dressed in black,
Shouldered it, each with bending back,
And carried it out. . . I sat apart
And wiped my eyes and broke my heart —
Oh, yes! and each 'Poor Punch!' he said
As he saw me weep and bow my head.

Well, sirs, it may seem strange to you
But I was sad, for a day or two —
I thought of Judy and all she'd been,
How young she was, and then my sin
Came in a nightmare to my brain
And shook my hand with a palsy pain.
Superstition be damned! said I —
There's no use moping — we all must die —
And what does it matter how it's done?
Weep in roses, or hang in fun!
And so it happened, and not long after,
Strutting around with a crooked laughter,
I met this girl named Polly Prim,
Dark and devilish, red-lipped, slim,
A virgin harlot, the fame of the place,
Because no man had kissed her face.

Now I'm not handsome, as you can see,
But I've a power with girls in me —
I take no credit, it's something given,
Sent to the womb by hell or heaven —
A trick, a knack, a stab of the eye,
A twist of the lip, malicious, sly,
Soft in persuasion, bold in the act —
No nut's so hard that it can't be cracked!
You wouldn't think, with a nose like mine,
Purple and gorgeous with too much wine,
And a bony hump like a pedlar's pack
Pushing the coat up off my back,
You wouldn't think that a man like this,
Short of murder, could steal a kiss . . .
And yet I swear, by the devil's dame,
There's many a girl I've called by name,
And when I called, by gad, she came!

This Polly, well, she was like them all —
Ripe red fruit and ready to fall;
Love her — me? God bless you, no!
But nevertheless I told her so —
I smiled to her — whispered, in the street,
Two words — enough! we arranged to meet
At the willow tree by the churchyard wall
As soon as the proper dark should fall.
Well, I was late — I kept her waiting —
Nothing better than a bit of baiting —
And she was vexed and started to go.
'Polly,' said I, 'I love you so!
You won't desert me, — now we've started, —
And leave your poor Punch broken-hearted? . . .
Now look! By Judy's green grave there
There's none so pretty as you, I swear!' —
At this she trembled and clung to me
And rose tip-toe by the wall, to see
Where Judy's grave was . . . Meanwhile I

Pretended, furtive, to wipe my eye.
'Poor Punch!' she sighed, 'your Judy's dead . . .
Did you love her — much?' I shook my head.
'Not half as much as you,' I said . . .
'Why do you cry, then?' 'Because I'm lonely.
Polly I love you, love you only.'
At this she frowned. 'No doubt,' said she,
'You said to her what you say to me.'
She took two steps toward the town, —
I caught her backward by her gown;
And what do you think I told her then?
Oh, there's no limit to the wit of men!
I told her straight if she'd be brave,
I'd prove my love by Judy's grave.
She looked at me with a sudden scare.
'Come to the grave — I'll kiss you there!'

The night was thick. No moon there was.
The wind made whickerings in the grass.
The willows tapped at the churchyard wall
And we saw, like ghosts, the dead leaves fall.
'What's that?' said Polly. 'Dead leaves!' said I.
Close to our heads a bat whizzed by.
She clung to my arm, her hand was weak,
She opened her lips but could not speak.
I stooped and caught her under the knees
And lifted her up, as light as you please,
Over the wall; but just as I climbed
To the cold stone top the church clock chimed,
Then boomed the hour with a thunder-sound:
And a gravestone keeled with a clap to the ground . . .
Well, I'm not easily scared, but that,
Take my word for it, knocked me flat!
I've danced at murders, laughed at duels —
But at this my sweat rolled off in jewels!
Polly looked up at the starless sky
And covered her face and began to cry;

She leaned against me and clung and trembled;
But I, though scared, of course dissembled, —
I took her arm, and led her then
Over the weed-wet tombs of men.
Once, we stumbled upon a spade —
Thrust in the earth by a vault new-made;
Once, in the dark, I heard her moan
As she touched with her hand a dew-cold stone.
But we came to Judy's grave, and there
I kissed her eyelids, loosed her hair,
Swore there was no such thing as sin, —
And she, being frightened, soon gave in.
You know I'm honest; I won't pretend
That I wasn't scared, nor recommend, —
At least not wholly, to all, — such fashion
For most enjoying an evening's passion.
For more than once, at the wail in the trees,
The heart in my body seemed to freeze;
And I half expected, — bless my eyes! —
To see a ghost from the cold grass rise.

So much for Polly. I here pass over
The days that followed, — days of clover!
But all things end, and the trouble came
When Polly died, — with me to blame.
There lived a constable in that town,
An insolent bully, a red-necked clown,
With small pig's eyes and stupid face,
A fool, the laughing-stock of the place.
He hated me, as I did him,
Because he loved this Polly Prim . . .
Why does the good Lord make such fellows?
He rolled his head and blew like a bellows
Whenever, as often, he chanced to see,
On a clear evening, Polly and me
Walking together along the lane:
Upon my honour, it gave him pain! . . .

And once, one evening, as we lay
With much to do and little to say
In deep grass by the churchyard wall, —
We suddenly heard a pebble fall;
And there he crept in the darkness, groping
From stone to stone with loud steps, hoping
To catch us out . . . How still we kept!
This way and that in the dark he stept,
Heavily breathing, bending, peering;
And when at last he was out of hearing,
Lord how we laughed; and how like flame
Our kisses after that fright became! —
Well, on the night that Polly died,
I sat in the inn, alone. Outside
The rain came down in glassy sheets,
I heard it sing and seethe in the streets,
Green lightning through the windows flashed,
Thunder along the treetops crashed,
A shrill wind whistled; and once it seemed
I heard through the wind a voice that screamed . . .
I knew right well that Pol was dying,
I stopped my ears, but still that crying
Rang like a nightmare through my brain.
Then all at once, through the window-pane,
I saw this constable's white face stare,
Stare and vanish. I left my chair,
My flesh turned cold, for I knew well
The news the constable came to tell:
I knew, as well as that light is light,
Murder had come to town that night.
The door flew open: in he came,
With his mouth like wax and his eyes like flame.
'Good evening, officer,' then said I:
'Is it raining still?' — There was no reply, —
For a breath or two; and then he said
'I suppose you know your whore is dead?' —
He stared at me: I stared at him . . .

'I suppose you allude to — Polly Prim?'
'Allude? You know damned well I do.'
'A whore is a whore. What's that to you?'
'You know damned well what it is to me —
And now you'll settle . . .' A knife flashed free,
Flashed in an arc, I ducked, he lunged,
Down to the floor like an ox he plunged
With me on top: I caught his wrist,
Snapped it sharp with a sudden twist,
His fingers loosened, the knife fell out,
I caught the haft up, turned about,
And struck him twice. He gave one moan,
Clutched once, — and then lay still as stone.

Now, this was folly. . . I'm free to admit
For once — h'm — anger outran my wit.
Murder will out! I was straightway tried
By a jealous judge, and would have died
Had not my cunning returned to me,
At the gallows foot, and set me free.
There was a hangman there, poor wretch,
A morbid soul by the name of Ketch —
Jack Ketch; a corpse with a slow green eye
That only lit when he saw men die.
No sooner was I condemned, than he
Conceived a peculiar joy in me:
Watched me, talked to me; to and fro
Before my window he would go, —
Forever touching, as he spoke,
Hand to gullet, his little joke!
Now, when the day for the hanging fell,
He came to the court outside my cell,
And set up, under my very eyes,
The gallows! . . . Well, sirs, being wise,
And having pretended, many days,
To be a fool, I began to praise . . .
'Oh, what a pretty tree!' said I,

And clapped my hands. He rolled one eye
With a dubious tilt toward me then
And grinned, and slouched away again.
Back he came, in a whisper's time,
With rope and ladder, and started to climb
To the gallows-top. At this I ran
To the small cell-window, and began
To cry 'Stop, thief! — There's a thief out here!
Robbing the fruit-tree!' — shrill and clear
I sang this out: Jack Ketch spun round
And stared at me with never a sound . . .
He looked at me with a pitying look,
Then once or twice his head he shook,
Tapped his forehead, tied up his noose,
Leaving it swinging large and loose,
Climbed down, and sauntered off once more . . .
This time, when he came back, he bore,
(He and the sheriff, on their heads,)
A coffin, all lapped round with leads . . .
'Aha!' I cried, with a knowing air;
'The thieves have fetched a basket there!' —
Down they dropped it upon the stones —
Thump! and a shudder thrilled my bones.

Ketch came to me. 'Now, Punch, step out!'
'Oh, no!' cried I: 'What's this about?'
'Come out, sir, and be hanged!' said he, —
'A pretty fruit for a pretty tree!' —
'Hanged on a tree — what's that?' said I.
'Hanged by the neck until you die!'
At this I wept and beat the stones,
A mortal terror froze my bones;
I cried aloud as I was led
To the gallows foot, already dead . . .
Jack Ketch began to shine with glee.
— 'Put up your pretty head!' said he —
'Inside the noose!' — I began to quake,

The rope came dangling like a snake,
I touched it, shivered, touched again,
And took it in my hands, and then, —
Once more pretending lack of wit, —
Thrust up my head — outside of it . . .
'Oh, no!' said Ketch — 'inside, inside!'
'Inside of what?' — Again I tried,
And failed again. At this he swore.
'Now, Punch, watch me, and try once more!'
He held the noose above his crown
And then with his two hands dropped it down, —
And quick as a wink I hauled him high,
Hauled him dangling against the sky,
Knocked down the sheriff, turned and ran,
Once more a free and happy man!

Oh, Lord, oh, Lord, what things I've done!
What tricks have played, what devil's fun!
With many a death my hands are red;
Many a heart for me has bled;
Many a tear has fallen for me
From woman's golden praying-tree!
I will not say I've not at times
Fled from the darkness of my crimes:
Sometimes with sin and sickness faint,
On my poor knees, before some saint,
I've wept the blackness of my heart
And vowed a better life to start . . .
Yet I confess each saint was human,
Some not too proud or holy woman, —
And not too proud for earthly blisses,
Laughter, and moonlight sport, and kisses! —
What girls have held their hands to me!
What mouths to touch, what eyes to see!
Yet something's in me, something strange,
That drives me on to seek for change;
I love for a little and not for long —

And walk my ways then with a song.
Some hold — and I will not deny —
It's not of a mortal birth am I:
I wailed not from a woman's womb,
Nor am I destined for the tomb . . .
Some hold, who've known the things I've done,
I am the devil's only son . . .
But this I doubt . . . For once I saw
Old Nick himself with tail and claw,
On a green hillside in the dusk
Where the wild roses were in musk.
With Doctor Faustus by him there, —
Bearing a black book, pale as care, —
He paced the grass; his eyes were coal;
He sought to snare my immortal soul.

It was, I say, as evening fell.
The sky was green. A silver bell
Sang in the vale, and all fell still
As Satan smoked across that hill.
I lay in the grass and sucked a straw
And schemed how I might thwart the law,
When suddenly, lifting up my eyes,
I saw him red against the skies.
Lord, what a start it gave to me!
'Good evening, Mr. Punch!' said he . . .
And at those words, like whips of flame,
A dark cloud on that hillside came,
The shapes of rocks began to change,
The trees seemed sinister and strange,
They stirred upon their stems, and eyes
Peered out from under leaves, and cries
Flew bodiless upon that air
In angry jargon everywhere;
And though I looked a long while down
I saw no valley, saw no town.
Old Nick himself was nowhere then,

Although I heard his voice again
Out of the dark in swollen tones
Like fall of subterranean stones:
'Consider well what you shall see
And make your bargain here with me!' —
Then Faustus, with a hand that shook,
Turned the great pages of his book,
As if he turned the stars; and first
A flood of light around me burst;
And in a valley by a sea
Bound by invisible veins to me
All in the twinkling of an eye
A town went glistening towards the sky,
With walls and towers and clustered trees
And swarms of men there thick as bees . . .
Then Faustus, tremulous with age,
Turned like a sheaf of sky that page, —
Valley and sea were rolled away . . .
I saw myself, at the end of day,
Climb up a peaked and verdant hill
Beside the twinklings of a rill;
And there a rock I saw; and there
A voice was heard upon that air
Saying, 'Smite once!' and in my hand
There grew, as out of the air, a wand,
And once I smote. And straight there came
Out of the rock a crimson flame,
And out of the flame, naked and fair,
Venus herself, with golden hair.
Upon white daisies there she stepped
And first she shivered, and then she wept,
And then through her hair she smiled at me,
And sidelong came; but suddenly
Like time itself that luminous page
Flashed, and I saw that archimage
Spread out his ancient hands, and look
Grimacing upward from his book.

'You see now, Mr. Punch,' he said,
'What power we hold. Even the dead
Rise upward through the trammelled grass
If we command. All comes to pass,
As we desire!' — 'Then let me see,'
Said I, 'if such a thing can be!' —
He turned his huge page once again . . .
And now I saw a level plain
Far as the eye could see, and there
Were graves and tombstones everywhere.
And all those graves and tombs were still,
Motionless as the dead, until
There rose, as out of the earth, a cry
Wavering slowly to the sky;
And suddenly then, but without sound,
Those stones fell softly to the ground,
Millions of tombs divulged their dead . . .
With clapping arm and pallid head
Against a sky of sunset flame
Out of the trammelled grass they came,
Stirred like a forest in the wind,
Flourished their bones, till, somehow thinned,
They seemed to blow along that sky
Like hosts of withered leaves, that fly
Before a stream of air; and then
Dwindled, fell down, lay still again . . .
Then Faustus said: 'The time has come:
Sign here your name, set here your thumb!
All power will Satan give to you
If, dying, you will repay the due.'
'My soul, you mean?' — 'I mean your soul!'
'Then may my heart turn black as coal
Before I serve, eternally,
Any such tyrant fiend as he!' —
At this a roiling cloud of smoke
Burst from the grass, and Satan spoke
And burned before me on that hill.

'Surrender now,' he cried, 'your will!'
I reached to earth, and seized a stone,
And flung it straight; and, all alone,
Saw how he melted in that air
With ancient Faustus by him there;
Before it struck I saw him pass;
The stone fell softly to the grass . . .
And there in the grass I sucked a straw
And schemed how I might thwart the law.

What is it, in a woman's skin,
So surely drives a man to sin?
What is it, in a woman's eyes,
No sooner laughed in than it dies? . . .
The loveliest lady in that town
Was she, who wore a green silk gown,
The baker's wife, a haughty dame, —
And it was sweet to bring her shame!
The first time, when I smiled at her,
She curled her lip and did not stir . . .
The second time, she gleamed at me
Through narrowed eyes, amusedly.
The third time — she went quickly by,
But there was laughter in her eye.
I turned to look and she turned too —
And she was surely mine I knew.
The fourth, I met her by a stream
Reading a book, but half in dream:
It was an afternoon in spring —
We might have heard the blackbird sing.
She talked uneasily, laughed at me,
Picked up her book, but let me see
She more than liked to have me there:
And dropped her book and primped her hair.
I leaned and caught one fingertip,
Playfully squeezed it, let it slip
Into the grass again . . . We lay

And breathed and smiled, no word to say.
The fifth — I met her late at night.
Her eyes were dark in lantern-light.
I caught her arm and pressed it twice
And felt her hand as cold as ice . . .
'Pauline, come out to walk with me!'
She shook her head. 'Oh, no!' said she —
Her opened lips were grey with pain,
Backward and forward along the lane
She looked, afraid lest we be seen.
'Oh, no!' said she — but did she mean
No with her voice, yes with her heart? . . .
I took her hand as if to start
And suddenly she began to cry, —
Yet came with me . . . 'Pauline,' said I,
'Lift up your mouth!' Once more, at this,
She shook her head . . . yet took my kiss,
Shut both her eyes, clung hard to me,
And closer leaned with breast and knee . . .
Above black trees the moon swam high
And small white clouds were in the sky;
The lilac-heads were sweet; we crept
Past houses where the good folk slept
Into a garden; a silver light
Flared through the trees, and dimly bright
Were pool and grass and garden walk;
And there we sat to kiss and talk;
And there, beneath that poplar tree,
She gave her trembling heart to me . . .
The sixth, by all odds, was the best —
By this her conscience was at rest;
She smiled at me as if to say
'Do not persuade, — but have your way.'
It was a sun-stilled afternoon,
The brook flashed fire. A sliver of moon
Seemed, like an icy ghost, to melt
In warm blue sky . . . Her heart I felt

Thumping beneath my palm. We stayed
A sweet while there in the poplar shade:
She told her secrets, every one,
And of her husband we made fun.
The seventh — she began to cling, —
And fiddled with her wedding ring . . .
'O! we were monstrous sinners both,
And we should part!' But she was loth
To come to this; so clung to me
Almost, perhaps, too tenderly . . .
The eighth and ninth — my joy was mixed.
Our kisses over, straight she fixed
Her blue eyes on my heart, to say,
Since I had led her so astray,
And made her loathe her husband — why,
If I should leave her she would die!
At this, you'll easily conceive,
My one wish was, of course, to leave . . .
And though I kissed her, stroked her, smiled,
Tickled her chin, and called her 'child,'
Sidelong she peered askance at me,
Her eyes grew dark, — and she could see
Plainly as pebbles in the brook
The secret thoughts beneath my look.
'What are you thinking, girl?' I said, —
Sharply she turned away her head,
Compressed her lips, was still a space
Put up one hand against her face, —
And then in a queer tone, forced and low,
Said, 'Nothing — only, it's time to go.'
And then cold fury rose in me
And we walked homeward silently.

Well, sirs, it was that very night,
Brooding alone by candlelight,
My queerest of all adventures came . . .
I sat and sulked. My thoughts, like flame,

Licked up my memories of Pauline,
Calling her vulgar, plain, obscene,
Coarse-fleshed, a dull and nagging thing,
Conquered only to crawl and cling.
Why do they change? . . . Why lags desire? . . .
Resentment in me like a fire
Roared on the tinsel of those days,
Consumed them all. I walked those ways
By every leaf and stone again,
And every leaf was a leaf of pain,
And every stone lay cold in me
Or fell through depths of agony.
Was there in all this wide world never
One woman I might love for ever?
Or if that miracle could not be,
One woman who might tire of me
Before I tired, and fling me by:
One woman lustrous as the sky,
Girdled with stars, set round with light,
Whose heart was music, whose eyes were night?
Who moved like a sea wave in the wind;
Transfiguring all things when she sinned?
This was absurd — I laughed at this!
What woman would dare to refuse my kiss?
What queen, indeed, could tire of me? —
And yet, if such a queen might be . . .
Beautiful, haughty, perilous, wise . . .
What rarer sport, what nobler prize?
At this I must have slept; for when
My puzzled eyes unclosed again
The room seemed darker, — large, and strange;
Even as I looked, it seemed to change;
And as I marvelled, straight I heard
Close to my ears one whispered word —
'Sheba!' — said once. And then I saw
Old Nick himself with tail and claw
Come back again. Beside me there

He marvellously emerged from air
First horns and head, then tail and limb,
Upward, as one might softly swim
From ocean's depths . . . One gleaming hand,
Even before I saw him stand,
Still bodiless, he stretched to me . . .
'So, Punch, you've called my name,' said he, —
'And here I am!' — His dark mouth grinned.
Within those walls was a tempest wind.
The candle guttered. His glowing face
Filled with a ghostly shine that place.
'Listen!' said he . . . and as he spoke
Those walls, no solider than smoke,
Seemed slowly streaming on dark air . . .
'There is one woman wise and fair,
More marvellous than her you dream.
This is my bargain — this my scheme.
You shall be borne through time and space
To feed your soul upon this face:
If you can win her you are free;
But if you fail, — you come to me!' —
My heart beat loudly. 'Done!' said I . . .
From all the elements rose a cry,
Water and fire and wind and earth
Joined in a frenzied scream of mirth.
Punch or the Devil — they should see
Which was the better man to be! . . .

All in the twinkling of his eye
I crossed blue seas of whistling sky.
The clamor died behind me. Soon
By Sheba's gate, under a moon, —
Against which palm-trees black as jet
Fringed in a giant silhouette, —
Along a path of silver sand
I walked, with stars on either hand.
Beneath the palm-trees fountains spattered,

Luminous fishes flashed and scattered,
Leaving behind them streaks of fire
And bubbles of light. . . The moon pushed higher,
And through black branches, quick as flame,
Luminous parrots went and came,
And fiery feathers drifted down . . .
Lord, what a place for me, a clown!
I skipped along that path; and there
Flew marvellous music on that air, —
Slow horns and cymbals, and the sound
Of many dancers whirling round.
And then my heart stood still in me:
By the flaming doorway I could see,
Two giants, black as stone, and tall
As pine trees, one by either wall.
Like fiery moons their eyes they rolled;
They roared at me; my brain went cold;
But in between them, nothing daunted,
I capered up those stairs, and flaunted,
Wagging the hump upon my back,
Into the court . . . Lord, what a pack
Of men and women jostled there!
Sheba sat in a golden chair
Set high upon a glittering throne
Of jewelled and silvered ivory-bone.
A fan of peacocks' feathers waved
Before her eyes. The floor was paved
With golden moons and stars of blue;
Vermilion birds about her flew;
And out of the air dissolving sweet
Fell music with persuasive beat.
And then I saw how one by one
Great mages filed before that throne, —
Upon their knees went humbly down
Scholar and prince with book and crown;
To all she smiled, denied them all,
Vainly before her did they fall.

The Duke of Lorraine trembled there;
King Solomon, too, with snow-white hair;
Herod the Great hung down his head,
And Virgil, pallid as the dead;
Judas Iscariot, dark of eye,
Pulled at his chin and shuffled by . . .
And last of all that host came I! —
Lord, how I shook! She smiled at me . . .
And in her eyes as in a sea
Of fire and darkness I went down:
In froth of moonlight seemed to drown:
Whirled in a wave of music, spun
In ravelling fiery threads of sun!
Where was I? . . . Was I shivering there? . . .
A roar of laughter smote that air,
The mages shook their sides with glee,
Queens and madmen laughed at me.
Solomon laid his crown aside
And clapped his hands: and Judas cried;
And Heliogabalus sobbed aloud . . .
White anger froze my veins. I bowed
Coldly, to all — and all fell still,
Except one laugh that trailed out shrill
Then died away. 'Great queen!' I said —
And paused. She leaned her golden head,
With one white hand beside her ear:
'Louder!' she said — 'I cannot hear!' —
And slowly smiled — and as she smiled
Smaller and foolisher than a child
I seemed. I cleared my voice, and then —
'Great queen!' began, — and once again
Forward she leaned and smiled at me,
In grave and sweet perplexity,
And raised one small hand, crystal-clear,
Once more to touch her jewelled ear.
And then, behind my back, I heard
Laughter subdued, a tittered word,

A stir of mirth . . . I turned and glared, —
Saw solemn faces ill prepared;
Saw twisting mouth and shifting eye.
So Sheba's deafness was a lie!
And quick as a wink I turned, I climbed
Those ivory steps. Clear laughter chimed,
Confusion rose. Beside her throne
I leaned, I roared in a tempest tone
'Sheba, my name is Punch! I stand
With power of darkness in my hand, —
Power to shake your kingdom down,
To crack your heart and break your crown!'
And then as I stood quaking there,
Feeding upon her eyes, her hair,
Amazing drunkenness waved in me:
I gallantly hopped upon her knee,
I kissed her mouth! and straight arose
A clamour of cries, and silence froze,
And Sheba, quivering backward, weak,
Tried once, and twice, and thrice, to speak;
And flushed; and stared; and laughed; and then —
Put up her mouth to kiss again! . . .

At once sweet music thrilled the air!
Heliogabalus tore his hair!
Solomon raged and broke his crown,
Vermilion birds flew singing down,
Horns and cymbals stormed at the wall
And a dancing madness took them all.
All night they danced . . . and all night through
Vermilion parrots clanged and flew . . .
The walls were shaken with song and glee
While Sheba lay and smiled at me.
And through her eyes I went and came
Now like an ice-thing, now like flame,
A thousand times . . . Before us waved
A peacock fan . . . the floor was paved

With golden moons and stars of blue . . .
And dancers danced there, all night through.

And day by day and night by night
I dwelt there in amazed delight,
King of that golden mountain-land
With slaves to bless my least command.
Take this! fetch that! . . . An old guitar,
The blue dust falling from a star,
Pearls for Sheba or wine for me,
Or coral bleeding from the sea, —
No matter what; for quick as a wink
It came, before I'd time to think.
How Sheba smiled! and how she laughed!
And oh, what cups of wine she quaffed,
And how we danced and how we sang,
And how that glittering palace rang
With music under the rosy moon
Of horn and cymbal and bassoon!
Heliogabalus was my slave,
And Judas nightly from his grave
Rose with a sheet about his loins
To dance before us for copper coins,
Weeping, weeping for his sins
To a cheerful tune from violins . . .
Mermaids came with rainbow fins,
Sea-weed-bearded kings of the sea
Showered rich tribute there for me, —
Dead men's treasure of gold and stones
Was swept away before our thrones.
And once — one evening — tired of this,
Yes, tired for once of Sheba's kiss,
Tired of purple and gold, and cries
Of parokeets with crimson eyes,
Musicians beating perpetual drums
And diamonds brushed away like crumbs,
Tired of this, with joy I listened

To a mermaid's voice; her blue eyes glistened,
Cold as the sea were her eyes, and deep,
And walking like one who walks in sleep
I went with her, I followed her down
Great stairs of stone to a royal town
With towers of sea-shell filigree
By glow-worms lit in the gloom of the sea;
And amber walls, and streets of sand . . .
The blue-eyed mermaid took my hand:
Silver dolphins with eyes of flame
Snoring fountains about us came,
Crabs whose backs were pearl-encrusted
And ancient turtles diamond-dusted;
All the dark kingdom came to rout us
And oh! what a dance was danced about us! . . .
Until, at the break of the blue sea-day,
Up coral stairs I hurried away,
Once more to Sheba, the scarlet queen,
Who danced with bells and a tambourine,
Who poured black wine, and sang to me
Till I forgot that queen of the sea. . .

Well, sirs, all things will come to an end, —
Old Nick, you know, is no man's friend . . .
How long I stayed, I don't know now — ;
But back I came, — I don't know how, —
To go my daily rounds again
With red birds darting through my brain . . .
Yes, sirs, there's many a thing I've done —
I've had my fling, I've had my fun:
No man or devil has bested me, —
Clap me in jail, I soon go free!
Even the inquisition came
And marked a cross against my name,
And locked me howling into a prison
Because I denied their Christ had risen!
But did I stay there? . . . Not a bit.

There's always a way for nerve and wit!
A man's wit is a golden key
To open the door and set him free . . .
And Death — how many times I've fought him! —
How many lessons I have taught him!
The first time — I was in my bed:
Naked I fought him, cracked his head,
And drove him, moaning, into the street . . .
Death! Do you think he's hard to beat?
Why once, when I was young and strong,
I chased the varlet all day long, —
Up hill and down, by vale and shore,
And into the sea! It made me roar
To see those lean shanks rise and fall,
To hear him rattle across a wall, —
To hear him crying aloud for breath . . .
Even old Nick is worse than Death! . . .
And want and weariness — well, these too
Will somewhere lie in wait for you;
And sickness like a black dog comes
To whine at the table and beg for crumbs . . .
Yet here you see me — a mortal man:
And what I've conquered, — all men can!

. . . A mortal man . . . Though I'll not say
That some time, after the end of day,
You might not see me, a giant size,
Hurling a shadow against the skies . . .
Blotting the stars . . . at one step taking
A hill or a town . . . the whole earth shaking . . .
And I'll not say that the time must come
When Death will find me, and leave me dumb!

WHAT POLLY ONCE CONFESSED

Since you insist, you fool, why then, I'll tell you . . .
Love Punch? Good Lord! I hope I'm not so silly!

Red-nosed, with hands like hams, humpbacked and bandy, —
And small green rheumy eyes! I'd sooner love
The wildman that they showed us in the circus!
Him with the ring in his nose, and the leaves in his hair,
And the long arms like a gorilla's always dragging!
Love him! . . . Don't make me laugh. I'll crack the mirror.
But since you insist (and I can see you're hungry
As all men are, sooner or later, in love,
To root among my muddy secrets, snuffling
Above them with a leering satisfaction)
Why then, I'll tell you. Hate me if you want to.
The whole thing comes to one word — jealousy! . . .
And I won't say that as I look back on it,
And all that came from it of lies and hatred,
I don't, sometimes, feel fifty kinds of fool . . .
You've heard of jealousy? How wise you are!
Well, then, you know how blind and cruel it is,
How like a cramp it shuts about the heart
And turns the blood to poison, and so sends it
Creeping into the brain for schemes of torture.
Judy and I were jealous — that's the story.
Why were we? God knows! ask me something easy.
We do things, feel things, sometimes, without knowing
The reason why. As far as I remember
I hated Judy — Judy hated me.
At five years old she stuck her tongue out at me;
At ten years old we pulled each other's hair;
At fifteen — well — she stole my sweetheart from me.
We had a way of smiling at each other —
So innocent it seemed, and oh so sweet! —
That had the basilisk beaten to a frazzle.
Look, I can do it still, I've had such practice! —
We lowered our lids — like this — ; and smiled — like this! . . .

So, we grew up. And one fine day this Punch
Came roaring into town, with all his stories
Of women weeping for him, dying for him,

And all the rest. Of course, no one believed him —
No one, that is, but Judy! We all saw
The coward that he was, — a mouse for courage,
Ran if you raised your voice! But Judy, somehow,
(Though, to be sure, she never was too clever)
Believed him: yes, she thought him *so* romantic,
Oh, so unusual! And she lost no time
In setting after him . . . Oh, well, you know
What fools men are — (you're one yourself) — and Punch
Was no exception, rather worse than most:
Crazy for love, went smirking around women
Tongue hanging out, his little eyes revolving
In search of titbits — fawning, leering, sidling;
And knowing this, of course, we laughed at him . . .
So Judy found him easy: though I won't say
She didn't use the few wits God had lent her.
Before he knew it, Punch had been seduced, —
Trussed up and married . . . Gone — another hero!

Now for confession. And it's not so easy
As kissing under aspen leaves in moonlight.
First, as for Punch, I will confess I liked him —
Well, more than half! Repulsive, ugly, bestial,
Coward and sneak — I knew him all these things,
As who could not. But still, there was about him
When he was young, as then he was, some presence,
Some swagger of the flesh, vivid and subtle,
That could not help but make a woman's body
Tingle with secret pleasure. There you have it!
You see us now, girls, spinsters, and old women,
Watching behind our shutters when he passed:
Shuddering with a pleased ecstatic horror
If he should speak to us or smile to us;
And yet, oh, hating him! Sometimes I think
It's not the saint we love men for, but satyr:
The mouth too loose with constant lippish thinking
Of fevered kisses, and the little eyes

Malicious and provocative that smear you
With drivel of desire. It's true we hate him,
Yet hate, sometimes, is not so unlike love:
We try to scorn him out, to laugh him down,
Yet feel our features changing, under his,
To mirror him . . . our mouths grow loose as his,
Corruption thrills the flesh. Unless we shriek
And break the spell, we're one more atom lost
In the terrific maelstrom of the blood.
Punch had the satyr's face, the satyr's body,
The twinkle of shrewd eyes, the wag of the leg,
That stiffens flesh. I hated him — and liked him.
You see then how I felt, when Judy came
And sighed, and smiled, and whisperingly confided
(All to enrage me!) how she'd caught her monster —
Limed the leaves, led him into the chamber . . .
You see then how I laughed and tweaked her ear,
Patted her hand and said 'You clever Judy,'
With furies in my heart: I could have killed her . . .
Poor fool! she might as well have said in words
What with her snaky smile she said so plainly —
'I've beaten you at last!' —

                     I smiled, of course . . .
But none the less revenge was coiling in me
With watchful eyes. And while the vixen snickered
Secretly there beside me, I was thinking
Already of this satyr, Punch, her husband,
And of her ruin through him. Give me credit!
Oh, give me credit! I am sometimes clever.
I saw the whole thing through from start to finish!
I saw a moonlit garden in my mind,
With Punch there, like a satyr, trampling lilies,
Wallowing among lilac leaves, and snorting, —
Or whining, rather, — his bristly passion for me:
Lifting his great red hands up in the moonlight
Under my window: or coming over the wall

With one leg up, and anguish on his face,
And the moon behind his head — just like a halo!
Fantastic sight! I was already laughing.
The moon herself might well turn red to see it.
And as for Judy — I saw her at her window
Waiting for Punch, alone and cold in the moonlight,
With little hard-fixed eyes distilling poison . . .
Rapture! I almost loved her at that moment.

Why bore you with details? You need no telling
How women do such things. You know me well,
Know all my tricks, know how I laugh or twitter,
Smile timidly with dark eyes gleaming sidelong,
Let fall my hand, — as if in carelessness, —
Upon your arm; or lean one breast against you
To whisper you some most ingenuous secret!
H'm! . . . Magic! . . . Magic of flesh! You too have felt it
And thrilled to it. You've heard it in the evening
Shaking a devilish music in the darkness
Of passionate thought; bats are abroad in gardens;
The grass is soft to lie on; and the moonlight
Goes over you like hands. Can flesh resist it?
Poor foolish flesh! pour wine for pigs and bears,
Get them so drunk they cannot stand, but squeal
Lying upon their helpless backs, and blinking
At fifteen suns: their drunkenness is nothing
To the helpless lunacy of human flesh
Tipsy with lust. You've seen it crawl and slaver,
You've seen it dance its idiot dance in moonlight
With eyes upturned so imbecile and wistful:
And, oh, what caperings! . . . Well, then, for spite
And little else (except what I've confessed)
You see me, in a green gown, leaning slowly
To play on Punch these delicate fleshly harpings.
You see me dance with him while Judy watches,
Her blue eyes darting hatred among swift dancers,

Following us, in lazy convolutions,
Among the chords and discords . . . You can see
The panic heartbeats in those eyes of hers,
For all their cruelty . . . The girl is frightened . . .
She sees Punch smile at me — in a way she knows!
She sees the twitchings of his hand behind me —
Against my flesh! She sees his eyes turned upward
In an ecstatic misery all too plain . . .
Oh, Lord, those eyes of his! They gave me nightmares.
I almost spoiled the whole thing more than once,
By laughing in his face.
                                        Well — there's the story.
A few weeks passed and Punch was in my garden
Just as I thought he would be; trampling lilies,
Heaving his crooked shoulder over the wall
Against the moon, wallowing in my lilacs:
While Judy sat afar and waited for him.
Sweet triumph! How I laughed and told the neighbours!
See the red monster eating from my hand!
The wildman come from his cave, his bones and berries,
To waltz on his hindlegs in obedient circles!
I give him a fan to hold, he snuffs and paws it,
Goes home with the perfume on him, passion-draggled,
Grunts my name in his sleep . . . Too sweet a triumph! . . .
For now poor foolish Judy, struck with horror,
Failed to come forward fighting — what I hoped for:
Instead, with one scared look, she stepped down backward
Into the dark. I mean, she killed herself.
Not out of love for Punch! Oh, no. I'm certain.
But out of broken pride. Yes, simply that.
And left me feeling, somehow, somewhat foolish.

You see, then, how much truth is in his story —
You see how much I loved him . . . There! I've told you
The whole thing through, for you to sniff and snort on.
Isn't it pretty? . . . Romance, with all its graces!

Go on, be jealous now, — hate Punch! hate me!
Tear out my heart, defile the sacred image
Of Punch that's graven there! . . . And when you're finished —

How do you like the way I've done my hair?

HOW HE DIED

When Punch had roared at the inn for days
The walls went round in a ringing haze,
Miriam, through the splendour seen,
Twinkled and smiled like Sheba's Queen,
Jake was the devil himself, the host
Scratched in a book like a solemn Faust;
And the lights like birds went swiftly round
With a soft and feathery whistling sound.
He seized the table with one great hand
And a thousand people helped him stand,
'Good-night!' a thousand voices said,
The words like gongs assailed his head,
And out he reeled, most royally,
Singing, amid that company. —
Luminous clocks above him rolled,
Bells in the darkness heavily tolled,
The stars in the sky were smoothly beating
In a solemn chorus, all repeating
The tick of the great heart in his breast
That tore his body, and would not rest.

Singing, he climbed the elusive street,
And heard far off his footsteps beat;
Singing, they pushed him through the door,
And he fell full length on the darkened floor . . .
But his head struck sharply as he fell
And he heard a sound like a broken bell;
And then, in the half-light of the moon,
The twittering elvish light of June,

A host of folk came round him there, —
Sheba with diamonds in her hair,
Solomon thrumming a psaltery,
Judas Iscariot dark of eye,
Satan and Faustus and Lorraine,
And Heliogabalus with his train . . .
The air was sweet with a delicate sound
Of silk things rustling on the ground,
Jewels and silver twinkled, dim,
Voices and laughter circled him . . .

After a while the clock struck two,
A whisper among the audience flew,
And Judy before him came and knelt
And kissed him; and her lips, he felt,
Were wet with tears . . . She wore a crown,
And amethysts, and a pale green gown . . .
After a while the clock struck three
And Polly beside him, on one knee,
Leaned above him and softly cried,
Wearing a white veil like a bride.
One candle on the sill was burning,
And Faustus sat in the corner, turning
Page after page with solemn care
To count the immortal heartbeats there.
Slow was the heart, and quick the stroke
Of the pen, and never a word he spoke;
But watched the tears of pale wax run
Down from the long flame one by one.
Solomon in the moonlight bowed,
The Queen of Sheba sobbed aloud;
Like a madonna carved in stone
Judy in starlight stood alone:
Tears were glistening on her cheek,
Her lips were awry, she could not speak.
After a while the clock struck four,
And Faustus said 'I can write no more:

I've entered the heartbeats, every one,
And now the allotted time is done.'
He dipped his pen, made one more mark,
And clapped his book. The room grew dark.
At four o'clock Punch turned his head
And 'I forgive you all,' he said. . .

At five o'clock they found him dead.

Part II

Mountebank Carves His Puppet of Wood

HE CONCEIVES HIS PUPPET TO BE STRUGGLING
WITH A NET

1

As evening fell, and Punch crept out of the wood
And saw the valley before him (like my life,
Stretched out before me, waiting there? he thought)
And saw the sun go melting redly down
Behind bare oaks, and the long shadows, fanlike,
Whirling across the quiet fields, he pondered
On the simplicity, the tranquil beauty, even,
Of morning, twilight, afternoon, or noon, —
So clear by contrast to the nagging jangle
Of his own days! . . . Dry branches caught his feet,
The snapping of them teased his brain to folly,
He clawed at cobwebs that wiped across his cheek,
Inwardly snarled, was maddened, and once more thought, —
Letting his restless eyes rove, seeing nothing, —
His life was a buzzing fly, vainly struggling
To loose weak wings from the glutinous web of fate.
How was it other men could live so simply?
How was it they could love, yet go unscathed,
Walk freely, laugh, and make it all a story?

Or did they lie? — The red sun swelled and sank,
A huge red bubble poised upon the hilltop:
Vermilion clouds flew over it and faded:
The sky, from orange, turned pale green, faint blue;
And the bare boughs of trees, flung up against it,
Frozen and still and black, seemed like great claws.

2

Well, then, if others lied, he too would lie . . .
These faces of the smiling men he knew,
Baker and constable and mayor and hangman,
What did they mean? Were they, as they pretended,
Such gloating misers of illegal riches? . . .
As their imagined faces swam before him,
Ruddy or pale, they seemed to avert their eyes, —
Like those who close their windows to a burglar.
Ah! that was it — they lied. And they, like him,
Walked always warily, for fear of nets,
Ran hard in darkness when they thought none saw them,
And, in their secret chambers, wept for terror.
He laughed at this; because he saw so clearly
On a dark moonless night, along the street,
Half frantic, panting, with his mouth wide open,
The white-faced baker speeding from his shadow.
Yes, they were liars, all, — and he would lie . . .
Although, of course, some things might be accomplished —
Even by him . . . even by him, indeed! —
He picked a stick up, cracked it with his hands,
Smiled at his conscious strength, pressed hard his feet
Into the withered grass, and heard life singing;
Lights came out of the darkened earth like flowers
And swam on the lustrous air . . . they were the lights
Of windows in the village, candles behind them . . .
And as for women . . . but at the thought of women
He thought of Judy only, pale-haired Judy . . .
Judy with wide blue eyes, eternal Judy! . . .

There was a grave for Judy, and he would dig it;
Or had he dug it, — was he digging now,
With every thought? — He paused, with step suspended,
In a cool sort of horror; he seemed to feel
Himself a shovel, used by relentless fate,
To dig that grave . . . was lifted up and thrust,
Lifted again . . . He shivered and then stepped forward,
Seeing the face of Judy eddying down
On a black coiling current into darkness.
This was a kind of madness, and he forbade it.

3

Judy! — Lying beside her in the moonlight
He feigned a sleep, and turned, and through the window
Watched how the crooked moon went slowly up
Among black elm-boughs, driving out the stars.
And here was Judy sleeping so beside him
While fate in him, as in a cup, mixed poison.
Black thoughts, like webs, he softly put around her,
Quietly back and forth. On her white skin, —
The moonlight touched one shoulder, made it dazzle —
He seemed to see these thoughts, like black webs, falling,
Knitting her fast for death . . . And who, above her,
Hung like the bearded spider . . . he, or fate?
And why was she so marked for death at all?
Of course, if he had nerve, as heroes should have,
He'd kill her now, — smother her with a pillow,
Strangle her with his hands, or cut her throat . . .
But thinking this, his lips grew dry, his hands
Weakened, his breath was hurried, he closed his eyes
To shut the hideous room out, known too well,
And all that went with it . . . himself and Judy . . .
How would the baker do it, or the hangman?
Poison? He licked his lips and poured it slowly,
Saw the green bubbles sliding . . . No, not poison . . .
Judy would know, accuse him before she died,

Or what was worse, stare at him, in her writhings,
With new-found horror . . . Darkness closed him in,
No door of light there was, he seemed imprisoned:
Chained and encircled . . . He, himself, was helpless.
All that could help him now was what most bound him —
Fate . . . and fate, as always, seemed just grinning.

The village clock struck suddenly into his musings . . .
Twelve molten golden plummets of slow sound
Plunged heavily downward in a void of silence,
Leaving a surge of air . . . He saw the tombstones
Glistening in the moonlight, ghostly rows,
And felt, as it were, the earth creep up about him . . .
Was he a shovel in the hands of fate,
Digging a grave? Digging a grave for Judy?
Well, it was strange to think that he had loved her —
Perhaps still loved her — yet desired her buried!
When she caressed him next, or stood on tiptoe
To prim her lips for his, he'd think of this;
It would be hard, he thought, to meet her eyes . . .

The moon, by now, had climbed above the elm-tree, —
Swam freely; though black claws reached after it.
The stars hummed round it still, though at a distance.
Would he be ever as free as the moon was, even?
After a while he slept, and in his sleep
Dreamed of a grave that opened, — without shovels.

4

Judy in sunlight combed her hair out slowly,
Tossing her small head backwards. Now her elbows
Flashed in the sun; her blue eyes, in the mirror,
Sought for his eyes, and smiled; the streaming hair
Dazzled him. Yet, desiring so to kill her,
And being afraid, his hatred only hardened,
His hands, that dared not hurt her, could not touch.

Did she perceive this? Did some whisper reach her,
Chilling her blood? She smiled, and went on combing,
The smile died slowly, meeting no smile for answer,
The silence deepened, prolonged, seemed fraught with meanings.
If she could know the dream he had dreamed last night,
Of an earthy grave that dug itself beneath her,
And swallowed her without sound — what would she say?
Laugh for a moment, perplexed, and hide her trouble, —
Or think the thing a trifle? — pat his cheek,
Abuse him, mockingly, for sleeping treason?
He watched her elbows moving, watched the comb
Gliding the golden length of hair, and thought
(First with a start, but after with composure)
If she could only know one instant, clearly,
How much he hated her and wished her dead —
Would she not die, or — even — kill herself?
Just here, half laughing, Judy turned towards him
With something on her lips to say: but seeing
A cold glare in his eyes grew suddenly grave
And cried 'Why, what's the matter? — ' He, surprised,
Guilty, caught with a red knife in his hands,
Lowered his eyes, and laughed and said 'Oh, nothing!';
And left her staring, large-eyed, after him.
Even as he left, his guilt had changed to anger.
Yes, there it was — that everlasting net
Falling upon his brain! He could not move
But it was there before him, softly tangling,
Meshing his hands and eyes. He hated Judy, —
The more because she now intruded on him,
Blundered among his poisons . . . His, or fate's?
He raged a while. The sunlight was detested.
Freedom! Who had the thing? This net came softly
On all he thought and did; desires and hatreds,
These were the fevers of too-mortal flesh,
Insuppressible flesh . . . Why love? Why hate? . . .
Or could one play, with skill, a music on them? . . .
No, not if one was (as he was) a coward . . .

He walked on grass, stared at the intricate blades,
Saw all was interwoven. 'So my frailties!'
He thought, 'are interwoven. I am helpless.'
Yet, with a teasing half-smile, he remembered
That though one might not conquer, one might lie.

5

Polly had waited for him by the brook —
Pretending not to. When she saw him coming
She turned her back and sang . . . Confound the girl!
Was she avoiding him, or only teasing?
He stood, half hesitating, looking downward;
Wondered if she had seen him. His flesh quickened,
The blood sang brawling melodies in his brain,
He thought, with lips apart, his chance had come
To do as other men did (if they did) —
Fling prudence to the wind and take his pleasure.
The blood sang ribald melodies in his brain.
His coward heart was hammering at his ribs.
The sky was blue and birds were singing in it,
Polly was singing, sunlight flashed on the water,
And he alone seemed sinister under the sky . . .
Would she resent his hump, make fun of him? . . .
Desire was strong in him, and he stepped downward.

Polly (the witch) played devil's music on him;
Teased at the darker currents of his blood
While seeming not to tease. She chattered, simpered,
Narrowed her black eyes on him in dark questions,
Plucked at her dress with lazy fingers, sighed,
And when she saw the half-cowed tiger rising
Behind his eyes, leered sidelong at his hump
(She knew he watched) and froze him to the marrow.
Basking in sunlight, somehow she contrived
To strip her body bare, — to lie before him
In naked loveliness: her clothes were vapour,

Her beauty burned them off, her flesh sang through them,
The white skin flashed before him . . . When, half frantic,
With hearing, seeing, feeling such clear music,
And blind with a sudden violence not his own
He flushed, and caught her hand, and tried to kiss her,
She suddenly laughed. 'Now, hunchback, don't be silly!'
She smoothed her hair, looked at him coldly, frowned, —
Then rose and walked away . . . He felt like crawling.

6

The throbbing music she so played upon him
Grew, in his dream, to a beauty past all bearing!
A bright and baleful light in shafts from heaven
Slanted upon a green hill; trees were shaken,
The leaves flew down upon it and whirled upon it
As if it were a wind; it swept and thrilled him.
There, as he built a wall to keep the sea out,
A mist-white sea that flashed without wave or sound,
She came before him and lifted her hands and laughed,
Naked and fair . . . But just as he leaned to take her
Black webs like rain came ravelling out of the sky,
Fastened upon her, meshed her, bound her helpless,
And whirled her away on air. He woke in horror:
Half doubting if it were Polly after all — ;
Half hoping, half believing, it might be Judy.

7

Waking from this his life seemed somehow changed! . . .
His body was light; the air seemed singing about him,
Moonlight roared through the elm-trees like a river,
The trees seemed ready to walk; even the houses
Seemed only to pause on earth for a moment, ready
To tilt on the stellar air and soar away.
Bewitched again! this time by Polly Prim.
He desired to dance, and sat up straight in bed

With gnomes and elves cavorting in his brain;
And then he remembered how absurd he was,
And felt his hump, and the stiffness of his legs.
Well, — whatever the outcome, — this was music, —
Spring with a million green leaves glistened in him:
His hate of Judy rose in a smoke of laughter . . .
Whether she lived or died he could avoid her —
Why waste his thoughts upon her? Love was better.
And was it sure the girl was laughing at him?
Had he, in fact, seemed so ridiculous?
One instant, he was hot with a throbbed confusion,
His hands were tight. He heard her laughing coldly,
Saw the clear devilish eyes, and felt like crawling . . .
With a slight turn and shrug, though, these reflections
Vanished . . . He felt instead her cool skin touch him,
And saw himself, the next time at the inn,
Winking, slapping his knee, and confiding slyly
To the baker or the hangman how he, Punch,
(Despite his ugliness — so all too obvious!)
Had half seduced that Polly Prim already, —
Boldly touched her knee with his hand, and kissed her, —
In fact, could have the rest of her for the asking! . . .
Warm preludes started murmurings in his brain.

8

'No doubt' (he thought) 'this web is still around me;
But Polly weaves it now, and so it glistens,
It sings about me, I can dance within it . . .'
He put his hands out, thinking he might feel it
Shimmering on the air. If net this was
It was a pleasant net, and well worth having.
Wherever it touched it burned . . . He walked within it,
Remembering, with a bland astonishment,
How he had railed so, railed at hell and heaven,
For spreading snares for him. . . And here was Polly!
Polly, with sombre hair, — and pale hands lifted

To play such music on him! — Feeling this,
(As, swimming, one might feel the cool of water
In streaks and whorls translucent flowing round him,
With a slight seethe of bubbles,) he walked gaily,
Forgetting much. Blue days like flowers gigantic
Opened above his head, flashed far above him,
Were slowly closed. Birds hung suspended in them,
Burned in the blue, revolved, or lazily sailed,
Glided away, were lost. Faint voices thrilled him
Seeming to echo voices once familiar
Now half-forgotten, vague, and strange in meaning . . .
The moon itself, — (blown like a silver bubble
In the blue air) — seemed but an idle symbol
Of time and fate, as idle. It passed slowly,
Merged in a foam of cloud, was softly lost . . .
Bound as a victim in such web of music,
Spun to his end in skeins of sound like fire —
This fate was sweet! It hardly seemed like fate . . .
Thinking these things, and always seeing Polly
Dancing before him in a clear depth of sunlight
(Uncaptured yet — he shivered —) he kissed Judy
And touched her arm, and smiled, and never winced . . .
He had forgotten, now, his dream of shovels.

9

One morning, meeting Judy on the stairway,
He noticed, — for the first time, — something strange:
She eyed him palely, raised one hand, seemed shrinking
Faintly upon herself to let him pass . . .
Some threat there was in this — he went more slowly,
Probing that look . . . What was the woman thinking? . . .
It was as if, in some way, death were in her
And looked out through her eyes. It was as if
He had glanced in through the open door of a tomb
And seen cold shadow there . . . Was Judy planning
The death which he himself, in thought, had hoped for?

Terror came down upon him, his feet were heavy,
The sunlight darkened, he suddenly saw his fate
(That fate which he himself had set in motion!)
Moving with sinister speed, looming above him,
Roaring among his trees! — His hands fell weak,
His cowardly eyes found nothing they could look at,
He sat among withered leaves . . . Judy was dying!
Judy was killing herself! Judy was dead!
The leaves flew round his feet, dust whirled among them,
The sun went over the sky, and swelled and sank,
The hours were struck, all things went on, resistless,
And he was whirled along with them . . . Well, truly,
Had he desired her dead, or hinted at it? . . .
Had he been murderous, even in words? . . .
Had he looked at her with a look of hatred? . . .
When he found heart at length, and slowly limped
Across grey fields, and saw the house, it seemed
Quietly changed. It seemed to keep a secret.
Its secret lay on the kitchen floor, in darkness.
He held a light above her, stared, was speechless.
Judy had taken poison and was dead.

10

Polly, upon his anguished summons, came
To dress his Judy, lay her out in satin,
And spend the night. He sat, and heard her moving,
Moving to and fro in the room above him,
Pulling the curtains down, opening drawers:
Moving, when she remembered to, on tiptoe . . .
What was she doing, all this time, up there? . . .
He wished the floor were glass, that he might see her . . .
And Judy lying there! He thought of Polly,
Living — and Judy, dead. This living body,
Turning there in the presence of the dead,
Bending above it, touching it with warm hands,
Rising to move away, with clear dark eyes —

Its beauty dazzled him; his flesh was quickened,
The blood sang teasing melodies in his brain,
Provoked a silent cry. Where was he drifting?
Where was he — rather — being swept, and helpless?
A gesture of struggle passed like a ghost before him,
He sank back weakly, knowing his efforts useless;
And hearing the soft steps ring once more above him
Surrendered to their music. Flares of pain
Rose in his heart, but through the pain that music
Steadily sang . . . He knew himself most ugly,
And closed his eyes for a moment not to see it.
Red-faced, lascivious, hump-backed, and a coward!
Where the strings pulled, he moved. He was a puppet.

When all was still — (still pond and no more moving! —
The phrase flew into his mind and laughed at him)
He went upstairs to bed; and the dread thing happened.
Faint fragrance stirred on the quiet air. At first
He heard no sound. He found his door and opened,
And stood there, silent. And as he stood there, trembling,
(Or was he shivering? for the air was cool)
Thinking how gross he was, how red and ugly,
And wondering if he dared to do this thing, —
With Judy lying dead, there, in her room;
Or if he had the courage; well, just then,
Polly came into the hall, and smiled at him,
Combing her hair . . . She combed her hair and smiled,
Lazily smiled, tilting her dark head backward,
Bending her smooth white arms. He stood transfixed . . .
Slow savage chords throbbed in his brain: his mouth
Too dry for speech, his feet too weak for moving . . .
'What is it?' Polly asked. His smile was foolish.
He did not know what answer was intended, —
Whether she knew what music clashed within him,
Pretending not to hear it (hearing perhaps
The same great cymbals in her own dark veins)
Or whether, if she knew, she only teased him, —

And hearing him confess, would feign a horror! . . .
He was afraid . . . 'Judy is dead' (he thought)
'I am alone . . .' he raised his hands to his eyes,
Pretending a wave of grief. Polly, at this,
Came to him quickly, stood before him, touched him . . .
'Now don't be foolish!' — He looked up, saw her smile,
(That slow soft smile again! What did it mean?)
And as he looked she took a slight step backward . . .
Silence came down upon them. He felt a net
Falling between them. He desired to move, to break it,
To touch her warm white body that sang before him,
But could not stir. If he could lift his hand —
What could prevent his touching her arms, her hair,
Her round white throat? . . . Then, as the silence deepened,
Smiling a little again, she walked back slowly,
Paused at her doorway — or seemed to pause — one instant,
To gleam through narrowed eyelids darkly at him, —
And softly closed her door . . . What did she mean? . . .
Should he go after her — knock at the door? . . .
The loud blood hammered and swelled against his temples,
Desire and fear confused him. He stood helpless.
He entered his room, sank wearily on his bed,
Stared through the window at a night of starlight
And cursed his fate; and all about was silence . . .

Judy herself was not more dead than he.

                                    11

'Is this the house where Judy lived?'
'Yes, — long ago.'
'The house where Judy lived and died?'
'Ah! . . . long ago.' . . .
He lay in the dark. Why did this idiot jingle
Keep running in his head? What did it mean?
Had he grown old already? — He clutched the pillow
And looked out through the pale blue square of window

Between black twisted branches at the stars.
Yes. There they were, just as they were before,
Silver and blue and green and twinkling crimson,
Yellow and white . . . they danced and laughed and trembled,
Pirouetted and sang, yet never moved.
And there was Judy, dead, in a darkened room,
Never to comb her hair again, or, laughing
Run down the stairs, or snap the stems of violets. . .
And here was he, hump-backed and red and bestial,
Driving her through his thoughts; and there was Polly
Sleeping, — or lying awake, perhaps, to smile!
He watched a thin bough, thrust against his window,
Dipping upon the air against the stars
As if it caught them and let them go again . . .
It was a claw. Fate itself was a claw.
His life was full of claws. He was a shovel
Held in such claws . . . and made to dig a grave,
A grave for Judy. And there was Judy waiting . . .
Or was it himself had died and would be buried? . . .
The earth piled up above him, he could not breathe.

'Is this the house where Judy lived?'
'Yes — long ago.'
'The house where Judy lived and died?'
'Ah! — long ago.'

12

Polly, he thought, was lying in her room
Stretched out upon the white bed, straight and slender;
Her long dark hair spread out upon the pillow.
Perhaps she lay awake still, gazing vaguely
Down that white length, and through the tall blue window
At these same stars . . . perhaps she turned her head
And lazily closed her eyes, to shut them out . . .
These thoughts played through his mind like a melody, —
Glissandos, shimmering downward from the treble

Sharply to crash among deep chords of passion . . .
And through these tones the thought of Judy came
Like freezing silence . . . Judy! . . . Judy! . . . Judy! . . .
What did the word mean? What had it ever stood for? . . .
Judy lying alone in a darkened room,
Her eyelids closed, her hands upon her breast!
If she could rise, and live again, — he'd hate her . . .
But dead? . . . He closed his eyes, and in the darkness
That roiled his mind ran fast through a wind of voices . . .
If he had killed her it had been unwitting.

13

Unravelling in his dream from vague beginnings,
Like a melody evolved from muttered tunings,
These things grew strange in size. Against a wall
Quivering in a light's unsteady yellow,
A shadow fell; and Polly stood before him
Naked and fair. He moved and caught and kissed her,
She half averted her face, she strained away,
Delirium fused his veins. Then down the stairs,
Bringing a sort of darkness as they came,
He heard the steps of Judy ring, — each step
Spreading a darkness and reverberating.
Polly was gone. He trembled, he desired to hide,
He stood by the wall. . . When Judy came at last,
Standing before him suddenly, — warm and young, —
He saw that she was pregnant; and remorse
Stifled his heart. Ashamed and shy and awkward
He hesitated towards her, touched her, kissed her,
Said (what he had not said so long) 'I love you!' — ;
Then leaned against the wall and cried like a child.
She looked at him surprised, — and tenderly, —
And slowly walked away.

Later, his dream
(But after he had waked and stared in anguish

At the dark ceiling above him, vaguely white)
Brought him a hidden sound of Polly's laughter,
The clear notes blown from nowhere. There he seemed
To run from some one, some one with a knife —
The constable? — he did not turn to see,
But ran; till suddenly, thinking he was safe,
He saw the man before him in a chair
With his back turned; and stabbed him, then, and killed him . . .
As the man moved his head to look, he woke.

14

He walked in a rain to see his Judy buried.
The sky was filled with the slanting spears of rain,
Grey spears of rain. Over the tops of trees
Whistled the wind-torn clouds. The ruts were gleaming,
Puddles were ringed and rippled. At the churchyard
They found the grave already dug, raw earth
Heaped up beside it, pitted and dark with rain.
This was the last injustice! This was monstrous.
They lowered the coffin awkwardly into the grave,
On the bare resonant boards that hid his Judy
The rain drummed monotones, wet earth was shovelled;
And suddenly, able to bear the thing no longer,
He turned his back, stared at the rain-lashed grass,
And saw how cruel was life. The church-bell tolled,
The tones were whirled away as soon as struck,
Tumbled upon the wind, and lost in rain,
Or beaten down to the ground. Among worn grass-blades
Rain-bubbles winked and ran with delicate seething,
Bare trees whipped in the wind . . . the day was madness.

Dusk fell. He crossed the fields alone. His house
Looked old and cold and small and time-forgotten.
'Is this the house where Judy lived?'
'Yes, — long ago. . .'

'The house where Judy lived and died?'
'Ah! — long ago.'

He thrust the door, stood in the silent hallway,
And heard no sound save whir and splash of rain
And tick of clocks; alone and loud and foolish
In the slow mouldering and decay of time.

15

Through the tall window, on the brown curve of the hill,
He watched pale silvery arrows of rain descending;
Slow long arpeggios thrilled and chimed in his heart.
The soft drops brushed on the window and were muted.
The grey-white sky above him whirled with rain.
'Well, then . . . if Polly refused me . . . Judy tricked me . . .
But *did* they now, — or did I misinterpret? . . .
No! I should wrong myself if I should think so . . .
Have I not half seduced the girl already?
Did I not . . . kill the other?' — Thinking this
He seemed to feel that horrible net once more,
But thrust it harshly aside. 'No, I am free:
No man or law or fate can change my purpose,
No god defeat my will! If, on that hillside,
Old Nick himself, and Doctor Faustus with him,
Should spread the world before me, for my soul —
Setting before me Venus with bright hair,
Towers of silver, walls inlaid with sapphires, —
I should refuse. No fate shall take my soul! . . .
And where is she so proud, who, to my cunning,
Shall not surrender her crown, her heart, and all? . . .'
He was tired, he bowed his head; and in a dream
The Queen of Sheba smiled on a throne before him,
A far faint clashing of music reached his ears,
A ghostly pageant of crimson shimmered and smouldered
And swayingly died away. . . And death itself

Went dwindling into the grey rain, only pausing
At the sky's edge to lift one menacing arm . . .
Or was it only a gaunt tree, silhouetted,
Flinging a long black branch out, one great claw? . . .

.   .   .   .

The dark dream spread before him, like a valley
Made strange with music. Birds flew upward from it;
Far down flashed moving lights. He closed his eyes
And smiled, and took one step, and then another;
And groping raised his hands. . . The air was warm.

This was the valley of forgetfulness
Where painful thoughts and frustrate deeds would fade . . .
He saw an orange moon rise, strangely large,
Above soft trees. Among the unbroken vineyards
Maenads came out to dance, he heard them singing,
The leaves swished back behind them, laughter descended . . .
This was the valley of love and lawlessness;
Where thirst was quenched, with no satiety,
And flesh and stream and tree were all immortal.
Cymbals softly clashed in the moonlit forest
Far down before him, the undulant air was fragrant
With flight of ghostly roses; out of the silence, voices
Rose faint and clear. . . He slowly descended the hill.

HE IMAGINES THAT HIS PUPPET HAS A DARK
DREAM AND HEARS VOICES

First Voice

Pave the sky with stars for Punch!
And snare in flowers a moon for him
With white rose-trees and apple trees
And cherubim and seraphim!

Second Voice

Look! he comes! how tall he is!
A crown of fire is on his head;
The sky unrolls before his feet,
Green mountains fear his tread.

The meteors now like dolphins dive
Into the white wave of the sky,
Blue moons and stars around him sing
And suns triumphant cry!

Third Voice

Build a house of gold for Punch,
Of gold without and silk within,
With floors of glass, and let there be
For ever there a silver din

Of music's many instruments
In slow and low amazement heard:
In every window-niche a cage,
In every cage a singing-bird.

Build it in a kingdom far;
In a forest green and deep;
Where no tears nor sorrows are,
But only song and sleep.

There to the noise of wind in trees
And many rivers winding down,
Let him forget the cares of earth
And nod a kingly crown!

Fourth Voice

Like a tower of brass is Punch,
And great and stately is his pace;

There is no other as tall as he, —
None with so fair a face.

Fall down, fall down, you kings of men,
Fall down before him! This is he
For whom the moon pursues her ghost
And demons bend the knee.

Woe unto you, you miscreants
Who dare the lightnings of his eyes!
His hand, how strong! His wrath, how just!
His brow, how white and wise!

Fifth Voice

Solomon, clown, put by your crown,
And Judas, break your tree:
Seal up your tomb and burn your cross,
Jesus of Galilee!

For here walks one who makes you seem
But atoms that creep in grass;
You are the pageant of his dream,
And he will bid you pass.

Let Rome go over the earth in gold
With trumpets harshly blown!
For here comes one whose splendour burns
More gloriously, alone.

Heliogabalus, laugh your last!
Queen Sappho, lie you down!
Punch the immortal shakes the seas
And takes the sun for crown.

Sixth Voice

Sheba, now let down your hair,
And play upon it with your hands,
While girls from Tal and Mozambique
Parade before in sarabands, —

Play him songs inaudible
With white hands braceleted and slim,
Or shake your hair and let it fall
And softly darken him.

Cling to him, while cymbals far
Are sweetly smitten in the dusk,
And maenads, under a haughty star,
Break the white rose for its musk:

Cling to him, and with your lips
Feed his heart on crumbs of fire
That shall, perpetually, delight,
But never slay desire!

Seventh Voice

Open a window on the world
With all its sorrow, and then
When he has heard that sound a space,
Close it fast again. . .

Sweet will it be, lapped round with ease
And music-troubled air,
To hear for a moment on the wind
A sound of far despair:

And then, to turn to lights again,
And fingers soft on strings,
While Sheba slips her bracelets off
And spreads her arms and sings. . .

Sweet will it be, to hear far off
That gusty sound of pain,
And to remember, far away,
A world of death and rain:

And then, to close the window fast,
And laugh, and clap soft hands,
While girls from Tal and Mozambique
Parade in sarabands. . .

Close now the window! Close it well! . . .
That slow lament of pain
Was but the dissonance that makes
Dull music sweet again.

Eighth Voice

Death, you will wear a chain of gold,
And wreaths of roses white and red,
And nightlong will you dance for him
With garlands on your head.

Bring a cup and pour him wine,
And dance for him; for this is he
Who plays a jocund tune for you
But will not set you free.

Or go with thongs to scourge the world
And lay it waste; and then come back
To sorrow before him in a cage
And garb yourself in black.

A cage of gold he keeps for you! . . .
There he will watch you dance,
And fill his cup, immortally,
And laugh at circumstance.

Ninth Voice

There is a fountain in a wood
Where wavering lies a moon:
It plays to the slowly falling leaves
A sleepy tune.

. . . The peach-trees lean upon a wall
Of gold and ivory:
The peacock spreads his tail, the leaves
Fall silently. . .

There, amid silken sounds and wine
And music idly broken,
The drowsy god observes his world
With no word spoken.

Arcturus, rise! Orion, fall! . . .
The white-winged stars obey . . .
Or else he greets his Fellow-God;
And there, in the dusk, they play

A game of chess with stars for pawns
And a silver moon for queen:
Immeasurable as clouds above
A chess-board world they lean,

And thrust their hands amid their beards,
And utter words profound
That shake the star-swung firmament
With a fateful sound! . . .

. . . The peach-trees lean upon a wall
Of gold and ivory;
The peacock spreads his tail; the leaves
Fall silently. . .

*

MOUNTEBANK FEELS THE STRINGS AT HIS HEART

In the blue twilight the puller of strings, half-tenderly
Tumbling his puppets away, — Punch, Judy, and Polly, —
Into the darkness again; Jack Ketch and Faustus,
Solomon, crowned with a crown of tinsel and silver,
Sheba with small hands lifted; Judas Iscariot
With a noose of frayed thin silk about his neck,
And the Devil himself in scarlet with white eyes leering, —
Tumbling them into their box, the cords relaxed,
The small world darkened, whereupon they danced and
    squeaked, —
Leaving them there in the dusk pell-mell together;
And turning away, at last, to look from a window
At a darker and greater world, ring beyond ring
Of houses and trees and stars, sky upon sky,
Space beyond silent space of clouds and planets:

Suddenly, there, as he stood at the darkening window
Watching the glimmer of uncounted worlds in the twilight,
A world so vast, so piercingly chorded with beauty,
Blown and glowing in the long-drawn wind of time, —
He saw himself, — though a god, — the puppet of gods;
Revolving in antics the dream of a greater dreamer;
Flung up from a sea of chaos one futile instant,
To look on a welter of water whirling with crimson;
And then, in an instant, drawn back once more into chaos.

. . . Was it enough, to remember that in that instant
He had cried out in a cry of rapture and anguish? . . .
Was it enough to believe, — if he could believe it! —
That the faint voice crying abruptly and strangely its anguish

Was the voice of himself? . . . Or only the voice of the gods? . . .
Was he no better than Judy, or Polly, — or Punch,
Capering about his cage of twittering dreams? . . .

Strange! As he looked from the height of the darkened window
At the glimmer of immortal worlds below and above,
Star beyond star, house beyond house, — soul beyond soul? —
He imagined that Judy, there in the box behind him,
Stirred her fellows aside and rose in the darkness
And quavered to him . . . 'Listen! you puller of strings!
Do you think it just to call me into existence, —
To give me a name, — and give me so little beside? . . .
To Polly you give her laughter, to Punch his illusions, —
To me you give nothing but death!'

She wept after this,
Resting her small white elbows there on the box-edge,
And waited in silence. He, meanwhile, not turning towards her,
But resting, like her, his arms on the sill of the window,
Watched the dark world.

'How shall I answer you, Judy? . . .
It is true you have little but sorrow and death at my hands —
It is true you seem hardly a shadow for Polly and Punch, —
And this I regret! You step for a moment from darkness
Turning, bewildered, your face in a twinkle of lamplight,
Lift sharply your hand, — and vanish once more, and for ever.
But Judy, — how else could I find you, — how even console you?
I too am a puppet. And as you are a symbol for me
(As Punch is, and Sheba — bright symbols of intricate meanings,
Atoms of soul — who move, and are moved by, me —)
So I am a symbol, a puppet drawn out upon strings,
Helpless, well-coloured, with a fixed and unchanging expression
(As though one said "heartache" or "laughter"!) of some one who
        leans
Above me, as I above you. . . And even this Some one, —

Who knows what compulsion he suffers, what hands out of dark-
      ness
Play sharp chords upon him! . . . Who knows if those hands are
      not ours! . . .

'Look then at my mind: this tiny old stage, dimly lighted,
Whereon, — and without my permission, — you symbols parade,
Saying and meaning such things! You, now, with your death,
Crying out into my heart, if for only a moment!
Punch with his devils about him, his terror of darkness!
And Polly there laughing beside him — look now how you walk
On the nerve-strings of all I can know, to delight me, to torture,
To pass in a nightmare of gesture before me, how heedless
Of me, — whom our gods have ordained to exist as your world!
Think, now! I can never escape you. Did you call me a tyrant?
I desire to change you — and cannot! . . . I desire to see you
Under a pear-tree — (we'll say that the tree is in blossom —)
A warm day of sunlight, and laughing, — at nothing what-
      ever! . . .
A green hill's behind you; a cloud like a dome tops the hill;
A poplar tree, like a vain girl, leans over a mirror
Trying on silver, then green, perplexed, but in pleasure;
And you there, alone in the sunlight, watch bees in the pear-tree,
Dipping the leaves; and you laugh — for no reason whatever!
Delightful! One moment, at least, no Punch can disturb you,
No Polly whirl dead leaves about you! You stand there un-
      troubled . . .
Thus, then, I desire to see you, to have you exist
If only an instant; yet down come the shadows between us,
And all they have left me is — Judy, to whom I have given
A name, and so little beside!'

                                    . . . There was silence a moment;
And when he turned back, expecting, perhaps, to see Judy
Leaning her small white elbows there on the box-edge, —
No, not a sign. The puppets lay huddled together,
Arms over heads, contorted, just where he had dropped them;

Inscrutable, silent, terrific, like those made eternal
Who stare, without thought, at a motionless world without mean-
ing.

Seven Twilights

I

The ragged pilgrim, on the road to nowhere,
Waits at the granite milestone. It grows dark.
Willows lean by the water. Pleas of water
Cry through the trees. And on the boles and boughs
Green water-lights make rings, already paling.
Leaves speak everywhere. The willow leaves
Silverly stir on the breath of moving water,
Birch-leaves, beyond them, twinkle, and there on the hill,
And the hills beyond again, and the highest hill,
Serrated pines, in the dusk, grow almost black.
By the eighth milestone on the road to nowhere
He drops his sack and lights once more the pipe
There often lighted. In the dusk-sharpened sky
A pair of night-hawks windily sweep, or fall,
Booming, toward the trees. Thus had it been
Last year, and the year before, and many years:
Ever the same. . . 'Thus turns the human track
Backward upon itself, I stand once more
By this small stream. . .' Now the rich sound of leaves,
Turning in air to sway their heavy boughs,
Burns in his heart, sings in his veins, as spring
Flowers in veins of trees; bringing such peace
As comes to seamen when they dream of seas.
'O trees! exquisite dancers in grey twilight!
Witches! fairies! elves! who wait for the moon
To thrust her golden horn, like a golden snail,
Above that mountain! — arch your green benediction
Once more over my heart. Muffle the sound of bells,
Mournfully human, that cries from the darkening valley;

Close, with your leaves, about the sound of water;
Take me among your hearts as you take the mist
Among your boughs!' . . . Now by the granite milestone,
On the ancient human road that leads to nowhere,
The pilgrim listens, as the night air brings
The murmured echo, perpetual, from the gorge
Of barren rock far down the valley. Now,
Though twilight here, it may be starlight there;
Mist makes elfin lakes in the hollow fields;
The dark wood stands in the mist like a sombre island
With one red star above it. . . 'This I should see,
Should I go on, follow the falling road, —
This I have often seen. . . But I shall stay
Here, where the ancient milestone, like a watchman,
Lifts up its figure eight, its one grey knowledge,
Into the twilight; as a watchman lifts
A lantern, which he does not know is out.'

II

Now by the wall of the little town I lean
Myself, like ancient wall and dust and sky,
And the purple dusk, grown old, grown old in heart.
Shadows of clouds flow inward from the sea.
The mottled fields grow dark. The golden wall
Grows grey again, turns stone again; the tower,
No longer kindled, darkens against a cloud.
Old is the world, old as the world am I;
The cries of sheep rise upward from the fields,
Forlorn and strange; and wake an ancient echo
In fields my blood has known, but has not seen.
'These fields' — (an unknown voice beyond the wall
Murmurs) — 'were once the province of the sea.
Where now the sheep graze, mermaids were at play;
Sea-horses galloped; and the great jewelled tortoise
Walked slowly, looking upward at the waves,
Bearing upon his back a thousand barnacles,

A white acropolis. . .' The ancient tower
Sends out, above the houses and the trees,
And the flat fields below the mouldered walls,
A measured phrase of bells. And in the silence
I hear a woman's voice make answer then:
'Well, they are green, although no ship can sail them.
Sky-larks rest in the grass, and start up singing
Before the girl who stoops to pick sea-poppies.
Spiny, the poppies are, and oh how yellow!
And the brown clay is runnelled by the rain.'
A moment since, the sheep that crop the grass
Had long blue shadows, and the grass-tips sparkled:
Now all grows old. . . O voices strangely speaking,
Voices of man and woman, voices of bells,
Diversely making comment on our time
Which flows and bears us with it into dark, —
Repeat the things you say! Repeat them slowly
Upon this air, make them an incantation
For ancient tower, old wall, the purple twilight,
This dust, and me! . . . But all I hear is silence,
And something that may be leaves or may be sea.

III

When the tree bares, the music of it changes:
Hard and keen is the sound, long and mournful;
Pale are the poplar boughs in the evening light
Above my house, against a slate-cold cloud.
When the house ages, and the tenants leave it,
Cricket sings in the tall grass by the threshold;
Spider, by the cold mantel, hangs his web.
Here, in a hundred years from that clear season
When first I came here bearing lights and music,
To this old ghostly house my ghost will come, —
Pause in the half-light, turn by the poplar, glide
Above tall grasses through the broken door.
Who will say that he saw — or the dusk deceived him —

A mist with hands of mist blow down from the tree
And open the door and enter and close it after?
Who will say that he saw, as midnight struck
Its tremulous golden twelve, a light in the window,
And first heard music, as of an old piano,
Music remote, as if it came from the earth,
Far down; and then, in the quiet, eager voices?
'. . . Houses grow old and die, houses have ghosts —
Once in a hundred years we return, old house,
And live once more.' . . . And then the ancient answer,
In a voice not human, but more like creak of boards
Or rattle of panes in the wind — 'Not as the owner,
But as a guest you come, to fires not lit
By hands of yours. . . Through these long-silent chambers
Move slowly, turn, return, and bring once more
Your lights and music. It will be good to talk.'

                                    IV

'This is the hour,' she said, 'of transmutation:
It is the eucharist of the evening, changing
All things to beauty. Now the ancient river,
That all day under the arch was polished jade,
Becomes the ghost of a river, thinly gleaming
Under a silver cloud. It is not water:
It is that azure stream in which the stars
Bathe at the daybreak and become immortal.'
'And the moon,' said I — not thus to be outdone —
'What of the moon? Over the dusty plane-trees,
Which crouch in the dusk above their feeble lanterns,
Each coldly lighted by his tiny faith;
The moon, the waxen moon, now almost full,
Creeps whitely up. . . Westward the waves of cloud,
Vermilion, crimson, violet, stream on the air,
Shatter to golden flakes in the icy green
Translucency of twilight. And the moon
Drinks up their light, and as they fade or darken,

Brightens. O monstrous miracle of the twilight,
That one should live because the others die!'
'Strange too,' she answered, 'that upon this azure
Pale-gleaming ghostly stream, impalpable —
So faint, so fine, that scarcely it bears up
The petals that the lantern strews upon it, —
These great black barges float like apparitions,
Loom in the silver of it, beat upon it,
Moving upon it as dragons move on air!'
'Thus always,' then I answered, — looking never
Toward her face, so beautiful and strange
It grew, with feeding on the evening light, —
'The gross is given, by inscrutable God,
Power to beat wide wings upon the subtle.
Thus we ourselves, so fleshly, fallible, mortal,
Stand here, for all our foolishness, transfigured:
Hung over nothing in an arch of light;
While one more evening, like a wave of silence,
Gathers the stars together and goes out.'

v

Now the great wheel of darkness and low clouds
Whirs and whirls in heaven with dipping rim;
Against the ice-white wall of light in the west
Skeleton trees bow down in a stream of air.
Leaves, black leaves and smoke, are blown on the wind;
Mount upward past my window; swoop again;
In a sharp silence, loudly, loudly falls
The first cold drop, striking a shrivelled leaf.
Doom and dusk for the earth! Upward I reach
To draw chill curtains and shut out the dark,
Pausing an instant, with uplifted hand,
To watch, between black ruined portals of cloud,
One star, — the tottering portals fall and crush it.
Here are a thousand books! here is the wisdom
Alembicked out of dust, or out of nothing;

Choose now the weightiest word, most golden page,
Most sombrely musicked line; hold up these lanterns, —
These paltry lanterns, wisdoms, philosophies, —
Above your eyes, against this wall of darkness;
And you'll see — what? One hanging strand of cobweb;
A window-sill a half-inch deep in dust.
Speak out, old wise-men! Now, if ever, we need you.
Cry loudly, lift shrill voices like magicians
Against this baleful dusk, this wail of rain!
But you are nothing. Your pages turn to water
Under my fingers: cold, cold and gleaming,
Arrowy in the darkness, rippling, dripping —
All things are rain. Myself, this lighted room,
What are we but a murmurous pool of rain?
The slow arpeggios of it, liquid, sibilant,
Thrill and thrill in the dark. World-deep I lie
Under a sky of rain. Thus lies the sea-shell
Under the rustling twilight of the sea;
No gods remember it; no understanding
Cleaves the long darkness with a sword of light.

VI

Heaven, you say, will be a field in April,
A friendly field, a long green wave of earth,
With one domed cloud above it. There you'll lie
In noon's delight, with bees to flash above you,
Drown amid buttercups that blaze in the wind,
Forgetting all save beauty. There you'll see
With sun-filled eyes your one great dome of cloud
Adding fantastic towers and spires of light,
Ascending, like a ghost, to melt in the blue.
Heaven enough, in truth, if you were there!
Could I be with you, I would choose your noon,
Drown amid buttercups, laugh with the intimate grass,
Dream there forever. . . But, being older, sadder,
Having not you, nor aught save thought of you,

It is not spring I'll choose, but fading summer;
Not noon I'll choose, but the charmed hour of dusk.
Poppies? A few! And a moon almost as red.
But most I'll choose that subtler dusk that comes
Into the mind — into the heart, you say —
When, as we look bewildered at lovely things,
Striving to give their loveliness a name,
They are forgotten; and other things, remembered,
Flower in the heart with the fragrance we call grief.

VII

In the long silence of the sea, the seaman
Strikes twice his bell of bronze. The short note wavers
And loses itself in the blue realm of water.
One sea-gull, paired with a shadow, wheels, wheels;
Circles the lonely ship by wave and trough;
Lets down his feet, strikes at the breaking water,
Draws up his golden feet, beats wings, and rises
Over the mast. Light from a crimson cloud
Crimsons the sluggishly creeping foams of waves;
The seaman, poised in the bow, rises, falls,
As the deep forefoot finds a way through waves;
And there below him, steadily gazing westward, —
Facing the wind, the sunset, the long cloud, —
The goddess of the ship, proud figurehead,
Smiles inscrutably, plunges to crying waters,
Emerges streaming, gleaming, with jewels falling
Fierily from carved wings and golden breasts;
Steadily glides a moment, then swoops again.
Carved by the hand of man, grieved by the wind;
Worn by the tumult of the tragic seas,
Yet smiling still, unchanging, smiling still
Inscrutably, with calm eyes and golden brow —
What is it that she sees and follows always,
Beyond the molten and ruined west, beyond
The light-rimmed sea, the sky itself? What secret

Gives wisdom to her purpose? Now the cloud
In final conflagration pales and crumbles
Into the darkening water. Now the stars
Burn softly through the dusk. The seaman strikes
His small lost bell again, watching the west
As she below him watches. . . O pale goddess,
Whom not the darkness, even, or rain or storm,
Changes; whose great wings are bright with foam,
Whose breasts are cold as the sea, whose eyes forever
Inscrutably take that light whereon they look —
Speak to us! Make us certain, as you are,
That somewhere, beyond wave and wave and wave,
That dreamed-of harbour lies which we would find.

Exile

These hills are sandy. Trees are dwarfed here. Crows
Caw dismally in skies of an arid brilliance,
Complain in dusty pine-trees. Yellow daybreak
Lights on the long brown slopes a frost-like dew,
Dew as heavy as rain; the rabbit tracks
Show sharply in it, as they might in snow.
But it's soon gone in the sun — what good does it do?
The houses, on the slope, or among brown trees,
Are grey and shrivelled. And the men who live here
Are small and withered, spider-like, with large eyes.

Bring water with you if you come to live here —
Cold tinkling cisterns, or else wells so deep
That one looks down to Ganges or Himalayas.
Yes, and bring mountains with you, white, moon-bearing,
Mountains of ice. You will have need of these
Profundities and peaks of wet and cold.

Bring also, in a cage of wire or osier,
Birds of a golden colour, who will sing
Of leaves that do not wither, watery fruits

That heavily hang on long melodious boughs
In the blue-silver forests of deep valleys.

I have now been here — how many years? Years unnumbered.
My hands grow clawlike. My eyes are large and starved.
I brought no bird with me, I have no cistern
Where I might find the moon, or river, or snow.
Some day, for lack of these, I'll spin a web
Between two dusty pine-tree tops, and hang there
Face downward, like a spider, blown as lightly
As ghost of leaf. Crows will caw about me.
Morning and evening I snall drink the dew.

Samadhi

Take then the music; plunge in the thickest of it, —
Thickest, darkest, richest; call it a forest,
A million boles of trees, with leaves, leaves,
Golden and green, flashing like scales in the sun,
Tossed and torn in the tempest, whirling and streaming,
With the terrible sound, beneath, of boughs that crack.
. . . Again, a hush comes; and the wind's a whisper.
One leaf goes pirouetting. You stand in the dusk
In the misty shaft of light the sun flings faintly
Through planes of green; and suddenly, out of the darkest
And deepest and farthest of the forest, wavers
That golden horn, *cor anglais,* husky-timbred,
Sending through all this gloom of trees and silence
Its faint half-mute nostalgia. . . How the soul
Flies from the dungeon of you to the very portals
To meet that sound! There, there, is the secret
Singing out of the darkness, — shining, too,
For all we know, if we could only see!
But if we steal by footpaths, warily, —
Snap not a twig, nor crush a single leaf;
Or if, in a kind of panic, like wild beasts,
We rend our violent way through vines and briars,

Crash through a coppice, tear our flesh, come bleeding
To a still pool, encircled, brooded over
By ancient trees — all's one! We reach but silence,
We find no horn, no hornsman. . . There the beeches
Out of the lower dark of ferns and mosses
Lift, far above, their tremulous tops to the light.
Only an echo hear we of that horn,
Cor anglais, golden, husky-timbred, crying
Half-mute nostalgia from the dark of things. . .
Then, as we stand bewildered in that wood,
With leaves above us in sibilant confusion,
And the ancient ghosts of leaves about our feet —
Listen! — the horn once more, but farther now,
Sings in the evening for a wing-beat space;
Makes the leaves murmur, as it makes the blood
Burn in the heart and all its radiant veins;
And we turn inward, to seek it once again.

Or, it's a morning in the blue portal of summer.
White shoals of little clouds, like heavenly fish,
Swim softly off the sun, who rains his light
On the vast hurrying earth. The giant poplar
Sings in the light with a thousand sensitive leaves,
Root-tip to leaf-tip he is all delight:
And, at the golden core of all that joy,
One sinister grackle with a thievish eye
Scrapes a harsh cynic comment. How he laughs,
Flaunting amid that green his coffin-colour!
We, in the garden a million miles below him,
At paltry tasks of pruning, spading, watching
Black-stripèd bees crawl into foxglove bells
Half-filled with dew — look! we are lightly startled
By sense or sound; are moved; lose touch with earth;
And, in the twinkling of the grackle's eye,
Swing in the infinite on a spider's cable.
What is our world? It is a poplar tree
Immense and solitary, with leaves a thousand,

Or million, countless, flashing in a light
For them alone intended. He is great,
His trunk is solid, and his roots deceive us.
We shade our eyes with hands and upward look
To see if all those leaves indeed be leaves,
So rich they are in a choiring down of joy,
Or stars. And as we stand so, small and dumb,
We hear again that harsh derisive comment,
The grackle's laughter; and again we see
His thievish eye, aware amid green boughs.
Touch earth again: take up your shovel: dig
In the wormy ground. That tree magnificent
Sways like a giant dancer in a garment
Whose gold and green are naught but tricks of light.
And at the heart of all that drunken beauty
Is a small lively cynic bird who laughs.

Who sees the vision coming? Who can tell
What moment out of time will be the seed
To root itself, as swift as lightning roots
Into a cloud, and grow, swifter than thought,
And flower gigantic in the infinite?
Walk softly through your forest, and be ready
To hear the horn of horns. Or in your garden
Stoop, but upon your back be ever conscious
Of sunlight, and a shadow that may grow.

Poverty Grass

First, blow the trumpets: call the people hither!
Not merely in the township! Send them further.
Set hornsmen at all cross roads: send out horsemen
With horns, a man's length, bound in brass,
Far to the north, the west. Bid them to blow
Unceasing summons, shatter the air, shake leaves
From trees decrepit. I would have the world
Sound with a bugle music from end to end.

Lead then the people hither, have the roads
Black with the mass of them at night and noon.
And when you have them, see them banked about me,
Row behind row — (how shine already the faces!) —
Like angels in Angelico's vision of heaven.
Those that were horsemen first will now be ushers —
'Stand there!' they'll cry, 'no crowding! — Those behind
Will hear, feel, understand, as well as those
Who rest their chins upon him, prop their elbows
Against the coffin-lid! Stand still! be patient!'
As for the house — that must be fit as well.
Thus, as it now stands — no! it is too meagre.
The stage is bare. First, the approach is bad.
The hill, behind, that for a thousand years
Has washed its loam and leaves against these walls, —
The hill must go. So, let a thousand axes
Flash against bark: let fall a thousand oaks
With all their crying birds, small scolding squirrels,
Bees' nests and birds' nests, hornets, wasps, and snakes.
A thousand carts, then, each with a quaking tree
Outstretched in ignominy, chained and helpless, —
These, going hence, will be our first procession:
We'll bear to the sea our captives. Next, an army
With spades and picks a thousand, have them led
To music, up the hill, and then like ants
Devour him: gash him first, and swarm in the gash,
Eat inward till he's maggoty with men, —
A hollow seething shell, — and lastly, nothing.
As for the house, its walls must be of glass.
And no partitions! one vast room that's walled
And roofed with clearest crystal. There at night
We'll have great light, ten thousand flames of candles,
Ten thousand clear-eyed flames in a crystal casket:
The folk on the utmost hill will see, and cry
'Look, how the moon's caught in a crystal coffin!'
And last, myself, there in that crystal coffin,
Flooded with light, reclining half, half sitting

Propped up amid soft silks in a little box
Of brilliant glass, yet lidless. There I'll sit
Like prophet at a tomb's edge, open-mouthed,
Pale, old, obscene, white-bearded — see! my beard
Hangs on the coffin as a snow-drift hangs
On a wall of ice . . . And there, at last, I'll speak.

So, then! You see it clearly. It is night-time.
The house is bright. And I, — in an open coffin
Of glass, that's in the house, a larger coffin, —
(That, too, in the coffin that we call the world,
Large, airy, lucent, lighted with lights of stars, —)
Peer from the luminous grave's-edge into darkness
That's filled from hub to marge with staring faces.
Beautiful! Is the world here? Let it gaze, then,
And fill its idiot eyes to overflowing
With a sight not known before. Step closer, kings, —
Emperors, use your elbows as the plebs do.
Steam, if you like, with your ambitious breath
These walls that tell no lies. I'd have you hear me,
You most of all; though I forget not either
The vast grey hungry maggot-mass of men:
The little wedge-shaped darlings, in their broth
Of carrion illusions! . . . How they rot
The air they breathe, turn the green earth to poison,
People the sky with pestilence of sick fancies!
See how the whole sky swarms with dirty wings! . . .

O Man, who so corrupt all things you feed on;
Whose meditation slimes the thing it thinks;
Vile borer into the core of the universe;
Spoiler and destroyer; you, ambitious,
Crawling upon your admirable belly
For nothing but that at last your tube-shaped mouth
Should blindly thrust and suck at the innermost heart
Of the world, or god, or infinite overthrown;
Foulest and most dishonest of all creatures;

Sole traitorous worm of all things living, you
Who crown your horrible head with a dream of glory
And call yourself a king! Come closer, hear me,
I am the prophet who, as through these walls
Of innocent glass, see all things deep and clear,
The after and before, revealed or hid:
Partly among you living, partly dead,
I see your hungry mouths, but also see
With my dead eye, — (one cold eye underground
Beneath the earth's black coffin-lid, —) the dead.
Ha! You would have my secret? You would hear
The one bright shattering trumpet whose long blast
Blows like a whirlwind myriad ghosts from tombs?
You cry to the prophet, do you, for a vision —
You'd have me, with one sombre word of magic,
Cry beauty back from dust, and set to singing
This catacomb of graves you call a world?
Press closer, kings! Swarm over me, you plebs!
Feed your rapacious eyes on me, devour
With mouths and nerves and nostrils and raw brains
This bloodless carcass that contains your secret:
Have out my heart, hold up above it candles,
Pass it among you, squeak and growl and jabber,
Stamp it beneath your feet — it's an old leaf
Will turn to a little dust . . . For there's the wonder!
I am but poverty grass; a dry grey weed;
A trifling dusty moss, fine-branched as coral — ;
One footstep makes it powder. And my secret, —
Which all my horsemen brought you here to learn, —
Is nought but this: this singing world of yours
Is but a heap of bones. Sound once the trumpet
And you shall see them, tier upon tier, profound
As God himself! Sound twice the trumpet, then,
And I shall add my bone or two. And after,
At the third blast, will all these lights puff out, —
And you may grope in the darkness, as you came.
Sound the bright horn. Shut, coffin! I am dead.

Psychomachia

I

Tent-caterpillars, as you see, (he said)
Have nested in these cherry-trees, and stripped
All sound of leaves from them. You see their webs
Like broken harp-strings, of a fairy kind,
Shine in the moonlight.

And then I to him:
But is this why, when all the houses sleep,
You meet me here, — to tell me only this,
That caterpillars weave their webs in trees?
This road I know. I have walked many times
These sandy ruts. I know these starveling trees,
Their gestures of stiff agony in winter,
And the sharp conscious pain that gnaws them now.
But there is mystery, a message learned,
A word flung down from nowhere, caught by you,
And hither brought for me. How shines that word,
From what star comes it? . . . This is what I seek.

And he in answer: Can you hear the blood
Cry out like jangled bells from all these twigs;
Or feel the ghosts of blossom touch your face?
Walk you amid these trees as one who walks
Upon a field where lie the newly slain
And those who darkly die? And hear you crying?
Flesh here is torn from flesh. The tongue's plucked out.
What speech then would you have, where speech is tongueless,
And nothing, nothing, but a welling up of pain?

I answered: You may say these smitten trees,
Being leafless, have no tongues and cannot speak.
How comforts that my question? . . . You have come,
I know, as you come always, with a meaning.

What, then, is in your darkness of hurt trees;
What bird, sequestered in that wilderness
Of inarticulate pain, wrong ill-endured,
And death not understood, but bides his time
To sing a piercing phrase? Why sings he not?
I am familiar, long, with pain and death,
Endure as all do, lift dumb eyes to question
Uncomprehended wounds; I have my forest
Of injured trees, whose bare twigs show the moon
Their shameful floating webs; and I have walked,
As now we walk, to listen there to bells
Of pain, bubbles of blood, and ached to feel
The ghosts of blossom pass. But is there not
The mystery, the fugitive shape that sings
A sudden beauty there that comes like peace?

You know this road, he said, and how it leads
Beyond starved trees to bare grey poverty grass;
Then lies the marsh beyond, and then the beach,
With dry curled waves of sea-weed, and the sea.
There, in the fog, you hear the row-locks thump,
And there you see the fisherman come in
From insubstantial nothing to a shore
As dim and insubstantial. He is old,
His boat is old and grey, the oars are worn.
You know this, — you have seen this?

                                    And then I:
I know, have seen this, and have felt the shore
As dim and thin as mist; and I have wondered
That it upheld me, did not let me fall
Through nothing into nothing . . . And the oars,
Worn down like human nerves against the world;
And the worn road that leads to sleeping houses
And weeping trees. But is this all you say?
For there is mystery, a word you have
That shines within your mind. Now speak that word.

And he in answer: So you have the landscape
With all its nerves and voices. It is yours.
Do with it what you will. But never try
To go away from it, for that is death.
Dwell in it, know its houses, and cursed trees,
And call it sorrow. Is this not enough?
Love you not shameful webs? It is enough.
There is no need for bird, or sudden peace.

II

The plain no herbage had, but all was bare
And swollen livid sand in ridges heaped;
And in the sharp cold light that filled the east
Beneath one cloud that was a bird with wings
I saw a figure shape itself, as whirling
It took up sand and moved across the sand.
A man it was, and here and there he ran
Beating his arms, now falling, rising now,
Struggling, for so it seemed, against the air.
But, as I watched, the cloud that was a bird
Lifted its wings; and the white light intense
Poured down upon him. Then I saw him, naked,
Amid that waste, at war with a strange beast
Or monster, many-armed and ever-changing;
That now was like an octopus of air,
Now like a spider with a woman's hair
And woman's hands, and now was like a vine
That wrapped him round with leaves and sudden flowers,
And now was like a huge white thistledown
Floating; and with this changing shape he fought
Furious and exhausted, till at length
I saw him fall upon it in the sand
And strangle it. Its tentacles of leaves
Fell weakly downward from his back, its flowers
Turned black. And then, as he had whirled at first,
So whirled he now again, and with his feet

Drew out the sand, and made a pit, and flung
The scorpion-woman-vine therein, and heaped
The sand above.

              And then I heard him sing
And saw him dance; and all that swollen plain
Where no herb grew, became a paradise
Of flowers, and smoking grass, and blowing trees
That shook out birds and song of birds. And he
In power and beauty shining like a demon
Danced there, until that cloud that was a bird
Let fall its wings and darkened him, and hid
The shining fields. But still for long I heard
His voice, and bird-song bells about him chiming,
And knew him dancing there above that grave.

III

Said he: Thus draw your secret sorrow forth,
Whether it wear a woman's face or not;
Walk there at dusk beside that grove of trees,
And sing, and she will come. For while she haunts
Your shameful wood with all its webs and wounds
And darkly broods and works her mischief there,
No peace you'll have, but snares, and poisonous flowers
And trees in lamentation. Call her out
As memory cries the white ghost from the tomb.
Play the sharp lyric flute, for that she loves,
With topaz phrases for her vanity.

And I in answer: She is dear to me,
Dearer that in my mind she makes a dark
Of woods and rocks and thorns and venomous flowers.
What matter that I seldom see her face,
Or have her beauty never? She is there,
It is her voice I hear in cries of trees.
This may be misery, but it is blest.

Then he: And when you have her, strongly take
Her protean fiery body and lithe arms
And wailing mouth and growing vines of hair
And leaves that turn to hands, and bear her forth
Into that landscape that is rightly yours
And dig a grave for her, and thrust her in
All writhing, and so cover her with earth.
Then will the two, as should be, fuse in one.
The landscape, that was dead, will straightway shine
And sing and flower about you, trees will grow
Where desert was, water will flash from dust,
And rocks grow out in leaves. And you, this grief
Torn from your heart and planted in your world,
Will know yourself at peace.

                 But will it be, —
I asked, — as bright a joy to see that landscape
Put on diffused her wonder, sing her name,
Burn with the vital secret of her body
There locked in earth like fire, as now to have
Her single beauty fugitive in my mind?
If she is lost, will flowering rocks give peace?

And he in answer: So you have the landscape
With all her nerves and voices . . . She is yours.

Chiaroscuro: Rose

He

Fill your bowl with roses: the bowl, too, have of crystal.
Sit at the western window. Take the sun
Between your hands like a ball of flaming crystal,
Poise it to let it fall, but hold it still,
And meditate on the beauty of your existence;
The beauty of this, that you exist at all.

She

The sun goes down, — but without lamentation.
I close my eyes, and the stream of my sensation
In this, at least, grows clear to me:
Beauty is a word that has no meaning.
Beauty is naught to me.

He

The last blurred raindrops fall from the half-clear sky,
Eddying lightly, rose-tinged, in the windless wake of the sun.
The swallow ascending against cold walls of cloud
Seems winging upward over huge bleak stairs of stone.
The raindrop finds its way to the heart of the leaf-bud.
But no word finds its way to the heart of you.

She

This also is clear in the stream of my sensation:
That I am content, for the moment . . . Let me be.
How light the new grass looks with the rain-dust on it!
But heart is a word that has no meaning,
Heart means nothing to me.

He

To the end of the world I pass and back again
In flights of the mind; yet always find you here,
Remote, pale, unattached . . . O Circe too-clear-eyed,
Watching amused your fawning tiger-thoughts,
Your wolves, your grotesque apes — relent, relent!
Be less wary for once: it is the evening.

She

But if I close my eyes what howlings greet me!
Do not persuade. Be tranquil. Here is flesh

With all its demons. Take it, sate yourself.
But leave my thoughts to me.

Priapus and the Pool

. . . Was God, then, so derisive as to shape us
In the image of Priapus? . . .
(Priapus? Who was he?)
Are we never to be left by our desires,
But forever try to warm our foolish hearts
At these illusory fires?
(Priapus! . . . do you mean a terminal figure
In a garden by a sea?)
It is strange! for one so easily conceives
A quieter world, in which the flesh and dust
Are contented, do not hunger, or thirst, or lust. . .

(Priapus! . . . But, I don't know who you mean.
Do you intimate God played some trick upon us? . . .
I will tell you about a pool that I have seen!

It is very old, it is very deep and clear,
No one knows how deep it is,
The ancient trees are about it in an ancient forest,
It is a pool of mysteries!)

. . . It is puzzling, none the less, to understand
How God, if he is less or more than flesh,
Could have devised for us, walking in his garden,
The delicate imperfections of this mesh. . .

(When it is clear, the pool reflects the trees —
Look down, and you will see the flight of a bird
Among the wavering boughs! But when a breeze
Comes slowly from that wood, the pool is stirred,
And a shadow like the skeleton of a cloud
Shivers like a ghost across it, puffs and passes. . .

When it is still, the sky comes back again,
And at the fringes it reflects the grasses.)

. . . Must we always, like Priapus in a wood,
In the underbrush of our perplexities,
Pursue our maidens — pursuer and pursued? . . .

(I will not say it is not sometimes troubled!
It is very old; strange things are imaged there.
Out of its depths at night the stars have bubbled;
And into its depths maidens have hung their hair.
Leaves have fallen into it without number
And never been found again.
Birds have sung above it in the ancient trees.
And sometimes raindrops fall upon it, and then
There are rings of silver upon it, spreading and fading,
Delicately intersecting. . .
But if you return again when the sky is cloudless,
You will find it clear again, and coldly reflecting.
Reflecting the ancient trees of the ancient forest,
And the ancient leaves, ready to fall once more,
And the blue sky under the leaves, old and empty,
And the savage grasses along the shore.)

. . . Priapus, himself, was never disenchanted. . .
Why, then, did God permit us to be haunted
By this sense of imperfections? . . .

(But can a pool remember its reflections?
That is the thing that troubles me!
Does it remember the cloud that falls upon it,
Or the indignation of a tree?
Or suppose that once the image of Priapus
Fell quivering in ferocious sunshine there
As he came suddenly upon it from his forest
With fir-cones in his hair —
Would the pool, through the silences thereafter,

Recall that visitation and be stirred
Any more than it would hear and heed the laughter
Of a swinging ape, or the singing of a bird?)

. . . Was God, then, so derisive as to shape us
In the image of Priapus? . . .

(It is very old, it is very deep and clear,
No one knows how deep it is!
The ancient trees are about it in an ancient forest,
It is a pool of mysteries.)

I

The viola ceased its resonant throbbing, the violin
Was silent, the flute was still.
The voice of the singer was suddenly hushed. Only
The silence seemed to thrill

With the last echo of music, hovering over
The nodding heads of the listeners bowed and few;
And I became aware of the long light through a window,
Of the beauty of silence, of the beauty of you

Never so sharply known as when, beside you,
I dared not look to see
What thought shone out of your face, or if, like marble,
It hid its thought from me.

Never so lovely had music seemed, as when
Its lips were closed, its beauty said,
Its arrow of sound lost forever in the singing of the infinite;
And I could not turn my head,

In the motionless azure of silence that descended upon us,
Lest, somehow, you should not be there,
Or shine too much or little with the momentary beauty
Of which I was bitterly aware.

It was as if the mingled clear voices of the music,
Which the heart for a moment happily knew,
Had somehow, in the instant of their cessation,
Falling from air, become the beauty of you.

O white-flamed chord of many notes miraculously sung
In the blue universe of silence there for me:
I shall remember you thus when you are old and I am saddened;
And continents darken between us, or the silence of the sea.

II

In the moonlight I cry out, in the sunlight I bitterly exclaim,
I curse myself, turning my eyes upon my wretchedness;
Lamentable it is to be caught once more in the net of red flame;
Only in the darkness without stars I at last lie still.

I have despised the universe that could so scheme to capture
The ridiculous sparrow in its futile red net of desire.
Now I despise no more. The city shines suddenly with rapture.
The sky burns bright, the trees bend their heads in a dream.

Voices of delight rise out of the stones beneath my feet,
Azure the dusk is, the waters are singing. Wondering I stand
While the universe deepens about me. Sword-sharp-sweet,
Your voice, that I remember faintly, pierces my heart.

O light of the clear blue sky, for the first time known:
I am the solitary leaf that burns and falls
Shrivelled under your immensity, ecstatically blown
Down to the dust and darkness. Forget not me.

III

When trout swim down Great Ormond Street,
And sea-gulls cry above them lightly,
And hawthorns heave cold flagstones up
To blossom whitely,

Against old walls of houses there,
Gustily shaking out in moonlight
Their country sweetness on sweet air;
And in the sunlight,

By the green margin of that water,
Children dip white feet and shout,
Casting nets in the braided water
To catch the trout:

Then I shall hold my breath and die,
Swearing I never loved you; no,
'You were not lovely!' I shall cry,
'I never loved you so.'

IV

This is the shape of the leaf, and this of the flower,
And this the pale bole of the tree
Which watches its bough in a pool of unwavering water
In a land we never shall see.

The thrush on the bough is silent, the dew falls softly,
In the evening is hardly a sound.
And the three beautiful pilgrims who come here together
Touch lightly the dust of the ground,

Touch it with feet that trouble the dust but as wings do,
Come shyly together, are still,
Like dancers who wait, in a pause of the music, for music
The exquisite silence to fill.

This is the thought of the first, and this of the second,
And this the grave thought of the third:
'Linger we thus for a moment, palely expectant,
And silence will end, and the bird

'Sing the pure phrase, sweet phrase, clear phrase in the twilight
To fill the blue bell of the world;
And we, who on music so leaflike have drifted together,
Leaflike apart shall be whirled

'Into what but the beauty of silence, silence forever?' . . .
. . . This is the shape of the tree,
And the flower, and the leaf, and the three pale beautiful pilgrims;
This is what you are to me.

v

And already the minutes, the hours, the days,
Separate thoughts and separate ways,
Fall whitely and silently and slowly between us,
Fall between us like phantasmal rain and snow.
And we, who were thrust for an instant so sharply together,
Under changing skies to alien destinies go.

Melody heard in the midnight on the wind, —
Orange poppy of fire seen in a dream, —
Vainly I try to keep you. How the sky,
A great blue wind, with a gigantic laugh,
Scorns us apart like chaff.
Like a bird blown to sea am I.

O let us hold, amid these immensities,
The blinding blaze of the hostile infinite,
To the one clear phrase we knew and still may know:
Walls rise daily and darkly between us
But love has seen us,
Wherever we go love too must go.

Beautiful, twilight, mysterious, bird-haunted land
Seen from the ship, with the far pale shore of sand,
And the blue deep folds of hills inviting the stars to rest,
Though I shall never set foot there, nor explore you,

Nor hear your angelus of bells about me, I shall adore you
And know you still the best.

VI

Why is it, as I enter at last the panelled room,
And pause, having opened the door,
And turning my eyes from wall to wall in the gloom
Find all as it was before, —

Something, a slow, grave, passionless wave of grief,
So whelms me in silence there,
That I listen, like one who loses his only belief,
In vain to the voiceless air?

Did I expect, in my absence, that you had come —
You, or a sign from you —
To lend a voice to a beauty that else was dumb?
But alas, there is nothing new,

The room is the same, the same, there has been no change,
The table, the chairs are the same,
Nothing has altered, nothing is singing and strange,
No hover of light or flame;

And the walls have not, as in an illusion of spring,
Blossomed, nor the oaken chair
Put forth pale leaves, nor is there a bird to sing
In the mystically widened air.

Yet if you had come, and stood for an instant dreaming,
And thought my name and gone,
Leaving behind you hardly a stir of seeming,
I should no less have known;

For this would have been no longer the hated room
Whose walls imprison me now,

But the infinite heavens, and one white bough in bloom,
And a bird to sing on the bough.

VII

There is nothing moving there, in that desert of silence,
Nothing living there, not even a blade of grass.
The morning there is as silent as the evening,
The nights and days with an equal horror pass.

Nothing moving except the cold, slow shadow
Thrown on sand by a boulder, or by the cliff
Whose rock not even a lichen comes to cover,
To hide — from what? — time's ancient hieroglyph.

The sun, at noon, sings like a flaming cymbal
Above that waste: but the waste makes no reply.
In all that desolation of rock and gravel
There is no water, no answer to the sky.

Sometimes, perhaps, from other lands more happy,
A faint wind, slow, exhausted, ventures there,
And loses itself in silence, like a music.
And then — who knows? — beneath that alien air,

Which moves mysteriously as memory over
Forlorn abysms and peaks of stone and sand,
Ghosts of delight awake for a shining moment,
And all is troubled, and that desolate land

Remembers grass and flowers, and birds that sang there
Their miracles of song in lovely trees,
And waters that poured, or stood, in dreaming azure,
Praising the sky. Perhaps once more it sees

The rose, the moon, the pool, in the blue evening,
And knows that silence in which one bird will sing

Slowly and sleepily his praise of gardens.
Perhaps once more, for a moment, it remembers spring.

VIII

The mirror says: Condole not too profoundly
With the pale thing you see yourself to be.
Do not recall that dead men sleep so soundly,
Nor wanly see

The sad procession passing, as a symbol
Of your so-much-to-be-pitied state of mind.
What you would shut in a coffin is too nimble
To be confined.

Look! as you search these depths, gleefully seeing
The atomy spectral coffin darkly pass,
Far off flashes a gesture of someone fleeing;
Across the glass,

In that small circle of shadow (which I show you
Your introspective eye is) goes the ghost
Of a delightful grief which seems to know you
Yet counts you lost.

She turns her dark young beautiful head toward you,
Sombrely looks at you, and, least foreseen,
Dazzlingly smiles at you, as if to reward you —
Most generous queen! —

For the one word not said, the light betrayed not;
And turning upon the dusk is vaguely gone
Out of that world of yours she sought not, made not,
Nor would have known.

O rain of light! Ten times a day you stand here
To watch that brown-eyed ghost of delight escape,

Happy in knowing you now forever command here
That lovely shape.

IX

I shut my eyes, I try to remember you.
But as a diver plunging down through sunlight
To meet his azure shadow on the wide water
Shatters through it and is gone,
Thus I, coming suddenly upon your ghost,
See it but cannot grasp it: it is lost.
I stand in the dark and call you. I am alone.

Come to me: stand before me: turn your head
Sharply against the light: put forth one hand
Holding an amber bead: then let it fall.
Say 'It is nothing!' Slowly rise and move,
Darkened, against the open window; against the wall
Pause, with the sombre gesture that I love,
And slowly say, 'I do not understand.'

How I have seen you! How I have drunk of you!
Now, when I most would have you, you escape.
Thus is your mouth? or thus? I do not know.
But see, I ignore you now, bewildering shape,
Flee in the darkness from you . . . And you come
Laughing before me, saying, 'I love you so!'

X

Now over the grass you come,
Gravely you come with a slow step
Into the azure world I call my heart:
Tardily you approach me.

Butterflies of the sun flicker about you —
Who could have foreseen it?

Moths of the moon at your finger-tips
Melt like flakes of snow.

Is it not too late that you come?
Are you not merely a ghost?
Behold, before you once speak my name,
Wind whirls us apart like leaves.

Never again, after this dream, shall I have peace.
In my heart is nothing but the crying of snow.
The grass over which I seek you is white with frost.
You have left upon it no footstep.

I place my most secret thought
Like a bough of magnolia
Where perhaps you will find it and remember.
It withers, and you do not come.

XI

Suddenly, as I gaze at the sombre land in the picture,
The bridge, the enchanted stream, the long, long watery plain,
And the dark wood, and the small far houses, and the blue hills
Flashing like dolphins under a light like rain;

Look! The picture has opened! the sounds come in,
Broad, rich streaming, in the late light of the sun,
The whole wide land is a flood of mysterious sound! . . .
O this is the land where you have gone,

Your voice floats up to me from that bridge, I hear
The tiny words out of dusk like a gnat-song come —
'Stay! stay where you are! You will be happier there!
I will at last, perhaps, come home!'

O voice, crying the ineffable, face invisible,
Beauty intangibly gone like a tracery out of the sky!

Come back! . . . But the window closes. Bridge, stream, houses,
      hills,
Are silent. Small is the picture. None stirs in the world save I.

XII

There was an island in the sea
That out of immortal chaos reared
Towers of topaz, trees of pearl,
For maidens adored and warriors feared.

Long ago it sunk in the sea;
And now, a thousand fathoms deep,
Sea-worms above it whirl their lamps,
Crabs on the pale mosaic creep.

Voyagers over that haunted sea
Hear from the waters under the keel
A sound that is not wave or foam;
Nor do they only hear, but feel

The timbers quiver, as eerily comes
Up from the dark an elfin singing
Of voices happy as none can be,
And bells an ethereal anthem ringing.

Thereafter, where they go or come,
They will be silent; they have heard
Out of the infinite of the soul
An incommunicable word;

Thereafter, they are as lovers who
Over an infinite brightness lean:
'It is Atlantis!', all their speech;
'To lost Atlantis have we been.'

XIII

See, as the carver carves a rose,
A wing, a toad, a serpent's eye,
In cruel granite, to disclose
The soft things that in hardness lie,

So this one, taking up his heart,
Which time and change had made a stone,
Carved out of it with dolorous art,
Labouring yearlong and alone,

The thing there hidden — rose, toad, wing?
A frog's hand on a lily pad?
Bees in a cobweb — ? No such thing!
A girl's head was the thing he had,

Small, shapely, richly crowned with hair,
Drowsy, with eyes half closed, as they
Looked through you and beyond you, clear
To something farther than Cathay:

Saw you, yet counted you not worth
The seeing, thinking all the while
How, flower-like, beauty comes to birth;
And thinking this, began to smile.

Medusa! For she could not see
The world she turned to stone and ash.
Only herself she saw, a tree
That flowered beneath a lightning-flash.

Thus dreamed her face — a lovely thing,
To worship, weep for, or to break.
Better to carve a claw, a wing,
Or, if the heart provide, a snake.

XIV

Fade, then, — die, depart, and come no more —
You, whose beauty I abhor —
Out of my brain
Take back your voice that lodges there in pain,
Tear out your thousand golden roots
That thrust their tentacles in my heart
But bear no fruits.

Now like an exquisite but sterile tree
Your beauty grows in me
And feeds on light
Its lifted arms of leaves and blossoms white.
Come birds, come bees,
And marry flower with flower that it may bear
Like other trees.

Or else let hatred like a lightning come,
And flash, and strike it numb,
And strew on rock
These singing leaves, that, singing, seem to mock.
Thus let my heart once more be naked stone,
Bare under wind and hard with grief,
And leave not in a single crevice
A single leaf.

JOHN DETH

A METAPHYSICAL LEGEND

*

I: The Star-Tree Inn

1

John Deth and his doxies came to town.
By the weeping-cross they sank them down.
They were in rags, in rags was he.
A branch of blossom, across his knee,
Spun, in the drifting smoke of the moon,
A hawthorn sweetness. It was June.
'Go now, you, Millicent Piggistaile,'
Said Deth, 'to find an inn, and ale.
You, — Juliana Goatibed, —
Carve the black rock, and rest your head.
This night, with Millicent I lie;
You, like the mind, once more put by.
Hurry! and at the Star-Tree tavern
Rouse the musicians; have the seven
Fiddles playing, and devil's drum,
To jig to . . . Tell them that I come.'

2

Then, in the smoke of the moonlight, rose
Bitter of mouth and weary, those
Tall gypsies: she whose eyes were flame,
And she who bore the shameful name:
The golden-haired, who loved her lord,
And the dark demon, who abhorred.

Pat-patter went they; and the moon
Dipped in a cloud and they were gone.
And Deth, with chin in palm, sat on,
Staring; and in his musing saw
The crablike moon thrust out a claw,
Wave at a sea-weed cloud, and swim
In a blue pool; then dive and dim.

3

Above the churchyard wall he leaned.
Under a wet stone, lichen-greened,
The cricket sang. How slept they now, —
Madeline, of the golden brow;
Elaine, whose eyes were swift to speak;
And Petronilla, of satin cheek?
The laughing mouth, the greedy hand —
What found they now? Deth raised his wand,
And held its flowers above the dead.
'Take this — and this — and this — ' he said;
With each quick hiss a blossom fell
Softly in moonlight, slow and pale,
Upon the dark ungarnered grass;
And lo: each grave became of glass;
Each coffin was of crystal bright;
Wherein glowed sadly a blue light.

4

'Elaine, how sleep you? Madeline,
Where works the worm whose name is sin?
What dreams hard Petronilla, there,
Under her cobweb tent of hair?'
He leaned, he stared, he laughed a little.
Bare under glass the bones lay brittle,
The bones lay mute; but at his word
In the queer light they loosely stirred;

The jointed fingers clenched and turned;
The deep eye-sockets filmed and burned;
Over black rib and pelvis went
A flush of breathing color, blent
Of pearl and Shiraz, fiery mesh,
Dim heart, and insubstantial flesh;
And Petronilla touched her hair;
And Madeline opened eyes, to stare
Upward, beneath the coffin-pane;
And softly, betwixt the two, Elaine
Woke, weeping . . . 'Ah! you remember — wake
Once more — to anguish — for my sake? . . .
You'd live once more, to dance with me, —
To kiss my claw, — to feel my knee? . . .
Sleep, now! but at the stroke of ten
Run to the Star-Tree Inn again:
You'll have, before this night is past,
Your one dance more; but this the last.'
He leaned, he stared, he laughed a little.
There under glass the bones lay brittle,
Lay still; and softly died the light
That made those coffins greenly bright.

5

Under the moon the yard lay dark,
With tilted moss-grown stones, to mark
Where slept in earth his weeping slaves:
A wilderness of rusted graves.
He twirled his wand. He limped, he moved
Beyond the lych-gate, loathed and loved.
St. Mary's laboring clock he saw;
Measuring hard the double law
Of life and death; life and death;
Dust and breath; dust and breath
This too would end; would sink and pass,
Like other dead things, under grass.

The choirs, humming in candle-light,
Stirring carved aisles with scented white,
Would pace, with golden books, away;
And the stone tower be sunk in clay.
Darkly dreaming, he caused to fall
One pebble from the rotting wall.
He felt it strike, in his deep brain;
And shrank, as one who shrinks from pain.

6

And turning, so, he heard begin,
On throbbing air, a violin
Prelusive; then a ticking drum. . .
'So! the musicians now have come,
And I must hurry; they wait for me. . .
Be healed now, ancient foot and knee!
Be strong and young, poor bird-claw hand,
And fit to hold this youthful wand! . . .
Heart, be heartless! . . . Dropping rags,
Be burning satin! . . . You, my hags,
Be queens for me, your wretched king!
God hides his eyes behind a wing.'
And stately then, and wrapped in flame,
King Deth before the tavern came
And angrily smote the hated door
Beneath the magic sign that bore
The bright-eyed Tree, whose branches shone
With winking star and staring moon.
'Come now,' he cried, 'and bid me in, —
All you who groan at life and sin!
Queen Millicent, and Parson Prude!
Queen Juliana, and Doctor Lewd! —
You, Farmer Trufit! with your dame
And silly son and daughter lame! —
You, Gardy Finch, with your two girls
Whose small white necks are crisp with curls. . .

Open the door! For John Deth comes
To beat his feet to the beating drums.'

7

Then, as the Inn door opened, he
Proud as a god stept merrily
With golden feet and wand of thorn,
Dark ivy fringing eyes of scorn.
Barlyng, the Host, before him stood,
Ruddy Silenus carved of wood,
His ringed hands plump upon his paunch.
'Welcome!' he sang, 'a friend so staunch!
Come in, and sing, and dance, and drink,
And, if you like' (a watery wink)
'Make love, among the trilling glasses
To our poor simpering country lasses!
Take whom you will! Be welcomed, lord!
By Barlyng, your old host, a bawd.'
The girl-faced flute-player tipped his flute;
And while the rout stood chilled and mute,
Blew across it a gleeful note
Like rainy eve in blackbird's throat;
And straight the dancers seemed to float,
Beating the air with feet like wings:
The fiddlers struck the buzzing strings,
And sang, and nodded polished skulls,
While round them frolicked the frumps and trulls.
The Bishop passed them with a caper,
Waving aloft a learnèd paper.
Behind him tripped the sad-eyed vicar
Who beamed on Millicent, the liquor
Seething his blood to frothy ichor.
'Come, Millicent, my spangled queen!
Come thump your shivering tambourine —
And dance me to the realm unseen!'
But Millicent gave his arm a shove:

'No, no! it's not the dead I love!
This youth I'll take; his lips are sweet;
I'll ripen him for a winding-sheet;
I'll wrap him for the Paraclete!'
He kicked the drummer's brass a clang,
And swore. Queen Juliana sang
With far-fixed eyes, red thumbs on hips,
Treading a measure, while her lips
Grew savage; and then led away
Into the dark, to kiss and play,
Old Farmer Trufit's gaping son,
The smiling simple-hearted one.
'My lord,' the rosy Bishop cried,
'Take me! Long since I should have died!
And in this treatise I have read
That flesh, corrupt, no sooner dead,
Grows up in beauty like a flower!'
'Bide, then,' said Deth, 'until that hour.'
'But I am tired, and I would die!
Be merciful, and let me lie
In earth, among your blessed host,
Forgetful of the Holy Ghost.
When slowlier the thin blood flows
Than sap in brown November rose; —
The house of life a dwindling storm
Of sunset clouds, and not so warm —
When ice creeps over heart and eye —
What use to live, lord? Let me die!'
'Dance, then; and you may come with me.'

8

The clock struck ten. And those pale three
Who slept beneath untended grass
In coffins blown of lucid glass,
Came laughing through the open door,
Joined hands, and danced across the floor

To Deth, and kissed him. Madeline
In scarlet gown and slippers green;
Petronilla in amethyst, —
A white owl winking on her wrist;
And last, in black, demure Elaine
Bearing a peacock-silver train.
Madeline touched, ere he could speak,
The frosty sparkle on his cheek.
Pale Petronilla kissed the hand
That held the many-flowered wand.
Elaine was shy, Elaine was grave.
'My lord!' she said, 'such joy you have! —
What pleasure can you have in me?' . . .
Deth smiled, and took her on his knee,
And kissed her mouth. Her eyes grew dim
As shyly she looked up at him.

9

'Of all the lovely dead,' said Deth,
'That weep twixt here and Nazareth;
Of all who once had shining hair
But now in dungeon lie and stare
And, if they dream of braiding, must
Consign the braiding unto dust;
Unthinking, unremembering, —
Or stirred by bird-song in the spring:
No, there is none so fair as you;
A mouth so sweet I never knew. . .
Look up — lift up your eyes, Elaine — !
That down them I may pass again
Into that sad eternal light
Where still you treasure, phantom-bright,
Our night of love, your bridal night!'
She murmured softly, like one chidden:
'My lord, I did as I was bidden. . .
Would you have less? Or is there more?'

Deth's eyes strove darkly to explore
Her eyes. 'Ah! — there I see you still —
There, as at night I climbed the hill.
Clearly, as in a crystal ball,
I saw you, behind door and wall.
What black dream flowered in your brain?
What wormy vision, deep Elaine?
That you uncoiled, then coiled again,
In the small room, your shining hair?
What made you lift the flame, and stare
Into your eyes so long a while —
Your mirrored eyes — and sadly smile?
Did you hear footsteps on the hill?
And hearing footsteps were you still?
Did they come subtly up your blood, —
As there in candlelight you stood — :
The soft, the whispering, gold-shod feet
That nearer, clearer, louder, beat,
So loud at last they made you start —
Lest they should tread upon your heart? . . .
And tread they did; and tread they did.'
'As you are bidden, so you bid,
My lord,' Elaine said; 'Flower and bird
Fall down before the instant word. . .
My hair uncoiled I coiled again
Because I heard your summons plain;
Yet though I loved you, lord, I grieved:
And gladly longer would have lived.'
Each gravely smiled; and smiling still
Each kissed the other's smile; until
Their sad eyes closed, as in excess
Of dark, unhappy, blessedness.

10

But Petronilla, owl on wrist,
Laughed down upon them as they kissed:

'See how these lovers keep their tryst
With string and cymbal loud about them
And coffin-maidens come to rout them!
Is this our lord who rules the dead?
And have his lips too often fed
Upon the living, that he wakes
This coffin-girl, Elaine, and takes
Her insubstantial heart again?'
She laughed; and as she laughed, Elaine
With opened eyes stood up; and tall
Behind her, Deth, against the wall
In scarlet rising, seemed to change
Into something still and strange:
Clawlike again became the hand
That stiffly held the flowering wand.
'What Petronilla says is true!
Go now, Elaine! I've done with you.
Go mark your victims with a kiss
And dance them out, while cymbals hiss,
Dance them down the moonlit street
To opened grave and winding-sheet.
In the beginning is the Word!
You, Petronilla, with your bird,
Lead out the Bishop, make him spring
Like a rheumatic goat, and sing
Such carols as will wake the dead
To laughter in their rooty bed.
You, Barlyng! Open now your door —
You'll fleece poor travelers no more;
This night I'll cancel out your score;
Come with me — dance! Here's Juliana
To take your hand and sing hosanna!'
'My lord — ' said Barylng, 'I! your friend!
And must I come so soon to end?
Is this, at last, a just reward?
Have mercy on your servant, lord!'
'What words are these — unjust and just?

Sing now! By midnight you are dust.'
Deth grazed the angry brow; and straight
Old Barlyng, shrinking, seemed elate
And wildly laughed, his face gone white,
His eyes become divinely bright.
He kicked his heels on the petaled floor
And spun, and opened wide the door.

11

In wavering row the rout came dancing;
Now backwards drawn, and now advancing;
And Deth, with delicate wand, caressed
Each, as he came, on brow or breast:
And those, foreseeing, who wept before
Went lightly laughing through the door —
Old Trufit and his nodding dame
And silly son and daughter lame:
Gardy Finch; and his sweet girls
Whose small white necks were crisp with curls;
Juliana and aproned Barlyng;
The toothless Vicar; and his darling
Millicent, the spangled queen,
Beating aloft her tambourine;
And after them a score of others;
Fair boys and girls; and smiling mothers;
And last of all, with Doctor Lewd,
Elaine; who, weeping as he wooed, —
Led out in his obscene embrace, —
Covered with shameful hands her'face.
Then stepped the drummer with his drum;
The fiddlers fiddling Kingdom Come;
The staring flutist, short of breath;
After them all, gaunt-shadowed Deth.

12

Above his head the Star-Tree swung.
The ragged chorus now was sung —
'Day of wrath, upon that day,
When (as David and Sibyl say,)
Time, dishonored, comes to clay! . . .'
'Dies Iræ!' whispered Deth.
Upon the Argus tree his breath
Rose like a vapor to deflower;
And softly fell an elfin shower
Of tinily winking stars and moon
Upon his cloak, and dimmed as soon
As snowflakes die in April air;
Twinkled, and left the Star-Tree bare.
'Day of wrath — upon that day!'
With angry claw he waved away
The Star-Tree sign, the Star-Tree Inn;
And laughed, to see his feet begin
Themselves the dance so deeply learned:
The dance of bones that beat and burned.

13

The lych-gate green was opened wide.
The dancers rocked from side to side.
Fairy lights burned in the grass.
The churchyard now was roofed with glass.
And down a crystal stairway, bright
With goblin candle and glow-worm light,
Under the ground the dancers went:
Juliana, and Millicent,
And Parson Prude and Doctor Lewd
With small Elaine whom still he wooed;
Gardy Finch; rapt Madeline
Bearing a light beneath her chin;
The Bishop hale; tall Petronilla,

Who loudly sang the *'dies illa';*
Two by two Deth saw them pass
Under the catacomb of glass;
Watched them wind far down, and go
Among the cells, in honeyed row,
Till each had found his crystal bed
And stretched his length and propped his head:
Each with his hands upon his breast,
There, singing still, they lay at rest.

'Horn of wonders, scattering sound
Through all dead regions underground!'
Deth raised once more the clawlike hand
That bore the moon-white-flowered wand;
And held its blossoms above the dead.
'Take this! and this! and this!' he said.
With each sharp hiss a petal dropped
In withered grass. The singing stopped.
The crystal roof, the lights, grew dimmer.
And nought was left but a wannish glimmer
Where Petronilla, with upward stare,
A last time, drowsily, touched her hair;
And Elaine lay weeping; and Madeline
Breathed out the light that warmed her chin.

14

Above the churchyard wall Deth leaned,
Counting the tombstones, carved and greened,
In pallid rows; whence slowly came
Those two; the one with eyes of flame,
And she who bore the shameful name —
The golden-haired, who loved her lord,
And the wise demon, who abhorred.
Loud-whirring wings in Mary's tower
Foretold the striking of the hour.
High up, the hidden small-voiced bell

Shook out twelve silver birds, that fell
Slowly to earth on whizzing wings
Among the churchyard whisperings.
And lo, commingled with the ringing,
Were heard five ghostly voices singing:
'*The quick to church, the dead to grave,*
We ring: such usage let us have.
Who here, therefore, doth damn, or swear,
Or quarrel, though no blood appear:
Who wears a spur, o'erturns a bell,
Or, being unskilful, spoils a peal;
He'll sixpence pay for every crime,
To warn him 'gainst another time.
Let all in friendship hither come
While Treble sings to Thundering Tom;
And since bells are for recreation,
Let's ring, and fall to admiration.'

II: Millicent Piggistaile

1

'My lord,' said Millicent, 'now rest
Your head on this exhausted breast,
This breast that is a ruined world.
Here rocks decay, and seas are whirled
To nothingness; here God is not;
And all things living are forgot.
Dark Juliana, on her tomb,
Angrily stares against her doom;
There, like the robin, leans her head
To hear the whispers of the dead:
She loves you not. Come, lord, and rest
Your head on this exhausted breast.'

Under the churchyard yew they lay,
In shade, those two. Not far away
Dark Juliana stretched herself
Along a narrow marble shelf,
Watching, with wide unfathomed eye,
The bat at caper. . . 'Come and lie
In this cold grass, your arm above me,
Once more, and tell me that you love me.
Here, in this breast, all things are dead.
All is at peace. Here make your bed.'
'This night,' said Deth, 'I lie with you:
Our deathless sorrow we renew.
I'll see once more, through your deep face,
The horror huge of ruined space —
Where all that grew no longer grows;
The tomb, wherein the whirlwind blows.
There will I lie! there slowly thrust
Dead roots, to crack that sterile dust.'
'Look deep, my lord! And do you see
The whirlwind-besomed tomb in me?
This is not flesh! This is a world
In which no living seed is furled;
No anguished root, to threaten spring;
No bough, to bear; no bird, to sing.
Come now, my lord; and be a tree;
And grow with pitiless roots in me.'

2

The sidling crab-moon plunged itself
In weedy cloud. And from her shelf
Among the tombs the demon saw
The silver-jointed awkward claw
Wave at a vapor and withdraw.
The churchyard drowsed, without a breath;
Save there, where Millicent and Deth,
In the black yew-tree shadow, strove

To warm in bone and rock their love.
There Millicent lay back, and pressed
Deth's scythe-sharp chin against her breast
As though to cut, with that bright bone,
Into her heart of hollow stone.
'Now, lord, at last we are alone, —
Alone in all the world,' she said:
'There are no living and no dead.
The graves, that were your torment, gone,
All graves at last become but one;
And that grave shapes itself in me
For you to grow on like a tree.
Grow here! Here thrust and knot your roots.
Tower to leaves and flowers and fruits!
God hides his eyes behind his wing
While we perform this sacred thing.'

From the dark labor of his love
Deth rested then, and did not move.
Downward he brooded on that face
Below his own, which now like space
Grew vast and meaningless and strange
And eyeless. Then he felt the change
Come upward through him; cold and deep;
Like clotting water felt it drip
Into his heart; there saplike spread.
On the black stone he dropped his head.

3

And now the moon-white petalled wand,
Fallen down from the rootlike hand,
Alone in darkness breathed and glowed
And writhed its living leaves, and showed,
Like a live thing of wounded light
That wreathed its anguish, how the night
Emptied itself of shape and sound,

A horror deep that had no bound;
Within whose glimmering hollow was
An island of tall churchyard grass;
And there, upthrust in dripping gloom,
A black, dishonored, cracking tomb.
And on the tomb there grew a tree
Which moved its white roots rapidly
Now here, now there, from side to side,
Like vipers blind that struck and pried
Over the stone, until a crack
Was found upon the vaulted back;
Wherethrough a taproot whistling thrust
Into the sighing vault of dust
And swelled and reddened and rived apart
The aching stones and pierced the heart;
While hissed the other roots, a crowd,
And fed and throve. Then cried aloud
The injured tomb: 'Your roots have found
The core of anguish, underground!
My inward walls they search and scrape
And I am blest! . . . My lord, what shape
Take you above? And do you grow?'
The dark tree answered: 'Grief I know,
And feed on; my increasing leaves
Are syllables of one who grieves.
Swiftly I grow! My branches turn
Like burning boughs that as they burn
Twist upward through the twisting fire
And feed upon it as on desire.'
The tomb made answer to the tree:
'Queen Juliana — where is she? . . .
Does she, like Sybil, read her book
Angrily, — and forbear to look?
Or does she watch the furious root
That brings its misery to fruit?'
The dark tree clashed its leaves and said:
'Queen Juliana preens her head

Beneath my bough, against a knee
Of gnarly root twixt you and me.
She stares and dreams. Her chin is propped
Upon her palms. Her book is dropped.'
'What is it that she stares at? What
Is that she dreams of?' 'Things forgot
By you and me. All hideous things.
Root-rived mouths; and festered wings.
Petronilla, whose hair is rotten;
Elaine, who weeps alone, forgotten;
And Madeline; whose breasts are gnawed
By the sharp worm that was a bawd.'

4

Five chains of moonlight shot the gloom
Of swelling leaves; and showed the tomb
Wrapt every way with roots, that gript
The falling stones; and slid and slipt
Through grinning cracks, as though to smother
And coil and bruise and crush each other
In slippery knots convulsed. And there
Among live roots that made a chair
Dark Juliana sat to stare
A gold crown winking in her hair;
Beneath her chin strong knuckles folded;
Eyes black; and forehead fury-moulded.
Her opened book that lay in grass
Mirrored the crab-moon like a glass
And a wheel of cobweb; staring down
She saw her knuckles, saw her crown;
And under, moon-shot, swirling, dense,
Swollen each second more immense,
The frightful tree, world-bearing tree,
The tree that cracked infinity.
And now she watched the slow roots tighten
Against the shrinking tomb and brighten

With what they fed on. Now she heard
Out of the tomb, word mixed with word,
A windy murmur, sighed complaint,
Deep underground, confused and faint;
As though, far down, the host of dead,
Imprisoned in a mighty bed,
Cried out in sleep, or babbled words
Misshapen, like sleep-charmèd birds
Who feel the snake among them pass
And dare not wake. And now with glass
That wilderness was paved. And there
Came running up the crystal stair,
Naked and small, with rose-wreathed hair,
Miriam Finch, who bore a light
And thrust it against the leafy night
And 'Father!' echoing called, and then
Turned, and fled down deep stairs again. . .
Then all grew dark. And through the book
Queen Juliana leaned to look;
And saw, far down, a long root reach
And wrap the child, who without speech,
Let fall the light. Then spoke the tomb:
'My lord, strange voices fill this gloom;
Make haste; unpeople my deep womb;
For I am tired, I would be still!'
'Voices? Then let them have their will.'

5

Then spoke the tomb: 'Thus ends the world!
Now, with the last of roots uncurled,
You hale away these ghosts from me. . .
Now I am still. Now buds the tree,
That soon will strangely bloom, and bear
A fiery world in phantom air. . .
Make haste, great tree! And break me, now.
Shatter my vault for bud and bough.

Let the last breath of my foul bosom
Rise bubbling through you, break in blossom,
And magically bloom and blanch,
A moon, upon your topmost branch! . . .'

The tree no answer made. No bird
Among its maze of boughs was heard.
But it grew vast. Its massed leaves shook.
And Juliana, in her book,
Saw how it raged, a world in size,
And filled with thrusting boughs the skies;
Vast boughs that leaned as if to breach
The glassy infinite, and reach
Across the ridgy ice of time
To the vague God who hung sublime,
Like a great cloud, enfolding space,
With bright wings tall before his face,
Unmoving, rapid, rapt in light.
And a soft roaring filled the night
Of boughs. A whistling wind came through them;
A wave of chaos blind, and blew them;
Till buds of planets winked and shone
And burned the boughs, and fiercely blown,
Opened enormous staring flowers,
And dropped hot petals, blazing showers,
A rain of flame. The demon saw
The tightening roots, a griffon's claw,
Crush the weak tomb; it sighed; it spoke
'Peace!' and was lost; a puff of smoke
Thinned from the clutching roots, was gone;
Nothing but powder left of stone.

Then cracked the tree. The branches split.
Ripe moons and pale suns swelled in it
And bore it over. The branches sagged
With heavy stars that blazing dragged
The treetop down. And swift, and strange,

The tree itself began to change:
Shriveled: along each palsied limb
Crawled a flame: the suns grew dim,
And dwindled showering; bubble moon
Burst, and hovered in sparkles down;
The leaves exhaled, the small tree shrunk,
Twisted and wizened, writhed and sunk,
In a soft blaze like tinsel melting;
Till nought was left but a flimsy pelting
Of firefly glints on the brow and hair
Of dark Juliana who brooded there . . .
It died, like snow in April air.

6

Then all was still. No sound there was.
The cricket slept in dripping grass.
Nought was breathing, nought was stirring:
Until from the ivy came a whirring
And waking wings in Mary's tower
Foretold the striking of the hour.
Slowly, the little small-voiced bell
Shook out four silver birds, that fell
Softly to grass, on whizzing wings,
Among the churchyard whisperings.
Dark Juliana closed her eyes
And nodded among her mysteries;
While there, beneath the churchyard yew,
In chilly shade they stirred, those two,
And heavily rose, as if from sleep
Of passion fathomlessly deep.
'Come Millicent — my doxy queen!
Come upward from the vast obscene.
Swim swiftly upward — breathe; escape
The fetid tomb; resume your shape!
Day creeps; and Juliana sleeps;
Deep in her sleep the demon weeps

For us, and for all suffering things —
Root-rived mouths, and rat-gnawed wings;
The broken tomb; the phantom tree;
Herself, a part of you and me.
Look, how the spasm takes her face
For dreaming deep of God's disgrace!'

Queen Millicent no answer made,
But palely rose in the yew-tree shade;
Among the pallid tombs they stept,
And watched, where Juliana slept,
And in her slumber shook and wept.
So brooding stood. Then with quick wand,
Gently he touched the sleeping hand;
And Juliana sucked her breath
Opening wing-filled eyes at Deth;
Profound, estranged. 'And has day come?
And are you from your wanderings home?'
Deth answered: 'Home from tomb and tree.
The day has come.' They turned, those three:
Out of the churchyard darkly went
Juliana and Millicent:
And Deth, in twilight, loitering after,
Stifled in heart a rabid laughter;
Insane, the raging laugh of grief;
Hysteria of the withered leaf.

III: The Falling of the Birds

1

'Come birds! Come chirp, come laugh, come sing!
Come goudspink, whirl your flimsy wing!
Come teewhaup cry, come nightingale
And mourn for Millicent Piggistaile!
Eagle and heron, blackbird, lark,

Hurrying sparrow, and booming hawk —
Come, stumbling owl, and blink and stare
Caught in the sunlight's blinding hair!
Tuwhoo cry out! red robin come,
Where Deth's hand flings your daily crumb!'

In a sun-shot flash of powdery rain
Deth singing sped down Dead Man's Lane,
Where murdered warriors, long since dead,
Lay bones akimbo, heel to head.
The spider's trembling web he broke
That burned in air twixt thorn and oak;
The rain-bright wheel sunk softly, broken,
The spider swung, with no word spoken;
And Deth, with dripping wand, went on
While birds above him sang for dawn.
'See how they mount,' he cried, 'and fill
The sky with flickering wings, until
High up a swarm of gnats they seem,
Waver, and hover and flash, and gleam
And weave, like motes in a fever-dream! . . .
Come birds! Come cry! Come moan! Come rage!
Come weep that heaven is but a cage!'

2

He was in rags; a pilgrim, he
Sang down the deep lane merrily,
Struck off, with whizzing wand, a leaf,
Shook showers of drops, and hid his grief;
While murdered men, behind his back,
Moved tongues of clay, and clucked 'Alack,
That Deth must take the harmless birds,
Who have but song, who have no swords!
See how they come, poor darlings, come
To sing their souls out and be dumb!
Go back, bright feathers! Eyes of light,

Be hooded, lest you're clay to-night!
Look not beneath the serpent's lid
To see what seed-pearl there is hid:
What blood-drop stone, what topaz clear,
Or frozen amethystine tear!
It is the stone of light that kills:
The stone that thrills: the stone that stills.'
The red sun sent a stinging shaft
Through the wet boughs; wherein Deth laughed
And whirled his rags, to skip and frisk
With a scudding shadow, ribbed, grotesque;
Three oak-leaves tore; one twig was shattered;
A hundred scarlet drops were scattered;
A bee cried out in a foxglove bell,
Both slain in the grass; and Deth stood still.
'Stoop, birds! Stoop, feather-brains! and say —
Shall I come as bird or snake to-day?
You, Miriam Robin, on your nest —
Warming five eggs beneath your breast, —
Command now: how would you like me best?
With beak and claw? Or were it better
With rainbow rings and eyes that glitter?'
Lifting a rag he flashed a wing
And hawklike screamed and swerved, to fling
A gliding shadow. Winged and blue
It hung with sickle edge, and grew
Enormous, roaring, shook a cry
From Miriam Robin, dull of eye —
'Pity! Pity! Not I, not I!'
Deth laughed; and coiled him like a spring.
The laugh became a hiss; the wing
Wizened, and winked with rainbow scale;
By quivering primrose slid the tail;
The eyes were sparkles; flat the head;
Deep the thin mouth; the tongue of thread
Flicked out and in; and, hushed, the bird, —
Lids drooped, beak open, — spoke no word.

Then croaked the dead men underground —
'Sing, Miriam, sing!' . . . The bright snake wound
On a gray-footed ivy-stem;
Dropped head and opal diadem;
The tiny eyes, red seeds of fire,
Unwinking, glowed their shrewd desire.
And dead men clucked their tongues of clay:
'Sing, Miriam, sing! and fly away!'
Miriam whispered: 'The eyes are red:
Smiling, they leave the smiled-on dead.
Poppy, let fall one silken petal
Upon the jeweled head to settle!
One petal drop! your hour is come!
Die now, and save me from the worm!'
Gauzy-throated, the poppy sung —
'Spare Miriam, lord! for she is young!'
One petal dropped. The scarlet hood
Mantled the cunning head like blood.

3

With myriad voices grass was filled.
A beetle clicked. A cricket shrilled.
A host of ants, deep underground,
Murmured in earth a mournful sound,
Sang slowly, rolling grains of sand.
The scarlet eft, with scarlet hand
Clutching a twig, and small dark eye,
Under an oak-leaf ticked his cry.
And buttercups, like sea-surf swinging,
Their countless gentle gold-bells ringing,
Tinkled for gnats and tolled for bees
And chimed for dragon-flies. Vast trees
Flung down their blossoms green that fell
Roaring through air, each clanging bell
Quenched in the grass. White moth on thistle

Fanned with his wings and made them whistle . . .
And Deth, deep-sunk in the surf of tune
That seethed the flowering sea of June,
Drunk with the voices, bells, and zithers,
Passionate choir of all that withers,
Flickered his tongue and arched his head
From Miriam's nest and Miriam dead.
Horned mouth and jeweled pate he thrust
Through twanging web and lichen crust;
A red-furred spider caught, that trilled
Loud as a fly; then all was stilled.

4

'Come birds! Come cry! Come moan! Come rage!
Come weep that heaven is but a cage!'
Deth, on the hilltop, flung his cry
Hard as a flint against the sky.
In grass he sat. The birds, a cloud,
Darkened the hill. Their wings were loud.
No voices had they — tongues were still;
Like falling leaves they touched the hill;
Winnowed the grass with fanning wings;
Among the daisies fell in rings;
While Deth, unsmiling, never stirring
Amid the fluttering and the whirring
That blew his rags and fanned his face,
Sat stonelike, staring, in that place.
Between his knees in nodding grass
A golden cage of osier was;
Shaped like a bell, no bird inside;
The door of osier opened wide.
This twice he turned. With nodding head,
Sadly, at last: 'Speak, birds!' he said.
'Miriam on her nest lies dead.
Five eggs beneath her breast grow cold.

This is the day of wrath foretold.
Who knows my secret? . . . Whose bright eyes
Have seen in the wood the light that flies?
That bird who tells me, he shall have
This cage of osier, he shall live;
Think well! for all who do not know
Shall melt upon this hill like snow.
Within my humming web are heard
Caught worlds that cry. What means a bird?'
Bubbled the clay in Dead Man's Lane:
'For him, within whose net complain
Suns that whistle and moons that die,
What means, alas, the sparrow's cry?
Miriam on her nest lies dead,
A poppy petal hoods her head.
The wormfly dances in the sun
And sings; her sexton work is done. . .'
'Think birds! Think deeply! Think! Recall!
One lives, one only, of you all!'

                              5

Tranced were the birds in tree and grass.
Their lively eyes were still as glass.
They looked at Deth. They hunched. They stared.
Their bright wings drooped; they all despaired.
'Come, birds!' cried Deth. 'Can no one speak? . . .
You there, Mag Oolie — feather-beak!
You — bloody-claws! — round-amber-eyes!
Old howlet, you who look so wise —
Tuwhoo! cry out, and sing it plain —
Where flies the light in wind or rain?
Where's beauty fled? Where's brightness lying?
Where runs the nymph with tresses flying? . . .
What hollow oak-tree hides her now
Till twilight? By what singing bough
Leans she her head to twist her hair

And stands, with bright eyes, listening there? . . .
Speak, owl!' . . .

                         Then spoke the owl: 'Tuwhoo! . . .
Last night by China Wall I flew.
I saw Confucius lapt in red
Among the brown Cataian dead.
"Beauty is in the mind," he said —
"Beauty is in the eternal way."
The lips that spoke were deep in clay.
. . . Rank grass above his bones was tangled.
Wild herds above him pawed and jangled.
The Tree of Heaven pierced him through
With one deep pillar-root. It grew
With arrowy leaves; twelve fathom high;
With massy column toward the sky.
"Beauty is in the mind!" said he —
Five carrion crows were in the tree.
One of them slipped and gave a caw.
And there I fed. And there I saw
A horde of phantoms pale, like waves
Break softly on that land of graves.
Rapid and soundless lap and glide;
Over the wall; to deserts wide:
Through gorges; among grassy seas;
By jingling streets; and under trees
And into hovels and out again,
Through walls, with neither sound nor pain.
Your slaves, my lord! Cataians dead. . .
"Beauty is in the mind!" he said —
In seven silver bubbles broke
The clay-bound syllables he spoke.
The moonlight, white and cold as snow
On Tree of Heaven and carrion crow,
Made all seem strange. — The fool said "Caw!" —
And the rapt carrion answered "Law!" '

6

The owl was still. Then cried Moll Hern —
'Is beauty, thus, a thing to learn? . . .
No, lord! It is a thing to see. —
Thrice has the vision come to me!
It is a golden eel that weaves
Twined light beneath dark water-leaves.
By Nile Bank I have seen it twice:
And once beneath Kamchatka's ice!'

Low laughter flew among the birds
Derisive of the heron's words:
Of golden minnow; golden gnat;
And jeweled frog; and silver rat;
And pearly newt; and ruby ant;
'And ivory fish!' cried cormorant,
'Inlaid with gold!' 'And silver lark,'
The merlin laughed; 'a pretty mark
For sluggish claw or greedy beak!'
'And golden mouse!' said owl, 'with squeak
Melodious, shining soft and sleek!'
They laughed, they ruffed their throats and crests,
And shook their tails and puffed their breasts;
And nudged each other with their wings
And chuckled throaty obscene things
And trilled and clucked with mirth-shut eyes.
But Deth was sad. 'Is none more wise
Than plump Mag Oolie, skinny Hern?
Let Whistling Dick now have his turn.
Think well, poor thrush! and be more sage
Than these, if you would win the cage.'

7

Then sang the thrush: 'A wasp-filled thorn
Twists from the heart of dead King Horn;

Where, half the year, the snow lies deep
On aching bones that never sleep.
There have I sung: and there have heard
Defiant of my voice, the word
Of Horn, who once a pilgrim came
To Rimenhild, white heart of flame.
She, she was beauty! She has still
On April evenings green and chill,
Blown on the wind, the power to thrill
The agued bones of that poor king.
Twice in the tomb he tries to sing.
Twice he cries: "The dream was strange
That bade the king to fisher change! . . .
I flung my net, and in it drew
No fish; but that gold ring you knew.
Pour me no ale, but fill a cup
With mead; and I will drink it up,
And leave the ring; thus may you see
That I am Horn, and welcome me. . .
. . . Horn, the son of Murry, am I! . . ."
Twice in the thorntree shakes his cry;
And stammered praise of Rimenhild;
And a curse on Mody and Fikenhild . . .
She, lord, is beauty, who can make
So grievously dead earth to wake!'

8

The pipit, from the swinging tree
Dropped briefly singing, 'Can it be
That beauty is so basely born?
Then beauty were a thing to scorn!
Is beauty prisoner to the flesh —
A gold-bird in a leaden mesh?'
Deth turned the cage; from idle hand
He dropped in daisied grass the wand.
'Speak, Crow! Speak, Heedy Royston! tell
Of beauty in a parable!'

'Ha!' said the Crow. 'The silly pipit! . . .
I'll paraphrase him! *Hic incipit!*
. . . When the green damsel, with sad pace,
Came at dusk to the trysting-place;
And saw in the blue pool, mirrored fair,
White hands, and golden wavering hair;
And thought of the seven kisses given,
And seven nights of sin unshriven, —
Of beauty's lips that age with the kiss,
The burning body that dulls with bliss:
She broke her girdle, and flung it down,
And stained with dust her green silk gown;
She looked at ripples, and longed to flow
As clearly bright as the waters go.
She sighed; she stooped; she filled her hand
With tinily twinkling grains of sand;
She spread five fingers in grasses green —
The dark little blades looked up between;
And tears made doubly bright her eyes
As long she stared at hills and skies,
Thinking how once she had walked with these
In young clear innocent daybreak ease. . .
She dropped three pebbles: they broke the stream, —
The wandering ripples ringed her dream.
White, among leaves, she desired to go,
Like grass to quiver, like wind to blow. . .
Alas! of a sudden her lover came
And stood by a tree and sang her name;
And she, forgetting her moment's whim,
Jumped up, and laughed, and ran to him.'

9

'Ah, heedless Royston, cynic bird, —
And cynic still with your last word!
On heaven's blue stone you whet your laughter,
Your scornful "haar!"; and what comes after, —

What under, or before, might go, —
You flout . . . Good, brave, deluded crow —
You shall be made as white as snow! . . .
You, little goudspink, chalandire, —
Where's beauty? Where's my heart's desire?
Where sleeps she now?' Sad-voiced was he;
And smiled at gold-finch listlessly;
As one who sees, yet sees not, dreaming
Of secrets dark beneath the seeming:
The speck of blackness in the seed
That gulfs infinity in its greed:
The yawning ruin, in the flower,
Whence Hinnom vale will come to power.
And sad-voiced was the gold-finch too;
And slow; as he in midnight flew;
And knew his flight the last; and knew
His error destined. 'Ah, my lord, —
What wisdom can a finch afford, —
Who only knows the thistle well?
Is beauty in the thistle bell?
The thistle seed on my small tongue?
Of this, this mostly, have I sung;
Yet wise enough am I to know
This is not beauty. What may show
As beauty's golden seed to me
For you a mite of dust may be.
I yield my will; I sadly guess
What may, for you, be loveliness.

10

'By Nanking pool, I saw one ghost
Speak with another; of that host
Mag Oolie knew. — Cried Yuan P'ien:
"Alas — among the dead, again
We meet, old friend! unresting blown
On the dry wind that whirls us on

To Nowhere out of Nothing! Speak! —
Before the wind his hatred wreak
And part our hands!" . . . Then Hao Shih Chin,
Poet and potter, old and thin:
"To what can hands of vapor cling? . . .
How fly the hawk without a wing? . . .
Yet sweet it is twixt gust and gust,
To pause with you, remembering dust, —
Long since, poor garment, laid away. . .
My Teapot Cottage, made of clay —
Alas is gone; barbarians dwell
Above the buried temple bell;
The wine-cup that I loved the most —
Deep in the nine-bend stream is lost."

'Then Yuan P'ien: "And do you think, —
As I do, — of the Forest of Ink?
Talking, we sat at tea for hours.
Half-opened, frail, hibiscus flowers —
Our tinted cups! . . . My friend, we knew
The temple fair at Pao Ssu;
The curio-dealer in his stall
Beside the damp Nine-Dragon Wall,
And all his curious treasures laid
On orange silk in mulberry shade.
Rouge-boxes like persimmons ripe
With lustrous glaze and juicy stripe
And covering leaf: a cricket cage
Of Hsiu, the cunning archimage:
Globed bursting peony cups of Chun;
A perfume box by Hsiu's son. . .
What beauty have we seen, my friend!"

' "Beauty is that which has an end!"
Said Hao Shih Chin. "The lovely face —
Tao, that suffers time and space!
Let it from space and time escape —

It is eternal, has no shape.
Ghosts here — what have we? Dead and wise,
We know but feel not; have no eyes
For beauty: beauty is that which dies
To-morrow; but is not yet dead.
It is the whiteness in the red. . .
Beauty we knew, but know not now —
The ice-white bowls of Yueh-Chow;
And those of Hsing-Chow, white as snow.
Like snow, like ice, they come, they go.
These had the beauty of the leaf;
Which comes from Nothing, and has a brief
Delight in Being; and weeping goes
Once more to Nothing, and Nothing knows.
Beauty is briefness: it is the death
That cries 'I live!' twixt breath and breath.
It is the softly taken breath
That mourns 'Alas!' twixt death and death."

' "Beauty is life!" cried Yuan P'ien:
"How gladly would I live again! . . .
How gladly give the All for Little,
And the Enduring for the Brittle! . . ."

". . . I think of Chen Chung Mei; who died
Because with his weak soul he tried
To make the Little say the All.
He shaped a Kuan-yin white and tall,
Mixing his soul with soulless clay.
Divine, she smiled! But Chen Chung Mei —
Dropped down before her, senseless lay,
Died in his dream. He knew her not.
Potter had turned himself to pot!"
Thus Hao Shih Chin. And Yuan P'ien
Opened sad lips to speak: but then
The long wind blew their hands apart
And whirled their white beards. "Have good heart!"

Each cried to other; and their ghosts
Flew off, like leaves, with Tao's hosts.'

11

. . . The goldfinch ceased. And Deth was still;
And kindly, gravely smiled; until
The cormorant (head sunk and dozing)
Stirred from his dream (one eye unclosing)
And shook a wing, and chuckled — 'Krell!
I like the goudspink's story well!
But what, pray, is it all about?
Here's neither beauty, no, nor trout! . . .
What's this of ghosts, and sunset-bowls,
Where potters mix with clay their souls?
Moll Hern's a fool; but we might learn
Something, I think, from fool Moll Hern.
Beauty is food, — food, beauty! there
Is all we know, and all our care!'
He sunk his head and closed his eye.

'Here,' said the sparrow, 'speaks the sty:
Malodorous chords from bubbling ooze.
Vermin and worms will have their views.
My lord, last night I fed, at Rome,
In grass where once was Lesbia's tomb.
There chickweed creeps, and clover red, —
Above that once transcendent head;
And there, amid the bindweed, grows
One tulip lovelier than a rose.
There sleeps the bee at night; and there,
I heard, or dreamed, in that sweet air,
A voice — whose voice I do not know —
Murmuring out of the ground below:
"Tulips, freaked in pink and white,
Are lifted for the heart's delight. . .
Raindrops, pelting on broad leaves, —

Loosening silver from black eaves, —
Fall in the secret heart; and sing
A nameless and bewildering thing . . .
Sparrows — though of little voice —
May make the tired heart rejoice;
Winnowing quick-winged from the brain
Web and windlestraw of pain;
Even in shadow, there may be
Beauty for you, beauty for me . . .
Be glad to think — when we are dead —
Great clouds will still sail overhead;
Scattering slowly, as they pass,
Jewels of rain, to light the grass:
To lift, for other men's delight,
These tulips, freaked in pink and white." '

12

The sparrow ceased, and one brown wing
Preened and ruffled. Not answering,
Deth closed his eyes; the birds were still.
Then Philomel: 'To Sanchi Hill,
Seeing the heavens smoke with shame,
At night great King Asoka came.
The moon rose: and the moon was red.
Then cried the king: "Ten thousand dead,
Kalinga sunk in crimson mud,
And Ganges like a vein of blood.
The moon is scarlet, for my sake.
The war must end! And I will make
A temple here, where men may read
The eight-fold path, Nirvana's creed.
Here build a stupa! here enshrine
The relics of Gautama's line.
Groves, here; beneath whose wings may rest
The singing pilgrims; east and west,
Four gates of granite, huge, to show

Where everlasting peace may grow. . .
Carve in the Eastern Gate a tree
With mangos hung; and let there be
The caryatic nymph, to cling,
With bracelet ring, and anklet ring,
Beneath its boughs; the fruits above:
The Buddha's mother, Sacred Love.
Cut deeply in each architrave
The story of dead Chandra. Grave
The Peacock with his thousand eyes,
Brief emblem of our dynasties;
The massive stone-ends be volute;
And all the rest with flower and fruit
And beast and man and bird designed,
In blessed harmony entwined.
Henceforth forever is no war;
But peace; and rest; and Buddha's lore."
Thus cried Asoka to the moon.
Alas! what is brute Time, that soon
Must dynasties, as men, devour?
Wise King Asoka spoke his hour;
His dream is vanished; like a flower.'

'Often at night,' said Deth, 'have I,
Under a forest's leafy sky
Heard in the listening dark your cry,
And thought it beauty, Philomel,
And mourned. But, ah, this tale you tell,
Of King Asoka, gone to dust,
With drums and dreams and gates that rust —
Here's nothing, no! . . . Speak now, some bird —
Where's Beauty, Beauty? . . .'

13

No wing stirred,
No beak was opened. Then was heard

The squeaking bat, who flapped in grass,
Awkward and purblind. 'Let me pass,
Sisters!' And they with shudders drew
Aside, and let the creature through,
Who, stumbling, fell before the cage;
And squeaked: 'My lord! I am not sage!
Yet, used to darkness, know some things
Hidden from timid daylight wings.
No virtue, truly, that I rove,
Moon or no moon, the haunted grove — !
Why should I either blame or praise
My sisters, Lord! — to each her ways.
Yet happened it that last night, dancing
Out of a well, in starlight glancing
From oak to willow, hunting food
From Saxon vale to Wickham wood —
Beyond Dumb Woman's Lane I found
A cavern, slanting underground,
Hid in a thicket; the beechen grove
Showered a moon-pierced shade above,
Where, all unwitting, Philomel
Sang to the dark. And there befell
That as I dropped my hands to see
This cave, — before unknown to me, —
Venus Anadyomene,
Foam-born Venus, goddess of Love,
Came from the vault, and in that grove
Stared at the moon. Naked was she,
Whiter than shell her breast and knee,
Cold as the moon her fair face shone,
Her hair like frost in the light of the moon.
The leaves about her a sea-sound made,
Seethed, seethed. And the beechen shade
Was dark and cold as shade must be
In moonlit cavern beneath the sea.
She, lord, is beauty! Seek her there!
Strangle the goddess with her bright hair!'

The cage was open. The bat flew in.
The air grew loud with a whistling din
Of wings. A thousand birds as one
Went from the hill against the sun.
Beneath the multitudinous cloud
Deth raised his wand, and cried aloud:
'Be snow, bright birds!' . . .

                                   Then fell the snow;
The hill was white. And bent, and slow,
His shoulders bright with frost, one hand
Clutching the cage, and one the wand,
Deth stooped down from the voiceless hill.
The sun broke forth. The bat was still —
Head downward in the cage he swung;
The cage a bell and he the tongue.

IV: *Venus Anadyomene*

1

'My lord,' said Juliana, 'wake!
The hour of peace is coming. Take
The osier cage, and let the mouse
Guide us once more to Venus' house.
All things, as heretofore, have run:
The tamarisk devoured the sun:
Burning, the snake-fed buzzard flew
And screamed by Fairlight Cliff. Thrice crew
The roosting cock. The forest was,
With all its acorn-cups and grass,
And forkèd boughs, a sound of singing;
The myriad bells of goblins ringing . . .
Wake, lord, and come!'

2

John Deth awoke,
And shook the dew, and no word spoke,
And at the demon, long and hard,
Stared, and the heavens thickly starred,
As though he comprehended nought;
But in his eyes deep-coiling thought
Struggled, like pitchy smoke; and soon
Memory rose there, like the moon.
Darkly he rose; and taller grown
By starlight carved of granite stone,
Towered above his doxies, bent
A clouded brow on Millicent,
Murmured: 'The birds — like snow they went.
The sky was dark. The cold flakes fell
Loud on the leaden grass. The bell
Of osier, that before has sung,
Was shut upon its living tongue . . .
And down the hill I came to sleep. . .'

3

Then Millicent, who seemed to weep,
Where on a forest-stone she sat,
Cried out: 'My lord, now take the bat,
The rere-mouse foul who guides our way,
And do this thing! Soon comes the day.
Speak to your servant, lord!' she said.
(The cage hung dark above her head,
Deep-lodged within a holly tree.)
'Speak to your servant, lord!' said she;
And upward, weeping, looked, and saw
The vampire, hanging by a claw;
Fox-eared; and still; with burning eyes.
'You who alone,' cried Deth, 'were wise,
And knew the goddess of all blood —

Now guide us to the shameful wood
That hides the torment! Speak, foul moth, —
Whose wings are webs of Stygian cloth! . . .
Speak, and forever live . . .'

4

Thereat
Made answer slow the weak-voiced bat:
'My lord, your power this osier shows;
As on the hilltop showed the snows.
My life is yours; your will is law.
And yet, eternal wing and claw, —
Franchise for everlasting grief, —
These seek I not! Better the brief
And dumb existence of the leaf.
Who knows naught — let him live forever!
Who knows and mourns — pity! and sever
From the blind sap that bears him, lord;
Deep death alone is his reward. . .
— And yet, forgive! I do you wrong?
Not over all things are you strong:
And I am he you cannot kill; —
I cannot die.' The bat was still,
And dark amid his osier hung.
Then found the cage again its tongue:
'But you must go! The way is plain.
Hurry. And by Dumb Woman's Lane,
Betwixt two silver birches, break
The spider's wheel; and you will take
Venus, who twists her frost-white hair
And stands, with bright eyes, listening there.'

5

The bat-voice dropped. The moon behind
A small fog flew; the night was blind.

And Deth unhooked the cage, and bent
With Juliana and Millicent
Beneath dead boughs; across a wall;
And up the lane, where chill and tall
The wych-elms whispered. Now the singing
Of myriad leaves began; the ringing
Of goblin heart-bells softly thrilled
Deep in the haunted wood, and filled
The night with grief. In Deth's left hand
Glowed like a snake of light the wand,
And showed how Juliana stept:
How, in his cage the vampire slept:
While Millicent, in silence, wept.

Between two branching birches hung
The cobweb wheel. Against it swung
The cage, and tore the little thread.
Silent, with unuplifted head,
Staring at dead leaves, swiftly came
Behind their master's cloak of flame
The hurrying two; pursued the hand,
Clawlike and bright, that clutched the wand:
And stopped, where moonlight poured to pave
A floor of bluebells. Black, the cave
Yawned at the moon; and moonlit, there
Venus, twisting her flowered hair,
Venus Anadyomene,
Foam-born Venus, cold as the sea,
Shone like frost. Loud in the wood
The goblin heart-beats rang, while stood
The three before her. And she quavered,
Frightened — like flame that backward wavered —
Her long hair slipping against her knee:
'Lord Deth, what seek you here with me?
You, Millicent, what do you here —
Your deep eyes thronged with wings of fear?
And you, black gypsy, all things knowing —

Where, among ruins and starlight going?
To what can copse and cavern lead you?
What weed-grown shameful grave can need you?
This grove is mine. The hour is late.
What brings you here to break my gate?'
Then Deth: 'Here in this wood you die.
And we have come to crucify.'
The goddess stared. 'The birds, — ' she said,
'Will blind you, save me!' 'Birds are dead,'
The other answered, 'all save one,
Who slumbers in this cage, alone.
The bat betrayed. The rest are snow.'
Venus was still. Then deep and low,
Angry, the bell-like laughter rang,
Lovely derision; and she sang
'The foxes, then!' and hid a star
Behind one finger. Near and far,
Deep-mingled with the goblin singing,
They heard the bells of foxes ringing;
And footsteps pattered, thick as rain,
The leaves that strewed Dumb Woman's Lane.

6

'Foxes!' Deth hissed. The word was chill.
He raised the wand. They listened. Still
Were bells and footsteps. Dark the wood
Leaned in on Venus where she stood. . .
'Pity!' she cried. The petalled bough
Lightly caressed her, breast and brow:
The eyelids closed; breath shuddered deep;
She swayed, like one who stands in sleep.
'And are you, — Venus, — bound at last?'
— Over the white face strongly passed
A sleeping grief. The drowsy lips
Murmured slow, in the moon's eclipse;
The shut eyes wept; the golden head

Fallen forward as it were dead:
'Caught, as it was predestined, lord!
In the beginning was the word.
Hang the bat in the hemlock tree.
Nail my hands. Crucify me.'
'You call me lord, and master?' 'Yes:
You burn my body to nothingness.'
He touched the fluttering eyelids. Sleep
Burned in the white god, sinking deep.

7

Dark Juliana above her bent
Evilly smiling. Millicent
Shrank back and leant against a tree,
Hiding her white face, not to see;
Yet heard the goddess, overthrown,
Fall among stifled bluebells, moan
Once, twice, and weep; the demon wove
A crown of flowers, under, above,
Fast as poison about the head;
Venus in moonlight slept as dead.
The palms were pierced. The feet were bound.
Millicent heard the mallet pound:
And the goddess cry; and, then, from Deth,
Whistling, a sharply taken breath:
And footsteps going; and farther, after,
Deep-ringing, rich, the demon's laughter,
And laughter again, with no word spoken;
And swish of leaves, and a tree-branch broken.
And suddenly, in the hidden cage,
With prophet's cry began to rage
The folded bat: 'Turn, Millicent!
And see the god's white ichor spent!
Daughter of Venus, turn and see
Venus nailed to the hawthorn tree . . .
The foam-white goddess, forever young,

There like a bat in a cage is hung;
Death and the Demon crucify
Venus, that you and Deth may die. . .
Vision of blindness! Empty illusion!
Error! error! and sad confusion. . .
Millicent, turn! your eyes uncover!
Regard the demon, the demon lover:
See what cruelty Deth can fashion,
Bloody device of hands of passion!
Triumph was dreamed, and folly born,
And Deth for his own brow weaves the thorn.'

8

Then, in the moonlight, Millicent, turning,
Saw in the thorn tree, golden, burning,
Radiant, white, a body of snow,
Where veins of fire began to glow,
The immortal god, her wounded bosom
Burning whiter than white-thorn blossom,
Her arms outstretched amid leaves, her hair
Caught among thorns, her white flanks bare.
Burning brighter than moon in cloud
Or lamp in tomb or torch in shroud,
Her eyes wide open and fair to see,
Her beauty burned in the hawthorn tree.
White among boughs the white doves came
And beat white wings against the flame;
Circling and crying, their wings were bright
Against the burning body's light.
Foxes crept in the wood, green-eyed,
Crouched in a ring. And Venus cried,
Lifting once more the fallen head:
'Think not, my people, the god is dead,
Who in this hawthorn seems to die!
Twisting in death, and burning, I
Live in the hearts that crucify. . .'

She ceased. The head fell forward. Light
Coiled from her eyes. The forest night
Leaned closer about her. Breast and limb, —
Their brightness swarmed with leaves, — grew dim,
Darkened, were lost. The haunted wood
Devoured the Goddess of All Blood.
Densely, about the hawthorn, grew
A poisoned thicket: where vainly threw
The moon her breaking spears of blue. . .

And Deth, and the Demons, turning slowly,
Tongueless went from the wood unholy:
Climbed up the westward hill, and saw
The moon go down: one red-tipped claw
Waved at a vapour and withdrew:
They sank, were nothing, and nothing knew.

Save Juliana; who stared at space
Till deep as the world became her face:
She and the world became but one.
Stone was the world: she lay like stone.

V: *Juliana Goatibed*

Then Juliana Goatibed,
Carving the rock beneath her head,
Carved it vast, with hammering thought
Out of terrific vision wrought.
It was the world. Nought else there was;
No living voice; no cloud; no grass;
Only the rock, whereon, in space,
She sat, with dark all-knowing face.
No shape it had: it had no bound.
Mist was beneath it: mist around.
No sun woke there; no star, to light
That ship of granite infinite.

But there the demon (chin on breast)
Who crouched and stared and found no rest; —
From laboring dream found no escape; —
Hewed of the world a tombstone shape;
And then, with deep-thrust hands of thought
Drew darkly upward, out of nought,
The carver's self. Old, old was he,
Old as the world itself might be;
Swam slowly upward, kept a gleam,
Still dripping, from the dark of dream;
And sat, cross-legged, an atom size,
Unconscious of the demon's eyes.
'Carve, now!' said she. And he, unhearing,
Unhurried, old, and nothing caring,
Conscious of stone and nought but stone,
Stone to be cut by brittle bone,
With tiny chisel and mallet smote
The ancient base of rock; and wrote
Small words thereon: Deep words that first
Glimmered in darkness, budded, burst
Like lilies in the demon's brain:
Then in immortal rock made plain:
'Here lies John Deth; and by his side
Millicent Piggistaile, his bride.
Creator and destroyer keep
Henceforth their everlasting sleep.
And she, — the flame between, — who drove
Their anguish on, accursèd Love, —
Who died before, that they might cease; —
Shares with them their eternal peace.
Dated: heart of the timeless word
Before and after the sundered Lord.'

The Carver nodded; nodded; slept;
Yet in his hand the chisel kept . . .
And Juliana, who leaned to laugh
Above the dusty epitaph,

Looked through the stone. And there she saw
The moon go down with red-tipped claw;
Dumb Woman's Lane; the Westward Hill;
And in the charred grass, — shrunk and still, —
Deth sleeping, but about to wake;
Millicent, weeping for his sake;
Herself, beside them, wide-eyed, weaving
Vision of peace beyond believing. . .
The birds behind them, in the wood
Still flapped about the burning rood. . .
'Peace now!' she cried. She dropped her head,
Her mind grew dark. The world was dead.
She dreamed. The Carver and she, alone,
Would sleep forever upon the stone.

King Borborigmi

You say you heard King Borborigmi laugh?
Say how it was. Some heavenly body moved him?
The moon laughed first? Dark earth put up a finger
Of honeysuckle, through his moonlit window,
And tickled him?

        — King Borborigmi laughed
Alone, walking alone in an empty room,
Thinking, and yet not thinking, seeing, yet blind.
One hand was on his chin, feeling the beard
That razors could not stay; the other groped;
For it was dark, and in the dark were chairs;
Midnight, or almost midnight; Aldebaran
Hanging among the dews.

        — King Borborigmi
Laughed once or twice at nothing, just as midnight
Released a flock of bells?
        — Not this alone;
Not bells in flight toward Aldebaran;

Nor the immitigable beard; nor dews
Heavily pattering on the pent-house roof;
Nor chairs in shadow which his foot disturbed.
Yet it was all of these, and more: the air
Twirling the curtain where a red moth hung:
The one bell flying later than the others
Into the starstrung silence: the garden breaking
To let a thousand seedlings have their way:
An eye-tooth aching, and the pendulum
That heavily ticked upon the leftward swing.

— These trifles woke the laughter of a king?

— Much less than these, and more! He softly stepped
Among the webby world, and felt it shudder.
Under the earth — a strand or two of web —
He saw his father's bones, fallen apart,
The jawbone sunken and the skull caved in.
Among his mother's bones a cactus rooted,
And two moles crept, and ants held carnival.
Above the obscene tomb an aloe blossomed;
Dew glistened on the marble. This he saw,
And at the selfsame moment heard the cook
Wind the alarm-clock in her bedroom, yawn,
And creak the bed. And it was then, surprised,
He touched a chair, and laughed, and twitched the curtain, —
And the moth flew out.

          — Alas, poor Borborigmi,
That it should be so little, and so sorry
A thing to make him laugh!

          — Young Borborigmi,
Saw more than this. The infinite octopus
With eyes of chaos and long arms of stars,
And belly of void and darkness, became clear
About him, and he saw himself embraced

And swept along a vein, with chairs and teeth,
Houses and bones and gardens, cooks and clocks;
The midnight bell, a snoring cook, and he,
Mingled and flowed like atoms.

        — It was this
That made him laugh — to see himself as one
Corpuscle in the infinite octopus? . . .
And was this all, old fool, old turner of leaves? . . .

— Alone, thinking alone in an empty room
Where moonlight and the mouse were met together,
And pulse and clock together ticked, and dew
Made contrapuntal patter, Borborigmi
Fathomed in his own viscera the world,
Went downward, sounding like a diver, holding
His peakèd nose; and when he came up, laughed.
These things and others saw. But last of all,
Ultimate or penultimate, he saw
The one thing that undid him!

       — What was this?
The one grotesquer thing among grotesques?
Carrion, offal, or the toothbrush ready
For carnal fangs? Cancer, that grasps the heart,
Or fungus, whitely swelling in the brain?
Some gargoyle of the thought?

       — King Borborigmi,
Twitching the curtain as the last bell flew
Melodious to Aldebaran, beheld
The moth fly also. Downward dropped it softly
Among dropped petals, white. And there one rose
Was open in the moonlight! Dew was on it;
The bat, with ragged wing, cavorting, sidling,
Snapped there a sleeping bee —

— And crunched the moth? . . .

— It was the rose in moonlight, crimson, yet
Blanched by the moon; the bee asleep; the bat
And fallen moth — but most the guileless rose.
Guileless! . . . King Borborigmi struck his foot
Against a chair, and saw the guileless rose
Joining himself (King Bubblegut), and all
Those others — the immitigable beard;
Razors and teeth; his mother's bones; the tomb:
The yawning cook; the clock; the dew; the bells
Bursting upward like bubbles — ; all so swept
Along one vein of the infinite octopus
With eyes of chaos and long arms of stars
And belly of void and darkness. It was then
He laughed; as he would never laugh again.
For he saw everything; and, in the centre
Of corrupt change, one guileless rose; and laughed
For puzzlement and sorrow.

                              Ah, poor man,
Poor Borborigmi, young, to be so wise!

— Wise? No. For what he laughed at was just this:
That to see all, to know all, is to rot.
So went to bed; and slept; is sleeping still,
If none has waked him.

                    — Dead? King Borborigmi
Is dead? Died laughing? Sleeps a dreamless sleep
Till cook's alarm clock wakes him?

                              — Sleeps like Hamlet,
King of infinite space in a walnut shell —
But has bad dreams; I fear he has bad dreams.

And in the Hanging Gardens

And in the hanging gardens there is rain
From midnight until one, striking the leaves
And bells of flowers, and stroking boles of planes,
And drawing slow arpeggios over pools,
And stretching strings of sound from eaves to ferns.
The princess reads. The knave of diamonds sleeps.
The king is drunk, and flings a golden goblet
Down from the turret window (curtained with rain)
Into the lilacs.

                    And at one o'clock
The vulcan under the garden wakes and beats
The gong upon his anvil. Then the rain
Ceases, but gently ceases, dripping still,
And sound of falling water fills the dark
As leaves grow bold and upright, and as eaves
Part with water. The princess turns the page
Beside the candle, and between two braids
Of golden hair. And reads: 'From there I went
Northward a journey of four days, and came
To a wild village in the hills, where none
Was living save the vulture and the rat,
And one old man, who laughed, but could not speak.
The roofs were fallen in; the well grown over
With weed; and it was there my father died.
Then eight days further, bearing slightly west,
The cold wind blowing sand against our faces,
The food tasting of sand. And as we stood
By the dry rock that marks the highest point
My brother said: "Not too late is it yet
To turn, remembering home." And we were silent
Thinking of home.' The princess shuts her eyes
And feels the tears forming beneath her eyelids
And opens them, and tears fall on the page.

The knave of diamonds in the darkened room
Throws off his covers, sleeps, and snores again.
The king goes slowly down the turret stairs
To find the goblet.

                                    And at two o'clock
The vulcan in his smithy underground
Under the hanging gardens, where the drip
Of rain among the clematis and ivy
Still falls from sipping flower to purple flower,
Smites twice his anvil, and the murmur comes
Among the roots and vines. The princess reads:
'As I am sick, and cannot write you more,
Nor have not long to live, I give this letter
To him, my brother, who will bear it south
And tell you how I died. Ask how it was,
There in the northern desert, where the grass
Was withered, and the horses, all but one,
Perished' . . . The princess drops her golden head
Upon the page between her two white arms
And golden braids. The knave of diamonds wakes
And at his window in the darkened room
Watches the lilacs tossing, where the king
Seeks for the goblet.

                                    And at three o'clock
The moon inflames the lilac heads, and thrice
The vulcan, in his root-bound smithy, clangs
His anvil; and the sounds creep softly up
Among the vines and walls. The moon is round,
Round as a shield above the turret top.
The princess blows her candle out, and weeps
In the pale room, where scent of lilac comes,
Weeping, with hands across her eyelids, thinking
Of withered grass, withered by sandy wind.
The knave of diamonds, in his darkened room,
Holds in his hands a key, and softly steps

Along the corridor, and slides the key
Into the door that guards her. Meanwhile, slowly,
The king, with raindrops on his beard and hands,
And dripping sleeves, climbs up the turret stairs,
Holding the goblet upright in one hand;
And pauses on the midmost step, to taste
One drop of wine, wherewith wild rain has mixed.

The Wedding

At noon, Tithonus, withered by his singing,
Climbing the oatstalk with his hairy legs,
Met grey Arachne, poisoned and shrunk down
By her own beauty; pride had shrivelled both.
In the white web — where seven flies hung wrapped —
She heard his footstep; hurried to him; bound him;
Enshrouded him in silk; then poisoned him.
Twice shrieked Tithonus, feebly; then was still.
Arachne loved him. Did he love Arachne?
She watched him with red eyes, venomous sparks,
And the furred claws outspread . . . 'O sweet Tithonus!
Darling! Be kind, and sing that song again!
Shake the bright web again with that deep fiddling!
Are you much poisoned? sleeping? do you dream?
Darling Tithonus!'

        And Tithonus, weakly
Moving one hairy shin against the other
Within the silken sack, contrived to fiddle
A little tune, half-hearted: 'Shrewd Arachne!
Whom pride in beauty withered to this shape
As pride in singing shrivelled me to mine —
Unwrap me, let me go — and let me limp,
With what poor strength your venom leaves me, down
This oatstalk, and away.'

                        Arachne, angry,
Stung him again, twirling him with rough paws,
The red eyes keen. 'What! You would dare to leave me?
Unkind Tithonus! Sooner I'll kill and eat you
Than let you go. But sing that tune again —
So plaintive was it!'

                        And Tithonus faintly
Moved the poor fiddles, which were growing cold,
And sang: 'Arachne, goddess envied of gods,
Beauty's eclipse eclipsed by angry beauty,
Have pity, do not ask the withered heart
To sing too long for you! My strength goes out,
Too late we meet for love. O be content
With friendship, which the noon sun once may kindle
To give one flash of passion, like a dewdrop,
Before it goes! . . . Be reasonable, — Arachne!'

Arachne heard the song grow weaker, dwindle
To first a rustle, and then half a rustle,
And last a tick, so small no ear could hear it
Save hers, a spider's ear. And her small heart,
(Rusted away, like his, to a pinch of dust,)
Gleamed once, like his, and died. She clasped him tightly
And sunk her fangs in him. Tithonus dead,
She slept awhile, her last sensation gone;
Woke from the nap, forgetting him; and ate him.

God's Acre

In Memory Of. In Fondest Recollection Of.
In Loving Memory Of. In Fond
Remembrance. Died in October. Died at Sea.
Who died at sea? The name of the seaport
Escapes her, gone, blown with the eastwind, over
The tombs and yews, into the apple orchard,

Over the road, where gleams a wagon-top,
And gone. The eastwind gallops up from sea
Bringing salt and gulls. The marsh smell, too,
Strong in September; mud and reeds, the reeds
Rattling like bones.

            She shifts the grass-clipper
From right to left hand, clips and clips the grass.
The broken column, carefully broken, on which
The blackbird hen is laughing — in fondest memory.
Burden! Who was this Burden, to be remembered?
Or Potter? The Potter rejected by the Pot.
'Here lies Josephus Burden, who departed
This life the fourth of August, nineteen hundred.
"And He Said Come." ' Josephus Burden, forty,
Gross, ribald, with strong hands on which grew hair,
And red ears kinked with hair, and northblue eyes,
Held in one hand a hammer, in the other
A nail. He drove the nail. . . This was enough?
Or — also — did he love?

            She changes back
The clipper. The blades are dull. The grass is wet
And gums the blades. In Loving Recollection.
Four chains, heavy, hang round the vault. What chance
For skeletons? The dead men rise at night,
Rattle the links. 'Too heavy! can't be budged . . .
Try once.again — together — NOW! . . . no use.'
They sit in moonless shadow, gently talking.
'Old Jones it must have been, who made those chains.
I'd like to see him lift them now!' . . . The owl
That hunts in Wickham Wood comes over, mewing.
'An owl,' says one. 'Most likely,' says another.
They turn grey heads.

            The seawind brings a breaking
Bell sound among the yews and tombstones, ringing

The twisted whorls of bronze on sunlit stones.
Sacred . . . memory . . . affectionate . . . O God
What travesty is this — the blackbird soils
The broken column; the worm at work in the skull
Feasts on medulla; and the lewd thrush cracks
A snailshell on the vault. He died on shipboard —
Sea-burial, then, were better?

                                On her knees
She clips and clips, kneeling against the sod,
Holding the world between her two knees, pondering
Downward, as if her thought, like men or apples,
Fell ripely into earth. Seablue, her eyes
Turn to the sea. Sea-gulls are scavengers,
Cruel of face, but lovely. By the dykes
The reeds rattle, leaping in eastwind, rattling
Like bones. In Fond Remembrance Of. O God,
That life is what it is, and does not change.
You there in earth, and I above you kneeling.
You dead, and I alive.

                        She prods a plantain
Of too ambitious root. That largest yew-tree,
Clutching the hill —

                        She rises from stiff knees,
Stiffly, and treads the pebble path, that leads
Downward, to sea and town. The marsh smell comes
Healthy and salt, and fills her nostrils. Reeds
Dance in the eastwind, rattling; warblers dart
Flashing, from swaying reed to reed, and sing.

The Road

Three then came forward out of darkness, one
An old man bearded, his old eyes red with weeping,

A peasant, with hard hands. 'Come now,' he said,
'And see the road, for which our people die.
Twelve miles of road we've made, a little only,
Westward winding. Of human blood and stone
We build; and in a thousand years will come
Beyond the hills to sea.'

              I went with them,
Taking a lantern, which upon their faces
Showed years and grief; and in a time we came
To the wild road which wound among wild hills
Westward; and so along this road we stooped,
Silent, thinking of all the dead men, there
Compounded with sad clay. Slowly we moved:
For they were old and weak, had given all
Their life, to build this twelve poor miles of road,
Muddy, under the rain. And in my hand
Turning the lantern, here or there, I saw
Deep holes of water where the raindrop splashed,
And rainfilled footprints in the grass, and heaps
Of broken stone, and rusted spades and picks,
And helves of axes. And the old man spoke,
Holding my wrist: 'Three hundred years it took
To build these miles of road: three hundred years;
And human lives unnumbered. But the day
Will come when it is done.' Then spoke another,
One not so old, but old, whose face was wrinkled:
'And when it comes, our people will all sing
For joy, passing from east to west, or west
To east, returning, with the light behind them;
All meeting in the road and singing there.'
And the third said: 'The road will be their life;
A heritage of blood. Grief will be in it,
And beauty out of grief. And I can see
How all the women's faces will be bright.
In that time, laughing, they will remember us.
Blow out your lantern now, for day is coming.'

My lantern blown out, in a little while
We climbed in long light up a hill, where climbed
The dwindling road, and ended in a field.
Peasants were working in the field, bowed down
With unrewarded work, and grief, and years
Of pain. And as we passed them, one man fell
Into a furrow that was bright with water
And gave a cry that was half cry half song —
'The road . . . the road . . . the road . . .' And all then fell
Upon their knees and sang.

                    We four passed on
Over the hill, to westward. Then I felt
How tears ran down my face, tears without number;
And knew that all my life henceforth was weeping,
Weeping, thinking of human grief, and human
Endeavour fruitless in a world of pain.
And when I held my hands up they were old;
I knew my face would not be young again.

Dead Leaf in May

One skeleton-leaf, white-ribbed, a last year's leaf,
Skipped in a paltry gust, whizzed from the dust,
Leapt the small dusty puddle; and sailing then
Merrily in the sunlight, lodged itself
Between two blossoms in a hawthorn tree.
That was the moment: and the world was changed.
With that insane gay skeleton of a leaf
A world of dead worlds flew to hawthorn trees,
Lodged in the green forks, rattled, rattled their ribs
(As loudly as a dead leaf's ribs can rattle)
Blithely, among bees and blossoms. I cursed,
I shook my stick, dislodged it. To what end?
Its ribs, and all the ribs of all dead worlds,

Would house them now forever as death should:
Cheek by jowl with May.

That was the moment: and my brain flew open
Like a ripe bursting pod. The seed sprang out,
And I was withered, and had given all.
Ripeness at top means rottenness beneath:
The brain divulging seed, the heart is empty:
The little blood goes through it like quicksilver:
The hand is leather, and the world is lost.

Human, who trudge the road from Here to There:
Lock the dry oak-leaf's flimsy skeleton
In auricle or ventricle; sail it
Like a gay ship down red Aorta's flood.
Be the paired blossoms with dead ribs between.
Thirst in the There, that you may drink the Here.

Cliff Meeting

Met on the westworn cliff, where the short grass
Blew on the sea-rock edge, with crowded sea-pinks
And heather, she and I stood face to face,
Strangers, and stared. What's in a face or eye
That gives its secret, when the moment comes,
For nothing, less than nothing? We but looked,
Looked once, looked hard, looked deep; the sea-wind spared
The blue still waters of her soul; far down
I saw the ghost I loved. Did she see also,
In my wan eyes, a depth, and a swimming ghost?
Tranced so at cliff's-edge, stood and stared; then laughed;
Then sat together in chilly sunlight, watching
The moving brows of foam come round the headland,
And rabbits daring the cliff.

Her hand, in grass —
(A sea-pink nodded betwixt thumb and finger)
I touched and lifted: she but smiled. Her arm
I scratched with a tiny fork of heather, drawing
A pair of furrows from elbow down to wrist,
White and sharp; she smiled at first, then frowned.
Her mouth, which said no word and gave no name,
I kissed; and as I kissed it, with eyes open,
I saw the sea-pink (caught twixt thumb and finger)
Plucked up unmercifully.

                    The sun went down
Between two waves; and as it went, she rose,
Shaking her dress. To-morrow (so she said)
Here by the cliff's-edge we might meet again.
What's in a face or eye that gives its secret
So lightly, when the moment comes? She saw
Weariness in me, love gone down like the sun,
The fleet ghost gone; and as she saw, she drooped.
Beauty waned out of her; the light drained out
From her deep eyes; pathetic seemed she; I
Discomfited, leering upon her, angry
That I had thought I loved her. So, she went:
Miserable, small, self-pitying, down to darkness.
I watched her go, thinking it strange that she —
Meagre, unlovely — should have captured me.

And on the morrow, when she did not come,
There by the cliff's edge, staked, I found a letter
Mystic, insoluble, with few words written,
Saying — (and it was strange, and like a dream,
For, as I read, the words seemed only marks
Of bird-claws in the sand —) that she was gone
Down to the village, darkness, gone forever;
But left this bird for me, that I might know —
What I should know. And in the short grass lay,
There with the sea-pinks, a blue cormorant,

White eyelids closed, and dying. Her I lifted
Between my hands, and laid against my breast,
Striving to warm her heart. The bird was starved;
The eyes drooped open, and the livid beak
Opened a little; and I gave my hands
To her to eat, having no other food;
Thrusting a finger in the beak, that she
Might eat my flesh and live. But she was dying,
And could not move the purple beak, falling
Against my hand, inert; and then I thought
That, seeking to make her eat, I did but hasten
Her death. For in a moment, then, she died.

Along the cliff I walked, taking the bird,
Holding it in my hands. . . What had she meant
In leaving this blue cormorant for me?
Was she not coming? Everywhere I looked;
By rock and tree; in coigns of heather; even
Down where the moving brows of foam came in.
Nowhere — nowhere. The sun went west behind
Two waves. It was the hour of parting. Would
She come not now for that?

                    The darkness gathered.
The sea-pinks lost their colour. And I walked
Along the cliff's-edge, losing all power of thought,
Taking the cormorant into the dark with me.

Sea Holly

Begotten by the meeting of rock with rock,
The mating of rock and rock, rocks gnashing together;
Created so, and yet forgetful, walks
The seaward path, puts up her left hand, shades
Blue eyes, the eyes of rock, to see better
In slanting light the ancient sheep (which kneels

Biting the grass) the while her other hand,
Hooking the wicker handle, turns the basket
Of eggs. The sea is high to-day. The eggs
Are cheaper. The sea is blown from the southwest,
Confused, taking up sand and mud in waves,
The waves break, sluggish, in brown foam, the wind
Disperses (on the sheep and hawthorn) spray, —
And on her cheeks, the cheeks engendered of rock,
And eyes, the colour of rock. The left hand
Falls from the eyes, and undecided slides
Over the left breast on which muslin lightly
Rests, touching the nipple, and then down
The hollow side, virgin as rock, and bitterly
Caresses the blue hip.

                It was for this,
This obtuse taking of the seaward path,
This stupid hearing of larks, this hooking
Of wicker, this absent observation of sheep
Kneeling in harsh sea-grass, the cool hand shading
The spray-stung eyes — it was for this the rock
Smote itself. The sea is higher to-day,
And eggs are cheaper. The eyes of rock take in
The seaward path that winds toward the sea,
The thistle-prodder, old woman under a bonnet,
Forking the thistles, her back against the sea,
Pausing, with hard hands on the handle, peering
With rock eyes from her bonnet.

                It was for this,
This rock-lipped facing of brown waves, half sand
And half water, this tentative hand that slides
Over the breast of rock, and into the hollow
Soft side of muslin rock, and then fiercely
Almost as rock against the hip of rock —
It was for this in midnight the rocks met,
And dithered together, cracking and smoking.

It was for this
Barren beauty, barrenness of rock that aches
On the seaward path, seeing the fruitful sea,
Hearing the lark of rock that sings, smelling
The rock-flower of hawthorn, sweetness of rock —
It was for this, stone pain in the stony heart,
The rock loved and laboured; and all is lost.

Elder Tree

'The sensual will have its moment? The brain
Sleep? . . . You can prophesy? . . .'

        — Thus laughed the woman,
Tall, thin, and bitter as an elder tree,
Lifting her white face like a crown of bloom.
And so I swore by darkness, trees, and blood,
And rivers underground, and felt my brain,
(Thus challenged by her brain) fall steeply down
Like a dead leaf upon the rushing flood.
'Yes, I can prophesy,' I laughed in answer;
And lost my life in hers, which brighter shone,
Radiant and derisive. 'Never yet,'
She darkly smiled, 'has voice of man flown in
To break my chords of being. You but waste
The evening, with its bank of clouds, where stars
Plunge down to swim . . . Look, how the lights now come
Like perforations in that wall of trees —
Wherethrough the Ultimate winks!'

        And she was still,
Clasping long hands around her lifted knee.
These touched I twice, with teasing finger-tip,
Three times and four, then wearied. But the darkness
And that profounder sound where rushed the river,
Nocturnal, under all, and moving all, —

Took both of us, annulled the brain, devoured
The elder tree, with white faint face of bloom,
And me, who sat beneath it.

               Then my blood
Was filled with elder blossom cold and white,
My arms embraced the tree of singing wood,
My hands took leaves and broke them. We were lost,
Thus mingled, in the world. No speech we had.
Till suddenly (as at the end of death,
The darkness being silent) we stood up
Once more; the woman hushed, an elder tree,
And I a voice. And then she smiled, and said —
'Ah, it is true! The sensual has its moment.
The trickster brain — thank God — can be deposed . . .'

Then I, 'Look now! how all the trees rush back
From the dark stream! and every blade of grass
New-washed in starlight!'

          'Starlight?' . . . She laughed, rustling, —
Rustling, nodding her elder-blossom face, —
'Not starlight, no! The trees, the grass, the brain,
Come back again from blood; and they are strong.'

The Room

Through that window — all else being extinct
Except itself and me — I saw the struggle
Of darkness against darkness. Within the room
It turned and turned, dived downward. Then I saw
How order might — if chaos wished — become:
And saw the darkness crush upon itself,
Contracting powerfully; it was as if
It killed itself: slowly: and with much pain.
Pain. The scene was pain, and nothing but pain.

What else, when chaos draws all forces inward
To shape a single leaf? . . .

          For the leaf came,
Alone and shining in the empty room;
After a while the twig shot downward from it;
And from the twig a bough; and then the trunk,
Massive and coarse; and last the one black root.
The black root cracked the walls. Boughs burst the window:
The great tree took possession.

          Tree of trees!
Remember (when time comes) how chaos died
To shape the shining leaf. Then turn, have courage,
Wrap arms and roots together, be convulsed
With grief, and bring back chaos out of shape.
I will be watching then as I watch now.
I will praise darkness now, but then the leaf.

Sound of Breaking

Why do you cry out, why do I like to hear you
Cry out, here in the dewless evening, sitting
Close, close together, so close that the heart stops beating
And the brain its thought? Wordless, worthless mortals
Stumbling, exhausted, in this wilderness
Of our conjoint destruction! Hear the grass
Raging about us! Hear the worms applaud!
Hear how the ripples make a sound of chaos!
Hear now, in these and the other sounds of evening,
The first brute step of God!

          About your elbow,
Making a ring of thumb and finger, I
Slide the walled blood against the less-walled blood,
Move down your arm, surmount the wrist-bone, shut

Your long slim hand in mine. Each finger-tip
Is then saluted by a finger-tip;
The hands meet back to back, then face to face;
Then lock together. And we, with eyes averted,
Smile at the evening sky of alabaster,
See nothing, lose our souls in the maelstrom, turning
Downward in rapid circles.

                       Bitter woman,
Bitter of heart and brain and blood, bitter as I
Who drink your bitterness — can this be beauty?
Do you cry out because the beauty is cruel?
Terror, because we downward sweep so swiftly?
Terror of darkness?

               It is a sound of breaking,
The world is breaking, the world is a sound of breaking,
Many-harmonied, diverse, profound,
A shattering beauty. See, how together we break,
Hear what a crashing of disordered chords and discords
Fills the world with falling, when we thus lean
Our two mad bodies together!

                    It is a sound
Of everlasting grief, the sound of weeping,
The sound of disaster and misery, the sound
Of passionate heartbreak at the centre of the world.

An Old Man Weeping

How can she say this misery? A hand
Of gold, with fingers of brass, plucking
At random, murderously and harshly, among
The stretched strings of the soul? A hand cruel
Yet loved? Deep in the soul it plunges

Twanging and snapping; murderous graceful hand
On which she fawns and weeps.

And yet not this
Nor nothing like this. It is a burning tree
Grotesque of shape, yet many-leaved, wherethrough
The wind makes melody.

Nor yet this,
It is a music powerful and visible
Shaped like an octopus, each arm a beak,
Each beak a murder.

Nor yet this, but love
Taloned, with red on talons, and redder mouth,
Singing and striking.

You, through whom love comes,
Hideous, gaunt, large-boned, arid of face,
Ravaged by sorrow — say why it is that love
Flies to you as the bat flies to its cavern!
Hated woman of wormwood, body steeped
In Lethe, tasting of death!

The carven priest
Gilded and small, with one gilt hand uplifted
And gilded forehead smooth, and coronet
Gilded, and the black eyelashes lowered
To hide the eyes, and passive suffering mouth,
Woodenly murmurs: Tao, the way, the way,
The region Way!

And the red crusted bowl
Shaped by the fleeing potter, eyes intent
On dragons, cries — Give form to formless, shape
The flying chaos!

And last the imprisoned blood,
Pouring darkly from cell to cell of the heart,
Upseethes: Go near her, break her walls down, pour
Blood into blood, embed your brain in hers,
Root your gross thought in her no-less-gross thought!
Music with music mingles, be you music
Mingled, let the dissonance, clashed and dissolved,
Pierce with reality the too-smooth song!

(. . . Thus looked she at me on a summer evening
With cornflower eyes, sad brow, and aging mouth,
And smiled askance, miserable, dumb, ashamed,
And moved the pathetic bones toward me sadly,
And locked me in her heart, as one might lock
An old man, weeping, in a rusted cage.)

Electra

I

The little princess, on her eleventh birthday,
Trapped a blue butterfly in a net of gauze,
Where it was sunning on a speckled stone.
The blue wings fluttered in the silkworm net.
'What voice, Blue Butterfly,' (the Princess cried)
'Is voice of butterfly? . . . You scream in fury
Close to my ear; yet hear I not a sound.'
She caught it down against the stone, and pressed
A royal finger on each round blue wing;
And as one tears apart a folded leaf
By pushing right and left, so tore she, smiling,
The azure fly. . . Her eyes were bright and blue,
Her teeth were sharp; the sunlight streaked her hair
With twining gold along two braids. She frowned
As might a chemist at a test-tube-drop
(Bright, poisonous and pendent) when she saw
Cerulean dust upon each finger tip.

This, being rubbed against a tulip-mouth,
(A glutted bee dislodged) she sat demurely:
Opened her book, on which leaf-shadows winked;
And blew a dart toward a scarlet bird
In bright green tropics of the Amazon.

II

Dressing the naked doll of redded wax,
(The white cheeks rouged), she feather-stitched a square
Of scarlet silk with golden staggering stitches;
Chain-lightninged all its edges. After this,
A square of azure silk, a square of purple,
Superimposed; and then a tinfoil crown,
Massive, of divers colours; this, compounded
(Relics of Beaune, of Jerez, and Oporto)
Blazed the wax brow. A bed of cottonwool
Was smoothed; and thrice-anointed Ferdinand
(First pressed against her thigh for nourishment)
Was covered with a soiled green handkerchief
And closed his eyes: exchanging glass for wax.

This was the seventh year. Between the eighth
And ninth, the form of nourishment was changed.
The doll was clasped between her knees. She held
A knife in one hand, while the other lifted
A paper bird. The neck of this was severed.
And Ferdinand had passed from milk to blood.

III

'Your soul' (so said her father in the spring
That brought her sixteenth year) 'turns smaller, as
Your body waxes to ripe beauty. Dwarfs
(As you have seen in circuses, or tumbling
Through scarlet-papered hoops, at vaudeville)
Bear on the brow, though mouth and eyes be fair,

A drawn and arid look, of suffering.
Dwarfed, and as blue and arid, peers the soul
Like a starved nymph from your bright eyes. Your mouth
Though beautiful, and, yes, desirable, —
(Even to me, who like a wizard shaped it), —
Is much too red; too cruelly downward curved,
It hides a tooth too sharp. You will do murder —
Laughing and weeping; hear the song of blood;
The gnome in you will laugh; the nymph will weep.'

She locked strong hands around his neck and kissed him.
Lifting a naked knee to press him subtly
She hurt him consciously; kissed till he laughed;
Unlocked her hands, then, sobered; moved away;
Shook down the golden skirt; whistled a tune;
And read the morning paper, coiled like a cat.

IV

'Under this water-lily knee' (she said)
'Blood intricately flows, corpuscle creeps,
The white like sliced cucumber, and the red
Like poker-chip! Along dark mains they flow
As wafts the sponging heart. The water-lily,
Subtle in seeming, bland to lover's hand
Upthrust exploring, is in essence gross,
Multiple and corrupt. Thus, in the moonlight'
(She hooked a curtain and disclosed the moon)
'How cold and lucent! And this naked breast,
Whereon a blue vein writes Diana's secret,
How simple! How seductive of the palm
That flatters with the finest tact of flesh!
Not silver is this flank, nor ivory,
Gold it is not, not copper, but distilled
Of lust in moonlight, and my own hand strays
To touch it in this moonlight, whence it came.'
Naked in moonlight, like a doll of wax,

On the stone floor nocturnal, she stood still
But moved her hands. The cruel mouth was curved,
Smiling a little; and her eyes were fixed,
In wonder, on Diana's hieroglyph.
And it was then (her nineteenth autumn come)
She heard at last, so often prophesied,
The singing of the blood. Her beauty broke
To sound beneath her hands, which moved from breast
To knee and back again, and bruised the flank
That was not gold or copper, but became
A throbbing sound beneath palpating palms.
Thus stood awhile; then sighed; then dropped her hands
And wept, as he (who loved her) had foretold.

v

It was the twentieth birthday, or the moon,
Which flung a careless net upon the house
Trapping the stone (as she had trapped the fly);
These, or the emptied heart of night, which filled
The house with weeping. In the room they lay
Weeping together. 'Like a harp it is'
(She said) 'which but to sound, but once to sound,
Snaps every string. Better to die, than be
Conjointly now, henceforth, a broken thing
Where sound of life was once.' She pressed his hand
Against her side, where once the doll was pressed,
Prince Ferdinand; but she was hungry still.
So then she held him hard between her knees
And heard the song of blood, outrageously,
And cried, 'Shut eyes and kiss me!' 'O, Arachne!
What web is this you weave, dear poison-mouth?'
'The web, alas, is cut as soon as woven,'
She answered. And the word she spoke was true.

VI

The moonlight and the house then sang together,
Yet not the house, but something in the house,
As if together they once more distilled
(Of blood and moonlight) ivory or gold,
Copper or silver; or, if not quite these
Something of which the moon contrived the surface
While blood beneath supplied the essence gross.
Useless! for it was spilled as soon as brimmed.
Prince Ferdinand was dead, Arachne dead,
The blood unmoving, and the moonlight vain.

Goya

Goya drew a pig on a wall.
The five-year-old hairdresser's son
Saw, graved on a silver tray,
The lion; and sunsets were begun.

Goya smelt the bull-fight blood.
The pupil of the Carmelite
Gave his hands to a goldsmith, learned
To gild an aureole aright.

Goya saw the Puzzel's eyes:
Sang in the street (with a guitar)
And climbed the balcony; but Keats
(Under the halyards) wrote 'Bright star.'

Goya saw the Great Slut pick
The chirping human puppets up,
And laugh, with pendulous mountain lip,
And drown them in a coffee cup;

Or squeeze their little juices out
In arid hands, insensitive,

To make them gibber . . . Goya went
Among the catacombs to live.

He saw gross Ronyons of the air,
Harelipped and goitered, raped in flight
By hairless pimps, umbrella-winged:
Tumult above Madrid at night.

He heard the seconds in his clock
Crack like seeds, divulge, and pour
Abysmal filth of Nothingness
Between the pendulum and the floor:

Torrents of dead veins, rotted cells,
Tonsils decayed, and fingernails:
Dead hair, dead fur, dead claws, dead skin:
Nostrils and lids; and cauls and veils;

And eyes that still, in death, remained
(Unlidded and unlashed) aware
Of the foul core, and, fouler yet,
The region worm that ravins there.

Stench flowed out of the second's tick.
And Goya swam with it through Space,
Sweating the fetor from his limbs,
And stared upon the unfeatured face

That did not see, and sheltered naught,
But was, and is. The second gone,
Goya returned, and drew the face;
And scrawled beneath it, 'This I have known' . . .

And drew four slatterns, in an attic,
Heavy, with heads on arms, asleep:
And underscribed it, 'Let them slumber,
Who, if they woke, could only weep' . . .

Sonnets

I

Broad on the sunburnt hill the bright moon comes,
And cuts with silver horn the hurrying cloud,
And the cold Pole Star, in the dusk, resumes
His last night's light, which light alone could shroud.
And legion other stars, that torch pursuing,
Take each their stations in the deepening night,
Lifting pale tapers for the Watch, renewing
Their glorious foreheads in the infinite.
Never before had night so many eyes.
Never was darkness so divinely thronged
As now — my love! bright star! — when you arise,
Giving me back that night which I had wronged.
Now with your voice sings all the immortal host,
This god of myriad stars whom I thought lost.

II

What music's devious voice can say, beguiling
The flattered spirit, your voice can richlier say,
Moving the happy creature to such smiling
As the young sun brings flowers at break of day.
Nor can the southwest wind, which turns green boughs,
Or sings in watery reeds, outvie your voice,
No, though the whole wide world of birds he rouse,
And boughs and birds together all rejoice.
Not water's self, shy singer among stones,
Vowelling softly of his secret love,
Can murmur to green roots such undertones,
Nor with low laughter have such power to move.
No rival — none. There is no help for us.
Be it confessed: I am idolatrous.

III

Think, when a starry night of bitter frost
Is ended, and the small pale winter sun
Shines on the garden trellis, ice-embossed,
And the stiff frozen flower-stalks, every one,
And turns their fine embroideries of ice
Into a loosening silver, skein by skein,
Warming cold sticks and stones, till, in a trice,
The garden sighs, and smiles, and breathes again:
And further think how the poor frozen snail
Creeps out with trembling horn to feel that heat,
And thaws the snowy mildew from his mail,
Stretching with all his length from his retreat:
Will he not praise, with his whole heart, the sun?
Then think at last I too am such an one.

IV

My love, I have betrayed you seventy times
In this brief period since our stars were met:
Against your ghost announced unnumbered crimes,
And many times its image overset;
Forgot you, worshipped others, flung a flower
To meaner beauty, proved an infidel;
Showing my heart not loyal beyond an hour,
Betraying Paradise, and invoking Hell.
Alas! what chain of thought can thinking bind?
It is in thought alone that I have faltered,
It is my fugitive and quicksilver mind,
By every chance and change too lightly altered.
Can I absolve, from this all-staining sin,
The angelic love who sits, ashamed, within?

V

IMPRIMIS: I forgot all day your face,
Eyes, eyebrows, gentle mouth, and cheek, all faded;
Nor could I, in the mind's dark forest, trace
The haunted path whereby that dream evaded.
Secundus: I forgot all night your laughter,
In vain evoked it by strong charms of thought:
Gone, like a cry that leaves no image after,
Phoenix of sound which no hand ever caught.
Tertius: my wanton mind and heart, together,
Forgetting you, you absent, have delighted
For no more cause than bright or stormy weather,
Singing for joy; in truth, I am benighted.
Yet, when I home once more from breach of faith,
Love there awaits me with a joy like death.

VI

What lunacy is this, that night-long tries,
With seven or seventy or ten thousand words,
To compass God in heaven, the loved one's eyes?
Alas! were the whole language turned to birds,
And I Prince Prospero to set them free,
Though I should hide all heaven with beating wings,
Still the essential would escape, still be
Unspoken, dumb, like all essential things.
Love, let me be the beginning world, and grow
To Time from Timelessness, and out of Time
Create magnificent Chaos, and there sow
The immortal stars, and teach those stars to rhyme —
Even so, alas, I could in no sense move
From the begin-all-end-all phrase, 'I love.'

VII

My love, my love, take back that word, unsay
The heavy sentence that confronts us now:
Check Time: and let today be yesterday,
The fallen flower again upon its bough.
Say you deceived yourself — say you mistook —
Say you were angry, though you were not so —
And I'll believe you as the boy his book,
Taking your no for yes, your yes for no.
Christ! Is it possible this shadow weighs
So grievously upon you? And must I
Find comfort in this secondary praise, —
Outshone, by him, in your appraising eye?
Were love magnanimous, then I might speak
Nobly of this and him; but I am weak.

VIII

Here's Nature: it's a spider in a flower,
Poison in honey, darkness in delight,
Disastrous doom that tolls delirium's hour,
The arrow of mischief in the brightest light.
What's love, with doubt's slow venom mixed, unless
It be a most ecstatic hue of hate?
Joy, in the heart, grows dumb with bitterness;
The serpent coils bright rings by Eden gate.
Nor can the eye, or cunning brain, remove
Loathing from love, or honor from mistrust;
Horror with beauty wrangles in this love,
The angel wrestles with the fiend of lust.
Not here, not here, will Eros rest his head,
Nor sleep, and smile in sleep, till we be dead.

IX

Here's daffodil — here's tulip — here's the leaf
Of new-sprung hawthorn in the bird-loud wood;
And sunlight trumpeting at our coil of grief,
While busy murder hammers at his Rood.
You are not all I thought you might be; I
Am not the god my rival was; and so,
We stare, we tremble, hopeless to deny
The chaos that we know, and know we know.
Here is no tragedy, if it were not
That more I love you as you worse appear;
Here is no poison could you be forgot,
And that grim shadow which you hold so dear.
But since you loved him, love, he lives in you;
And since I hate him, I must hate you too.

The Pomecitron Tree

Here the skeleton leaf, between
Eglantine and celandine,
Harries an hour (that seems an age)
The snail's deliberate pilgrimage.
And in that same stupendous hour,
While royally unfolds the flower
Magniloquent in the sunlight, She
Dreams by the pomecitron tree.

Not lust alone is in her mind,
Nor the sad shapes of humankind.
What ant is this, with horns, who comes
Exploring huge geraniums?
Up the green-jointed column stalks,
And into halls of scarlet walks;
Boldly intrudes, partakes, then goes
— Alas! — to eat her favorite rose.

Not lust alone; yet this was lust,
And lust was that deliberate gust
That warmly roused the leaves, caressed
The lawn, and on her open breast
Blew, from the pomecitron tree,
One ravished petal, and a bee . . .
Into her bosom flew, from this,
The fiery-wingèd wounding kiss.

Into her bosom. Deeper then,
It startles to that world of men,
Who, in the kingdom of her mind,
Awake, arise, begin to wind
Along the subterranean road
That leads from their abhorred abode. . .
They move and murmur, while the ant
Climbs an enormous rhubarb plant.

And then it is her voice that cries,
While still beneath the tree she lies:
Maker of gardens, let me be
Turned to a pomecitron tree!
Within his veins no longings rise;
He turns no concupiscent eyes;
Nor hears, in the infernal mind,
The lustful army wake and wind.

He, though his roots are in the grave,
Is placid and unconscious, save
Of burning light, or rain, that slides
On dripping leaves and down his sides.
In his cool thought the sparrow nests;
A leaf, among more leaves she rests;
Or, if she sings, her watery voice
Is joined with countless that rejoice.

What bliss is his! what deep delight!
To face, with his own dark, the night!
With his own sunrise meet the sun!
Or whistle with the wind, and run!
Why, Lord, was it ordained that I
Must turn an inward-roving eye?
Why must I know, unlike this tree,
What lusts and murders nourish me?

To him, no doubt, most innocent
Seems, in this sunlight, my intent:
No primrose ever lightlier breathed
Than my tall body, flower-enwreathed.
Soft as lilies the sunlight rests
Upon my pollen-powdered breasts.
My two hands, of their own sweet will,
Can stir like leaves, or stand as still.

What stems can match this throat of gold
And ivory? What stalks uphold
So lightly, in this garden, such
Delirious flowers to taste and touch?
What pistilled mouth can rival here
My mouth, what leaves outvie my hair
In mindless beauty? . . . Yet, behind
This mindless beauty lurks a mind.

Ah, while the rhubarb leaf is spread
Broad as a salver by my head:
And the green aphis pastures on
This tall green tower of Solomon:
The mind, within my flower's bell,
Conceals its black concentric hell.
There at this minute swarms the host,
And lewd ghost speaks with furious ghost.

There the sad shapes of humankind
Through brown defiles in sorrow wind;
And, if they speak, their arid speech
Is of that land they cannot reach.
There the defeated warrior lies,
And westward turns defrauded eyes.
Deformed and monstrous are those men:
They climb, and do not turn again.

It is to me each lifts his face!
It is to me, with footsore pace,
Summoned once more, they creep and come,
Pointing toward me as to home.
What love is in their eyes! Alas,
That love so soon to lust should pass!
The hands they lift are stumps; they stir
The rank leaves where their faces were.

Maker of gardens, let me be
Turned to a pomecitron tree;
Or let me be this rhubarb plant,
Whose lavish love is ignorant;
Or let me be this daffodil,
Which lusts and murders, yet is still
All-in-itself, a golden All
Concentred in one burning ball!

. . . She sighs; and it is in her thought
That grief so desperate may be fraught
With tears; and tears were sweet, displayed
Here, in the pomecitron shade;
And grief is pleasant, when beguiled
By mindless garden, or a child;
But the few tears are thought, not shed;
She claps her hands, and laughs, instead.

Annihilation

While the blue noon above us arches,
And the poplar sheds disconsolate leaves,
Tell me again why love bewitches,
And what love gives.

Is it the trembling finger that traces
The eyebrow's curve, the curve of the cheek?
The mouth that quivers, when the hand caresses,
But cannot speak?

No, not these, not in these is hidden
The secret, more than in other things:
Not only the touch of a hand can gladden
Till the blood sings.

It is the leaf that falls between us,
The bells that murmur, the shadows that move,
The autumnal sunlight that fades upon us:
These things are love.

It is the 'No, let us sit here longer,'
The 'Wait till tomorrow,' the 'Once I knew — '
These trifles, said as I touch your finger,
And the clock strikes two.

The world is intricate, and we are nothing.
It is the complex world of grass,
A twig on the path, a look of loathing,
Feelings that pass —

These are the secret! And I could hate you,
When, as I lean for another kiss,
I see in your eyes that I do not meet you,
And that love is this.

Rock meeting rock can know love better
Than eyes that stare or lips that touch.
All that we know in love is bitter,
And it is not much.

Meeting

Why do I look at you? Why do I touch you? What do I seek in you,
      woman,
That I should hurry to meet you again?
Why must I sound once more your abysmal nothingness,
And draw up only pain?

Hard, hard, I stare at your watery eyes; yet am not convinced,
Now no more than ever before,
That they are only two mirrors reflecting the sky's blank light,
That, and nothing more.

And I press my body against your body, as though I hoped to break
Clean through to another sphere;
And I strive to speak to you with a speech beyond my speech,
In which all things are clear;

Till exhausted I drown once more in your abysmal nothingness,
And the cold nothingness of me:
You, laughing and crying in this ridiculous room,
With your hand upon my knee;

Crying because you think me perverse and unhappy; and laughing
To find our love so strange;
Our eyes fixed hard on each other in a last blind desperate hope
That the whole world might change.

At a Concert of Music

Be still, while the music rises about us; the deep enchantment
Towers, like a forest of singing leaves and birds,
Built, for an instant, by the heart's troubled beating,
Beyond all power of words.

And while you are listening, silent, I escape you;
And I run by a secret path through that dark wood
To another time, long past, and another woman,
And another mood.

Then, too, the music's cold algebra of enchantment
Wrought all about us a bird-voice-haunted grove;
Then, too, I escaped, as now, to an earlier moment,
And a brighter love.

Alas! Can I never have peace in the shining instant?
The hard bright crystal of being, in time and space?
Must I always touch, in the moment, an earlier moment,
And an earlier face?

Absolve me. I would adore you, had I the secret,
With all this music's power, for yourself alone;
I would try to answer, in the world's chaotic symphony,
Your one clear tone:

But alas, alas, being everything you are nothing —
The history of all my life is in your face:
And all I can know is an earlier, more haunted moment,
And a happier place.

The Argument

First Voice

Do not believe this mighty grief
Is more than breaking of a leaf.
Summer can tear the elder blossom
To redder pain than wounds a bosom.
The numbed bee climbs, and climbs again,
And faints at foot of window-pane.
The sparrow, trammelled in tall grass,
Knows terror deep as Jesus' was.

Second Voice

How wider, how much deeper then,
The comprehensive grief of men,
Who, in the universe of mind,
The law itself of sorrow find!
Although you catch the fainting bee
And on Hymettus set her free,
The multitudes remain, who die
Alone, unheard, on Calvary.

These, though they be unseen, we know:
They help our prize of grief to grow.
How, then, can pain of mindless flowers,
Or panic bird, be great as ours?
Each aching leaf and claw is part
Of that all-sympathizing heart.
All griefs it knows; and then knows too
The grief of knowing that grief is true.

First Voice

Do not believe this argument
Whose rays of light are water-bent!

Alas, each humble suffering thing
Meets, in the hurting of the wing,
As much of pain as it can bear;
The smoke of Hinnom greets it there;
Or, if the pain be more, its eyes
Are closed, the bird or flower dies.

But you, who say your grief is great,
Can still, with wisdom, contemplate!
How can the living know a grief
As sharp as that which killed the leaf?
Ah, when I hear you yield the cry
Of loss itself, and see you die,
Then I will hail that Night in you
Which, as it died, the dead leaf knew.

Second Voice

But I have seen in living eyes,
And under foreheads calm and wise,
Such caves of suffering as shame
The omnipotent creator's name.
They know and see; they feel; yet bear
What none but humankind would dare;
To world's end look, and back again,
And see in all things only pain.

There, in the one bewildered face,
Is sorrow of an outcast race.
Darkness too deep for human tongue
Is there miraculously sung.
Look, how the barren poet's style
Seems, in the act of death, to smile!
He tries to laugh, this creature made
Of pain, and born in sorrow's shade.

Ah! I have seen in one short page
Such sorrow as would fill an age,
And in a scribbled letter known
Anguish would burn an empire down.
Here's Shakespeare — look! — whose heart grows numb,
And his angelic power dumb,
When the one drop of weeping blood
Upon his page becomes a flood.

First Voice

Do not believe your Shakespeare's grief
Is more than tearing of a leaf.
Tread on an ant, he knows a pain
Cruel and red and broad as Spain.
Starving mice and weeping trees
The hemlock drink with Socrates.
The lark, defeated, knows a loss
As black as hangs upon a cross.

The Quarrel

Suddenly, after the quarrel, while we waited,
Disheartened, silent, with downcast looks, nor stirred
Eyelid nor finger, hopeless both, yet hoping
Against all hope to unsay the sundering word:

While the room's stillness deepened, deepened about us,
And each of us crept his thought's way to discover
How, with as little sound as the fall of a leaf,
The shadow had fallen, and lover quarrelled with lover;

And while, in the quiet, I marvelled — alas, alas —
At your deep beauty, your tragic beauty, torn
As the pale flower is torn by the wanton sparrow —
This beauty, pitied and loved, and now forsworn;

It was then, when the instant darkened to its darkest, —
When faith was lost with hope, and the rain conspired
To strike its gay arpeggios against our heartstrings, —
When love no longer dared, and scarcely desired:

It was then that suddenly, in the neighbor's room,
The music started: that brave quartette of strings
Breaking out of the stillness, as out of our stillness,
Like the indomitable heart of life that sings

When all is lost; and startled from our sorrow,
Tranced from our grief by that diviner grief,
We raised remembering eyes, each looked at other,
Blinded with tears of joy; and another leaf

Fell silently as that first; and in the instant
The shadow had gone, our quarrel became absurd;
And we rose, to the angelic voices of the music,
And I touched your hand, and we kissed, without a word.

Twelve Good Men

I

Yawning orchids, with lilac throats,
Burning lilies and dahlias, deep
Tulips (the tropic steams with fragrance),
Violets mooned and huge with dew;
Carnations, colour-of-cowrie, sharp
With jointed stems . . . Lord, what flowers!
The glass at the front of the shop is fogged,
Rippled, confused, the light drips through, —
Crooked peonies, wrinkled phlox,
Green in jungles, and red in waves.
Sweet peas, lapped in a pearly tissue,
Glow through the dimness, coral and jade . . .

High over all, in a copper cage,
Yellowbird swings with live black eyes,
Darts to his perch, flaps at the wires,
Fills his throat with bubbles, and sings.

The murderess wears on her breast today
A small white rose: . . . bends her head,
Crushing the stamens against her lips . . .
How can she hear the evidence now? . . .
The man is saying 'At one, I walked
In the Public Garden, and met her there . . .'
The murderess listens, hints a smile
Smelling the rose . . . She killed his wife?
Perhaps she was right! 'At half-past two —
She went to the station to catch a train . . .'
Half-past two! and will they remember
To put fresh roses behind the door?
The low voice murmurs 'At five o'clock
I walked to the house . . . My wife was dead.'
. . . Dead! More flowers! — a hearse of flowers!
Carriages packed to the roof with flowers!
The raw-turned clay with flowers smothered,
Roses in wreaths with well-wired leaves,
Crosses of ivy, dripping moss,
Arums, cannas, and dense tuberoses! . . .
All of them dead next day!

II

Figures and figures and figures and figures
This to the debit, that to the credit,
Inked forefinger and left eye blurred;
One more entry to make . . . The florist
Sighs, leans forward, a woman's voice
Quavers 'I went to the porch, to shake
My long-handled mop, — in the afternoon, —
And saw this girl' — The voice proceeds,

Babbles of murder, the twelfth of June,
The girl who asked 'Is his wife's hair grey?'
'No, that's his mother . . .' the voice flows on,
The murderess tilts her eyes to the jury,
Muses; ponders; with idle finger
Turns, on the thin white wrist, her bracelet,
Slips it upward, then downward, wonders
Darkly, at bottom of eyes grown deep . . .
Ah, she is pretty; looks like — who?
Someone, on the hot beach, in summer.
Gloucester: Edith! the eyes are the same;
And the sombre mouth; and the braided hair!
Could Edith have dared a thing like this — ?
No! — incredible! . . . There, by the sea,
She laughed, and scooped blue wells in the sand,
Splashed in the shallows, ran and screeched
When gravel and undertow dragged her feet . . .
The widow, who lives in the flat upstairs,
Flushes; flutes 'I had just come down
To scour my kettle; and there in the yard
I saw this woman. Her dress was brown,
She wore a toque of a lemonish yellow,
With small squat flowers. Queer, she said,
He lived — so rich! — in a house like that . . .
Well, it's true, I might have forgotten
The face, — but then, I'm sure of the hat! . . .'
Figures, figures, figures, figures;
Red ink, blue ink, pages and pages:
Columns and lines . . . The clock ticks slowly;
And always, one more entry to make.

III

The murderess, lifting her hatrim, burning,
Burns straight at him! Her eyes are blue,
The young mouth tired and disillusioned,
Worn, as a pebble is worn by the sea.

To think what hatred devoured this body,
Gnawed her to nothing! There she is,
Pale and lovely, a sea-blanched root,
Flung to the horror of sun . . . The judge
Rules out the witness's 'indisposure.'
The voice is raised: 'I smelt the smoke
And knocked at the door, but got no answer;
Stooped; looked through the keyhole; saw
Her sitting, leaning, propped on the table,
Her head bent down in a curious way —
Perfectly still! — I forced the door
And saw she was dead: the pistol lying
Just inside the crook of her arm . . .'
An officer brings *'exhibit five.'*
'This is the morning-gown she wore?'
'Yes; it is' . . . The dark green satin
Is lifted; whispers; the audience stirs;
The murderess lowers her chin, and stares
Tranquilly at it; as though she saw
A curious thing, and far away . . .

Noon is struck; the court adjourns.
. . . Will Paul remember to wind the clocks?
. . . He lifts in tweezers a tiny ruby,
(Glittering blood-stained grain of sand;)
Peers through the microscope at his eye;
And drops it cunningly into the socket,
Seeing it huge as a damson plum.
The delicate spring, like a breathing thing,
Dilates and closes, dilates again;
A chorus of tickings, loud and soft,
Nervous and light or solemn and slow,
Thin and metallic, or like faint music,
Teases the air; hung on the wall
Are watches and watches and clocks and clocks
Nibbling at time; spread on the counter
Are smouldering opals in velvet trays,

Diamonds winking with points of blue,
Crimson and saffron, coral in heaps,
A ring like a snake with small sharp eyes,
And a *'lavalliere* of pearls, well graded,
With one in the centre, a large pink pearl,
Slightly buttoned.' He picks with tweezers
The glittering ruby, a lizard's eye,
And tips it tinily into its place . . .
Lord what a ticking! the air is fevered
With seconds coming to consciousness.

                            IV

The 'cello' waxes the worn white bow;
The 'oboe' drops a plummeted string
To pull the cloth through the oboe's length;
Luvic, smiling, struts out to sing, —
With clouds of powder on shoulders and arms,
Emeralds lighting her thick white hands.
He strikes three chords: she licks coarse lips:
White, in the pool of fire, she stands,
Fills the magnificent throat, and sings.
Pearls in a hailstorm flash to grass;
Cold clouds melt in a cobalt sky;
Birds through the thick boughs trill and pass.

Hearing the husband murmur — 'Yes!
I gave her a ring, and told her lies!' —
The murderess touches a scarlet check
Leans slowly, covers her face, and cries.
The voice goes on: 'Ten months ago, —
One afternoon, — because I had said
That I was 'through,' — she poisoned herself;
And later, I found her nearly dead . . .'
Poisoned herself — for a man like him! —
Well! — The murderess stares at the floor,

Dabs at her cheek . . . Half-past two:
Luvic opens the piano-score.

v

Seventy fir-trees flung in waves
On frozen grass, to lop with an axe,
And nail to the pole for a Christmas Tree!
The fresh chips leap, the wood is sweet,
The blue edge smears and dulls with pitch;
And now with a hammer the nails are driven
In sharply ascending scales of sound, —
Blows on a great dull xylophone . . .
Nail the star to the top of the tree
Jewelled with small red bulbs! . . . Sea wind
Wails in the boughs, the pigeons fly,
Hover above him with whimper of wings,
Clapping wide wings in white and blue,
Or wheeling away when the hammer falls . . .

The old pawnbroker fawns at the rail
Rubs pale hands, and slides his eyes
Like little green beads from side to side
And scratches his beard . . . 'Yes, I am sure
That is the woman I sold it to . . .
She wore a veil, but I noticed her eyes . . .
The fifth of June: a gun pearl-handled;
The calibre — yes — was thirty-two . . .'
The murderess glares, a fury cries
'How can you stand there, you, a man,
Who never saw me, never before,
And swear my life away!' . . . The judge
Raps for order; the old Jew grins
And rubs his mouth with his hand. 'Strike out
That speech from the record! — You, of the jury,
Pay no attention to that! — Proceed.'

Pay no attention! You might as well
Shut your ears to a thunder-clap!
By George, the hussy was fine! And look
At the husband, furtive and sheepish there!
The rotten loafer! if men like him
Were only given more work to do . . . !
Say, won't the boys be keen on this? . . .
And Annie will spoil the dinner, to hear it! —

VI

June the twentieth: ten o'clock.
The moon just rising . . . Strange, that love,
Of all things, is so hard to remember.
The warmth of a hand, a sigh, a kiss,
The ring of a voice among still trees,
Old apple-trees, poor frightened ghosts —
Gone, all gone! — And meanwhile, there,
Two miles away at a farmhouse door,
A lantern whirling its ominous shadows
Of scissored legs on a wall of mist,
A knock at the door, a drowsy woman,
Death in a question, death in an answer, —
And vivid now as if carved in stone.
Strange, that love should be carved in mist,
And death, with a slow hand, carved in stone.

Blossoms sink in the moonlit fern.
Tree-toads trill in the misty trees.
The murderess straightens, pale and tired,
Smooths her hair (an eye on the clock)
And the voice proceeds: 'At half-past ten
We knocked at the farm-door, found her there
Half undressed and going to bed.
She spoke; was calm; confessed she knew
As soon as she saw us why we came . . .'
The husband hides his face with his hands . . .

The murderess smiles and strokes her knee . . .
. . . June the twentieth, ten o'clock.
Love-in-a-mist, and death in stone.

VII

The floor is sweet with trodden shavings,
Twisted shavings and musk of pine;
He lays the plane aside, and saws
Steadily through the pencilled line;
The streaked saw hums, the sawdust sifts
A lazy dust; before him lies
The delicate blue-print pinned to the board;
A knot in the wood, the hot saw cries
Perplexed and shrill . . . His back is tired;
He stands for a moment; sees her there
Smiling, laughing, far away,
Grey-eyed and pale, with haloed hair, —
Her fingers dusted white with flour,
Her sleeves rolled up to the elbows, — far
In space and time, her small face shining
Coldly and steadily as a star.
Christmas is coming: He will fashion
A box of teakwood, small and fine;
And carve the top with leaves and roses,
And rub with oils to make it shine.
One in the center, opened flat,
Petal and pistil carved with care,
Soft as the flesh of the rose itself;
Leaves curled back to reveal it there.

The officer shows *exhibit four* —
The bullet chipped from the parlour wall;
Turns the lead between finger and thumb.
The doctor is summoned; takes the stand;
Cynic; opened the woman's skull;
Dissected; found two bullets; one

'Undoubtedly caused unconsciousness — .
It lodged in the brain above the ear . . .'
The eyes of the murderess rove like moths,
Rove like moths in the courtroom, rest
Profound with mystery; and he sees
The world she lives in, like his own, —
Hovels, black streets, wet walls and trees;
Deadfaced people who creep and cry
Through chequered shadows of day and night;
Wind in the tulips; wind at the windows;
Vagrant music, and pain, and light.
Labyrinths all! and in us slumber
The scarlet angels we do not know —
The furious demon who whets a knife;
The eye in the dark that aims a blow.

VIII

Christmas is coming — time to change,
Arrange new prints and casts in the window! —
What was the one that sold last year? . . .
Ah, that one of queans in a harem
Shooting craps by a marble pool;
Columns, and doves, and a blind flute-player!
The wingèd goddess; the Lincoln imp;
And then, that print that has sold for years, —
Dante (you know, — the sour-faced poet!)
Glooming, mute, by the bridge in Florence;
Sulking aloof; while Beatrice comes
Along the wall by the old brown river,
Languid in satin, sniffing a flower,
Musing, with half-shut, sea-bright eyes . . .
That tinted etching — an old cathedral —
The one great sun-shot rich rose-window,
With dusky ladder of sunlight, lighting
Tiny people and stone-bright floor . . .
And the one in blue; the slim sharp maenad

Dancing, white, on a wind-swept headland, —
Dancing (with arms raised) toward the sea.
And the faun with pipes by a twisted pine;
And the long green wave with glittering edge,
Mottled with creamfoam, ready to crash!

Downward, through this whirl, Medusa
Stares, unlidded, sombre, saddens
Cold to the heart, draws inward sleep,
And slumbers all, dull eyelids dropt . . .
The suicide note (*exhibit two*)
Intoned; the expert mounts the stand.
'It is my view, this note was written
By the murdered woman' . . . Suicide note . . . !
So: the murderess must have glared
Pistol in hand; commanded: 'write!'
And shot her twice, while the ink was wet . . .
Just like her, too: easy to see
How ripe she'd be for a thing like that —
Shoot her, slap the hot gun down
Reeking with smoke, and walk right out
And slam the door as if nothing had happened! —

IX

. . . Judas! if Janes were all like her —
How many men would, like this husband,
Cringe in a chair in a buzzing court
And watch their spotted lives unravelled! . . .
Poor wretch! He did what all fools do —
And here he was, in a greenish glare,
Sprawled on the slide of a microscope!
And all because that damned fool chit
(Who after all was as bad as he)
Believed a passion could last forever! . . .
Suppose, now, Grace should find it out
That he was not, as he told her, married; —

She'd drag him into the courts — to-morrow! . . .
Or if she was half-mad (like this woman),
Shoot him! — No, no, the woman is guilty!
And high time, too, these harpies learned
That you can't revenge yourself on fate
For a broken heart by berserk killing!
Think, now; if Grace should read the papers,
And see this harebrained fool acquitted . . .
My God! Who knows? She might go running
To have her photograph newly taken —
(Venus born from a foam of tulle!)
And buy a pistol and sprint, hot-foot,
To nail him with bullets against a wall! . . .
And afterwards, on the witness-stand,
Confess with sobs, — poor innocent thing, —
How he had come, an older man,
And led her astray! — Led her astray!

                              x

Lemons in bowls, chopped ice in vats,
Syrups in rows of sticky jars,
Venomous green and bloodstone red,
Orange, chocolate, lustre of lights
In slippery marble, flash of glass
And moan of fans. Banana flips,
Sundaes with syrups and ladled nuts,
Sherbets in alps, ice cream, an egg
Cracked in a glass . . . and a voice is saying
'You mean to tell me, — in spite of that,
And after you knew this man was married, —
You loved him still, and wore his ring? . . .
Although you knew he had lied to you —
You still could trust him?' 'Yes, I did.'
'And you believed him, when he said
As soon as his first wife was divorced

He'd marry you — you believed in this?'
'Yes.' — 'And this ring he gave to you —
How was it marked?' — 'From Tom to Joan.'
'Nothing else?' — 'No, nothing else.'
'You did not know the divorce was granted
Until he had married his second wife —
The murdered woman?' — 'No, I did not.'
'How did you feel when you found this out?'
'I was surprised — but that was all . . .
My love had died, — some time ago.'
'Your love had died? . . . Why did it die?'
'Well, — because he was cruel to me' . . .

The low voice trembles; tears streak down
The scarlet cheeks, are burned away.
Drugged and ravished and kicked and beaten,
Threatened with death — and loved him still!
A man like that — and loved him still!

XI

Pools of pale light wash on the ceiling,
Whorl and quiver and swirl and vanish,
Ripple to brilliance or splay in green . . .
Delicate bubbles flow from the pipe
Voluting upward in fluted silver;
And slowly among them shimmer and fall,
Glide and glisten, or gleam and drowse,
Breathing globules among black weeds,
Vermilion fish with fire-rimmed eyes.
The tortoise sleeps, the lizard listens,
The red frog dives, the white sand stirs . . .
Ah, to pass from a world like this
Cool and quiet, submerged from time,
To horror and lust and the glare of death! —
There on the sill of the court-room window

Pigeons sidle and coo in the sun;
Here, in the silence, slowly and clearly,
Dull words drip like drops of blood.

The judge is charging the jury at last:
He lifts his finger, the words are slow.
'The law says . . .' Ah, who cares for the law?
What does it matter? — A girl sits there,
An atom horror in gravedeep eyes,
Victim of fate that is greater than laws.
Guilty? Of course. But then — who's not?
Look at her there! is she worse than these,
These twelve good men who weigh her heart? . . .

He closes his eyes: the voice recedes
With talk of 'does the evidence show'
And 'if it does you will have to say' . . .
Florist, jeweller, clerk and all
Fade, dislimn; far off he sees
This girl, who never has known a home,
Walking to work in a mill at ten —
Measuring thread and folding cloth —
Through webby windows seeing the sky.
Ten huge years she creeps like this;
Eyes and hands grow hard at the loom.
And then this salesman takes her heart,
Makes it a charm for his watch, entices
The child, half drunk with dizzy laughter,
From year to year, promise to promise;
Now in Green Street, now in Main,
Secretly now in Gordon Square, —
Hurrying into lamplit cabs,
Nervously walking in midnight streets;
From house to house, and city to city;
Flowers and theatres, kisses and blows,
Betrayal, lust, death wooed in vain, —
And life going past her all the while,

Slipping away like the hills and fields
Seen from a train; the man found vile,
Divorced, and married again in secret,
And suddenly — gone on his honeymoon! . . .
Is it a woman, or is it a girl,
Who sits there, sits in the dark, and stares,
Eyeless, searching the jury's eyes? . . .
A girl who wails and strikes with her hands
The monstrous gate that clangs in her face;
Beats on the brass with impotent hands!
Just such a girl as climbs his knee,
And begs for a story — Aladdin's Lamp;
Kay; Rapunzel; The Forty Thieves;
Sindbad; the feathery arrowed ghost
Who rose from the coffin, crossed the choir,
Climbed stone stairs to the pulpit, screamed
'Horror!' and he by the waves who sang
'Fishgirl, fishgirl, in the sea,
Come to the shore and listen to me! . . .'
Just such a girl, by the spider caught,
Tangled in scarlet and captive there! . . .

XII

The clang of hammers on purple steel
Dies; and the flash of lilac fades;
As he stands with sweating hands on the rail
Facing the mob that faces him
(Such eyes! They are ready to burn his heart!)
And brings from the dark the two sharp words
That open the wall and show the sky.

PRELUDES FOR MEMNON

O R

PRELUDES TO ATTITUDE

I

Winter for a moment takes the mind; the snow
Falls past the arclight; icicles guard a wall;
The wind moans through a crack in the window;
A keen sparkle of frost is on the sill.
Only for a moment; as spring too might engage it,
With a single crocus in the loam, or a pair of birds;
Or summer with hot grass; or autumn with a yellow leaf.
Winter is there, outside, is here in me:
Drapes the planets with snow, deepens the ice on the moon,
Darkens the darkness that was already darkness.
The mind too has its snows, its slippery paths,
Walls bayonetted with ice, leaves ice-encased.
Here is the in-drawn room, to which you return
When the wind blows from Arcturus: here is the fire
At which you warm your hands and glaze your eyes;
The piano, on which you touch the cold treble;
Five notes like breaking icicles; and then silence.

The alarm-clock ticks, the pulse keeps time with it,
Night and the mind are full of sounds. I walk
From the fire-place, with its imaginary fire,
To the window, with its imaginary view.
Darkness, and snow ticking the window: silence,
And the knocking of chains on a motor-car, the tolling
Of a bronze bell, dedicated to Christ.
And then the uprush of angelic wings, the beating

Of wings demonic, from the abyss of the mind:
The darkness filled with a feathery whistling, wings
Numberless as the flakes of angelic snow,
The deep void swarming with wings and sound of wings,
The winnowing of chaos, the aliveness
Of depth and depth and depth dedicated to death.

Here are the bickerings of the inconsequential,
The chatterings of the ridiculous, the iterations
Of the meaningless. Memory, like a juggler,
Tosses its colored balls into the light, and again
Receives them into darkness. Here is the absurd,
Grinning like an idiot, and the omnivorous quotidian,
Which will have its day. A handful of coins,
Tickets, items from the news, a soiled handkerchief,
A letter to be answered, notice of a telephone call,
The petal of a flower in a volume of Shakspere,
The program of a concert. The photograph, too,
Propped on the mantel, and beneath it a dry rosebud;
The laundry bill, matches, an ash-tray, Utamaro's
Pearl-fishers. And the rug, on which are still the crumbs
Of yesterday's feast. These are the void, the night,
And the angelic wings that make it sound.

What is the flower? It is not a sigh of color,
Suspiration of purple, sibilation of saffron,
Nor aureate exhalation from the tomb.
Yet it is these because you think of these,
An emanation of emanations, fragile
As light, or glisten, or gleam, or coruscation,
Creature of brightness, and as brightness brief.
What is the frost? It is not the sparkle of death,
The flash of time's wing, seeds of eternity;
Yet it is these because you think of these.
And you, because you think of these, are both
Frost and flower, the bright ambiguous syllable
Of which the meaning is both no and yes.

Here is the tragic, the distorting mirror
In which your gesture becomes grandiose;
Tears form and fall from your magnificent eyes,
The brow is noble, and the mouth is God's.
Here is the God who seeks his mother, Chaos, —
Confusion seeking solution, and life seeking death.
Here is the rose that woos the icicle; the icicle
That woos the rose. Here is the silence of silences
Which dreams of becoming a sound, and the sound
Which will perfect itself in silence. And all
These things are only the uprush from the void,
The wings angelic and demonic, the sound of the abyss
Dedicated to death. And this is you.

II

Two coffees in the Español, the last
Bright drops of golden Barsac in a goblet,
Fig paste and candied nuts. . . Hardy is dead,
And James and Conrad dead, and Shakspere dead,
And old Moore ripens for an obscene grave,
And Yeats for an arid one; and I, and you —
What winding sheet for us, what boards and bricks,
What mummeries, candles, prayers, and pious frauds?
You shall be lapped in Syrian scarlet, woman,
And wear your pearls, and your bright bracelets, too,
Your agate ring, and round your neck shall hang
Your dark blue lapis with its specks of gold.
And I, beside you — ah! but will that be?
For there are dark streams in this dark world, lady,
Gulf Streams and Arctic currents of the soul;
And I may be, before our consummation
Beds us together, cheek by jowl, in earth,
Swept to another shore, where my white bones
Will lie unhonored, or defiled by gulls.

What dignity can death bestow on us,
Who kiss beneath a streetlamp, or hold hands

Half hidden in a taxi, or replete
With coffee, figs and Barsac make our way
To a dark bedroom in a wormworn house?
The aspidistra guards the door; we enter,
Per aspidistra — then — *ad astra* — is it? —
And lock ourselves securely in our gloom
And loose ourselves from terror. . . . Here's my hand,
The white scar on my thumb, and here's my mouth
To stop your murmur; speechless let us lie,
And think of Hardy, Shakspere, Yeats and James;
Comfort our panic hearts with magic names;
Stare at the ceiling, where the taxi lamps
Make ghosts of light; and see, beyond this bed,
That other bed in which we will not move;
And, whether joined or separate, will not love.

III

Sleep: and between the closed eyelids of sleep,
From the dark spirit's still unresting grief,
The one tear burns its way. O God, O God,
What monstrous world is this, whence no escape
Even in sleep? Between the fast-shut lids
This one tear comes, hangs on the lashes, falls:
Symbol of some gigantic dream, that shakes
The secret-sleeping soul. . . And I descend
By a green cliff that fronts the worldlong sea;
Disastrous shore; where bones of ships and rocks
Are mixed; and beating waves bring in the sails
Of unskilled mariners, ill-starred. The gulls
Fall in a cloud upon foul flotsam there;
The air resounds with cries of scavengers.

Dream: and between the close-locked lids of dream
The terrible infinite intrudes its blue:
Ice: silence: death: the abyss of Nothing.
O God, O God, let the sore soul have peace.
Deliver it from this bondage of harsh dreams.

Release this shadow from its object, this object
From its shadow. Let the fleet soul go nimbly, —
Down, — down, — from step to step of dark, —
From dark to deeper dark, from dark to rest.
And let no Theseus-thread of memory
Shine in that labyrinth, or on those stairs,
To guide her back; nor bring her, where she lies,
Remembrance of a torn world well forgot.

IV

Or say that in the middle comes a music
Suddenly out of silence, and delight
Brings all that chaos to one mood of wonder;
A seed of fire, fallen in a tinder world;
And instantly the whirling darkness fills
With conflagration; upspoutings of delirium;
Cracklings and seethings; the melting rocks, the bursts
Of flame smoke-stifled, twisting, smoke-inwreathed;
Magnificence; the whole dark filled with light;
And then a silence, as the world falls back
Consumed, devoured, its giant corolla shrivelled;
And in the waning light, the pistil glowing,
Glowing and fading; and on that shrinking stage —

Whisper it, how among the whispering ashes
Her pale bright beauty comes, the moon's dark daughter,
Lighting those ruins with her radiant madness;
How swiftly glides, and stoops, with what light steps
Touches the dead face of that desert, comes
Nearer, bending her face, her divine eyes
Bright with the brightness of the ineffable;
Seeking, and finding not; smiling at nothing,
Blessing the emptiness; her angelic face
Hopeful at first, then hopeless, and at last
Weeping; so standing, while her slow tears fall;
And the long silence begins, the silence that was

And is and will be; creeps round her; rises coldly;
And all is still; the world, her hope, and she.

V

Despair, that seeking for the ding-an-sich,
The feeling itself, the round bright dark emotion,
The color, the light, the depth, the feathery swiftness
Of you and the thought of you, I fall and fall
From precipice word to chasm word, and shatter
Heart, brain, and spirit on the maddening fact:
If poetry says it, it must speak with a symbol.

What is a symbol? It is the 'man stoops sharp
To clutch a paper that blows in the wind';
It is the 'bed of crocuses bending in the wind,' the
Light, that 'breaks on the water with waves,' the
Wings that 'achieve in the gust the unexpected.'
These, and less than these, and more than these.
The thought, the ghost of thought, the ghost in a mirror.

Catch a beam in your hands, a beam of light,
One bright golden beam, fledgling of dust,
Hold it a moment, and feel its heart, and feel
Ethereal pulse of light between your fingers:
Then let it escape from you, and find its home
In darkness, mother of light: and this will be
Symbol of symbol, clue to clue, auricle of heart.

The glass breaks, and the liquid is spilled; the string
Snaps, and the music stops; the moving cloud
Covers the sun, and the green field is dark.
These too are symbols: and as far and near
As those; they leave the silver core uneaten;
The golden leaf unplucked; the bitter calyx
Virginal; and the whirling You unknown.

VI

This is not you? these phrases are not you?
That pomegranate of verses was not you?
The green bright leaf not you, nor the gold fruit
Burning amongst the leaves, hot fruit of gold,
Nor bird, nor bough, nor bole, nor heaven's blue?
Alas, dear woman, I have sung in vain.

Let me dishevel then once more the leaves
Of Cupid's bright thesaurus, and there find
The word of words, the crimson seed of seeds,
The aureate sound of sounds; and out of this
Conceive once more your beauty, and in terms
Your feminine keen eye will not disdain.

For this is you: on April page it is,
Again on June, and once more on December:
On August page I find it twice, and March
Chronicles it in footnote, and July
Asserts it roundly; thus, from page to page,
I find you many times, in many terms.

It is a snowflake, which is like a star,
And melts upon the hand; it is a cobweb
Shot with silver that from the golden lip
Of April's dandelion hangs to the grass;
It is a raindrop, of tremendous worth,
Which slides the whole length of a lilac leaf.

This is not you? these symbols are not you?
Not snowflake, cobweb, raindrop? . . . Woman, woman,
You are too literal, too strict with me.
What would you have? Some simple copper coin —
I love you, you are lovely, I adore you?
Or, better still, dumb silence and a look?

No, no, this will not do; I am not one
For whom these silences are sovereign;
The pauses in the music are not music,
Although they make the music what it is.
Therefore I thumb once more the god's thesaurus,
For phrase and praise, and find it all for you.

It is a star which might be thought a snowflake,
Lost in a twinkling; it is a dandelion
Shrouded with silver brightness; it is a leaf
Which lets the raindrop go, but keeps its light.
It is the purple veining, in the white,
That makes the pure throat of the iris pure. . .

Yet you would have me say your hair is Helen's, —
Your gait angelic; while I turn from these
To the vast pages of that manuscript
On which the stars are stars, the world a world;
And there I find you written down, between
Arcturus and a primrose and the sea.

VII

Beloved, let us once more praise the rain.
Let us discover some new alphabet,
For this, the often-praised; and be ourselves
The rain, the chickweed, and the burdock leaf,
The green-white privet flower, the spotted stone,
And all that welcomes rain; the sparrow, too, —
Who watches with a hard eye, from seclusion,
Beneath the elm-tree bough, till rain is done.

There is an oriole who, upside down,
Hangs at his nest, and flicks an orange wing, —
Under a tree as dead and still as lead;
There is a single leaf, in all this heaven

Of leaves, which rain has loosened from its twig:
The stem breaks, and it falls, but it is caught
Upon a sister leaf, and thus she hangs;
There is an acorn cup, beside a mushroom,
Which catches three drops from the stooping cloud.

The timid bee goes back to hive; the fly
Under the broad leaf of the hollyhock
Perpends stupid with cold; the raindark snail
Surveys the wet world from a watery stone . . .
And still the syllables of water whisper:
The wheel of cloud whirs slowly: while we wait
In the dark room; and in your heart I find
One silver raindrop, — on a hawthorn leaf, —
Orion in a cobweb, and the World.

VIII

Conceive: be fecundated by the word.
Hang up your mind for the intrusion of the wind.
Be blown, be blown, like a handful of withered seed,
Or a handful of leaves in autumn. Blow, blow,
Careless of where you blow, or to what end,
Or whether living or dying. Go with the wind,
Whirl and return, lodge in a tree, detach,
Sail on a stream in scarlet for trout to stare at,
Comfortless, aimless, brilliant. There is nothing
So suits the soul as change.

                    You have no name:
And what you call yourself is but a whisper
Of that divine and deathless and empty word
Which breathed all things to motion. You are *you?*
But what is you? What is this thing called you?
A seed, a leaf? a singing congregation
Of molecules? an atom split in two?
Electrons dancing in a magic circle? . . .

A world, of which self-knowledge is the centre? . . .
Laugh, and forget yourself; despise, and change;
Hate, or do murder, love, beget, despair.
Go down and up again, go in and out,
Drink of the black and bright, bathe in the bitter,
Burn in the fiercest, and be light as ash.

You might have been a sparkle of clear sand.
You, who remember for a twinkling instant
All things, or what you think all things to be,
Whose miseries consume you, or whose joys
Hoist you to heaven, such heaven as you will:
You might have been a dream dreamed in a dream
By some one dreaming of God and dreamed by God.
You might indeed have been a God, a star,
A world of stars and Gods, a web of time;
You might have been the word that breathed the world.

You are all things, and nothing. Ah poor being,
Sad ghost of wind, dead leaf of autumnal God,
Bright seed of brief disaster, changing shape:
Go with the wind, be untenacious, yet
Tenacious too; touch quickly what you may;
Remember and forget; and all transact
As if each touch were fatal and the last.
You are all things, and all things are your soul.

IX

All this is nothing: all that we said is nothing:
Your eyes, your hair, are nothing, your grief, your tears, —
Your laughter, too, that filled the room with laughter,
And your quick step, as quickly gone as come;
Nothing, nothing, as goldenrod is nothing,
Withered in season, and from it gone the web,
And the poor spider gone, and all his flies.
What's goldenrod to Deneb, that bright star?

What means the spider to the moon? what means
This lecherous human, with his loves and griefs,
To such rank vegetation as Venus knows,
Or the cold chasms of snow that mantle Mars?
Nothing: they do not know us. We dispense
With all authority; and what we are,
Or what we have, are what we have and are
In our own godhead, and in that alone.

And all is meaningless? . . . Or all means nothing?
Your hand is but a claw for clutching food,
Food for the heart or belly? . . . Your two eyes
But sharpened senses for the just perception
Of this? . . . So come we to our mother chaos.
But there is, — so you tell me, — music, too:
Music and beauty, and the love of love,
Music and love and beauty, and all that.
There is this moment, this unsubstantial moment,
Which has a substance deep as God is deep:
Deeper, in fact, than thought of God can be.
You there, I here, — the rug of wool between us,
Four pictures on the wall, a room, a house,
Water in pipes, brought from the hills for us,
An ash-tray, and a table, and three chairs:
All this devised for man by man; all this,
And our communion through them, and our speech.
You there, I here, who half-perceive each other. . .

Woman, the thing is madness, we are mad.
You are not Helen, nor I Solomon.
Bathsheba you are not, nor am I Troy.

X

But you and I, Charybdis, are not new;
And all that flows between us is the dead. . .
— Thus Scylla, the scarred rock, sad child of time,

Benumbed with barnacles and hung with weed,
With urchins at her feet, and on her brow
Foul nests of cormorants, addressed her moan
To hoar Charybdis, who, beyond the whirlpool,
Lifted a hornèd crag to God and Nothing.
And still the salt sea sucked between them, bearing
The bones of ships and bones of humans, white
The one as other, and as little worth.

Where is this corner of the crumbling world:
Where are these rocks, beloved, that cry out
Their hate and fear of time, their bitter sadness
At past, and passing, and the sense of past?
It is between ourselves these waters flow.
It is ourselves who are these self-same rocks, —
And we it is whom time has cracked and hung
With frost and filth. The sea-gull's is our voice;
The wail of mariners; the cry of wind.
And all that flows between us is the dead.

No need to go to Lethe, nor to Sibyl,
To memory, or forgetfulness, or both,
To find such horror, or such richness, mixed,
As we can find who smile here face to face.
The waters of the human soul are deep.
We are the rocks that rot above those waters.
We are the rocks on whom the times have written.
We, the recorded sadness of the world.

What marvels, then, for us, who know already
All that the waters of the godhead give?
Let us desist from this forlorn attempt
To wring strange beauty from a world well known.
Patience is all: so Shakspere might have said.
Let us be patient, then, and hear at night
The flux and reflux of the whirlpool, borne
Restless between us; submit, since needs we must,

To sad remembrance; but remember also
That there was nought before remembrance was.

XI

Address him how you will, this golden fly, —
This dung-fed gildling of a summer's day:
He'll have his time, will buzz and come and go,
Visit the queenliest flowers, suck his fill,
Fatten himself to glory, and be dead.
He's Beowulf, is he? give him Grendel, then,
And Grendel's mother also, and the rest.
He'll strut, by God, as well upon a grass-blade
As any other ant; and we will praise him.

At midnight, when the graves all yawned together,
A pestilential sigh; again at noon,
When all the graves, with a smug sound of silence,
Closed up their chops against the light of day;
He heard — or so he'll have us think — a cry.
It was old Adam's cry; it was the cry
Of human flesh, delivered out of time,
Untimely ripped from chaos; it was anguish
Phrased in a white and red of flesh, as flowers
Phrase in a white and red a something else.
And he, this gildling, heard it, and was moved;
He mimicked it; he learned its naked vowels;
He spoke it, sang it, shouted it, although
Its meaning still escaped him.

                                        O just God,
Teach us how justice may be done to him.
Remind us, with the mirror and the sea,
With ice, and the bright parrot, and the moon,
And the dear dream that shakes our limbs in sleep,
How all of nature is shot through with this
Sweet mimicry. This fault, if fault it be,

Is Godlike; as all other things are Godlike.
What matter that this cry, this cry of woe,
This cry so precious to us, so our own,
Our inarticulate and immortal grief,
Should be, by this poor gildling, overheard,
And twice and thrice and many times rehearsed?
He too is God. Divine and empty, he
Repeats, unknowing, the disastrous word;
A fool, a pool of water, speaks the star;
Heartless and ignorant, drunkard of language, he
Deflowers the immortal heartbreak for his bride.

XII

Poor fool, deluded toy, brief anthropomorph,
You who depend at centre of your web,
Thinking the web projected from yourself,
With all its silver spokes and drops of dew,
Its antic flies and frantic wings, and such, —
Consider now if you yourself are not
Created by the web. The spokes and dewdrops,
The flies and wings, gigantic web of the world:
This whirling wheel, concentring on itself:
Produced and sought you; you yourself, poor spider,
Dreamed of by chaos and of chaos born.

Poor fool, sad anthropomorph, give up this notion
Centrifugal; perpend awhile, instead,
The world centripetal, and see yourself
As the last comer in this world of shapes.
You dream the world? Alas, the world dreamed you.
And you but give it back, distorted much
By the poor brain-digestion, which you call
Intelligence, or vision, or the truth.

Here's morning, with its flooding of the world,
Not what the evening was; and here is evening

Come with its multitude of golden flies,
Which is not as the morning was; and here
Is noon, which is not either. And for each
You meditate profoundly. This is morning?
All hail to selfhood, who is come refreshed
From nightlong dark digestion of the things
He trapped from chaos of the yesterday.
And here is noon, and rest; and here is evening,
With all those golden flies which yet remain
For conquest by the cunning. Self is strong:
He shapes the world as should be. He is wise:
He understands the world as food. He spins
The broken rim anew, and calls it good.

XIII

And how begin, when there is no beginning?
How end, when there's no ending? How cut off
One drop of blood from other, break the stream
Which, with such subtlety, such magnificent power,
Binds the vast windflower to its throbbing world?
. . . Shall we be bold, and say, then, 'at this point
The world begins, the windflower ends?' rip out
One bleeding atom, pretend it has no kin? . . .
Or shall we, with the powerful mind, hold off
The sky from earth, the earth from sky, to see
Each perish into nothing?

           They will perish:
The drop of blood, the windflower, and the world;
Sound will be silence; meaning will have no meaning.
The blade of grass, in such a light, will grow
Monstrous as Minotaur; the tick of the clock, —
Should it be taken as the clock's dark secret, —
Is chaos and catastrophe; the heart
Cries like a portent in a world of portents,
All meaningless and mad.

Softly, together,
We tread our little arcs upon our star;
Stare at each other's eyes, and see them thinking;
Lay hands upon our hearts and feel them beating;
But what precedes the luminous thought, or what
Unnumbered heartbeats timed the beat we feel, —
What burnings up of suns, or deaths of moons,
Shaped them, or what wreckage in time's stream, —
Ignore. . . And are our footsteps parallel?
Or runs your blood as slow as mine? or comes
The golden crocus, of this April's fiction,
As hotly to your thought as mine? The birds
That throng imagination's boughs, and sing,
Or flash from sward to leaf, for the sheer joy
Of mounting or descending in thought's air;
Or mate in ecstasy, and from that flame
Breed constellations of flame-colored flight:
Come they and go they, love, in your green tree
As swiftly as in mine? was there such singing
In mine as yours, or at the self-same season?
Have I such boughs as you, in the same place;
Or such a surf of leaves, when the wind blows;
Or such a fountain of bright flame, when birds
All skyward mount together? —

So we pace
From here to there, from there to here, — touch hands
As alien each to each as leaf and stone,
One chaos and another. Have good heart!
Your chaos is my world; perhaps my chaos
Is world enough for you. For what's unguessed
Will have such shape and sweetness as the knowing
Ruins with pour of knowledge. From one bird
We guess the tree, and hear the song; but if
Miraculous vision gives us, all at once,
The universe of birds and boughs, and all
The trees and birds from which their time has come, —

The world is lost. . .

        Love, let us rest in this.

XIV

— You went to the verge, you say, and come back safely?
Some have not been so fortunate, — some have fallen.
Children go lightly there, from crag to crag,
And coign to coign, — where even the goat is wary, —
And make a sport of it. . . They fling down pebbles,
Following, with eyes undizzied, the long curve,
The long slow outward curve, into the abyss,
As far as eye can follow; and they themselves
Turn back, unworried, to the here and now. . .
But you have been there, too? —

                 — I saw at length
The space-defying pine, that on the last
Outjutting rock has cramped its powerful roots.
There stood I too: under that tree I stood:
My hand against its resinous bark: my face
Turned out and downward to the fourfold kingdom.
The wind roared from all quarters. The waterfall
Came down, it seemed, from Heaven. The mighty sound
Of pouring elements, — earth, air, and water, —
The cry of eagles, chatter of falling stones, —
These were the frightful language of that place.
I understood it ill, but understood. —

— You understood it? Tell me, then, its meaning.
It was an all, a nothing, or a something?
Chaos, or divine love, or emptiness?
Water and earth and air and the sun's fire?
Or else, a question, simply? —

                — Water and fire were there,
And air and earth; there too was emptiness;

All, and nothing, and something too, and love.
But these poor words, these squeaks of ours, in which
We strive to mimic, with strained throats and tongues,
The spawning and outrageous elements —
Alas, how paltry are they! For I saw —

— What did you see?

      — I saw myself and God.
I saw the ruin in which godhead lives:
Shapeless and vast: the strewn wreck of the world:
Sadness unplumbed: misery without bound.
Wailing I heard, but also I heard joy.
Wreckage I saw, but also I saw flowers.
Hatred I saw, but also I saw love . . .
And thus, I saw myself.

      — And this alone?

— And this alone awaits you, when you dare
To that sheer verge where horror hangs, and tremble
Against the falling rock; and, looking down,
Search the dark kingdom. It is to self you come, —
And that is God. It is the seed of seeds:
Seed for disastrous and immortal worlds.

It is the answer that no question asked.

XV

Dead man: dead brother: sad mouth stopped with clay:
Reed for the rice-bird's wing, shade for the fly:
This thousand years dissolved, yet living still,
Here standing, in this clay, which your hand fashioned;
Here brooding, thinking, giving, in this room:

Dead heart: dead brain: sad spirit lost in weather:
Blown to the southwest in a rattle of leaves,

Cracked under foot, and all, all gone together:
Yet here still standing, by this mirror, facing
Whoever sees this porcelain girl, — this figure
Devout, serene, where now I meet your soul:

Dead hand, you touched the heart of time, you knew
Whispers of silence, the mute path of God;
Hot chaos knew, with its rank arteries,
And anguish, with its blood. You heard the ticking
Of bruisèd minutes from the wall of night,
Suspiration of stars, the bitter cry
Of atoms grooved in orbit. You were living:
Sunlight had packed your heart. Living, were dead:
Darkness had packed your thought. You knew desire:
Love had gilded the moonlight on your eyes.

And now, — all gone, all gone; except this figure, —
This porcelain girl, — whose head is bowed, whose hands
Await a service, and whose heart is meek. . .
If there are gods inhabiting in chaos:
If there is justice, or a tithe of justice:
See that the mind that dreamed this thing be safe.

XVI

Coruscation of glass — so said he, sharply —
It is not, nor alembic tongued with flame;
Nor is it molten gold, nor a blue light,
Nor brass, nor silver; no, not one of these.
The water-drop, that hangs, and quakes, and falls,
Quivering with all heaven before it falls, —
No, no, although it take the sky's whole azure,
This it is not. . . It is a little flame,
Smaller than eye can think; tinier even
Than the frail twinkle of a thought, which burns
One atom in the brain . . .

And yet this thing —
This iridescence, this coruscation, this twinkle —
This lizard's eye, this fly's wing — !

Merciful heaven,
Give me a language that will say this thing,
And having said, destroy! Give me a freedom
To scorn this thing! Am I a slave? Must I
Deliver up my body, dwarf my mind,
Swaddle my spirit and crucify my heart,
Because this lizard's eye, infinitesimal,
Has struck me somewhere? Must I walk a madman?
Grow pale? be melancholy? have bad dreams?
Renounce my food, hating mankind, and all
Because this lizard's eye has *looked* at me?

Absurd! It is an indigestion, merely.
Disorder of the blood. . . Mistaken diet.
Or too much looking at the moon, too little
Upon the sun. The print I read's too small:
I will get larger books, with larger margins.
I will cut down the tree that shades my window.
And I will go to music —

No, not music!
The thing itself — by God, the thing is music.
For when she touches me, or when she speaks — !
Then comes the little fly's wing of a flame:
Then the brain lights and dizzies: then the body
Grows light as brightness. . . And the thing is music.
It is a sound of many instruments —
Complex, diverse, an alchemy of voices —
Brass melting into silver, silver smoothly
Dissolving into gold; and then the harsh
And thickening discord: as if chaos yawned
Suddenly and magnificently for a forest;

Swallowed its tangle of too gorgeous bloom;
Devoured its beauty, derisively, and clashed
A brassy gloating after. . . . Is it this?
Yes; and the chaos, then — the chaos, then, —
Ah, what a heaven of sweetness of pure sound
It yields to God! A clear voice, like a star, —
And farther off another, — then another, —
Each, like an angel, taking his own station — ;
As if a thousand tapers, one by one,
Were lighted, all the way from Here to Nothing;
As if a thousand angels, one by one,
Walked over heaven singing . . .

                           Merciful God —
This is a wondrous thing; that if she touch
My fingernail with but her fingernail, —
Or if she look at me, for but the time
It takes a leaf to fall from leaf to leaf, —
I become music, chaos, light, and sound;
I am no longer I: I am a world.

                      XVII

And thus Narcissus, cunning with a hand-glass,
Preening a curl, and smirking, had his say.
God's pity on us all! he cried (half laughing)
That we must die: that Lesbia's curl be lost,
And Shakspere's wit forgotten; and the potter —
Who saw, one instant, all humanity,
And phrased its passion in a single figure —
That he be sunk in clay, and dumb as clay.

God's pity on us all! he cried, and turned
The guileful mirror in a guileful light;
Smiled at the fair-curved cheek, the golden hair;
The lip, the nostril, the broad brow, the hand;
Smiled at the young bright smile. . . Alas, alas,

To think that so great beauty should be lost!
This gold, and scarlet, and flushed ivory,
Be made a sport for worms!

                But then a wonder
Deepened his gazing eyes, darkened the pupils,
Shaded his face, as if a cloud had passed.
The mirror spoke the truth. A shape he saw
Unknown before, — obscene, disastrous, huge, —
Huge as the world, and formless. . . Was this he?
This dumb, tumultuous, all-including horror?
This Caliban of rocks? this steaming pit
Of foisting hells, — circle on darker circle, —
With worlds in rings to right and left, and other
Starbearing hells within them, other heavens
Arched over chaos? . . .

              He pondered the vast vision:
Saw the mad order, the inhuman god;
And his poor pity, with the mirror dropped,
Wore a new face: such brightness and such darkness,
Pitiless, as a moonblanched desert wears.

XVIII

In the beginning, nothing; and in the end,
Nothing; and in between these useless nothings,
Brightness, music, God, one's self. . . My love, —
Heart that beats for my heart, breast on which I sleep, —
Be brightness, music, God, my self, for me.

In the beginning, silence, and in the end
Silence; and in between these silences,
The sound of one white flower, opening, closing.
My love, my love, be that white flower for me:
Open and close: that sound will be my world.

In the beginning, chaos, and in the end
Chaos; and the vast wonder come between, —
Glory, bewilderment, all sense of brightness.
Love, be that glory and that sense of brightness.
You are what chaos yielded. Be my star.

XIX

Watch long enough, and you will see the leaf
Fall from the bough. Without a sound it falls:
And soundless meets the grass. . . And so you have
A bare bough, and a dead leaf in dead grass.
Something has come and gone. And that is all.

But what were all the tumults in this action?
What wars of atoms in the twig, what ruins,
Fiery and disastrous, in the leaf?
Timeless the tumult was, but gave no sign.
Only, the leaf fell, and the bough is bare.

This is the world: there is no more than this.
The unseen and disastrous prelude, shaking
The trivial act from the terrific action.
Speak: and the ghosts of change, past and to come,
Throng the brief word. The maelstrom has us all.

XX

So, in the evening, to the simple cloister:
This place of boughs, where sounds of water, softly,
Lap on the stones. And this is what you are:
Here, in this dusty room, to which you climb
By four steep flights of stairs. The door is closed:
The furies of the city howl behind you:
The last bell plunges rock-like to the sea:
The horns of taxis wail in vain. You come

Once more, at evening, to this simple cloister;
Hushed by the quiet walls, you stand at peace.

What ferns of thought are these, the cool and green,
Dripping with moisture, that festoon these walls?
What water-lights are these, whose pallid rings
Dance with the leaves, or speckle the pale stones?
What spring is this, that bubbles the cold sand,
Urging the sluggish grains of white and gold? . . .
Peace. The delicious silence throngs with ghosts
Of wingèd sound and shadow. These are you.

Now in the evening, in the simple cloister,
You stand and wait; you stand and listen, waiting
For wingèd sounds and wingèd silences,
And long-remembered shadows. Here the rock
Lets down its vine of many colored flowers:
Waiting for you, or waiting for the lizard
To move his lifted claw, or shift his eye
Quick as a jewel. Here the lizard waits
For the slow snake to slide among cold leaves.
And, on the bough that arches the deep pool,
Lapped in a sound of water, the brown thrush
Waits, too, and listens, till his silence makes
Silence as deep as song. And time becomes
A timeless crystal, an eternity,
In which the gone and coming are at peace.

What bird is this, whose silence fills the trees
With rich delight? What leaves and boughs are these,
What lizard, and what snake? . . . The bird is gone:
And while you wait, another comes and goes, —
Another and another; yet your eye,
Although it has not moved, can scarcely say
If birds have come and gone, — so quick, so brief, —
Or if the thrush who waits there is the same . . .
The snake and lizard change, yet are the same:

The flowers, many-colored, on the vine,
Open and close their multitude of stars, —
Yet are the same. . . And all these things are you.

Thus in the evening, in the simple cloister,
Eternity adds ring to ring, the darker
Beyond the brighter; and your silence fills
With such a world of worlds, — so still, so deep, —
As never voice could speak, whether it were
The ocean's or the bird's. The night comes on:
You wait and listen, in the darkened room,
To all these ghosts of change. And they are you.

XXI

The first note, simple; the second note, distinct;
The third note, harsh; the fourth, an innuendo;
The fifth, a humble triad; and the sixth —
Suddenly — is the chord of chords, that breaks
The evening; and from evening calls the angel,
One voice divinely singing.

                Thus, at random,
This coil of worlds in which we grope; and thus
Our comings and our goings. So the twilight
Deepens the hour from rose to purple; so
One bell-note is the death-note, and completes
The half-remembered with the soon-forgotten.
The threes and fives compute our day; we move
To doom with all things moving.

                You and I
Are things compounded of time's heart-beats, stretching
The vascular instant from the vascular past;
You, with forgotten worlds, and I with worlds
Forgotten and remembered. Yet the leaf,
With all its bleeding veins, is not more torn

Than you are torn, this moment, from the last.
Can you rejoin it? Is it here, or there?
Where is that drop of blood you knew last year?
Where is that image which you loved, that frame
Of ghostly apparitions in your thought,
Alchemic mystery of your childhood, lost
With all its dizzy colors? . . . It is gone.
Only the echo's echo can be heard.
Thrice-mirrored, the ghost pales.

                    You plunge, poor soul,
From time's colossal brink into that chasm
Of change and limbo and immortal flux;
And bring up only, in your blood-stained hands,
One grain of sand that sparkles. Plunge again,
Poor diver, among weeds and death! and bring
The pearl of brightness up. It is this instant
When all is well with us: when hell and heaven
Arch in a chord of glory over madness;
When Pole Star sings to Sirius; and the wave
Of ultimate Ether breaks on ultimate Nothing.
The world's a rose which comes this night to flower:
This evening is its light. And it is we,
Who, with our harmonies and discords, woven
Of myriad things forgotten and remembered,
Urge the vast twilight to immortal bloom.

XXII

And if this heart go back again to earth,
Taking his anguish with him to make roots,
And his delight for flowers, — as if a laugh
Should grimly quench itself in rock and grass;
Or if the soul, like the last breath, should go
Thinning away in air, a smoke of frost;
What is there strange, then, in this myth of thought, —
That I should take the tulip's bell, and crush it,

And from its broken beauty make a heart?
Look, I will catch in air the frost's bright sparkle,
And warm it in my hands to make a soul.
What better stuff than hoarfrost for a soul? . . .
What better blood, — than anguish, — for a heart? . . .
Thus comes my angel, all complete, from myth;
And weeps, as angels should.

                                                      And I will shake
Such darkness over music as will send her
From sound to silence back again. The night
Will beat her down and quench her. Thus, bewitched,
She will coil home confused, with all her marvels,
Draw in her pulse of colors, wings of light,
Contract, assume an agony, and be
Once more the mind that made her.

                                                      Is this strange?
Or is it strange that always we should go
Bewildered, in this dance from blood to beauty, —
From beauty back to blood? . . . I am a man:
Sentience wrung from the rock. And in a twinkling
The rock is wrung from sentience.

                                                      Love, it is time
We called to huge assembly the bright stars, —
Those luminous hearts that are our kin in blood.
We will confer; with such huge majesty
As stars and men may bring to conference;
With oratory of lightning and of gravel
Propound and legislate upon this matter;
And keep our minutes in a book of sand.
Here, we will say, that man is but a leaf, —
Veined like the leaf, and thrilled, and vascular,
And blown as lightly down. He drinks the light, —
Yet in his veins the sap is full of death;
And his own darkness meets him from within.

Here, we will say, and with a thousand tongues, —
The tongues of leaves and stars, and men and rocks, —
That we are all blood-brothers, and but change
From one to other. And this instant speech,
Now in the sunlight as we walk together,
(Summoning to our thought all hell and heaven),
This too we see, in the brief act of speech,
Gone back again to stone. The thing I said
Was the last flicker of a dying star;
The falling of a tree before a glacier;
The fly in resin caught, and turned to amber;
The fossil dug from earth. The thing I said
Was in the moving grass, before it came
With all its false complexity upon
The current of my blood; and it is gone
Back to simplicity as soon as spoken. . .

Here is the star upon our tongues, and here
Our consciousness, with all its wonders, falls
From its bright moment, like a cobweb, broken,
Once more into the whirl of rock. And we, —
With all our hot complexity of passion,
Our cool and intricate questionings, — are only
Histories told in stone, and, once told, lost. . .
Did we admire the evening? feel the light
Upon our eyes and hands? . . . But this was only
Rock that whispered of rock; and it is gone.

XXIII

The clouds flow slowly across the sky, the idea
Slowly takes shape, and slowly passes, and changes
Its shape in passing. It is a shape of grief,
Plangent and poignant. It is a comic gesture.
It is a wound in air. It is last year.
It is the notion, — flippantly held and lost, —
Of next year, with a burden of coarse disasters,

Or the year after, with a burden of boredom.
The leaf has come and gone — it was hard, bright, brittle,
Bore thorns, sparkled in light, and now is lost, —
Find it, love, if you can. It was the scene
Of Tristan, firefly, and Isolde, firefly; they glowed
With timeless rapture upon it, gilded its edges,
And they and it are gone.

                    The clouds flow slowly,
The idea is slowly changing, like the cloud,
The mind is changing, like a heaven of clouds,
The 'I' changes, and with it the 'you.' The sea
Brings its flotsam, and takes it away again,
Or leaves a bewildering fragment on the sand,
A pebble, a splinter of wood, a cork, a bottle,
Which other tides will devour. The wind alters,
And the cloud, moving, becomes a bird, a dolphin,
The skeleton of a leaf, a curve, a nothing.
The blood changes, and the idea becomes
A wish, or half a wish, a fear, a chuckle, —
Vision of winking bubbles, — or a nothing.

The year moves on, and with it I become
Something less and something more.
The window breaks, and the light in the room is changed.
The cobweb alters it anew. The rain
Darkens the corners beyond recognition,
Evokes what ghosts they have. The southwest wind
Fills them suddenly with blossom. The snow
Throngs them with memories. . .

                        Excellent woman,
Rock over water, field beneath cloud shadow,
Fixed above the changing,
Take comfort if you can in this mad waste.
I am the leaf that dies upon your hand:
Dismiss me with my dying. We are undone

With permanence in impermanence, the flowing
Of shape to shape which means all shapelessness.
Is this my hand in yours? ah, no such thing.
It is the fog which curtsies to the fog:
The god who finds himself a fraud: the wind
From nowhere blown to nowhere.

XXIV

I

And so you poise yourself, magnificent angel, —
Bird of bright dream, brief soul of briefer knowledge, —
In the pure æther of a thought, unthinking
Of endings or beginnings. And the light
Of change and unknown purpose hues your wings.
The cloud, that hangs between you and the moon,
Darkening all things, darkens also you.
The sunrise burns you to an incandescence.
And sleep, annihilator of the all and nothing,
Makes of your wings a demon's wings, that winnow
The freezing airs of chaos.

              So, unconscious,
You beat the winds of nescience, and sustain, —
Magnificent angel, treader of bright thought, —
Your being, which is nothing, in a nothing;
And yet, are something, and are glorious;
And make the godhead great.

              How shall we name
This instant, which is you, and make it rich? . . .
To what rank origins,
In memory's dung or rock, trace out its seed? . . .
It is the clover that is cropped and gone.
It is the frostflower on the fern, that melts
At daybreak, and no trace of it is left.
It is the shadow of the fern, on grass,

Dispersed among a multitude of grassblades,
Shaken by wind, all unobserved by ants,
And ended with the day.

II

Majestic instant, —
Great golden sum of dream whose truth is zero,
Zero of thought whose truth is god, and life, —
Pause in your flight, as if the arrow paused.
Be for our purpose as a rainbow, frozen.
Hang betwixt zenith and the nadir, as
A drop of rain might hang. And is this truth?
Or is the grassblade, by itself, the grass?

It is a moment between moments, passing
From one to other; is a syllable,
Meaningless in itself, which lights a word;
The pause, between two words, which makes a meaning;
The gulf between two stones which makes a world.

III

Upward he soars from nothing, and his wings
Are marvellous with dew; or downward plunges
To that sublime Gehenna whence we came.
There too his wings are wide; and there he hangs,
Magnificent, in madness and corruption,
Master of outrage, and at home in shame.
Yet knows he this? He is a kind of fool;
A mote that dances in a beam; aware
Of selfhood only, but not selfhood's roots.
He sings, but knows no cause for singing; laughs,
For laughter's sake, as if the dead leaf laughed;
His agony is causeless; and his tears
Fall like a frozen sleet from his blind eyes,
Forgotten soon as fallen. . .

                                     Thus we reach
The mystery with hot and vascular hands,
Insensitive; it perishes as we touch,
Perishes like the snowflake. Thus we wear
A brightness on the forehead of our terror,
A hopeless smile upon the ruin we hide.

And meanwhile, as we sit here in the evening, —
And listen, and remember, and are still, —
Upward or downward borne upon wide wings,
From Heaven to Hell and back again, — we know
We are but lightning on a sea of chaos;
The flash on sad confusion which is god.

                          XXV

And in the darkness touched a face, and knew
Beyond all knowledge of the hands or senses
The truth that only one such face can tell.
The wind was there, the cold, the sound of snow;
Terror was there, the mystic door unopened;
The golden doge was there, with robe and ring,
The hour-glass, and the spider; and he came
Despite these things, and most of all despite
The skeleton, with the lantern in his hand,
To that one face whose message was the truth.

But what is truth? — Is it a sum of surds?
The lamp towards a locus moving? time,
Measured in agonies of the ventricle? —
Why, let us be pedantic, and proclaim
That truth is what it seems, or seems to us;
It is the two plus two that makes a four;
It is the falling of a leaf, the death
Of holiest mystery upon a cross;
It is the coughing of an old man's blood;
It is the human face he thought was God.

But in the darkness touching it, he thought
All terror solved, all wonder sounded, all
Asperities of desert or of mountain,
Remotest miseries of Aldebaran, or
Immediate tortures of the pulse, dissolved.
The skeleton was broken, and the spider
Reduced to such a minion as will weave
Dainty devices for a doge's dress;
The snow, the cold, were gone, the wind was gone;
And in a sudden glory he was lost.

XXVI

There was one drop of blood came down his thigh
Between the hairs, as a slow brook might go,
And slipped across the knee, and backward then
(I watched it) streaked the calf, thence fell to ground.
The grass received it twice: two blades were red.

And as I saw it, I was moved to speak;
Profundities were on my tongue, but vague;
Whence come these miracles? whence flows this blood?
Is there a god? — But still, I did not speak;
Stared at the wet grass; and then raised my eyes:

And looked a long while at the west, where clouds
Darkened with blood above the slaughtered sun.
I saw a tree, which stood up, like a cross,
Against that brightness; and I thought 'a tree
Will come to agony as sure as god';

And thinking this, was studious not to turn
Toward that agony which behind me hung.
But why was this? And as I further thought,
And downward turned my eyes, and in the grass
Saw the small daisy, which the night had closed:

I laughed a little to myself, for so
(At least to others) might my own heart seem:
Afraid of darkness. And as thus I stood,
With downcast eyes, at sunset, in that place,
Secretly laughing to myself, he died.

I heard him die: I knew that he had died.
And instantly I stooped and touched the grass,
Tenderly, yet with hands self-conscious too,
And with one finger touched the daisy, moved
Its frightened face against a chickweed leaf.

And all the while I smiled. — But why was this?
Was there no rash profundity to say?
— Instead, I walked a few feet to the west,
And looked across the vineyards and hard hills
To the last light that smouldered in a cloud;

And kept my back toward that agony,
Which now no more was agony; and said
With a loud voice (because I was alone):
Take from this heart its mean profundities;
And make it simple in the face of death.

Then came away; and left that effigy
Of godhead and myself and my dear friend
Alone and cold and lofty in cold light;
And downward went to misery renewed;
To that same god, in agony of birth.

XXVII

So, death being dead, and love to hatred changed,
The fern to marble, and the hour to snow;
Music become the noise of worms, and all
This dance of stars a senseless rout of atoms;

Come: we will break our hearts with no compunction:
And make a sad beginning of our ends.

Out of corruption the bright daffodil
Lifts up her brave preposterous loveliness;
The bee comes forth, again, from the thawed hive;
And we, with numbèd wings of sense, crawl out
To stretch our sickly bodies in the sun;
And to confer with what it is we have.

Was there a sunset once, of divers colors?
Pale purple, gold, portals of broken light,
Whence rose a heavenly harmony of sound?
Such as believing hearts might prophet-wise
Summon from darkness, or from tombs? — This light,
This heavenly sound, we now no longer know;

Yet know we knew it once; and keep therefrom
A kind of warmth on our remembering eyes.
The hands we held against that light still sparkle;
And if we turn them now to humbler use, —
Reshaping the dark earth which is ourselves, —
This is false glory we may well indulge.

Beauty there was in the first song we sang,
Before the fire had touched our tongues; again,
Beauty will grace our last of songs, the more
Because we know that beauty meaningless.
Is there a god who knows and mourns himself?
It is Narcissus and his glass is truth.

The sunset comes again, with opened doorways;
And if we see beyond it what we know,
And not that fairyland at which we guessed;
If we see horrors there, in a bright light, —
A misery of waves, — a majesty
Of incandescent and defrauding void, —

Yet, let us break our hearts with no compunction,
And find what music senseless courage yields;
We will applaud illusion, smiling still
At wisdom, which applauds itself; and go
Once more towards the dreadful west, to ask
Whence the bright colors of the sunset come.

XXVIII

The time has come, the clock says time has come.
Here in the mid-waste of my life I pause,
The hour is in my hand, and in my heart
Miscellany of shards and shreds. The clock
Ticks its iambics, and the heart its spondees,
Time has come, time has come and gone,
Winter has taken its toll, summer its harvest,
Spring has brought and taken away its illusion.

What is time, the clock says what is time,
Never the past, never the future, always the now,
What is time, the seed says it is all
Fertility turned deep by the foot of the plow.

The hour has added to the spirit's peace,
Seed has added to minute, and world to flower,
Tears have flowed to the heart till it is rotted,
Hands have worn the hand till it is hard.
Why, I have seen the all, have seen the nothing,
Have heard the monosyllable of the tomb,
Have buried stars and resurrected them,
And watched the shadow moving across a wall.

What is time, the stitch says what is time,
Always the future, never the past, never the now;
Only the seam foresees the future, but even
The longest seam will feel the foot of the plow.

Stand, take off the garments time has lent you,
The watch, the coins, the handkerchief, the shoes,
Take out your heart and prop it on the mantel,
Your soul, also, and wrap it in a thought;
Display your shards and shreds on the windowsill
Among geraniums and aspidistras,
The week before, and the week before the last,
Ridiculous chronicle, taste, touch, and smell.

What is time, the heart says what is time.
The heart is ticking on the mantelpiece.
The heart says all is past and nothing future.
The heart says heart will never cease.

XXIX

What shall we do — what shall we think — what shall we say — ?
Why, as the crocus does, on a March morning,
With just such shape and brightness; such fragility;
Such white and gold, and out of just such earth.
Or as the cloud does on the northeast wind —
Fluent and formless; or as the tree that withers.
What are we made of, strumpet, but of these?
Nothing. We are the sum of all these accidents —
Compounded all our days of idiot trifles, —
The this, the that, the other, and the next;
What x or y said, or old uncle thought;
Whether it rained or not, and at what hour;
Whether the pudding had two eggs or three,
And those we loved were ladies. . . Were they ladies?
And did they read the proper books, and simper
With proper persons, at the proper teas?
O Christ and God and all deciduous things —
Let us void out this nonsense and be healed.

There is no doubt that we shall do, as always,
Just what the crocus does. There is no doubt

Your Helen of Troy is all that she has seen, —
All filth, all beauty, all honor and deceit.
The spider's web will hang in her bright mind, —
The dead fly die there doubly; and the rat
Find sewers to his liking. She will walk
In such a world as this alone could give —
This of the moment, this mad world of mirrors
And of corrosive memory. She will know
The lecheries of the cockroach and the worm,
The chemistry of the sunset, the foul seeds
Laid by the intellect in the simple heart . . .
And knowing all these things, she will be she.

She will be also the sunrise on the grassblade —
But pay no heed to that. She will be also
The infinite tenderness of the voice of morning —
But pay no heed to that. She will be also
The grain of elmwood, and the ply of water,
Whirlings in sand and smoke, wind in the ferns,
The fixed bright eyes of dolls. . . And this is all.

XXX

You trust the heart? far better trust the sea.
Or swear, with Romeo, by the inconstant moon.
Believe that ripening acorns will not fall.
Turn a dull eye on heaven, a trustful eye,
And think the clouds will keep their rain forever.
She will be faithless to you: will have smiles,
Deep from the heart, for other men than you;
Will touch them with the wings of her wide spirit;
Delight and madden them; lead them to darkness;
And all with such a fraction of soul's mischief
As a dropped eyelid covers. . . In a twinkling
The deed is done: and she is lost, is lost,
Farther than ever imagination's power
Will sound or soar in chaos.

Hurry after,
If so you will, with hatred's furious wings,
And strike her like the hawk; she will be numb,
And stupid too, and hang defenseless under,
And die or live with the slow rage of betrayal.
Strike her till she be dead: and it is you
Who will lie dead, with the world's ruin about you.
Tell her that she is faithless and a wanton.
Rip auricle from ventricle, and shred
The sore affections out; but better blame
The ignoble blood — or so you'd say — that comes
From god himself.

For so it comes, from god.
It is the sovereign stream, the source of all;
Bears with it false and true, and dead and dying:
The seed, the seedling; worlds, and worlds to come.
Is there a treason here that is not you?
Accept this logic, this dark blood of things.
There is no treason here that is not you.

XXXI

Where is that noble mind that knows no evil,
Gay insubordinations of the worm?
Discords of mishap, rash disharmonies
Sprung from disorders in the spirit's state?
If there is such, we'll have him out in public,
And have his heart out too. There is no good,
No sweet, no noble, no divine, no right,
But it is bred of rich economy
Amongst the hothead factions of the soul.
Show me that virtuous and intolerable woman
Who swears, and doubly swears, that she is good,
And feeds her virtue on a daily lie;
That simple soul who wears simplicity
As if it were a god's cloak dropped from heaven;

Who has no secrets, no, not one, and minces
Sunrise to sunset with a sunlit smile,
Her little brain and little heart wide open;
By god, we'll rip such foulness from that angel
As never charnel knew!

        But if we find
In some rank purlieu of our rotting world
That stinking wretch whose rot is worse than worst:
That natural marsh of nature, in which evil
Is light as hawk to wing, and with such grace:
Him whom the noble scorn, whose eye is dark,
Who wears proud rags around a Hinnom heart:
Why, in that heart will come such power as never
Visits the virtuous, and such sweetness too
As god reserves for chaos.

XXXII

Such as you saw, on such and such a day, —
The word you spoke, at such and such an hour, —
Such feeling, or such vision, or such thought — !

What is this suchness that we talk of, lady?
What is a 'such,' that we should make it speak?
It is a sound by tongue and wonder made —

Delirium of the surface of the earth;
Shudder of air . . .

        And it is less than this — :
It is the flame, dropped on a wet leaf;
The blood-drop on the pillow; the breath blown
On the cold windowpane which winter weaves.

It is the history, in item told,
Of ichthyosaurus in a marsh of time;
Of Grimm's law in the forest leaf . . .

And yet,
Comes the dark forest, which no heart foretells,
No mind foresees, no will forestalls, and takes
This suchness, all its beautiful abstraction, —

And you, bright flash of time, whose gentle hands
Touch the divine in melody; and me
Who waste my hour, comparing such with so.

XXXIII

Then came I to the shoreless shore of silence,
Where never summer was nor shade of tree,
Nor sound of water, nor sweet light of sun,
But only nothing and the shore of nothing,
Above, below, around, and in my heart:

Where day was not, not night, nor space, nor time,
Where no bird sang, save him of memory,
Nor footstep marked upon the marl, to guide
My halting footstep; and I turned for terror,
Seeking in vain the Pole Star of my thought;

Where it was blown among the shapeless clouds,
And gone as soon as seen, and scarce recalled,
Its image lost and I directionless;
Alone upon the brown sad edge of chaos,
In the wan evening that was evening always;

Then closed my eyes upon the sea of nothing
While memory brought back a sea more bright,
With long, long waves of light, and the swift sun,
And the good trees that bowed upon the wind;
And stood until grown dizzy with that dream;

Seeking in all that joy of things remembered
One image, one the dearest, one most bright,

One face, one star, one daisy, one delight,
One hour with wings most heavenly and swift,
One hand the tenderest upon my heart;

But still no image came, save of that sea,
No tenderer thing than thought of tenderness,
No heart or daisy brighter than the rest;
And only sadness at the bright sea lost,
And mournfulness that all had not been praised.

O lords of chaos, atoms of desire,
Whirlwind of fruitfulness, destruction's seed,
Hear now upon the void my late delight,
The quick brief cry of memory, that knows
At the dark's edge how great the darkness is.

XXXIV

After the yes and no, the light denial,
The gesture noted, the eyelids veiled,
The fierce bright light of horror in the eyes,
Avoided, stared at, sounded, where it swarms
With heavy-wingèd and half monstrous things, —
Then is it that the moment falls between us,
Wide as the spangled nothingness that hangs
Between Canopus and Aldebaran.

Woman, and I am lost to you, I go
Downward and inward to such coils of light,
Such speed, such fierceness, and such glooms of filth,
Such labyrinths of change, such laboratories
Of obscene shape incessant in the mind,
As never woman knew. There, like the worm,
Coiling amidst the coils, I make my home;
Eat of the filth, am blessed; digest my name;
Spawn; am spawned; exult; and am spewed forth;
And so come back again, to you, and time —

To find you, with your finger on the clock,
One minute gone, no less, no more, and still
Deceit's unconscious horror in your eye . . .
So, to your smile, I give Gehenna's smile;
And to your kiss, the kiss that breeds a world.

XXXV

This was the gentlest creature that we knew,
This lamia of men, this sensitive
Sad soul, so poisoned, and so poisoning.
God take his bowels out, and break his bones,
And show him in the market as he is:
An angel with a peacock's heart, a fraud
With such a gilding on him as is gold.

This was the nimblest of the necromancers,
This lodestar of the mind, this tentative
Quick thought, so injured, and so injuring.
God take his conscience out, and set him free,
And break his mind to rapture, and delight
Those that would murder him, and those that love,
And those that love mankind.

XXXVI

Good virtuous son, adviser to the poor,
Getter of children on your father's dower,
Usher at weddings, and at churches too,
Chairman of clubs, and Madam here's your pew;
Uxorious simple sensuous and impassioned,
Rebel for once, when drunk, but now old-fashioned;
Remember how you took the harlot's hand,
And saw one instant hell's dark hinterland.

All's relative: the slow at last make haste:
Rash friends of rebel days have gone to waste;
Blackballed by clubs in which your voice is power,

And cut down like the clover in its hour.
While you, from state to state, move on in pride
With your lubricious madam at your side;
Upright and right, and freshly bathed, and pure;
Insurance paid, and god outside your door.

Remember that fierce atom in your blood
Which bade you stand in hell, where once you stood;
Remember the good friend who stands there still,
And thinks of you, and smiles, and thinks no ill.
Let that dark flame come once again between
Hypocrisy and hell's bright sabbath-green;
There we will dance once more, and in our hour
Worship the god who honors our poor floor.

XXXVII

Come let us take another's words and change the meaning,
Come let us take another's meaning, change the words,
Rebuild the house that Adam built, with opals,
Redecorate Eve's bedroom. We were born
With words, but they were not our words, but others',
Smacked of the kitchen, or of gods, or devils,
Worn and stained with the blood of centuries,
The sweat of peasants, the raw gold of kings.
Shall we be slaves to such inheritance?
No; let us sweep these skeleton leaves away,
Blow them beyond the moon; and from our anger,
Our pride, our bitterness, our sweetness too,
And what our kidneys say, and what our hearts,
Speak with such voice as never Babel heard;
And bring the curtain down on desolation.

Was this rich tongue of ours shaped by our mothers?
Has it no virtue of its own? says nothing
Not said before at church or between sheets?
Must Shakspere, with his phrase for the stormed heaven,

Hot midnight veined with lightning, babble only
Such mother's milk as one time wet his cheek?
Then let's be dumb: Walk in the little garden:
Watch the wise thrush delight as once in Egypt;
And hear the echoes of Thermopylæ.

And this is peace; to know our knowledge known;
To know ourselves but as old stones that sleep
In God's midstream of wreckage, worn as smooth.
All's commonplace: the jewel with the rest.
The demon truth, sharp as a maggot, works
His destined passage through the Absolute.

XXXVIII

When you come back from Memnon, when you come
Into the shadow, the green land of evening,
And hear the leaves above you, and the water
Falling, falling, in fountains;
When you remember Memnon, and the sand,
The stone lips crying to the desert, the stone eyes
Red with the daybreak not yet seen by you;

When you shake out the desert from your shoes
And laugh amongst you, and are refreshed,
And go about your business, now secure
Against the mockery of the all-changing moon;
And most of all, oh sly ones, when you sell
So dearly to the poor your grains of wisdom,
Or barter to the ignorant your belief;

Oh think of this belief and think it evil,
Evil for you because you heard it only
From a stone god whose prophecies you mocked;
Evil for them because their hunger buys it;
Evil for both of you, poor pitiful slaves,
Who had no heart, when chaos came again,
Who had no love, to make the chaos bright.

Go back again, and find the divine dark;
Seal up your eyes once more, and be as tombs;
See that yourselves shall be as Memnon was.
Then, if you have the strength to curse the darkness,
And praise a world of light, remember Memnon —
Stone feet in sand, stone eyes, stone heart, stone lips,
Who sang the day before the daybreak came.

XXXIX

Came down by night with voices in his heart,
Came down from the high altar of the mountain
Where the white eagle clutched the sheep, and stones
Rattled dislodged by wind; there the wet rock
Had burned before his eyes, so bright the angel
Who beat upon it many-wondered wings,
Beating his wings, yet moveless in that place;

So that the grass a little space about
Was lighted as by lightning, and he saw
The mountain flower at the angel's feet,
The drops of water on the hanging fern,
The daisy like a star against the moss,
A circle of pale green about the rock;

And he came down again, but had heard nothing;
Nor heard the village bell, nor heard his friend;
But entered his own house; and in the dark
Stood by the window, looking out at darkness;
Looking again toward the mountain altar,
Where now was darkness also; but his ears

Were filled with voices, filled with a sound of singing,
The wind's voice from the mountain, and his heart
Radiant in his breast was like a lamp. . .
And from that time his house was dark no more,
But housed an angel who was silent there,

Beating bright wings, yet moveless; and the light
Went forth from him; although he said no word.

XL

I

And this, the life-line, means — why, you are brief;
Briefer than Shakspere's candle; like the fly
You know one sunrise only. Here's the grassblade —
But maybe too the spider — and it's gone,
And you too gone; a drop of dew as huge
As Deneb to a fly; and you are gone.
Did you remember much? You saw a sparkle,
You saw a wing that made a shadow; crept
Under a hooked leaf like a scythe; dropped then
Against an acorn cup; lay still; curled feet;
But all in vain, the shadow got you. Thus
Good butcher destiny must knife us all.
And this, the heart-line, means —

                            Romeo, Romeo,
And wherefor art thou Romeo? Not for love,
Which takes but gives not, gives but takes not, lends
At such a usurer's rate as ruins the heart.
Generous, yes; magnanimous, sometimes; greedy,
Ah far too often; cautious, too, but not
When caution saves you; fool, fool, always fool,
Grasper at nothing, when the grasping nothing
Might well have saved you for another nothing;
And so to bed. . . Alas, and so to bed.

The head-line? It is deep. Deep, very deep.
You have thought west and north, and northwest too,
And boxed the compass of the smaller notions;
Scanned the far clouds with sextants, lacking sun;
Caught the faint star in mercury at midnight,

Pursued magnetic Poles. You have seen heartbeats
Beating in light in the plethismograph —
Was this in Camberwell? at Brooklyn Bridge? —
And found the scream and whisper much alike.
But truth is truth, although it change its time.

II

And let it change its time, and let us come
To rich dishevelment of truth, and find
A multitude of Pole Stars in its fall.
Here's one in Denmark Hill, so bright, so bright
That hatred melts like frost; and here's another
Plucked like a crocus on the hill at Belmont;
And here's a third, a slow and creeping truth,
Which swims along the bloodstream to the heart.
Oh god, let us move backward from this thing —
Truth is a lie when worshipped as the truth;
The lie a truth when worshipped as a lie.

So, let the venom swim toward the heart
And Romeo hold his breath. Ah here you have
Poor wretch, poor wretch, the essence of it all:
Catch here in agony the golden fragment:
Be conscious, for a fraction of the world:
Hate, love, desire, suffer with mouth and eye;
Bruise the poor body that is soon to die;
And so to bed. . . Alas, and so to bed.

And this, the life-line — means — what does it mean?
Why, you are brief; you have no meaning; you;
The clock's tick on the mantel; the heart's heavy
Dictatorial tick that guides your thought;
The world beneath the heart that makes you die. . .
Come, let us hold our hands out to the cloud,
And ask him if our destinies are just.

XLI

Or daylong watched, in the kaleidoscope,
While the rain beat the window, and the smoke
Blew down along the roof, how the clear fragments
Clicked subtly inward to new patterns, seeming
To melt from rose to crystal, moon to star,
Snowflake to asphodel, the bright white shrinking
To let the ruby vein its way like blood,
The violet opening like an eye, the pearl
Gone like a raindrop. Never twice the same,
Never remembered. The carpet there, the table
On which the dog's-eared Euclid with fixed stars,
The cardboard battleship, the tops, the jackstones,
And the long window lustred with changing rain,
And the long day, profound and termless.

                                                    Or
The ship's deck, midnight, winter, and the stars
Swung in a long curve starboard above the mast,
And bow-ward then as the sea hoists the bow,
And back to port, in a vast dance of atoms,
Poured down like snow about you, or again
Steady above the mast-light, the wide span
Of brilliant worlds, not meaningless, watched bravely
By him who guards the lighted binnacle, and him
Dark in the swaying crow's nest, who beats his arms
Against the cold. What mind of stars is this?
What changing thought that takes its ever-changing
Pattern in burning worlds, worlds dying, named
Sirius or Vega or the Pleiades?
What voyage this beneath them, termless, but
Not aimless wholly, trackless in the trackless
Changing of thought in that wide mind of stars?

Back from that bitter voyage to this moment:
Where the clock's tick marks hunger from disgust,

And the hour strikes for laughter, causeless, caused
By one strayed particle, unseen, between
The heart's Nile and the brain's unknown Sahara:
Rolando's fissure and the Island of Reil.
Who watches here, oh mariners and surgeons?
What Pole Star lights these shores? The atom grows,
If so it will, much like a tree, its light
Orion's now, and now the Bear's, the clock
Seeking in vain its time. We will go on,
Since go we must, bending our eyes above
The little space of light we know, watching
Thought come from news, love come from thought, desire
Come to fulfilment or defeat; and all
Swinging beneath us like that mind of stars,
Which alters when it must, alters for nothing,
In the long night that guides the ship to death.

XLII

Keep in the heart the journal nature keeps;
Mark down the limp nasturtium leaf with frost;
See that the hawthorn bough is ice-embossed,
And that the snail, in season, has his grief;
Design the winter on the window pane;
Admit pale sun through cobwebs left from autumn;
Remember summer when the flies are stilled;
Remember spring, when the cold spider sleeps.

Such diary, too, set down as this: the heart
Beat twice or thrice this day for no good reason;
For friends and sweethearts dead before their season;
For wisdom come too late, and come to naught.
Put down 'the hand that shakes,' 'the eye that glazes';
The 'step that falters betwixt thence and hence';
Observe that hips and haws burn brightest red
When the North Pole and sun are most apart.

Note that the moon is here, as cold as ever,
With ages on her face, and ice and snow;
Such as the freezing mind alone can know,
When loves and hates are only twigs that shiver.
Add in a postscript that the rain is over,
The wind from southwest backing to the south,
Disasters all forgotten, hurts forgiven;
And that the North Star, altered, shines forever.

Then say: I was a part of nature's plan;
Knew her cold heart, for I was consciousness;
Came first to hate her, and at last to bless;
Believed in her; doubted; believed again.
My love the lichen had such roots as I, —
The snowflake was my father; I return,
After this interval of faith and question,
To nature's heart, in pain, as I began.

XLIII

Not with despair, nor with rash hardihood,
And yet with both, salute the grassblade, take
The terrible thistledown between your hands, assume
Divinity, and ride the cloud. Come boldly
Upon the rock and count his scars, number
The ants that raid the pear, and be yourself
The multitude you are. We are destroyed
Daily. We meet the arrows of the sun,
Corruption, ruin, decay, time in the seed,
Usury in the flesh, death in the heart.
This band of sunlight on the frost — mistrust it.
This frost that measures blades against the sun —
Mistrust it. Look with meanest scrutiny on
This little clock, your slave. You, yourself —
Put up your plumes and crow, you are a clock
Unique, absolved, ridiculous, profound,
The clock that knows, if but it will, its tick

To be a tick, and nothing but a tick.
Walk then among the shadows with your measure
Of long and short and good and evil, mark
The come and go that leaves you — as you think —
Much as you were, or as you thought you were;
And when the spring breaks, stop.

                    Divine time-heart
That beats the violet to fragrance, turns
The planet westward to his fruitful death,
Gives the young sun his season, or compels
The hand to seek the cheek —

                I saw the evening
Giving her daily bread, and heard the prayers
Of proud weeds answered, saw the ritual
With which indifferent moss and tree were married,
The steeples pointed to the absolute,
Man avoided man, star avoided star,
The rocks were single in hard humbleness;
And thought alone it was that in its weakness
Sought answering thought.

             Divine time-thought
That brings the dead man home to underground,
Blessing the resurrection for no reason;
Giving the child his candlelight of love,
Briefly and snatched away, that he be wise —
And know in time, the dark —

               I saw the morning
Promise his daily bread, heard the Lord's Prayer
Whispered by sea-grass for the Lord himself:
That thought be thought no more, that heart be heart
Henceforward, timeless; and I was deceived,
Wishing to be deceived; and wise in this;
And touched a rock, and became rock forever.

XLIV

When you have done your murder, and the word
Lies bleeding, and the hangman's noose
Coils like a snake and hisses against your neck —
When the beloved, the adored, the word
Brought from the sunrise at the rainbow's foot
Lies dead, the first of all things now the last —

Rejoice, gay fool, laugh at the pit's edge, now
Heaven is come again, you are yourself
As once you were, the sunrise word has gone
Into the heart again, all's well with you,
Now for an instant's rapture you are only
The sunrise word, naught else, and you have wings
Lost from your second day.

                          Wisdom of wings,
Angelic power, divinity, destruction
Perfect in itself — the sword is heartshaped,
The word is bloodshaped, the flower is a coffin,
The world is everlasting —

                          But for a moment only,
The sunrise sunset moment at the pit's edge,
The night in day, timeless for a time:
Childhood is old age, youth is maturity,
Simplicity is power, the single heart
Cries like Memnon for the sun, his giant hand
Lifting the sun from the eastern hill, and then
Handing it to the west —

                          And in that moment
All known, all good, all beautiful; the child
Ruling his god, as god intends he should.

XLV

The dead man spoke to me and begged a penny,
For god's sake, and for yours and mine, he said,
Slowly under the streetlamp turned his head,
I saw his eyes wide open and he stared
Through me as if my bones and flesh were nothing,
Through me and through the earth and through the void,
His eyes were dark and wide and cold and empty
As if his vision had become a grave
Larger than bones of any world could fill,
But crystal clear and deep and deeply still.

Poor devil — why, he wants to close his eyes,
He wants a charity to close his eyes,
And follows me with outstretched palm, from world to world
And house to house and street to street,
Under the streetlamps and along dark alleys,
And sits beside me in my room, and sleeps
Upright with eyes wide open by my bed,
Circles the Pleiades with a glance, returns
From cold Orion with a slow turn of the head,
Looks north and south at once, and all the while
Holds, in that void of an unfocussed stare,
My own poor footsteps, saying

                I have read
Time in the rock and in the human heart,
Space in the bloodstream, and those lesser works
Written by rose and windflower on the summer, sung
By water and snow, deciphered by the eye,
Translated by the slaves of memory,
And all that you be you, and I be I,
Or all that by imagination, aping
God, the supreme poet of despair,
I may be you, you me, before our time

Knowing the rank intolerable taste of death,
And walking dead on the still living earth.

. . . I rose and dressed and descended the stair
Into the sunlight, and he came with me,
Staring the skeleton from the daffodil,
Freezing the snowflake in the blackbird's whistle,
And with that cold profound unhating eye
He moved the universe from east to west,
Slowly, disastrously, — but with such splendor
As god, the supreme poet of delight, might envy, —
To the magnificent sepulchre of sleep.

XLVI

But there were houses in the intermediate
Voyage from dark to dark, resting-places
Known to this homeless child that is the spirit,
Something remembered, something dearly loved,
The well-known door, the doorstep, the small window,
The face behind the window, the clock clacking
Comfortable time, time for sleep,
Time for the coming of the beloved's footstep,
Time for the firelight on the wall,
For the simple voice that says —

                              Here I am,
Here is a letter from the other world,
Here is news from the land of everlasting,
Here is the yellow nasturtium picked in the garden, with purple
Bloodstains in its throat, the marks where the bee
Plunged in the pollen, remember these, take them
With you when you set out again, this flower
Will be your passport —

                              And so this little room
With four walls and a ceiling and a floor,

A picturebook in which myself am picture,
The clock that strikes at a minute past the hour,
Moth in the carpet, corruption in the doorpost,
The visitor who comes and sits too long,
Angels who come too seldom, the little box
Worn down with affectionate use, and the air
So always, so particularly, in this place,
My own, my spirit's —

              Come, it is time to move,
There are so many places we must see,
So many other houses we must visit,
Doorsteps and windows, so many faces too
Behind those windows, other clocks with other
Errors in time, other carpets, other chairs,
And we must hurry, or we will miss the ship
With clearance papers for the Milky Way —

Deluded sentimentalist, will you stay
In this one room forever, and hold only
One withered flower in your withered hand? . . .
This is the ship that goes to No Man's Land.

XLVII

O Daughters of Jerusalem, weep for me;
Weep for yourselves, and for your children's children;
Weep for the world, that it should still bear fruit,
The fly that still it breeds, the oak that still
Lets fall its acorns on the prophet's breast;
Weep for the weed and campion, that they bloom, despite
The priest's anathema. That day has come
Which impotent and dying men desired.
Blessèd, they cried, the barren, and the wombs
That never bare, the paps that give no suck;
Blessèd to die, thrice blessèd the unborn.

O pitiful servants of a servant's servant,
Eaters of myth, devourers of filth, cowards
Who flee the word's edge as you flee the sword,
Slaves of the clock's heart, serfs of history,
Low minions of the worm —

                     Children, forget them, —
Forget the proud in wisdom, those who fear
To know the things they do. We are the sons
Of that bright light that knows no turning back;
We the prometheans who never die;
The crucified, who scorn our crucifixion,
Because we know our fate was in ourselves;
We are the Jesus and the Judas too.

Nor will we be in paradise together,
To-day, to-morrow, or in other years;
Nor eat of milk and honey, save of that
Which now we have in seeing what we have.
Our mothers know us, and we know our mothers;
Our fathers got us, and we know our fathers;
No gods abandon us, for we are gods;
We thirst not, nor are finished, nor commend
Our spirits to another's hands,

                     But walk
Upright, unholy, graceless, swift and proud,
From cloud to sunlight and from sun to cloud,
And take our ease in death. . . O slow of heart,
O fools that still believe the half-dead prophets, —
Move south, avoid the North Star, shun the frost.

XLVIII

Pawn to king four; pawn to king four; pawn
To king's knight four — the gambit is declined.
The obvious is declined; and we adventure

For stranger mishap than would here have fallen.
Where would the victory have led us, what
New square might thus have witnessed our defeat?
The king is murdered in his counting-house;
Or at the table, where he carves a fowl;
Stabbed by his light-of-love; drowned in his bath;
And all that he might know —

                Why, something new;
Such sport of nature as deforms a leaf
Or gives the toad a wing. Thus we find
The afternoon, for all its honeyed light
On gilded lawns, is monstrous grown, profound
Induction to such hell as Blake himself
Had never guessed. Suddenly comes the Queen
Dressed like a playing-card; a wind of fear
Flutters the courtiers; and the garden strewn
With the blown wreckage of our flimsy world.
And the poor king, bewildered, stops his heart
On the loud note of doubt.

              Yet, let us risk
This tame avoidance of the obvious.
Inward or outward, let the maze invite
The poor mind, avid of complexities,
And wrap it in confusion. It is here,
When tearing web from web, that we most answer
The insistent question of the will-to-be;
The eternal challenge of the absolute;
And it is here

          most brightly comes false nature in a mask,
The mincing queen of loveliness, and smiles
Witchery, through her painted smile of hate.
Shall we succumb? or through the garden gate
Make such an exit as no trumpets sound?
Shall we be mannered, and let manners lead us

Through nimble mockery and dance of wits
Which we know well that only death will end?
O take her hand, poor king, make love to her;
Praise her false beauty, which is richly true;
Walk in the coverts with her, kiss that mask
Whose poison kills the subject it inflames;
And when you feel the venom chill your blood,
Then look about you, then with leisure smile
At all denied you and at all you know;
Count the bright minutes; pick a flower and smell it;
Observe the lights and shadows; theorize
Magnificently of life and death; propound
The subtle thesis of pure consciousness . . .
And bow, and leave the world one wit the less.

XLIX

But if you search in vain the book of words,
And Christ and all his prophets beat their wings
Vainly before you — if the word of words
Set down in gold by fiery seraphim
Means nothing, less than nothing, to your heart —
Then take your heart out and devour it, mortal,
Eat out its shreds of bitterness, and taste
The god you were before dishonor hid you.
Jesus is not the spokesman of the Lord:
Confucius neither, nor Nietzsche, no, nor Blake;
But you yourself. Hold out your hand, and stare
At fingers, palm and fingernails, the wrist
Supple and strong, and wonder whence it comes,
And what its purpose is.

                            Its aim is murder:
Murder in fact, in effigy, or both.
Kill what you hate: hate what you will: love
Only what you would kill. And if you love,
Kill slowly, subtly, O invoke the power

Of Shakspere, nimblest murderer, for your art.
He was a 'man of wax' — moulded and melted
The things he loved and hated, lest he melt
His own heart's tallow . . .

                Yet, despite his skill,
Perished, in the fierce furnace of his will.
Emulate Shakspere, then, in all but this;
Prorogue your murder, and protract your bliss.

L

The world is intricate, and we are nothing.
The world is nothing: we are intricate.
Alas, how simple to invert the world
Inverting phrases! And, alas, how simple
To fool the foolish heart to his topmost bent
With flattery of the moment! Add, subtract,
Divide or subdivide with verbs and adverbs,
Multiply adjectives like cockatoos
That scream lewd colors in a phrase of trees;
Or else, with watery parentheses,
Dilute the current of your pain, divert
The red Nile's anguish till at last it waste
In sleepy deltas of slow anodyne:
Turn, with a word, the hæmorrhage to a glacier;
And all that — fools! — we may enjoy (this moment).
Precisely what we are.

                Despair, delight,
That we should be thus trapped in our own minds!
O this ambiguous nature in the blood
That wills and wills not, thinks and thinks not, hates
What it most loves, destroys what it desires,
Dissects, with skeleton's algebra, the heart!
Which will we keep? the heart? the algebra?
Will Euclid guide us safely to our tombs?

Must we renew man's venture round the Poles —
Seek, through the brain, some colder Northwest Passage —
Reason our way by inches to the frost
And frozen die in triumph? This were death
Noble indeed, enjoined of god, for those
Who think it noble and enjoined of god.
Thus let us perish. We have been round the Cape
With Freud, the sea-gull, Einstein, and the Bear;
Lived on the sea-moss of the absolute;
And died in wisdom, and been glad to die.

But let us die as gladly for such reasons
As have no reason: let us die as fools,
If so we will; explore the rash heart's folly;
The marshes of the Congo of the blood.
Here are such wisdoms — who knows? — as pure wisdom
Knows nothing of. Such birds of Paradise, —
Delusory, — as Euclid never knew, —
Colors of our own madness, and of god's. . .
O humans! Let us venture still, and die,
Alternately, of madness and of truth.

LI

O god, that down the shaftway of the sun,
Or down the mistway of the moon, should come
As in the ghost miasma of the marsh
Or in the dream that haunts the swamps of sleep
Or in those waking thoughts of gleaming madness
Disowned as soon as owned — that we should see
Such wonders, such wonders —

                       What did you see?
Was it a shape that has no shape in words?

Time has no terror, and space no delight,
The sense no horror, and the pulse no stop,
Reason no Chinese Wall —

                                      Yet you have paused
Here at the northeast corner of the world
To ask a question of the goldenrod.
Here's quartz, to sparkle in the sun; here's clover
Which sometimes has four leaves; and here the dream
And here the marsh, above which Hiroshige
Has drawn his ghosts of fog, and in the fog
The kingfisher — You hear his voice? You know
The flash of blue that is the flight of god?
Here, where you pause to ask your foolish question,
Here at the turning of the wind, here
Where somewhere leads to nowhere, and the wind
Blows north and south at once —

                              Here I remember —
Wait, wait, I have forgotten — I remember —
Everything. . . And everything is nothing.
Your father's whisper in the garden. The evening
Light through the bedroom window, the slow sound
Of steps on the stair —

                              O it is more than this
It was a house — it was a face —

                              What did you love? . . .
It was a shape that has no shape in fact.

                              LII

Stood, at the closed door, and remembered —
Hand on the doorpost faltered, and remembered —
The long ago, the far away, the near
With its absurdities — the calendar,
The one-eyed calendar upon the wall,
And time dispersed, and in a thousand ways,
Calendars torn, appointments made and kept,
Or made and broken, and the shoes worn out

Going and coming, street and stair and street,
Lamplight and starlight, fog and northeast wind,
St. Mary's ringing the angelus at six —

And it was there, at eight o'clock, I saw
Vivien and the infinite, together,
And it was here I signed my name in pencil
Against the doorpost, and later saw the snow
Left by the messenger, and here were voices —
Come back later, do come back later, if you can,
And tell us what it was, tell us what you saw,
Put your heart on the table with your hand
And tell us all those secrets that are known
In the profound interstices of time —
The glee, the wickedness, the smirk, the sudden
Divine delight — do come back and tell us,
The clock has stopped, sunset is on the snow,
Midnight is far away, and morning farther —

And then the trains that cried at night, the ships
That mourned in fog, the days whose gift was rain,
June's daisy, and she loved me not, the skull
Brought from the tomb — and I was there, and saw
The bright spade break the bone, the trumpet-vine
Bugled with bees, and on my knees I picked
One small white clover in the cactus shade,
Put it in water and took it to that room
Where blinds were drawn and all was still —

                                        Neighbors, I have come
From a vast everything whose sum is nothing,
From a complexity whose speech is simple,
Here are my hands and heart, and I have brought
Nothing you do not know, and do not fear.
Here is the evening paper at your door —
Here are your letters, I have brought the tickets,

The hour is early, and the speech is late.
Come, we are gods, — let us discourse as gods;
And weigh the grain of sand with Socrates;
Before we fall to kissing, and to bed.

LIII

Nothing to say, you say? Then we'll say nothing:
But step from rug to rug and hold our breaths.
Count the green ivy-strings against the window,
The pictures on the wall. Let us exchange
Pennies of gossip, news from nowhere, names
Held in despite or honor; we have seen
The weather-vanes veer westward, and the clouds
Obedient to the wind; have walked in snow;
Forgotten and remembered —

                     But we are strangers;
Came here by paths which never crossed; and stare
At the blind mystery of each to each.
You've seen the sea and mountains? taken ether?
And slept in hospitals from Rome to Cairo?
Why so have I; and lost my tonsils, too;
And drunk the waters of the absolute.
But is it this we meet for, of an evening,
Is it this —

        O come, like Shelley,
For god's sake let us sit on honest ground
And tell harsh stories of the deaths of kings!
Have out our hearts, confess our blood,
Our foulness and our virtue! I have known
Such sunsets of despair as god himself
Might weep for of a Sunday; and then slept
As dreamlessly as Jesus in his tomb.
I have had time in one hand, space in the other,

And mixed them to no purpose. I have seen
More in a woman's eye than can be liked,
And less than can be known. And as for you —

O creature of the frost and sunlight, worm
Uplifted by the atom's joy, receiver
Of stolen goods, unconscious thief of god —
Tell me upon this sofa how you came
From darkness to this darkness, from what terror
You found this restless pause in terror, learned
The bitter light you follow. We will talk —

But it is time to go, and I must go;
And what we thought, and silenced, none shall know.

LIV

And if the child goes out at evening, stands
Cold in the cobbled street, and claps cold hands
To frighten pigeons, so that they will fly
Against the sunset —

                 And the sky is red,
The hills are blue, the pigeons black —

If, from an opened window, music falls
And touches him with hands, stroking his hair
Gently, as if to say Why here we are, —
The ivy leaves are green, the earth is brown,
The sky is red, but darkens — and if hearing
Suddenly he is frightened — for no reason —
Something mysterious has chilled him, left
Somewhere an open door to darkness —

                     Bells have pealed
For smaller things than this, for battles lost
Far out at sea, kings dead, weak princes born,

Republics drowned in blood — thunder has clapped
His clouds together over fields of wheat —
Trees cracked in lightning and died slowly —

                                  Close the door
Against the sunset and the flying pigeons,
Against the child who brings his terror home,
Against the music in the vines, that asks
Questions we cannot answer, against the night
That eats the blood of worlds poured in the west,
And all the terrible doubts that rise like smoke
From evening fires —

                  We will shut ourselves
Into such darkness as we know is ours;
We'll warm our hands above our private terrors;
And whisper to our hearts

                    Which whisper back —

Go, clap your hands against the sunset, children!
Invoke dark memory; the witch will tell you
How god was frightened, when a pebble fell:
Covered his eyes, because the plum-tree blossomed:
And weeps for you, his sons, who fear to live.

                  LV

Indulge your terror: let him have his claws,
His goblin snout, his fangs, his huge grimaces
Which eat the fog, your house, your heart, yourself;
Entice him; let the cold mist creep upon you;
Let him lie down beside you in your bed
And stretch his foul and sweaty reptile body
Against you, hip and thigh, and close cold hands
About your throat; feel well his scales and horns;
And the wet marsh-breath on your cheek. So only

You'll keep the little candle of your wits,
And rise at daybreak —

                 To another terror;
And this is better still. This is the prince,
The prime, the very fashion-plate of horrors;
The ghost that walks by day; the unpaid debt
Which time himself presents, with interest,
And space collects, with spades. You must go
A slow mile with him; he will tell you much;
Is learnèd in the lore of seasons, knows
The dogwood from the daisy; entertains you
With dates and measurements of kings and comets,
And syzygies of satellites long dead,
(But still an object-lesson) and all such.
A necromancer, too — for he will change
An acorn to an oak tree in a twinkling;
An oak-tree to an ash; and laugh, and say
'What's dead to-morrow is not dreamed to-day.'

It is our terrors that delight us, lead
Downward to such Golcondas of soft gold
As warm the thought with thinking. It is these
That light the dogwood in the spring, the daisy
When summer dries the roof, the aster
When autumn kills the fly. . . If we have made
Contract with time and space, and with the spade,
Had ourselves measured with the falling leaf —
We'll snap our thumb-bones, then, at frost and rime,
And be, like wise men, ghosts before our time.

LVI

Rimbaud and Verlaine, precious pair of poets,
Genius in both (but what is genius?) playing
Chess on a marble table at an inn
With chestnut blossom falling in blond beer

And on their hair and between knight and bishop —
Sunlight squared between them on the chess-board
Cirrus in heaven, and a squeal of music
Blown from the leathern door of Ste. Sulpice —

Discussing, between moves, iamb and spondee
Anacoluthon and the open vowel
God the great peacock with his angel peacocks
And his dependent peacocks the bright stars:
Disputing too of fate as Plato loved it,
Or Sophocles, who hated and admired,
Or Socrates, who loved and was amused:

Verlaine puts down his pawn upon a leaf
And closes his long eyes, which are dishonest,
And says 'Rimbaud, there is one thing to do:
We must take rhetoric, and wring its neck! . . .
Rimbaud considers gravely, moves his Queen;
And then removes himself to Timbuctoo.

And Verlaine dead, — with all his jades and mauves;
And Rimbaud dead in Marseilles with a vision,
His leg cut off, as once before his heart;
And all reported by a later lackey,
Whose virtue is his tardiness in time.

Let us describe the evening as it is: —
The stars disposed in heaven as they are:
Verlaine and Shakspere rotting, where they rot,
Rimbaud remembered, and too soon forgot;

Order in all things, logic in the dark;
Arrangement in the atom and the spark;
Time in the heart and sequence in the brain —

Such as destroyed Rimbaud and fooled Verlaine.
And let us then take godhead by the neck —

And strangle it, and with it, rhetoric.

LVII

One star fell and another as we walked.
Lifting his hand toward the west, he said —
— How prodigal that sky is of its stars!
They fall and fall, and still the sky is sky.
Two more have gone, but heaven is heaven still.

Then let us not be precious of our thought,
Nor of our words, nor hoard them up as though
We thought our minds a heaven which might change
And lose its virtue when the word had fallen.
Let us be prodigal, as heaven is;
Lose what we lose, and give what we may give, —
Ourselves are still the same. Lost you a planet — ?
Is Saturn gone? Then let him take his rings
Into the Limbo of forgotten things.

O little foplings of the pride of mind,
Who wrap the phrase in lavender, and keep it
In order to display it: and you, who save your loves
As if we had not worlds of love enough — :

Let us be reckless of our words and worlds,
And spend them freely as the tree his leaves;
And give them where the giving is most blest.
What should we save them for, — a night of frost . . . ?
All lost for nothing, and ourselves a ghost.

LVIII

The dead man spoke to me and turned a page
Wide as the world, with stars upon its forehead,
And Genesis and Kings and Acts in gold,
And Chronicles and Numbers; and he said —

Slowly as in the lamplight turns my head,
Slowly as in the starlight turns the world,
So slowly comes the end.

                    And then he turned
Another page, — the moon was on its margin, —
Another with a golden crab outstretched, —
A third with twins of granite, — and a fourth
Where Alpha was at war with Omega,
The word on fire; and there stood Socrates,
Disputing with a walnut for the world;
The pros and cons were hacked like arms and thighs;
The hewed words bled their vowels. Socrates
Perished for truth; the walnut throve and grew.
Where wisdom was, now grew a walnut grove.
Then Jesus sowed the dragon's teeth, and then
The dead man turned again —

                    And Jesus, dead,
Became the star-tree, became Igdrasil
That murdered all mankind with powerful roots;
Only the rock lived, and unblemished still
Smoothed its brow in the sun.

                    The dead man said —
More pages have I yet, more worlds to come.
Resist this little frost of evil! turn
To death more dreadful than the death of flesh.
Turn now, and drink time's poison, before time
Drink you; and learn the alphabet of change
Before the omega has come, and know
Leviathan himself; and be himself;
And rage, no larger than a leaf, against
The world that's smaller still —

                    Here is the page!
Here, look! the wing is written of that word

Not spoken yet, — O angel still unborn.
Come turn it, Thought! and see the splendor there, —
The emptiness that knowledge cannot dare.

LIX

This biped botanist, this man of eyes,
This microscope with legs, who turns the seasons
Under his lens, one grassblade to another,
Pursuing god from leaf to spore, and seed
To calyx, all his world become a world
Of chlorophyl as green as any greenfly —

With daffodils mad footnotes for the spring,
And asters purple asterisks for autumn —
Reads the vast page of *idems* and *quem vides,*
Confers, collects, collates, compares, concludes;
And one day walks, his pocket full of seeds,
Into the forcing-bed prepared for him.

Where, like a bulb, he swells, and grows, and thrusts
Inquiry upward, and inquiry downward,
To find if light is lighter than the dark,
Or dark less dark than light; to watch the worm
Crawl on small hands and knees between the rootlets;
Or see the sun unfold his flower at dawn.

O peeping god, what secret would you have?
Here on spring's margin sings the daffodil,
Such precious nonsense as no god foresaw.
Pick it, dissect and analyze its root:
It is your heart; then laugh, with fool's delight,
That heavenly folly made this world so bright.

LX

He smiled, remembering this simple thing.
Forgot the book, which had recalled it. Smiled

At floor and ceiling and the four good walls,
The window and the sun. It was a notion
As gentle as a primrose. And he felt
As gentle too as if he too had leaves
And made the most of what poor light there is
In iron December.

         . . . And at this moment,
She chose to speak her hate. Thereat the angel, —
That had been he, smiling at morts and trifles,
Preening its silver feathers in delight,
Remembering little and forgetting much,
As love intends we should, — at her first word,
Became as foul a tomb as hoards a worm.

That day, he read no more.

LXI

Shall we, then, play the sentimental stop,
And flute the soft nostalgic note, and pray
Dead men and women to remember us,
Imaginary gods to pity us?

Saying
We are unworthy, father, to be remembered,
We are unworthy to be remembered, mother,
Remember us, O clods from whom we come —

Shall we make altars of the grass and wind
Implore the evening:
Shall we make altars of water and sand
Invoke the changing:
Shall we desire the unknown to speak
Forget the knowing?

We came together through the meadow of shadows,
Clouds crossed us, birds sang above us, grasshoppers

Chirred through the warm air, the southwest wind
Brought the hot smell of goldenrod, you found
Four kinds of goldenrod, all in one field,
Hornets sang in the orchard, the painted turtle
Straddled the dry rock by the river —

O Christ, and are we drowning men, to clutch
At straws and leaves? must we remember each
Frolic of dust along the road that led us
From there to here? Idiots, must we ask
The cobweb to recall just where we sat —
Are we Caligulas, that we command
Even our privies to remember us?
Here is a letter with a cancelled stamp —
Decipherably dated. Must it weep
Black tears of ink because it bears our name?
Or must our calendars abase themselves?
Shakspere would spit on this: let us spit also. . .
Good god, we are not come to such weak softness
That we must beg our very origins
To bless us from the past! What we remember,
Why that's ourselves; and if ourselves be honest,
We'll know this world of straws and leaves and hearts
Too well to give it power.

LXII

I read the primrose and the sea
                    and remember nothing
I read Arcturus and the snow
                    and remember nothing
I read the green and white book of spring
                    and remember nothing
I read the hatred in a man's eye
                    Lord, I remember nothing.

Scorn spat at me and spoke
                I remember it not
The river was frozen round the ship
                I remember it not
I found a secret message in a blade of grass
                and it is forgotten
I called my lovers by their sweet names
                they are all forgotten.

Where are my lovers now?
                buried in me.
The blades of grass, the ships, the scorners?
                here in me
The haters in the spring, snow and Arcturus?
                here in me
The primrose and the sea?
                here in me.

I know what humans know
                no less no more
I know how the summer breaks
                on Neptune's shore
I know how winter freezes
                the Milky Way
My heart's home is in Limbo
                and there I stay.

Praise Limbo, heart, and praise
                forgetfulness
We know what the tiger knows
                no more no less
We know what the primrose thinks
                and think it too
We walk when the snail walks
                across the dew.

I was a rash man in my time
                    but now I am still
I spoke with god's voice once
                    now I am still
Evil made my right hand strong
                    which now is still
Wisdom gave me pride once,
                    but it is still.

Lie down poor heart at last
                    and have your rest
Remember to forget
                    and have your rest
Think of yourself as once you were
                    at your best
And then lie down alone
                    and have your rest.

These things are as time weaves them
                    on his loom
Forgot, forgetting, we survive not
                    mortal bloom
Let us give thanks, to space,
                    for a little room
Space is our face and time our death
                    two poles of doom

Come dance around the compass
                    pointing north
Before, face downward, frozen,
                    we go forth.

LXIII

Thus systole addressed diastole, —
The heart contracting, with its grief of burden,
To the lax heart, with grief of burden gone.

Thus star to dead leaf speaks; thus cliff to sea;
And thus the spider, on a summer's day,
To the bright thistledown, trapped in the web.

No language leaps this chasm like a lightning:
Here is no message of assuagement, blown
From Ecuador to Greenland; here is only

A trumpet blast, that calls dead men to arms;
The granite's pity for the cloud; the whisper
Of time to space.

THE COMING FORTH BY DAY
OF OSIRIS JONES

*

Stage Direction

It is a shabby backdrop of bright stars:
one of the small interstices of time:
the worn out north star northward, and Orion
to westward spread in ruined light. Eastward,
the other stars disposed, — or indisposed; —
x-ward or y-ward, the sick sun inflamed;
and all his drunken planets growing pale.
We watch them, and our watching is this hour.

It is a stage of ether, without space, —
a space of limbo without time, —
a faceless clock that never strikes;

and it is bloodstream at its priestlike task, —
the indeterminate and determined heart,
that beats, and beats, and does not know it beats.

Here the dark synapse between nerve and nerve;
the void, between two atoms in the brain;
darkness, without term or form, that sinks
between two thoughts.

                              Here we have sounded, angel! —
O angel soul, O memory of man! —
And felt the nothing that sustains our wings.
And here have seen the catalogue of things —

All in the maelstrom of the limbo caught,
and whirled concentric to the funnel's end,
sans number, and sans meaning, and sans purpose;
save that the lack of purpose bears a name
the lack of meaning has a heart-beat, and
the lack of number wears a cloak of stars.

The Things

The house in Broad Street, red brick, with nine rooms
the weedgrown graveyard with its rows of tombs
the jail from which imprisoned faces grinned
at stiff palmettos flashing in the wind

the engine-house, with engines, and a tank
in which young alligators swam and stank,
the bell-tower, of red iron, where the bell
gonged of the fires in a tone from hell

magnolia trees with whitehot torch of bud
the yellow river between banks of mud
the tall striped lighthouse like a barber's pole
snake in the bog and locust in the hole

worn cigarette cards, of white battleships,
or flags, or chorus girls with scarlet lips,
jackstones of copper, peach tree in the yard
splashing ripe peaches on an earth baked hard

children beneath the arc-light in a romp
with Run sheep Run, and rice-birds in the swamp,
the organ-grinder's monkey, dancing bears,
okras in baskets, Psyche on the stairs —

and then the north star nearer, and the snow
silent between the now and long ago

time like a train that roared from place to place
new crowds, new faces, for a single face

no longer then the chinaberry tree
nor the dark mockingbird to sing his glee
nor prawns nor catfish; icicles instead
and Indian-pipes, and cider in the shed

arbutus under pinewoods in the spring
and death remembered as a tropic thing
with picture postcard angels to upraise it
and·trumpet vines and hummingbirds to phrase it

then wisdom come, and Shakspere's voice far off,
to be or not, upon the teacher's cough,
the latent heat of melting ice, the brief
hypotenuse from ecstasy to grief

amo amas, and then the *cras amet,*
the new-found eyes no slumber could forget,
Vivien, the affliction of the senses,
and conjugation of historic tenses

and Shakspere nearer come, and louder heard,
and the disparateness of flesh and word,
time growing swifter, and the pendulums
in shorter savage arcs that beat like drums —

hands held, relinquished, faces come and gone,
kissed and forgotten, and become but one,
old shoes worn out, and new ones bought, the gloves
soiled, and so lost in limbo, like the loves —

then Shakspere in the heart, the instant speech
parting the conscious terrors each from each —
wisdom's dishevelment, the purpose lamed,
and purposeless the footsteps eastward aimed

the bloodstream always slower, while the clock
followed the tired heart with louder knock,
fatigue upon the eye, the tardy springs
inviting to no longer longed-for things —

the birdsong nearer now than Shakspere's voice,
whispers of comfort — Death is near, rejoice! —
remember now the red house with nine rooms
the graveyard with its trumpetvines and tombs —

play jackstones now and let your jackstones be
the stars that make Orion's galaxy
so to deceive yourself until you move
into that house whose tenants do not love.

The Costumes

Bought from an old clothes man who rang a bell
licence three hundred sixty-five, to sell

Item: a pair of infant's socks two inches long
a dozen diapers, a woolen shawl of blue
a linen dress embroidered by a spinster aunt
ditto, ditto, a bonnet of angora (ribbons for chin)
a pair of white kid shoes for dress occasions
a rubber sheet, a long cloak of white fur

Item: a dozen bibs, another dozen of diapers,
a pair of drawers made of thin rubber
a pair of woolen mittens
and a pair ditto of aluminum (perforated)
to prevent thumb-sucking

Item: a dozen pairs of shorts
shirts, stockings, sandals, and a sailor's cap

Item: six sailor blouses, with appropriate ties
anchors embroidered on sleeves, whistles attached by cords,
with short sailor trousers of serge
a black velvet jacket with trousers to match
neckties and various shoes

Item: long trousers
collar buttons, cufflinks of silver,
a large watch with a loud tick, much heard at night
a sweater, a woolen coat with brass buttons
and woolen gloves almost impervious to snowballs

Item: a dinner jacket, three stiff shirts, collars,
pumps for dancing, a derby hat,
a dress suit, white flannels, a bathing-suit,
a raincoat with plaid lining

Item: a pair of rubbers

Item: a pair of moccasins

Item: a tweed hat bought in England, green,
goloshes, silk shirts, collars of increasing sizes,
and assorted neckties, mostly blue

Item: pyjamas, linen for summer, woolen for winter
with tasseled cords and pockets in the jackets

Item: sundry felt hats

Item: a coffin.

Characteristic Comments

The nursery clock
tick . . . tock

The face
mmmmmmm . . . mmmmmmm

The sleeves
put your arms in

The shoes
don't break the laces

The handkerchief
change me

The hat
shape of your head

The necktie
wrinkled

The fire
your hands are cold

Shakspere
to lie in cold obstruction and to rot

Vivien
but Darling!

The rain
look at the streaked light on the window-pane

The other faces
we are smiling

The shoes
polish us

The pencils
sharpen us

The desk
>   work

The peach
>   eat me in sunlight

The prostitute
>   follow me

The coffin
>   I also serve who only lie in wait

The heart
>   I will

Four Speeches Made by an Obelisk

North

>   Northward, the nothing that we give a name,
>   southward, the selfsame nothing without fame,
>   westward, the sunset over sterile sands
>   eastward, the stone Memnon with hollowed hands.

South

>   Little is life, with love, or without love,
>   with or without wings, bones can scarcely move,
>   rain will destroy the flesh, the eyes go blind,
>   and stone will not remember much the mind.

East

>   Memorials erected by our slaves
>   will close their eyes to time like humbler graves,
>   Cheops and Jones indifferent grass will cover,
>   the ant or worm will be the final lover.

West
>Speak if you will, it is as Memnon speaks
>of that supernal dawn that never breaks,
>or as I speak, on north south east and west
>of kings now useless who have gone to rest.

Remarks on the Person of Mr. Jones

The trained nurse
>it's a fine boy, not a blemish, God bless him

The face
>mmmmmmmmmm . . . mmmmmm

Other boys
>hey bricktop hey carrots

The teacher
>an appearance as of strength in reserve

The girl
>who let you out? are you wet behind the ears?

The music
>your heart is beating, your will is strong
>you are walking in a hall of clouds
>your hand is cunning and the gods are young

Picture of a mountain
>you too

The horses in the field
>you are swift

The leaf
>you are brief

The snow
> centuries hence, it will be long ago

The mirror
> lights, lights, more lights!

Memory
> this is a roiled reflection of the face

Vivien
> If you had wings you would be less an angel
> and more the devil that you sometimes are
> but you're an angel and a devil, too
> and amateur at both

Pride
> Look at that biceps! measure it with your hand.
> Was ever such a consciousness as this?
> here's wisdom that would break behemoth's heart
> and such a passion as could shape the world
> to better purpose

Shame
> Foulest, foulest, foulest,
> digester of filth, excreter of filth,
> unwashed effluvium of this rotting world,
> sickly beginning and more sickly end,
> cut out that natural heart that beats your blood
> and with it shed your life

The sun
> rejoice

The rain
> weep

Inscriptions in Sundry Places

On a billboard
   smoke Sweet Caporals

In a street-car
   do not speak to the motorman

On a vending machine
   insert one cent then press the rod
   push push push push

On a weighing machine
   give yourself a weigh

On the schoolhouse
   Morton Grammar School Founded 1886

In gilt letters on a swinging black sign
   Dr. William F. Jones M.D.

On a tombstone
   memento mori

On a coin
   e pluribus unum

On the fence of a vacant lot
   commit no nuisance

In a library
   silence

At the entrance to a graveyard
   dogs admitted only on leash

At a zoo
> do not feed the animals

On a cotton wharf
> no smoking

On a crocheted bookmarker in a Bible
> time is short

On a sailor cap
> U. S. S. Oregon

At a railway-crossing
> stop look and listen

At the end of a road
> private way dangerous passing

Beside a pond
> no fishing

In a park
> keep off the grass

In a train
> spitting prohibited $100 fine

On a celluloid button
> remember the Maine

On a brick wall
> trespassers will be prosecuted to the full extent of the law

Outside a theatre
> standing room only

At the foot of a companionway leading to the bridge of a ship
> officers only

In a subway
>   the cough and sneeze
>   both spread disease
>   and so does spit
>   take care of it

Over the gateway to a college yard
>   What is man that thou art mindful of him?

Ditto
>   enter to grow in wisdom

On a sign hung with two lanterns beside a frozen river
>   no skating

Beside a wood
>   no shooting

Behind a building in a dark alley
>   No sir, carry your water up the street

In a public lavatory
>   fools' names and fools' faces
>   always show in public places
>   and this I'll add if you don't know it
>   that Shakspere was no backhouse poet

Ditto
>   Mabel Waters 26 John Street

Ditto
>   do not deface

Ditto
>   say when you'll meet me

Ditto
>   it was down in the Lehigh Valley — me and my saucy Sue

In a museum
> visitors are requested not to touch the objects

In a concert hall
> no admission after doors are closed

On an office door
> Peter Jones

In a saloon
> no treating allowed

Laundry-mark on linen
> B69

In a window
> board and room

On a ship
> first class passengers not allowed aft of this sign

In a train
> ne pas se pencher au dehors

On an apartment-house door
> all deliveries must be made at side entrance

Over a door in a hospital
> staff only

Various Rooms

The nursery
> High on the southern wall the clock
> tick — tock — tick — tock —
> and on the western wall the rain

flashing claws on the window pane
the ceiling white the walls blue
the shawl above you is blue too
here is the place where comes the face
and murmurs mmmmmmm — mmmmmmm.

The walls are changed and papered well
with peacock and red tulip bell
here is a desk with pen and ink
and here at night you sit and think
of Jesus and the Holy Ghost
the fisherman whose wife was lost
the genii in the bottle, and
Julius Cæsar and fairyland
and two plus two and four plus four
and footsteps pause behind the door —

The dining-room
Porridge and cream for breakfast, sugar-bowls,
soft bibs and soft-boiled eggs, and salt-cellars
of crusted silver, tiny silver spoons,
the chandelier that fell, the silver bell,
nasturtiums in a cut-glass bowl that sparkled.

The hall
here once was Waterloo, and here the great
Napoleon deployed a hundred tents;
and cannons shot dried peas against the wall.

Father's office
a verb is an action being or state of being;
the articles are 'the' and 'an' or 'a';
around the rugged rock the ragged rascal ran

The schoolroom
these desks, all carved with names, once saw him rise
and in his trouser-pocket put the prize

Kitchen
> tin mug of coffee on an oilcloth table;
> advertisements of pills for female ills

Sunday school
> the fatherhood of God, the brotherhood of man —

Another schoolroom
> let me see that paper. Did you cheat?

A room in a school hospital
> so the three caravels to westward veiling
> foamworthy frows and able seamnen seething
> southward in soft altlantic saw you sinking
> depe depe and deeper darkly down and drown
> drenched and despatched and drunk with more than ether
> ceiling concentric to a funnel flaring
> sounds of wide froth and sea-surge softly hearing
> whispers of space and time and nothing caring
> the silver bubbles blinkt and you an oyster
> dark smells of oakum, far above three shadows
> Columbus gone, America discovered
> down drown down drown down drown and you too soon
> for what you know already and forget
> put up your hands and touch the keels Columbus

A lecture-room
> Focus a little experience —

A bedroom
> Quick — stand behind the door — don't make a sound
> don't breathe. Sorry the towels are so dirty.
> When you go down, carry your shoes in your hand!

Another bedroom
> Darling darling darling darling darling

Another bedroom
> It's only a handkerchief — see?
> I've got the flowers. Honest I didn't know it.

Another bedroom
> Give me another sovereign and I will

Another bedroom
> I never knew, I never knew.
> I didn't either.
> Look — it's beginning to snow.
> Perhaps you'd better close the window, do you think?

An office
> Well, I'll meet you half way

Another bedroom
> Is that you Vivien?
> This is the face I saw, this is the face
> the trumpetvine the tombstone and the place
> This is what music said
> look, you are walking in a hall of clouds
> your hand is cunning, the gods are young

A drawing-room
> Lovely weather isn't it? How do you do

A ballroom
> One, two, three-and-slide; one, two, three-and-slide;
> down by the stream where I first met Rebecca

An office
> In reply to your inquiry of the 16th instant —

A stateroom
> Creak — and a wash of sea — bells and a bugle,
> the north star drowned, a majesty of waves

washing the heart, and memory but a night
in which at last a single face is bright

Bedroom in a hospital
   Now if you'll roll your sleeve up, I will give you
   this little shot of morphine, which will help you
   you'll be surprised, it will be very easy
   lie still and close your eyes.

Mr. Jones Addresses a Looking-Glass

Mr. Jones
   So this is you

The mirror
   yes this is me

Mr. Jones
   but I am more
   than what I see

The mirror
   what are you then
   if more than that?
   a coat a collar
   and a hat

Mr. Jones
   also a heart
   also a soul
   also a will
   that knows its goal

The mirror
   you are a razor
   in a claw

       and more than that
       I never saw

Mr. Jones
       far more than that
       I am a mind
       whose wanderings
       are unconfined
       north south and east
       and west I go
       and all things under god
       I know

The mirror
       speak if you must
       but I distrust
       and all that glitters
       is but dust

Mr. Jones
       but I remember
       what I see
       and that, in mirrors,
       cannot be

The mirror
       well, Mr. Jones, perhaps it's better
       to be, like me, a good forgetter

Mr. Jones
       how can you know what here goes on
       behind this flesh-bright frontal bone?
       here are the world and god, become
       for all their depth a simple *Sum.*

The mirror
       well, keep the change, then, Mr. Jones,

and, if you can, keep brains and bones,
but as for me I'd rather be
unconscious, except when I see.

The Face

The blue shawl first, a canopy of blue,
blue sky, blue ceiling, the bewildering light
that comes and goes, and in it formless forms
and then the form of forms the shape of shapes
the darkness with the face, the face with eyes,
the face with stars, the leaning face, the murmur,

sweet food, sweet softness, incalculable depth
unassailable but protective height
the tower among the stars, great Igdrasil,
and so the sounds grown slower, more distinct,
one from another clear, the murmur shaking
deeply the chords of being, and the voice

speaking or singing, with notes far apart —
so far apart that terror folds his wings
between one syllable of sweetest sound
and its successor, — but so slow, so slow,
that terror downward, on delicious wings,
floats, — falls in the darkness, — in the silence, —

then upward beats his wings, when the word sings,
is gone away, into the blue of heaven,
up to the shawl of stars — and here the instant voice
murmurs into the heart, into the throat,
till all the blood is radiant in the veins
whispers the secret, the lost secret, far away

and it is bird song, it is boughs of trees,
the flight of light among palmetto leaves,

the wave of wind across the field of daisies,
the voice of water fluctuant in the night,
and the street-vendor, the old negress, singing
'yea, prawns, yea, okras,' in the bright blue morning —

and then the face withdrawn, farther withdrawn,
into the sunset red behind the lighthouse,
beyond the river's mouth, beyond the marsh,
far out at sea, or stars between two clouds,
farther and farther, till it lives again
only in nearer things — and it is now

the sunlight on the hand and on cold grass,
the acorn cup half filled with rain, the locust
unfolding irised wings of isinglass
the hummingbird above the flower's mouth
on an invisible cord of purest gold —
wing shadows on the wall of an old house —

and now in speed recaptured, now in strength,
and now in words dissembled, or half seen,
as when strange syllables with sudden brightness
open dark eyes, and all the page of words
becomes a field of flowers, moving and fragrant,
clover and tulip in deep grass and leaves —

all stirred and stirring in a wind from somewhere
far off and half remembered — from that sky,
that ceiling, that bewildering light, that shawl
of stars from which the voice of voices came;
then lost once more, and half seen farther on,
glimpsed in the lightning, heard in a peal of thunder —

diffused, and more diffused, till music speaks
under a hundred lights, with violins,
soft horns, nostalgic oboes, where again
the terror comes between one sound and other,

floats, — falls in the darkness, — in the silence, —
then upward beats his wings when the voice sings —

and it is life, but it is also death,
it is the whisper of the always lost
but always known, it is the first and last
of heaven's light, the end and the beginning,
follows the moving memory like a shadow,
and only rests, at last, when that too comes to rest.

Unofficial Report Made by Divers Trysting Places

A lamp-post
> He stood here. It was the hour of the dog.
> His hat pulled down to shield his face,
> his dirty raincoat on his arm, his hand
> holding his watch.

Bench in an avenue
> He sat here, in the dark, watching the cars
> feel through the night-fog with long bright antennae
> then rose, walked off a little, and came back,
> and sat and rose again. Then Vivien came —
> Vivien and the infinite together!
> St. Mary's rang the angelus in the fog.
> I heard them laughing as he took her hand,
> and the night swallowed them.

Library in a hotel
> The prostitute sat here beside the table.
> He was late: he kept her waiting.
> She was pale, her dress was shabby,
> she smoked three cigarettes, crossed, and uncrossed her knees,
> looked at her wrist watch, angrily,

and read a magazine of Christian Science.
When he came, they scarcely spoke.

Entrance to a subway
He waited almost an hour, in the snow;
but no one came.

Lobby of a hotel
Every Wednesday, at two o'clock,
he stood here, smoking, waiting;
he called her Gwen.

A tree on a hill
Three times he met his Vivien here:
three times I gave them blessing.

A park bench
It was the hour of Venus and the sailor.
They sat here eating popcorn. She was a Jewess.
The arc-light, shining through the cottonwood,
showed trampled mud and peanut shells
and a discarded garter. The swans were asleep,
dead matches floated in the dirty water,
and the gardens filled with whispered laughter.
Afterwards, when they smoked,
she laughed, and said she had a son in Troy.

A lamp-post
He stood here. It was the hour of the wolf,
his hat pulled down, his raincoat on;
but when she came, it was a different girl.

Bench in an avenue
They quarrelled here. He rose and walked away.
She sat here crying.

Entrance to a subway
> He stood beside his suitcase, reading a paper.
> When they met, they were both embarrassed.

A tree on a hill
> They will remember me.

Bench in an avenue
> For many days she came and sat alone.

Lobby of a dingy hotel
> I knew him well.

Report Made by a Medical Student to Whom Was Assigned for Inspection the Case of Mr. Jones

Facies
> sallow and somewhat haggard; thin and pallid;
> intelligent; with no marked cyanosis;
> the lips however pale and slightly blueish.
> No prominent veins, no jaundice, no oedema.
> The eyes are sunken, broad dark rings around them;
> conjunctivae, pale; gums, not affected;
> no blue line, and no sponginess. Tongue, — moist;
> with yellow coat . . . The right ear shows
> a small herpetic cluster on the lobule.

Neck
> no enlargement; normal pulsation.

Chest
> as a whole, symmetrical in outline.
> respiratory movements, uniform.
> Supra-clavicular (and infra-clavicular) regions

no more depressed than anaemia warrants.
No heart-impulse visible. Apex beat not seen.

Abdomen
   the skin, deeply pigmented. The abdomen
   somewhat distended; uniform in shape.
   Found only one small spot that might be thought
   a rose-spot: no abdominal pulsation.

Extremities
   forearms and thighs, dotted with small spots —
   average about a pinhead size (some larger) —
   varying from the color of fresh blood
   to almost black. Are not removed by pressure, —
   not raised above the surface, sharply outlined:
   appear (on close inspection) as minute
   haemorrhages beneath the epidermis . . .
   The skin, harsh, scaly. Follicles, not prominent.
   Muscles, somewhat flaccid. No oedema.

Palpation
   confirmed throughout the character of the skin.
   No evidence of enlarged glands on the neck.
   None found in the groin or the axillae.
   The heart impulse not felt; nor apex beat.
   Could not determine lower border of liver.
   Over a considerable area, and bilateral,
   marked tenderness, most marked in lower portion.
   Recti contracted — spasmodically — under pressure.

Percussion
   the lungs gave normal resonance throughout.
   The area of cardiac dulness
   came half an inch within the mammary line.
   The abdomen, throughout, was tympanitic, —
   flat on the flanks well back; dull on the pubes; —
   which I attribute to contracted recti.

The upper limit of the negative dulness
was opposite fifth rib in mammary line.
Flatness began at sixth rib. Lower border
seemed normal in position. Splenic enlargement
could not be well determined; normal dulness
not easily distinguished, partly owing
to tympany of stomach and intestines.

Auscultation

negative as regards the chest; nothing abnormal
was audible in either lung.
The apex beat was heard (equally well)
in interspaces four and five.
The heart-sounds feeble: difficult to hear;
the first sound, valvular; the second, clicking.
No murmur. In the neck, no venous hum.
No friction sounds were heard above the liver.
Did not examine spleen for friction sounds.

The eruption

first noticed with the first abdominal pains.
On radial side of forearm, near the wrist,
a bruise-like spot, size of a dime;
which passed through various shades of red and blue;
then brown and black; scaled off; and disappeared.

Speeches Made by Books, Stars, Things and People

The books

Everyman I will go with thee and be thy guide,
in thy most need
to go by thy side.

The people

Hi there Jones

say did you mean that?
well, telling him won't make him, will it
when I saw you you were sitting at the café table, thinking

The stars
> Look at us

Shakspere
> And death being dead there's no more dying then

The people
> Hi there Jones!

The stars
> Light-years!

The books
> Homage to thee, o great God, lord of truth.
> O lord I come to thee to see thy kindness
> I know thee and I know thy name, and know
> the names of all those gods who dwell with thee.

The people
> He must go westward to the outer darkness
> and die, and pick the deathless asphodels.

The stars
> We are eyes

The books
> Behold I have come to thee, and I bring truth
> sin I destroyed for thee, I have not sinned
> against mankind, nor yet against my kin
> nor wronged the place of truth, nor known the worthless.
> I wrought no evil, nor cheated the oppressed,
> nor did those things the gods abominate
> nor vilified the servant to his lord.

The people
> He's a liar.

The stars
> Winter is coming.

The books
> Never have I caused pain, nor let man hunger
> made man or woman weep, nor children weep,
> have not committed murder, nor commanded
> others to do my murder. I have not
> stolen the offerings to departed spirits
> nor robbed the gods of their oblations, nor
> committed fornication.

The people
> Hey bricktop hey carrots
> who let you out? are you wet behind the ears?
> his hands are covered with blood.

The stars
> Nebular hypothesis.

The books
> Have not polluted myself in holy places
> diminished from the bushel, taken from
> nor added to the acre-measure, nor
> encroached on fields of others. Nor have I
> misread the pointers of the scales, nor added weight,
> I have not taken milk from mouths of children,
> nor caught the fish with fish of their own kind.

The people
> The sycamores will have no food for this guy
> he lies in his throat
> lynch him

The stars
> Square of the distance?

The books
> I have not put out a fire when it should burn
> I have not driven cattle from their pastures
> I have not cut the dam of a canal
> I have not shunned the god at his appearance
> I am pure. I am pure. I am pure. I am pure. I am pure.

The people
> Outside, outside!
> close the door after you, will you?
> who let him in anyway?
> hi there Jones

The pendulums
> Pain — pang — pain — pang — pain —pang.

The stars
> First degree! second degree! third degree! forever.

The things
> We know better

A clock
> *Cuckoo! cuckoo! cuckoo!*

The beds
> Foul enseamèd sheets

A girl
> Hello Peter — do you remember me?

A dollar-bill
> He'd steal a penny from a dead man's eye

A grave
    Enter, to grow in wisdom

A cat
    He kicked me

The peach-tree
    He broke me

Waste-basket
    Filled me with circulars and unpaid bills

The hands of a clock
    Here we go round the mulberry bush
    mulberry bush mulberry bush

Jackstone
    I am still here in the yard, under a brick

Psyche
    He drew a moustache on me with an indelible pencil

The locusts
    Look out for the wasps

The swamp
    Beware the snake

The books
    Homage to you who dwell in the hall of truth
    I know you and I know your names. Let me not fall
    under the slaughtering knives, bring not my wickedness
    to the notice of the god whom you all follow;
    speak ye the truth concerning me to god.
    I have not done an evil thing, but live
    on truth, and feed on truth, and have performed
    behests of men, and things that please the gods.

The things
>Pull out the plug.

Broad street
>Hot asphalt!

Ricebirds in the swamp
>Gunshot!

The organ
>Please give a penny to the poor blind man —
>poor blind man — poor blind man —

Shakspere
>Walk you thus westward you will see the west
>grown colder but still west: or march you east
>why eastward still the sun will blanch before you,
>with ice upon his eyes, but still the sun.

Picture-postcard angels
>Harp the herald tribune sings

The music
>Angel of nothing in a world of nothings,
>palmetto leaf in sunlight, time and tide
>divinely moving, and the lighthouse bright
>against the golden western sunset light —
>O phrase of beauty, in the darkness born,
>spoken and stilled; swiftness against the cloud;
>cloud against starlight, heartbeat in the blood,
>memory of the dust and gods of dust:
>weak hand that touched, strong hand that held, weak hand
>   that touched,
>eyes that forgetting saw, and saw recalling,
>and saw again forgetting; memory moving
>from wonder to disaster, and to wonder,
>the bloodstream full of twilight, and the twilight

inflamed with sunsets of remembered birth;
O death, in shape of change, in shape of time,
in flash of leaf and murmur, delighting god
whose godhead is a vapour, whose delight
is icicles in summer, and arbutus
under the snowdrift, and the river flowing
westward among the reeds and flying birds
beyond the obelisks and hieroglyphs —
whisper of whence and why, question in darkness
answered in silence, but such silence, angel,
as answers only gods who seek for gods —
rejoice, for we are come to such a world
as no thought sounded.

The desk
    I'll meet you half way, he said.
    I'll meet you half way, he said.
    I'll meet you half way, he said.

The people
    Hi there Jones.
    where's your bankbook?
    well, he's a good egg, at that.

Vivien
    If I were less the face and more myself
    if you were less the face and more yourself
    if we were less the face and more ourselves
    and time turned backward, but our knowledge kept —

The operating-table
    Now if you'll roll your sleeve up I will give you —

The stars
    Open your mouth and shut your eyes —
    and I will give you a great surprise.
    Eclipse

obscuration
transit

A basket of okras
    Childhood! sunshine!

The shoes
    Laces broken, worn out

The books
    I gave a boat to him who needed one.
    I have made holy offerings to the gods.
    Be ye my saviours, be ye my protectors,
    and make no accusations before God.
    Look, I am pure of mouth, and clean of hands,
    therefore it hath been said by those who saw me
    come in peace, come in peace, come in peace.

The graveyard
    Come to pieces! bones to you, old bonetrap

The snow
    Poor Pete's a-cold

The books
    My heart of my mother — my heart of my mother — my heart
        of my being, —
    make no stand against me when testifying, —
    thrust me not back to darkness!

The face
    My little son!

Truth
    Tell me: who is he whose roof is fire,
    whose walls are living serpents, and whose floor
    a stream of water?

Hypotenuse
>   The shortest distance — ha ha — between two points

The people
>   Dirty dog — !
>   look at the cut of his trousers.
>   Hi there Jones!

The books
>   In very truth this heart has now been weighed
>   this soul born testimony concerning him
>   this that comes from his mouth has been confirmed
>   he has not sinned, his name stinks not before us
>   let him go forth into the field of flowers
>   let him go forth into the field of offerings
>   let him go forth into the field of reeds.

The people
>   Bribery! simony! perjury! blasphemy!

The stars
>   Chaos — hurray! — is come again

The face
>   Divinest of divine and love of loves
>   daybreak of brightest light and morning star
>   murmur of music in the fairest flower
>   o cloven sweetest fruit, and tenderest vine
>   dear timelessness of time and heavenly face
>   and dearest clover in the darkest place —

A lamp-post
>   Here he spat

A document
>   Here is his name, perjured

A ditch
>   Here he stooped

The face
>   Wonder of wonders in a world of worlds
>   o heart that beats beneath a larger heart
>   quick hands to beauty born in helplessness
>   and love of loveliness with tenderest touch —

The stars
>   Great Circle!

The outer darkness
>   Airless! Waterless! Lightless!

The books
>   In god's name, and god's image, let him die

The clock
>   Tock.

Landscape With Figures

The birches
>   tell the tale silverly

The larches
>   whisper it — hush

The pines
>   who was it? who?

The junipers
>   the bird in the bush

The brook
> Demosthenes' pebbles

The wind
> where was it? when?

The grass
> she? who was she?

The echo
> tell it again

The hillside
> warm sun upon these frozen bones of granite —
> I stretched my ribs and thawed —

The haunted house
> another frost like that, the chimney'll fall —
> there was ice by the pond's edge.

The cricket
> zeek . . . zeek . . . zeek

The wind
> who did you say she was? who?

The brook
> she babbled, she laughed, half weeping she loitered,
> she laughed without laughter, wept without tearfall —

The echo
> laughed and laughed laughed and laughed

The wind
> why did she? where? . . .

The pines
> seek her and soothe her!

The birches
>   tale-telling tell-tale!
>   this frost makes me tinkle.

The cricket
>   seek . . . seek . . . seek . . . seek . . .

The hillside
>   slowly the hard earth, from these cusps of granite
>   softly in sunlight released —

The bell-tower
>   doomed in hell, domed in hell, doomed.

The brook
>   she, she was querulous:
>   he, he was quarrelsome:

The echo
>   he he! — she she!

The haunted house
>   alas, alas how this cold autumn-wind
>   moans through old rib-bones! whines through old clapboards!

The grass
>   they? who were they? . . .
>   sure, surely I saw them . . .

The pines
>   who saw them? you?

The brook
>   babblers and wind-bibbers
>   leave love alone!

The echo
>   fling the first stone

The brook
       wept she then? walked she then? whither.

The hillside
       warm sun upon these frosted bones of granite —
       I stretch my ribs and thaw beneath the lichens —
       the drip from hoarfrost tickles at my sides
       and runs toward that chattering brook —

The haunted house
       I knew it — that brick at the top is loose.

The cricket
       seek . . . see . . . seek . . . see . . .

The bell-tower
       doom doing, doomsday, doom done, doom.

The larches
       where are they vanished to?

The brook
       what was that word that so hurt her? what hurt her so?

The birches
       whisper it

The larches
       soothesay

The pines
       where and when? who and why?

The grass
       shhhhhhhhh! . . . shhhhhhh!

BLUES FOR RUBY MATRIX

Where's Ruby, where has she gone this evening?
what has her heart done, is it enlarged,
is she so flown with sombre magnificence,
is the web wrapped round her and she mad?
Why, she should have been here hours ago
and this a snowy night too and the soul starving —

Where's Ruby where has she gone today?
is she so glorious, is she so beautiful,
has she wings that thus abruptly she has gone?
come back Ruby, you are my light-of-love
(and her with a carbuncle too and no money)
where has she gone where has she gone?

I saw her once at a soda fountain,
you don't believe it you don't believe it do you?
I saw her once at a soda fountain
strangling sarsaparilla through a paper straw.
Where's Ruby gone where is she gone this evening —
incandescence has stopped, the night is dark.

I was a driver once and knew a thing or two,
the rails were right but everything else was wrong,
come back Ruby I will unwrap the web around you,
Oh I will blow the snow off your brain tonight
and polish your conscience for you and give you a tip
and show you the stairs to the bright door of hell.

Come Ruby, I will undo your rubber goloshes,
come Ruby, I will undo the clasps,

let us walk along the track of ice a little way
and talk a little way of ice and icicles
for you too knew the way the hoarfrost grew
on God's terrific wings —

how in the heart's horn comes the prince of pauses,
the peace between the agonies — O you
who found the stepping stone and brought it back,
gave it to me because I stood and loved you,
you who stood, when others stood no more,
on the abandoned and unprosperous shore.

Why. it was you I loved and knew, and you
it was, the speechless and inalterable you
the one of the Aprils and the one of June,
O undiscoverable and unpursuable one
and one that was not one but two and three
or three that was not three but you and me.

Thus it comes, thus it comes Ruby,
woman who art not woman but a wound,
wound who art not wound but indeed a word,
word that art not word but truly a world
sprung spoken speaking spoiled and spent
in the brief darkness that the darkness meant.

II

But I was not convinced and said so too,
there among marigolds with Easter coming,
no I was not convinced had no convictions
and she was not convincing in the spring,
it was the wrong time, it was spring.

What I said was nobody's business, no,
nobody's business, I said the words straight out

and made no mention of the nightingale
nor of the willow buds or pines or palms
nor of the pleasure parks on Coney Isle
which Ikey Cohn decreed,

but I was blue and made no bones about it,
I was blue and said so to her face
there by the hot dog stand beneath the lamp
and not so far from the filling-station
I held her hand and told her face to face —

What did I tell her? Oh ask me something easy
why should I say the primrose has an eye,
why should I say the goldenrod is dusty
or the railroad long as hell from here to there,
why should I make remarks about her hair?

Tell me, brother, the little word to whisper,
tell me, brother, the little word to say,
tell me, sisters, the grand technique of love
or how to speak of beauty when you see it,
for what I said was angry that was all,
I told her to go to hell and well-damned stay there.

She made no mention of the nightingale,
why should she with no nightingales about,
nor of that other bird that burns to death.
The sidewalk was red brick beneath our feet,
the hot dog stand bright as the mouth of hell

but she was part and parcel of the brightness
that hell is said to have,
swallowed the night and smiled it back again,
laughed like a million lights, spoke like a cannon
she was a scenic railway crashing downward,
my straw hat blew away.

Pennies dimes nickels and quarters gone
and midnight come and the last boat so bright
so bright so light so cheap and full of people
all with their mouths and hands — Oh come and see
the world that lies behind the primrose eye
under the gilded teeth of Ikey Cohn —

come and see the water beside the ship,
see the white lines of foam that cross the brain
and break against the skulltop and are bitter,
come and join us in the convincing spring
and learn how sad it is to stay out late.

Good-bye, Ruby, I am fed up with you,
good-bye Ruby, your nose needs powder,
I've got that midnight feeling in my heart,
I'll hate you till breakfast-time, till the poached eggs
make peace between us —

but you were behind the primrose eye and saw
the sunrise world and all the wings — and you
had known the ultimate and called it nothing
and you have sightseen God with tired eyes
and now come back to toast our daily bread.

III

What she had was something with no name,
if she were dead I'd carve it on a stone,
it was as right as rain as true as time,
necessary as rhythm in a tune,
what she had was only a word or two
spoken under the clock.

Delay was precious and we both delayed,
come on, Ruby, and hold on clock,
but there were springs unsprung or half-sprung, still

compelling mechanism to its stillness
and in the reading-room we read the word,
the silent word that silent spoke of meaning —

it was the now, it was the then, it was the when,
it was the snow, the rain, the wind,
the name and then the where, the name, the street,
the hearse, the cradle, the all-knowing judge —
and I unerring knew the pressing word
and she receptive knew it —

the midnight took my meaning, and the noon
engulfed it in broad sunlight, the swift cloud
carried it northward like a handkerchief
to lose it in the eventualness of time
while I with equal steps climbed up the stairs
away from the remembered, to descend —

and she ascending too, with equal steps,
and she descending too, before and after,
bearing the blossom, her angelic heart,
the thurible, the incense, her quick eyes
knowing the known and guessing the unknown
searching the shadow which my mind betrayed.

Why, we were here before, but now remember
you at your time and I at mine,
both of us here to know this selfsame thing —
and now together know it, now together,
and in this pause together of the wings

touch the feathers, let the snow touch snow,
whisper recoil from whisper, frost shun frost,
that we may know what we have known already
but never with each other in this place,
or at this time, or even in this world,
and never with remembrance of before.

What she had was an evening paper, a purse,
a hat, a cape, and what I had was purpose,
but now, the purpose gone, I have — what have I Ruby,
if not a phrase of ice to carve on stone,
ambiguous skeleton of a whisper, gone
as soon as spoken, and myself alone?

IV

Boy, if I told you half of what I know —
the gulfs we cross by day to meet at night,
the Lincoln Highway and the Big Rock Candy mountains,
the deserts of the Gulf of Mexico,
boy, if I told you how I spend my time
at night-school learning all the stars of love

propound the constellations of her heart,
the North Star and the Southern Cross,
voyage to regions of the albatross
and come back spangled with bright frost of death —
boy, if you carved with me the curves I carve
against the dark undaunted ice of time

and knew those curves of hers that curve beyond
geometry of hand or eye or mind
into the bloodstream and above again,
westward under the sea with setting suns,
oblique dishonest and profound as hell,
corrupt, unchanging, changing, choice as steel —

Boy, if you went with me along her streets
under the windows of her lighted eyes,
saw the foul doors, the purlieus and the cats,
the filth put out the food received the money
the evil music grinning all its teeth,
cachinnations above the sauerkraut!

This is where she lives and loves, that Ruby,
this is where she lives and pays her way
among the unborn and the dead and dying,
the dirty and the sweating, pays her way
with sweat and guile and triumph and deceit
burning the empty paper bags and scraps.

Boy, if I told you where the money comes from
out of a silver mine in Colorado,
the unrefined refined and the bright goddess
brought all the way from chaos to Mike's Alley
and on her hand at noon to pay the rent
roof to prevent the rage of heaven's tent —

but if I told you half of what I know
I'd have to be the Gulf of Mexico
the Big Rock Candy Mountains in the spring
and every other big or little thing.
I'd wear the Milky Way out with my walking,
wear out my shoes with the walking blues.

Hush Ruby, I meant these words for someone else,
hush Ruby, it's all right now,
only a little student of geometry
who wanted to know the why and where of curves
went out and came back frozen by the stars
with geometric frostbite in his brain.

Take him in with you and warm him Ruby,
take him in with you, put him to sleep,
tell him the difference between truth and lying,
tell him where you've been and what you mean,
the clock, the closet, horror's cloaca too —
and wake him, when his heart is fed and dead.

V

But this was nothing boy, and I said nothing,
no leaf or love was born but it took time.
Come on and shake the cosmic dice, come seven,
come on and shake the bones for odd or even
but this was nothing and no one said a word.

I saw the palm leaf and I took it down, Ruby,
I saw the gold leaf and I took it down.
I saw the heaven leaf and I took it down, honey,
I saw the dead leaf and I took it down.

I saw the word that shaped the lips of water,
I saw the idea that shaped the mind of water,
I saw the thought of time that shaped the face,
I saw the face that brought disgrace to space.

But this was nothing, girl, and I said nothing,
nothing I thought, what could I think but nothing?
who nothing knew and was the seed of nothing,
the conscious No One watching Naught from Nowhere.

Take the palm leaf for what it is no other,
take the gold-leaf and put it down,
take the heaven-leaf and put it down, Ruby,
take the dead leaf and put it down —

for what is wisdom, wisdom is only this —
history of the world in a deathbed kiss,
past and to be in agony brought home,
and kingdom of darkness come.

VI

No use hanging round we must be going,
no use waiting before the evening altar

green screen of evening sky between paired stars
where the cloud worships and the wind is bowed,
there's no use waiting Ruby we must be moving.

You are a rock like that blue mountain too
jagged and scarred like that where the snow lingers
and I have seen the sunrise on white shoulders,
the orchid among the boulders,
the edelweiss and ewigkeit
and the retreating armies of the night.

No use waiting, Ruby, we will not hear,
the proud hosanna of the stars is not for us,
we will not hear them sing the silver word
nor see the angelic wings ascend between
the silver trumpets against a sky of icy green.

This we abandon, and though this have seen
see it no more, but take our evening down
along dark streets that you have made your own,
the wretched streets that in-and-out are you,
there where the cry of pain is in the bone

and where your darkness prowls around us nightlong,
approaches and retreats, confronts us snarling,
devours the hours — is this your house Ruby,
are these your stairs, is that your window open,
is there a bed a ceiling above the bed?

do voices come and go and slam of doors?
Smells of fecundity, the human spawn,
far off the cries of trains, the taxi's ticking
is all coincidence that thus together
everything meets upon this tip of time —

your hand that murdered men or drew the morning
out of the seventh vial, or rolled the mountains

against the tombs of all the gods, or poured
the zeros one on other and destroyed
the indestructible to create the new —

came like a flame from sand, reentered water,
was braided like the ice, became a wall
sang through the trumpet of eternity
and now, descended, holds a greasy key
and presses it against a greasy lock —

Farewell Ruby, for this is where I leave you
your hand releases me its filth is on me,
the holy filth of long corruption comes
coldly upon me as an absolution,
sharply we flower in this foul farewell.

VII

But God's terrific wing that day came down,
loud on the world as loud and white as snow
out of the blue the white and then the silence.
O Ruby, come again and turn the time.

Ruby, your name is matrix, rock of ages
cloven by lightning, smitten by thunder,
the surged upon deep shore interminable,
the long, the nebulous waves, the foam of time,

beating upon you, breaking upon you foaming,
the worldlong fruitfulness of assuaging sea,
hammers of foam, O Ruby come again
be broken for our simple coming forth —

let the rocks fall upon us with fearful sound,
the long bright glacier of the stars be broken,
the beginning and the final word be spoken,
come again, come again, and turn the world.

This world that is your turning and returning,
matrix mother mistress menstrual moon,
wafer of scarlet in the virgin void,
O come again and turn the world to thought.

But God's terrific wing that day came down
snow on the world, and Ruby you were snow,
deceitful whiteness and the blood concealed
so that the world might know how worlds will end.

LANDSCAPE WEST OF EDEN

I

It was of a deck, the prow of a ship, uplifted
by the wide wave of blue and whiteness, swung
towards the star-side by a long wave from the west,
then earthward dropped. And there I, not alone,
westward facing,

            and with me the two children,
Eve and Adam, from Eden come with flowerbuds,
and roots of flowers, and acorns in their hands,
and words for worms and flies; and the long slow sunset
bridled the redfoamed sea, from north across to south,
touching each wavetop with a crimson feather,
and the seabirds too were red;

            and as I lay, rising and falling
as rose the crimsoned waterwaves, remembering
seas, seas, and other seas, and seas before them,
above earth, under, and in this kind of dream, —
and those too fainter that with waves of less than nothing
chill the faint cheeks of stars, — so I watched
how, in a later age, the long clouds of brilliant scarlet
with openings of light from the last lost sun
were but as trains of human purpose, that weakly cross
from one frail island to another island, farther.
And so I said (but Eve and Adam were silent):
'It is the death and daybreak, all in one;
sow your seeds in the dark, and they will prosper.'

I smiled at them, but they smiled not at me.
They held with small hard hands their buds and flowers
and precious seeds from Eden, — but how could they believe
— poor darlings, angels of the daybreak! how could they think
to plant the bright gold solid seeds of Eden, and the bright shoots,
in something less than Eden or more than earth?

Nor could I persuade them; nor, not being God, would wish
to alter the inalterable, save for my own poor pleasure,
— and that perhaps were pleasure enough? to see the change
alter historic eyes, with all the fallen stars removed?
the constellations clearer, those I know?
But ah, poor children, to make them the victims
of such ideal delight! that they should see their flowers
wither, or worse, worse still, grow to strange shapes!
And am I a father, that I should beat my children for this?
No, no, my darlings, do your murder in your own way,
as I in mine; and at the end of the world's evening,
when the harvest of stars has been gathered and stored for nothing,
then we will sit together, and understand, and exchange
the husks of seeds which we vainly planted under the rainbow;
and you will say, 'You went farther,' and I will say,
'But to no purpose' . . .

       But now we sail
westward together, and say nothing, hostile to each other,
and the world is good, and old, and deep.

II

And then the minstrel fellow, whom I hated,
came softly stepping, harp in hand, from wave to wave,
with such a brightness, such a lightness, such delight
in his own wave-flight across seas of chaos,
and such assurance, and such eyes of wisdom's colour,
and wings of the sea-eagle or the angel,
touching his heart to such deep chords of heaven-praise,

that I was ashamed, but also jealous. And I saw
how well and swiftly from wave to wave he came,
making such sport of it as swallow makes of summer-flight
for his own joy in motion. And 'O curst man,' he sang,
'you will know nothing, you will waste your life
in desperate voyages to the unknown coasts, —
turn back and listen; but you cannot, cannot listen;
nor, if you listened, could I sing to you with such power.'

Poised then upon the prow a moment, westward pointing,
his eyes contemptuous of the west as of the east,
he struck his heart and sang a southward song.
What comfort there? And Eve and Adam heard him, smiling, —
dear children, how they loved that sweetest heaven-praise!
And I too loved it, and I wept, but still I looked
beyond his heart and harp and wings to westward;
but for no reason, save my purpose there.

And southward then he flew, from crimson wave to wave,
with such a lightness, such delight, such heavenly brightness,
his eagle wings spread out in fiery light,
and in the winds of heaven his heart-harp making songs
of such divine and sorrowful home-going
as might have turned the ship's prow southward too.
But I too, like the children, Adam and Eve,
held in hard hands my stubborn seeds and shoots;
and closed my ears and eyes; and sailed to the shoreless
sunset land whose cliffs were only clouds.

III

And this dream-ship dissolved into evening light,
galleys of gold and crimson galleons and fiery caravels
sunk and consumed in fire with wrack of red clouds,
and the one island left that was myself —
this sunset-thought, here at the western window, looking
across the red marsh, where the dark birds fly homeward

athwart the day-end light, — as now my thoughts
bring back those images of Eve and Adam
to me once more, who sent them forth; and the angel too
who was myself come home.

       The little road, far off,
turns up the hill, winding among tall trees,
loses itself among black shadowed houses
and there, forthgoing from the window in my thought's power,
I climb the hill in sunset light, going westward;
but soon my purpose flags, or I forget it;
and here again am standing before the open window,
remembering.

       Remembering the 'out there' and the 'here within,'
this little coral island of the mind,
broken upon with all the foams of nescience;
now bared and glittering, now almost overwhelmed and drowned;
with its little memories of weeds, mosses, shells and sands,
left for a moment between one wave and other,
felt, noticed, hardly known through the hardness,
and swept away again.

       Remembering also
the memories of these things, and the deep magic
wrought upon them by the falsenesses of memory:
the shell become a jewel, the sand become a desert,
the waves become the ineluctable hatred of chaos,
the weeds and mosses become as bridges of delight
wonderfully windswept, archangelically designed,
fairylifted and void-defying, between
one fever of darkness and the next; wherever
nimbly I send my messengers, and they return, swiftly,
with that fantastic nonsense which feeds the soul.

Thou art, thou art, thou hast, thou hast —
miraculously nothing, that miracle

which breathes out life and breathes in death;
say no more of it then than this, lost island soul,
no more than this; thou art and hast.

IV

But in the friendly night, walking in night's womb,
to first warm darkness again born back, and gladly
comforted by the mother-dark, feeling
the thick pulse, the cord of stars, and the far heart
beating its slow and heavy diastole
so that my being trembled, well knowing itself
to be where it was, and nowhere else, to be
the dull half-anguished resistance-joy of being:
and on the soft path walking toward a faint light
heartless myself but needing no heart, and following
the quick lights of firefly memories, gone and come,
so close that they touched me as I moved —

                    what need I more than this,
what need I, laughter, more than this, — you, voice of weeping,
what need I more than this? Then the angel with the lantern
held his light against my eyes so that I shrank back,
my eyes hurt by the cold full horror of light,
but too late turning back, for the light held me.
And he with hard strong hands grasped me and drew me forth
under the question of his lantern, marking
with shrewd eyes, my eyes, what my answers were.

'And come, coward,' he said, 'learn to give another answer
than pain! Learn now to dishevel the simplicities,
and to rejoice in the bitter dishevelment!'
And so I went with him, bewildered, to a mean room
squared out of time and space, and with their coldness,
and saw, for the first time, the almighty clock.

v

The morning oak I praised, whose wide grey branches spread
hardily against a sky of blue and white
dipping his leaves to the wind and a frolic of rain
and in this summer-season as tolerant of jackdaws
as in the winter of snow. In the deep grass I stood,
under the singing circle of leaves and lichens,
watching the alternate colours of sky go over,
and hearing and feeling the wind among my flashing leaves:
raising the eastern boughs, and solemnly dipping the western;
whirling concentric a moment, and then still.
O mindless delight! the words had half escaped me,
as the oak too half escaped me: but the shadow
shifted and caught me, and I stood in shade to my knees,
remembering the foursquare room, and all my roots.

Then, when the wind pulled, I pulled a rock,
then gave a handful of leaves, a patter of acorns,
wasted on rock, or doomed to be stifled in grass;
and, the wind shifting, pulled at another rock,
gave him a branch of fresh-torn leaves and mast,
felt the birds gone. Is this the dishevelment
foreseen?

But I am walking again
naked of thought as an angel without wings, rejoicing
at nothing, or rejoicing that one can so rejoice
at nothing, and I am already again in my cold room
where now the oak-tree bursts the walls and ceiling.
Clock, here's an acorn for you! Here will be oaks.
Adam and Eve, dear children, will sit beneath you gladly
and tell each other the lovely lies of Eden;
while I, their humble father, ignored, will lean from the window,
and send to the sunset a powerful thought of death.

VI

Nevertheless, my dilapidated angel-self, with ragged wings,
pursued my flight into the far too purple west
and brought me back laughing from the sentimental sunset,
and slapped my hands to make them let go of the dirt of death,
and stood me in a corner, still laughing, and walked to and fro
half beating his wings, so that the room was windy;
and I, the oak-tree, whispered, and gave him two leaves.
'You, with your powerful sunset thought of death!' he said,
'You always westward going, as if in the west alone
the rainbow buried its golden claws! you with this longing
for many-coloured annihilation, sacrifice
for something, everything, or even nothing, if only
you go there with wings and come back with a halo!
Why, are we so desperate yet? Must we die suddenly?
or is the North Star hero of a melodrama?
Is paper snow falling from the empyrean
on your poor soul, cast as the abandoned heroine?
Must we have bells and cannons and trumpets
and flowers flung for bones, garlands for skeletons,
harp-songs for *rigor mortis*? This were an insult to us.
Let us be quiet, and examine the causes as we may;
the rainbow's foot is in dishevelment;
the veriest fools and idiots can recognize the novel;
only the gods can know and praise the good.
And we are gods.'

            Whereat I dissembled chagrin,
from this, my angel self, I concealed my sorest shame,
and for a while pretended to be a mindless tree.
Beneath me the two children exchanged trinkets of trove,
and kissed many times with increasing boldness,
and began, without knowing it, to plan a world.
I too was as simple as that: I could have moved
at one step into the fruitful south of worldmake
and spawned a rainbowed world like any fish.

Nor was the impulse lacking. I looked forth greedily
and saw where best this new magnificence might be:
there, there, it was; not shaped like any other world;
never before conceived as now my blood conceived it;
but now checked, with hatred, contempt, affection and laughter.
'Look!' I said to Eve and Adam, 'there is a world lost!'

And the satirical angel, with brightened wings, glowing,
with wisdom-coloured eyes, and a delightful stillness, said:
'We are still far from wisdom, still with pain and joy
accept the pure simplicities of the soul.'

VII

Sleepless lying many nights I thought of these things,
humble, hopeless yet, but with the mind's godlike eye
seeing always farther and deeper into the night-world,
myself seen also in a little hammock, swung
darkly parallel with the earth's dark surface,
absurd cocoon of consciousness, hung in the void,
ridiculous little worm-prism of the darkly known.
With my hand I reached then upward and took Polaris
and flung him southward into the night, there to start
a new world, and to leave the old world new;
now should be no more north for prophets and mariners.
And I scattered the Seven Sisters, so that I might laugh
watching them run like lost ants hither and thither
— but all this in a dream.

                        It was myself I thus dispersed,
thus with a thought altered to new pattern
for the delight in change, and the delight in knowing
the old order now forever fixed and inalterable;
fixed in the memory, but changed by thought of change;
for nothing changes but thinking makes it change.
As one would move the vases on the mantelpiece,
the right to left, the left to right; and shift the clock,

and perhaps also shift its meaningless measure of time,
so that this profound void interval we call a second
has become instead a long and transverse wind,
a tide of space; down which we altered plunge
to a new knowledge of sublime forgetfulness.
Then, like angelic salmon, to reascend
up the long cataract of strange re-ordered order,
to a new shape of dream, a new design of God.
So, having moved the vases (only with a thought of moving)
and made the clock (which was an ear) an eye,
the room grown shapeless, and myself shapeless, then
delighted came I back to the world of memory;
as a swimmer, long submerged, beaten by waves,
comes up at last triumphant from long darkness,
and sees the cliffs above him, and his own tree,
birds with white bright feathers, the shore of warm pebbles,
an oak leaf, close to his cheek, in sea-froth, whirling,
the seal shining on the wet rock, and all these things
vivid and hard as metal in the bright sunlight;
and himself too as hard and clear as they.

Thus I renewed
the world within, the world without, world without end.

VIII

Not for long will man walk in this world
before death speaks to him and dread deflects him
from child's delight in flowers; and time is doom,
and sounds and sights of dolour, come with the clucking clock,
strike the heart's midnight. Nor is it far,
as ravens and buzzards fly, from the cradle to the grave.
Thou hast, thou art, and then thou hast not, art not.
Look how the sunlight blazes on red blooms
whether they be in garden, or in field, or in the mind,
or on the undiscoverable and unremembered grave.
And thus I saw (walking forth) the crumbling stones

heavy with honeysuckle; and forthwith I remembered,
though still a child, the bones that gave me birth.

This was the west wind, over flowers, that softly came
whispering whys and whithers, wherefrom I went
kneedeep in goldenrod and became drunk with sun.
There the first angel came, flying from tomb to tomb,
winnowing grass and flowers, slowly, with indifferent wings,
and followed, smiling, as I went in doubt from stone to stone,
perching on each in turn, and holding in his hand
a withered flower. And at first I avoided him
and moved away, ashamed, and with sly pretence of leisure
went to another grave, another tomb, another vault,
and saw the bones.

       And then he gave me
the withered flower, and this I held in my hand,
stared at, and thought long, and it was he
who spoke. 'This is your father,' he said, 'this is your mother,
and here are east and west, and downward-flowing water,
and the upward-going thought!'

            And thereupon I pondered
of upward-going thought; and cast away the flower;
and deep in hot goldenrod buried my face and wept;
and thrust my hands amid the stalks and earth.

IX

Spreading my boughs above the children, Eve and Adam,
the daylight warm and windless, and wisdom yet
not come to find the peril in wisdom's source,
they sleeping, he with pebbles in his hands, and she
with daisies in her hands, and in her hair —
so, with deliberate dream, I foresaw god.
It was as clear a feeling, and as cool,
as east wind brings to underside of oak-leaf,

precise and precious, dislodging raindrops,
and making ants to stumble . . . Dreaming thus I saw
the god of wrong, the downward-going god, which Eve and Adam
were doomed to be; and for myself alas I saw
the upward-going thought, but powerless to change these guilty
    lives.

But from this vision waking
I spoke to them, walking angrily before them,
and asked them (who were ashamed and frightened)
whether they were awake, and what they knew of god,
and which of us was god, and which of us least godlike,
and whether indeed (considering all things)
we needed gods at all.

Far off I saw the angel,
no larger than a mosquito above the trees;
and with discomfort I knew (but concealed it from the children)
the satiric laughter in his wisdom-coloured eyes.
And so I walked apart, my questions unanswered,
and left them puzzled, with the flowers and the pebbles,
and waited, in the little darkness of my own chagrin,
to see if he would come. And he came lightly,
but not derisively, nor with satire, rather with pity,
and this I suffered more; and before me, gravely,
stood for a moment silent, and then softly asked
which of us was god and which of us least godlike
and (if we needed gods) where we might find them?
Nor did he smile then; nor did I answer; and we stood
face to face for a long time, my eyes downcast
and his unwavering; until at last
I looked at him; and then he smiled, and as he smiled
I knew myself forgiven and foreseen, and my foreknowing
foreknown, and all the world I knew foredoomed.

x

Ignorant I pitied myself, I went humbly
among stupendous fanfares and hornblasts of wisdom,
and none there were who knew less than I, and many
who sent their words with flags to the very ramparts of time.
Only the questioner I loved, the hemlock-lover,
him whom bitterness made sweet and humbleness made wise;
and not that poet who thought himself (alas) a god.
This much I learned from the tomb-seeing angel.
And this too I concealed from the children.

And as I sat
there with the publican drinking bitter beer,
while the coarse clock ticked centuries for stupid stars,
calendars coming and going from dying printers of words,
planets cooling and changing as men change minds,
it was there the two men came from east and west,
wise men from west and east, and spoke their wisdom;
while the publican with wings laughed in the corner.

And first the first one said, his face like sea-moss,
his hands the claws of gulls: 'Good fellow, I have been,
from here to there, from dust to water, and have known
all languages, and spoken them, and known also
the god withheld in each, the wisdom lost; but lastly
found, at the end of life — as now I am — this wonder:
this tongue, in which the meaning is so dispersed,
into such tiny particles, such fragments
of meaningless glitter, such infinitesimal surds,
that (on a careful estimate) it will take
a thousand years to assemble (of such sounds)
enough to make one meaning . . .'

Hearing this, I went forth and laboured
a thousand years; and slowly gathered, in my carts and barrows,
at last enough of sounds to make a meaning.

Proudly I brought them back, before the publican, and drank
his bitter beer again; and now the second sage
had just begun to speak. He pulled his beard, and said
(gently scorning the other sage, and also scorning
the carts and barrows which had brought my meaning):
'So say you? . . . Why, this is nothing. I have been
from there to here, and here to there, and found
at last the tongue of tongues; now, at the end of life, I know
what no philologist has known before me.'

At this the publican laughed, beating his wings,
'And what is this?' he said, 'another wonder?
One more of these, by God, and we shall have no sense, no sense
      at all!'
But the sage answered:

                    'It is a language
in which the meaning is so concentrated, so terrible, so godlike! —
that one quick syllable is a thousand years.'

And with that clap of thunder we were changed.

XI

Nevertheless many times temptation of wisdom-pride
came to me, nor perhaps will I ever escape
that shameful fault, which is the folly of all fools;
as one day in the garden, under a tree, sleeping,
I woke and heard the voices of Eve and Adam beneath me.
They lay in languor, by love exhausted, laughing,
and idly (thinking me asleep) began to talk.
And Adam said: 'But if there are these things, Eve, —
the things we know, and know delightful, — may there not be
outside us, and beyond, in another world,
things more delightful still?'

                    I partly opened my eyes,
and watched how Eve, sitting in grass with idle hands,

touched in her thought, with those small hands relaxed,
unimagined wonders, in a world as yet unknown.
Sombre, with downcast eyes, she thought of these;
effortful; and with deliberate puzzlement;
and said: 'But Adam; who knows; may it not be
the new things might be dreadful?'

             'Foolish woman!' he said,
'perhaps they are. Perhaps they are! But even so
(not that I think it likely) we could come
homeward again; if there are terrors in that world, —
devils, goblins, ghosts, the seven-sworded rainbow,
or ice that kills the heart, — think, think, how escaping these,
this garden would rejoice us!'

             Thereupon I awoke,
and walked before them with my accustomed anger,
turning my back for a moment, only to glare at them between the
    leaves,
contemptuous as much of Adam's childish boldness
as of Eve's timidity and tenderness. Will I never learn
the wisdom that is aware, and watches, and gladly waits?
But I was impatient, and chided their impertinence,
and their small foolish foresight. 'Why!' I said, —
'What can you know of life, who are not yet dead?'
And then I boasted of all my bales and blessings,
my many times repeated death, wisdom of tombs,
horrors of chaos from which, again and again,
emerging godlike I made a man-shape of my misery.
'What can you know, who are young as the yellow primrose?
Will you cast horoscopes at the age of pollen?
Learn first to wither!'

             As I walked, I watched warily,
for fear my sceptic angel might in secret slyness
be hiding near. It was not he, but Adam,
who chastened me. For Adam said:

'Forgive my foolishness, —
but is not pollen the seed of dead plants, and of death?'

Then suddenly, before him, I was ashamed.
For in his eyes, lowered, abashed, I clearly saw
wisdom and innocence, and innocence in wisdom,
the death of shame; and knew him destined, in his time,
to be my angel . . .

But I was proud, and turned my back, and said no word.

XII

Were one to know the world as a wide wanhope of web
such as with shrouded eye the hornet sees, when death-caught,
then, when he hears only the humming of his own wingbeat,
naught answering, naught pitying, no reply
from hornet-gods, — only the dreadful silent shape
approaching abruptly, he, the enemy, the unknown —
why this were something, too, to know, this plane of silken
treachery, in which the wing is worse than worthless!
Are gods exempt? is the cold cloud exempt? the wind,
is he exempt? At sunset the wind dies, slowly,
the cold cloud dies of snow, the world is a tomb
of dead gods. But this is simple, this simplicity
of cruelty, intelligible and terrible,
godlike and therefor good!

Thus, as I watched the water
on a black night of bitter star and frost,
first freezing in small fans and ferns of glass,
clicking and tinkling, then with sullen creakings closing, —
the leaf encased, the floating twig, the stick, the straw,
at the white edge the pebbles too embraced in claws of ice —
and, at last, groaning, the whole pond imprisoned —
thus, I thought of the many deaths and murders by which we
        live —

how one thought slays another, itself then slain;
and frost creeps over feelings, and time destroys
what frost has spared.

Above the hill I saw
the moon's dead beauty come; trees snapped in the cold,
wounded forever; and in my heart I knew
the children's quarrel, in which hard words are flung
and murder done in play, which will at last be earnest . . .
And so I clenched my murderous hands and laughed.

XIII

The peach-tree being in bloom, beneath it I waited,
centuries, between the falling of light pink petals;
one fell upon my hand, another in my hair;
one was dislodged by a sparrow, another by a bee;
a third the wind flung down; the fourth and fifth fell of their
own weight; and I awoke from sleep
to find the sixth beside me in warm grass.
Far off below me, on a long slope of hill, I saw various
new furrows in a field, sleeked by the ploughshare,
so that they glistened in the May sunlight, —
new waves of earth, and bright as waves of sea.
There the birds foraged, cried as they settled,
alarmed went chattering westward, where they waited;
till quiet came again, and they returned to earth.

But what I waited for, unless it were earth-wisdom,
or warm persuasion of the slow spring-season-sunlight;
or what the peach-tree blossoms (leisurely falling) had to say —
who will interpret this, in words of quartz and crystal?
laziness was my light, delight was less in laughter;
slow was the pulse, and penitent, for past foolishness;
pollen blood went frothily in my veins, and sluggishly;
and I lay still as tree-root . . .

I watched the cloud
(carved by the peach-tree into shapes no cloud should know),
pass slowly over, blossoms dark against its white,
westward; until it cleared the tree, and sank gravely
into the sunset and a red resurrection.
And I thought of Eve and Adam, changed by morning and eve-
        ning;
myself, by the blossoms changed; blossom, by birdsong;
shadow, by time; and the heart happy with nonsense . . .
And so lay smiling until the seventh blossom fell.

XIV

'Strange, strange it is,' I said to the dark angel —
he, darkened by his thought, as I by mine,
and as the field we sat in was darkened by a cloud —
'strange that the body should be unfaithful to the mind,
the mind unfaithful to the body! will the soul wander
witless among the waters and hills which are her own?
This peach-blossom is visited by innumerable
bees and flies and butterflies (faithless wantons);
it is their faithlessness that makes them welcome.
Thus, she is fertile; thus, the mind is fertile; why then
must love be sterile, in pure faithfulness?'

'Why indeed?' the angel said.

'Let Eve love Satan, and Adam adore Lilith then,' I answered:
'Eve will learn much from Satan, and Adam from Lilith, —
and how delicious, how new, this wisdom will be!
Satan disguising himself — needlessly — quite needlessly! —
as the insinuating, the insidious, the all-knowing serpent!
and Lilith — what will Lilith be? what will Lilith be?'

'Là, là!' the angel said.

'But then' — I pondered aloud — 'will Eve love Adam? or Adam

love Eve? will they bring back their wisdoms?
will each receive from the other the new wisdoms?
will they be angry?'

'They will be angry,' the angel said.

'Ah! Just as I thought! . . . Rain is unfaithful to field,
ocean to air, lover to lover,
mind to body and body to mind. The thought
runs westward, while the body leches eastward!
Thought will want fractions, body will want flesh!
Here are no conclusions?'

'Thou sayest it? Thou knowest? Then thou growest!
And soon, thou wilt learn to laugh.'

Whereat he rose, and spread angelic wings,
and eastward went to Eden; while in the grass I wondered
at the disparateness — or so it seemed — of thought and flesh;
and held the blossom in my hand, and in a vision
saw the world ending in a laughter of pure delight.

XV

The tired hand, the tired eye, — these too will have place
in thought's constellation, which sags slowly
earthward and sleepward, and as it sinks grows brighter,
brighter and larger; so grow the setting stars,
magnified to magnificence in earth's miasma.
Thus fever inflames the infinitesimal;
the seed becomes a world, terrors become gods;
and thus fatigue makes prophecies and portents
of its own weariness.

        Or so I thought, while evening
brightened above the marsh-mist the first planet-light;
and, tired, I felt my tiredness turn to tired thought;

tired thought to sadness; sadness to bitter despair,
despair to wisdom, backward-looking, but such wisdom
as lives on nightshade, and the moonlight in waste places.
Ruin of thought? ruin of gods and worlds? ruin
of man's brief empire?

　　　　　　I saw Adam sleeping, Eve
sleeping beside him; her hand was on his shoulder,
the buttercups half-fallen from it, some of them fallen,
behind him fallen, her hand relaxed and sleeping too —
and Adam's hand, asleep also, was on her hip;
the caress arrested, poised, postponed. And so they waited
(not knowing that they waited) for the renewal
of loves exhausted, and beliefs destroyed.
But in the morning — how new their love would be!
the world, how young! the buttercups, how many!
and Eve so strange to Adam, and Adam so strange to Eve!

Where then, — I said to the moon, — is honesty?
can thought be trusted, if it change its tune
as weariness, or weather, time or space or mood,
dictate the theme? If so, here's chaos come.
If thought must change, as changing seasons change,
change to the dictates of the blood and moon, the mind
moving to measures of the mere unmeaning —
is honesty the best policy, or policy
the only honesty? Surely the latter, like a bright fixed star,
will guide us firmly, ineluctably,
variants overruled, safely to nowhere?
Choosing a thought, we'll sail to it, and die, —
somewhere between the thought and nought . . . But if
we choose for honesty itself, why then, we'll change
minute by minute the bewildered compass;
we'll change our minds, as change our moods; and die still chang-
　　　ing.
And wisdom will be change, and faith in change . . .

Thus in the evening, as I watched the moon enlarge,
westward sinking, with a rim of golden cloud,
myself went westward too, in enlarged thought;
and sank in somnolent magnificence, slowly,
in grandiose gradualness, to divinest sleep.

XVI

'Daybreak?' the angel said. 'But what is daybreak, god?
do you mean night-break? do you mean dark-break?
or else, poor dreamer, do you mean that sullen waking
from sleep's omniscient nescience to sad thought?
Why, would you have, flung from the eastern mountain-top,
three stars, an arrow of light, and a rose-petal?
Is this so precious? is this a harbinger of joy?
O come and climb with me; eastward we fare from Eden;
thus we will speed the dawn; and thus — ah, think of this —
will speed the sunset too.'

   He spread angelic wings,
wide as the valley seemed they in the darkness, beating,
and whirled the air and rose; and with him, I, unwilling,
beat my new wings, which ill sustained me eastward,
already burdened with foredoom and feel of night.
Eastward we went, and Eden fell behind us;
until our eastward thought so far outran us
that we were there, before our wings were there.
Hung on our wings, then, in the empyrean,
we waited, for such dawn as never comes.
And as we hung there, in the foreday whisper,
the first warm currents of air intermingling with the cold,
the birds beneath us singing in still-dark trees,
he said, and smiled:

    'Mortal god, it is given to no mortal
to see his birth. Go further eastward yet;
your birth is still before you. Seek it, yes!

But ah, my friend, though there is warmth in sunrise, it is not such
as warms the hand; and if it warms the heart,
or gives the mind's eye vision, or brings comfort
to those weak gods who long to know their birth,
it gives no joy to you.'

           Thereat he turned,
and westward went; easily; with slow wingbeat, floating
on westward flowing light. For now the sun
had thrust a golden limb above the mountain-top;
and all the eastern trees were edged with brightness,
and my own wings were bright before my eyes;
so bright that all the east was dim with light;
and that dark world, from which I came, obscured.
Marvellous was it, warm in colour, rose-bright, and deep;
wonders came up from it, whirling, and went westward;
the sun rose, the earth and stars all changed,
my wings I stilled, eastward eagerly staring.
But though I saw the gashes of bright light,
the depths of terror, the void, the vividness, the wonder,
horror of trees outlined against the brightness,
I saw no more.

           And so at last, wiser only
in facing the unknown, I flew past Eden.

XVII

And then the minstrel fellow, whom I hated,
him of the harp, the Hermes-heeled, the southward
sybarite, wide-winged, and with such ease of flight
as made my new wings heavy, came from the south,
touching angelic laughter from his heart-strings,
so sweet a song that all the birds were still.
Then, beneath the shadow of his wider wings,
shadowed by them, and sheltered, and also shamed,
and in the stillness hung beneath him, hearing

his heavenly voice, I held my speech, and speechless
waited until he spoke.

               'O infant god,' he said,
'empty-handed you come from east and west,
took not my warning, followed me not,
saw not, or heeded not, the wisdom-colour of my eyes,
nor heard my song; heed now, and bend your flight
southward with me, and sleep in heart-warmth there.'

Softly the song fell, his shadow against the sun
was cool and great, nor would it have been hard
to follow in his wake, when, with slow measure,
he separated light from dark, and flew
southward once more; and from him, as he went,
came the soft harp-strings of his southern heart.
With even flight he flew, and left the sky
as cold and bright above me as before;
no shadow sheltered me; so that I longed
to go with him, as longed my wings to follow
the current of his wings; which still, in the cold air,
fanned at my feathers.

               But I hung still, above
the oak-tree; and beneath the oak-tree saw
Adam and Eve, whose eyes were eastward turned.

                    XVIII

Thus from the window eastward faring in thought I went,
no longer now by footpaths humbly content to go
but spreading imagination's widening wings;
and saw the origin, the east-light, the red daybreak,
the void of the unknowable, whence we come.
And must we know — I thought sadly — the unknown?
why must we seek it?

Eastward again I laboured,
this time on foot, slowly, through dew-bright grass,
and saw the morning-glory untwist his white and purple.
Why must I watch this? why must I seek this cold beginning?
why must I know myself — alas, alas, — or try
to think I know myself? Here is that nescience,
that edge of clashing darkness, where I had birth.
Hence come my hand and heart. Hence comes the subtle thought
which, seeing chaos, knows itself, no more.
What comfort here? And if indeed this be
desire for first unconsciousness again;
if here, in daybreak's horror, I would drown;
if here in chaos I would sink my thought and drown;
were it not better, as the angel says,
to drown in sunset, having known the west?
Or is it better to have seen the east, before
we westward fly, with a westward dying world?
The morning-glory opened; the east was bright; the clouds
northward and southward parted before the sun;
the mountains brightened, east of Eden;
shafts of new light flew westward;
and westward I too returned, on lagging feet,
uncomforted, unthinking, sad, unseeing;
and felt my folded wings teased by the wind;
and homeward come in sadness, stood once more at the window;
marvelling at this great world which was myself.

XIX

Between the snow and summer, I heard Adam's anger
bitterly spoken, to Eve, and listened in secret, laughing,
while the spring fog was soft in the apple orchard.
And 'Woman,' he said, 'would you know nothing? would you be
ignorant all your days? dawdle here forever?
You saw our god go eastward — would you not go
eastward also, to see the things god saw?
Why, this is cowardice!' He glared at Eve;

but she smiled back with such impertinence,
that I was angry; although I knew her right.

'But what is eastward, Adam?' she said, laughing.
'Will we find there the rainbow's foot? or learn
why god is god? or why ourselves are mortal?
must we forever forage in the dark, with Eden
so close at hand? . . . Let us return to Eden!'

Then Adam took an oakbranch,
and broke it in his hands, in pride of strength;
and glared, and spoke again.

                    And 'Fool!' he said,
'what now is Eden? Eden was for our childhood.
Are we forever children? do we grow?
have you learned nothing, in this journey westward,
save that you want once more the fruits of Eden?
must you go back and play with acorns, grassblades, fernleaves?
Is nothing learned, with loss of innocence?
Eastward (I heard the gods say) lies that chaos
which groaned, and gave us birth. Are we such children, still,
that we must fear the darkness whence we come?'

'Eden is better,' said Eve. 'I want no chaos.'

'Would you remain a fool?'

                    'Why not?' said Eve.

'Ah, but you will not!' said Adam; 'for I will take you
eastward with me. There we will face the rock,
and learn the filthy roots that make us evil!
Come!'

              And he took her hand, and dragged her forth
a perilous journey (a mile or two) eastward, climbing

the hard hill, in the fog; and Eve protested
alarm, despair, and clung to him, and pleaded
and begged for Eden, and wept; but in her heart
laughed; for she knew how soon this work would end.

And I, who followed them, with soft and secret flight,
pitying both, and pleased with both, but angry also
that they should mimic thus so soon, unwitting,
the agonies of gods, waited, and watched;
knowing how soon fatigue would end this flight;
and knowing, too, that Eve knew; and that Adam,
after this show of courage, would relinquish
this splendid thirst for knowledge, and would sleep.

And thus it was. And when at last they rested, —
quarrelled and wept and slept, — I spread my wings
gladly above them; as an oak-tree might.

XX

Playing chess in the sunlight with the angel,
suddenly the angel's wing shadowed the pieces, curving
a sharp shadow forthright between the queen and bishop.
Then all was changed. That world of logic changed.
Eclipse was on me, a line of darkness dreadfully drawn;
and such a vision I had as sometimes comes in sleep.
Suppose — and this I thought, lifting upward
the shadowed bishop, so that his mitre was in the light —
suppose this board, in which all logic so clearly lies
in one bright plane, though now by shadow altered —
suppose this board, this game, had other dimensions?
If kings and queens had wings —

                    I moved my piece, pondered,
downward and upward into a world unguessed
by rooks and pawns; and said, more to myself
than to the angel, whose fingers lightly touched his king:

'If all were on one plane, how easy! If sorrow
were sorrow only for a single reason, not for
a thousand things! And if, for but a moment,
alas, for but a moment, we might know
the countless planes of feeling, or of knowledge, or of guess,
of which a moment's awareness is the intersection!
If we could see, — all in an instant, —
the lost flower, the tired hand, the slowed heartbeat, the cry
of water on rock, the sad history of the sand;
the tragedy of the half-remembered, the half-longed-for;
perceptions of time, of distance; self-distrust, self-praise;
simplicity of removal, and the wound it gives;
simplicity of approach, and the blessing it gives;
absence or presence of warmth, the come and go of light!
If we might know, at the instant itself of speech,
the atom's disaster in the blood, the new decision
made in the nerve-cell!'

        The angel moved his king,
stared through me, said: 'Why not go farther still?
what of the kidneys, the liver, the heart, the stomach?
Your speech is these: it is the sum, also, of these:
you are the sum of worlds within and worlds without.'
I took my knight by the ears, and lifted him,
and placed him in the sunlight, where he sparkled.
'Now I am changed,' I said; 'for by this action, surely,
I am a seedling's root that thrusts against a stone;
Eve with delight by Adam touched; the planet urging
his dying heat against the dying sun;
whispers returning, after touching the rock's face;
water returning, in a whisper, to the cloud.
And ah what hatreds, what furies, what deliriums,
moved to their end in this obliquity!
What loves, too, which the atom still remembers,
but I myself forget!'

       'And deaths,' the angel said.

XXI

It was when Lilith became an angel that I learned
(as before from Eve I guessed) how language too
leads one perforce into the south of worldmake.
She, with new wings, and vanity of wings,
preening her snow-plumes, smiling, fanning them slowly
for the new joy and power, lifting herself
a wing's width from the grass, and softly alighting
on winnowed flowers again, came to me, tempting.
Bringing her wings before her eyes, she smiled darkly,
hiding her face she laughed a little, and spoke
with such soft speech that I, distrusting, listened.
'Now that I have these wings which are my birthright,
these wings, of which Eve's innocence deprived me,
I shall again explore the world of darkness!
Come, god, and see how evil can flower in purple!
Come with me, I will teach you how the kiss
creates such kingdoms as your pure Adam never dreamed.'

Strange, too, the imaginations that she gave me
out of her voice and eyes, while, daylong and nightlong,
under the farthest nothing, we hung embraced.
One day and then another, with level flood of light,
far, far below us, poured the stars to westward;
and still we beat wide wings upon the ether;
and still I kissed the world-deep eyes and mouth.
Such wordless words she spoke as passed my knowledge:
said nothing, whispered, murmured, wept, caressed;
yet in my blood, and in my brain, began to build
fantastic worlds, and false too as fantastic.
Were the sun moved, and black as any cinder;
were the moon cleft, and blood poured down from it;
were darkness shed by stars, and in the darkness demons
swimming with wings of fire, their eyes like mouths;
and were I there, omnipotent in wonder,
now man, now woman, all alike pursuing,

and all alike embracing with swift wings,
drinking the darkness of innumerable mouths —

I trembled with the beginnings of this new power;
already half distinct I saw that fevered world;
inchoate lewdnesses becoming shapes,
shadows becoming lurid delicious lights,
all whirling, mad, and with delirium's wonder,
splendours of foulness. I withdrew my lips
from Lilith's lips, beat my right wing, and turned
to stare more soberly at this world of evil.

And so, my hand against her hair, I knew
how false this world, how true, and what its power;
and so, returning, brought its darkness back;
and built its splendid ramparts against Eden.

THE POET IN GRANADA

*

Homage to Lorca

I

Chickweed, gorse, pink cistus; and the white cistus with furry
        leaves;
    blue pimpernel, and the purple poppy;
the cork tree, half hawthorn and half oak, color of olive;
    and the smoky olive with sparse shade;
broom, blue lupin, the tiny daisy; bee-orchis and wild violet;
    golden-eyed orchis, rooted by snouts of pigs;
the barren red rocks of the campo santo, among whose stones
    clings the dwarf wild lavender, aromatic as bay.
Red soil, red rock, red clay, and the clay hard-crusted,
    runneled into arroyos by the winter rains:
but now baked hard, worn smooth, shiny and resisting the foot;
    . . . and the white Sierras;
the white Sierras above the foothills, red foothills plumed with
    olive;
    like those red stippled hills,
burnt sienna, bright blue, hard green, of Hokusai.

The goats browse on the slope in the shadow, by the water-course,
    goats and black sheep and lean pigs;
the officious dog, and the woman with child, far-seeing,
    and a boy with an olive-switch.
Bells are tinkling, bells are clashing and clinking,
    Japanese wind-bells in spring wind;
tinkle tonkle (bells saying the slow words)
        tonkle tunk (casual bells of beasts.)

Far off the blue hills, blue waves, tremble in the heat,
      dissolve in a gauzy sky;
up the deep road of the Sagramonte, the Sacred Mountain,
      upward through the heat-waves,
stumbles the paniered donkey-train, striking the cobbles,
      four boys beating three donkeys;
downward, down the red-gullied road, the stench by the Winter
      Palace,
      clatters the mule-train, whacked by men.

Take your choice! The streets of Granada, too, stink with filth;
      in the street of the Poet Zacatin
the small boys howl round the body of a dead cat, waterlogged,
      and then drag over it, this being *Fiesta,*
clattering and thumping, a string of junk, old pails, old pots,
      scrap-iron and broken bedsprings;
whereas in the morning papers, at the cafés, the aesthetes read
      of the spiritual regeneration of Spain, flinging
scornful phrases at the practical buccaneering Englishman,
      and the Yanqui millionaire.

II

Palm Sunday, the rain intermitting, rain intermitting
      for the parched Sierras,
the Poet entered Granada, riding a milk-white ass,
      the foal trotting after under flowering Judas.
The procession was expected at four. It was already six
      in the Plaza, by the Café Royal,
when the four trumpeters drew abreast of the tables
      on the dapple-grey Arabs
and set the plumed horns to their lips, the leader blowing a solo,
      shrill, fierce, and precarious,
while glasses clinked on indifferent tables, and small boys,
      derisive, blew an answering summons.

And then the procession: disorderly: the hooded and masked
            rows of men and boys with palms,
tall yellow branches against the evening, waving and rattling,
            dry rattle of dead leaves;
two and two the priests sauntering and gossiping, bold priests
            turning black eyes under low hat-rims:
the palms tall and bright in the evening light.
            At the corner, by the Café,
the procession halted, drew back on itself, huddled together,
            then again awkwardly started.
Hoods and masks, slotted eyes, and then the Sacred Float,
            mantled in plaited leaves,
teetering, without dignity, ridiculous; and the peasants bowed,
            doffing their high-crowned hats,
and the priests murmured and shuffled, their low voices
            half-amused, unconcerned.
The enthusiast plucked a leaf from the float, as a souvenir,
            and children were lifted to see.
Taaa-ta-ra-taaa! The cracked high bugle screeched,
            hysterical and sobbing;
and Jesus, the poet, the condemned man, self-condemned,
            had entered the Street of the Catholic Kings, riding
to Pilate, to Judas, to the agony in the Public Gardens,
            foreseeing violence; foreseeing death.

III

(In the *Paseo del Invierno*, the Winter Walk,
            under the chestnut trees, the Judas trees,
by the red baroque barracks, the twisted red columns,
            it is there he will walk in the evening,
pulling at the scant Spanish beard, while children
            beg him for pennies. *Perrrrrito! Uno perrrrrrito!*
A little dog! Pennies and half-pennies,
            plucking at his coat-sleeves
while he thinks, or tries to think.

What is this that we are about to do? what
misery of indecision before the certainty of fact? is it
        for mankind that we suffer, propose to suffer?
or for ourselves? Is it for these children,
        that we shall give our lives, the ignorant and innocent,
these who make faces and beg pennies? Or is it for
        ourselves only, the unquiet, the unstable,
who are ourselves still children, that all men
        may know their childishness? And this voice, —
the voice from the heart which tells us we are chosen, —
        shall we believe it — ? —
and must we, therefore, die? —

        From the red baroque barracks to the Fountain,
the fountain of the Four Upright Lions, eyes downward,
        walking softly, walking slowly;
from the Fountain to the low parapet by the muddy river,
        where mule-teams wait in the shallows for gravel;
regarding, from the bed of purple irises,
        the snow-covered Sierras, and again turning,
seeing everything, forgetting his guitar, seeing nothing.

        Father, if it be Thy will,
decide these things for us, let not these decisions
        be left to simple men, put Thy wisdom
into our hearts, bring to pass by Thyself
        whatever things seem good to Thee.)

                        IV

Good Friday, the Friday of God, and in the evening
        the streets jammed with people,
crowds pushing under the blossoming Judas, crowds
        packing the streets for the sacred procession,
strolling beside the Genil's dirty water, the women
        passing unconcerned

through the heavy carbolic smell of the men's urinals,
        and the human filth of streets:
flamboyant nursemaids, arms akimbo, carrying
        beribboned and velveted infants,
bantering jeering phrases with the impudent soldiers,
        they with the shapeless uniforms,
while other infants, humbler, bare-bottomed,
        squat shameless among mud and cobbles.

The festival of the seed, the burial; the offering made
        to the gods of harvest. Prickly pear
spreads its great palms of spines, blue-green, glaucous,
        above the caves cut in the rock.
The aloe with golden bells glows in late sun, and the gipsy woman
        smiles as she offers a lucky fortune, for silver,
or a dance, in which she will be clad in a single shawl, or —
        and the smile becomes castanets.

Eight: and the clamor of bells: and the procession
        starts. The Cross, the Scarf, mummers in peaked hats,
masked mimes in scarlet gowns, scarlet and saffron, the candles
        uplifted fluttering in red cups like tulips,
the trumpeters bursting the still twilight with shrill sound.
        And the crowd of combs and shawls,
mantillas and laces, gaudy uniforms and Toledo blades,
        presses inward toward the procession.
Hail to Priapus, to Bacchus!
        Hail too to Dionysus and Adonis! Hail, hail!
The gross priests pass, with great bellies, the wine-bibbers,
        and the guards on their horses,
and then the float bearing the sacred casket
        glass and gilt and tortoise-shell,
lighted by toppling candelabra without and within,
        the sheeted recumbent corpse,
the poet borne to the burial. *Tormento, su tormento* — ah his
        agony!
        The zealot sings to the crowd

his wingèd arrow of song, white-faced, and the crowd
        lifts him and cheers him — Olé!
And then come the centurions; the Roman eagle;
        the imperial guards, with leg-straps and breast-plates;
and again more tulips.
        The men in the cafés, rising,
leave their brandies for a moment:
        the women stare down from their balconies.
And so to the church of Santa Anna, the catafalque
        lifted up the stairs through the door,
while peaked hats sneak aside in the gathering darkness,
        by the river-wall of the church,
to light cigarettes, or for other purposes. Top-hatted,
        three officials light cigarettes in the portals;
across the street, two old women, bowing and muttering,
        crawl towards the church on their knees.

Io! The seed is planted, planted in earth,
        and we shall have harvest,
harvest of hatred and thistles. The superb centurions
        marching proudly, drums thudding,
withdraw, disappear; the crowd bursts into the church,
        and the reek of incense;
and boys lift up the red skirts of the catafalque
        to see how the thing was propelled.
The candelabra are removed, and the candles extinguished,
        by the sacristan in shirt-sleeves,
and once more, for another year, the recumbent, the corpse, is in
        darkness:
        alone: the crowd leaves him.
The poet, the veiled recumbent, lies sleeping, lies solitary,
        while human returns to human;
the god, the veiled mystery, lies watchful, lies waiting;
        lies fertile, while the human sleeps.

V

On Easter, what? The bells of Santa Anna, the bells
                among the cactus in the gipsy quarter,
the Albaicin, the bells of the squat red tower
                of the Alcazar, where the ghosts
of the Moors keep watch in moonlight.
                In the gardens of the Summer Palace
the Hundred Fountains are turned on at eleven
                for the tourist, the artist with his sketch-book,
the quarrelling honeymoon couple, and the photographer,
                with his hooded camera.
The sky cloudless and hot, clouds of white dust
                floating from the beaten roads,
dust-clouds veiling the olive trees, where the donkeys
                sway with their double baskets.
Goats, from the crest of the red hill, skip down to the shadow,
                shadow of cork trees, rank grass and myrtle,
by the stone watercourse, dried by the sun. Goatherds sing
                like grasshoppers. In the Alhambra,
crowds patter like rain through the arabesqued arcades;
                counting the arches; reading the inscriptions
cut in the stone by the French troops, in eighteen-eleven. . .
                Then too the resurrection, the harvest, —
harvest of hatred and murder! On the Sagramonte,
                the olive tree shades the cave dug in rock;
and there the gipsy woman dips the water-jars, and hands them
                dripping to the boy and girl, barefooted:
there the clay chimneys thrust out of the warm rock:
                there too, at evening,
the priests, in the seminary, alternate their prayers
                with ascensions of rockets and abrupt clamor of bells,
                        while
old women gather their linen
                from the spines of the prickly pear.

On Easter, what? Six fine Andalusian bulls for the bullfight,
      and the bullring packed with people;
six fine bulls, four blacks, two calicos, and a dozen
      Rosinantes, poor scarecrows of horses;
the white shawls spread on the parapet,
      embroidered with scarlet roses;
and the sinister mule-team, plumed with red, jingling its bells.
      Olé! Olé! The stately procession
advances gravely across the bullring,
      advances on the smooth sand,
the *alguaciles* on proud horses, the *toreros* behind them
      walking like dancers in their delicate slippers,
walking gracefully, their tight small-clothes gleaming,
      doffing their tricornes stiffly.
The Key is given and taken, the men scatter, the trumpet
      sounds out over *sol y sombra;*
high, clear, sharp, and noble the trumpet sounds,
      the dread door is opened:
it is the dedication to death, the consecration
      of the living and the undying to death,
the sowing of blood whence shall come the resurrection,
      the red flower of the illusion.
The horses die bravely but ignobly, their own hooves
      chopping their entrails, smelling death;
the bulls die bravely but stupidly, bewildered
      by the dance of lightning, eyes blind with sun and blood,
the red flower of the illusion. The great voices, bugling,
      dominate for a hushed moment the vulgar hubbub,
dominate the hissed swear-words of the sweating men,
      the butterfly capes, the quivering red flags:
the great voices speak shrilly and superbly of death, then are lost
      in the sunlight, the confusion, the shouts,
the flinging of hats and orange-peel. A drunkard falls into the ring
      and is arrested, the galloping mule-team
drags out the dead bull, his muzzle spurting up the sand in a wave,
      turning it like a plough; and then once more

high, clear, sharp, and noble, the trumpet calls for the opening
        of the dread door, the dedication of the undying
to death; once more, while already the butcher dismembers
        the carcase, sells the warm tongue and testicles,
the trumpet sounds for the sowing of the seed of blood, the living
        seed of blood, whence shall come
the harvest of murder, the resurrection, the red flower
        of the illusion, the dreadful and desperate dream.

                                    VI

Chickweed, gorse, pink cistus — white cistus, with furry leaves:
        blue pimpernel and purple poppy;
the spiny cork tree, half hawthorn and half oak;
        and the olive tree with sparse shade;
broom, blue lupin, daisy — bee-orchis and small wild violet;
        yellow-eyed orchis rooted by snouts of pigs for the bulbs;
the red rocky slope by the campo santo, with loose stones,
        and dwarf wild lavender, aromatic as bay:
red soil, red clay — ah, but not yet with blood —
        runneled into arroyos by the winter rains,
now baked hard, and resisting the foot.
        And the white Sierras,
and the red foothills, tufted with the grey olive,
        like those red stippled hills,
burnt sienna, and azure, and hard green, of Hokusai:

these shall remain when the harvest has been scythed,
        the red flower of the illusion
plucked, broken, and forgotten,
        the hatred and murder
finished: a hard land of sure rock and sweet orchard, the wide air
        blameless as soulless, and wholesome as a handful of
            thyme.

The Four Appearances

I

It is the sunlight only, the pure shape
of shapelessness, the moonlight only;
the moving light on the moving wall;
the shadow indistinguishable from light,
and time's beat, heart's beat, so that each from all
only as falling leaf from falling leaf might fall,
one from another, and into another, escape,
flight and fear on the quick tongue of delight:

and the soft hand folding the soft other,
which with a breath is gone and come,
surrounding, or by miracle surrounded,
forgetting or forgotten, known, unknown;
deeply implanted in the budding bone,
bedded in the eye, profoundly founded
in light, the father, and dark, the mother,
seed in impermanence softly sown —

and the harp breaking all its strings at once,
icicles tinkling from a frozen wall,
snapped ecstasy of time for time renewed;
while the disparate loves, with desperate eyes,
search their own shapes for such as might delude,
(lest the whole splendid mythos fall)
to feed the rainbow on its daily food
of self-engendered lies.

II

And then the change, as if the wind had changed,
the slight quicksilver breeze in a field of clouds,
the golden shudder in a field of golden wheat,

that lustrous and anchored smoke so lightly shifted
and the leaves silverly lifted;
or as the familiar wall, by frost estranged,
waits white and blindfold in the frightened street
till the sun's fingers and the blind ice meet:

and suddenly your hand is new before you,
as new and sharp as the stone beside the sea:
transparent — look! — as you lift it against the sun:
and there you watch the blood, like ichor, run
in aureate radiance round the skeleton:
it is the sunlight running round the bone,
the gilded lie of living that runs around the stone,
and your own isolation, come to adore you!

Cold as a monolith beside the sea you stand,
a separate thing between the sun and sand,
alien to each, and with hard eyes perceive
staring, to hate, and hating, to believe,
how, all about you, crystal, foam and grain,
tiny and vast, seaweed and weather, cruelly enchain
each the other's aborted and smoothworn self,
the indifferent pattern of the hour to weave.

III

Next out of sunlight the sphere globed and sleek,
such as the sunlight of a dream might break,
and the sphered godlike image there contained,
its violent and human beauty strained
into that sudden size, that sudden shape,
whirling concentric, never to escape,
the beautiful face toward you turned, but pained,
and all that golden strength so bound, so weak —

and your own elbows against your sides hard pressed
and your own heart mutinous in your breast,

as like maimed gods, or gods defamed,
powerless and sad, with sad self-pitying eyes,
from tortured world to tortured world you glare,
each measuring ruin in the other's stare,
each in the other to see the godhead named,
but prisoner, too, and lamed —

and so, each in his sphere of sunlight, blown
bubble-like away in time, the thistledown
that meets in air, touches, and lightly parts,
lost as soon as found and known,
separated with constrainèd hearts,
and the face backward turning still to see
that violent beauty by selfhood overthrown,
and, in the noble eyes, the look of agony.

IV

Then again change, as if the wind had changed;
or the eyelids closed, and the dream opened, the dream
turning a silver leaf, showing a silver seam;
as if in a garden the wind touched a tree,
and suddenly all was stirred and estranged,
all motion and commotion, all flurry and hurry,
leaf against blossom moving, blossom over blossom,
shadow and twinkle, and something that seems to be
a moving face, eyes, a hand, a bosom —

yes, and the white shoulder, then, and the quick mouth
laughing under the quick dark eyes, the bright face
turning with the wind — as if a wind had come from the south
bringing with it the whole tree of silver metal —
the wreathed goddess in her whirl of petal
opening her arms to the night,
winding the stars about her shoulders in delight,
turning and turning, yet motionless in that place —

yourself motionless, too, and as if not there,
yet under the closed eyelids in a dream aware
of the changed tree, and yourself changed, the confusion
as of leaves and arms, leaves and hair,
and your own hands on the cold blossoms bare,
and in your powerful vision the illusion
of the divine blossom miraculously become one
with the dark tree of sight it buds upon.

The Temptation

It was not gross, it was not sudden, it came subtly;
was not harsh, was not brazen, but dwelt softly;
like a moist evening drew a golden ring around the moon;
withdrew, and then, withdrawn, went speaking —
not as the world speaks, not as a voice
comes from another, but as a voice hidden,
confused and diffused in one's own blood:
murmur, but less than murmur, the divine sound
of the blood itself that warms from vein to vein,
bearing assuagement from the heart to the hand,
the hand to the heart, the thought to the will —

as if with the softest of footsteps walking
in a wide landscape of dispersed hills and trees,
with the far ring of brightest light in which the clouds
from nowhere coming dissolve to nowhere —
as if there walking with softest footstep
it was not the far, not the ultimate, not the bright
horizon's ring you saw, nor the dim clouds,
nor the night falling, the small moon's golden ring,
nor the sound of the wind in the distant trees
turning and turning the helpless leaves —

no, nor the sense of these that drew your thought,
not those, not those far off, not those engaged

the senses expert in the expert flesh:
no quickening of ear was quick to hear,
nor was the hand raised, or the finger pointed;
but close before you, and beneath your feet,
the small grass singly laced and cold, the sharp
point of a flower, and yet not sharp, but gently
come from the earth, come from a dream,
and soundless as dreamed hands and faces seem —

ringed by the instant and immediate thus,
as if in a gentleness gone mad the flowers and grass
danced in a ring around you, came closer dancing,
and you turned, but they came closer still —
not menacingly, but tenderly, yourself
whispering the softest secret to yourself, yourself
the outer and inner rings, the voice and the ear,
the hand and the heart, the world and the eye;
and turning away you turned again, and saw
with what amazement and what delight

that these, the grassblades, and these, the flowers,
the instant world that ringed about your feet,
were your own language not yet spoken —
your own words, there, of this, and this, and that!
Why, it was this you meant, and it was this
you would have said, if given time, if given also
the need and place to say these things; you would have found
just such phrases, these rhythms of grass, the wind
quick among flowers, loud among leaves —
and this pattern, and this grace! —

Ah, but suddenly, at this very instant,
flowered from that shape of loveliness a shape
shadowy and ominous; as if death's comment
upon the flower might flower from the flower itself;
the shadowy echo, golden but shadowy extension
into another and more dreadful dimension;

and yourself, speaking to self, the inner and outer rings,
only the first voice of the paired and golden echo,
the echo from the unknown, the still-to-come;
magnificent unshaped thunder of divine doom;

ah, but suddenly, at this very moment,
cried from the grass itself death's careless comment,
cried from the little flower its hidden torment,
and the ringed world, ring beyond ring of light,
widened to nothing, became intolerably bright,
gave back its silence to the infinite;
remote and cold as stars were flower and meadow —
silent in sunlight was the rock's delight;
and on that mystic marriage fell a shadow,
and the aloneness of the soul was right.

Then with what shame, and with what shamed obeisance,
and harsh self-knowledge, as in tempestuous Eden,
you saw, beyond the serpent's hour, the mind's hour,
the hand's hour, the heart's hour,
gathering all around you, inward and outward,
the untamed wave of the world:
flashing an easy crest along the firmament,
downward opening to chaos with soft and worldlong thunder;
yourself, in that hand of water, flung like a seashell
beyond temptation, beyond your dream.

TIME IN THE ROCK
O R
P R E L U D E S   T O   D E F I N I T I O N

I

And there I saw the seed upon the mountain
but it was not a seed it was a star
but it was not a star it was a world
but it was not a world it was a god
but it was not a god it was a laughter

blood red within and lightning for its rind
the root came out like gold and it was anger
the root came out like fire and it was fury
the root came out like horn and it was purpose
but it was not a root it was a hand

destructive strong and eager full of blood
and broke the rocks and set them on eath other
and broke the waters into shafts of light
and set them end to end and made them seas
and out of laughter wrung a grief of water

and thus beneath the web of mind I saw
under the west and east of web I saw
under the bloodshot spawn of stars I saw
under the water and the inarticulate laughter
the coiling down the coiling in the coiling

mean and intense and furious and secret
profound and evil and despatched in darkness

shot homeward foully in a filth of effort
clotted and quick and thick and without aim
spasm of concentration of the sea

and there I saw the seed upon the shore
but it was not a seed it was a man
but it was not a man it was a god
magnificent and humble in the morning
with angels poised upon his either hand.

II

We need a theme? then let that be our theme:
that we, poor grovellers between faith and doubt,
the sun and north star lost, and compass out,
the heart's weak engine all but stopped, the time
timeless in this chaos of our wills —
that we must ask a theme, something to think,
something to say, between dawn and dark,
something to hold to, something to love —

Medusa of the northern sky, shine upon us,
and if we fear to think, then turn that fear to stone,
that we may learn unconsciousness alone;
but freeze not the uplifted prayer of hands
that hope for the unknown.

Give us this day our daily death, that we
may learn to live;
teach us that we trespass; that we may learn,
in wisdom, not in kindness, to forgive;
and in the granite of our own bones seal us daily.

O neighbors, in this world of dooms and omens,
participators in the crime of god,
seekers of self amid the ruins of space:
jurors and guilty men, who, face to face,
discover you but judge yourselves to death,

and for such guilt as god himself prepared, —
dreamed in the atom, and so brought to birth
between one zero and another, —

            turn again
to the cold violet that braves the snow,
the murder in the tiger's eye, the pure
indifference in the star. Why, we are come
at last to that bright verge where god himself
dares for the first time, with unfaltering foot.
And can we falter, who ourselves are god?

III

Envy is holy. Let us envy those
bright angels whose bright wings are stronger far
than the bare arms we lift toward the star.
And hate them too; until our hate has grown
to wings more powerful than angels' wings;
when with a vaulting step, from the bare mountain,
we'll breathe the empyrean; and so wheel
gladly to earth again.

            Then we shall see
and love that humbleness which was ourselves;
it will be home to us; until such time
as our strong wings, in their own majesty,
themselves will lift us to another world;
from which is no return.

            But in that world,
there too burn higher angels, whose wide wings
outspan us, shadow us hugely, and outsoar us;
rainbows of such magnificent height
as hide the stars; and under these we'll cower
envious and hateful; and we will envy,
till once again, with contumacious wings,

ourselves will mount to a new terror, wheel
slowly once more, but gratefully, and gladly,
to home in limbo.

And thus North forever.

IV

Woman, woman, let us say these things to each other
as slowly as if we were stones in a field
with centuries of rain in which to say them —
let us say in the morning
     'we do not hear each other'
and in the evening
     'we do not hear each other'
and let us be bewildered by the yes and the no,
the plus and minus, the where and there,
the hour in the thistledown, the acre in the seed —

and walk distracted in the world of men,
bow to all voices,
see ourselves in the mirrors of all minds,
smile at all faces,
and in the beneficent evening, once more, always,
sleep in all peacefulness.

V

Out of your sickness let your sickness speak —
the bile must have his way — the blood his froth —
poison will come to the tongue. Is hell your kingdom?
you know its privies and its purlieus? keep
sad record of its filth? Why this is health:
there is no other, save what angels know.

Ravel the pattern backward, to no pattern:
reduce the granite downward, to no stone:

unhinge the rainbow to his sun and rain:
dissolve the blood to water and to salt:
is this dishevelment we cannot bear?
The angel is the one who knows his wings!

You came from darkness, and you now remember
darkness, terror, windows to a world,
horror of light, cold hands in violence thrust,
tyrants diastole and systole.
O cling to warmth, poor child, and press your mouth
against the warm all-poisoning side of the world.

She's there, she's there, — whispering at all hours —
defending and deluding and defending —
she's in your heart, she's in your traitor blood,
arches your eyebrow and contracts your eye.
Alas, what help for you, poor orphan fool,
who creep from rib to rib, and lose your way?

Let poison spit its blister from your tongue:
let horror break the left side of your heart,
the brightest syllable be drowned in blood — :
thus to the knowledge of your wings you come,
O angel, man! and thus to wisdom bring
terror from terror, and the Thing from thing.

VI

This too to know, the moment of disruption —
the cloud broken, the rain falling, the mind
emptied in foulness and disaster, the hand
trembling, and closing forlornly on the dark —
while the clock ticks, and the heart beats,
and all goes on, all goes on, as always —
this too to know, O wingèd one, you who sit
under the praying-tree —

and I am dead,
I that was laughing am alone and dead
the hands stiff in a gesture of reaching
the eyes sightless in the act of seeing
the heart filled with cold blood in the act of beating
the brain chilled at the instant of delight —

and you gone, grassblade, my sister —
and you gone, pain, my brother, you who measured
milestone and tombstone, sleep and dream —

this too to know, death before death, sleep before sleep,
the edge before the sword, poison poured
before the cup is filled — O wingèd one,
you who ascend, you who descend, who know
rankness and rightness and the equal terror
and worldlong fly in fear from each to other —
comfort me, bring the pause which we call peace.

This too to know, the despair with heavy wings
the blind angel, the one that is oneself
the face of panic, the mouth relaxed from desire
whirlwind of speed that centers on itself —

and in this room from wall to wall to walk,
to split the hour in minutes,
separate the leaves, crush the seeds,
and in one's hands break the treasonable heart —

this, too, angelic knowledge, — this, too, angelic!

VII

How seldom speaks the one who unwitting rouses
passion's blood, the heart that sleeps daylong,
nightlong too — how seldom speaks the one
bitter too, bitter as ourselves, bitterer even,

the one who has tasted bitterness, keeps
that hard taste on his tongue —

Where did he walk that he got this taste,
who was it, what woman, whom he loved,
who was it that died beforetime,
what rain or wind was it that came untimely?

Let him come in and warm himself at this hearth
and spread his wares of bitterness upon this hearth
I will welcome his bitterness and not give him my own
save by knowing and admitting the taste of bitterness.

VIII

Ah poor fellow, he has been hurt, he remembers
the scene that hurt him, remembers the sound
of her that was hurt, the caught animal, the eye
shut for fear of darkness, not of light, —
writhing within he is, ah poor fellow, he knows.

In the one word he spoke I knew he knew,
that salty syllable, the bitter accent's pause —
in that one word I sounded the human blood:
came to my own b!ack heart again, and knew.

Where shall he go for healing, — to what bright flood?
Is there a cloud we can clap against this wound?
Is there a world we can press against this word?
O human walls tell us what we can do:
and bring us, out of human history,
wisdom of walls, wisdom of windows, wisdom of roofs, —
the something solid and peaceful in a stone,
such as can mend or break.

                    He was standing here —
he that was hurt, he that remembered;

stood here, thought of the thing that hurt him,
the word, the world, the wound —
and I thought with him, remembered with him, knowing
nothing of his own word or world or wound,
only my own wound that I could share,
my own world that I could give.

O God, is it less than this or more,
that we must give — ?

O word is it more than this or less,
that we can say — ?

                    Rashly we give them both, —
the wound, the word; and stand ashamed of shame.

IX

Thus boasting thus grandiloquent he stood
thus eloquent thus orotund he spoke
thus posing like an acrobat he paused
thus like an actor loosed his syllable
the bright the brief the brave, the seeming certain,
and smirked

          upon that stage of his own making
there in the dirty wings on dirty sawdust
against the trumpets of a vivid world.

X

True inwardness — ah! there is such a phrase — ?
the truth is inward, and not outward — the oak tree
false in the bark, false in leaf or mast,
true only in the root? and you, poor biped,
who rise in the morning to walk and talk —

are the shoes that await you by the chair
less true than the dreams from which you wake, the hat
that hangs in the hall less true than memory
which remembers it, reaches a hand to it, —
the door less true than the hand that shuts it?

Move outward, and you only move, poor biped,
an atom's atom from here to here, never
from here to there — again your 'self' you meet,
it is yourself that waits outside the door,
salutes you on the waking side of dream —

hands you your coat, your collar, the new necktie,
directs your appetite, chooses an egg,
says, as you read the morning paper, act
or do not act, reflect, do not reflect,
love viciously, love wisely, love not at all —

this is 'you,' this headline in the news,
the news is 'you,' is old already, undiscovered
is 'you,' too, long discovered. Greet your face —
dispersed in some such terms, phrased, rephrased;
speak to that farthest star, which is yourself!

Are these less 'you' than the decayed molar?
the lost appendix? the leaky heart? the mind
too much delayed by daily bread of sex?
Learn the true outwardness of inner truth!
time will at last bring both at once to end.

For at one stroke — no matter whence it come —
lightning or ice or blood — inward and outward
will singularly cease, and be the same.
Then history will give to both a name;
and so at last those things so bravely done
will be at peace with what was merely known.

XI

Mysticism, but let us have no words,
angels, but let us have no fantasies,
churches, but let us have no creeds,
no dead gods hung on crosses in a shop,
nor beads nor prayers nor faith nor sin nor penance:
and yet, let us believe, let us believe.

Let it be the flower
seen by the child for the first time, plucked without thought
broken for love and as soon forgotten:

and the angels, let them be our friends,
used for our needs with selfish simplicity,
broken for love and as soon forgotten;

and let the churches be our houses
defiled daily, loud with discord, —
where the dead gods that were our selves may hang,
our outgrown gods on every wall;
Christ on the mantelpiece, with downcast eyes;
Buddha above the stove;
the Holy Ghost by the hatrack, and God himself
staring like Narcissus from the mirror,
clad in a raincoat, and with hat and gloves.

Mysticism, but let it be a flower,
let it be the hand that reaches for the flower,
let it be the flower that imagined the first hand,
let it be the space that removed itself to give place
for the hand that reaches, the flower to be reached —

let it be self displacing self
as quietly as a child lifts a pebble,
as softly as a flower decides to fall, —
self replacing self
as seed follows flower to earth.

XII

One cricket said to another —
come, let us be ridiculous, and say love!
love love love love love
let us be absurd, woman, and say hate!
hate hate hate hate hate
and then let us be angelic and say nothing.

And the other cricket said to the first —
fool! fool! speak! speak! speak!
speak if you must, but speaking speaking speaking
what does it get us, what does it get us, what?
act act act act give
giving is love, giving is love, give!

One cricket said to another —
what is love what is love what is love
act — speak — act — speak — act — speak —
give — take — give — take — give — take —
more slowly as the autumn comes, but giving
and taking still, — you taking, and I giving!

And the other cricket said to the first —
yes! yes! yes! you give your word!
words words but what at the end are words
speech speech what is the use of speech
give me love give me love
love!

One cricket said to another —
in the beginning — I forget — in the beginning —
fool fool fool fool fool
too late to remember and too late to teach —
in the beginning was the word, the speech,
and in the end the word, the word, the word. . .

But while they quarrelled, these two foolish crickets,
and bandied act with word, denying each,
weighing their actions out in terms of speech,
the frost came whitely down and furred them both,
the speech grew slower, and the action nil,
and, at the end, even the word was still;
and god began again.

XIII

As if god were a gypsy in a tent,
the smeared mask in the smoky light,
smiling with concealed intent —
pointing to the bag of fortunes from which you choose —
his hand like a claw, a tiger's claw,
the claw with stripes —

                (as if one thus, in the twilight,
at the hour of the bat, the hour of the moth,
when night-eyes open and day-eyes close,
saw, in the flitting betwixt light and light,
the half-knowledge which is more than knowledge, —)

saying choose now — the time is come — put in your hand —
take out the card that tells your future —
five words or six in vast calligraphy
spaced paused and pointed as they should be, printed
in words of Alpha, in words of Omega
or in such words as are not words at all —
thunder, harsh lightning, the fierce asterisk
that stars the word for footnote to dead worlds —
choose now, be doomed, take out the phrase
that calls you king, that calls you fool,
brings the fat klondyke to too greedy hands —

                        as if you saw
the crass inevitable and stupid finger

thrust then among the alien cards, alien phrases,
your finger, injured by life, already willing
to turn one way, rather than another —

                    and saw it choose
one phrase, one idiot round of idiot words
(how can you say your scorn for this deception)
one phrase, one sullen phrase, to be the symbol
of all you are — to be the ambassador
of all you are to all that is not you —

if life were this, if soul were only this,
as well it might be, should be, must be, is —
god the proud gypsy in his tent at twilight
yourself the fool that darkling takes a card — :
your life thus blindfold dedicate to folly,
murder become a hand, hand become murder
by patient evolution —

              Think of this,
and laugh, at moth's hour, bat's hour, or at wolf's hour, —
that moth be moth, bat be bat, wolf be wolf, —
that gypsy be a god;
shuffler of cards, and cozener of fools.

XIV

       'In secret place where once I stood
       Close by the banks of lacrym flood' —
                     — Anne Bradstreet

When madness comes with yellow eye
and thrusts with thumbs the skull awry
so that its crooked scenes destroy
the one hope left from childhood's joy:
then *har har har har har* cry
and give the fig to madman's day.

When nightmare shrieks at midnight stroke
and sours the word that sunrise struck —
the starlight on the madman's eye
quick as a spider on a fly —
then harsh-come let your merriment be,
and thumb the fig at madman's day.

Let snow on leaf lie hot as blood
and angel scream by lacrym flood
and out of sickness the new day
come glibly as the curd from whey —
then *ho hum* yawn and let time pass
and give the fig to madman's ass.

The angel laughs as angel should
if he be found by lacrym flood:
the starlight on the madman's eye
twists like a spider on a fly:
and if it speaks the sunrise word
sours all day to midnight's curd.

Be then of madness all compact —
singular soul whose word is act —
singular act whose word is sole
embassy of angelic whole — !
— be but a beam that wounds a sound
on unforeknowing indifferent ground.

What's gone is here, what's here is going —
time but a feather upon the flowing —
and madness come, with golden eye,
to good end thrusts the skull awry — :
so *fee fi fo fum* merrily cry
and give the fig to madman's day.

XV

At the first stepping-stone, the past of water —
the thought with blunt nose swimming against the stream —
the tail and fins rigid, the water cold,
the scales cold, the past cold and perfect —

at the second stepping-stone, the present of water,
fluid memory surrounding the cold wish —
weeds borne downward on the changing stream
thoughts in a dream on the scarred stones —

at the third stepping-stone, the stillborn step —
suspended poise of the becoming soul —
I was there, I am here, I will be there and gone,
not yet gone, but waiting to be gone —

at the third stepping-stone, the sense of water,
the perfect stream, breakless unchanging all — :
let us wait here, in the timelessness of un-willing,
and watch the past and present perpend the future . . .

At the fourth stepping-stone, it is another, —
that other, not ourself, who stands and remembers
the departed one, who stayed at the third stone,
who is now present with us like a ghost —

ghost of water, ghost of stone, ghost of weed,
that other, alas, who is but is not, was
and is, is dead but will be, will be borne
downstream forever past the later comers —

those who reach the fifth stone, or the sixth,
who wait there poised, remembering, the dead men
whose deaths will take us on from stone to stone
further across the perfect stream of water —

but never across, never to reach the last,
the final remembrance, the all-knowing shore —
where death looks backward from the shading tree,
and perfect stillness stares at perfect stream.

XVI

Went home so, laughing, the foolish one, who knew
(or thought he knew, and thinking is to know)
the bitter, brief, and bright, the morning's madness,
the evening's folly. So took home with him
a card, a glove, a letter, and the word
spoken and laughed at and denied, the word
born in the heart, but stillborn: the denial
of grassblade's heart.

                    Has the grassblade a heart?
morning a pulse? the human hand a meaning?
was there a purpose in my name this morning?
This is a day of dreadful commonplace;
of news and newspapers and date and action;
I brushed my teeth, and drank my coffee, saw
sunlight among the dishes, spoke the word
that breakfast dictates; saw the immortal worm
under the table and beneath the world,
working his comic passage toward death.

How there, old fellow, and have you come again,
you that I saw beneath my fingernail,
who ate my sweetheart's eyelid and her eye —
who ruin the daylight and delight in dark,
follow me to my birth and to my death,
sit in my breath and chuckle in my heart —

must you be always where delight is brightest
let fall your seed beneath the hawthorn blossom,
scream behind rainbows? I have seen your wings.

Know you. You are that fellow who was born
under my name, but with a different meaning:

you are that fellow whose precocious death
leads me to graveyards in the glare of noon,
and murmurs murder in the bridal bed.
Lie down: we are absolved: we go from here
to wider emptiness, and such dispersals
of death, and cruelty, and the death of pain,
as no life knew before, or will know after.

XVII

Sad softness of control, unceasing censor,
multiple ghost, white Cerberus of the soul
whose melancholy baying guards the moon
above the sleeping eye —

               must we be angry
as the tree is angry, angry with the wind,
the leaves angry, borne down or up
striving in vain for rest

                   are the roots angry
thrusting in agony against the stone
urging their grief against the dark, waiting,
and yet not waiting, for inconceivable rest

must we be angry with the wind and stone
exert the blood against the permanent horror
wind inward, downward, upward, without pause,
resist resistance, and all for nothing?

Sad softness of control, unceasing censor
what is your purpose in perpetual midnight
you who say wait, you who say pause,
whose word, whose only word is always no-yes,

the ambiguity, the evasion, the dishonesty
which is the sum of all our honesties

the sifting one, ambivalent one, the honesty
which is the sum of all dishonesties —
total of stars which is a thought of darkness
total of darkness which is a thought of stars —

must we be angry, that we at last be still
violently move that we at last find peace
be restless that we know the price of pause?
where is the sleep we came from, where the sleep —
midnight, without irritant of stars —
knowledge without memory?

                              Let us be angry
wake and be angry with the wind and stone
and know the loneliness of being alone.

XVIII

And God said to Adam —

Breath will be breath, the in the out,
        the cold the warm,
word will be word, the agony,
        the time, the stone;
I will stand here nor seldom move,
        see nothing new,
tree without root, the unfixed thought
        wandering with the unmoving you.

Beach will be beach while sea returns
        meaning be nothing
nothing will mean what the world means, no more,
        the time, the stone —
I will wait here nor ever stir
        think nothing strange

while the heart's clock works round the dial
    of human and predicted range.

Where you have been, what seen, will mean
    but dark but bright
time but a dream, the seem but gleam,
    no time, no stone
no bloodfilled heart that swarms with shapes
    no hands that clutch
only the lonely self that thinks
    of inaccessible to touch.

Stand there and wait, stand there and think,
    unbroken will,
handful of light, delirium's brain,
    the strong the brave —
seed left by light whose fading seed
    is darker light
O patient watcher whose faithful watch
    makes of the night more dreadful night.

XIX

This image or another, this quick choosing,
raindrop choosing a path through grains of sand
the blood-drop choosing its way, that the dead world
may wake and think or sleep and dream

This gesture or another, this quick action
the bough broken by the wind and flung down
the hand striking or touching, that the dead world
may know itself and forget itself

This memory or another, this brief picture
sunbeam on the shrivelled and frosted leaf
a world of selves trying to remember the self
before the idea of self is lost —

Walk with me world, upon my right hand walk,
speak to me Babel, that I may strive to assemble
of all these syllables a single word
before the purpose of speech is gone.

XX

And you who love, you who attach yourselves
to another mouth, who in the depth of night
speak without speech act without conscious action
in all that lamentable struggle to be another
to make that other yourself, to find that other,
to make two one

        who would be tree and earth
cloud and ocean, movement and stillness,
object and shadow

        what can we learn from you
pathetic ones, poor victims of the will,
wingless angels who beat with violent arms,
what can we learn from your tragic effort

is there a secret here, an unambiguous
message, a leaf blown from another star,
that thus all stand and watch you, thus all envy,
all emulate? must we be violent too?

O patience, let us be patient and discern
in this lost leaf all that can be discerned;
and let us learn, from this sad violence learn,
all that in midst of violence can be learned.

XXI

Deep violet, deep snow-cloud, deep despair,
deep root, deep pain, deep morning — must we say
deepness in all things, find our lives in deepness?

we too are deep? the breakfast salutation,
that too is deep? Alas, poor Arabel,
poor woman, poor deluded human, you
who finick with a fork and eat an egg,
are you as deep as thought of you is deep?

Timeless. The morning is not deep as thought.
Spaceless. The noon is not as deep as dream.
Formless. The night is not as deep as death.
And I defer the notion of the infinite,
the thought of you, the thought of morning,
idea of evening, idea of noon.

XXII

If man, that angel of bright consciousness,
that wingless mind and brief epitome
of god's forgetfulness, will be going forth
into the treacherous envelope of sunlight —
why, the poor fool, does he expect, does he expect
to return at evening? or to return the same?
Those who have put on, in the morning,
that cloak of light, that sheath of air,
wrapped themselves suddenly, on the exit,
in the wild wave of daybreak, which has come
from cruel Alpha, — what has become of them?
They will return as the sons of darkness.

If woman, that demon of unconsciousness,
that wingèd body of delightful chaos,
that quick embodied treason and deceit,
will go forth sinuously from the opening door
and take to herself the garment of daylight —
who will vouch for her, go her surety,
who will her bondsman be, or swear by the cloud
that she, who thus went forth, will thus come back?
If she took darkness with her, will she return

with luminous heart, and a soft light within?
For that which goes forth comes back changed or dead.

If the child, that frail mirror of the sky,
that little room of foolish laughter and grief,
transient toucher and taster of the surface,
assembler and scatterer of light, — if he go forth
into the simple street to count its stones,
its walls, its houses, its weeds and grassblades,
so, in the numbered, to sum the infinite —
infant compendium of the terrible — :
will the changed man, and the changed woman,
await him, with full knowledge, in the evening —
salute him gravely, with a kiss or handshake,
oblique embrace of the young wingless shoulders —
will they, unknowing, unknown, know this Unknown?

All three at evening, when they return once more
from the black ocean of dark Omega,
by those wild waves washed up with stars and hours,
brought home at last from nowhere to nothing —
all three will pause in the simple light,
and speak to each other, slowly, with such queer speech
as dead men use among the asphodels;
nor know each other; nor understand each other;
but tread apart on the wind, like dancers
borne by unearthly music to unearthly peace.

The house of evening, the house of clouds, vast hall
of which the walls are walls of everywhere,
enfolds them, like a wind which blows out lights.
And they are there, lying apart, lying alone,
those three who went forth suddenly in the morning
and now return, estranged and changed;
each is alone, with his extinguished lamp;
each one would weep, if he had time to weep;
but, before tears can fall, they are asleep.

XXIII

What the moon says is moon, and all compact;
what the act says is act, and only act;
what the clock says, with algebra's cold face,
is times and time, spaces and space.

Ah but the phrase, the phrase that sprouts to phrase,
and dulls or brightens as the moon its phase,
is the bright always bright, dull always dull,
ugly or beautiful,

must the phrase too have flesh or plume or scale,
be hard or soft, sensual or epicene,
and must we choose voluptuously between
female and male,

even here, even here, in the wide world of dream,
dismiss the abstract and pursue the gleam,
woo the soft syllable and scorn the hard,
the young desire, the old discard,

touch with a lover's hand that word or this,
take her to bed with us to clip and kiss,
while her poor sister pleads alas in vain
being chaste and plain?

Defrauded! Let these nuns be nuns no more,
but all alike be angel, or else whore;
and let us know each single syllable
is ringed with heaven and hell;

sums all, means all, says all, states the vast end
and vast beginning, where the pure forms descend
from dark to dark with one quick curve of gleam,
in time's huge dream;

thus, in the that or this, the such or so,
the silent pinnacle of the world to know
where glory and horror are only thought, the word
now and forever unheard.

XXIV

If one voice, not another, must speak first,
out of the silence, the stillness, the preceding —
speaking clearly, speaking slowly, measuring calmly
the heavy syllables of doubt, or of despair —
speaking passionately, speaking bitterly, hunger or hope
ordering the words, that are like sounds of flame — :
if one speaks first, before that other or the third,
out of the silence bringing the dark message,
the grave and great acceptance of the rock,
the huge world, held in the huge hand of faith:

and if it says, I hold the world like this;
here in the light, amid these crumbling walls;
here in the half-light, the deceptive moment,
here in the darkness like a candle lifted — :
take it, relieve me of it, bear it away;
have it, now and forever, for your own;
this that was mine, this that my voice made mine,
this that my word has shaped for you —

if this voice speaks before us, speaks before
ourselves can speak, challenging thus the dark;
waking the sleeping watcher from his sleep,
altering the dreamer's dream while still he dreams;
so that on waking — ah, what despair he knows!
to learn that while he slept the world was made —
made by that voice, and himself made no less,
and now inalterably curved forever —

yes, if to wake, to cease to dream, be this,
to face a self made ready while we slept,

shaped in the world's shape by the single voice —
if thus we wake too late and find ourselves
already weeping, already upon the road
that climbs past shame and pain to crucifixion —
seeing at once, with eyes, just opened, the world,
vast, bright, and cruciform, on which so soon
ascending we must die —

                          and to look backward,
but know no turning back; to go forward,
even as we turn our faces to the past;
still gazing downward from the hill we climb,
searching the dark for that strange dream we had,
which the voice altered and broke —

                          ah, can it comfort us,
us helpless, us thus shaped by a word,
sleepwalking shadows in the voice-shaped world,
ah, can it comfort us that we ourselves
will bear the word with us, we too, we too
to speak, again, again, again, again, —
ourselves the voice for those not yet awakened, —
altering the dreams of those who dream, and shaping,
while still they sleep, their inescapable pain — ?

XXV

The picture world, that falls apart, and leaves
a snowflake on the hand, a star of ice,
a hillside, a dead leaf

                        the picture world,
the lost and broken child's book, whence we treasure
one picture, torn and soiled, the faded colours
precious because dimmed, clear because faded,
the picture world, which is ourselves, speaking
of yesterday, and yesterday, and yesterday,
the huge world promised in the bud of May,

the leaf, the stone, the rain, the cloud,
the face most loved, the hand most clung to —

must we go back to this and have this always:
remember what was lost or what was torn:
replace the missing with a better dream
built from the broken fabric of our wills —
thus to admit our present is our past,
and in one picture find unaltered heaven —

or, shall we be angelic, close brave wings,
fall through the fathomless, feel the cold void,
and sound the darkness of the newly known? —
To face the terror in this rain that comes
across the drowned world to the drowning window;
be ignorant of rain, this unknown rain;
unknown and wild as the world was to god
when first he opened eyes — ah surely this
were nobler answer than the glib speech of habit,
the well-worn words and ready phrase, that build
comfortable walls against the wilderness?
Seeing, to know the terror of seeing: being,
to know the terror of being: knowing, to know
the dreadfulness of knowledge:

                              Come, let us drown in rain,
cry out and drown in this wild single drop,
sound the pure terror on steadfast wings, and find
in death itself the retrospective joy
held, like a picture-book, in a drowned hand.

XXVI

Has the Jew spent his farthing? the weed
frolicked his seed? the cloud dispersed his rain,
never to know his bellyful again?
is the soul bankrupt? the mind emptied? the mouth
dried up of speech? no words to come? no thought

yet undelivered in all this world of thought?
why there are bricks and stones, and therefor walls;
sand, and therefor mortar; there is space,
still uncircumferenced by demons' wings,
or angels' either; and to sum the world, —

but who will sum the world? what god will add
digit to digit, sandgrain to sandgrain,
amuse himself, on the last wall of knowledge,
laugh there, be boisterous, sum all things up
in one vast thunderclap of synthesis —
speak his own sentence, and be dead?

> Beloved, there is time,
between this morning's instant and that wall,
for such infinitudes of delight and grief,
such patient addings and subtractions, such
new sentences, each wider than the last,
new knowledges, new visions and revisions,
that we ourselves are like that god; each moment
is the last wall from which our laughter rings;
the world summed up; and then a new world found,
vaster and richer; a new synthesis,
under the sandgrain, and above the star.
Come, let us read the book, look up each word,
say dark or bright, be frightened, pick our way
through the fierce multitude of thoughts and things —
from god to chaos, and chaos to god again —
in the unending glossary of the world.
Was that a bell that struck? a moment gone?
a voice that spoke, a bird that flew?
They were the shadows of a speech to come.

XXVII

This mountebank, this saltimbanque, this leaper
of mortal benches and immortal hoops,

this saltatory fool, who would as soon
fling you his quacksalve dogma from the moon
as from the circus tent — the cunning one,
the laughing one, who thrives in half-lights, makes
his laughter ring among white ribs of graves —

he, who of bitterness makes the healing word,
sells crucifixes to the crucified,
or crucifixions to the not yet dead —
claps on his mask, laughs out of terror,
sings like a bird in the thunderbolt itself —

nimble comer and goer, haunter of crypts and cells,
quicksilver heels, who tells his lies for love,
reads you your fortune in the thistledown
and draws such magic out, from fine belief,
as almost makes the dead man rise again —

praise him, fools, follow him, for he goes
by the bright path that only godhead knows;
cross his palm with silver, for he will give
gaily, out of his heart (for that is he)
the one thing the heart needs, the need to live.

XXVIII

And this digester, this digester of food,
this killer and eater and digester of food,
the one with teeth and tongue, insatiable belly,
him of the gut and appetite and murder,
the one with claws, the one with a quick eye,
whose footstep — ah — is soft as treason —
this foul embodied greed, this blind intestine —
this human, you or me —

                                    look sharply at him
and measure him, digesters! hear his speech,

woven deceit, colossal dream, so shaped
of food and search for food — oh believe him
whose hunger shapes itself as gods and rainbows

is he not perfect, walks he not divinely
with a light step among the stars his fathers
with a quick thought among the seeds his sons
is he not graceful, is he not gentle,
this foul receiver and expeller of food,
this channel of corruption,

                     is he not
the harbinger, the angel, the bright prophet
who knows the right from wrong, whose thought is pure,
dissects the angles, numbers pains and pleasures,
dreams like an algebra among waste worlds —
can we not trust him, sees he not the sure,
disposes time and space, condemns the evil-doer —
is his digestion not an ample measure?

Come, rooted ones, come radicals, come trees,
whose powerful tentacles suck earth, and join
the murderous angels; and let us dance together
the dance of joyful cruelty, whence thrives
this world of qualities which filth ordained.

XXIX

How is it, flower, at the bitterest minute
when we have committed murder with the heart
when we have willed it, and hold up our hands
red to ourselves, though white to others
how is it, flower, you who must share with us
this transient glory, this beauty, this delight

how is it, daybreak, you who light the worlds,
careless of one or other, living or dead,

the cold rock lighted, or the living grass,
the eyes opened, or the long snow melted,
how is it daybreak are you conscienceless
are you indifferent to all your murders

must we absolve ourselves, is there no other
who will absolve us bless us give us peace
are we the angels who must heal ourselves
condemn ourselves and then reprieve ourselves
is it ourselves who must give absolution
to hand to claw to root to leaf

why we are lonely then and have no help
we who walk only because we walk
we who think only because we think
feel for no reason and reason of what we feel —
why we are purposeless, who have a purpose
alas, because we are blind have eyes

how is it, courage, at the moment of failure
when we have dared to die but are not dead
when we have feared to live but are still living —
are we but flowers, who have such thoughts, flowers
who make such nightmares out of simple things?
flowers who die because we understand?

XXX

The word coming, with the long cloud of evening
the coffin cloud of stone, the cloud of blood
the action coming, the word spoken, the hand
lifted, fallen again, held out, withdrawn —

the word, loaded with a dead world of meaning,
the speaker only a summary of that world —
himself all meaningless, the word forgotten
as soon as spoken, its meaning lost —

the action, only a summary of force —
the blow struck, the gift given, the kiss
surrendered and received, snow over rock,
rock under snow, and the sun soon risen —

where are we come, if neither word nor action
speak for ourselves? O angel, bear us still
into this realm of freezing nothingness —
teach us still to act and speak —

teach us to know the action from the word —
to act simply, but knowing that we act;
to speak simply, but knowing that we speak;
never to confuse the one with other —

and to know also that the word is action,
the word is murder,
to know also that the act is speech,
the kiss a word:

O angel, guide us still, lend us brave wings
that we may mount wide circles through confusion:
seeing, in today's action, tomorrow's word;
knowing, in tomorrow's word, the seed of death.

XXXI

And time comes in that is a ball of crystal
time comes in that is a sheaf of wheat
time comes in that is a cloud of thunder
time comes in that is a drop of rain

the blood drop centres in the ball of crystal
the blood drop hurries down the sheaf of wheat
the blood drop opens to the voice of thunder
the blood drop drowns beneath the drop of rain

where is the blood drop gone and where the whisper
where is the mouth of blood that sang the song
where is the heart that broke within the crystal
time that came life that went

here in the blind almighty hand is god
rain thunder wheat and crystal mixed with blood
the broken heart the broken mouth that sings
the god who hates himself but dies for love

and time goes out that was a drop of blood
and time goes out that was a song of blood
and time goes out that was a death of rock
to peace at last love's kingdom come.

XXXII

Then the red edge of sunlight spoke alone
graving the stars until their granite grieved
and groves of grandeur grew along those grooves

then the red edge of sunlight spoke alone
and graved the stars and etched upon them voices
voices of leaves and then the voice of hands
the cry of murder answering to that edge

then the red cry of murder spoke alone
and carved the silence into shapes of meaning
out of the blood magnificent cry of meaning
silence and speech silence and speech silence

then the one meaning arose alone arising
huge as the world, daybreak vaster than daybreak,
the song the hate the praise the love the fear
terrible hope that is the hand's despair

then the vast hand of meaning lifted up
itself alone against the fearful nothing

touched and trembled touched again and held
the last the lost the lonesome the idea

and the idea was greater than the hand
that held it, the hand greater than the murder,
murder was greater than the injured granite
the injured granite greater than the sun

but the red edge of sunlight died alone
and grieved the stars and hushed upon them voices
the voice of hands and then the voice of leaves

the red edge of sunlight failed alone
and grieved the stars until their granite groaned, —
and itself lost at last, the lost idea,
greater than everything, now less than nothing.

XXXIII

But let us praise the voice the lonely voice
but let us praise the leaf that is the first
but let us praise the syllable the only
that syllable which is the seed of worlds

why we are walking and our lives are speech
you with a word and I with answering word
here we are walking in a world of omens
the leaves are in our hands and we exchange

what was it that you said what word was that
what sound was that my tongue gave back in answer
what touch was this of rock that brought a meaning
here in this field that is a gift of stars

here in this grass that is a gift of tongues
here in this light that is a gift of suns
here in this nearness that is a gift of space
here in this love that is a gift of face

love let us praise the voice and then deny it
let us adore denial and revile it
cross the field of stars and then forget it
love the face in space the space in face

let us adore together the vile atom
that fetched us here and gives us words to say it
simple simplicities in simple nothing
walking together in the field of death

love let us cross the field and then absolve it
despise our human moment and forgive it
revere our fear of godhead and remove it
rejoice in voice and then rejoice in sleep.

XXXIV

Ah but all meaning, and all delight in meaning,
has gone from me —

            — The evening took it, Monster?

— Took it, and closed her curtains round the moon.
Walked westward on the moon-blanched cheek of earth
and took all meaning with her. She is gone.

— Then set a trap for evening: set it thus:
weave hopes as grassblades and beliefs as wattles:
and lay them crosswise on the dew: and wait
in the green penance of a broken heart.
When she comes back, then have your meaning back.
It will be what it was.

            — Ah yes, I know.
It will make wings of hands, and hands of wings!
the syllable will fall to blood and stone:
and I shall walk, as once I walked, alone.

— Why not? the footstep should be footstep only:
echo against the infinite: and come
in dew, or frost, or snow, to its own nothing.
Thus, you will sleep at home.

XXXV

Go out in fog go out in snow go out in hoarfrost
break down the autumnal web that bars your path
gather your leaves and berries seeds and torments
your hours and minutes and all you save therefrom
assemble in all weathers the world's wonder
that tapestry of consciousness and stars
which grows from cabbage roots and sines and cosines
sing as you walk sing as you gather nonsense
sing as you make your meaning out of nonsense

and bring them home to us and spread them out,
your treasures, and assure us of the pattern
in which they fall — it must be thus and thus
only and always in such shape as this
this is the curve that sought them this wild curve
bending the waves of water or of light
shaping the alpha to the shape of the world
the shape of the word

                    and thence your meaning
pitiful child pitiful crystal
you with your four o'clocks and half-past threes
your fingernails, your wound, your simple disbeliefs,
your glass of water and your wine and mirrors,
english for poetry, french for prose,
your books, your box of letters —

                    love and believe them
since so you must, poor victim of the curve,
collect your odds and ends and build your meaning

and then conceive that vaster form which moves
along the beaches of a vaster ocean,
the naked shape of an unwilling will:
who finds such odds and ends as you and me,
and puzzles out the meaning of our loves,
and gives his world the meaning that we mean,
and so forgets us.

XXXVI

But I have speech saved up against that demon
and I will fend her off and keep her from me
say to her from the deathbed's edge — back monster —
back to your shadow, you who are shadow only
— yes yes and should this adjuration fail me
why from the hell of memory I'll summon
the lightning word, the word of fire, and speak
once and once only —

                    then will that foulness falter,
grovel, fall down, and on low haunches crawl,
slink, become one with the shadow beside the wall
back to her nether world of nether nature —
ah that low shape who has usurped our wings
to be an angel too —

                    but it is not like this.
No, for the lightning word,
that word of wings which silence gave a mouth,
unspoken which was spoken, unbreakable broken,
darkness made wild with light —

                    O pitiful self,
who of these shapes and shames make all thy meaning
and draw thy being from disease of chaos
who of disasters makest thy quick joy
and now so fearest the womb of night that bore thee:

who when called back would exorcise thy mother,
would hate her, fear her, spit contempt upon her,
disown the shadow that gave thee shape —

speak from the bed's edge, fool, your lightning word:
she will expect it as the earth expects it:
she will expect you as the earth expects you:
your word was only self, and this she knew;
it is the lightning's speech; but darkness, too,
has words; and these await you, when you come
into the rock that is your home.

XXXVII

Where we were walking in the day's light, seeing
the flight of bones to the stars, the voyage of dead men,
those who go forth like dead leaves on the air
in the long journey, those who are swept
on the last current, the cold and shoreless ones,
who do not speak, do not answer, have no names,
nor are assembled again by any thought, but voyage
in the wide circle, the great circle

where we were talking, in the day's light, watching
even as I took your hand, even as I kissed you,
ah the unspeakable voyage of the dead men
those who go up from the grass without laughter
who take leave of the wheat and water without speech
who pass us without memory and without murmur
as they begin the endless voyage

                        where we stood
in the little round of colour, perilously poised
in the bright instant between two instant deaths,
whispering yes, whispering no, greeting and permitting,
touching and recalling, and with our eyes
looking into the past to see if there the future

might grow like a leaf, might grow like a bough with flowers,
might grow like a tree with beneficent shade

but what delight that was, O wave who broke
out of the long dark nothing against my breast,
you who lifted me violently so that we rose together,
what delight that was, in that clear instant,
even as we shone thus, the first, the last,
to see the flight of bones, the everlasting,
the noiseless unhurrying flight
of the cold and shoreless ones, the ones who no more
answer to any names, whose voyage in space
does not remember the earth or stars
nor is recalled by any spider, or any flower,
the joyless and deathless dancers —

                                        speak once, speak twice,
before we join them, lady, and speak no more.

XXXVIII

Then it was that the child first spoke to me
the innocent the clear in the clear morning
the young voice finding the first sounds of joy
first sounds of grief of terror of despair
the weak hand holding mine, that was no stronger,
as if for guidance, who was my guide, though younger

so that we walked together in the cool garden
he that was innocent but knew it not
who in the thrush's song heard terror and delight
and a wide fear in the wide wave of light
joy and sorrow in the coolness of the shade
strength in my hand my hand that was afraid

myself the guilty one alas who tried to learn
new innocence by giving back my shame

into those eyes of laughter which became
guilty and frightened as I learned new joy
alas alas that thus the garden way
leads the old footstep with the young astray

he into a cloud walking I into a sun
forgive me child that thus we become one
forgive the things that teach us thus to cherish
the dread exchange by which we love and perish
forgive us trees forgive us garden path
that grief buys happiness and love buys wrath

under the thrush's voice walking back slowly
the holy innocence became unholy
the younger hand grew older and stronger
the world-stained hand grew fairer and younger
together sharing the adulterous union
which is the dreadful secret of communion

now let the murderer hide shameful eyes
behind young wings new-come from paradise
and let this angel take and hold the knife
bewildered by the murder which is life
thus in the middle noon to come together
stained hand and immaculate feather.

XXXIX

On that wild verge in the late light he stood,
the last one, who was alone, the naked one,
wingless unhappy one who had climbed there,
bruised foot and bruised hand,
first beholder of the indecipherable land,

the nameless land, the selfless land,
stood and beheld it from the granite cliff
the far beneath, the far beyond, the far above,

water and wind, the cry of the alone
his own the valley, his own the unthinking stone

and said — as I with labor have shaped this,
out of a cloud this world of rock and water,
as I have wrought with thought, or unthinking wrought,
so that a dream is brought
in agony and joy to such a realm as this

let now some god take also me and mould me
some vast and dreadful or divine dream hold me
and shape me suddenly beyond my purpose
beyond my power
to a new wilderness of hour

that I may be to him as this to me,
out of a cloud made shore and sea,
instant agony and then the splendid shape
in which is his escape,
myself at last only a well-made dream to be —

and as he spoke, his own divine dream took
sudden kingdom of the wide world, and broke
the orders into rainbows, the numbers down,
all things to nothing; and he himself became
a cloud, in which the lightning dreamed a name.

XL

And when he saw the cloud, the little cloud,
moon-coloured, melting, on a summer's day —

False beginnings will lead you to false endings;
here's nothing; the cloud is gone; moon-coloured
or nacreous, pearl-shaped or shape of self,
gone now since you are gone. The cloud still there,
bearing its little ghost of rain, shifting

from north to east, silvered under the star,
distraught in sunlight, swollen, or while you sleep
divulged. Have you forgotten? alas, no.
Goes with you: on your right hand walks the heavens:
swims like a fish above your memory's eyebrow,
there, there, and again there, beyond, above,
touched with the mind's hand once, and now so lost.
O have him back. O take him with you, infant,
whose edge was on the moon, take again birds
to mark their flight diagonal across him,
let tongue or eye accept the raindrop. Space,
with all her wonders, why, can you keep them here
in this small smoky hut of time?

                      Desultory,
the changing of the wind, but to have back
even that simple evening, that simple flight,
the cloud advancing on the wall of night,
the rain advancing on the wall of wind,
the mind advancing on the world of sight —
what will you do, what wild precautions take,
with what wild love, as rock of snow, remember,
marry what leaf with ice, what death with daybreak,
or how unhinge your heart — ?

                      desultory
the image in the mind, desultory
the moon behind the cloud's edge, the rain
streaked in the west against the whorl of light
and every tree and leaf so clear, so near —

                      desultory
even the simple faith that keeps you there:
the heart that breaks before the passage of space;
memory that breaks before the gift of time.
Let the cloud go, let the world go, let the poor heart
pause when it will, lie down and sleep.

XLI

In the clear shaft of light the child so standing
alone, but his aloneness yet unknown,
all things accepting, all things at random heeding,
nearest pebble and farthest star commanding,
sorrow and joy his own
to do his bidding

In the clear shaft of light, whether the tree
were moved by the wind or still,
alone on the flowered hill
there with the birdsong and the time song
day song and wind song
all things himself to be

So that the leaves himself became
and the green hill made answer to his name
and all things knew him who himself knew all —
so that, the sun obscured by clouds, the light
absent, he too was absent with delight,
thus went, thus came

He with the pebble in his lifted hand
whose footsteps might be traced
by flower or grass displaced —
now gone, now here, now far, now near,
now fallen in shadow beyond the rim of death
again brought homeward by lightly taken breath —

O simple one, happy one, vague one, nimble one,
has time come over your hill
has time with long bells told you, told
and do you stand there still,
among dead flowers, the sunlight gone,
your hill grown old?

In the clear shaft of light the man so standing
alone, but his aloneness known,
all things accepting, all things gladly heeding,
the heart beating, the hand bleeding,
the lost world now again his own
and marvellous with understanding.

XLII

Who would carve words must carve himself
first carve himself —

              O carpenter,
you whose hand held nails
who knew the plane tree and the oak tree
                    with heavy adze
hardening the muscle that became the word

and you, the sculptor, who made of hemlock wood
the little doll, or cut blind eyes in stone,
                habitual stroke
hammering the memory to rock precision,
god and logos, well-tempered question in the chisel,
who knew the kindness of fatigue —

              rising or stooping
these angels of mankind these devils of wit
sifters of habit and deceivers only
as the trained muscle deceives the mind, or feeds with custom:
these who were often tired
strengthening backs for weight of tree or stone,
or what might else of burden come from man —

who would carve words must carve himself,
first carve himself; and then alas
finds, too late, that Word is only Hand.

XLIII

Ask the wind in, the night too, and the stars,
we'll have a dance with clouds, our friends the clouds, —
as known as you, and as much wedded. What did we wed
but a handful of stars far off, a flight of fog,
sound of wind that turns with the falling world?
Go out woman and ask them in. Ask them in.

And so, with a simple gesture of abnegation,
the wind went out and asked the woman in;
the cloud went out and asked the woman in;
the star went out and asked the woman in;
night went out like a priest. And the man, waiting,
turned inward on himself, in his own room,

and heard his anger stride away in darkness;
spoke once, one word, Woman! to hear the silence;
then stood, and closed his eyes, and thought of time;
time, and its waves of bells that beat the mind;
time, that is born of mind, destroying mind;
measure of the forgotten, measure of the remembered;

so learned the quick simplicity of knowing;
touched his hand to his forehead, and so found
the history of the world, and of all thought —
there, in the warmth of bloodfilled hand on brow,
all the dishonest history of the world:
cruelty become cunning, cunning becoming idea —

and the defeated self, self torn from death — !
alas alas! for now, as thus he walked, —
measuring steps in the careful room, —
he saw, in self, the history of love;
in the defeated self, the birth of love;
and so lay down, and slept.

XLIV

Where without speech the angel walked I went
and strove as silently as he to move
seeking in his deep kindness my content
and in his grace my love

walked without word and held my arms as wings
from stone to stone as gently stepped as he
observed humility with humble things
as I himself might be:

till he it was at last who stood and spoke —
Be man, if man you be! Or be ashamed.
And turned and strode away. And on that stroke,
(as if now I were named)

in my own heart I looked, and saw the plan
for murder unadmitted. Then I knew
how mean the angel is who apes the man,
or man to man untrue

if he enact the angel. In that hour,
I did the murder I had planned; and then
sought out that fellow, my own dream of power,
and mimicked him again.

XLV

Still the same function, still the same habit come,
the endless algebra that marks the mind.
A leads to b and b to c; we wait
in vain for change. No sudden Clytemnestra
walks from the scene and with her takes the world —

or so the sentry said. And watched the moon
pull half the desert downward as she went,

involved in silvered trees and dunes and towers
shadows of spears and whatnot. Moons and moons —
all gone in one, and all the tides gone too,
salt blood, salt water. What's left but dark. What's left
but night, night which is function of the day;
which is in turn a function of the night!
Or so the sentry said.

              And saw his feet,
sandalled, and semi-prehensile, on the sand,
gripping the moonchilled sand and then releasing,
forward and back along the wall's foot, turning
under the fig-tree. Lately it had a shadow,
but now had none. And 'a-prime' leads to 'b-prime,'
build how you will. Nuisance, that there should be
no wildness left in nature — no chance of dicethrow
to change the world, or changed then change it back —
the two plus two makes eight — !

                 Clytemnestra
walked on the terrace when the moon had sunk,
and licked her little finger. Tasted blood.
Addressed herself: Woman, you've changed the world,
you should have been a man. And henceforth men —
use them, use them! Smiled, and walked in the dark,
and heard, below the wall, the sentry's cough.

XLVI

What without speech we knew and could not say
what without thought we did and could not change
violence of the hand which the mind thought strange
let us take these things into another world,
             another dream

what without love we touched pronouncing good
what without touch we loved and gave no sign

violence of spirit which only spirit knew divine
let us take these things into another world,
           another sleep

walk with me heliotrope fly with me sparrow
come beating of my heart and learn how life is narrow
how little, and ill, will be remembered by tomorrow
let us give our lives into another world
           another hand

where like old rocks we shall be heaped forgetful;
or waste away like stars in fiery stillness;
no clock with mortal cry to speak our illness;
let us take our deaths into another time
           another god

come girl, come golden-breasted girl, and walk
on the so silent and sun-sandalled path
between the foremath and the aftermath
let us hurl our joy into another chaos, another wrath
           and make it love

what without speech we know we then shall say
and all our violence will there be gay
what without thought we do will be but play
and our unspoken love as bright as day
           and we shall live.

XLVII

Not with the noting of a private hate,
as if one put a mark down in a book;
nor with the chronicling of a private love,
as if one cut a vein and let it bleed;
nor the observing of peculiar light,
ringed round with what refractions peace can bring —
give it up, phrase-maker! your note is nothing:
the sum is everything.

Who walks attended by delight will feel it,
whom sudden sorrow hushes, he will know.
But you, who mark the drooping of an eyelid
or in a wrinkled cheek set out a reason —
sainted! But only if you see —

                    and only then —

why, that the sum of all your notes is nothing . . .
Make a rich note of this — and start again.

XLVIII

Surround the thing with phrases, and perceptions;
master it with all that muscle gives
of mastery to mind, — all strengths, all graces,
flexes and hardnesses; the hand, the foot;
quick touch of delight, recoil of disgust;
and the deep anguish too, the profound anguish,
which bursts its giddy phrase. Surround the thing
with the whole body's wisdom, the whole body's
cunning; all that the fingers have found out,
the palm touched of smoothness or roughness;
the face felt, of coolness or stillness;
the eye known, of mystery in darkness;
the ear found in silence.

Surround the thing with words, mark the thing out
passionately, with all your gestures become words,
patiently, with all your caution become words,
your body a single phrase —

                    And what do you say — ?
O simple animal, twisted by simple light — !
do you tell space or time what the thing is?
Or do you tell the 'thing' that it is you!

XLIX

Tired of the long soliloquy of the mind
he walked in the wind and heard
his own soliloquy magnificently abroad
the wild original word around him flowing
the word uttered without knowing
framed by no mind, flung from no mouth

the drowning one balanced breathless in the wind
lost in speech
striving in haste to know the every from the each
in vain to find
the leaf of leaves the wave of waves
the meaning of meaning

and then came back from the soliloquy of the wind
and listened again to the long soliloquy of the mind;
the spirit humbled, and shaped, and at last resigned,
to the four walls that confined.

L

And the child said to me in a dream —
habitual strength is no stronger than habitual weakness:
the habitual hero is no hero:
the habitual weakling has found his marvellous level:
who knows, for another, good from evil?
the only strong one is the angel who is half devil.

And then I stooped, and saw
under our footsteps the imponderable law,
the vast and shapeless and bloodbeating Thing —
inestimable ruin which conceived a wing,
unspeakable glory which conceived a claw —
and hung my head in shame

that I should blame
these indecipherable and unintelligible notes
scrawled on the nearest margin of the world —
these mites, these men, these motes.

LI

The miracle said 'I' and then was still,
lost in the wing-bright sphere of his own wonder:
as if the river paused to say a river,
or thunder to self said thunder.

As once the voice had spoken, now the mind
uttered itself, and gave itself a name;
and in the instant all was changed, the world
two separate worlds became —

The indivisible unalterably divided;
the rock forever sundered from the eye;
henceforth the lonely self, by self anointed,
hostile to earth and sky.

Alas, good angel, loneliest of heroes!
pity your coward children, who become
afraid of loneliness, and long for rock
as sick men long for home.

LII

But how it came from earth this little white
this waxen edge this that is sharp and white
this that is mortal and bright the petals bent
and all so curved as if for lovers meant
and why the earth unfolded in this shape
as coldly as words from the warm mouth escape

Or what it is that made the blood so speak
or what it was it wanted that made this

breath of curled air this hyacinth this word
this that is deeply seen profoundly heard
miracle of quick device
from fire and ice

Or why the snail puts out a horn to see
or the brave heart puts up a hand to take
or why the mind, as if to agonize,
will close, a century ahead, its eyes —
a hundred years put on the clock
its own mortality to mock —

Christ come, Confucius come, and tell us why
the mind delights before its death to die
embracing nothing as a lover might
in a terrific ecstasy of night —
and tell us why the hyacinth is sprung
from the world's dull tongue.

Did death so dream of life, is this its dream?
does the rock think of flowers in its sleep?
Then words and flowers are only thoughts of stone
unconscious of the joy it thinks upon;
and we ourselves are only the rock's words
stammered in a dark dream of men and birds.

LIII

Pretend no more, admit there is no sunrise:
the ice and dark must stay, the heart must sleep:
love without love need now no longer weep,
nor the dead man remember;

Deceive the hand, it will be undeceived;
deceive the mind, it will recall disproof;
love betrayed is a house without a roof
but you must live there.

No, without phrase of comfort or deceit, —
no quondam star admitted by despair, —
go forth poor fellow to that inward air
which is your spirit's courage;

The outward Pole Star lost, your own is truer:
break the bright icicles that fringe your north,
those that now hang against your going forth
as at your coming hither;

And still no haste to die, when deathward, always,
decipherably, with footsteps clear, you creep
nearer, but always consciously, to sleep
like one who climbs a hill —

With shortening, but always sharper, breath
to the desired and all-forgetful nothing;
the bright, the brave, the brief, that ends with breathing,
the moment's death.

Learn these things now? No need to learn, we know them:
came with the heart, whose pride is but the beat
between absurd extremes of frost and heat:
why this is childsplay;

And here before us, all that chart of wonder,
infinitesimal and divine gradations —
stations, and nobler stations, and still stations,
before the thunder.

LIV

Thus far coming and at this cliff arrived
the unimagined become this world this shore
the unknown become these rocks and this invisible
pathway of waters
comfortless child let us turn back
let the known become again unknown

Did you bring with you a heart to eat
shall we sit now upon these rocks and eat our hearts
shall we remember
what there is no difficulty in remembering
or shall we forget
what it is so easy to forget
the shape of your hand your name
the shape of other rocks and the shame
is there time yet

To reveal to ourselves what was by ourselves concealed
to conceal from ourselves what was by ourselves revealed
is it too late to change
strange to familiar familiar to strange
can we reverse
backwards from Omega to Alpha, rehearse
our little alphabet of sand
our little alphabet of flowers
fingers touching and dividing the cruel hours
can we undo the done unknow the known
unshape the shaped
suffer the crucifixions we so devoutly escaped

It is a disaster to think of this
our death that we should think of this
already we have turned back and returned
who only thought of turning
but we do not die
for already returning from the past we have hoisted sail,
already our ship creates new islands
where again we shall land and fail.

LV

Did you too see it see with your own eyes
the horror the shape of rocks beneath the snow
or was it another shape a monstrous cloud

or the sound of wind in a haunted room
did you too touch it touch it with your hand

Was someone else there too or were you alone
and was there a clock to cry the time aloud
a minute to or a minute past the hour
and did the wave of revelation break
over your head and hands the wave of sky

Was it the colour of terror was it blue
and were you drowned in the wild blue the blue wave
whistled aloft on terror and then flung down
and then alone again and standing still
standing alone and still as a dead man stands — ?

The innumerable wonder that escapes
the immeasurable terror that escapes
afterwards only a grain of sand
in a dead hand
dying memory that slowly relinquishes
dying shapes.

LVI

Or else a room, and in the room five voices
speaking at once and what delicious babble
'sherbet' and 'velvet' and 'purple' and 'fragrant' and 'loud'—
the window gives on winter, the cold light
high up and cold, and in the pipes a knocking
that brings the firelight upward from earth's furnace —
and here are pictures too and rows of books
pictures of lakes and boats harpoons and faces
cold leaves bright flowers a beach an eye that watches
one eye that watches and in the books are notes —
compare page so and so, idem and ibid.,
names names and other names, and here a rhyme
such as reclaims a bell resumes a time —

words words and other words, like leaves, like leaves
some that are sounds some that are deep as wounds
some that are hands, some that are wings or claws —
and over all, assuming all, five voices
speaking at once in what a rich confusion —

Who put the window there what says the window
is there a nothing there or is it something
is someone looking in was it a cloud
is someone looking in was it a star
is someone looking in was it a god
had it a face and did you see its eyes
did it go past and will it come again
was it the thunder stooping? call it back —
listen — look — smell it — taste it — touch —
nothing, no; the voices speak again
murmur or shout, or whisper, or are sad —
'sherbet' 'velvet' 'purple' 'fragrant' 'shrill' —
and then at last, when the dark comes, are still.

LVII

Escape the pattern to another pattern:
avoid the ending for another ending:
hate the face now, you fool, to love it later —
or love it now to hate.

               Here's the magician
come for his evening tricks with bags and sleeves
marked cards and easy fingers. Here's the illusion
come for the morning with an eye of sunrise
and every grassblade golden. Here's the deception
who framed our hearts and minds and dwells there now
as naturally as blood. Here's the division
between one truth and other which is false
between one lie and other which is true
between one hour and other which is nothing

between one eye and other which is hell.
What will you have, be angry with your hand,
despise your eye, dissect your fancy,
shed out the broad humanity that lies
foul, rich, dishonest, and profound, in blood?
will you say yes to the heart, no to the belly?
and who says yes or no?

     Cry down to the dark
which is below you and is waiting for you,
and ask her for an answer. She is a pattern
begot of patterns and begetting patterns;
mad beyond madness, will tease you on
from false to false forever.

LVIII

Why should we care what this absurd child does,
follow him idly, watch the doll
laid in the grass and covered with dead leaves —
fingers tenderly lacing the dead leaves —
pathetic solicitude of the foolish for the unknowing?
why should we stand here, and watch this travesty,
we, the wise and old, the hardened, the disillusioned
from our window of bright despair looking downward
at the little contemptible street of human affairs —
and the child there, unconscious, tender, preoccupied,
bending in the dust above his beloved fragment?

Or the old men and women going up and down:
those with tired feet, or bent hands; those who see
dimly before them as indeed dimly behind them:
who greet one another stupidly and kindly:
is this not too to be dreadfully despised,
that thus we stand, secretly, behind curtains,
pitying the children, who were ourselves,
and the old, who will be ourselves —

pitying and despising, who will ourselves be pitied and despised:
but feeling, in memory and foresight, a kind of power?

But what else can we do, we who wait here between
one wall and another one clock and another
who can neither play happily in the dust, nor lie still?
too late for the one, too soon for the other,
what can we do but hide behind curtains, and spy?
Spying joyfully on the two blessings, beginning and end?

LIX

Who said the blandishment of the moon, who said
study the interstices to know the evening
who called the heart a faulty measure of time
weighed the stars in a scale of eyesight? descend
from that poor altitude, and find a way
simple as the bee finds to a flower
plain as the sand in the palm of a child's hand
easy as the alphabet. Morning opens
noon is the full round blue of the sea
dandelion is the first and last of flowers
defies the winter as it defies autumn
evening closes like the shutter of a camera,
sleep closes the eye but not the mind,
for then the dreams come. What is your dream,
concentric algebrist? a compound only
of moons, flowers, times, mornings, noons, evenings.

As this you had, that grief was unbearable,
as this you had, that truth was untellable,
this of the clover, with nine leaves, this
of the face with wings.

               The blandishment of the mind
silvers all things with ghostly delight
abhors all things with profound horror

or else, in an ecstasy of terror
cancels the world out and is dead. The blandishment
of the pure dream is a single hand
which takes the life up broken and makes it whole
fills the desert with dandelions, weighs the stars
with the opening of an eye. Its divine madness
hears the swift sound of time but without fear
makes its approach and passage as slow as a footfall
brings the past backward and the future forward;
bids all stand still. You, without wings, walk here;
the world is beneath you like a seed,
how will you have it grow. Will you have now
spaces, emptinesses? a net of bloodvessels
eaten by the cancer of thought? but fear to think
deliberately, for deliberation is poison.
Leave all to the sovereign blandishment of dream.

LX

The chairback will cast a shadow on the white wall,
you can observe its shape, the square of paper
will receive and record the impulse of the pencil
and keep it too till time rubs it out
the seed will arrange as suits it the shape of the earth
to right or left thrusting, and the old clock
goes fast or slow as it rusts or is oiled.
These things or others for your consideration
these changes or others, these records
or others less permanent. Come if you will
to the sea's edge, the beach of hard sand,
notice how the wave designs itself in quick bubbles
the wave's ghost etched in bubbles and then gone,
froth of a suggestion, and then gone.
Notice too the path of the wind in a field of wheat,
the motion indicated. Notice in a mirror
how the lips smile, so little, and for so little while.
Notice how little, and how seldom, you notice

the movement of the eyes in your own face, reflection
of a moment's reflection. What were you thinking
to deliver to the glass this instant of change, what margin
belonged only to the expectation of echo
and was calculated perhaps to that end, what was left
essential or immortal?

                    Your hand too,
gloved perhaps, encased, but none the less
already bone, already a skeleton,
sharp as a fingerpost that points to time —
what record does it leave, and where, what paper
does it inscribe with an immortal message?
where, and with what permanence, does it say 'I'?
Perhaps giving itself to the lover's hand
or in a farewell, or in a blow,
or in a theft, which will pay interest.
Perhaps in your own pocket, jingling coins,
or against a woman's breast. Perhaps holding
the pencil dictated by another's thought.

These things do not perplex, these things are simple, —
but what of the heart that wishes to survive change
and cannot, its love lost in confusions and dismay — ?
what of the thought dispersed in its own algebras,
hypothesis proved fallacy? what of the will
which finds its aim unworthy? Are these, too, simple?

LXI

The evening comes, the evening comes as always
with the dissimulations of fatigue
as that you are tired as that you forget as that you hesitate
between one thought and another one wish and another
as that you welcome darkness but wish for light
stare at the darkening light from the window, hating
the night in the room at your back, the lamp unlighted,

the unpeopled room which the light will people
known things which will ask again to be known —
the book left open the single flower in the vase
the newspaper the basket of letters the clock
which she whom you love she whom you hate
has forgotten to wind

                          and how does it come
this wave of the will how does it enter the blood
that thus with your hand you feel it and clutch it
thus against your throat press and make it beat
with such a gorgeous violence? how does it enter
the idea, which is angelic, and remain pure?
how does the angel of the idea remain pure?

There is nothing pure — alas, too easy it is
to answer one's own questions, to give left hand to right
or to match leaf with leaf as children do.
What do you say to yourself but your own confusion —
items and idioms of your own prolonged fatigue;
what do you think when darkness comes?
You wish yourself a sentimental farewell,
but not quite truthful not quite loving — no,
it is the farewell of an unbeliever
the farewell of a dishonest man, who knows
with what delicacy to weigh the deceptions
even when dealing with himself: it is the evening
which says to itself, why, it's another evening,
no worse, no better, but god's hand in it — it is the man
who says to himself, for the thousandth time,
be honest now, or die; and falls asleep.

                          LXII

The bird flying past my head said previous previous
the clock too said previous
I was warned, I was too soon, but I went on

taking with me a buzzing headful of omens
as this, and that, and the other, all to no good
turn back, go to the right, no no go forward,
under that tree, under that cliff, through that man's house
his wife will tell you, ask her the way

I went and asked, it was all as I had foreseen,
one thing and then another all as if planned
the bird saying previous previous and the clock croaking
the cliff and the tree and the house and the wife
the husband looking askance at me over his work
why it is all a dream I said and hurried
with leaden or golden steps in dream's bravado
past bird clock cliff tree wife and husband

into the beyond — but what was the beyond but nothing
nothing nothing — a shore a shape a silence
an edge a falling off — a loaf of fog
sliced by a knife. It was then that I turned back,
and found the past was changed and strange as future —
cliff tree wife and husband changed and strange;
and the same or a different bird flew past my head
saying previous previous, as if I were again too soon.

LXIII

Design the tombstone of the usual one.
Have it on earth or have it not at all.
Carve it in leaves or carve it in a cloud.
Who was it (whispering) where did death take him?
what did he do? what name did he have?
now lies he there rotting for birds to decipher.

Design it like this; with questions of words,
or questions of music or questions of wind —
here lies the dishonest one who sought so for honesty
here lies the impure one who sought so for purity

here lies he unconscious who fought so for consciousness
honest and pure, but unconscious as well.

Too simple this ending: the bird flew across
the window was open he saw the bird fly
he crooked up a finger but the bird it had flown
the window was closed and the daylight was gone —
carve a quick word on a shadow and say
that the man who knew nothing has lain down alone.

Design the tombstone of the usual one.
Have it in grass or have it not at all.
Carve it in water or carve it in a cloud.
Where is his purity where is his honesty
what did he know with his passion for consciousness?
now lies he there prone for the worm to decipher —

As weight and as water as blood upon bone
as rags for the merchant as quarrels for heirs
deep sleep for his widow her hands on her belly
his children are free there is joy for his friends
empty his boxes and burn up his letters
empty he started and empty he ends

As weight and as water as space within space
this huddle of thought which has lifted a face —
too simple this ending the bird has been seen
the word has been stripped to what words cannot mean —
carve a quick thought on a window, remember
that the man who knew nothing had nothing to say.

LXIV

Insist on formality if you will, let the skeleton
insist on formality if it will
allow it the hat the spats the gloves
and let it observe its exquisite decorum
at weddings or funerals, even at christenings

Let it say yes and no and hum and haw
give it an eyeglass and a programme of the music
something to do with hand and eye
it will embrace you pat you on the back
say it remembers you and knew your father

Let it observe its exquisite decorum
in the manipulation of decay —
and sing too — with hearty sepulchral voice —
in celebration of those rituals
which make a formal of the absolute

As if it were better, at the end of time,
when time runs faster, to mark the minutes out
with gold or diamonds, even with cannonshot —
the intervals more regular and precise
— and decorated too — to give them dignity!

Precisely what is this? that we should face
with such a putting on of airs and gloves
the bone, already formal in itself?
as if to minimize or decorate
the bone in bone, the order of skeleton!

For god's sake men, for god's sake women,
let the wild love too have its moment
let us forget the bone that flesh is heir to
and be informal — if never again —
at weddings and funerals, if not at birth.

LXV

We do not know we do not remember
we shall not know we shall not remember
a single flower
you will not remember the shape of a single mouth

this that first touched you
   and with a heaven of light
this that last touched you
   when touch was no longer known
this that you first touched
   broken flower bruised mouth
this that you last touched
   the all-symbolizing wall

you do not know do not remember
you shall not know shall not remember
a single leaf
you will not remember the shape of a single word.

LXVI

Brought them with him and put them down, as if
to come from nowhere with a random burden
of odd and ends, and quids and quods and surds,
whatnots and whiches — as if to put them down
were tantamount to saying he had thought them
and thought the bringing and thought the putting down
and thought himself who thought he brought them there

as if such randomness were part of nature
as if such casualness were part of nature
or the mad separateness of such an action
whether it served a purpose or served none
were the precise bright plume of God's own madness

but not that either, no, a different thing —
the always bringing, the always putting down
the odds and ends and quids and quods and surds
but never new, never the bright beginning,
as if the beginning were always at the middle
and never rememberable the sunrise words

who was it brought them with him and put them down
who was it came from nowhere and dropped his burden
the nondescript purveyor of nondescriptions
exhausted speaker of the exhausted word
wind outblown the word that died with speaking
the helplessness of helpless thought.

LXVII

Walk man on the stage of your own imagining
peel an orange or dust your shoe, take from your pocket
the soiled handkerchief and blow your nose
as if it were indeed necessary to be natural
and speak too if an idea should recommend itself
speak to the large bright imaginary audience
that flattering multiplication of yourself
so handsomely deployed and so expectant
tell them between flingings of orange peel
or such other necessary details of your rôle
precisely what they are, or what you are
since — lamentably — they are so much the same thing.
Decrepit inheritor of the initial star!
do you yourself sometimes imagine
or even perhaps say to that peculiar audience
something of this? as that yourself and they
comprise one statement? supercilious
the actor may be, often is, to those who hear him
but to be supercilious to one's self
even in one's dramatic moments! — marvellous
decay of what in God's first declaration
might have been good.

LXVIII

What you have said and cannot say again
prevented word that would have said your pain

idea prevented by the forbidden word
deliver us from this, bright alphabet

what you have thought and cannot think again
prevented thought that would have found its word —
word prevented by the forbidden thought —
deliver us from this, deep alphabet

the word walks with us, is a ghost of word —
the thought walks with us, is a ghost of thought
thus to the world's end in a silence brought
and to a babel our dark alphabet

come heart, invent a new word a new thought:
feel with new heat, new brightness, *a* and *b*
may thus become a glass through which we'll see
new worlds lost in the old world's alphabet

the sudden light, the sudden breaking, the sudden whirl —
come light, come light, let the heart be a bird
whose single being is a single word
brightness beyond soul or alphabet.

LXIX

I saw all these things and they meant nothing
I touched all these hands and they meant nothing
I saw all these faces Lord and they meant nothing
Lord Zero they meant nothing

accept my worship Zero for these devotions
for all these sins and for their absolutions
remit my guilt and wash my hands Lord Zero
for yours was the conception

and I will teach you in another world
out of my misery I will learn and teach you

I will teach you Lord in another world
I will give you my heart

the heart that the sailor gives to the broken ship
or the wheelwright to the turning wheel
the heart that the farmer gives to the frozen furrow
a stubborn heart like that

and I will also teach you by giving you my hands
look how they are injured Lord, see how hard they are
see how their beauty has been marred and scarred
I will teach you by giving you my hands

Christ had not hands like these, his hands were perfect
Christ's heart was great, not small like mine,
I do not believe in Christ, he is our dream,
and you too are our dream, Lord Zero

but we will defeat you, we will convert you,
we will teach you to laugh as the unhappy do
you will become human and broken like ourselves
you will become One with us, Lord Zero

(It is here that the little doubt comes in from the window
like a cold wind fluttering the leaves
and we ourselves go forth again on that wind
to become Lord Zero.)

LXX

Misery has no shape
you cannot define it you cannot say it
agony has no name
you cannot speak it

easier to see the colour of the air
and to taste the wind

unhappy one give up your grief
as if it were a child

let it grow beside you
as if indeed it were your shadow
let it walk from you
and have shadows of its own

misery has no meaning
it has no syllables it is nothing
it is the stupid face of apprehension
open mouth that has no word

easier to watch, in your own breast,
the fearful balancing of the heart
systole and then diastole
held breath between death and death

let the heart decide it
as if indeed it were yourself
let it talk with you
have arguments of its own

o life defend us from this agony
deliver us from grief again
show us once more that it is only
our child conceived in pain.

LXXI

Disaster is no disaster on a starlit night.
Look how the planets move. Look there, look there,
how when the tree shakes the loosed star comes forth
as impudent as ever! How can you keep
poor fool in such an angelic presence
your handful of pain? Look at that world
so young so fiery so swift and so intent —

and deny if you can that you, too, once,
ran forth as splendidly as that. And how long since?
Yesterday? this morning? Even as you look
that swift conviction burns once more — it is this instant;
and all your life sums up one fiery thought,
bright as that loosed star, and begins again.

LXXII

Shape the shapeless with your strong thumb woman
in the grey light shape the shapeless
and we will watch you we the anonymous will watch you
anonymous shoulders anonymous eyes

you, bent amongst the boulders, bent amongst the ferns
you the grey animal the shapeless mother
while we the shaped ones watch you between your fingers
suffering as you shape us
(but this was not the image, it was another,
it was a dream of a face as wide as snow.)

LXXIII

Destiny comes in as softly as a sunbeam
greets you with the subtlety of thistledown
smiles with all light and as nimbly as light
is here and there and nowhere all at once:
the air that enfolds you when you open the window
the speck of dust that drops from your sleeve
the sound of a dove on the roof.

                      Destiny
moves as deliberately and as delightfully
as imperceptibly and as freely
as the clot of blood which releases
the wounded side of the vein. It creeps
on a sure stream to the heart: it will speak

once, and suddenly; say death or birth;
or both together. It will surprise you
with a ribbed rainbow of which the ribs are pain
the false colours translated from the blood
or else, and as easily, make you a daybreak;
where at a single step from the white hill
all angels rise like snowflakes out of snow
and the pure light is yours.

                        Make it, mortal,
as you would have it — lift your hands and take
the sunbeam into your palm, imagine
the white light which is yours.

                    LXXIV

This flower, she said to the child, you may have,
this with the little veins in the throat, and this
white one with the three purple spots, this too
take in your hand and watch it fade, forget
how it stood in the grass and cast a shadow
before it died. But this other flower
no, that is for later, that must be saved,
it must be left here, clinging to the side of the star
like a child at his mother's breast,
with the plantain leaves at the right and the grassblades
crisscrossed about the cool strong stem, and the green acorn
lying on the earth beside it at the left.
Of this you may keep only what you remember.
And it will live still, with an intense light,
when the others are dead.

                        The child walked westward
with the whole evening round him like a bell,
clear and deep and full of stars, the slow fading
of the green twilight like a fading flower, the stars
brightening in the huge arch. He counted them,

turned in a circle and counted others, and still others,
saw how the lower were the larger and brighter,
then stood at fault; walked back to ask again;
but she was gone. Now he would never know
which one, of all these stars, now he would never know
which star it was the flower had clung to —
flower and star and voice were gone — ;
while the whole evening seemed to him like a hand
defending him, — forbidding, but defending.
Yet in the darkness was something new, something bright,
which was neither in the cold grass at his feet
nor in the sky: it was the simple image
of the star with the flower on its breast;
this he could have, this he could keep.

LXXV

And that grin, the grin of the unfaithful,
the secret grin of self-congratulation
facing the mirror at midnight, when all has gone well,
when the returning footstep has not been heard,
nor the errand guessed, nor the change of heart perceived,
nor the eye's secret discovered, nor the rank perfume
smelled on hand or mouth

                    that grin like a flower
which opens voluptuously amid poisons and darkness
at the mere sight of itself as if to say
courage you have done it let now bravado
match in its brazenness the mercurial deception
go forth and kiss the cheek of her you have deceived

you too have known this and failed to be ashamed
have brazened it out and grinned at your own grin
holding the candle nearer that you might see
the essential horror.

Yes, and you have noted
how then the chemistry of the soul at midnight
secretes peculiar virtue from such poisons:
you have been pleased: rubbed metaphoric hands:
saying to yourself that the suffering, the shame,
the pity, and the self-pity, and the horror,
that all these things refine love's angel,
filth in flame made perfect.

LXXVI

Alas, if among these volcanic ruins, moonchild,
you find the foothold more precarious, the reward
less certain, and if in the vague light
you stoop less often to find among cold ashes
the trove that delights your hand, your heart —
(you moving there like a habitual shadow
among shadows, and shadows of shadows, and all of them
only the whispers and echoes of your own past —
you groping there, on the dead planet, which is yourself)

And if you are not pleased,
(as self-lovers can be, even with their own ruins)
nor turn, like the moon, a delighted face to the sun,
flattered by so much splendour,

If it has come to this,
that you are a ghost among ghosts, and the ghosts
are yourself, and yourself a guest
among ghosts, so that the reality and the shadow
are alike to unfeeling fingers —

Why, then, let the autumn suggest
the falling of a leaf, the changing of a colour,
the bending of a bough, the contraction

of the young bud against the north, all with a view
to further and other landscapes. Remember the delicate
Quaker Lady, who lets fall a petal, the better
to explore another season, stepping with giant simplicity
across death to another time, yet without moving;
remember the little spider, whose final web,
shaken by the wind, broken by the rain,
dislodges him, to shrink and sleep beneath a frozen leaf,
but with conviction; and remember too
how, even when death surrounds you, as if you were a field
lamentable with dying men, how even then
the one man still alive will hug his wounds
and dream with intolerable brightness of a single thing.

LXXVII

The great one who collects the sea shells I beheld
he was like the fog with long fingers he was like a cloud
stooping over the mean fields and the salt beaches
brushing the sad trees with kind shoulders
but again he had no shape, his shape was my imagination
and I beneath his foot like a dry pebble.

The fog went above me with long hands and a soft face
above the ships with a cold breath above the sails
what he loved he took and kept well, beyond death,
but I noticed that especially he loved little things
the seaweed, the starflower, the mussel, the bones of a small fish on
    the sand

I separate from him, but not separate, because I loved him
thinking of him among the marshes, the wet woodpaths, the grasses,
thinking of him who was myself but who was more loving than
    myself
alas that the pebble cannot move or be moved
nevertheless I imagined him, he was my creation

O god of my imagination, god of my creation,
whom thus I impersonate, my father, my mother,
whom I create out of the visible world, as you created me
out of the invisible, let me be the one
who loves the seaweed, the starflower, the mussel, the bones of a
     small fish on the beath
and I among them like a smooth pebble.

LXXVIII

But having seen the shape, having heard
the voice, do not relate the phantom image
too nearly to yourself, leave the bright margin
between the text and page, a little room
for the unimagined. What's here, beneath your hand,
is less and more than what you see or feel;
deeper than air or water; deeper than thought
can dive, whether between stars or between gods;
deeper than the sound of your heart. Walk right or left
it is no matter, whether in room or field,
under a tree, beside a road, the shape
will be deciphered only to elude you.
Is the fog only the shape of yourself, idiot?
and the fog an idiot too? is the god
your own vast fog of folly projected?
Think better of your love than this!

                          She reads a book:
her hands are on the table: the bright light
falls on the opened pages, the two pages,
and on the ordered words. And while she breathes
the braids upon her bosom rise and fall
as slowly as her eyes recite the lines, —
from left to right, from right to left, softly
reshaping from that sight a world of sound.
There with her ears, but not with ears, she learns
how leaves can make an aureate grace of air

weaving a visual pattern, but in sound;
moved by the wind, heard by the poet's ear,
and now in visual sign transcribed again.
What miracle is this? that she who reads
here in a simple room of time and chairs,
can watch a bough dissect an arc of sky?
can feel the current of the wind that lifts it?
can hear, and see, and feel, that wound in air?
As the bough dips and flurries, she reads and breathes;
as move the leaves, her hands upon the page;
as lives the tree, or as the poet lives
in living with the tree, so lives her eye;
and as the poem lives, her woman's grace.
But which lives first? and who is living?

        God
is such a margin as thus lies between
the poem and the page's edge, a space
between the known and the imagined, between
the reported and the real. He is your fancy.
And you are his.

LXXIX

Look! with what lustre, what light, what lightning, the daybreak
strikes the bronzed cobweb, so that it quickens with gold —
or the dark window, so that it shows in the morning
the daffodil's yellow in a landscape of snow!

The bronze, or the darkness, transmuted, transfigured, the glory
shot through the meanness, each strand of the web become living —
or the window in winter become, to the sleep-laden eye,
the daffodil nodding by a margin of dream.

Admit it! what chance of escape? poor mortal, whose terror
accepts such disproof with the heart before reason can change it:
whose waking to light is a joy, whose waking is love,
greet your love and accept it.

That you opened your eye with delight is a proof of your love;
do not deny it, but keep it, and hold to it hard;
you love, for your nature is love; your joy in the daylight is proof
that love without reason is love without end.

LXXX

Lady, you are a character in a play, you walk
westward towards the window with just such taking
of the strange light upon your face, the effect
conscious and calculated, but none the less
deep in the evening's beauty. Who could have known
that the sunset would be of these wild colours,
making the room, the walls, your face, a strange
description, such a sharpening of the fact,
or such a lighting of it, as gives it new
wonders and disorders? You have seen meadows
changed by the evening light, striped and brightened,
or a single oakleaf burning like a miracle
in casual sunlight, each vein and mole and wound
become as real and vascular as the warm tissue
of your own hand, lifted against the sun.
Thus now your face, at the open window,
against the dying madness of a simple day:
your calculations fall in with those of god:
your deceptions are his: and what was meant to be
a clever figment, a designed action, becomes
something the hand cannot touch, nor the mind follow,
nor the heart withhold. Your lie becomes a truth:
so beautiful, so burning, that he believes, —
he, the deceived one, looks, and loves, and believes.

LXXXI

Assurance can come from nothing, or almost nothing;
the imperceptible accretion of trifles;
the mistaken speech, acknowledged, or unacknowledged,

the penetration of a deception; it can come
from observation of what has been unobserved:
new knowledge of an old history, new sight
of a known face, a known field; the path
familiar to the foot, but with surprises,
a raw pebble, dislodged by rain, a scarlet leaf
drowned in a puddle, a branch of maple to brush the sleeve,
or such other casuals. It can come
with a change of weather, the sundrawn mist
exaggerating softly the shape of a tree, snow
altering the face of a house, so that you guess
but do not know, yet triumph in knowing. Or can come,
and this is best, from the renewed inspection
of a known thing, and long loved; something small,
something tiny, but loved. The pimpernel,
hidden, with dusty petals, in deep grass,
obscure but always remembered, clear and
delicate, but with something obtuse as well,
obtuse and infinitesimal — this is the sort
of well-loving, and well-knowing, that changes
Tuesday to Wednesday.

Why not, or why,
have Wednesday for Tuesday? This is a question
which neither the heart nor calendar can answer.
But if assurance can feed itself on change,
change, then, and be assured.

LXXXII

As if you were a child again; you smooth
a little space of sand, with careful fingers,
pick out a twig, a stone, a scrap of paper
or other obstacle; then, all prepared,
make in that space of yellow sand a poem:
with first a golden shell, and then a white,
a fern leaf after, then a twig, and then

a row of pebbles, each of different size,
one after other, a parade of soldiers:
a brown and then a yellow, each one larger
than that before; and, at the last, as captain,
white as the foam, a carapace of crab.
Behind you, as you work, you hear the reeds
seethe in the little wind, the crows fly over,
a ragged caravan; and these you hear
cawing among the corn; the smell of waves
comes upward from the beach, part froth, part sound;
and while you stoop and work, you know these things.

But there is also at your back the sea;
this too you know; this too you fear; that wide
unaltering but always altered laughter;
which the wind's hands will change, to change again;
which bears the seagull's shadow and the ship
with equal ease. What will you do with this?
Will it be mentioned? You stoop once more to add
a shark's egg to your poem of sand, a frond
of purple vetch with curled end, the fine tendril
curled like a watchspring. Now the poem is perfect,
now it says everything. You rise and turn
proud of your handiwork, and walk beside
the margin of the sea. The long waves come
to drown their fading rims of foam in sand
white arcs on intersected arcs of white
with all their sound, and all their power; you see
the wilderness; and in the face of this
your poem becomes the perfect shape it is;
the sea left out!

And thus, you know the world.
Thus, with a phrase, exclude the absolute.

LXXXIII

Music will more nimbly move
than quick wit can order word
words can point or speaking prove
but music heard

How with successions it can take
time in change and change in time
and all reorder, all remake
with no recourse to rhyme!

Let us in joy, let us in love,
surrender speech to music, tell
what music so much more can prove
nor talking say so well:

Love with delight may move away
Love with delight may forward come
Or else will hesitate and stay
finger at lip, at home,

But verse can never say these things;
only in music may be heard
the subtle touching of such strings,
never in word.

LXXXIV

What face she put on it, we will not discuss:
she went hence an hour since. Where she went,
is another matter. To the north, to the south,
as the man whistled, or the whim bade, she went,
or even — who can say — following a star.
Her heart is like an hourglass, from which the sand runs —
no sooner run than tilted to run again;

her mind, a mirror, which reflects always the last moment;
her face, you would know it anywhere, it gives you back
your own light, like the moon. Tell her a lie,
threefold she reflects it; tell her the truth,
and its returned brilliance will strike you dead.
She is of quicksilver. You might as well
pillow your head on a cloud, as on that breast,
or strive to sleep with a meteor: when you wake,
she is gone, your own hand is under your cheek.

Yet she is of the material that earth is made of:
will breed as quick as a fly: bloom like the cherry,
fearless of frost: and has a nimble fancy
as tropic in pattern as a fernleaf. She walks
as naturally as a young tree might walk:
with no pretence: picks up her roots and goes
out of your world, and into the secret darkness,
as a lady with lifted train will leave a ballroom,
and who knows why.

                 Wherefor do you love her, gentlemen?
Because, like the spring earth, she is fruitfulness?
and you are seed? you need no other reason?
and she no other than her perpetual season.

LXXXV

Observe yourself, but placidly: the mirror
is well placed, with the light behind you: Narcissus
could ask no more. This is the face you shave,
at morning, tenderly, with care for moles
or small excrescences more temporal:
you know, have felt, time and again, its cheeks,
their roughnesses and hollows; the fat chin;
the corners of the mouth, each different;
one melancholy, one weak. You know the eyes,
the faded blue, which cannot meet your gaze,

and the drooped eyelid, after dissipation,
hung low upon a large unseeing pupil.
The earlobes too you love, your fingers love —
scooped, like the nostrils, for crisp lather; the nose,
you disregard, provided it can breathe.
The brow — what of the brow? You press your hand
against that span of bone and flesh, to feel
its ache grow deeper, if it aches; the bone
resists the hand, with deep surprise to both,
that its own hand should rise against the brain.
And the hand wonders what the sore brain thinks.

The hand wonders, but the dull eye also:
questions the mirrored eye and eyelid: stares
more painfully, in that glazed and lidded pupil,
than ever proud Narcissus in his pool.
What's there? what virtue, or what truth? Hatred
glares back at you; the dulled eye is stupid;
but not too stupid, or too dull, for hate. ·
You hate each other; you lean and hate; the light
shows deeply into hate. Who is that man?
His face is meanness, and should be destroyed!
But then the mouth —

             For suddenly the mouth
begins to smile; and smiles and smiles; and grins
maudlin affection; unless it be divine.
Is it divine? or maudlin? The two faces
glare at each other; sober; become still.
There is a truce, there is a silence: you lean
toward each other, into mystery.
Who is that man? His face is strange, and good!
unknown, and therefor god. . .

             And so, once more,
eternity makes heartbreak peace with time.

LXXXVI

What the hands touch is true; if blood
bind up the wound, yours or another's,
and wash your fingers, and let it heal.
Afterwards, you will see the scar,
the white mark in the flesh, stigmata.
The eyes, seeing, imagine Christ.
The seal is permanent in the flesh.

What the mind touches is a ghost
impermanent as wound in air
which active memory cannot fill:
ghostly image of ghostly tree
etched on the eyelid when it closes:
the hands, reaching, imagine god;
the truth is permanent in the mind.

Have what you will, let mind or hand
touch and distinguish blood or tree
bleeding anguish of sap or vein:
dissever world from self, dissever
falling leaf from beating heart.
The world, creating, imagined you.
You are impermanent, the world will change.

LXXXVII

The old man leaned upon the eagle's wings
above the golden wings and the wide book
Socrates with the flame looking down above the leaves,
falcon eye over toothless mouth
smiling at time and at us his shadows
                              while we whispered
he began with a crooked hand his lecture.

My darlings my murderers my little echoes
today let us not begin as the poets do
with a sharp sensuous picture, the obvious
design on weak credulities:
let us not say, to take an example,
that the old man leaned on an eagled lectern
above the brazen wings, and the wide book;
nor yet with a waste landscape, or the sea.
                                        Instead,
let us say that destiny leans above us
in the shape of an old man, a humble and disorderly
citizen, with faded clothes and hair, whose wife
neglects him as much as he neglects himself.
Thus to reverse the process.

                        Better still,
for I hear murmurs from my shadows,
let us be as abstract as we may, begin with pure
nothing, and from nothing dryly proceed
to something. Destiny leans above us
like nothing: we know nothing: how can we say
therefor that it leans? it is not an old man,
nor a young one, wears no clothes, and reads no book,
nor delivers lectures; nor has it a lectern,
nor an eagle under his hands with wings of violent brass;
none of these things; not even a voice;
it is as if there were not even a wind;
nor a space for wind; or any space at all;
my darlings, my echoes, we are nothing:
and yet we speak.

                        And thus in speaking come
to something, which is yourselves;
you in a row waiting for words, you who listen
with round mouths to the round words;
and I who speak them, an old man leaning forward,
an old man learning from the open mouth.

LXXXVIII

And look and remember well, as with an actor,
how each moment is that brilliant and particular
stepping forward from shadow to the stage
where all will be seen; the lights are beneath you
and beyond the lights the crowd, a silence;
so that the flexing of your knee is noted;
the arch of your hand, or the turn of your cheek
burned away from you as soon as seen.
The eyelid droops only to be torn from you;
your smile, your tears, your heart,
exist only to be devoured. Courage
must bear you swiftly, each moment must carry you
to the next safe gesture: each expression
must take you quickly from the last, it is a race
with anonymous hatred and innumerable eyes.
What you were, they have eaten, and already
they eat what you are. You must hurry
like a magician from trick to trick; the smile
is flung like a handkerchief, the frown is dropped
rapidly to take its place, next you must turn
with a dancer's grace, angrily
stoop to tie a shoelace, or else again
stand with your finger to chin as in thought.
It is all seen, it is all eaten, nothing
escapes that mouth of hungry light, only
the extreme of agility and practice will find you
a safe exit into the wings.
If applauded, perhaps you have been a practiced actor;
swift in mimicry, an adjustable ape,
quick as a typewriter or a telegraph,
and perhaps no better. If received in silence,
it may be that you were an honest man.

LXXXIX

1

It was the departure, the sun was risen,
the light came across the flat sea, yellow blades
fell like swords on the small white houses
the half hoisted sail creaked on the ship
the seagulls hovered in circles and cried
on the foredeck the sailors stood at the capstan

the moving light made the land look as if it were moving
the houses shifted the windows changed
cocks crew and the hens strutted into the street
and you went down the path of shells, carrying
a box on your shoulder, a bundle in your hand
I followed hearing ahead the sound of your feet

but you carried also the invisible
you carried also the unspoken
what we could not say what we had not said
what we had not lived and could never live
what we had lived but could not be forgotten
where will you remember it where again will you sit down

at a little foreign table reading a paper
the news a month old and our hearts a month dead
with a strange clock above you and a bird in a cage
chirping in another language
but not yet now it is still the daybreak
look they are hoisting the sail and singing

the moving light makes the land seem to move
it is we who are going away and not you
we take away with us an indecipherable heritage
time is broken in our hands
it is we who leave you here in a motionless ship
as we begin the immeasurable circle

say goodbye to us make your farewells
the earth is leaving you the earth is going
never again shall we come to this permanent ship
or you everlasting with your box on your shoulder
it will always be daybreak with us, the beginning,
we shall never be older, or wiser, or dead.

2

Too simple. It was not like that.
The day was an ordinary day, the milk
came at seven, the newspaper at eight,
the milkman woke us we heard the angelus
and turned to each other knee to knee
you with indigestion I with a backache
the melting snow dripping at the window
and pigeons making a flutter

                    Confucius says
what did we read last night about Confucius
what was my dream of Anna Livia
the drowned mermaid who powdered her nose, before
submitting languidly to the river, the landscape
carefully embossed with flowers. Primroses
with pink tips I saw, and the spinach-green
mythic meadows, and other small flowers,
and the allegorical trees,
and Virgil before me, guiding.

                    Not thus to hell
was Dante led, not thus to heaven,
the entrance to neither is so simple. Sounds of the world
come upward confusedly but pertinently
to us who lie here, struggling awake
from dulled angers and dimmed perceptions. My love,
your slippers are under the bed, and the glass of water,
it is Tuesday already, we must begin again.

3

Into the gulf between
bellsound and waiting and bellsound and then
the unfilled silence which sets a term to time
into the void the opening of the eye
into the eye the entrance of wild light
and the slow forgetting of the night
the dreams shifted from left to right
the hand moved and right foot to left foot shifted

in the dark interval between what is it we have seen
who were those shadows, who were those others
those whom the ship took down with farewell cries and hands
whose cries and whose last laughter we heard
the cloud broken by the sun
the light broken by rain
the sea broken by pouring water

into that nameless space
which is the awaking face
waiting and then no memory and then an image
while the hand yet is still
and the mouth does not know if it will smile
let the division come
let the pure separation come

let the division come
in this serene bewilderment this leaving
of the half known for the half known
before there is conceiving or believing
or with self-knowledge the eyes are done
or the hands remember each other
while yet our south and north are sleeping
let us both stay and go forth,
let this be our home, our keeping.

XC

And in the wide world full of sounds and nothings
of faces and no faces and no sounds
of words and wounds and in the words no world
but only you whose face we cannot fathom
and you whose word is what a word is only —

the evening breaking what the morning brought
the morning ending what the evening thought
bee deceived by flower and heart by hour —

precious chameleon of the human soul,
what colour will you match in this disaster?
of all the hues which choose?

shake your hand and say this hand is honest —
turn your kaleidoscope, the broken glass
will shape your fancy to a truer shape
than ever destiny — but what is destiny — ?
spied from god's shoulder.

XCI

In heavenly stillness when the evening stands
deep as a world above your lifted hands —
deep as a world above your lifted face
the profound ocean of unspoken space —

look, as the darkness deepens, your arms reach farther
godlike and fisherlike the world to gather;
but still the streaming waters elude your meshes,
weeds and flotsam outnumbering the fishes.

Nothing is there? But again the stillness comes;
once more against the dark your godhead looms;
the vaster net of a vaster self you fling,
and draw toward you the innumerable Thing.

What god with angry face would you find there?
or what immortal food or end of care?
Greatly your own greatness the net brings back;
or, weakly dared and flung, your own soul's lack.

XCII

But no, the familiar symbol, as that the
curtain lifts on a current of air, the rain
drips at the window, the green leaves seen in the
lamplight are bright against the darkness, these
will no longer serve your appetite, you must have
something fresh, something sharp —

The coarse grassblade, such as will cut
a careless finger, the silver pencil
lying straight along the crack in the table
in its pure rondure a multitude of reflections
or else your own thumbnail suddenly seen
and as if for the first time

Strongly ridged, warm-coloured as flesh but cool,
the pale moon at the base, and the fleck of scar
which grows slowly towards the tip — you think of a river
down which a single dead leaf perhaps is carried
or you think of a glacier in which
an acorn has been frozen —

But these too are familiar, it is not these
which will say your thought, you lift desperately
your eyes to the wall — the smooth surface
awaits them as precisely and coldly
as the paper awaits the gleaming pencil, giving
nothing, not even a resistance —

Where will you turn now if not to the rain,
to the curtain in the wind, the leaf tapping the window,

these are the wilderness, these are beyond
your pencil with its reflections
your thumbnail with its suggestion of rivers and glaciers
now you must go abroad

To the wild night which everywhere awaits you
and the deep darkness full of sounds
to the deep terror in which shines for a moment
a single light, far-off, which is suddenly quenched
this is the meaning for which you seek a phrase
this is your phrase.

XCIII

Or else, in an afternoon of minor reflection,
the savage sunset tamed, and in your garden
the bright stripes beneath your feet, fool
you think from footstep to footstep how easily
man's genius can compose an ode to death.
The honeysuckle puts down its tendrils from the wall
and seeks to embrace you, the seedlings
break the earth as you watch and seem to approach,
the thrush clings with cold claws of a serpent
to his favourite bough and sings. What can you say
that these have not said, are not saying,
you with your consciousness of time? time
swings with the tendril, sings in the birdsong, clings
with the bird-claw, it is time
which thrusts like the leaf's eye from the cold earth.
These already know death, in the mere adventure
in the mere going forth they know and seek it gladly,
they embrace it tightly, what can you say
that is not known to the cold claws of the thrush?
Your ode to death is not in a phrase,
nor in a hymn to darkness, nor in a knowledge
of timelessness, or the sad iteration

of time. Your ode to death is in the lifting
of a single eyelash. Lift it and see.

XCIV

Or in duplicity, in ambiguity: as at the circus
when the cards have double meanings, or the flame
is deceptive, and the clown comes through it
unhurt: his face comes through the flame,
but the flame was perhaps unreal, was not there.
The white bright face, with the red mouth, comes grinning
alive towards you, and the flaming hoop, the ring of fire,
falls to the grass, goes out. Perhaps like this
is the profound duplicity, the ambiguity
which appeared your easy theme: of this you hoped,
walking on the bright stripes of your tamed sunset,
to phrase your ode to death: in this falseness
was something simple, in this doubleness
something disposable, as of two voices
which, in equivocation, make a chord.
But death, like life, is simpler still. Live it and see.

XCV

And it is you: toward the light you move
as silently, as gravely, as a ship
counters the evening tide: the silver forefoot
divides the winedark water: lights may be
where land may be: the darkened shore may hide
who knows what orchards; and behind those boughs —

And it is you: toward the face you move
as smoothly and as lightly as a gull
counters the evening air: the silver wingtip
divides the winedark dusk: belief may be
where rest may be: what thought you had, when restless,
who knows what wisdom it will lean to now —

And it is you: against the night you walk
with one hand lifted up and like a lamp
to guide and fend off evil: eyeless, eyeless
your courage, like a cloud, assumes the wall;
presumes and mounts it; is unbroken still;
proceeds to find what further waits, what other —

And it is you: who passed, but stay here still;
you, like a chair, which someone else has made;
you, like a rug, which someone else has woven;
you, like a wall, which someone else has mortared;
a book, some hand left open; a face, seen once,
not liked, or disliked, but remembered: you.

XCVI

It is the other, it is the separate, it is the one
whose touch was strange, who with an eyeglance
sounded and wounded you, who went then
quickly to another world, who was gone
before you had guessed, before you had known,
quick as the shadow of a whip over grass
or the shadow of falling water on a rock —
he who said yes, but with a separate meaning,
who said no with an air of profound acceptance,
he who was other, he who was separate —

That precious thing is gone, that bright grassblade
suddenly by the frost's fierce tongue
was silvered and melted, how will you have it back —
there is no having it unless you had it,
lament your selfishness in vain, be sentimental
and hug the lost image, it is in vain,
he remains in another world —

                    Simple one, simpleton,
when will you learn the flower's simplicity —

lie open to all comers, permit yourself
to be rifled — fruitfully too — by other selves?
Self, and other self — permit them, permit them —
it is summer still, winter can do no more
who brings them together in death, let them come
murderously now together, it is the lifelong
season of meeting, speak your secret.

AND IN THE HUMAN HEART

I

Bend as the bow bends, and let fly the shaft,
the strong cord loose its word as light as flame;
speak without cunning, love, as without craft,
careless of answer, as of shame or blame:
this to be known, that love is love, despite
knowledge or ignorance, truth, untruth, despair;
careless of all things, if that love be bright,
careless of hate and fate, careless of care.
Spring the word as it must, the leaf or flower
broken or bruised, yet let it, broken, speak
of time transcending this too transient hour,
and space that finds the beating heart too weak:
thus, and thus only, will our tempest come
by continents of snow to find a home.

II

As salvage is too slow, and dives too deep,
and brings to light too little, at such length,
a coin or two at most, where fortunes sleep,
a golden ingot for that iron strength,
so is this parsimoniousness of love
which wastes a life of care for relics lost,
neglects a golden sunrise, here above,
for sunken summers, gone, nor counts the cost.
Break the poor pattern that would count and scheme;
add web to web; or, spider-like, devise
the slow-encroaching all-embracing dream,
a golden universe of golden flies:
let the one thing be one and one alone —
the hand fling once, once only, and one stone.

III

Then winter will speak well for you, as spring;
darkness will chide the brightness down, and tell
such wonders as no migrant bird could sing;
and timelessness itself will be a bell
to end all skeins and schemes and schisms of time,
and lovelessness, translated, will be song;
hatred and ice will not escape that rhyme,
the right will flaunt the plumage of the wrong.
Fear will be fear, still, but his stars how good —
such as will guide lost mariners aright —
the frost and felspar be your holy food,
and journey's end the all-benignant night.
If love can do such things, and more, for us,
what can we be, love, if not generous?

IV

And this, your hand, is but an easy measure
of such wide wealths of space as beggar counting,
a summer summed up in a moment's pleasure,
touch, and a touch again, the total mounting
beyond compute, beyond compare, each finger
the planet's easy pace from time to terror:
chaos, within this palm, finds time to linger,
and, without recompense, work out his error.
Touch, and a touch again — each fingernail
is mooned and starred, in each a cosmos turns:
there the defeated and exhausted fail;
there in his holy fire the martyr burns;
and there, in ecstasy, the god makes bright
his own projected and applauding night.

V

As on a stage the backdrop makes the scene —
the light or bright, against which dark is shown;
or the black nothingness, the world-between,
whereon false cycloramic stars are thrown:
that emptiness, that space, for which the action
is a brief foreplay, and of small importance:
poor trifles, as of fiction, passion, faction,
before the indifferent hand lets fall the curtains —
so must our love be, love — a candle raised
against the darkness of divine neglect;
only against that void can be appraised
sureness of heart, or the heart's intellect;
yes will be yes a thousandfold; the kiss
a flower brought back broken from the abyss.

VI

This body must my only altar make;
there will I burn the miracle, and there
the bread and wine of strict communion take,
beating my heart as a deliberate prayer.
There the pure knowledge, and the only, hymns
of the divine and only Known-Unknown:
O Altitudo in the bloodstream swims,
the god of love sings in the very bone.
Here is your praise, and all of it; what more
has this sacrarium of flesh to offer?
A whisper in the brain, yet, like a shore,
wide as the sea, with all the sea can proffer:
a mystery, confined in little space:
the whole world's wonder in a single face.

VII

And search the senses — ah, but not too well!
To search the senses is to search the roots,
and the dark-loving knowledge needs its hell
to send the simple bough its simple fruits.
Not search them, no: but let them windows be
for the unsifted and untroubled light —
the great choir flooded by infinity,
the holy body like a fane made bright.
In such a light, our knowledges will meet,
nimbler than light itself, cunning as air;
our worlds, conjoined, beat with the same wingbeat,
and that divine vibration everywhere;
the body, cruciform, by godhead stilled,
like a poor church with golden rumor filled.

VIII

Or shall we turn it, turn it like the weather,
turn sunlight outward, turn the snow back north,
turn back the snow, on land and sea together,
bring from the south a cone of dazzle forth,
sweep the whole hemisphere of darkness, turn
the swimming land and sea to brilliance down —
and all that in the instant we may learn
strict interval between a laugh and frown?
No — but to better purpose let us move
the worlds that we, like light-givers, dispose:
not in our fantasy, but in our love,
shall ring the orbits of the moon, the rose;
our outward love the gods and suns to bless,
but the small sandgrain and the ant no less.

IX

Nor can time hinder us, or space embarrass,
ourselves the victor-victims of them both,
who, in a thought, deny them power to harass,
and, in a kiss, accept them, nothing loth!
What unknown circles have they, or lost regions,
wideness, or emptiness, or desolation,
what zeros of despair, in which our legions
are not already camped, and keep their station?
Their strength is our strength — how can we be weak,
who the whole wildness of the world inherit?
In us, the fierce words of creation speak;
we but give back its undiminished spirit.
Let us remember this, when we embrace:
in us are met the powers of time and space.

X

If we must speak, then let us humbly speak;
humbly becomes the great, and great we are;
ice is the silent language of the peak;
and fire the silent language of the star;
the sun is silent, the moon silent, too —
only the wind gives voice to ice or flame;
let us be modest, then, of I and You,
and give them back the hugeness whence they came.
Shadow to you, the subtle — light to me,
the nimble — and the twilight soul between,
in which, embracing, we may learn to be,
and having learned to be, may learn to mean;
then we shall speak, as the moon speaks, with snow,
our words already frozen, long ago.

XI

Blue, blue, and blue again, and blue once more,
the autumn breaks on the unbroken sea —
the blue sea breaks on the unbroken shore,
yet without breaking, ringed infinity —
blue, blue, and blue again, and blue once more,
wide as this orchard is, and wider yet —
wide as this kingdom, whose reverberant shore
is all about by clanging seas beset —
blue, blue, and blue again, and bluer still,
all-overarching heaven, fierce dome of azure,
which can outstare the eagle's eye, or kill
the intemperate heart that vaunts too much its pleasure:
this is our color, love, for it is fate;
and we will match with love that deathless hate.

XII

Time ticks, time flows, time runs, time pours his sand,
time blows his stellar flute, and with each note
touches, and so dismisses, with sure hand,
love that was precious in the blackbird's throat —
and life, more precious in the blackbird's heart,
and still more precious in his sweetheart's breast —
time, as indifferent to the blackbird's art
as to the orphaned fledglings in the nest.
Yet in this wrist that I hold out is time;
his murder here, as in your cheek; and you,
alas, my love, embody too his crime,
to whom alone you will at last be true.
Father am I of all then — you the mother;
for we embrace time who embrace each other.

XIII

And if we kiss, remember too how time
so many fools with flattering tongue has kissed —
so many kings and kingdoms praised in rhyme,
whose names no more now than the rhymes are missed.
What mountains has he not undone to dust!
What rivers rendered into sea! What space
not changed, obscured, and withered, with his lust,
which, like a hot breath, blasts the beloved face!
My love, what comfort in this dereliction,
for us, who know the ruin which we build —
we, the creative and created fiction,
this fiction by ourselves both willed and killed —
except to know, and in the knowing cherish,
that we, the loved and loving, must both perish.

XIV

How shall we phrase the all-unphraseable —
how, without tongues of flower or angel, speak?
Or, without voice of flame or glacier, tell
such silent truths as make our angel weak?
The angel is our own projected soul.
Oh, treat him tenderly; he brings us back
the little foolishness that makes us whole,
the splendid lunacy we love and lack.
How shall we praise the all-unpraisable —
my love, my love, how shall we praise this flower,
whose virtue is his scorn of heaven and hell
and his indifferent mastery of the hour?
His is a courage that dismisses seasons,
and a magnificence that scorns all reasons.

XV

Snowflake on asphodel, clear ice on rose,
frost over thistledown, the instant death
that speaks Time's judgment, turning verse to prose,
or withering June to blackness in a breath —
icicle, cheek by jowl with goldenrod,
and on the purple aster silver rime,
a web of death, bright as the web of god,
spun on these simple themes and schemes by time:
snowflake on asphodel — how clear, how bright
the blue burns through the melting star! how brave
the dying flower, and the snow how light
that on the dying flower makes his grave!
Snow's death on dying flower, yet both immortal —
love, these are you and I — enter this portal.

XVI

But these are greater names. The humbler, too,
shall suit as well: the twisted morning-glory,
its tender tip wet with the morning dew;
or the harsh plantain leaf; these tell our story.
Humble and good, are these — dog mercury
of pure simplicity and furtive blossom,
burdock and bindweed and good fumitory,
tansy and thyme, wild carrot's bleeding bosom —
and dandelion, the first and last of flowers,
and pimpernel, that must so secret be,
the small white clover, which is rightly ours,
dear to the bee, dearest to you and me —
in these our language speaks, outwitting doom;
in these pure petals is our kindom come.

XVII

As this: that I shall speak, being first to die,
in all these worlds which we have known together,
skylark in heaven, or the primrose eye,
or the wild streams and strains of April weather;
bugle of cock-crow at the daybreak blowing —
how brave that cry in darkness, how forlorn! —
these we have known together; these, still knowing,
yourself alone must greet. The selfsame horn
will sound its cheerful summons on that day
when you alone must wake, and I alone
begin the long sleep in my bed of clay,
adding earth's simple sum of stone to stone.
Yet, though I speak, and though you hear me speak,
let not the dead heart, nor the living, break.

XVIII

For brief as water falling will be death,
and brief as flower falling, or a leaf;
brief as the taking, and the giving, breath;
thus natural, thus brief, my love, is grief.
Let this too fall, as all things fall, to earth —
your grief with me be buried; let me be
the grave of all things that with me had birth —
sorrow and vanity be dead with me.
For our magnificence and kingdom is
vaster than shoreless time or hourless space:
here and forever blaze our histories
in the once-known and unforgotten face:
you, and the world, shall this bright ghost inherit:
Love, the four-wingèd and inviolate spirit.

XIX

Time will dismiss such subject shapes as these:
the thistledown, that flicks and clocks an hour;
the clock, that ticks industrious obsequies,
marking indifferent deaths of soul and flower;
the leaf, that in its time will shrink and shrivel;
the yes, that in its hour will be denied;
the soul that seeks in evil its own level,
as if for virtue none had ever died.
Time will dismiss such subject shapes as this:
the water that must dry away to nothing;
green fields laid waste in barren sand; the kiss
given and taken to an end of loathing.
Time will dismiss? But love dismisses time,
and knots him tightly in this love-knot rhyme.

XX

Snowflake, snowflower, on plum and pear, wild apple
shyest of trees, in shy and lovely blossom;
Diana, in the sun-and-shadow dapple,
blue eye, blue heaven, the half-glimpsed virgin bosom —
almighty sun, how turn the flowers all
humbly in little ranks their faces up,
following in adoration till thy fall,
each proffering to thy love his turning cup —
turning as thou turnest, and the season turns,
see how devout, in unison, they move,
while in last blue delight the skylark burns
and the rapt countryside hymns thee her love!
Yes, and to thee we turn our faces, too,
by thy rich lightning, like the year, made new.

XXI

Love, count the wildflowers on this golden bank —
count all these branchèd and leaf-bearing stems,
where, in the sun, a many-musicked rank,
they wear their white and golden diadems —
round as the sun is, as the moon is, round,
bearing them proudly, with no genuflection,
each with his starlike shadow, his own ground,
how still they stand, and yet still keep direction — !
Moon-dial or sun-dial could no truer tell
outrageous majesty of tide or hour:
the god's great violent heart beats in this bell;
eternity spreads time-rings in this flower:
and you, your hands among the blossoms counting,
are but another time and measure mounting.

XXII

And how dismember or dishevel this,
dissever item from atom, shred apart
angelic instancies that build the kiss,
dissimilate the accents of the heart,
break leaf from branch, or bough from bole, or bole
from root — distrain, or levy a distress,
on the poor minutes that compound a soul —
save for disaster, and to dispossess?
Ah, but not so. The kiss tastes bitter best
when it is solved, or partly, in despair:
nowhere shall love's head rest upon love's breast
so deeply, or so mercifully, as where
that agony of counting, lost in numbers,
worships, despairs, and kisses — and then slumbers.

XXIII

So, in the morning, when the east is strung
with the bright harp-strings of another day:
against whose glistening golden cords are sung
all things that birds can sing or words can say:
like a great page of music, whereto leaning
even the dark trees with their cordage sing,
each harbored bird and leaf with separate meaning,
the world's innumerable words for every string:
all things at praise or gaze, peach-bloom, oak-gall,
the greasy cricket waking, the quick ant
stepping in gold against that lightning, all
turned in that sudden fire to adamant:
so, as unnumbered, varied so as this,
the unresumable world that sums our kiss.

XXIV

The unresumable world that sums our kiss —
my love, if we could all that fortune summon,
which wastes its substance in the abstract 'this,'
or is dismissed as substance, or as common:
what cousin said in April, or the rain
washed from the morning; what the spider wrote
in dusty gossamer on a sun-warmed pane,
words that the sunset or the moonrise quote:
filaments, fragments, fractions — such as fever
can disarrange and disarray: the sum
of loves unowned, disowned, yet loves forever,
these that our bloodstream are, and kingdom come:
these, the unnumbered, let us love and·cherish;
which, like ourselves, if not remembered, perish.

XXV

Single and double, treble and multiple,
the flowermouth simple, or else fanged and honied,
snowflake and sun, of the same ichor full,
each as the other poor, or richly moneyed —
each with the same largesse, the immortal stream,
divine, unknowable, never-to-be-ended treasure,
the pouring texture that fulfills a dream,
or blooms a world, or points a moment's pleasure:
the flowermouth simple as a ring, and yet
how ringed with terror too, its silent bell
in the vast Nothing like a funnel set,
engulfing vortex between heaven and hell:
here is your hand, love, and the morning-glory;
which, though they differ, tell the selfsame story.

XXVI

Shape has no shape, nor will your thinking shape it,
space has no confines, and no borders time;
and yet, to think the abyss is to escape it,
or fix that horror's margin in a rhyme;
wind blows from heaven, the worlds from chaos pour,
pour into chaos, gone again; the night
foams on an emptiness that has no shore;
and all infinity like leaves in flight —
all flowing, passing, like the bloodstream, here,
that shapes its whispered moment in your hand,
shapes too the hand that holds this moment dear,
itself already pouring into sand;
yet, in the instant that we think it, will
that chaos shape our kiss, and so be still.

XXVII

How then the wingèd splendors round us tower!
Ourselves enthroned amid a hushed dominion
where rock and voice speak of the selfsame hour,
and time, like space, stoops to become our minion:
angelic presences of fire and ice,
the humbler presences of tick and mote,
whisper of thunder to the oriole's voice,
evening and morning in a single note.
There past and future, for ourselves conjoined,
are the vast vault that shadows our embrace;
for us, that heavenly arch of stars was groined,
god's waste and wreckage builded for your face:
all things despised, dispersed, in us unite,
and shape a glory of the Infinite.

XXVIII

Green, green, and green again, and greener still,
spring towards summer bends the immortal bow,
and northward breaks the wave of daffodil,
and northward breaks the wave of summer's snow:
green, green, and green again, and greener yet,
wide as this forest is, which counts its leaves,
wide as this kingdom, in a green sea set,
which round its shores perpetual blossom weaves —
green, green, and green again, and green once more,
the season finds its term — then greenest, even,
when frost at twilight on the leaf lies hoar,
and one cold star shines bright in greenest heaven:
but love, like music, keeps no seasons ever;
like music, too, once known is known forever.

XXIX

How many clouds must wraith-like rise from ocean,
shine and assemble towards the drag-net sun —
how vast and slow, how subtle, all that motion,
before the darkening, and the rain begun!
How many nights of rain to end this drouth,
the dark sky laboring on earth's laboring breast!
How many kisses, love, to brim that mouth,
and lead the goddess to her fruitful rest!
O southwest wind, bring back the rain, and bring
propitious darkness to my love and me:
though love no season knows, let this be spring,
and in my shadow let her fruitful be.
Trefoil and cinquefoil shine on earth's bare bosom;
this be our omen, that we too may blossom.

XXX

Sun-born and moon-born, sun-birth and moon-birth, we
like the twinned stars were twinned, and twinned to dance,
each in the other's flame, the Gemini,
circling and changing for each change and chance:
flame-light and swift, our steps divinely vary,
yet never farther than each circle rings;
thus to time's end we dance our alfridary,
bringing to pass, and pace, predicted things.
As the great Ptolemy, proud chronocrat,
plumbed the Chaldean tables, drew his chart,
set out his watery moon, marked this from that,
the cabalistic housings of his heart,
so we these names and numbers, all foreseeing,
dance, like the day his weather, into being.

XXXI

These items in our chronicle therefore set:
first, the wide sunrise, and the idiot's stare,
in the pale east one bright star loitering yet,
thereto the rooftops leaning hard and bare;
then, the strung sound of birdsong, and the east
like a vast theater ablaze with light,
the music louder, and the light increased,
and the plucked sound of harpstrings bright and tight —
the idiot's stare with golden wonder filled,
grass then to shiver, stone and stream to glisten,
the leaves, and the strung sound of birdsong, stilled,
all the arched night turned back, and hushed, to listen;
and then the heartbeat, and the dream — and then
fanfare of cock-crow, and our sun again.

XXXII

These items, too, put down. The golden spokes
whirl over heaven from the bright axletree,
on that fierce rim a curlèd vapor smokes,
and then the dazzling hub too swift to see —
the clouds, like horses rayed and rifted, breaking
unnumbered lightnings upward, the soft thunder
rolled through the shadows and the curtains, waking
all the earth's creeping kind for savage wonder.
Dragons of sleep and dream mount up that air —
these are our monsters and our demons, love —
our angels, too. And we, already there,
over the firmament to Nothing move;
yet hear the fly buzz on the ceiling, too,
and, with a handclasp, keep the I and You.

XXXIII

Yet, despite splendor, on the margin kept,
as might the wildflowers be that fledge a stream,
cowslip and blue flag, faithful while we slept,
the pouring texture that fulfills a dream:
your elbow touching mine; your iris flecked
with knotted light, golden-and-amber stitches,
like that with which the jewel-weed is checked,
or purple flag with veinèd throat enriches;
the ladybird, across your finger walking,
who parts the spotted wing-case, shows a wing,
as softly furls it back, while we are talking,
then, like a jewel, sits upon your ring;
these on the margin of our sunrise be,
lest time be faceless in eternity.

XXXIV

As leaf from wood, the dream will grow from being;
when the east opens, the eyes open too;
when the night opens, then begins our seeing:
we wake, we separate, for I and You,
look back on night, and all by night confounded,
all life, all love, all time; and then, reborn,
rejoice to find our love by love surrounded,
the same world waking to the selfsame horn —
all to be loved anew, and with the loving
shaped to our dream, ourselves too shaped therewith,
the worlds-in-worlds, of dream and being, moving
greatly together in a single myth:
thus, with each step we measure towards the east,
is the horizon of our love increased.

XXXV

High on those toppling balconies of cloud
that eastward from the world to nothing lean,
over starred Yggdrasill, the many-boughed,
at daybreak to the world's end we have seen —
upon those glittering terraces set foot
where rainbow's foot was never softlier set,
nor the bright lightning's swift and fiery root,
that dreamlike splits the golden parapet —
topples, reforms — yet walk securely there,
all the wide morning in one river spread,
a dragon caught in daybreak's yellow hair,
the stars like silver javelins downward shed —
a phantom, gone, which we can see, and love,
who on our firmament like godhead move.

XXXVI

Yet inward look as well, where bloodstream beats
intolerable pain, and therein seek
islands and kingdoms, source of frosts and heats,
cancer and chaos; where the fissures reek,
and time's slow drainage downward is to death,
atom from atom dripping, drop from drop;
a world, in the vast mystery of breath,
upheld by breath, which when that stops must stop.
Here, too, we steep our hands and hearts; and hence,
as from the marigold of magnificent day,
bring back, renewed and rich, magnificence,
still the more sumptuous that it will not stay;
here, too, our balconies, from which to see
end and beginning, and the star-bearing tree.

XXXVII

Sunrise or moonrise, outward or inward, love
bends as the dream bends to the curving wish,
shapes to the trembling and tender shape above
as to the dark world of his stream the fish,
bends as the seed bends to the vault of shell,
curves as the thought curves to the arch of mind,
in heaven an angel and a fiend in hell,
all things delighted in, all things divined —
and see how heavenward on these notes that make
a simple tune, as if by stepping-stones,
the halcyon path to subtler airs we take,
shedding like thistledown this flesh, these bones —
and yet even there, in that diviner voice,
hear the twinned 'you' speak softly, and rejoice!

XXXVIII

Separate, we join; and joined, we separate,
thus to rejoin once more, but bringing news —
you, of the morning rose by heaven's gate,
and I, from hell, the nightshade's poisonous dews —
each with that separate knowledge, the twinned star
hidden and secret in the hand, the heart,
each day devotion brought of strange and far,
each day, each morning, a new world to start.
How without wonder can we wake, to see
each in the other that unknown abyss —
time winding backward to infinity,
or at vast standstill in this touch, this kiss?
Nor will that morning come which is not strange,
who have, each day, such wonders to exchange.

XXXIX

Bird's eye or snake's eye, bright through leaves; the leaf
inscribed by sun with an all-cryptic message;
downflash of raindrop, no less slight and brief
than these; or snake or bird in soundless passage;
or as the cloud's rim, golden against the moon,
golden and bronze, swimming like foam to vanish,
fire-phosphor seethed on sand, and gone as soon,
immortal light to burnish or replenish;
one secret shape of cloud; one look; one mark
hurriedly notched on the all-hurrying sun;
bird's eye and snake's eye seen; then instant dark;
but not before the unplumbed world there known:
how swiftly turn the pages of this book,
whose secrets flash and vanish, even as we look!

XL

Look! In your eyes, the image of a cloud
tinily flecks the far-off blue, and moves
slowly away, and gone — a ghost, a shroud,
dispersed in heaven, and gone . . . Meanwhile, our loves
stare round it, stare beyond it, there to see
the multitudes of joy that choir this hour:
handclasp and morning star, the secret glee
that shapes a cheek, an eyebrow, or a flower:
the brazen bee, and the seven-banded light
that blades with bronze the oaktops — all at once
blending and binding, the whole world grown bright,
almost intolerably with joy the sun's:
how rich, how good — and yet, how richer, even
knowing all this, to watch that cloud cross heaven.

XLI

Here is life's handiwork — a page inscribed,
the name, forgotten, in the title set —
as if one said, The moonlit sky is ribbed
with golden clouds which sky will soon forget:
here too life's handiwork — a line corrected,
the secret cypher in the margin noted —
as if one said, The blue flag, when dissected,
is many-marked, gold-veined, and crow's-foot-throated:
and yet, anonymous — unknown alike
he that in clouds his name on heaven wrote,
and he whose pencil could so finely strike
gold vein from purple in the blue flag's throat:
my love, we too, like these, shall leave no name:
but have, like them, in flower or heaven, our fame.

XLII

Yesterday was another world, that broke
its leagues of furious space before our feet;
yesterday was another word, that spoke
magnificent chaos, where all meanings meet.
Tomorrow has its furious leagues to come,
all the dark shore where break the stars like foam;
tomorrow's thunder speaks the word of doom
under whose lightning we shall find a home.
Gaily over the phantom bridge we climb
from chaos past to chaos yet to be —
mountains and rivers, spellbound in our rhyme,
under our feet the empyrean sea —
kingfisher souls, wind-borne, the wingèd race,
whose flight shall knit together time and space.

XLIII

Whip up the horses of the Yes and No!
Day ends, time hurries, we have worlds to see,
our chariot be these winds of thought that blow
magniloquent meanings betwixt you and me:
if the void sunders downward, let us fall,
nethermost whistling Nothing there to find —
these but our nightmares, our own dragons, all,
who through the chaos but extend the mind.
Now shall our daybreaks hammered be of gold —
of love our empire, who all things shall love:
morning and evening are at hand, behold,
and to one measure, by our blessing, move:
all's here that is, or will be, or has been.
Rejoice, my love, our histories begin!

BROWNSTONE ECLOGUES

Sursum Corda

Speak to us only with the killer's tongue,
the animal madness of the fierce and young:
and from that agony we'll learn to break
our human hearts, but for thy suffering's sake.

Then will the mind, exploring passion, learn
through all this burning world how thou dost burn:
in every particle, and hour, thy death,
in every painful leaf the creative breath.

And thy stone's hardness, we will learn this too,
with our wet flesh, our flesh as soft as dew;
through this small looking-glass to guess at length
the savage knowledges beyond our strength.

Wherever death's red hand unhusks a heart,
or tiger ice rips the meek hills apart,
there we lie down alone, and lonely spend
the spirit's silence to the spirit's end.

Lost from thy rock-face to thy last abyss,
we faint in darkness for an age; yet this
ends in an hour; and in the sun with thee

we wear the rainbow and the rain, and see:
we break the numbers and the names, and see:
we are thyself, thy heart of light, and see.

Saint Ambrose: Early Morning

Daybreak, on slatting shutter and windowpane —
rise, and touch foot to floor.
Over your head the tin roof hums with rain,
Saint Ambrose tower peals four.

Now the slowed heart that all night long has beat
through yours and the body's slumber
seems, in the listening silence, to repeat
'without number, without number —'

yes, without number the things that come to end,
the idle promise broken;
in every tenement, in every room, a betrayed friend,
the deadly sentence spoken.

Down the dark street the faithless footfalls ring
where selfish to selfish moves,
as, to her treacherous end, turns one more spring,
and treason with cheat involves.

On your own hand how many deaths still bleed,
which the hand alone forgets!
Here, there, and everywhere, the unanswered need,
dead loves like unpaid debts.

Here the fly buzzes, and the fingernail
scrapes on the faded sheet:
there, through the sparkling window, the east grows pale;
and slowly upward beat

innumerable and anonymous as birds
on the dull void of air,
alas, the whole city's unhappy, unspoken words,
one vast and ragged prayer.

Stone to stone reaches, brick to brick is joined;
the votive candle shines
upward a little on arches grieved and groined
and shabbily twinkling shrines.

Stone to stone reaches, brick is joined to brick:
and along the sweating aisle,
look, at each Station of the Cross, the sick
kneel down; in a little while

who doubts but they will find an end to illness —
summer, and the long lost ships?
Or even a little love; or, out of stillness,
a blinding apocalypse!

But no. In darkness, behind the shaken church,
ribbed like the hurricane,
roars past the apse, while walls and windows lurch,
the first suburban train.

Doctors' Row

Snow falls on the cars in Doctors' Row and hoods the headlights;
snow piles on the brownstone steps, the basement deadlights;
fills up the letters and names and brass degrees
on the bright brass plates, and the bright brass holes for keys.

Snow hides, as if on purpose, the rows of bells
which open the doors to separate cells and hells:
to the waiting-rooms, where the famous prepare for headlines,
and humbler citizens for their humbler deadlines.

And in and out, and out and in, they go,
the lamentable devotees of Doctors' Row;
silent and circumspect — indeed, liturgical;
their cries and prayers prescribed, their penance surgical.

No one complains — no one presumes to shriek —
the walls are very thick, and the voices weak.
Or the cries are whisked away in noiseless cabs,
while nurse, in the alley, empties a pail of swabs.

Miserable street! — through which your sweetheart hurries,
lowers her chin, as the snow-cloud stings and flurries;
thinks of the flower-stall, by the church, where you
wait like a clock, for two, for half-past two;

thinks of the roses banked on the steps in snow,
of god in heaven, and the world above, below;
widens her vision beyond the storm, her sight
the infinite rings of an immense delight;

all to be lived and loved — O glorious All!
Eastward or westward, Plato's turning wall;
the sky's blue streets swept clean of silent birds
for an audience of gods, and superwords.

The Nameless Ones

Pity the nameless, and the unknown, where
bitter in heart they wait on the stonebuilt stair,
bend to a wall, forgotten, the freezing wind
no bitterer than the suburbs of the mind;

who from an iron porch lift sightless eyes,
a moment, hopeless, to inflaming skies;
shrink from the light as quickly as from pain,
twist round a corner, bend to the wall again;

are to be seen leaning against a rail
by ornamental waters where toy yachts sail;
glide down the granite steps, touch foot to float,
hate, and desire, the sunlight on the boat;

explore a sullen alley where ash-cans wait,
symbols of waste and want, at every gate;
emerge in sun to mingle with the crowd,
themselves most silent where the world most loud;

anonymous, furtive, shadows in shadow hidden;
who lurk at the garden's edge like guests unbidden;
stare through the leaves with hate, yet wait to listen
as bandstand music begins to rise and glisten;

the fierce, the solitary, divine of heart,
passionate, present, yet godlike and apart;
who, in the midst of traffic, see a vision;
and, on a park bench, come to a last decision.

North Infinity Street

The alarm clocks tick in a thousand furnished rooms,
tick and are wound for a thousand separate dooms;
all down both sides of North Infinity Street
you hear that contrapuntal pawnshop beat.

Hall bedrooms, attic rooms, where the gas-ring sings,
rooms in the basement where the loud doorbell rings;
carpeted or bare, by the rail at the head of the stair,
the curtains drawn, a mirror, a bed, and a chair,

in midnight darkness, when the last footfall creaks,
in northeast rain, when the broken window leaks,
at dawn, to the sound of dishes, the kitchen steam,
at dusk, when the muted radio croons a dream,

there, amid combs and the waiting shoes and socks,
and the bathrobes hung in closets, tick the clocks:
on the chest of drawers, on the table beside the bed,
facing the pillow, facing the recumbent head:

yes, from here to forever, from here to never,
one long sidereal curve of ticking fever,
all down both sides of North Infinity Street
you hear that contrapuntal pawnshop beat.

The Junk-cart

Some to pretence, and on proud knees pretend
knowledge of god, a prospect without end;
whisper a prayer in stained-glass-window-rose,
nod to the priest or presbyter, repose

in the loud organ's shuddering imprecision,
or even, in that spasm, beget a vision:
the thousand wings, and thousand eyes, of love,
become for them, and them alone, a dove.

Prettily banked, the peacock candles shine
in shrines of alabaster, serpentine;
dim in their gold, archaic saints look down,
or else look up, for holy cup and crown.

Here of a Sabbath fur and feather preen,
eager to see and eager to be seen;
above gilt hymnals the stone faces turn,
and, as they sing, in careful rapture burn.

Not this, nor here, the god our fathers knew —
those holiest fathers, the unknown, who grew
coldly as oaktrees in the north wind grow,
thus, as the tree his weather, the god to know:

not in these walls, but there, outside, he waits,
human and changeless by the city gates;
in the slight rain, symbol of crown and cross,
the junk-cart Jew and his quixotic horse.

Who Shapes a Balustrade?

Who shapes a balustrade, who but the sun?
By what hand carved or made, done and undone,
this angry tower where stand the angels four,
trumpet in hand, and waiting to adore?

Who the first granite laid, who but the light?
Cornerstone and keystone made, and placed aright,
rounded the golden dome, sharpened the spire,
the smooth arch curved for Rome, the column for Tyre?

Yes, from the sunlight sings each guise of stone,
each wingèd archway springs from sun alone;
he bids the rooftree soar, the stairway climb,
squares or exalts a door, steeples a chime.

As on a coast of rock the ocean breaks
so, at the sun's knock, cornice or louver wakes,
fretwork and filigree of sunborn rock
waking at dawn to be time's measure and mock.

See how with golden pace each tower in turn
he bids exist, and face, and then to burn!
Bids windows open wide, the entablature
above the column's pride blaze and be pure!

So, out of sunlight built, the city sings,
a reef of stone and gilt where the surf rings;
Atlantis under air, cloud-shadow-swept,
earth's wish, and the sun's prayer, in granite kept.

The Sounding

Blue sky, blue noon, and the secret line is flung:
once more, the Mariner his sounding takes;

from heaven's blue bridge once more the Lead is swung,
and downward through the ethereal Ocean breaks

the divine Plummet and the invisible cord
past sun-drowned Vega, and Orion's Belt.
Now the unfathomed is fathomed with a Word:
Earth, and this City, by their heartbeat felt.

Like a small lightning through the clouds' pale glooms,
at intervals unguessed by the faint sun,
down to this stony reef, the city, comes
that cord, unloosed so soundlessly to run;

and on the bridge that arches the unknown
the Master Mariner, his sounding sure,
carves in the ice: A kingdom overthrown —
man kills his children. But the birds endure.

Clearing and Colder

The mother church with twenty bells at seven
quarters in various voice our path to heaven,
the sleeping and the unsleeping rolled together
into the morning and the unknown weather.

East wind along a one-way street, we listen
for footfall, rainfall, see the talons glisten,
clutching at glass, invisible birds, and gone
to drip from fire-escape to muddied stone.

The postman's ring, and so-and-so steps out,
Kelly or Feibleman, to the newsboy's shout;
limps with a cane, planting the rubber tip
on bubbling brick, but careful not to slip.

The iceman's tongs, the milkman's bottles clink —
once more, now, it is later than you think;

the world's at war, the harbor fills with rain,
come all ye faithful, rise, to work again —

the desks are waiting in the tiers of sky,
the mother church strikes nine, hello, good-bye,
westward the turning world, and westward we,
for whom the evening papers may not be.

But meanwhile in the rain, and like a charm,
the morning paper folded beneath the arm,
the umbrella steadied against a sudden gust,
the hat-brim pulled hard down. In god we trust.

Two Visions

Between the curbstone and the brownstone stair,
where spiked iron railings enclose a grass parterre,
the red brick sidewalk blooms in midday sun.
One hour parking; we may park till one.

A pair of cedars fades in faded pots.
Recently watered, the forget-me-nots
droop in the parterre's border. A cigarette
twines its fume with the fume of mignonette.

Above these steps, the Art Show lifts grave portals
for fifty up-and-coming, but young, immortals.
In the plush *entresol,* in swift embrace,
a pale girl meets loud Bacchus face to face.

The tiger glares. The spavined whore leers up
with one eye rounded above a rounded cup.
Here the eclectics gather breast and bosom
as florists, for a bride's bouquet, dead blossom.

Vision! Who has it? The policeman on his beat.
Who, to the whistle, thrilling the nervous heat,

answers with sudden heart, a dream of red,
and sees on the sidewalk, haloed, a god fall dead.

Hatteras Calling

Southeast, and storm, and every weathervane
shivers and moans upon its dripping pin,
ragged on chimneys the cloud whips, the rain
howls at the flues and windows to get in,

the golden rooster claps his golden wings
and from the Baptist Chapel shrieks no more,
the golden arrow into the southeast sings
and hears on the roof the Atlantic Ocean roar.

Waves among wires, sea scudding over poles,
down every alley the magnificence of rain,
dead gutters live once more, the deep manholes
hollo in triumph a passage to the main.

Umbrellas, and in the Gardens one old man
hurries away along a dancing path,
listens to music on a watering-can,
observes among the tulips the sudden wrath,

pale willows thrashing to the needled lake,
and dinghies filled with water; while the sky
smashes the lilacs, swoops to shake and break,
till shattered branches shriek and railings cry.

Speak, Hatteras, your language of the sea:
scour with kelp and spindrift the stale street:
that man in terror may learn once more to be
child of that hour when rock and ocean meet.

The Habeas Corpus Blues

In the cathedral the acolytes are praying,
in the tavern the teamsters are drinking booze,
in his attic at dusk the poet is playing,
the poet is playing the Habeas Corpus Blues.

The poet prefers the black keys to the white,
he weaves himself a shroud of simple harmonics;
across the street a house burns, in its light
he skeins more skilfully his bland ironics.

All down the block the windows bloom with faces,
the paired eyes glisten in the turning glare;
and the engines throb, and up a ladder races
an angel with a helmet on his hair.

He cracks the window in with a golden axe,
crawls through the smoke and disappears forever;
the roof whams in, and the whole city shakes;
the faces at the windows say *ah!* and *never!*

And then the hour. And near and far are striking
the belfry clocks; and from the harbour mourn
the tugboat whistles, much to the poet's liking,
smoke-rings of bronze to the fevered heavens borne.

The hydrants are turned off, the hose rewound,
the dirty engines are no longer drumming;
the angel's golden helmet has been found,
the fire is out, the insurance man is coming.

And in the cathedral the acolytes are praying,
and in the tavern the teamsters are drinking booze,
and in his attic the poet is still playing,
the poet is playing the Habeas Corpus Blues.

Anaesthesia

This side, grey hospital; that side, grey jail.
The nurse, stiff-coifed, blue-uniformed, and pale,
buttons her cloak, decides to cross the Square,
and strolls by the Esplanade to take the air.

Whispers of ether and formaldehyde
blow from her hair along the riverside.
Under the hollowed wall the short waves splash,
and, among boats and floats, set ducks awash.

Ducks in a row; eyes down, tails up, they go;
like little steamers, or tug and barge in tow;
sparrows in chickweed at the water's edge;
pigeons picking at gravel, swans in the sedge;

and the police-boat, with a listless flag,
indolent in the sun, no corpse to drag,
shows off its polished brasses to the sky;
smoke in a wake of bubbles, it putt-putts by,

aimed at the bridge of arched and gothic stone,
where now the quick train rattles and is gone —
swoops down between the hospital and jail,
honing into the subway the curved rail.

And then the scream, the high scream of the steel;
as if together wheel and rail might feel,
sentient and soft, the agonies that thresh
the meeker mysteries of bone and flesh;

and as she hears, forbears to turn her head,
there, there behind her, to the silent bed,
where the true heart still tries, in vain, to keep
measure of pain and darkness, light and sleep.

Whisper Under Asphalt

Morning: the golden lava pours to stone.
The flesh is built of light, the structure bone.
Steel, stone, and brick, the surface burns away,
cornice and smooth façade, the face of clay:

burned off, burned down to dust by the blue sky,
powdered and burned: that magnifying eye
strips to forgotten earth all transient things.
Under the subway the mud lives and sings,

the flint cries sharply, the reed lifts its head,
the yellow iris springs beneath your tread;
and the long asphalt, in a gauze of heat,
falls from the river like a winding sheet.

Here water flows once more, and willows dream
with blossoms in their hair — the immortal stream
blest by the gods and nymphs; speech here is earth;
this is the granite where the blood had birth;

still living, fresh, as water lives, or stone,
the holy water to bless flesh and bone —
wakes under asphalt, as the morning wakes,
and once more into running laughter breaks.

Old Goody Two-Shoes

Turn from the Board Room; think of saintliness;
measure in stocks and bonds that humbleness;
sharpen a pencil, to give point to this
poor fool who wants no metamorphosis;

who guards all day, ill-clad, a freezing door;
or on her hands and knees scrubs a stone floor;
yet nothing envies or resents, but still
holds all of life as good, and nothing ill;

wastes a whole age in an absurd intent,
loveless, but from his purpose never bent;
adds to mad notes yet one more madder yet,
and with each note, and vision, an added debt;

denies herself, and those who trust her, food,
for greater glory of all mankind's good;
will not be hurt, by those who disbelieve,
nor in defeat, or doubt, will reconceive — :

these are the scholars of the love of life;
hope is their husband, and delight their wife;
simple parishioners of the daily stone,
to which they pledge the faithfulness of bone;

as, while you call a loan, endorse a note,
the weekend planned, and tickets for the boat,
old Goody Two-Shoes at the corner stands,
the tray of votive shoestrings in her hands.

The Lovers

In this glass palace are flowers in golden baskets.
In that grim brownstone castle are silver caskets.
The caskets watch and wait, and the baskets wait,
for a certain day and hour, and a certain gate.

Wonderfully glow the colors in this bright palace.
Superb the *flora,* in pyx and vase and chalice.
The glass is steamed with a stifling tuberose breath;
and lilies too, of the valley of the shadow of death.

The caskets are satin-lined, with silver handles;
and the janitor sings 'they'll soon be lighting candles.'
He sweeps the sidewalk, and as he sweeps he sings,
in praise of a hearse with completely noiseless springs.

Hush — the conspiracy works, it has crossed the street:
some day, and it's not far off, the lovers will meet:
casket and basket will soon set forth together
on a joyful journey, no matter how bleak the weather:

in a beautiful beetle-black hearse with noiseless tread,
basket and casket together will hie to bed;
and start on a pullman journey to a certain gate,
punctually, at a certain hour, on a certain date.

How to Accompany the Moon
Without Walking

Harsh, harsh, the maram grass on the salt dune,
seen by the cricket's eye against the harbor moon,
anchor-frost and seaward, the lighthouse moon —

the bellbuoy-beating moon, the tiderip bronze
ringing above deep channels and old bones,
the hawsehole moon, where blood and money runs —

foremast and mainmast moon, up harbor still,
island and smokestack moon, and the wind-spill
falling from the sail-throat for the moon to fill —

up harbor, the old wharf moon, the capstan moon,
and round it the capstan bars, the heeling tune,
India Wharf, we'll bring you to Rio soon —

the shipyard moon, the grain-elevator moon,
derrick and gantry, and the turbine croon
sweet under seafoam as a bird in June —

red-warehouse moon, yacht-basin moon, where spars
tangle and telegraph with stays and stars —
hi ho, the queen of accordions and guitars —

ship-chandler moon, sea-boots and Wharf Street shine,
the ropewalk moon that spins in turpentine,
sail-loft invaded with a pour of silver twine —

and high! up spinning! skyscraper tipped on purple!
skyscraper moon, and high! for the stare of people —
skysign and belltower moon, moon for the steeple —

bells breaking bronze, gold, down, the scattered tinkle,
silver-bell moon, cornice and rooftop twinkle,
Christmas and graveyard moon, the tinsel sprinkle —

and dead, the stockyard moon, where blood drips down,
dead longhorn and mute snout; the barrelhouse moon,
moonmusic doubling, rigadoon, jigadoon —

so down, and down, who will be darkened soon,
red and green lights, the pallid airport moon —
ah! on the flying field, the captive balloon!

and cold; for the rim of night, the earth's black arc,
swings up, blots out the stars, to the last spark;
while, underworld, the moon drowns dead and dark.

South End

The benches are broken, the grassplots brown and bare,
the laurels dejected, in this neglected square.
Dogs couple undisturbed. The roots of trees
heave up the bricks in the sidewalk as they please.

Nobody collects the papers from the grass,
nor the dead matches, nor the broken glass.

The elms are old and shabby; the houses, around,
stare lazily through paintless shutters at forgotten ground.

Out of the dusty fountain, with the dust,
the leaves fly up like birds on a sudden gust.
The leaves fly up like birds, and the papers flap,
or round the legs of benches wrap and unwrap.

Here, for the benefit of some secret sense,
warm-autumn-afternoon finds permanence.
No one will hurry, or wait too long, or die:
all is serenity, under a serene sky.

Dignity shines in old brick and old dirt,
in elms and houses now hurt beyond all hurt.
A broken square, where little lives or moves;
these are the city's earliest and tenderest loves.

Music

The calyx of the oboe breaks,
silver and soft the flower it makes.
And next, beyond, the flute-notes seen
now are white and now are green.

What are these sounds, what daft device,
mocking at flame, mimicking ice?
Musicians, will you never rest
from strange translation of the breast?

The heart, from which all horrors come,
grows like a vine, its gourd a drum;
the living pattern sprawls and climbs
eager to bear all worlds and times:

trilling leaf and tinkling grass
glide into darkness clear as glass;
then the musicians cease to play
and the world is waved away.

The Lady in Pink Pyjamas

The lady in pink pyjamas, in Pilgrim Place,
the lady with pencilled eyebrows and masquelike face.
all day, yes all day long, she is sitting there:
the lady with the yellow eyes, the platinum hair.

Outside her furnished room, on the brownstone stoop,
alone, yet one of the children, a changing group,
(children who come to play, and stare, and stay)
the lady in pink pyjamas waits all day.

She is older than the rocks on which she sits.
The yellow eyes, in the sunlight, shrink to slits.
The mouth is enamelled, it is serpentine;
the golden glare of the eyes is leonine.

The aged lioness dreams in the fly-loud zoo,
the amber eyes look down, they sift you through;
profound, contemptuous, a slow and amorous glare,
and something that melts, and sweetens, in that stare;

as of your death — half wished, and all foreseen;
as of your heart — unwashed, and all obscene;
as of your life — a thing of shreds and patches;
as of your love — a dance of beds and latches.

The lady in pink pyjamas knows them all,
the lady who sits in sun on the brownstone wall.
Deep is the welcome in those gilded eyes,
which know all hate, all love, and no surprise:

deep as a rock-cave in the starred Sahara
those golden hollows ambushed with mascara,
where, in all moonlit flight, is no oasis,
and no anabasis, only horror's stasis.

And — strange! — she has a bicycle, and this too,
somehow, in Pilgrim Place, looks old, though new.
She and the children mount it to ride in turns
as far as the Park, and the statue of Robert Burns.

Weather on Rooftrees

Summer, fall, winter, spring, the sky's blue waves
break and foam over the terrestrial architraves,
ruined bird's-nested cornices undone
by the alternate rage of frost and sun.

Rooftops pour down the shine, old gutters spout,
frayed eaves drip water or fire, day in, day out,
starlight whipped off warped saddleboards by rain,
fog torn by moonlight or the hurricane.

Where's North Wind gone, that froze the harbor's face?
Our one true love as old earth falls through space:
straight from the North Star like a trumpet blown,
earth, like the moon, a snowball packed on stone.

Summer, fall, winter, spring, the sky's lost leaves
blow, flash, drift, by roof-valleys, earth's mountain eaves,
pale shooting-stars, like exhalations, gone
past us and into nothing, forever down.

And we ourselves, cram full of dooms as this,
rich in possessions of ruin and the abyss,
sing to the North Star and the North Wind, sing
death and birth, summer, fall, winter, spring.

Clock and Compass

The clock, man's fear of time's short hour,
hums like a heart hung in a tower.
The weathervane, man's fear of the west,
hymns in terror that land of rest.

Together clock and weathervane
rejoice in pouring sun and rain.
It is in vain, and all in vain,
when man is gone, we shall remain.

Three Star Final

Wait here, and I'll be back, though the hours divide,
and the city streets, perplexed, perverse, delay
my hurrying footsteps, and the clocks deride
with grinning faces from the long wall of day:

wait here, beneath your narrow scrip of sky,
reading the headlines, while the snowflakes touch
on scarce-dried ink the news that thousands die,
die, and are not remembered overmuch:

yes, the unnumbered dead, whom none esteemed,
our other selves, too late or little loved;
now in the dust, proud eyes unknown, undreamed,
those who begged pity while we stood unmoved.

How can we patch our world up, now it's broken?
You, with your guilty heart, wait here and think,
while I strive back through lies and truths unspoken,
and, in the suburbs, the sunset snow turns pink:

you, in this dead-end street, which now we leave
for a more expansive, a more expensive, view;
snow falling, on a disastrous Christmas Eve,
and neon death at the end of the Avenue.

All the Radios

Far off, the yellow suburbs fade,
the winter dusk a bonfire made;
sunset grins through the balustrade
above the five-and-dime arcade;
listen — from every balcony
whispers the selfsame melody;
and prothalamiums begin
to touch the adulterous violin.

Inward escape: no more shall be
the druid loves of gale and tree;
wild air nor water rage no more
to death on this defeated shore.
Each heart the other with beauty wounds —
each must be hurt. The evening sounds
more freely now with pain and cry
as into love the lovers die.

Strike out the street-lights and the scene —
no mischief come these loves between;
towers and domes and silent roofs
bare to the starlight's crystal hoofs;
city and sky till break of day
thus to prolong their nuptial play;
till cries from every balcony
a morning-glory melody.

The Street That Took a Wrong Turning

Weep, for the street has lost its reputation.
They call it now the Alley of Assignation.
The houses, of peeling stucco, show their shame:
furnished apartments of ill, or little, fame.

Nightlong the doorbells cry, insistent thrill
through hot anatomies of stone and steel.
The doors grin open, and then hiss shut, all night,
in each lunette a discreetly hooded light.

Behind bead curtains the tipsy palmist sings,
waits for the telephone, slips off her rings,
then bathes her hands, and once more celebrates
the nightly encaenia of the heartless fates;

while overhead the changing footsteps pass
in endless recital of the *amo, amas,*
and laughter spurts down speaking-tubes, with clink
of ice in glasses as madam pours a drink.

Soothsay? No truth remains, here, to explore:
nothing unknown behind that whispering door.
Even the children guess, the few there are,
and wear their sacred knowledge like a scar.

The Census-Takers

Stranger, did you ever play ball in a vacant lot?
Will you lend us the loan of a match? or spare us a dime?
Did you hear of the murder? Would you like us to show you the
    spot?
Or like us to re-enact — on the spot — the crime?

Did you play ground-cricket by the light of the stars with a stick —
Tapped from the curb and tipped out of sight in the sky?
Was the street ever covered with straw when your mother was sick?
Will you visit the Funeral Home, and alone, when you die?

Over which shoulder, stranger, do you squint at the moon?
And where is the ferry, that meets you at half-past six?
What time is it now by the heart — too late? Too soon?
Will you hurry and tell us? That river, down there, is the Styx —

And we are the census-takers; the questions that ask
from corner and street, from lamp-post and sign and face;
The questions that later tonight will take you to task,
When you sit down alone, to think, in a lonely place.

Did you ever play blind-man's buff in the bat-flit light?
Stranger, whose heart did you break? and what else did you do? —
The census-takers are coming to ask you tonight;
The truth will be hurrying home, and it's time you knew.

Solitaire

And in the river the nameless body sifts
through stiffening fingers and the seaweed hair
this ultimate of agony, that drifts
the will beyond the point where sense can bear:

out of its world of tracks and telegrams,
the impedimenta of a choice and aim,
the marked time-tables and the diagrams,
inherited with birth and growth and name:

at the precise point of the hour unnoted,
alone, as all at such an hour must be,
severance made, the last cry horror-throated,
and sought deliverance — again — in a strange sea.

Who would be walking still, but for that choice,
yourself, with ten cents in your pocket left,
stood by the river wall, and found a voice,
of all but will to loss of will bereft;

and in the river the nameless body only,
with the short movements of the water moving,
the eyes open, and the white face lonely,
plaintiff no more, and done with the farce of loving.

Ballade d'Hiver: after Steinlen

Here at twilight, in December, long ago,
under the street-lamp, in the rain that turned to snow,
rain mixed with snow, the wet flakes soft and slow,
she said farewell, and turned away to go —

the small face shy in lamplight, and on the veil
a snowflake melting starlike — ah, how frail,
how burdened with the world's griefs, she seemed, how pale,
as the sad eyes lifted their 'All is of no avail!' —

To snow, and the world's darkness, she gave that look, —
and the long cruelty of time, she whom the world forsook;
to love, and loveliness, which the world so mistook,
and flame — the pure miracle! flame in the mountain brook!

Yes, it was this, in the secret room, she had sung to you,
pleading and piteous, as the deep song thrilled you through;
'sad song, sad singer, what will tomorrow do,
to you, to me, who denied the god we knew?'

Up the rich chords the rich voice slowly climbed:
sorrow, tomorrow — how sadly the words were rhymed!
Heartbreak so well prepared-for, so well-timed,
and the last cry with the last arpeggio chimed!

Thus, in the shuttered room (you see it still)
white hands on whiter keys wove out their skill,
that the pure song from hopelessness might distill
innocence, at least, and spring — 'One crystal daffodil!'

Yet, when that exaltation came to end,
and, waiting, you saw the pale brow slowly bend,
bend on the opened music-page, to lend
beauty to beauty, heard her cry, 'My friend — !'

how that false spring to falser summer turned,
and, with her trembling, the winter solstice burned!
Blind, blind, the others! You, only, had discerned,
known, after all, how desperately she yearned — !

And, yes, still yearned, still dreamed, though none should know,
sad, self-pitying, as she turned away to go — :
under the street-lamp, in the rain that turned to snow,
here at twilight, in December, long ago.

The Five-fifteen Farewell

Under the gantry, red-and-green-light-starred,
the last ailanthus in the railroad yard
lets fall to dust these fingers of yellow leaf.
The skeleton cries to cold, Be brief, be brief.

Look, in the sulphur sunset you will see it plain,
o traveller, you who peer from the evening train:
hard-knotted, bare, intense, at the edge of night,
it lifts fierce arms in prayer to the last of light.

Soon steam will freeze, the whistles mourn with frost;
the long rails, riveted and ice-embossed,
under the groaning wheels hear winter's beat,
the hot flange shrieking as it grinds the sleet.

The smoke slips cloudlike under the station roof,
spirals, and dissipates in heaven; the crystal hoof
of winter's horseman strikes, and strikes again,
as stars rush over the immense and solitary plain.

Farewell to street and tavern, the corner spa,
the newsboy yelling to the evening star!
Fixed now in winter, and faithful, we shall be,
as, in the trainyard, the last ailanthus tree.

Shaemus

We will go no more to Shaemus, at the Nip,
for sly innuendo and an Oporto Flip,
the rough but tender voice, the wide-mouthed grin,
the steady-unsteady hand that poured the gin:

memory, that flew back years to find a name,
found it, and fetched it up, still just the same;
the shaky footsteps, and then the shaky kidding:
you, the big business man, outbid, outbidding,

the mystery man, the man of deep affairs,
highbrow, and playboy, and friend of millionaires:
and you, the lovers, whose love was in your faces —
there you were, back once more — and still the traces! —

Yes, still the traces of that love he loved,
and re-examined, but as if unmoved;
the names fished up from time, or Singapore,
joined and repeated on his bar once more;

as if no let or hindrance were permitted;
as if both time and space could be outwitted;
endurance noted — in a protocol —
and then embalmed, of course, in alcohol.

And now himself, the immortal, lightly gone,
as if stepped out for a quick one — who had none.
And dead, his room inspected by his friends,
to find a will, adjust the odds and ends;

and there, the fifteen suits, the malacca cane,
the hats, and spats: in which he roved again,
far from the furnished room, the sacred bar,
immortal dandy, towards an immortal star.

All Death, All Love

Stand here at night in the shudder of the Elevated,
where moon and street-lamps mix, and the sudden trains
rock the black forest of steel, and the shadows, reticulated,
and the lights, reel over the housefronts from swift windowpanes.

No Forest of Arden, this! The corner drugstore
spills amber and blood down the granite curb; and the cemetery,
across the street, ponders in half-light, where no more
the famous dead come, and none to preach, or bury.

But the gate lies open, in violet light; and standing
here, in the hurrying evening, you will discover
meek rows of slate, there, with a marble tomb commanding;
and as you watch them, patient in moonlight, tell your lover

the delicious truth, which he knows too: that you lie there,
wrapt underground with death, and the ravished past;
your skull to dust crumbled, and the outspread fire of hair
with the hushed ecstasy of all history enlaced:

yes, you two, both, with that prone love embraced,
tugging at earth, like trees; while overhead
the train rocks shadows and steel; and here, two-faced,
your passion joins, and trembles, to accept the dead.

Nuit Blanche: North End

Red and green neon lights, the jazz hysteria,
for all-night movie and all-night cafeteria;
you feed all night in one, and sleep in the other,
and dream that a strip-tease queen was your sweetheart's mother.

A nickel for a coffee-half, a dime for a seat;
the blondes and the guns are streamlined and complete;
streamlined, dreamlined, with wide open cactus spaces
between the four-foot teeth in the ten-foot faces.

Hot trumpets and hot trombones for a soft-sole shuffle!
Sailors, bring in your tattoos, park your duffel!
There's a green-tailed blue-eyed mermaid stinging my shoulder,
and I've got to pass out before I'm a minute older.

Sawdust, spittoon, no smoking, please excuse —
afloat or ashore we mind our p's and q's.
Longhorn stand back, shorthorn stand close, is all
the circular eye makes out on the circular wall.

And still the red neon lights go round and around,
the red mouth opens and drinks with never a sound, —
red on the Square, red on the jingling Palace,
where all night long you rumbaed and drank with Alice —

red on the tattoo artist's sign, that shakes
anchors and flags together, ships and snakes,
roses, and a pink Venus, on a shell,
la la, all dancing fast in a neon hell —

while round and around the red beads wink, and faster
empty and open, pour and fill, disaster:
the red mouth opens and drinks, opens and winks,
drinks down the hotel wall, the drugstore, drinks

the Square, the statue, the bright red roofs of cabs,
and the cleaning-women, who arise with pails and swabs:
then stains the dawn, who, over the subway station,
steals in, with Sandals gray, but no elation.

The Visionaries

Come past these walls, these walls which enclose the sound
of violent wings, wild wings of sound, that beat
heavenward with man's heart, man's heart from underground,
lightward and godward, wings that refuse defeat;

where on bright strings quick bows concordant move
and heads and hands concordant bend or sway
obedient to the unknown, the unendurable, love,
which marries the here-and-now to the far-away;

past all the rows of those who simply listen —
mystics, who wait for their own hearts to break,
staring into that hatred, to see if — there! — might glisten
the beginning flower of light, all to remake;

leave these their vast enchanted dream, and come
across the car-tracks to the Grand Saloon,
where wrestlers glower or grin from smoky walls, and some
pick at an oyster to a juke-box tune;

where small-time race-track touts, pencil in hand,
study the form, live betwixt bar and phone,
drop the limp cigarette, trembling, to sawdust sand,
and with dry lips order one more, just one;

yes, here, with the house-plant on its golden stool,
and the one smooth plate-glass window, and the bar
jewelled with bottles, here too, at dusk, the haunted fool
comes for new wings and flight to the evening star:

draws in, as those to the wings of sound, to this
hot-honeyed heart of light, his dream distilled
through a glass brightly, brightly, the alembicked bliss
fierce in his brain, and the secret wish fulfilled.

Blind Date

No more the swanboat on the artificial lake
its paddled path throu͜ a neon light shall take;
the stars are turned out on the immortal ferris wheel,
dark and still are the cars of the Virginia Reel.
Baby, it is the last of all blind dates,
and this we keep with the keeper of the golden gates.

For the last time, my darling, the chute-the-chutes,
the Tunnel of Love, the cry 'all men are brutes,'
the sweaty dance-hall with the juke-box playing,
pretzels and beer, and our young love a-Maying:
baby, it is the last of all blind dates,
and this we keep with the keeper of the golden gates.

The radios in a thousand taxis die;
at last man's music fades from the inhuman sky;
as, short or long, fades out the impermanent wave
to find in the ether or the earth its grave.
Baby, it is the last of all blind dates,
and this we keep with the keeper of the golden gates.

Hold hands and kiss, it will never come again,
look in your own eyes and remember the deep pain,
how hollow the world is, like a bubble burst,
yes, and all beauty by some wretchedness accursed!
Baby, it is the last of all blind dates,
and this we keep with the keeper of the golden gates.

Love now the footworn grass, the trampled flowers,
and the divided man of crowds, for he is ours —

love him, yes, love him now, this sundered being,
who most himself seeks when himself most fleeing —
baby, it is the last of all blind dates,
and this we keep with the keeper of the golden gates.

But look — the scenic railway is flashed from red to green —
and swiftly beneath our feet as this machine
our old star plunges down the precipitous sky,
down the hurrahs of space! So soon to die! —
But baby, it is the last of all blind dates;
and we shall keep it with the keeper of the golden gates.

The Birdcage

The empty birdcage hangs with open door,
shadow of golden wires on golden floor;
Mavis's bird is gone, and Miriam's bird,
like Lesbia's, is a voice no longer heard.

A child remembers, as she thinks, with eyes.
So now, they follow the lost bird where it flies;
lift to the open window, the breadcrumbed sill,
soar to the clouds, remember, and are still;

drop back to an empty cage from empty sky,
flight and return, before they fill and cry;
Mavis and Miriam and Miranda too,
each with a bird, each with a bird that flew.

Molly hangs out an empty cage in moonlight —
luckier, this might be. May, in the sunlight,
purses her lips in a true birdcatcher's whistle.
Moppet sprinkles a leaf with seeds of thistle.

Children think with eyes, first, then with fingers;
both in the eyes and hands the knowledge lingers.

Marian's eyes and fingers suffer much,
remembering now how soft it was to touch.

All through the streets the empty cages hang,
bare little cells, where once the sweet birds sang.
Someone we loved has left this cage, the city.
Someone has left our hearts, and O the pity.

Dear Uncle Stranger

All my shortcomings, in this year of grace,
preach, and at midnight, from my mirrored face,
the arrogant, strict dishonesty, that lies
behind the animal forehead and the eyes;

the bloodstream coiling with its own intent,
never from passion or from pleasure bent;
the mouth and nostrils eager for their food,
indifferent to god, or to man's good.

Oh, how the horror rises from that look,
which is an open, and a dreadful, book!
much evil, and so little kindness, done,
selfish the loves, yes all, the selfless none;

illness and pain, ignored; the poor, forgotten;
the letters to the dying man, not written —
the many past, or passing, great or small,
from whom I took, nor ever gave at all!

Dear Uncle stranger, Cousin known too late,
sweet wife unkissed, come, we will celebrate
in this thronged mirror the uncelebrated dead,
good men and women gone too soon to bed.

Stone Too Can Pray

Lord, Lord — these miracles, the streets, all say —
bring to us soon thy best, most golden day,
that every stick and stone for thee may shine,
thy praise be sung in every shaft and line.

Lord, Lord — the steeples and the towers cry —
deepen beyond belief thy ancient sky,
deeper than time or terror be that blue
and we'll still praise thee by still pointing true.

Lord, Lord — the fountains weep — hear our delight,
these waters for birds and children we keep bright;
where children shout, and the stone dolphin sings,
bless with thy rainbow these holy eyes and wings.

Lord, Lord — all voices say, and all together,
stone, steel, and waking man, and waking weather —
give us thy day, that once more we may be
the endless miracle that embodies thee.

Spring Festival: The Taxis

Now in the spring the migrant taxis gather,
honking in lamplight to the sound of water;
listen — all night the song of the passionate meter
rises, as wandering taxis flock together.

The organ-grinder, too, comes out, old-fashioned,
to match his flute-notes with that reedier music.
The ailanthus trees, in the budding Square, are phthisic.
By the light of the moon, jackstones fly up impassioned.

Here, in the center of the footworn grassplat,
soldier and sailor, white and still, marmoreal,

marble in moonlight, the Civil War memorial,
stare at the picket fence, the dusty asphalt.

Blank the eye-sockets, in the shifting lamplight —
Victory, above them, holding wreaths, is moonblind;
but now, as the new leaves shift in the offshore east-wind,
the marble faces live and turn in the moonlight.

Look — the eyes darken, grow profound and tragic:
secret and deep, a momentary meaning
stares at the gathering taxis, glares at the greening
grassplat, while the meters pour out their music.

As if a delayed love, on the moonlight coming,
had turned the meters into hearts, fast-beating;
the marble soldier is now alive and waiting;
the marble musket stirs to the sound of drumming.

As if the blind eyes of the sculptured sailor
twinkled, twice, in the light of a falling jackstone;
and Victory's heart had ceased to be a tombstone;
and death, forever, world without end, a failure.

THE SOLDIER

*

I. *The Seasons*

More than a whisper, less than a sigh, perceptible
as breath in the mouth is silent and perceptible,
or the leaf on the dead stalk, rustling, rustling, to chatter
of time past and time to come: or the bird in the dusk,
iterating, iterating, his one phrase saying over
the all and the one, the all and the one, repeating
his knowledge of end and beginning:

                      so the river
of shapes and forms, termless and timeless, the nameless
river of the All-unending, murmurs to the dark
the history of things, the history of dreams, dissolving
the old in the new: solving, and then resolving,
claw shape and feather shape, the secret history of the rock,
fern-print and footprint, the quick dream in the heart, the
                        dream
breaking into the flower, and the cool flower breaking
slowly into the dream. We are aware, we hear it,
the voice whispering the name of life, the name of the
                      spirit,

              saying —
'Listen, soldier: forget for a moment the manual of arms:
the sweating out of a furlough, the fatigue, the hard bugle
              in the barracks:
forget too the business of bloodletting, your ancient
              profession:
yes, as old as that of the camp-followers: and listen:

there is something you don't remember: there is some-
                                        thing else.'
The wind rises at daybreak, drums round the eaves,
charges up the hillside, bayonetting the dog-grass,
whines down, ricochetting, through pasture walls, and then
runs swiftly over white waves to seaward. What does it
                                        bring,
what does it take, endless and invisible migrant?
Echoes and fragments, odours and visions: the traveller
bearing his tales and keepsakes from one land to another:
the yellow pine-pollen from the hilltop to the roadside:
sea fog, sea smell, salt smell of the kelp and shipworm
from the low-tide beach to the city street:
Widsith, the Far-traveller, the tale-bearer.

                                And as the wind
pours over mountains, over seas, northward, then eastward,
turns and returns, veers, pauses, backs through the compass,
breathless voyager and tale-teller, so too in all times,
and in all places, on the earth's surface and under the sea,
have the tides and currents, yes, and the seasons too,
changed and then changed again: whether of water or air,
fire or ice, sand or vapour. The seasons, yes:
soldier, think of the seasons: who more than you?
you who face sunstroke and frostbite, snow-squall and
                                        thunder,
flood-water, mud to the axletrees, the gale and the downpour.
The seasons affect warfare, the time for advance or retreat;
the seasons, altering rhythm, affect life and death.

In the country, you know how the birds come: March
                        blows their thousands
north from the Savannah and Chattahoochee, the Nile,
                                the Euphrates,
over brown steppes to Saskatchewan and Kamchatka, the
                                cuckoo crying
from the Arabian Desert to Yalta, the nightingale

winging to the Dover Straits from his Spanish garden.
Over the Gulf Stream, over the eastward-washing seaweed,
gregarious and cheerful, with his two or three poinsettia
                                                        words,
the robin arrives at the sands and fog of the Cape.
The silent fox-sparrow dances again in a litter of leaves,
and the red-winged blackbird shivers his chevrons.
The song-sparrow is heard at dawn, a spray of song
starlike in the leafless beach-plum; and the bright-eyed
                                                        chickadee
hides once more in the pinewood for his love and the secret
                                                        summer.
In the country, you know how they go: September blows
                                                        them
southward with the leaves, the early frost
white on the cornfield, frost like a groundswell.
The hour of departure has arrived: and they go their way.

The seasons, yes: for warrior and windflower alike:
for death and birth: for warfare of good and evil.
Dark is our past, secret and dark our future:
army struggles with army: only the maker
knows how the soul shall fare. A sudden glory
lodges the burning bird of steel in the breast,
as fish in water sift out their kind,
as flame sifts wood, as frost helms the bay with ice.
Time will unfetter the frost: but other and huger seasons
move over earth. Not those of the earth itself,
but of that elder Year, where the Plough and Pole
are motions in time, yet moveless and timeless.
The ice-age comes in like a wave, goes out like a wave,
brings with it its creatures and takes them away:
the fern-forests are gone, and the lizards: the waters
scream and subside. Long, long, the lamentation
sounded and sounds: creation and generation,
stagnation and slaughter and death, fruition and then
                                                        migration:

fire giving place to water, water to earth, the spirit
suffering darkness, suffering violence; in confusion,
shaping, or striving to shape, but lighter than air
mounting always.

          For the spirit admits no seasons:
to itself it admits no seasons. Dying or living,
deathless or momentary, invisible, indivisible,
the petal in water, the metal in flame,
under the hammerstroke of sunlight it changes its name:
yet, moving with the moving seasons, is always the same.

II. *The Migrants*

Dreams: signs: portents. The dream working in the rock,
in the ice, in the beating heart, in the spiral of the fern,
the sign showing, feeble in the firefly, brilliantly in the yellow
                                        leaf of death,
the portents creaking in the creative hollow of midnight.
Time speaks, time listens. The calendar's sun and stars,
aimed and prompt, relentless, inevitable,
flame through the emblazoned zodiac their hieratic courses:
the all is again eaten by the zero.

              And as the birds
and other creatures are borne on the immortal stream
to the north to the south to the east to the west,
lifting an anthem of life between dark and dark,
defeating heat and cold, or at last defeated;
fearful, always, of the instant of stealth or violence,
the cruel rapine of other birds, or creatures, or mankind;
so man, too, has his migrant and desperate history.
He too, like the birds, at the ghostly bidding of the cloud,
the omen of thunder, the surly summons of the sun,
the whirling dust in the summer fields, or savage
ice-floe and flood in the valley, the one

shrivelling the maize, and the pear on the bough, and the
                               cluster in the vine,
the other bearing deathward his dwelling, his stores, his
                               cattle;
he too has made his forced marches; hurriedly in the night
abandoning his cave, his tent, his hut,
the settlement by the wood's edge, his fire, his altar,
all that he has known and his fathers known; the square
                               field
which they and he have tilled; the women and children
captive perhaps; and a long and difficult journey
to be undertaken; solitude and misery endured;
yes, and death to many, before the new country is found
swimming under the rainbow.

                  And then, once again,
the mud hut, the settlement by the river,
the altar, the new beginning. Over and over,
immersed in the invisible stream, borne northward or
                               southward,
the eyes watchful, the ears listening, has he sought with
                               his seasons;
lifting his rush-light of love between one dark and other;
shaping with stern hands and heart a stern joy,
yet if need be entering into the death-silence of the mountains,
or descending to the yelping tumult of the sea,
to meet there and drive out those others, the strangers,
who have come, like the locust, driven by their own seasons,
to devour and spoil, like the locust. Over and over:
from age to age, from generation to generation:
man the unconquerable: you yourself: man the soldier.

Drums: oakleaves: eagles: the memorial arch, the
                               procession:
the tread of marching, soft and rhythmic, and the silent
                               hero's tomb.
Bronze: iron: steel: clatter of armour, glitter of helmet:

the well-touched drums quickening and thickening the
music:
the harmony warlike, to sound the note and accent
which the brave man utters in the hour of danger, the hour
when first he sees that his cause is failing, then when he
knows
that he marches to wounds and death, yet with firm step
and the steel-bright will to endure.
Listen, soldier: you know how the wars began:
far off, far back, in the sands and darks of time:
yet bright and clear as yesterday: you remember
how we the herdsmen fought for our rights in the pasturage:
how we, the hunters, proud of our skill,
swift-footed, ready with club or javelin, quick on the draw
with arrow or sling, and scornful of herdsmen,
or those others who tilled the soil, you remember how we —
yes, and how easy it was — made slaves of those weaklings.
Law sets the boundary of war, and war of law:
where the one is weak, the other is strong. With our arms
we established order, customs, classes: posted our edicts:
justly, as becomes the victor. We, the fire-bringers.

Fire-bringers, sons of Prometheus! On the banks of the
Nile,
history begins: there and by the filthy Euphrates, the
Tigris.
Fitted with all known conveniences for travel, the roads
stone-bright in the desert, suitable for the passage of vast
armies,
the wells properly designated, these two vast valleys
sounded to the barbarous flute. Shall we justify war —
migration and plunder and war? Shall we justify death?
Let me refresh your memory, you who fought
on the river bank with Darius, and lie there still —
you who stood with Leonidas at Thermopylae, the Hot
Gates,
died there, are buried there, yet still live:

you who rode by the wagon-train for Caesar,
whose voice is heard when the mistral whines in the grass
                                        of Gaul
or in the cry of the gull on Pevensey Beach:
dark is our past, secret and dark our future:
war and death are the natural lot of man:
effort and death, struggle and death, living and dying.
Does fire creep back to the spark that released her joy?
the tiger-lily of June sheathe up and enfold her flame?
the stream remount to her hidden source? Life strives
                                        with death,
warcraft shall wax in the hero: ever the wise man
ponders the strife of this world.

                            Justify death —
and justify war. Listen: wherever a people
has risen to greatness, and bred its children
as heroes to shine in greatness and in great deeds,
that glory was first engrossed, impanelled,
in bronze and bloodshed on the red field of battle;
there first that people became supreme. War winnows
                                        men —
war winnows nations. Saves or destroys. Destroys
'that which opposes progress.' Saves and extends
'that which advances progress.' Casts aside
'that which is contrary to civilization,' to be lost
to history's memory, or, if remembered at all,
recorded in a footnote only. The outlaw must die:
pay with his life for his crimes against mankind.

Wind blowing softly, softly, from the long blue corridor
of history: fair weather and fortune fetch hither
new wonders and wisdoms from far travels and trials:
baptised by new waters, our vision unsealed
by new light, new strangeness. Widsith, the Far-traveller,
descends from air with a headful of notions; Marco
                                        Polo

ribboned from Cathay; and the travelling salesman
home from Memphis with a new line of fancies.

III. *Antiphon of the Dead Soldiers*

'Tremendous before God, tremendous before time,
infinite in its gentleness, infinite in its greatness,
magnificent pour of stars we call the world
downward from nowhere forever to nothing:
the ceaseless fall of lights in the cold darkness
foam of knowledge and water of nescience
the barren shores of shadow to left and right
and the riddled cleavage of day and night:

'tremendous before space, tremendous before man,
infinite in its terribleness, infinite in its splendour,
magnificent pour of atoms we call the shape
the cry of form and the wail of substance:
footfall of substance and whisper of shadow
in the depth of the water and the twining of vine and rhyme
in the building of the flower the dissolving of the rock
alike in the mortal majesty of the heart and the clock:

'tremendous in creation, tremendous in cessation
infinite in its leisure infinite in its swiftness
magnificent lightning of the lifted hand
pitiful broken hand of fallen thunder:
who will voice it how are we brave to say
where one begins and another ends
where all ends and the one begins
how can we mark this map of chaos with broken pins:

'falter and alter must speech, and speechless become,
shaping to the shape or shapelessness of doom:
but how good it is how great it is and how it shines
like the light of mocking-birds on foaming trees

the bursting and burning of bells in the twilight air
or the turning of the heart in joy or prayer:
how good it is how great it is and how it shines
this world where death with the dogrose and birth with
                                    the wormwood twines.

'Who will voice it how are we brave to say
the meaning of the battle the meaning of the bloodstream
separate the star from the water the hour from the splinter
the tiger from the evening the serpent from the stone:
we who are only voices praising the wind
voices of wind praising the wind
who will ourselves be gone
when the world goes on.'

IV. *The Wars*

TWO SOLDIERS SPEAK

1

Dry leaves, soldier: dead leaves, dry leaves:
voices of leaves on the wind that bears them to de-
                                    struction,
impassioned prayer, impassioned hymn of delight
of the gladly doomed to die. Stridor of men,
stridor of beasts, praisers of lust and battle,
numberless as waves, the waves singing
to the wind that beats them down.

2

Under Osiris,
him of the Egyptian priests, Osymandyas the King,
eastward into Asia we passed, swarmed over Bactria,
three thousand years before Christ.

1

The history of war
is the history of mankind.

2

So many dead:
look at them there in the dark, look at them going,
the longest parade of all, the parade of the dead:
between then and now, seven thousand million dead:
dead on the field of battle.

1

The people which is not ready
to guard its gods, and its household gods, with the sword,
who knows but it will find itself with nothing
save honour to defend — ?

2

Consider soldier,
whatever name you go by, doughboy, dogface,
(*solidus,* a piece of silver, the soldier's pay),
marine or tommy, god's mercenary — consider our lot
in the days of the single combat. You have seen on the
                                              seabeach,
in the offshore wind blow backward, a wavecrest
windwhipped and quivering, borne helpless and briefly
to fall underfoot of an oncoming seawall, foam-smothered,
sea-trampled, lost; and the roar, and the foamslide re-
                                              gathered
once more to recede, wind-thwarted again. Thus deathward
the battle lines whelmed and divided. The darkling
                                              battalions
locked arms in chaos, the bravest, the heroes,

kept in the forefront; and this line once broken,
our army was done for.

1

            Numbers: our faith was in numbers:
drafts from all parts of the empire: the provinces levied:
each tribe with its native equipment: cane bows, naked
                                        arrows:
stakes pointed and hardened in flame: but also the sword-
                                    blade
hammered by the smiths of Phoenicia, the green-bronze
                                helmet
sprouting the horns and ears of the ox, the head-dress
carved from a horse-skull. Here flashed the golden
greaves of the Medes: spangled Scythians that starlike
fell through the hempstalks: and the huge blue Ethiops
whirling in lionskins. Over the battle,
confused and dreadful the clamour, the shouting, the dust-
                                        cloud
sifting to shadow the sun.

2

            Under the dustcloud,
the rumbling of wooden wheels, the cries of camels and
                                    elephants,
screaming of horses and braying of asses.

1

            Which side lost heart?
What mishap, mistake in an order, bad luck, first cleared
the disastrous field?

2

Some leaders, in battle sectors,
wondered what happened, when things went wrong with their
units.

1

A muleskinner lighted a lamp on his wagon, maybe.

2

There were not enough mounts for the slingers, the balistae.

1

Rumours were started.

2

And panic.

1

No trenches were dug.

2

What was the watchword, the password?

1

Discipline, discipline:
only when battle is joined, yes, and then only:
is the value of discipline proved. Minor infractions —
carelessness in dress, a dozen such minor offences —
ignore or permit them, because battle is imminent —

2

— and the outfit breaks, and the leaders are helpless.

1

This wasn't once; it happened again and again.
Shall we call the roll-call of times and places? ask them
to count off a cadence for us — ?

2

                    Item: the Great Wall of China:
on the northwest frontier, beating back the barbarians:
no message brought from the Emperor, cut off from supplies
for months on end, and the arrows falling like rain; each
                                                    day
a few more missing, our numbers dwindling; and all for lack
of the proper planning and foresight. It was there the
                                            captain
thanked his soldiers, and the ghosts of his soldiers, saying
'What here befell you, soldiers, will not be forgotten:
I will always remember how well you obeyed your orders.
Daybreak, hopeless again you went from the wall.
Nightfall, you come back fewer.'

1

                    Yes, call the roll-call:
the roll-call of names. Cyrus in Arabia. Marathon.
Brunanburh. Maldon. The world is a tomb for the
                                            soldier,
and what the stones say, no matter, it's always the same.

2

Look down in the weeds and read the inscription.

1

It says:
'Traveller, where we were ordered to stay, we stay:
these rocks are our names, wild thyme and the grass our
substance:
in Thapsacus, by the Euphrates: which none hitherto
had crossed on foot: it seemed by divine intervention:
as if it made way for Cyrus, our destined King.'

2

In the centre was Cyrus: and with him six hundred in
breastplates:
Cyrus alone bareheaded. The horses, on forehead and
breast,
wore armour: the horsemen had Grecian swords. Then
came
the chariots, those with scythes that shone from the axles,
cavalry and bowmen. And Cyrus, perceiving the King,
and knowing the omens propitious, rode at him and struck
him,
wounding him through the breastplate. Ctesias the surgeon
reports it, he himself having dressed the wound.

1

And Cyrus was dead, pierced under the eye, and with him
eight captains.

2

And Artapates, his servant and sceptre-bearer,
killed himself on his master's body. Gold chains and
bracelets
he wore, and a jewelled scimitar by his side:
so great the esteem in which Cyrus had held him.

And Cyrus's head lay pale in the dust: his sword-hand
                                                    also:
struck off by the King.

                                    1

                        As once, by the wall,
godlike Achilles, smiting the neck with his sword,
swept far both head and helm, and the marrow slowly
oozed from the spine, and the corpse lay prone on the earth.

                                    2

Dry bones, soldier.

                                    1

                    Dry bones in the singing sands.
The sands that chatter under the goatherd's footsteps.
What does the dry skull make of the perished garland,
the dust of a perished garland?

                                    2

                    The water-clock's chuckle
means nothing to him: nor the music of time, resolved
in a wider and darker interval. Listen to the voices,
                                    soldier —
these, yourself, still riding the ghost of the wind!

                                    1

Voices of men, the one and the many. You hear them
at dusk, for then it was that the battle was joined,
at moonrise too, for then it was, or again at cock-crow,
with dew and blood on the flint-corn. They speak —

2

— distinctly:
as now in the garden, the cricket's love-song
over the wall by the hollyhock. Distinctly
as the chirp of time on your wrist, or the singing
wings of your sweetheart's heart beneath your breast.
The air is alive with memory.

1

Breathing memory,
you breathe these ghosts.

2

Times, names, and places!

1

Here is Caligula, charging the Tyrrhenian Sea
for a handful of tritons, scooped in a helmet.

2

Here is Julius,
alone at night in a tent designing a bridge,
a bridge of oaks.

1

He will have his way, he will timber the ships.

1

And there, outside, in the fosse, he hears you talking,
you, Faber, you, Smith, the soldier —

2

— you, Jones, the legions — !

1

— or singing that ballad of Caesar, the bald-headed lecher!

2

Bridge spanned: ships timbered: the legions in winter
                                        quarters.
The mind turns southward, to mimosa, and the terrace of
                                        oranges.
Shall we say that war is an art? And that Greece was
                                its mother?
The most practical art — ?

1

                        And the least sublimated. You know
how the phalanx evolved: in Greece: how it altered our
                                        world.
Four-square: massive: erect: terrible in its effect:
the Spartan eight deep, the Theban still deeper:
the spears four fathom in length, and the lines at such
                                        distance
that the spears of the fifth rank protected the first:
before modern warfare, there was no such manoeuvre or
                                        weapon.

2

Athens was saved by it.

1

With the phalanx, Alexander
dreamed of that march that had for its compass a world.

2

Discipline, training — those were his business!

1

— As also
with the goose-step legions of Rome, who loosened the
phalanx
for open formation: those in the front rank, tired,
fell back, and the next line replaced them. The discipline
perfect,
the leadership faultless.

2

Count off, call the roll-call again,
speak the names in the dust, the great names, the little,
the remembered, the forgotten!

1

Attila, stricken at Chalons.

2

Attila, drunk at his wedding, and dead, and rolled down
the Danube.

1

Dead for a woman.

2

Rome sacked, Rome burned, Rome burning.
Who will believe it? that Rome goes to war, not for glory,
but in her own gates, her own walls, her own blood, for
her life?
The world sinks in ruins. All vanishes, all save our sins.
These alone flourish.

1

Rome pillaged by Vandals —

2

— and Bath by the Saxons. Roofs falling, gates breaking,
the red wall
crusted with lichen —

1

— the hoarfrost shines on the mortar,
the wall that sheltered the hall with its bright bosom,
where the baths stood hot in its heart!

2

Fast in the leafmold,
dreamless the heroes who built it. Far off, above them,
in the glass of shadows, the land of the living, the years
pass by in a whisper. In the glass of shadows,
the ghost of a ghost of a ghost, Gustavus Adolphus
masses his cannon to prepare an attack, his troops
in line formation, with muskets.

1

— new genius, new tactics!

2

— Leonardo writes to Milan he will build armoured wagons
to mount artillery, break through the heaviest ranks:
or in times of peace, adding, do as much too in painting
as anyone else!

1

And the Corsican corporal:
writes to his girl from Verona: 'I give you a thousand kisses.
We have had only ten men killed and a hundred wounded.'

2

Ten lives, ten leaves!

1

Ten leaves — or a hundred!

2

Ten years —

1

— or a thousand.

2

Who were they?

1

And what were their names?

2

Ourselves.

1

The infantry.

2

We who do all the dying.

1

Yes, it's the infantry always that does all the dying.

2

The poor bloody infantry.

1

The doughboy.

2

The dogface.

1

The tommy.

2

At Vimy, fanned out in a wave to break deathward
in a wave on the wire: and today in the fox-holes
at El Guettar, beating off tanks.

1

Other arms of the service
can do what they like to us, yes. But no ground will be gained
till the footsoldier takes it and holds it.

2

The queen of battles:
that's what they call us, and rightly.

1

A long road, soldier:
it's a long way back.

2

Yes: at Zabatus.
Three thousand stadia from home, and no one to guide us.
Impassable rivers before us, a false king behind us.
Alone, deserted, no horses, and the men disheartened.

1

Few were the watchfires.

2

None wanted food that night.
A handful only had bothered to stand at the arm-stacks.

1

Most of us lying alone, unable to sleep,
for sorrow and longing.

2

Thinking of home, our children,
our wives, our kinfolk, and the friends we never would see.

1

A dark hour, that was. It all seemed hopeless.

2

Hopeless.

1

And then — at midnight — sleepless too like the others —

2

— or roused by a dream, some said —

1

— the Foreigner called us:
the one they called the Foreigner, none knew the reason;
sitting in a ring round the fire, seeming to move in the
                                             firelight,
but this was illusion. And the Foreigner speaking:
'Soldiers, to abide in this place, given up to despair,
waking or sleeping, means death and death only.
I know you are heartsick and homesick. And so I
                              will say
what you know yourselves: that whoever wishes
to embrace his friends and children, why let him be
                              valiant:
not otherwise will he come to that day. Who wishes to
                                             live,

let him strive to conquer; for the conqueror lives,
but the conquered die.'

2

Few words: the men silent.

1

And the speech concluded, we rose up and burned our
tents,
and the wagons and baggage. Then, taking our arms,
the men drawn up in column of squads, we ordered
the long march back:

2

through desert and death:

1

to the sea.

V. *The Outpost*

The rocket furrows the dark, and falls, the red sparks
diminish falling, and die, the little rain
vanishes like a whisper, you hear for a deep moment
the night, the sound of night, the silence.
And another may rise, and another, you may see
other explosions, fantastic, far off, bright green
or violet or golden, and again the slow streams
of falling and silent fire.

There are clouds:
it is against these that the terror brightens,
these bring the terror nearer, bring it down.

But if there were moonlight, if there were stars,
how much farther, how much smaller, it would be:
like the lighting of a candle against the sunlight,
or the darkening of a room.

       Soldier, you move
with each brave footstep, yes, and each blunder,
forward to such a scene as this, in which
the artificial nearness of the sky
like a rich backdrop will flatter you,
deceives you into an intimate sense of closeness and safety,
the simple immediateness of your past, the slowness
of your little time. But if, suddenly,
the moon and stars come out, beware, for then
all in a glory of disaster may end at once:
past and future become you, and die.

VI. *The Unknown Soldier*

In the new city of marble and bright stone,
the city named for a captain: in the capital:
under the solemn echoing dome, in the still tomb:
lies an unknown soldier.

      (Concord: Valley Forge: the Wilderness
Antietam: Gettysburg: Shiloh.)

      In the brown city,
old and shabby, by the muddy Thames, in the gaunt avenue,
where Romans blessed with Latin the oyster and primrose,
the stone shaft speaks of another. Those who pass
bare their heads in the rain, pausing to listen.

      (Hastings: Blenheim: Waterloo:
Trafalgar: Balaklava: Gallipoli.)

Across grey water, red poppies on cliffs of chalk,
hidden under the arch, in the city of light,
the city beloved of Abelard, rests a third,
nameless as those, but the fluttering flame
substituting for a name.

          Three unknown soldiers:
three, let us say, out of many. On the proud arch
names shine like stars, the names of battles and victories,
but never the name of man, you, the unknown.
Down there runs the river, under dark walls of rock,
parapets of rock, stone steps that green to the water.
There, they fished up in the twilight another unknown,
the one they call *L'Inconnue de la Seine*. Drowned hands,
drowned hair, drowned eyes: masked like marble she
                            listens
to the drip-drop secret of silence; and the pale eyelids
enclose and disclose what they know, the illusion
found like fire under Lethe. Devotion here sainted,
the love here deathless. The strong purpose turns
from the daggered lamplight, from the little light to the
                            lesser,
from stone to stone stepping, from the next-to-the-last
heartbeat and footstep even to the sacred, the last.
Love: devotion: sacrifice: death: can we call her unknown
who was not unknown to herself? whose love lives still
as if death itself were alive and divine?

          And you, the soldier:
you who are dead: is it not so with you?
Love: devotion: sacrifice: death: can we call you unknown,
you, who knew what you did? The soldier is crystal:
crystal of man: clear heart, clear duty, clear purpose.
No soldier can be unknown. Only he is unknown
who is unknown to himself.

And you others, the living:
whatever your names are, Smith, Jones, Harris:
captain or corporal, private or top kick:
you who are now our hands, our arms, our hearts,
but most of all our arms, our shield: you who were
                                        once
something else — high-rigger, salesman, stone-mason,
soda-jerker or desk-man, broker or clerk in a store:
bear this in mind: you are neither alone nor unknown:
but one of ourselves, as we are yourselves. Bear it in mind
that we too are there, on the beach, in the field,
at mess or at drill; share with you discomfort, annoyance,
wet, pain, squalor, and filth. Bear it in mind
that before all else, from the very beginning,
we too were soldiers, we were all soldiers. This is our
                                        virtue:
seed in our hearts from the ones who perished before us:
that we should guard against every foeman
our lands, our faiths, our homes. From generation to
                                        generation:
man the unconquerable: you yourself: man the soldier.

Drums: eagles: drums: the crowds praying, the crowds
                                        watching:
the dead march softly touched, tears and pride for the one
who will never again give back his stand of arms,
the stand of arms that he chose for himself. The hero
lives in our watchful hearts.

                    Yes, but remember,
as he in our hearts would wish to remember,
even now, when oakleaves wither, and the generous bugles
praise him for the last time, remember also
those other heroes, his too and ours, who live or die
in another and deadlier warfare, the war of the spirit,
the war that wars beyond war itself. Shall we justify
                                        war?

Shall we justify life? Speak now, dead soldier:
after the mourning bugles, the perishing oakleaves:
shall we justify life?

                    And under your hand,
look, at the page of blood the book falls open,
and you read what you know already, the name of your
                                        heart,
the name and number appear and vanish, once, and once
                                        only,
in a moment of anguish. All men learn thus:
we come to our deaths like this, the mouth filled with blood,
and even as we read, of life accepted and given,
and ourselves given and accepted,

              the wings grow, the wings spread
the page deepens and darkens, darkens, then brightens,
serene shines the self, and beyond it, serener, the selfless.
Man's mind is a world, a sky full of stars, it embraces
the past and the future. O deep, deep and secret,
that miracle changing all, the light in the heart
impartible, implicit, the light in the hawthorn, the light
immane that works to flower in the dream, and pleads
on the bloody page! 'How strange, men of Athens,
my conduct would be, if I, who obeyed the command
at Delium and Potidea, and stood at my post
no less than my fellows, if now, when I hear
this summons, to search in myself and others for knowledge,
I forsook my post, fearing death. For sweet is that voice
as the flute in the ears of the mystic. And I must obey.
No evil afflicts the good man, living or dying.
Let us be of good heart about dying!'

              Remember the sail at Sunium
far down through fog at the cliff's edge seen,
curved and small as a gull's wing, death's wing
beating out of the sunlight —

remember the sail
that southward bore, past bird-foul Dungeness,
another, steadfast under a failing star,
who steered to Rome and to death foreknown, a soldier
marching against a battery —

remember him,
above shorn fields and the harvest at Heiligenstadt
who listened to silence, the first slow snowflakes of silence.
'One standing beside me said that he heard in the distance
a sound of fluting, and I heard nothing. One standing
                                          beside me
said that he heard in the distance a shepherd's song,
and I heard nothing.'

The agony of growing and knowing,
the agony and ecstasy and death of being and seeing,
genius of knowledge, that accepts, and makes all things
                                          good.
Violence: anger: hatred: power: the light changes,
                    the light alters,
the long light falls through adverse time, man's mind
becomes crystal, man's heart becomes crystal, even as
                                          the soldier
is crystal, was always crystal.

And the will turns
upward, up the spiral of light, ever to the brighter
stairway and doorway of light, unblinded seeking
the threshold itself of light, from the next-to-the-last
heartbeat and perception of pain and light even
to the unknown last, lost in the flame-sheath
of flowering glory, sheathed to unsheathe, unfolding
in love implicit impartible. The clear heart,
invisible and indivisible in its own clearness,
thou lookest upon, thou lookest into, O divine

guest and ghost of mankind, of whom mankind is the
guest:
guest and ghost, diviner and divined; thou knowest,
which is to say that we too know, at last
sheathed and unsheathed in knowledge, the love of earth
beyond man's love of himself, the love of life
in the simple knowing of death, the love of knowledge
in the knowing of pain.

In the last war of all
we conquer ourselves. Look home from the desert, soldier:
to the regenerate desert of the heart come home:
and know that this too needs heroes, and endurance, and
ardour.

THE KID

William Blackstone
(*Died 1675*)

Where now he roves, by wood or swamp whatever,
the always restless, always moving on,
his books burned, and his own book lost forever,
under the cold stars of New England, gone,

scholar who loved, and therefor left, the most,
secret and solitary, no Indian-giver,
who to his own cost played the generous host
and asked adventurers across his river:

what would he make of us, if he could see,
after so many tides have ringed this coast,
what manner of men his children's children be
to welcome home his still inquisitive ghost?

He, more than all, of individual grace,
the pilgrim innocence, self-knowledge sure,
stepped like an angel in this savage place,
and, in all nature, found no evil-doer.

A summer's freedom on a bramble shore
whose wild rose the Lords Bishop could not blight,
then the Lords Brethren saw him close his door,
bidding his orchards, and his house, good-night.

Now by the lamplit wall his friendly nod
salutes the late wayfarer on that hill
where wych-elms ward some semblance of the sod
he knew by Cam's side, and he measures still

the common field he found and kept aright,
setting his rose-trees and his fruit-trees out:
these, and his books, and truth, all his delight,
and the locked heart of man his only doubt.

I

The Witnesses

Who saw the Kid when he rose from the east
riding the bridled and fire-bright Beast?
heard him shout from the surf-gold, streaming
crupper and bit, the surcingle gleaming,
elbows sharp against daybreak sky,
the reins held light and the hands held high?
The clouds above him and the breakers below
blazed with glory, and the Kid also.
Who saw that hero, that pinto, come
like one indivisible Word from foam?

The horseshoe crab and the nighthawk did,
the quawk and the tern and the chickadee did,
yes, and the little green grasshopper did,
they saw the Kid, they heard the Kid.

Who heard that lad leap down from a cloud,
over the night hard hoofbeats pounding,
rapid and far or softer sounding,
nearer thudding, then sudden and loud?
The stars rode down, their hooves were bright:
they threshed the morning to sheaves of light.
Who heard from heaven that ghost tattoo,

down hyaline stairs of quartz and blue,
and then *yippee — yippee — halloo?*

    The bullbriar patch and the groundhog did,
    the Indian boy in the birch-tree hid,
    the solemn cricket and the fat katydid,
    these were the ones who saw the Kid.

To Old Man River from hoarse Monomoy
they eyed that pony, they admired that boy,
watched him skim over billows of oak
up before sunup and away like smoke.
He sped to the river, and they saw him span
wide water as only a rainbow can,
down the long valley a sun-ghost flinging,
lariat's whistle and a noose of singing.

    The catfish slick and the cunning 'possum,
    the hummingbird moth in the scuppernong blossom,
    the moccasin's braid in the bog-hole hid,
    they heard the Kid, they knew the Kid.

And these too knew him: a lynx of stone.
Rats' eyes, pricked in the blue of the moon.
Frogs' eyes, blinking like bubbles in ooze,
bedded by the creek in twos and twos.
The doe, turned tail, and the buck at stand,
shadows and eyes in the innocent land:
snuffings and shadows, the lone wolf howl,
and far in the Ozarks the quaver of an owl.

And westward, seaward, he drew the horizon,
following the Sioux, who followed the bison,
westward, along the Missouri no more,
far back remembered like Ohio's shore,
far back forgotten like the moosewood tree
and dust in the mouth on a prairie sea,

the watergap crossed, the chinquapins gone,
breast-high laurel, and still heading on.

I'm away, I'm away, I'm away to the west,
I'll stay no more on my mother's breast,
my sister can study the golden rule,
my little brothers can traipse to school,
my pa he can curse, my ma she can cry,
they'll all forgive me in the sweet by-and-by,
I come from heaven and to heaven I'll go,
but what's in between I'm a-wantin' to know!

Who picked up the words from the prophet's mouth?
Grizzly in the north, and longhorn south.
Who bore witness to that faring-forth?
Buzzard in the south, and eagle in the north.
Prairie-dog cities swarming in the sun,
golden in the evening, and then not one.
Buffalo spine. A high grass growing.
Rattlesnake rattle and tumbleweed blowing.

And these too witnessed: the sachem's daughter,
crouched by the creek for a pitcher of water:
riding like the wind — she cried as she ran —
that was no horse, and that was no man.
Forked from his fist came the lightning stroke,
the double thunder and a puff of smoke:
the double thunder and the lightning twice,
his hair like fire and his eyes like ice;
and a pinto pony, a wing of flame,
whinnying and gone as quick as it came.

The rain-god, sure! The little cloud rose
up the dark mountain and over pale snows,
thunder whizzed down from an eyried shelf,
and lo, the bright bird on the peak itself.
A flash through sunset, a meteor falling,

halloos and echoes in hollow rock calling,
halloos and echoes all night till dawn,
night stiff with rain, but the rain-god gone.

Who watched that spirit shoot down to the west,
sun going home to the sun-god's breast?
or praised that triumph, that last homecoming,
the pride, the glory, and the end of roaming?
The farewell darkness of night to love him,
a rainbow of stars for a crown above him,
who saw that pinto, that hero, go,
to the world forever, the world below?

   The old sequoia and the sea-hawk did,
   the barnacled lion in his sea-cave hid,
   the sand and the surge and the sea-fog did,
   they hailed the Kid, farewelled the Kid.

And these too hailed him: the high sierra:
desert, and rock, and the cordillera:
a glacier's leavings, a god's moraine,
a tower of ice, and a wall of rain.
They caught his hymn as it fell to the sea
from condor's shadow and sugarpine-tree:
of might in singleness, a crown in fate,
the everlasting of the golden gate.

II

The Land

The sun-cymbal strikes: and a land of voices
begins, and from ocean to ocean rejoices:
whispers of laughter: wave making mock
in glittering derision of water on rock:
the waterfall seethes: the pine-barren breathes:
cloud over watershed steams and wreathes:

fog slips down to drip into rain,
the cataract's secret loose on the plain:
grassland, swampland, the everglade sighing,
sighing in the rank sun, fetlocks drying.

And rivers: rivers with their proud hosanna:
Chattahoochee: Tallahassee: Susquehanna:
Savannah, high-yaller, and Arkansas, red:
Colorado bowling in a mile-deep bed:
Hendrik Hudson, with snow on his breast,
and Great Meridian that walls off the west.
What malice to rustle? what love-talk babbling?
Pebbles in a pool, and a freshet gabbling.
Drip-drop tinkle, an icicled fern,
honing of a rock, a bouldered churn,
and downward, sliding, with cliff-high roar,
merryflashed wave past a vanishing shore.
Who's there? who's here? The palmetto rattles.
The slow moss hisses. The cottonwood tattles.

Listen: the wind from the prairie is blowing:
listen: the harp-string whisper of snowing:
avalanche mutter: the granite scraped bare:
horn-cry of ice on the rime-bright air.
What leaves, what grasses, what reeds, what flowers?
Sun over cloud-cliff, cloud over showers.
And eastward, quartering, countering the sun,
a maze of lazy voices buzzing all as one.
River-mud slumping in a red lump, gone:
snag at the riverbend, blanched like bone:
moon-scented sweetgrass, a land unplowed:
whirled over sumach, the grasshopper cloud.

What sticks? what stones? what cavern? what briar?
Crag for the bighorn and the eagle's gyre.
The heat-song singing, the sun gone down,
and timberwolf hymn from the butte to the moon:

star for the firefly, stem for the thrush,
a fox on the sidehill, a bird in the bush.
South roar the rivers: east roars the weather:
all sounds gather in a vast wave together:
beast-cry and bird-song, a multitude of voices,
where, between oceans, the long land rejoices.
Leaf-step, rain-step: the canebrake rattles:
fog-step, dew-step: the silverleaf tattles.

III

The First Vision

Here, to be first, is not to find:
here, to be first, is the first mind.
Here, to be first, is not to claim,
but to give lonely truth a name.

He moved to the north, moved to the south,   *William*
camped on sand at the river's mouth,   *Blackstone*
camped in the sun, woke in the rain,
then struck his camp and moved it again.
Sticks for a fire, the fire put out,
fox-bark too close, or the owlet's shout:
a leaf displaced, the Observers near,
a secret company, but not to fear.
Stealth under stars, and stars to be read,
lying on his back, the Book overhead —
the Plow, the Pole, but positions strange,
direction altered, and a vaster range.
Who's there? who's here? The shades but shifted.
Eyes under leaves, and an oak-bough lifted.
Water-song, reed-song: and strange birds, too,
none, save one, with a voice he knew.
Was God's path here? By what to be known?
What trail, what blaze, in the wilderness shown?

Bullbriar, hacked for a snake-green lair:
snow on the leafmold, exceeding fair:
such to be studied, and for such, a prayer.
Morning and evening, Lord, I beseech Thee,
suffer my cry from this woode to reach Thee,
these are Thy presents, Thy heart I find
in the dark forest in sleet and winde.
As on the sea Thou sailedst before,
a cloud, that our shippe might see this shore,
so now Thou walkest, these trees Thy feet,
and in this brooke Thy heart doth beat.
Lorde, I am fearless, Thy mercy shown,
for where Thou art there is nought unknown:
what are these seemings save Thine own?
O grant Thy servant his grace of dayes
whose hours shall all be filled with praise:
here Thy newe workes must numb'red be
and fair names fitted to beast and tree.
All to be learned, all to be loved,
thus ever freshe Thy kingdom proved.

He moved to the north: by the harbor found
a sweet spring bubbling in open ground:
on a clear hill, by an oystred river,
and here, he thought, I shall dwell forever.
A plat of roses, a plot of trees,
apples, pears, and a skep of bees,
friends in the village, true Indian friends,
here Lord in joye my journey ends.
What should I want but bookes on shelf —
these few I have — and that dark selfe
that poures within me, a chartless sea,
where every landfall is named for Thee?
What other voyage could solace me?
Thou being pilot, Lord, I find
untrodden kingdoms in the minde:
freedom is all my coin: and these

humilities and simplicities,
Thy humblest creatures, birds and flowers,
instruct and ornament my hours.

. . . But the Lords Brethren came, and then
Lords Bishop also: the world of men
crossed his river. He moved again,
southward, a last time closed his door:
then to the wilderness once more.
Loud, loud, the savage sun: the sky
bright with pigeons: the jackal's cry
echoed the loon; and wolves, at night,
howled to the moon. But mind's delight
embracing these and all, he moved
deliberate in a world he loved.
Angelick pengwins trod that shore:
fearless he heard the lyon's roar:
pale honeysuckle ringed the page,
where, in a noon, he read an age.
What rills? what meads? what mast? what flowers,
to be inscribed in a Book of Hours?
What meditation, song, and prayer,
heard on the air and copied fair?
And love's green margin everywhere.
But house and book are burned and lost,
and death is one more river crossed:
shadow and voice together gone,
westward, southward, the ghost moves on.

IV

Second Vision: The Ambiguity

In secret wood, where once he stood,
hard by the banks of lacrym flood,[1]   *Anne*
two sister voices soft he heard   *Bradstreet*
dividing world in flesh and word:

as if two angels in his soul
leaned in debate from pole to pole:
argument, as of night and day,
whether 'twere wise to go or stay.
Sometimes the voices were as one,
then again broke that unison.
Both to be free they were agreed,
but challenged whose the greater need.
Was freedom of the heart? or hand?
of secret soul? or the wide land?
And were it better to stir or stand?
Thenceforth the traveler was possessed
by the two sibyls in his breast:
under the wood, beside the stream,
the changing voices shaped his dream.
Sometimes, to soothe that discontent,
to the soul's underworld he went,
cried his *O Altitudo* there,
but with the accents of despair:
for doubts and shades stood everywhere.
Was freedom but to be masterless?
not to be found in wilderness?
And then, which wilderness were best,
that of the world, or of the breast?
Sometimes in stillness the voice sings,
but loudly too when the broadaxe rings.
Shadow and voice together gone,
inward, outward, the ghost moves on.

V

The Martyrdom

He turned on his tracks: to the puritans came:
bore witness to bigots, was martyred in shame:
no church found for truth, and no house for faith,
but choir of the word, and the walls of breath:

an arbor of saplings, a shanty of wood,
for winter's whistlings, a river in flood.
This season, how grievous, how bitter this coast, *Lawrence,*
where love finds no chapel, no comfort a ghost! *Cassandra,*
Clap wings and begone, no lantern hangs here, *Josiah,*
but hatred and darkness, the dead of the year. *Daniel,*
Cry, cry, for New England, New Canaan indeed! *and Provided*
Dear ghosts of this forest, who suffer and bleed, *Southwick* 2
your names shall be chalice, your voices cry still,
who were whipped at a cart's-tail and hanged on a hill.
Lashed at a cart's-tail, through three towns driven,
hanged on a hill by the servants of heaven,
banished, or perished, or sold as a slave,
poor body unhoused, a hole for a grave —
cry, cry for New England! The true voices speak,
while granites of Norton and Endicott break.
This is my bodye: let it be my truth:
tear it in pieces, if ye have not ruth:
freely I give it, let it die, let it rot:
but as for your sentence, I matter it not.
Well know you the things we said in this place:
the enlargement of God we find in His grace:
come now what His wisdom and pleasure approve,
our rest and our life in His infinite love.
By the wills of men captive: made free by the Son:
chapter eight, in the Gospel according to John.

VI

The Kid

He turned to the land: forgot his name: *Hector*
changing and changeless went and came: *St. John de*
dreamed blood-knowledge as he slept in nature: *Crèvecoeur* 3
sucked blood-knowledge from the blood of the creature:
wing-thrust learned in the terror on face:
heartbeat probed in the heartbeat's place:

knew hummingbird fury: the hoof-hole still
clear under water, which sand would fill:
tension and torsion, snakes on the ground,
a mortal agony in combat bound:
tore leaves, broke ferns, for a word on the tongue: *John*
persimmon plucked for a new song sung: *James*
preached, as he killed: lived in a lair: *Audubon*
ate musquash, moosemeat, the fat of the bear:
spoke to his own soul, spoke to the stream,   *Henry*
Lord, lend me wisdom, Lord, let me dream: *David*
spent in thy heart was this sunshine day,   *Thoreau*
now in the evening a flute I'll play,
a flute in the forest, these pages to read,
a fly on the goldenrod, no more I'll need.
He trucked with the Indians: laid axe to root: *John*
packed his knapsack with the seed of fruit: *Chapman* 4
appleseed flung like flame in a wood:
fished pond and river, trod eels from mud;
framed a corncrib, and plowed up a field,
planted his corn and brought it to yield:
quit that clearing and a cabin of logs,
traded his store-goods and bought him some hogs;
and then, once more with an itching foot,
lashed a new raft, laying axe to root,
farewelled his folks, and floated down river,
to be home in the spring or else gone forever.

Said Tidewater Johnny to Bluewater Johnny,
you got to go west if you want to make money,
we built up the cities and filled them with people,
piled up a church and on top put a steeple,
and the cities are pretty, but the forest is best,
if you want to be private you got to go west.
Said Buckskin Johnny to Canebrake Johnny,
you got to climb trees if you want to eat honey,
the streets are well cobbled, the coaches are fine,
the ladies wear satin, the taverns have wine,

new immigrants skip from the packets each day,
set foot on the jetty, then up and away,
and the cities are pretty, but the prairie is best,
no money we'll need if we go to the west.
Said Catskill Johnny to Swannikan Johnny,
you fetch a horse and I'll find a pony,
we'll hitch Conestoga to a comet's tail
and hurry out west on the wilderness trail.
Nice manners and music are all very well,
and a college is fit for the son of a swell,
let moneybags tot up his slaves and his rum,
we're off to a place where a man has more room.
Go twing, go twang, go twang your guitar,
we'll roll all night to the prairie star,
there's no more Indians to fight, move on
where the Boone and Blackstone ghosts are gone:
you live but once, you're a long time dead —
who but a fool wants to die in bed?
And as for women, why, love 'em and leave 'em,
you got to love 'em but you got to grieve 'em.
Go twing your guitar, go twing, go twang,
I'm away to the coast on a wild mustang,
you need no ticket for the Golden Gate,
and the Big Rock Candy Mountains wait:
I've heard of a town named Snake-Eye Sue
with a bank and a bar and a damned fine view,
fourteen houses made of old tin cans,
but let me tell you that town is a man's:
that town is a man's, that's what they say,
and my name is the Kid, and I'm on my way!

Westward he rode, and the masks he wore:
southward he rode, and the names he bore.
Roared into town like a railroad train,
notched his gun, then notched it again.
He called his home the enchanted mesa:
came like a rustler, went like a greaser:

was twenty times shot and thirty times hung,
forty times captured and fifty times sprung:
ate mush and molasses with a long-handled spoon,
danced a square-dance from midnight to noon,
swing your partners, and now sashay,
do-se-do, give the gals away,
the promenade, and the allemande,
and pickin' posies on the Rio Grande:
kissed all the gals, and never missed one,
then rode out of town like a son-of-a-gun.
An old panhandler with the face of a moose   *Kit*
said, Chew terbaccer and swaller the juice,   *Carson*
I seen him with my own eyes, I did,
and I'm a horsethief if it wasn't the Kid.
Sandy and short, and his eyes was blue,
and what he looked at he looked right through.
A bindlestiff by the name of Joe
swore up and down it couldn't be so:
No sir, you ain't got the facts at all,
he wasn't freckled, and he wasn't small,
his name was Christopher, it wasn't Kit,
and he rode a pinto without no bit.
Said Bad Land Ike: It can't be the same.   *Billy*
I saw him in Pecos when he jumped my claim.   *the*
If a coffin nail's dead, then the Kid is dead.   *Kid*
His eyes were blue but his blood was red,
and they covered him up with an old bedspread.
No chick, no child, and no woman had he,
and they buried his body by a buckeye tree.

Rain-song and sun-song: rain from the sea:
here is my body, my truth let it be:
rain from the east and rain from the west
my body asleep in the deep earth's breast:
carve the stone tree, carve the stone urn,
the hourglass carve that never will turn,
the death's-head grinning, the willow-tree weeping,

my body asleep, and the raindrop dripping.
Stones! stones! stones! — and westward they face:
but thousands of miles have I been from this place:
thousands of waters my forefoot found,
in thousands of meadows my plow broke ground.
Here is my truth, and the page I turned:
but there, too, truth, and the wage I earned:
and the wisdom, also, that in rage I learned.
I drove the nails in the house I built: *Paul*
hammered a swordblade, and carved a hilt: *Revere*
blew the fine glass, poured lead in a mold,
and figured a ewer in pewter and gold:
for secret study, in sun and in shade,   *Benjamin*
I cast my type and my own book made,   *Franklin*
in subtler substance than silver wrought
the nerve of vision and the pulse of thought:
the verse of the hand, the verse of the eye,
the verse of the clear soul under the sky.
Stranger, as you are, so once was I.

What fiddles, what prayers, what dirge, what cry?
Skull in the desert and sand under sky.
Hands of cactus, and buffalo bones,
and a tassel of pine on a cairn of stones.
In the tall timber the true axe rings
where the ox draws wood and the woodsman sings:
a mountain of gold down the river is poured,
and a poppy's in bloom in praise of the Lord.
The praise is said, the prayer is done,
the fiddles are broken, but the ghost moves on.

VII

The Awakening

Dark was the forest, dark was the mind:
dark the trail that he stooped to find:

dark, dark, dark, in the midnight lost,
in self's own midnight, the seeking ghost.
Listen to the tree, press leaves apart:
listen to the blood, the evergreen heart:
deep, deep, deep, the water in the soul,
there will I baptize, and there be whole.
Dark, dark, dark, in this knowledge immersed,
by filth, by fire, and by frost aspersed,
in horror, in terror, in the depths of sleep,
I shudder, I grow, and my roots are deep.
The leaf is spoken: the granite is said:
now I am born, for the king is dead:
now I awake, for the father is dead.
Dark is the forest when false dawn looms —
darkest now, when the true day comes.
Now I am waking: now I begin:
writhe like a snake from the outworn skin:
and I open my eyes: and the world looks in!

VIII

The Last Vision

Said Railway Willy, O carry me back
on the golden engine and the silver track,
carry back east in a tall caboose
this broken-down body that's no more use.
I ain't seen Susie for sixteen years,
and the cinders are in my hair and ears,
I laid my rail and I drove my spike,
but the sound of the whistle is what I like:
all night I wait till I hear that freight,
and I set my watch, for it's never late.
We tunneled the mountain, we bridged the river,
we split the Rockies and they're split forever,
we coasted down to Pacific foam,
but now I'm dying and I want to go home.

Buffalo Gal, won't you come out tonight?
I'm headed east, and the signal's right.

O I'm headed for home, said Steamboat Bill,
on the Old Big River that shines uphill,
headed for the north from New Orleans,
feeding my fires on pork and beans.
I'll bowl through the chutes on the morning dew
and blow my whistle like I used to do,
blow my whistle and bowl through the chutes,
up from the bayous and away to the buttes.
O larboard leadsman, with your cry 'half twain!'
O Arkansas Traveler, with your rod and chain!
git aboard, it's time to go east again.
They've finished the cities, they're pretty to see,
and they're waiting to greet us with a golden key.

South poured the rivers: east went the dream:
east flew the glitter like a cloud of steam:
east coiled the dream like a wraith of smoke
on fields of clover that were forests of oak:
snow-song hovering, bird-song heard,
deep underground the shudder of the word:
death-knowledge whispered, death-knowledge guessed,
farewell the sunset, farewell the west:
rise up so early in the morn, my heart,
the road turns east and it's time to start:
rise up so early in the morn, my soul:
the roadstead's ready and the heart is whole.

He changed his name: Ahab became:
Ahab, and Ishmael, but the Kid just the same: *Herman*
his father's gods in a fury forswore   *Melville*
for a god more evil, but to worship more:
the god of hatred, of bland white evil,
the world incarnate as a blind white devil:
hurricane's wing: the capricious rage

that spares the pollen on the printed page
and then in frolic lays waste an age.
From the west returning, and the axe let be,
he turned, returning, to his mother, the sea:
islands, the foreshore, a gale in the Sound,
packets and whalers to the far east bound:
the full-moon tide, and the twin isles blest,
where Coffin and Daggett in God's Acre rest:
John and Lydia, that lovely payre,
a whale killed him, her body lyes here.

What thoughts? what hymns? what prayers? what altar?
Words out of tempest, and footsteps falter.
The sea-dark sounded, the dread descent
to fathom's meaning, a depth unmeant:
eyes to the self's black sea-heart turned,
the fouled line followed, the labyrinth learned.
Was God's path here? By what to be known?
What false channel-mark in the whale-path shown?
In Gulf Stream soul, or maelstrom heart,
what vortex to quarter, what shoals to chart?
Morning and evening, Lord, I reject Thee.
In fraud and fury, as in fire, I detect Thee.
In lust and in death I take and forsake Thee.
In breath and corruption I make Thee and break Thee.
In hate and despair I find Thee and lose Thee.
In breeding and bleeding I refuse Thee and use Thee.
In purposed or aimless I name Thee and shame Thee.
Wait Thou unknown, I'll seek Thee and claim Thee!

He plunged to the center, and found it vast.   *Willard*
Soared to the future, and found it past.   *Gibbs*
Always escaping the claws of clause,
inward or outward, the Laws and Cause:
mask under mask, face behind face,
name within name, place beneath place.
Ring within ring, he uncovered his pain:

found light in darkness, then darkness again: *Henry*
world whorled in world the whorl of his thought,   *Adams*
shape under series the godhead he sought:
for orbit's ritual and atom's cry   *Brooks*
he shot down the soul, saw it fall from the sky,   *Adams*
the invisible sighted, invisibly slain,
and darkly, in blood, resurrected again.
Working and weeping, Lord, I defy Thee.
In hurt and injustice I know and deny Thee.
Asleep in my slumber, I shake Thee and wake Thee,
in image, or number, or dream, to remake Thee.
Come terror, come horror, no need to escape Thee:
dipped in my death, I receive Thee and shape Thee!

Free flew the ghost: from the blood, from the land!   *Walt*
Hymned with the sea-voice on Paumanok sand!   *Whitman*
Broke like a billow, skimmed like a bird,
a rainbow on Greylock,[5] by Walden a word!
And sleeps in the churchyard, unlaureled the stone,   *Emily*
where lies the intrinsic, unknown, and alone.   *Dickinson*

SKYLIGHT ONE

*

The Orchard

Taking our time by the compass
    our direction by the clock
under the bough, where the windfall
    lies bitten by the frost and the squirrel,
through the jungle, in which imagination
    says 'time has fallen, time is falling,'
the immense jungle of crossed grasses
    and the green celandine of the heart:
who is it that steps like a leaf
    steps and then stops and then steps again
opening the door of cobweb
    to one mortal peril, then another?
who but the whole world in the heart,
    an apple full of seeds, dark seeds,
waiting for the living to be dead,
    and themselves, dead, to be resurrected!

Morning is blue as a child's globe
    on which no map has been drawn:
so, make a windmill of your arms
    and describe a pure circle:
thus the apple tree describes with her boughs
    the fatal fascination of sky,
while, with the same secret design,
    her roots feel the terror of earth.
Nothing divides your footstep
    from the world it rejects and rejoins:
you two are hurrying together

to the inevitable assignation.
The moon might have been your heart-beat,
    the sun a drop of blood in your hand,
circling forever in the tide
    of the ceaseless know-nothing.

Come, let us square out a space here,
    or have it round like a bird's nest,
a surface to scribble one word upon,
    or a box in which to find keepsakes:
or a room, very small, with one window,
    where sitting we can watch the shadows,
or a bed in which when we wish
    we can make believe that we sleep.
O something we can call our own,
    known and familiar for one moment:
A book that opens at a passage
    of which the meaning is 'maybe':
a face whose eyes have come back
    from the dreadful valley of nightfall:
a face whose eyes cannot stay
    from their holy love of forever.

Mayflower

I

Listen: the ancient voices hail us from the farther shore:
now, more than ever, in the New England spring,
we hear from the sea once more
the ghostly leave-takings, the hawser falling, the anchor weighing,
cries and farewells, the weeping on the quayside, and the praying:
and the devout fathers, with no thought to fail,
westward to unknown waters set joyless sail,
and at length, 'by God's providence,' 'by break of day espied
land, which we deemed to be Cape Cod.'

'It caused us to rejoice together and praise God,
seeing so goodly a land, and wooded to the brink of the sea.'
And still we share that providential tide,
the pleasant bay, wooded on every side
with 'oaks, pines, juniper, sassafras,' and the wild fowl rising
in clouds and numbers past surmising.
Yes: the ancient voices speak once more,
as spring, praised then by Will and Ben,
winds up our country clock again:
their spring, still living, now
when caterpillars tent the bough,
and seagulls speak
over the ale-wives running in Payne Creek.
The lyre-tree, seven-branched, the ancient plum, has cast
her sterile bloom, and the soft skin is cast
to glisten on the broken wall,
where the new snake sleeps in altered light;
and before sun-up, and late at night,
the pinkwinks shrill, the pinkwinks trill,
crying from the bog's edge to lost Sheepfold Hill.
Spring, spring, spring, spring, they cry,
water voice and reed voice,
spring, spring, spring, spring, they rejoice,
we who never die, never die!
But already the mayflower on the side hill is brown and dry,
Dry Hill is dry, the bog is drained,
and although for weeks it has not rained,
and the quick plough breaks dust,
yet towards summer the golden-rod and wormwood thrust.
The woodchuck is in the peas. And on his log,
the whip-poor-will shrieks and thumps in the bright May-morn-
     ing fog.

Three hundred years from Will and Ben,
and the crab-apple sage at Hawthornden;
and now they wind our country clock again,
themselves, whose will it was that wound it then.

Three hundred years of snow and change,
the Mermaid voices growing lost and strange;
heard at first clearly on this yellow sand,
ghost voices, shadow of ghost and whisper of ghost,
haunting us briefly in the bright and savage land,
heard in the sea-roar, then sunk in silence, lost.
Yet not lost wholly:
in deed, in charter, and in covenant sweetly kept,
in laws and ordinances, in the Quaker's Thee and Thou,
in the grave rites of birth and death, the marriage vow,
and the ballad's melancholy.
Sung by the driftwood fire or behind the plough,
in the summer-kitchen to the warm cricket-song,
sung at maying, sung at haying,
shouted at husking to the fiddle's playing,
murmured to the cradle's rocking,
and the wheel humming, the treadle knocking.
And in the names kept too: sorrel and purslane,
ground-ivy, catnip, elecampane,
burdock and spurge, and sultry tansy,
woad-waxen, and the johnny-jump-up pansy.
Yet even so, though in the observance kept,
here most of all where first our fathers stept,
was something of the spirit that became idle, and at last
lost all that love; and heard no more
the voices singing from a distant shore.
Intricately, into the present, sank the past:
or, dreaming only of the future, slept.

II

God's Acres once were plenty, the harvest good:
five churchyards, six, in this sparse neighbourhood,
each with its huddled parish of straight stones,
green rows of sod above neat rows of bones.
The weeping willow grieves above the urn,
the hour-glass with wings awaits its immortal turn:

on every slab a story and a glory,
the death's head grinning his *memento mori.*
All face the sunset, too: all face the west.
What dream was this of a more perfect rest — ?
One would have thought the east, that the first ray
might touch them out of darkness into day.
Or were they sceptics, and perforce, in doubt,
wistful to watch the last of light go out?
And in the sunset the names look westward, names like eyes:
the sweet-sounding and still watchful names. Here lies
Mercy or Thankful, here Amanda Clark,
the wife of Rufus; nor do they dread the dark,
but gaily now step down the road past Stony Brook,
call from the pasture as from the pages of a book,
their own book, by their own lives written,
each look and laugh and heartache, nothing forgotten.
Rufus it was who cleared of bullbriar the Long Field,
walled it with fieldstone, and brought to fabulous yield
the clay-damp corner plot, where wild grape twines.
Amanda planted the cedars, the trumpet-vines,
mint-beds, and matrimony vine, and columbines.
Each child set out and tended his own tree,
to each his name was given. Thus, they still live, still see:
Mercy, Deborah, Thankful, Rufus and Amanda Clark,
trees that praise sunlight, voices that praise the dark.
The houses are gone, the little shops are gone,
squirrels preach in the chapel. A row of stone
all now that's left of the cobbler's, or in tall grass
a scrap of harness where once the tannery was.
And the blue lilacs, the grey laylocks, take possession
round every haunted cellar-hole, like an obsession:
keep watch in the dead houses, on vanished stairs,
where Ephraim or Ahira mended chairs:
sneak up the slope where once the smoke-house stood
and herrings bronzed in smoke of sweet fernwood.
Lost, lost, lost, lost — the bells from Quivett Neck
sing through the Sabbath fog over ruin and wreck,

roofs sinking, walls falling, ploughland grown up to wood.
Five churchyards, six, in this sparse neighbourhood:
God's Acres once were plenty, the harvest good.

III

Three hundred years: in time's eye only a moment.
Time only for the catbird's wail,
from one June to another, flaunting his tail,
the joyful celebrant with his own mournful comment.
Time only for the single dream,
as, in this misty morning, all our generations seem,
seem only one, one face, one hope, one name:
those who first crossed the sea, first came,
and the newborn grandchild, crying, one and the same.
Yes now, now most of all, in the fateful glare
of mankind's hatred everywhere,
time yields its place, with its own bell
uncharms and then recharms its spell:
and time is gone, but everything else is here,
all is clear, all is one day, one year,
the many generations seem,
and are, one single purpose, one single name and dream.
Three hundred years from Will and Ben
our country clock's wound up again.
And as it chimes we hear ourselves still saying
the living words which they said then —
words for haying, words for maying,
love of earth, love of love, love of God,
but most the strong-rooted and sweet-smelling love of sod,
earth natural and native in the clay-red heart,
ourselves like pines in the sand growing, part
of the deep water underground,
the wild rose in the mouth, the sound
of leaves in surf and surf in leaves,
wind suffering in the chimney and round the eaves,
forgetfulness in the chattering brook, sleepiness in the sand,
forget-me-nots in the eyes, moonlight in the palm of the hand.

All's here, all's kept, for now
spring brings back the selfsame apple bough
that braved the sea three hundred years ago.
It is our heart, our love, which we had lost,
our very ghost,
forgotten in trouble on an alien coast.
Now, in the many-voiced country lane
which parts the fields of poverty grass and clover,
as the loud quail repeats twice over
Bob White, not quite, not quite, Bob White,
see it again and say it again,
world without end to love and have it,
bee-blossom heart to love and live it,
this holy land, our faith itself, to share again
with our godfathers, Will and Ben.

Evil Is the Palindrome

Perception is the beginning, sweetheart, perception
opens the window from which we view
terror fluttering toward us down an empty road
delight screaming on dark wings over the hill.
Shall we run? Shall we stand still?
O if we cannot live or love, let us forgive:
evil is the palindrome of live.

The first act is to open our eyes to the light,
the last act is to close them to inward night.
The first act, is it braver than the last,
when we surrender all that is left of us to sleep?
We close our hearts to terror, close them to weep.
If we cannot live or love, let us forgive:
evil is the palindrome of live.

Praise, praise, the dreadful fountain of all blaze,
the immense, cruel, dazzling, spouting source
of ethereal violent living and death-dealing powers:

clouds, sheaved lightnings, burning demonic forms
in angelic and ceaseless creation through the soul's storms.
If we cannot live or love, let us forgive:
evil is the palindrome of live.

Live for the frontier of the daily unknown, of terror,
for the darkness hidden in the striking hand,
the darkness opening in the thinking mind,
the darkness under the valve of the beating heart:
live for the borderland, the daybreak, whence we start
to live and love, and if we cannot live to forgive:
evil is the palindrome of live.

Crepe Myrtle
F. D. R.: April 12, 1945

i

Leaves, and waves, and years. Shadows of leaves, shadows of
waves, and shadows of years.
What will the boy recall of them
himself a leaf hurrying among leaves
planking of a lost whaler adrift among waves
washed and aspersed to the tolling of the years, until at length
the man remembers the boy, the man
drawing nostalgic pictures of the past with a stick?
'What have I seen? The leaves blown in harsh waves
waves scattered like leaves to leeward blown
leeward from the brave foolish heart, the intrepid mind,
but to be summoned again in a moment of vision
by waves no mind can control.'
Landward charge the white horses everlastingly
from the blinding notch of the sea-rim, numberless, calling
and falling, lapsing and collapsing, each at last
to become in substance one with another
or in motion with one and in substance with all:

seaward the charioteers the white manes riding
from the known shore to the unknown shoreless faring,
beyond the remembering vision of him who beholds
once for an instant the beginning of the endless.
Waves of leaves, waves of waves, waves of years:
but the sound at last silent, less than the chuckle
of the falling fountain of thought, the motion becoming
the symbol, only, of motion,
and simplified at last, and still.

ii

But look: the record of a handful of leaves
dances on the moonlit wall of an old house, opens
silent fingers, closes them again, points quickly,
and then is replaced by nothing, without comment
the slide removed from the magic lantern.
Perhaps to return again, altered, in sunlight, or yet again
to be altered anew, unrecognized, in leafless winter.
O blind dark darkness of self, blind dark brightness
of the surely not implacable, not unknowable, Other!
wave of the outer forever falling into the wave of the inner!
can we decipher here behind the quick shutter
in the single tremor of insight
the final meaning of shadow? The crepe myrtle
disowns its shadow on hard earth faded with blossom
designs a cemetery wall with echo of bloom
signals a moving message over the headstone, sliding
its cryptic stencil, life-and-death, between
old earth and new moon.

As here! reshaping
in the spring night! the lantern hung among tombs,
the pick striking a spark from granite, the spade
divulging the loose sub-tropic humus, the past!
and the old vault lies open,
empty to the fetid and aromatic night,

empty of all save the soft and silken dust,
dust as fine as hair or as passion, elusive
as moonlight on the shell road: empty of all
save a single gleam in the corner by the red wall:
and quickly as a heartbeat or cry unearthed,
shining again for the lantern after a hundred years,
the silver sword-hilt, the rusted sword-blade.
And behold, the hero walks again among men,
the living dead man salutes the dead men who still live,
and they stiffen, hearing the lost bugle of Eutaw Springs
across the cypress swamp in the dead of winter:
the voice of wisdom that trembles from the ground,
the voice of honour that trembles in rusted steel.

iii

The coffin of the great man travels slowly
through the applause of silence the applause of flags
the applause of tears and empty hearts, the applause
of the last and greatest loneliness, the speechless
loneliness of the great vision: the coffin of the great man
travels slowly over earth, slowly under sky,
slowly through the sun-sequined shadow, slowly through
     the shade,
slowly under the evening star and the faint new moon
and again now into the pre-dawn silence, and the first
pinewood voice of the mocking-bird, while eastward
under the Pole Star leans the world to the light
and the light falls on the pine-barrens like moss roses
and on the mountains like smoke. The coffin of the great man
travels under the arch of time without pausing
and without pausing under the arch of eternity
and without pausing under the arch of the infinite
travelling now as the earth travels, joining the earth,
turning to the right with the earth as it faces the Pole Star
they two becoming in substance one with another
in motion at one and in substance with all.

The coffin of the great man travels slowly
slowly and well through the seasons, the spring passing
over into the rich summer, and with the earth
revolves under the changing arch of the years.
And now the avenues of weeping are still, the applause
of silence itself is hushed, and the empty hearts
are again refilled with love, the limp flags
stiffen anew at the masthead. And it is he,
himself, the great man dead, who teaches us,
speaking from the coffin, already empty, and the grave
empty also. For the greatness is not there,
travelled not slowly thither with the slow coffin,
slowly to turn with earth under time's arch,
but is given to us to keep. The great man's name
walks again among us, the living greatness
speaks in ourselves. And we hear him saying
— as we heard the bugle of Eutaw Springs
sing in a sword-blade — *'Finis coronat opus* —
death crowns the work, not the man!' The voice of wisdom
trembling in our own hearts, the voice of honour
trembling in the broken sword.

                      Leaves, and waves, and years:
shadow of a handful of leaves that dances
on the wall of an empty house, the crepe myrtle
designing a cemetery wall with echo of bloom,
signalling a message over the headstone, sliding
her cryptic stencil, life-and death between
the old earth and new moon. And in our minds, now his,
where the waves are falling, falling, each at last
to become in substance one with another
or in motion with one and in substance with all,
seaward the charioteers the white manes riding
from the known shore to the unknown shoreless fare:
beyond the remembering vision of him who beheld
once and forever the beginning of the endless.

The Window

She looks out in the blue morning
and sees a whole wonderful world
she looks out in the morning
and sees a whole world

she leans out of the window
and this is what she sees
a wet rose singing to the sun
with a chorus of red bees

she leans out of the window
and laughs for the window is high
she is in it like a bird on a perch
and they scoop the blue sky

she and the window scooping
the morning as if it were air
scooping a green wave of leaves
above a stone stair

and an urn hung with leaden garlands
and girls holding hands in a ring
and raindrops on an iron railing
shining like a harp string

an old man draws with his ferrule
in wet sand a map of Spain
the marble soldier on his pedestal
draws a stiff diagram of pain

but the walls around her tremble
with the speed of the earth the floor
curves to the terrestrial centre
and behind her the door

opens darkly down to the beginning
far down to the first simple cry
and the animal waking in water
and the opening of the eye

she looks out in the blue morning
and sees a whole wonderful world
she looks out in the morning
and sees a whole world.

Summer

Absolute zero: the locust sings:
summer's caught in eternity's rings:
the rock explodes, the planet dies,
we shovel up our verities.

The razor rasps across the face
and in the glass our fleeting race
lit by infinity's lightning wink
under the thunder tries to think.

In this frail gourd the granite pours
the timeless howls like all outdoors
the sensuous moment builds a wall
open as wind, no wall at all:

while still obedient to valves and knobs
the vascular jukebox throbs and sobs
expounding hope propounding yearning
proposing love, but never learning

or only learning at zero's gate
like summer's locust the final hate
formless ice on a formless plain
that was and is and comes again.

Autumnal

Matrimony-vine, twin-starred, in the garden wall,
blooms where the last of sun-drowsed roses fall,
and the brown hollyhock's seed-purse breaks in rust
and drops her disks of seed to coin in dust.

O how to see and say, in these near things,
as much as heaven, where the hawk's scything wings
dissolve a curve less subtle than can delight
a lover's eye, or lover's hand invite!

Halcyon summer, heaven's-blue-chicory sky:
all, all above us that vast and open eye
which, like a lover's, sees and lights us through,
till we too burn with that cerulean blue.

My dear, my dearest, and oh too distant love,
let each to other be as that eye above,
gazing down love in all-day-long delight
until the closing of our hearts in night:

cherishing too these small, these much-loved things,
matrimony-vine, the hawk's gone westward wings,
all that compose for us a song of praise
dark as the night's delight, deep as the day's.

The Improvisation

i

The synthesis of spring once more, antique illusion:
the icicle slips from the eaves and is brilliantly shattered,
the dog-tooth violet pricks her ears under leaf-mould:

but not in April, and later than Indian Summer.
The bird, that we heard in our orchard,
let him remain unknown and nameless,
the fabulous harbinger of a chimerical season.
And who would have thought the hylas would wake November,
chant their plain-song in November?
Now systole and diastole should be hushed
mortally under snow, slowed to the rhythm
of water under ice on a night of planets.
Instead, comes the ragged celandine
brashly out of orbit, and the song-sparrow's rehearsed roulade
charms the breathless caesura of sunrise
wholesome and formal as a passage of Haydn.
Solecism of solstices: winter the dupe of spring:
or together the two in a dialectic
ghostly as moonlight at midday.

And the rituals, the formalities, the prepared language,
how inadequate to the occasion: for none exist.
The bloodroot unfolding under ice? the little Lady's Slipper
under snow? while the poor blue-bird,
lost between weathers, his time-sense confused as ours,
startles with colour the cavernous iceberg.
We were not born, surely,
to be thus confronted. The Great Astrologer's eyepiece
slipped from his eye for a moment, and the two particles
escaped all knowledge. And so, out of time,
and only of our own volition,
together drawn by an outlaw motion,
we reach the intangible, touch the inaccessible,
by our own privilege know the Unknown.

Yes, and with what precarious, hesitant, yet archangelic improvi-
    sation,
everything foreseeing, we make the slow footsteps
of love into music: as easily and naturally
as the sly catbird, luckiest of singers, builds his madrigal

into the nuptial nest. The approach, the half-meeting,
the hands eager to touch, almost touching, yet not touching,
the stillness, and the pause, the weighing of the laws
that move the measured footsteps towards obliteration,
and then at last, as if in air, sudden as a wing-beat,
the meeting itself —

                          whether through the eyes,
which can never have enough of light,
or through the hands, which can never have enough of touch,
or the voices, which, for joyful humility,
fall incredulous into silence —

these we compose intricately, with radiant certainty,
point counterpoint, the luminous algebra of love,
(it is as if our veins became skeins of light)
into our passacaglia, which now trembles
by right successions to its ecstasy.

And so the ending: for inevitably it ends.
Brightness falls from the air, and the moving dance
of the unseen dancers, who danced on light,
is over, and with it our shining.
The music is ended: yet after it falls
the wave of silence on which the music was written,
the moment of the music's wholeness, when we hear
the All in the single instant of time. Love ends
where it begins: the birth and the renunciation
are one, one and the same.

Fair indeed was the deceitful summer: halcyon the afterglow
in which we loose our thistledown towards winter:
August's fireflies are hurried to a phantom death
far from the rose-garden, by the metal rocks of Labrador:
and we die with them, they are ourselves.

ii

And of the bodies: the minds: the memories,
thus capriciously brought together: we who have neither
acquired nor inherited formulae for living, who love
from one soul's-instant to another, as we live:
always the giant step from island to island of being
terrified yet fearless over the infinite,
precisely as the celandine steps from November
to blind April, the season of death to the season of procreation:
what will they make of this unstellar conjunction?
propose what cavils and confusions? with what protocol
solemnize the meeting of self and not-self?
Hardened travellers, each with his own luggage
of habit and injury!

Let us not be afraid, for all is acceptable,
unknown past and unknown future alike acceptable:
the stepping-stones of the known to the past,
and the stepping-stones of the known to the future,
will lead us, item by sunlit item, till we drown in light.
Dear stranger, in whom the strangeness becomes dear,
and chaos familiar, what would I not know and love
of all your world that whispers back in time,
of all this time that images forth a world
to call itself the temporal 'you'!

iii

But the death is here, is now, twines its nightshade
with the first primrose, shines in our music
ironic and ephemeral as the firefly of summer.
The *moritura* is in the discovery, the farewell
is already prepared (with secret tears)
in the first ambiguous greeting, the divided voice
of love-and-death. And all the memories,

the luggage of habit and injury, yours and mine,
the loves, and the half-loves, and the self-loves,
beset us now as once they abetted, divide us now
as once they joined: the four-leafed clover
on the first page of childhood; the cricket
sunning himself on a pebble; the sad rain
on the long windowpanes of illness — you take back these,
as I take back my own. Slow histories recited;
agony projected as sunset on an evening of despair;
friends found and lost; and the dead leaf in the book
to mark the would-be-remembered phrase: all these,
the infinitesimal, or exaggerated, or ridiculous, but cherished:
all these rehearse our death, as if in a ritual
ourselves had prearranged. They reappear to bless us,
and vanish. Even our hatreds bless us and vanish.
Even our self-deceptions, which now, in the moment of sorrow,
we perceive were well-meant, and perhaps even angelic:
the desire to grow, to excel, to see ourselves in a mirror
of godlike beauty, apocalyptic power and wisdom:
even these avert their faces with a sly smile of blessing
and give us back to truth.
And the division, the separation, the first dreadful steps
toward separation and division,
oh, these too we must compose into a figure, a foreseen improvi-
        sation:
the valedictions transposed into the music,
but as if backward, as if the *aria da capo*
were really conceived at the end, and then cast back.
Scarcely perceptible, the first ghostly recession!
lighter than flute-song of an overtone,
or the quick choice whether to turn or not turn
the profile on a heartbeat of pain. And then, in succession,
half willed, half not, the 'half' separations, and the long back-
        ward look,
the net of not-yet-abandoned-hope flung softly out into the abyss,
but withdrawn again, unnoticed, untouched. And so, at last,
long since foreknown and endured, the dread chasm
of the separation itself —

                              whether discovered through the eyes,
which can never have enough of darkness,
or the hands, which would again become inviolable,
or the voices, which would again be still —

all these, already, we have known it from the beginning,
are the conceived and developed and concluded theme,
from signature to coda, of ourselves.
Dear stranger, our love was the music,
we held it for an instant in a handclasp of sunlight,
it is gone, and ourselves gone with it,
the best of us was there, died there.

Moritura

Three o'clock, and the surf of wind in the locusts
pours the quick moonlight through pooled or cascaded leaves:
O destructive and creative agony of the living leaves
at three o'clock in the morning of death in life.

For she has no heart, and I have no heart,
as we lie and listen to the agony of dying leaves:
it is our own rich agony we hear in the dying leaves
at three o'clock in the morning of death in life.

'There is ever,' she murmurs, 'a shadow of *moritura*
in anything really beautiful': and our love lies bleeding,
even in the first kiss our love lies bleeding,
at three o'clock in the morning of death in life.

Can we bid the image stay? or hold it trembling
in love's Narcissus pool for one shared moment?
O destructive and creative agony of the changing moment
at three o'clock in the morning of death in life.

The song-sparrow's song is fixed on the dawn like a pattern of
    silver

rises and falls in the dark like a pattern of silver
and the death of our love is fixed in a pattern of silver
at three o'clock in the morning of death in life.

Yes, in this deep embrace, we lie divided:
'For the death of all experience,' she murmurs again,
'is the shadow beside the experience, runs beside it,'
at three o'clock in the morning of death in life.

There, down the stairs of the blood, we hear it hurry,
light-footed ghost of change, the beautiful death,
and already our love is the moss torn away from the rockface
at three o'clock in the morning of death in life.

'Rest here, rest nowhere,' so says the surf in the trees.
'Rest here, rest nowhere,' says the heartless woman beside me.
For she has no heart, and I have no heart,
at three o'clock in the morning of death in love.

Plain Song

Best come in, the morning's bitter,
pollen float from stars is fatal,
everywhere the abyss lies open,
everywhere laugh dirt and death:

see the descending trap of sunlight
close alike on fly and flower,
membrane into membrane creeping,
vinelike for corruption thrust!

Impure heart that would be single,
multiple soul that would be simple,
watch your daybreak crash in atoms
on the world-coast named despair:

nothing's touched, and nothing's touching:
prey to love, you probe an abscess:
stillness in inebriate motion,
false and fecund fall apart:

even the secret self is faithless,
leers and lies when called to answer:
o divinest, o serenest,
man's invented dream of light!

thousandfold we find its mazes,
more we seek the more it crazes,
best come in, the morning's bitter,
shut the door and wait for night.

Voyage to Spring

i

Dry the grass this September, dry the whistle
of the quail searching the cranberry bog for water,
and the cicada's little helicopter
spins sadly down in sunlight, like a child's toy
running down at once in tone and time.
To be immersed now in a vision of rank spring again,
with all its powers and vicissitudes, its falseness too,
yet with its powers commensurate to its dream,
how inopportune, but with what persuasive logic
the notion shuttles (in, at last, the late afternoon rain)
through the warped summer! *We could have lived, we could
    live —*
so in susurrus whisper the perished grassblades
and the shrivelled plums that drop from the ancient plum-tree:
we could have loved, we could love —
rhythmic as the complaint of the crickets on a night of frost.
And the slow rain, the gentle resurrection of rain,

leaf-bobbing rain, twig-dripping rain,
walks down the road as if it were a vein
from which such visions might yet come again.

As so, indeed, they do. The natural magic
of natural things: the rain evokes the rain,
and that another. How the long quaver rises
in ghostly shimmer of fruitful deception.
Out of this, things came to pass — out of this,
the dream, the reality, the vision, and the fact.
I am what I was, I was what I am, I would like to be
what I am no longer. For the poor benefit
of a lost moment of sensual satisfaction,
the nymph-cry in the blood, the whimpered rainsong
of the beloved under one's kiss, the all-night-rainsong,
the *I-can-love, I-can-love,*
how one would sacrifice one's integrity, pretend
to be what one no longer is, envying those
who need no pretence, who in their natural spring
invent an April! Useless to remind the lovers
while still they are locked in undivided delight
in their self-woven chrysalis of night
that this is not an end or a beginning
nor a single birth nor a single death nor climax
nor an exploration nor a discovery nor a voyage
but the gross usufruct, indifferent and mechanical,
automatic as the bursting of a seed-pod,
of life itself, the source and sink of all.
Useless, too, to tell oneself. One looks and envies,
one listens and envies, longing only again to know
the accelerated heart-beat, the blind passion to touch,
the inexhaustible need for surrender, the suffocation
of anguish that one feels in separation,
and the unappeasable suffocation of desire
of each to be incorporated in the other.
False, false, false, all of it false,
the necessary inevitable illusion, chromatic deception

of the vernal and venereal equinox: the mere rubescence
of old whore earth in the spring.

ii

                    For the chromatic deception,
the viridescent treason, is everywhere: the blush
is merely the signal of deceit. How all nature
is riddled with design, yes, raddled with it too,
old harridan that she is. How with low cunning
she baits her trap with a young anxious body,
and that with agate eyes, and those with a radiance
beautiful and bent as sunlight through sea-foam:
and the small mouth, *bocca tremante,* trembling and timid,
that asks but says no, denies but says yes —
with what pathos, what tremulous empathy,
prefiguring all, foretasting all,
it offers to be shaped, or to shape itself, to yours —
which could have shaped itself to many, and in time
will find the time to do. For did you think
to have fidelity in nature? No such thing.
She is a broker, she must make money breed.
All her investments are short-term loans, callable
at notice. Let the young anxious body, the *bocca tremante,*
and the desired smile, *disiato riso,* fail in their purpose,
it is only for a moment, they will be tried again.

And with the necessary attributes, the requisite
décor, the illusory stage effects, all supplied
— as in a theatre programme — by yourself:
which is to say by Eros, the imagination.
Such sunsets, too. Sunsets to beggar description
and dissolve the reason, each with a chemical
affinity for the blood, and wired for sound
to the very psyche: while the off-stage aria
eerily haunts the wings with an evocation
of deus-ex-machina, the oracular, the all-too-divine.

Everything becomes of a texture exquisitely suited
to the lover's touch: preposterously precious:
the rock-surfaces are of silk, screened through desire,
and even the vulgarest landscape, mere terrestrial segment,
the broken billboard in a vacant lot,
is translated in a twinkling to translunar.

And then the music: the by-no-means
so incidental music — o god that music.
For what's in music that it so probes a lover's pain,
nesting even in the embolism? The threadbare scrape of catgut
tangles the gullible and hallucinated heart
with the music of the spheres, no less.

And what's to be treasured of this, what's kept
of the off-stage aria, the pinchbeck golden sunset
on a more than Roman scene? What's left of these
fine shades, and shades of shades, those o so delicate
distinctions and divinations, those rare tremors
projected by the lover's eye, his heart, his mind?
Nothing, or less than nothing: since it is something
chimerical as the blood-count in a raindrop:
and the wide arch of the deranged empire falls.
No, not in love comes summer from spring, no, never.
Nor is its dream, the dear dream (and we thought
its powers commensurate to its dream)
ever fulfilled. Not what the lover willed,
but something else, is kept: and while he slept.

iii

Yes, in the rain, in the autumn, in the memory,
the silence that follows the cicada's silence,
the footsteps of the rain gone down the lane
seeking a vision that will not come again
(or will it, do we find it now)
but most of all in memory, mine and yours,

the sad by-product of the sad by-product mind,
and most, most of all in the sad by-product mind —
o traitor love, perhaps in this we keep
something that will not fail us, even in sleep:

perhaps in the notation of the deception,
the riddling out of the illusory colours
with which old nature baits her trap, in the loving
and agonized appraisal of the young anxious body,
and the agate eyes, and the small mouth, *bocca tremante,*
that asks to shape itself to yours:
and in the knowing, and the pain of knowing, also,
the response, the answer, automatic in oneself:
yes, in this miserable knowledge, that destroys, as it learns,
heart-beat by heart-beat the passion it feeds on,
is our escape, our one escape. The mirage of spring
shatters about us in a broken prism of rainbows
never to be assembled again, or to be assembled
only in the ironic despair of a dream:
the false sunset has vanished under more than the sea:
the stage is suddenly vaster, there are no wings
for the off-stage voice of the pseudo-god:
instead, the silence and loneliness of self
become a new world, of which the shores
are faintly audible, faintly visible. We will go there.

The Lovers

This painful love dissect to the last shred:
abjure it, it will not be solved in bed:
agony of the senses, but compounded
of soul's dream, heart's wish, blood's will, all confounded
with hate, despair, distrust, the fear of each
for what the other brings of alien speech.
Self-love, my love, no farther goes than this,
that when we kiss, it is ourselves we kiss.

O eyes no eyes, but fountains fraught with tears,
o heart no heart, but cistern of the years,
how backward now to childhood's spring we thrust
there to uncover the green shoots of lust:
how forward then to the bare skull we look
to taste our passion dead in doomsday book!
Self-love is all we know, my love, and this
breeds all these worlds, and kills them, when we kiss.

Yet would I give, yet would you take, a time
where self-love were no criminal, no crime:
where the true godhead in each self discovers
that the self-lovers are both gods and lovers.
O love, of this wise love no word be said,
it will be solved in a diviner bed,
where the divine dance teaches self-love this,
that when we kiss it is a god we kiss.

The Clover

The tiger gash of daybreak rips the night
under palmetto leaves drips the first light
the dream is broken the word of water spoken
and the dream bursts with the golden scream
of the unknown bird in the fountained park
hark hark hark screaming beneath blind leaves
and the wild hour is strange and pain strange too
as also too that love to pain should change
the pure love-pattern into deep life-pattern change.
O love, o love, that in the mountains took
this simple heart beside the mountain brook
and broke the golden-rod for summer speech
brimming with water-gold the heart of each,
with what ascending footsteps carved in light
climbing the hyaline we have come to this
animal cry invented in a kiss!

And then the tiger gash of pain
the malicious bird screams in the park again
now at the window screams now at the breast
this breast that lives and loves.

Pray, time, what is our shame
or what this blessedness without a name
that the unknown of love should come to this
animal birth embodied in a kiss?
And this child born in pain of me
the small pale soul that wails in fear of light
what shall I be to him or he to me
now that the dual world is sundered into three?
All's lost in finding, we are swept away
like shoreless mariners, this bed our ship,
nor in this voyage shall we one harbour find,
but separately and alone, love as we may,
seek our own landfall under hostile day.
Farewell, dear voyager — already you depart
who but a moment since lay in my heart.

(And the red leaf turns, turns, in a circle of dust
in the shaft of light that has come and gone
and the light is turning, turning in a ring of darkness
in the mind of night that dreams of waking
and time is turned as sand by the hand is turned
circle in circle ring within ring
till again the finger writes in a circle of dust
in the shaft of light that has come and gone
and the world, my love, comes round
round as the ring of druid oaks in spring
or the ritual hymn the pinkwinks sing,
the world is round as a ring.)

For see, he brings you now his fourleafed clover
who is already (as you bear again) your lover:
and the clear pink-clawed blossoms too,

those that he loves,
clusters that smell like cloves.
As much as you, he loves — as much as you:
and as you turn your head,
on the pale pillow turn your head,
you see the something new
that lights (and listens) in your child, as if
your own eyes there gazed back at you:
and, if with love, yet with a different view.
For in that look, that probing interchange,
hovers the thought, perceptible to each,
shines between the eyes, but without speech,
that you surrender now your sovereignty,
but with a kind of acquiescent glee —
you whose thought-wings mount in wider gyre
over the world's wildness, yet know how soon
(time's gift, but also yours)
the child's must always further range, and higher.
This too is a departure, this accolade of clover:
but also, although no mention made,
without a kiss it is conveyed
(although perhaps each wished a kiss)
that now henceforward, far though the voyage take
each on his destined course, the child will keep
your heart, your mind, your love
enringed in his:
your flight, no matter where,
will be ensphered and safely move in his:
no matter, no, how far and faint it soar
or low and lost at last it fall,
his circling love embraces all.
Thus in silence, in the May-morning light,
the mutual accolade.

And o, you guessed, whose generous gesture made
his young thought feel the wing-beat's power
shuddering imagination in that hour

for flaming wheel and falcon tower
over the ruined infernos and gutted heavens
and obliterated purgatories of a world
overwhelmed and overwinged
in range and ring and rise of mind
by feather and ecstasy and blood —
and o, you knew, and meant,
if your own journey went
too early underground
and o poor love for only treason's reason,
too soon, too dark, in the alien spring,
the alien much-loved chinaberry season,
that he would join you there, his vision
flung down with the dust, and the windlost voice
chanting the last verse,
passionately in your grave. For there it stayed,
and there it stays, and there rejoined
to the lost heart, as the slow seasons made
their havoc, from ruin to ruin it too decayed,
fell with you lightly into earth, you two
becoming earth together. But not forgetful,
and not in sleep, if the dust sleeps, is thought to sleep:
for now his life was yours, dedicated to you:

who while he lives will be your lover
(listen, his footstep coming upon the whisper
buena ventura whisper of the Spanish moss)
and brings once more the clear-stemmed clover,
o lost love in this token
sharing with you again, but no word spoken,
that moment's magic, the May-bright morning,
when you evoked so long ago
beyond the chinaberry-shadowed wall
the rings and rituals of your light:
the leaf turning, turning in a circle of dust,
the finger writing, writing, in a ring of dust,
and the mind of night dreaming divine delight:

for the world, my love, comes round,
round as the dance of ancient oaks in spring
or the ritual song the enchanted pinkwinks sing,
the world is round as a ring.

Hallowe'en

I

All Saints', All Hallows',
All Souls', and Hallowe'en,
which is the evening of the last of October,
and the harvest moon full:
and the first of November, *Allerheiligen,*
and the second of November, *Allerseelen.*
The moon, dead brother, lights her bonfire
behind Sheepfold Hill, old corpse-fire
blazing through the oaktrees, the bone-fire
which, in the forests, the priests called *ignis ossium.*
And again you come to complain and to haunt me,
you and the others, the homeless: the bells
trill in the twilight, held by no fingers,
touched by no hand of the living, the voices
under the bronze cloud circle the bonfire,
wing-voice and bat-voice and tree-voice:
and the spotted pebble, flung hissing in flames,
is lost in the ashes, and with it your soul.
It is you at the fire's edge, grandfather — !
your skeleton dancing, the pumpkin-head glaring,
the corpse-light through the pierced eyes and slashed mouth,
you, past the gas-works and the power-plant drifting,
and the old car-tracks and the railroad crossing,
but not, no, not again to the Heath of Simmering
where you watched little rafts of gay candles
floating like fireflies down the Danube, the souls
of those who had drowned in the river! There you

with alien eyes saw the ancient god, there heard
with alien ears the *Allerseelen, Allerheiligen,*
the candles on grave-mounds, and the flowers,
the procession of the living with wreaths
to the hillside cemeteries in the mountains,
and, after dark, the processions of the dead
to the lost threshold, the lost hearthstone.
And now you come back to complain and to haunt me,
you, and my brother, and the others.
Was your vision of god not enough, that you come
for the vision of the not-yet-dead, and the cricket's
chirp on the still-warm hearthstone?

II

In the old time, the old country,
these two days, these two holy days,
were devoted to the dead. At the end of summer,
in the first haze of autumn stolen in from the sea,
at Samhain, the end of summer,
salt smell of kelp mixed with scent of the windfall
and whirled up the chalk path at daybreak,
we sacrificed a white horse to the sun-god
and kindled great fires on the hills
and nightlong we danced in circles
with straw-plaits blazing on pitchforks.
We sacrificed too to the moon-god,
an effigy, a simulacrum,
on this night, Hallowe'en, for we knew
the spirits of the dead were released, and would come
to rattle our latches and sit at the table. At Vespers,
in the dank churchyard, in the ossuary,
where the bones from an over-full graveyard were crammed,
we went in and knelt among bones. And the bones
(wing-voice and tree-voice and wind-voice)
suddenly were singing about us
joined in complaint and besought us

for prayers and more prayers, while the candles
flickered in the draft on grave-mounds.
Then on clean cloth we laid out the supper,
the hot pancakes, and the curds, and the cider,
and banked well the fire, and set the chairs round it,
said a prayer, and to bed.

In the old time, the old country:
but now none remembers, now they become
the forgotten, the lost and forgotten. O lost and forgotten,
you homeless and hearthless, you maskers and dancers,
masquerading as witches, as wild beasts, as robbers,
jack-o'-lantern leaping in the shadows of walls,
bells thrilling at the touch of bone fingers,
you come back to abuse and to haunt us,
you, grandfather, and my brother, and the others:
to the forgetful house, yourselves not forgetful,
(for the dead do not forget us, in our hearts
the dead never forget us)
you return to make mischief and to enter the house
you return once more to remind us.
The pumpkin-head lit with a candle, the cry
help the poor, help the poor, help the poor!
comminatory cry from door to door
and the obolos paid that the ghost be laid:
it is our ancestors and children who conspire against us
life unlived and unloved that conspires against us
our neglected hearts and hearths that conspire against us
for we have neglected not only our death
in forgetting our obligations to the dead
we have neglected our living and our children's living
in neglecting our love
for the dead who would still live within us.

                                  III

All summer it rained: day after day, from morning
to sodden noon and eave's-drop eve, it rained:

day after day the heavens and the clouds complained.
Heavy the honeysuckle poll with over-ripe blossom:
rank the myrtle by the doorstep: bleeding the bosom
of the rainsick rose who broke her heart on the tomb.
The dry wells filled, and the vaults, and the cisterns:
and the cellars with underground music: the furrows of clay
glittered with water: rotten under water the wheatfield lay.
In the drear suburb, beyond the greenhouse, and the stonema-
    son's,
on the Cove Road, among the marble shafts and porphyry basins,
and the cold eyeless angels with folded wings,
(there where we fished as children
looking over our shoulders at tombstones)
at last, undermined by water, the headstone fell,
sank softly, slowly, on the grave-mound,
and lay thus, a month neglected, on hollow ground.
And the spirit, the unappeased houseless spirit,
whose dwelling should be in ourselves, those who inherit,
even as our dwelling is in the tomb,
homeward once more looks now for prayer and praise
to be with laurels blest
and in our breast
live out his due bequest of nights and days.

IV

And so it is you at the dark's edge, grandfather,
revenant again to complain and to haunt me,
cavorting at the fire's edge, leaping through the flames,
while the moon, behind Sheepfold Hill,
lights her old bonfire, old bone-fire, and our ancestors
gather down from hillside, gather up from the sea-wall,
and come home to be warmed. You, from the Geissberg,
the 'Rhine full of molten gold, and the Neckar Valley
echoing the slow psalm of the curfew,'
from 'a lecture by Humboldt,' and a ship at sea
'which, as she took up the winds,
and rose in triumph over the waves,'

was a symbol to you of our relation to god:
'the absolute, the eternal, the infinite, a shoreless sea,
in unconscious rest, all its powers in repose,
to be used at man's will.' And the *Iphigenie
von Tauris,* at Heidelberg read with delight,
while the little Humboldt, 'his small face flushed,
eyes small, bright, and piercing,'
transcribed the last page of his *Kosmos.*
'And I thought, as he moved off, helped by his servant,
had I waited a twelvemonth, I would never have seen him.'

All Hallows' Even, Hallowe'en,
the evening of the last of October,
and the harvest in-gathered:
and the first of November, *Allerheiligen,*
and the second of November, *Allerseelen.*
Was your vision of god not enough, that you come
for the vision of the living, and the cricket's
small share of the hearthstone? Or is it some other,
some humbler, more human, news that you crave?
Your children? — long dead; and Cousin Abiel, the Quaker;
and the house with the hawthorns torn down;
and your own house a chapel; and the whaleships
departed: no more shines the eagle
on the pilot-house roof at the foot of the hill.
Yet no, not these are your loves, but the timeless and formless,
the laws and the vision: as you saw on the ship
how, like an angel, she subdued to her purpose
the confused power of ocean, the diffused power of wind,
translating them swiftly to beauty,
'so infinite ends, and finite begins, so man
may make the god finite and viable,
make conscious god's powers in action and being.'
Was it so? is it so? and the life so lived?
O you who made magic
under an oak-tree once in the sunlight
translating your acorns to green cups and saucers
for the grandchild mute at the tree's foot,

and died, alone, on a doorstep at midnight
your vision complete but your work undone,
with your dream of a world religion,
'a peace convention of religions, a worship
purified of myth and of dogma:'
dear scarecrow, dear pumpkin-head!
who masquerade now as my child, to assure
the continuing love, the continuing dream,
and the heart and the hearth and the wholeness —
it was so, it is so, and the life so lived
shines this night like the moon over Sheepfold Hill,
and he who interpreted the wonders of god
is himself dissolved and interpreted.
Rest: be at peace. It suffices to know and to rest.
For the singers, in rest, shall stand as a river
whose source is unending forever.

Everlasting

MESSAGE FOUND INSCRIBED ON U.S.S. NEW YORK
AFTER THE BOMBING AT BIKINI: *Kilroy Was Here.*

I

Immortal weather, and immortal mind,
gull's feather lost forever on the know-nothing wind,
death in the paring of a fingernail,
and our souls at fault or faultless:
silence, and pause, the imaginary laws
laws immane and immanent that imagine and create us
and that ourselves then create
or re-create or miscreate,
ourselves the helpless god that made us:
come, let us observe together, without comment,
this single but infinitely divisible moment:
a morning of dew, arrived without observation,
the leafling, there in the dew, arrived without notion or motion,
ourselves and the god in the simplicity of action.

II

'This is Skylight One, Skylight One,
coming up on simulated bomb-release.
Stand by.
Mark: end of the first practice run,
first practice run.

'This is Skylight One, Skylight One,
Predicted time of actual bomb-release
thirty minutes.
Predicted time of actual bomb-release
thirty minutes.'

'Skylight One,
this is Sadeyes.
Over.'

'Sadeyes,
this is Skylight One.
Over.'

'Skylight One,
this is Sadeyes. Interrogation:
will you say
how conditions were for bombing
on practice run?'

'Sadeyes,
this is Skylight One.
Bombing conditions were okay.
Over.'

'Sadeyes to Skylight One —
roger —
out.'

III

Sadeyes under Skylight One, waiting for the vision
to be fractured, refracted, atomized,
the giver and the receiver,
the recorder and the achiever,
two lovers awaiting the moment
when the unimaginable lightning will come over
and the flashfire of love join lover with lover:
see, as in a cathedral, the sad eyes raised
that the sky's sad mystery may be known and praised,
or known and understood,
o and that the vision may not be
such as will stain the white radiance of eternity —
light filtered through the blood.

Skylight One over Sadeyes, the wide arch
of the vast lens above the pacific sea,
indifferent and undeviating mind
that works its automatic way to find
wormlike in the dark, and yet not blind,
not blind to what it now must see and be:
the coral slowly crescent from the sea
from ocean midnight into light,
the mind that ringlike glows in night
from dark to fainter dark to bright,
until it is a lens
wide as the arch of the pacific sky —
and yet, projected by the blood.

Sadeyes under Skylight One, waiting
indifferent, unloving, and unhating,
for the always unknown, always new,
or partly known and partly new:
mind's necessity for knowing,
the palm-tree's and coral-reef's for growing,

towards the true or partly true,
pacific or unpacific,
specific or unspecific,
and the monstrous unknown, under the monstrous lens,
the infinite arch of mind's magnifying sky,
to be at last, perhaps, demonstrable and true,
although projected by the blood.

Sadeyes and Skylight One waiting for each other,
airplane and battleship together,
assignation of perception and destruction,
those who will violate to create,
sire and dam
of the new vision and division,
new fission, and new crucifixion,
imagined by the blood that built a brain,
out of the chain a chain conceived that will unchain
the chain itself, and yet a chain remain:
for the light that never was on land or sea
yet had to be,
and though not understood
predicted by the blood.

IV

And the moment moved:
as in a bed the lover to the loved,
as everywhere the lover to the loved,
in the winged membrane of the flame
all for a moment One became,
and in the brookside bamboo grove,
turning toward one love,
the Apocalypse above,
the ranked eyes of the little men
turned back to jellied dark again,
and the moment moved.

The moment moved,
as on the rock-face the dusty everlasting
its frost-faint shadow casting
for love of granite, love of gneiss,
and the north wind and the booming ice,
invisibly threaded
from pole to Pole Star, immortally wedded
to the curled rime of the eagle's feather
and the heart-dazzling glacier weather,
and already, in December, spins a lacelike shadow
beyond the snow to the green rock above the meadow,
and the moment moves.

The moment moves
outward and inward and with serene precision
to the appointed proliferation of division:
the eye sees itself, the light understands itself,
even to the dissolution of the vision
for the vision of vision:
as if ourselves and God became
o instantly and forever an innumerable name,
and time into itself gazed back again,
and all things were transfigured, and then again the same,
crying one cry the ecstasy and pain,
and the moment moves.

v

Yes, and we with it, godlike, everywhere,
the regicide, the Kilroy, always there:
ourselves — we know! — the god-destroyers and god-makers,
idol and soul-idol breakers:
we, the first fin wriggling up the beach,
we, the agony of coition O-ing the first speech:
ah, and in the ghost-womb of the first singing word,

division and subdivision into vision
already heard.

O joyous laughter and derision,
gaia scienza of the always first,
beach-climbing first invader,
iconoclastic newcomer, seed-bearing marauder —
and then the laugh blown back across the forbidden border,
heard again, sly and secret,
in the multifoliate unfolding of new order,
the new and more angelic design,
the new and more demonic design,
our god, ourselves, the through-and-through divine,
shaping itself in self-contemplative power:
and all anticipated, all in the same place and hour,
predictable and known, for everywhere
the god has left his name, the assassin's name —
Kilroy Was Here.

As here, as now, as this:
on the ephemeral and eternal rock-face of time
the dusty everlasting
her ragged shadow casting:
so might we be, so may we be,
faithful and true as this:
at home in the twin deaths of flame and ice,
invisibly and mortally threaded
from Pole to Pole Star, wedded
to the sun broken, the atom broken, and to the god broken,
and all that he has said or left unspoken:
true as the everlasting, who, in December,
sends her soft shadow
beyond the snow to an unknown meadow.

A LETTER FROM LI PO

A *Letter from Li Po*

I

Fanfare of northwest wind, a bluejay wind
announces autumn, and the equinox
rolls back blue bays to a far afternoon.
Somewhere beyond the Gorge Li Po is gone,
looking for friendship or an old love's sleeve
or writing letters to his children, lost,
and to his children's children, and to us.
What was his light? of lamp or moon or sun?
Say that it changed, for better or for worse,
sifted by leaves, sifted by snow; on mulberry silk
a slant of witch-light; on the pure text
a slant of genius; emptying mind and heart
for winecups and more winecups and more words.
What was his time? Say that it was a change,
but constant as a changing thing may be,
from chicory's moon-dark blue down the taut scale
to chicory's tenderest pink, in a pink field
such as imagination dreams of thought.
But of the heart beneath the winecup moon
the tears that fell beneath the winecup moon
for children lost, lost lovers, and lost friends,
what can we say but that it never ends?
Even for us it never ends, only begins.
Yet to spell down the poem on her page,
margining her phrases, parsing forth
the sevenfold prism of meaning, up the scale
from chicory pink to blue, is to assume
Li Po himself: as he before assumed

the poets and the sages who were his.
Like him, we too have eaten of the word:
with him are somewhere lost beyond the Gorge:
and write, in rain, a letter to lost children,
a letter long as time and brief as love.

II

And yet not love, not only love. Not caritas
or only that. Nor the pink chicory love,
deep as it may be, even to moon-dark blue,
in which the dragon of his meaning flew
for friends or children lost, or even
for the beloved horse, for Li Po's horse:
not these, in the self's circle so embraced:
too near, too dear, for pure assessment: no,
a letter crammed and creviced, crannied full,
storied and stored as the ripe honeycomb
with other faith than this.
                              As of sole pride
and holy loneliness, the intrinsic face
worn by the always changing shape between
end and beginning, birth and death.
How moves that line of daring on the map?
Where was it yesterday, or where this morning
when thunder struck at seven, and in the bay
the meteor made its dive, and shed its wings,
and with them one more Icarus? Where struck
that lightning-stroke which in your sleep you saw
wrinkling across the eyelid? Somewhere else?
But somewhere else is always here and now.
Each moment crawls that lightning on your eyelid:
each moment you must die. It was a tree
that this time died for you: it was a rock
and with it all its local web of love:
a chimney, spilling down historic bricks:
perhaps a skyful of Ben Franklin's kites.
And with them, us. For we must hear and bear

the news from everywhere: the hourly news,
infinitesimal or vast, from everywhere.

III

Sole pride and loneliness: it is the state
the kingdom rather of all things: we hear
news of the heart in weather of the Bear,
slide down the rungs of Cassiopeia's Chair,
still on the nursery floor, the Milky Way;
and, if we question one, must question all.
What is this 'man'? How far from him is 'me'?
Who, in this conch-shell, locked the sound of sea?
We are the tree, yet sit beneath the tree,
among the leaves we are the hidden bird,
we are the singer and are what is heard.
What is this 'world'? Not Li Po's Gorge alone,
and yet, this too might be. 'The wind was high
north of the White King City, by the fields
of whistling barley under cuckoo sky,'
where, as the silkworm drew her silk, Li Po
spun out his thoughts of us. 'Endless as silk'
(he said) 'these poems for lost loves, and us,'
and, 'for the peachtree, blooming in the ditch.'
Here is the divine loneliness in which
we greet, only to doubt, a voice, a word,
the smoke of a sweetfern after frost, a face
touched, and loved, but still unknown, and then
a body, still mysterious in embrace.
Taste lost as touch is lost, only to leave
dust on the doorsill or an ink-stained sleeve:
and yet, for the inadmissible, to grieve.
Of leaf and love, at last, only to doubt:
from world within or world without, kept out.

IV

Caucus of robins on an alien shore
as of the Ho-Ho birds at Jewel Gate
southward bound and who knows where and never late
or lost in a roar at sea. Rovers of chaos
each one the 'Rover of Chao,' whose slight bones
shall put to shame the swords. We fly with these,
have always flown, and they
stay with us here, stand still and stay,
while, exiled in the Land of Pa, Li Po
still at the Wine Spring stoops to drink the moon.
And northward now, for fall gives way to spring,
from Sandy Hook and Kitty Hawk they wing,
and he remembers, with the pipes and flutes,
drunk with joy, bewildered by the chance
that brought a friend, and friendship, how, in vain,
he strove to speak, 'and in long sentences,' his pain.
Exiled are we. Were exiles born. The 'far away,'
language of desert, language of ocean, language of sky,
as of the unfathomable worlds that lie
between the apple and the eye,
these are the only words we learn to say.
Each morning we devour the unknown. Each day
we find, and take, and spill, or spend, or lose,
a sunflower splendor of which none knows the source.
This cornucopia of air! This very heaven
of simple day! We do not know, can never know,
the alphabet to find us entrance there.
So, in the street, we stand and stare,
to greet a friend, and shake his hand,
yet know him beyond knowledge, like ourselves;
ocean unknowable by unknowable sand.

V

The locust tree spills sequins of pale gold
in spiral nebulae, borne on the Invisible
earthward and deathward, but in change to find
the cycles to new birth, new life. Li Po
allowed his autumn thoughts like these to flow,
and, from the Gorge, sends word of Chouang's dream.
Did Chouang dream he was a butterfly?
Or did the butterfly dream Chouang? If so,
why then all things can change, and change again,
the sea to brook, the brook to sea, and we
from man to butterfly; and back to man.
This 'I,' this moving 'I,' this focal 'I,'
which changes, when it dreams the butterfly,
into the thing it dreams of; liquid eye
in which the thing takes shape, but from within
as well as from without: this liquid 'I':
how many guises, and disguises, this
nimblest of actors takes, how many names
puts on and off, the costumes worn but once,
the player queen, the lover, or the dunce,
hero or poet, father or friend,
suiting the eloquence to the moment's end;
childlike, or bestial; the language of the kiss
sensual or simple; and the gestures, too,
as slight as that with which an empire falls,
or a great love's abjured; these feignings, sleights,
savants, or saints, or fly-by-nights,
the novice in her cell, or wearing tights
on the high wire above a hell of lights:
what's true in these, or false? which is the 'I'
of 'I's'? Is it the master of the cadence, who
transforms all things to a hoop of flame, where through
tigers of meaning leap? And are these true,
the language never old and never new,

such as the world wears on its wedding day,
the something borrowed with something chicory blue?
In every part we play, we play ourselves;
even the secret doubt to which we come
beneath the changing shapes of self and thing,
yes, even this, at last, if we should call
and dare to name it, we would find
the only voice that answers is our own.
We are once more defrauded by the mind.

Defrauded? No. It is the alchemy by which we grow.
It is the self becoming word, the word
becoming world. And with each part we play
we add to cosmic *Sum* and cosmic sum.
Who knows but one day we shall find,
hidden in the prism at the rainbow's foot,
the square root of the eccentric absolute,
and the concentric absolute to come.

                                    VI

The thousand eyes, the Argus 'I's' of love,
of these it was, in verse, that Li Po wove
the magic cloak for his last going forth,
into the Gorge for his adventure north.
What is not seen or said? The cloak of words
loves all, says all, sends back the word
whether from Green Spring, and the yellow bird
'that sings unceasing on the banks of Kiang,'
or 'from the Green Moss Path, that winds and winds,
nine turns for every hundred steps it winds,
up the Sword Parapet on the road to Shuh.'
'Dead pinetrees hang head-foremost from the cliff.
The cataract roars downward. Boulders fall
splitting the echoes from the mountain wall.
No voice, save when the nameless birds complain,
in stunted trees, female echoing male;
or, in the moonlight, the lost cuckoo's cry,

piercing the traveller's heart. Wayfarer from afar,
why are you here? what brings you here? why here?'

VII

Why here. Nor can we say why here. The peachtree bough
scrapes on the wall at midnight, the west wind
sculptures the wall of fog that slides
seaward, over the Gulf Stream.
                          The rat
comes through the wainscot, brings to his larder
the twinned acorn and chestnut burr. Our sleep
lights for a moment into dream, the eyes
turn under eyelids for a scene, a scene,
o and the music, too, of landscape lost.
And yet, not lost. For here savannahs wave
cressets of pampas, and the kingfisher
binds all that gold with blue.
                          Why here? why here?
Why does the dream keep only this, just this — ?
Yes, as the poem or the music do?

The timelessness of time takes form in rhyme:
the lotus and the locust tree rehearse
a four-form song, the quatrain of the year:
not in the clock's chime only do we hear
the passing of the Now into the past,
the passing into future of the Now:
but in the alteration of the bough
time becomes visible, becomes audible,
becomes the poem and the music too:
time becomes still, time becomes time, in rhyme.
Thus, in the Court of Aloes, Lady Yang
called the musicians from the Pear Tree Garden,
called for Li Po, in order that the spring,
tree-peony spring, might so be made immortal.
Li Po, brought drunk to court, took up his brush,
but washed his face among the lilies first,

then wrote the song of Lady Flying Swallow:
which Hsuang Sung, the emperor, forthwith played,
moving quick fingers on a flute of jade.
Who will forget that afternoon? Still, still,
the singer holds his phrase, the rising moon
remains unrisen. Even the fountain's falling blade
hangs in the air unbroken, and says: Wait!

VIII

Text into text, text out of text. Pretext
for scholars or for scholiasts. The living word
springs from the dying, as leaves in spring
spring from dead leaves, our birth from death.
And all is text, is holy text. Sheepfold Hill
becomes its name for us, and yet is still
unnamed, unnamable, a book of trees
before it was a book for men or sheep,
before it was a book for words. Words, words,
for it is scarlet now, and brown, and red,
and yellow where the birches have not shed,
where, in another week, the rocks will show.
And in this marriage of text and thing how can we know
where most the meaning lies? We climb the hill
through bullbriar thicket and the wild rose, climb
past poverty-grass and the sweet-scented bay
scaring the pheasant from his wall, but can we say
that it is only these, through these, we climb,
or through the words, the cadence, and the rhyme?
Chang Hsu, calligrapher of great renown,
needed to put but his three cupfuls down
to tip his brush with lightning. On the scroll,
wreaths of cloud rolled left and right, the sky
opened upon Forever. Which is which?
The poem? Or the peachtree in the ditch?
Or is all one? Yes, all is text, the immortal text,
Sheepfold Hill the poem, the poem Sheepfold Hill,
and we, Li Po, the man who sings, sings as he climbs,

transposing rhymes to rocks and rocks to rhymes.
The man who sings. What is this man who sings?
And finds this dedicated use for breath
for phrase and periphrase of praise between
the twin indignities of birth and death?
Li Yung, the master of the epitaph,
forgetting about meaning, who himself
had added 'meaning' to the book of 'things,'
lies who knows where, himself sans epitaph,
his text, too, lost, forever lost . . .

        And yet, no,
text lost and poet lost, these only flow
into that other text that knows no year.
The peachtree in the poem is still here.
The song is in the peachtree and the ear.

IX

The winds of doctrine blow both ways at once.
The wetted finger feels the wind each way,
presaging plums from north, and snow from south.
The dust-wind whistles from the eastern sea
to dry the nectarine and parch the mouth.
The west wind from the desert wreathes the rain
too late to fill our wells, but soon enough,
the four-day rain that bears the leaves away.
Song with the wind will change, but is still song
and pierces to the rightness in the wrong
or makes the wrong a rightness, a delight.
Where are the eager guests that yesterday
thronged at the gate? Like leaves, they could not stay,
the winds of doctrine blew their minds away,
and we shall have no loving-cup tonight.
No loving-cup: for not ourselves are here
to entertain us in that outer year,
where, so they say, we see the Greater Earth.
The winds of doctrine blow our minds away,
and we are absent till another birth.

X

Beyond the Sugar Loaf, in the far wood,
under the four-day rain, gunshot is heard
and with the falling leaf the falling bird
flutters her crimson at the huntsman's foot.
Life looks down at death, death looks up at life,
the eyes exchange the secret under rain,
rain all the way from heaven: and all three
know and are known, share and are shared, a silent
moment of union and communion.
                                        Have we come
this way before, and at some other time?
Is it the Wind Wheel Circle we have come?
We know the eye of death, and in it too
the eye of god, that closes as in sleep,
giving its light, giving its life, away:
clouding itself as consciousness from pain,
clouding itself, and then, the shutter shut.
And will this eye of god awake again?
Or is this what he loses, loses once,
but always loses, and forever lost?
It is the always and unredeemable cost
of his invention, his fatigue. The eye
closes, and no other takes its place.
It is the end of god, each time, each time.
Yet, though the leaves must fall, the galaxies
rattle, detach, and fall, each to his own
perplexed and individual death, Lady Yang
gone with the inkberry's vermilion stalk,
the peony face behind a fan of frost,
the blue-moon eyebrow behind a fan of rain,
beyond recall by any alchemist
or incantation from the Book of Change:
unresumable, as, on Sheepfold Hill,
the fir cone of a thousand years ago:
still, in the loving, and the saying so,

as when we name the hill, and, with the name,
bestow an essence, and a meaning, too:
do we endow them with our lives?
       They move
into another orbit: into a time
not theirs: and we become the bell to speak
this time: as we become new eyes
with which they see, the voice
in which they find duration, short or long,
the chthonic and hermetic song.
      Beyond Sheepfold Hill,
gunshot again, the bird flies forth to meet
predestined death, to look with conscious sight
into the eye of light
the light unflinching that understands and loves.
And Sheepfold Hill accepts them, and is still.

XI

The landscape and the language are the same.
And we ourselves are language and are land,
together grew with Sheepfold Hill, rock, and hand,
and mind, all taking substance in a thought
wrought out of mystery: birdflight and air
predestined from the first to be a pair:
as, in the atom, the living rhyme
invented her divisions, which in time,
and in the terms of time, would make and break
the text, the texture, and then all remake.
This powerful mind that can by thinking take
the order of the world and all remake,
will it, for joy in breaking, break instead
its own deep thought that thought itself be dead?
Already in our coil of rock and hand,
hidden in the cloud of mind, burning, fading,
under the waters, in the eyes of sand,
was that which in its time would understand.
Already in the Kingdom of the Dead

the scrolls were waiting for the names and dates
and what would there irrevocably be said.
The brush was in the hand, the poem was in the love,
the praise was in the word. The 'Book of Lives'
listed the name, Li Po, as an Immortal;
and it was time to travel. Not, this year,
north to the Damask City, or the Gorge,
but, by the phoenix borne, swift as the wind,
to the Jade Palace Portal. There
look through the clouded to the clear
and there watch evil like a brush-stroke disappear
in the last perfect rhyme
of the begin-all-end-all poem, time.

XII

Northwest by north. The grasshopper weathervane
bares to the moon his golden breastplate, swings
in his predicted circle, gilded legs and wings
bright with frost, predicting frost. The tide
scales with moon-silver, floods the marsh, fulfils
Payne Creek and Quivett Creek, rises to lift
the fishing-boats against a jetty wall;
and past them floods the plankton and the weed
and limp sea-lettuce for the horseshoe crab
who sleeps till daybreak in his nest of reed.
The hour is open as the mind is open.
Closed as the mind is closed. Opens as the hand opens
to receive the ghostly snowflakes of the moon, closes
to feel the sunbeams of the bloodstream warm
our human inheritance of touch. The air tonight
brings back, to the all-remembering world, its ghosts,
borne from the Great Year on the Wind Wheel Circle.
On that invisible wave we lift, we too,
and drag at secret moorings,
stirred by the ancient currents that gave us birth.

And they are here, Li Po and all the others,
our fathers and our mothers: the dead leaf's footstep
touches the grass: those who were lost at sea
and those the innocents the too-soon dead:

all mankind

and all it ever knew is here in-gathered,
held in our hands, and in the wind
breathed by the pines on Sheepfold Hill.

How still

the Quaker Graveyard, the Meeting House how still,
where Cousin Abiel, on a night like this,
now long since dead, but then how young, how young,
scuffing among the dead leaves after frost
looked up and saw the Wine Star, listened and heard
borne from all quarters the Wind Wheel Circle word:
the father within him, the mother within him, the self
coming to self through love of each for each.
In this small mute democracy of stones
is it Abiel or Li Po who lies
and lends us against death our speech?
They are the same, and it is both who teach.
The poets and the prophecies are ours:
and these are with us as we turn, in turn,
the leaves of love that fill the Book of Change.

The Logos in Fifth Avenue

i

September, and Fifth Avenue, you said,
and said it somehow as if we both were dead:
and then as in an afterthought you said
'The first word on the tongue is it of love
and is our language, then, all love, each word
a kind of kindness, a kind of blessing?

The heart, therefore,

was named the heart because we love the heart?

Or was it that the heart became the word?'
It is absurd: we look for meaning, find
that we are lost in an algebraic surd.
The hurricane between us, or, in the morning press,
reports of changes in the style of dress,
the breastless female or the sexless male —
o god but how our history grows stale
if it is this we come to at the end
of god's beginning! Anguish, did you say?
Anguish unjust? God's anguish?
               Play, play
the juke-box tunes of this unpopular day
the give-away and the say-hay-hay
forget the blind-man tapping with his cane
who will not see the autumn blue again
the newsboy with wet papers in the rain
the Big Board with its loss or gain:
excuse, or try to exorcise, the pain,
the anguish will remain.
               As it should do,
as it should do. What would we be
if when the wind blows we
were not, and always, broken with the tree
the christ in us so broken?
               What would we do
for fourth or fifth or heaventh avenue
and not with hope of recompense
or vanity of munificence
but with humility, and true?
Here is the locust tree, you see the thorns
it is the tree the tempest murdered, see
the starveling leaves stifled with soot
and suffer with the root
cramped under stinking asphalt!
               Come away
for we have front row seats at the latest play,
The Lilies of Gomorrah, The Bells of Sodom,
and we will save our sorrows till tomorrow.

ii

Knock knock: knock knock: ring ring:
what will the morning postman bring?
Sufficient unto the day the bills thereof
no valentine no harbinger of love
no mockingbird upon the video tree
to promise us the spring
       yet let him sing
above the neon lights in Ptomaine Row
sing for the library sing for the jail
yes and for all our lights that fail
as now they do. And we'll sing too
sing for the things we meant to do and be
the sunrise that we could not wake to see
the alms we did not give
      and the dear secret
found once, in the four-leafed clover, long since lost,
forgotten, or dissembled, or betrayed.

iii

     And now
take off the tarnished sock and go to bed
as if again we both were somehow dead
but as a prayer a remembered fraud of prayer
remember what you said.
       What did I say?
Save it for another day.
       What did I say?
Something of language, and of love, remember?
And something of September.
       I did not say,
I merely asked. Asking is all we seem
as in a waking dream
to be able or partly able

to do. We wait for knockings on a table
                    which when they come
are random false or meaningless or dull.
                    Better to knock on wood
as someone said!
                    And did he mean a tree?
Better to go to bed and *scream*
when nightmare rears its eyeless head
from the mythic waters of sleep.
                    Better to keep
even in sleep as now you do
the something that you said you thought was true
the something borrowed with something *blue.*
                    And yes,
blue was for the blind-man, blue was for the sky,
blue was for the eye —
                    I am not I.

                              iv

Morning empties the garbage pails of night
morning empties the sky of clouds the mind of dreams
and see, the dapple-grey coursers of the sun
beat up the dawn with their bright silver hooves.
It was not I who said this, was not you,
and yet we know it true.
                    For the dream kept,
as the dream always does, while still you slept,
under the quilt and under the guilt
and the starless waters of sleep,
what we could not endure and not forget
the perdurable time
which, as the telltale dream admits,
is of the nature of a crime.
                    Listen:
a bell unthinking in unthinking sky
mocks the resentful ear, as at the eye

teases the minatory light of morning.
                    Wake!
and face reality once more, reality
which in its finite wisdom permits us each to die
but will not die itself!
                    Return
out of the flight of dream to face
the fever and the fret, the sad St. Vitus
dance of the hours, the god's and ours,
amid the drear detritus
that blows along the one-way street
                    while at the corner
waits by the silver-wreathèd Cadillac
the undertaker's shiny black
                    sole mourner
for someone's Little Boy Blue or lost Jack Horner
and the meek body that was his share of god.
                    Today
we will again be circumspect
we know what to expect
the iceman with his fifty pounds of ice
nuns in a flutter at the convent door
                    the scattered rice
left for the pigeons from the wedding-day
and fifty sample bedrooms to inspect.
And in those fifty bedrooms who will sleep
as we this night or keep
vigil even in dream?
                    The tugboats mourn
in immemorial weather, the southeast wind
brings from the harbor rain, the clang
of ashcans rings on asphalt
                    but our dream our dream
with a timepiece precision seems to keep
its tiny tick of truth.
                    Take out your chalk
and on sidewalk as for hopscotch mark

the humble squares for devious progress: not
as in our childhood blossom root or leaf
nor rich man poor man beggarman thief
but drugstore movie bar and car
garage post office hospital morgue
subway and comfort station. Shall we play?
in this poor hierarchy find our way?
Listen to what they say: 'Gee mom my tongue is dirty.'
'How can it be? It's in your mouth.'
                        Or, 'Don't be stupid, kid,
dogs can't chew gum.'
                        Better to pray
remembering what you said.
                        What did I say?
And that was yesterday!
                        Better today
to take a taxi up Fifth Avenue
visit the sealions at the Zoo
stop for a beer at the Shamrock Bar and see
a baseball game or prizefight on TV.

                        v

The siren wails, but not from the far islands,
nor for divine Ulysses, but down the street
to fire or death. The bent cat in the alley
slinks his despair. Under the tree of heaven
cheep-cheep cheep-cheep the dusty sparrows
forage for gravel.
                        On his stoop the priest
blank-faced now takes the air
an interval of blankness between prayer
intonements for atonement without meaning.
But you too something said of prayer.
                        I did not say of prayer
but as a remembered fraud of prayer
ritual of beseeching from childhood's teaching.

Yet it was true if as a reaching
of mind and hand to understand beyond
what we were taught as true and, yes, still true.
                        And is still true, for you?
Still true, but in a different way.
                        What did you say?
What was it that you said and took to bed
so that we dreamed it both and loved it both
yes loved it knee to knee the I becoming we?
                        I said
each face of all we meet will soon be dead
I said the child is father to the corpse
I said the skeleton is in the womb
I said the city is a honeycomb
a honeycomb of tomb and there we move
or think we move who are already still
and there we love or think we love
                        and yet
perhaps we should not emphasize alone
the brevity of life the levity of stone.
Though this cathedral mausoleum fall
                        as fall it must and come to dust
and with its splendors us
                        still let us not forget
the nowness of the hand upon the bough,
the nowness of the now.
The living moment of the dream
with its timepiece precision watching truth
still keeps eternal youth
not only in the solar month and year
but always, and forever, here.
                        Stay, stay,
the hand upon the bough upon the heart
stand still o love o living art
that in the blood and in the sap and in the sun
as in our mythic dream last night
bids all remain unchanged:

urge now your love for all things demiurge
for that is he and that is we
and bid this pattern be.

A *Is for Alpha: Alpha Is for* A

i

Now it begins. Now the subaqueous evening
exemplary as the inalterable moon
begins again to begin. With slight starts
of organ-grinder music (if the scene
is of city) or of — '*dee-dee-dee* — !'
chickadee trill if (as it is) it is country.
The shadow, complex, seven-branched, of the ancient lyre-tree
prolongs itself on the sensual lawn and fades away
predicting a reverse shadow at daybreak. The star
(for look, love, there is a star)
trills through the sunset like a bird
diamond point in crimson word
and melts, and we are heard.
So, now, the casual evening begins, and its slow texture
weaves us into a casuistry. We, who were just now thoughtless,
or lost in a loss of thought,
come to a breaking and dissolving
sunset of our own. The world ends
and another begins. The love ends
— or does it? —
and another begins. But the light
lasts forever, there is no night.
The hands you lift are sunset, and the hands
are the exemplary moon. The eyes you lift
change with the texture of the evening,
Venus it might be one way, Sirius the other;
the lengthening shadow, so intricate, so various, of the lyre-tree
prolongs our listening nerves into the coming light

of tomorrow. My love, observe a moon
unobserved by any till now. Bland and bleak
as any lovestruck human. Such as we?
Such as we. We are the silver rind
of moonlight, for now it hardens, now is crystal,
on this tree, this virgin locust tree, and we
are moon and tree.

Fade, fade, all into darkness fade,
but also into light
since one the other closes.
The texture of the evening is of roses,
and we are, for the moment, roses too.
Love is not much: it is a touch: but it is true.

ii

Evening, which evens all things. Hand in hand
brindled by sunset thought we stand
prolonging our nerves, and with them nature, into another day.
We are the sacred players and the play:
we are the music, and what the musicians say:
and always our new title is Today.
Today, and yesterday; the divine dance
moves under heart and heaven, the wave of light
gathers its all for a breaking of time
and then falls inward. We are the rhyme
paired like two words in love, and move
in the twinned discord of a chord, our love
hidden in its own secret, like the rose.
Will the rose unclose, disclose?
finding — how naturally! — a reason for season?
It is ourselves that open, even
to the innermost heaven.
It is ourselves magically disguised
as harp-string and harp-song, birdsong and petal,
ice-metal, rain-metal,

ourselves curving the air with a wing
ourselves the air for the wing to find and follow
ourselves the sunlight and the swallow.
Divisibly indivisible we sing
the begin-all-end-all thing:
night becomes a god, and we the night,
for the unfolding and enfolding of our delight.

iii

Intervals and interstices of texture
enthrall us, bring us to a standstill, bemuse
fingertip and eyebeam, idea and eye;
while the mind fills with wonders. The voice
is of what? Who said to it, 'rejoice'?
You there, I here; you with your mountains of snow,
and your seven golden seas, and the woven Nile,
and the sky piled high with purple clouds;
and I with my rocky Sahara, ribbed with lapis lazuli,
and the last sail melting into sunset:
these are the language of interval, the interstices
subtle and gigantic, unfathomable, inaudible,
hieroglyphic and hieratic, by which we speak.
The exchange is golden. It is thesaurus. The exchange
beggars us only then to endow us again,
exhausts us only to replenish. The simple rain
walking before us down the country lane
shuttling before us down the country lane
says it with silver, syllables it slowly,
repeats its holy, holy,
and into it, and into night,
we weave this love, this light.

The Return

Dear tiger lily, fanged and striped! you are the bravest,
you as well as another will serve to chant

tongued with flame our vernal madrigal,
sowing among sequins of last year's locust
love's golden rhetoric:
you and the celandine
of immaculate green.
Wraiths of snow run from the stallion sun,
quicksilver lizards of water
flick their tails into cisterns,
and on the tarnished grass
where north wind sheered his drifts
in phantom edifice
melts the last sickle of pale ice:
and there, in a little while, where late was snow
the Indian Pipes will blow.
O darling, listen — from the orchised bog
chuckles the ancient and omniscient frog
his gross venereal hymn:
and the reed-scented wind, the bulrush-rattling wind,
dreams like memory through the mind.
Now love returns once more, our lost and antique love,
dear tiger lily! above
the sad detritus of death:
fling we then out of doors and into hearts,
where the year freshly starts,
and join the song-sparrow
in Hymen's favorite song:
for treason late and long,
yes, the sly shibboleth
of treason to death, and love, and another season!

The oak leaves rustle in the thicket,
loosen themselves, detach, and fall,
pale brown, pale purple, harsh still;
the hawk hangs over his beloved hill
as love hangs over the destined heart:
and once more joyfully we begin
the ancient dance of meet and part,

                                              wherein
each is in turn the hawk and each the heart.
We touch and meet, we touch and greet,
kiss gravely, tread apart,
next glance, and eye askance,
curtsey in courtship's bashful dance,
retreat, and then advance.
O unknown love
unknown and treacherous as that sky above
and as my own heart is,
what is the meaning of your kiss?
Each lover asks and answers this
in blinded bliss.
Glad, glad, the sound
of two hearts beating, together bound,
o but tumultuous the rest
of your face, love, that rests upon my breast,
tumultuous the rest
of each upon the other resting:
two worlds at war we are,
star dancing against star.
For each must learn in each
all the dark-rooted language under speech:
here, look! new love, the roots we did not know,
strong stems, deep stains, rich glories never guessed:
disparate origins and desperate sins,
acknowledged or unacknowledged, understood
or misunderstood; the labyrinthine windings
through the lewd galleries of the mind, to find
something or nothing; illusory findings
which vanish at the touch, or on exposure to the air,
and of which, only in default, are we aware;
hatred derived from love, love from terror,
the roots not knowing their own fruits;
the unpracticed, and then the all-too-practiced vices,
deliberate dishonesties and rehearsed voices;
purpose becoming mean, meanness purpose,

wants promoted to obsessions, and the obsessions
near to madness. Who am I, who are you,
that one to the other must be true, untrue,
or dissect untrue from true?
Who shall possess, or be possessed? possession
of how much? of what ecstasy, or for what duration?
Where, too, and in what characters shall we meet
playing what parts of the multitude we have played
wearing what masks and shabby costumes
on the strewn stage of habit? The attitudes
are predictable, and therefore false, they belong
to another situation, are the inheritance
of other loves and lusts. What beatitudes
can the wingèd god invoke from these? In what divine dance
instruct these stained and stinking puppets?
Out of such mouths what song, what song?

And yet the tiger lily, under the snow,
heedless alike of year ago or long ago,
and the endless history of her repeated love,
dares yet again to thrust above
the sad detritus of death, and grow:
and speaks with the song-sparrow the sly shibboleth
of another season, another treason!
Lost memory, lost love, lost to return,
can we, too, not be brave like these, relearn
o as if all were virginal and new
the hawk and heart of 'I' and 'You'?
O daring darling, can we not trust
once more that innocent sky
once more to break our hearts and die?

Comes now, comes she!
comes the unknown, the unpredictable,
she who is half spring, half summer,
between the lilac and the wrinkled apple blossom,
the unknown, all-unimagined newcomer,

birch foot, beech heart, myrtle hand,
and the indecipherable mind
and virgin bosom
and windflower grace
and timeless Etruscan pace
and the tiger's heart, cruel to be kind:
comes like the sunshot southwest wind
bidding the elm bough, soliciting
the fan of iris under the snow
for one more spring, one more spring:
while the hawk's wing
sickles the white-blossoming hill
with shadow of death, the scythe's shadow
shadowing the redwing into the meadow.
O innocence in guilt, and guilt in innocence,
she stoops, she hovers,
fiercest and subtlest, and yes, tenderest of lovers,
the ruthless one
whose eye is in the sun.

The Walk in the Garden

i

Noting in slow sequence by waterclock of rain
or dandelion clock of sun
the green hours of trees and white hours of flowers:
annotating again the 'flower-glory of the season,
a book that is never done,' never done:
savoring phrases of green-white, mock-white,
while the ancient lyre-tree, the ancient plum,
adds for another May its solar sum
in silent galaxies of bloom:
it is here, interpreting these, translating these,
stopping in the morning to study these,
touching affectionately the cold bark
of the seven-branched tree, where bees

stir the stars and scatter them down:
it is here, in these whitenesses of thought,
poring over these pages of white thought,
that we ponder anew the lifelong miracle:
the miracle that in these we best remember,
and in wisdom treasure best,
the lost snows of another December,
and the lost heart, and the lost love.
What matter that we are older, that we age?
Blest that we live this morning, blest
that still we read the immortal book
and in time's sunlight turn another page.

ii

Shall we call it, then, the walk in the garden?
the morning walk in the simple garden? But only if by this we
    mean
everything! The vast daybreak ascends the stairs of pale silver
above a murmur of acacias, the white crowns
shake dark and bright against that swift escalation of light,
and then, in intricate succession, the unfolding minutes and hours
are marked off by the slow and secret transactions
of ant and grassblade, mole and tree-root,
the shivering cascade of the cicada's downward cry, the visitation
(when the brazen noon invites) of that lightninged prism
the hummingbird, or the motionless hawkmoth.
Listen! The waterclock of sap in bough and bole,
in bud and twig, even in the dying
branch of the ancient plum-tree, this you hear, and clearly,
at eleven, or three, as the rusted rose-petal
drops softly, being bidden to do so, at the foot of the stem,
past the toad's unwinking eye! Call it
the voyage in the garden, too, for so it is:
the long voyage home, past cape and headland
of the forgotten or remembered: the mystic signal
is barely guessed in the spiderwort's golden eye, recognized

tardily, obscurely, in the quick bronze flash
from the little raindrop left to wither
in the hollow of a dead leaf, or a green fork
of celandine. For in this walk, this voyage,
it is yourself, the profound history of your 'self,'
that now as always you encounter. At eleven or three
it was past these folded capes and headlands, these decisions or
    refusals,
these little loves, or great,
that you once came. Did you love? did you hate?
did you murder, or refrain from murder, on an afternoon
of innocent cirrus in April? It is all recorded
(and with it man's history also)
in the garden syllables of dust and dew:
the crucifixions and betrayals,
the lying affirmations and conniving denials,
the cowardly assumptions, when you dared not face yourself,
the little deaths, and the great. Today
among these voluntary resumptions you walk a little way
toward tomorrow. What, then, will you choose to love or hate?
These leaves, these ants, these dews, these steadfast trifles, dictate
whether that further walk be little or great.
These waiting histories will have their say.

iii

But of those other trifles, the too intrusive,
the factual, the actual, that are too intrusive,
too near, too close, too gross, for deeper meaning:
what of these, what will memory make of these?
Will these too yield in time to the magic of translation?
The bobby-pins, the daily news, the paper-clips, even
the stuffed two-headed calf once seen in a pawnshop window;
as indeed also the crumpled letter, furtively
dropped in the ashcan at the corner,
yes, and the torn half of the movie ticket, bright pink,
found inadvertently in the breast-pocket, to remind you —

but meanly — of other days of afternoon rain:
how will you profitably rehearse these,
how will you (otherwise than here!) rehearse these,
        and to what end
of reconstruction? for what inspired reinterpretation
of the lost image, the lost touch?
Useless, here, the immediate, the factual, the actual:
the telephone remains silent when most you wish to hear it:
the May morning, or is it August or September,
remains empty, infertile, at precisely that instant
when your heart — if that is what you mean by heart —
would invoke a vision.
                        Blessing enough, indeed, it might have been,
but not under peach-tree or lyre-tree,
in the persistence of the radio's tremolo
and the listening silence of an empty room:
blessing enough if in these should quietly have spoken,
in answer to that invocation, the not-voice of voice,
the now almost unknown and unfamiliar voice,
the voice at first not recognized when heard:
blessing enough if in these
indifferent accidents and meaningless impromptus
the angelic not-you should open the door
and angelically enter, to take slow possession
of the room, the chairs, the walls, the windows,
the open piano with its waiting keys,
and the poor bed under the forgotten picture,
but possessing also
the divine touch that in the radiant fingertips
could at once create, with a magician's eloquence,
nothing from something, or something from nothing:
as, out of the untouched piano,
a shabby chord, a threadbare tune, the banal air
squealing from the midnight juke-box, where,
at the corner saloon, over the tepid beer,
you sit and stare,
remembering how the days have become years,

and the minutes hours,
and the false sunlight is distilled to tears
in the sentimental involutions of a shared sound:
yes, and the touch of the fingertip, once, on the back of the hand,
or, for a braver instant, tentatively, along the line of the cheek:
but no, these are all a broken imagination only,
the one and only heart remains lonely,
the morning remains silent, cannot speak,
muted by the ridiculous trifles, the preposterous trifles,
that stammer between the past and you.
Only, in the thinking hands, for a moment,
the persistent stupid bloodstream vaguely traces —
as if on air, as if on air —
the lost touch, the lost image, the chimerical future:
praying, now, for the illusion of an abstract love.

iv

The illusion of an abstract love? Say, rather,
it was the loves and hates that were illusion,
and all that accompanied them: items of fatigue
or of dubious regret, denials and acceptances,
these it is that are as clouds
gone deathward over the morning, lost, dislimned,
and now recoverable only, if at all,
in the remembered crevice in the remembered garden wall:
abstracted out of space, abstracted out of time,
but now reset, by the morning walk in the garden,
in crystal rhyme.
In these rich leaves, which are not only leaves
of lyre-tree or pomecitron, but also leaves
of a living book that is never done:
from winter to summer, from spring to fall:
in these we keep them all.
Here is that abstract love which we would find
wherein all things become imperishable mind:
the numberless becomes one, the brief becomes everlasting,

the everlasting opens to close
in the perishing of the raindrop on the rose:
violence is understood, and at last still,
evil is fixed and quiet as a tree or hill,
but all alike acceptable and one
and in one pattern made to move, or not to move,
by the illusion, if it is illusion,
of an abstract love.
Touch now again the serpent skin of the lyre-tree:
stoop now again, a hummingbird,
to the magic of the mock-orange:
count again by waterclock of rain
or dandelion clock of sun
the slow days of trees, the quick hours of flowers:
this time, this matin-song, this love, is yours, is ours,
a book that is never done, never done.

Overture to Today

i

This day is not as other days: will not be
a pale and stencilled pattern of those others:
the golden nexus of the dream
from which you woke at six in a thrill of rain
the golden wall from which an unknown woman leaned and spoke
calling your name, and then
put forth her hand to touch your face
saying, 'This day
will not be as those others, come, we will go away
into another world, another city, where
each avenue will be light, each house a prayer
and song the equivalent of breath!'
                              Fair, fair,
shines in the dream the dream's unfolding
from be to seem

from chaos into shape
from fear from death
yet with at first what slow and leaden step
we strive towards the wings of our escape
into that other country, where,
caught in a rarer pattern of intent,
we draw an exquisite and conscious breath!
                              Design,
as in the intricate dream, in us is woven:
and like the multiple meaning of the dream
which changes as it gleams, we too
are ravelled out in fiery threads:
under the very mind's-eye reappear
the thousand faces and the thousand eyes,
in every facet of the hour,
with which ourselves ourselves surprise.
                              Seed to flower:
and flower to seed. The hourglass turns
and pours its golden grains. The animal lives
mysteriously to himself, ordained, inviolable,
in a compulsive dream. The human child
so lives too without knowing,
innocent, living at one with the earth, the mother,
innocent participant of death and birth
and of begetting. Yet he must wake
and in the moment of his waking take
terrible knowledge of the miracle that is self.
See how he stands enringed
by the angelic and demonic powers, the winged
and fanged and finned and clawed!
And awed, and overawed,
now fades his song of innocence
                              and now begins
anthem of earth and heaven,
a new and richer counterpoint of praise,
that with experience is given:
henceforward he can sing

a fairer thing:
the radiant mysteries
that now are shared, and his.
                              Profound, profound,
celestial, or underground, or truly found
even in the hand's sore breadth, and the eye's beam,
as in the golden nexus of the dream,
the god of order like a golden worm
working in all things to his perfect term:
the golden rivet, reason, manifest
but only to our simple eyes in simplest form:
the mysteries
most impenetrable except in these, as these:
the pure simplicity of the flower
the little flower for the first time seen
above her shadow in her transparency of hour:
time taken transient shape in this, as time
takes shape in us who see
and in the foreforged word and chthonic rhyme
with which we bid it pause and be.
Who would not worship at the heart, the tree?
                              And we
who are the source of all delight and light
in which the meaning of the song stands still
are part and parcel of the mystery.

                              ii

And so, this day is not as others: no day
repeats the others. Yet what it brings
out of the instant past in its succession
for you the palimpsest of a dream, for the wild rose
time to open or to close,
time for the dead leaf to be crystal in the brook
for the opening or the shutting of the book
time for the oak to add another druid ring,
time to explore, time to explain

precisely why at six o'clock in a throb of rain
the cry of the pure heart was caught in a dream
precisely why
in the child's round vowel of song, or in the bird's
sleepy roulade, or in a myth, or a rune of words,
or on the blackboard in the school
where calligraphic chalk unfolds
a geometric golden rule;
design and the designer are the same,
the namer is the name.
                          We who divine,
waking or sleeping, or in the manifold dream,
define, then redefine,
by rule of thumb or harmony of number
seeking tomorrow's validity in curve or line or cosine
and in the eye that measures or in the thought
that through its own closed finite world of sense
                              takes measured flight
and always starting over, every day
brought to a standstill by the same or a different doubt,
the imagination like a kite reeled in
and then again reeled out:
                          we who divine
divine ourselves, divine our own divinity
                          it is the examination
of godhead by godhead
                          the imagination
of that which it is to be divine.

                          iii

Six o'clock. The tiger dream relinquishes
the traumatic heart. The tiger rain
claws at the windowpane
                          and before we sleep again
the bell strikes in the remembering heart
and as in a lightning-flash of time

                              we see
backward into the abyss of all we know and are.
Wings in the night fly left and right
swarm downward and away, and far,
only the cry of sky
                    floats upward, 'What am I?'
Yes, what am I? from what arriving? and into what
ascending or descending? The multiple dream
assembles its mythic fragments, like a kaleidoscope
clicks them into a pattern. We begin
to know, or think we know, to understand
or think we understand. Then sleep again.

                         iv

Before the unknown day which is to come
from east and past and earth and sky
arriving like the tumid tide that swells
under the precursive and magnetic moon
and bringing like the tide its ancient freight
of solar and human history, we wait
veiled in a hushed anticipation, conscious of the hour
and yet unconscious also since its power
not in the marker of the bell but in the swell
of tidal mystery without within
is ours as well as time's. In a pure state
of irresponsible expectancy, of pregnancy,
like those who wait to see
a theatre's curtain drawn and what is there to be,
we wait, and stare, and know
that this will be no ordinary show:
that something godlike here begins
                         and greater far
than our poor dream may have conception of:
                         and yet
it is ourselves who have conceived
and have believed

that what we see will be the work of love.
             This day
will be the enacting of that foredoomed play.

And now the musicians of the heart begin
with heartbeat drum and flute of truth
and tender violin, begin
the sacred overture:
                    at first the pure
song of the child the song of innocence
and daybreak air
                    and then the sober prayer
and anthem of experience
                    mature and sure
with contrapuntal weavings in and out
of love and wonder, faith and doubt,
                    and last
the many-voiced hymn of wisdom,
                    in which the past
of innocence and experience become one
the end implicit in the beginning
                    but all one . . .
                    And now the sun
divides the curtains of the night; our play,
of which the title is Today, will be begun.

What will it be? We do not know. But it will say:
love is the action which brings forth the day,
whether of will to love or will to live:
the necromancer's genius which brings forth
the golden All from the golden Nothing.
Love is poetry, the god's recreation,
his joy in *fiat*, the world becoming word.
It is creation and recreation, two words in one,
the poem always just begun
and never done.
             The world as word

this is the poem which the wise poet writes
in us and through us and around us writes
                          o and invites
all things created, and all things to come,
each to make tribute and contribution make
to what is never whole
                         or wholly heard.

Another Lycidas

I

Yet once more in the empty room review
the photomatic photo on the table
which years have faded but from which
still behind owlish glasses stubborn eyes
under an ancient hatbrim fix your own.
                         Which nevertheless are his
since it is at a camera that he gazes
there in the railway station, his own image
rounded in a lens in a curtained cubicle
while outside, along an echoing concourse,
passengers hurry for trains and trains depart
                   and overhead
the silent clock the electric clock
                     sans tick sans tock
with quivering hand pricks off another second
advancing for his life a last October.
                     Yet once more view
the silent face whose fierce regard for you
follows you like a conscience: stubborn, sober,
who after two martinis waits
and thus kills time till the opening of the gates.
What train it is he waits for we well know.
Leaving behind the evening suburbs it will go
south to the Islands and the pinewood Cape

where he was born, and grew, and knew
as if it were a legend learned by heart
each name each house each village, that ancient land
familiar to him as his face, the land
whence came with the ancestral name
inheritance of those steadfast eyes, the hand
salt-stung salt-harsh that for his forebears threw
the barbed harpoon or turned the wheel to windward
and kept it by the compass true.

II

Bequeathing us this gimcrack photo
as he himself would say *pictore ignoto*
for contemplation now that he is dead
bequeathing it by accident and not intent
yet speaking to us still and of that day:
what else would he have said or what else say?
       The massive head
and proud mustachios are not in his regard
and it is not at these he stares
who midway in his life no longer cares
(*nel mezzo del cammin di nostra vita*)
for vanity of self: what there he sees
and with his vision frees
beyond the Islands and the ancestral seas
and the hall bedroom the humble furnished room
in which he lived until he died:
       beyond all these
is what he sees he has himself become
and, with him, us: and further still
what, out of yeoman courage, country skill,
the ploughshare patience, the seafarer's will,
has come, as for the sailor homeward bound,
a change of course.
       Profound:
and yet not so, since simple must to complex grow.

And he who as a boy trapped muskrats in the creek
or through snow-stippled poverty-grass
tramped to the ringing pond to fish through ice
or rolled the barrel in, to salt the pork,
or sawed and split the pine and oak
in the pale sweetgrass by the cedar swamp
under a harvest moon that rose again
to silhouette the weathervane
above the meetinghouse: and who would say
year after year when he returned
the 'frost is on the punkin',' or 'I know
clam chowders on the backs of kitchen stoves
that have been there for nigh a hundred years':
                          or in the slate-cold churchyard,
where now unmarked he lies, point out the stone
on which appear these words alone:
'The Chinese woman, name unknown': then tell
her story, and a hundred others, which each house
bespoke for him along a mile of elm-tree-shaded road:
                          he who from this had grown
and all this wood-lot lore had known
and never had forgotten, nevertheless
with this rich knowledge also took
to Buenos Aires Cadiz and the rest
                          and Harvard too
his boyhood's book, the scholar's book,
the book that was his life. This was to be
his change of course. What his forefathers learned
of wisdom, courage, skill, on land or sea,
rounding the whalespout horn, or in a summer's 'tempest,'
or 'burning off' in spring or sanding down a bog
or making the strict entries in a log
beneath the swinging lamp, in a clear script
the latitude and longitude: this now would change
and the sea-change reverse. Chapter and verse
replace the log, and ripened scholarship
the island packet and the blue-water ship.

III

Humility was in that furnished room
as in the furnished room that was his mind.
The glass of sharpened pencils on the table
the pencil-sharpener on the windowsill
a row of well-worn books upon a bench
some Spanish and some French
the page-proofs spread out to be worked upon
a few whodunits and a lexicon

in a top drawer
a flask of bourbon or the full-ripened corn
for those who *might* be to the manner born

behind a curtain
the neatly folded clothes on hangers hung
an old guitar somewhat unstrung
and in its leather case upon the shelf
the top hat now no longer worn

tarnished for certain
but much used in more prosperous days.

An 'aluminium' kettle
sat in the corner behind his chair, for tea,

beside it a red apple.
And the tea-leaves went down the W.C.

Evening, by the Esplanade.
Sunset brindles the bridge, the evening star
pierces the cirrus over Chestnut Hill

and we are still
asking the twilight question. Where shall it be:
tonight, tonight again, where shall it be?

Down 'Mulberry' Street
beckon the streetlights, and our feet

through rain or snow or sleet
once more in unison to eastward turn
not to Priapus Garden or to view
what the 'poast' says is 'plaid' today

                              but if burlesque be on
to the Old Howard, or the Tam or Nip
the Oyster House or Silver Dollar Bar
then to the Athens, there once more to meet
with Piston's whole-tone wit or Wheelwright's neat
while the martinis flow and clams are sweet
and he himself our morning star
until Apollo's taxi ploughs the dawn.
                              Who would not mourn
for such a Lycidas? He did not know
himself to sing or build the lofty rhyme
or so he would himself have said: and yet
this was not true: for in him grew
the poet's vision like a tree of light
                         and leaves of light
were in him as the gift of tongues
                         and he was of those few
who, as he heard, reshaped the Word,
and made the poem or the music true:
and he was generous with what he knew.
                         Lightly, lightly, November,
the third unknown by him, with sunshot gale
from the Great Cove or Follins Pond bring home
the hawk and heron: while we remember
                         the untold wealth he took
into the grave with him, the open book
that lies beneath the grass
of all he knew and was:
                         composed by him
with calligraphic hand and curious eye
the pencil point unhurried, fine,
unfolding still its classic line
and waiting still for us to see:
and, at the end, the signet signature, 'G.B.'
Death's but a progress, or so Whitehead says.
The infant dies to childhood the child to boy
the boy to youth the youth to man.

                              Try as we can
if we should think to try or makeshift make
                              we cannot take
one age into another. Life is a span
which like the bridge the link not knowing link
comes to an end in earth as it began.
                      We cannot think
end and beginning all at once but only
in the broken beam of light recall
the instant prism in a recession of successions.
And it is only we, the living, who can see
in such another instant of successions
                              the span of such a man.

SHEEPFOLD HILL

*

The Crystal

I

What time is it now, brother Pythagoras, by the pale stone
set like a jewel in the brow of Sheepfold Hill?
There where the little spider, your geometrist,
shrinks from autumn in the curl of a leaf,
his torn world blown in the wind? What time, tonight,
under the motionless mill-wheel, in the pouring brook,
which bears to the sea — O *thalassa, thalassa,*
pasa thalassa, for the sea is still the sea —
the flickering fins, unnumbered, which will return thence
in April or May? By the dial in Samos what hour?
Or in Babylon among the Magi?
       Your forefoot ploughs
over the floating Pole Star, Ionian foam
wets once again the gemmed sandal, as westward still
the oars beat time, and the sail runs out, in the wake
of Samian Kolaios.
     Not you for bars of silver,
nor to trade wool or wine or raisins for tin,
and not to return to Samos, nor with regret, but rather —
listen! — as with these migrants who now above us
whirl the night air with clamor of wings and voices,
southward voyaging, the caucus of robins,
choosing, like you, a propitious hour.
       So the page turns
always in the middle of a sentence, the beginning of a meaning;
the poem breaks in two. So the prayer, the invocation,
and the revelation, are suspended in our lives,

suspended in a thought. Just as now,
still there in the dark at the prow of your galley,
your hand on the cleat, you observe the division of water,
the division of phosphor, yourself the divider,
and the law in the wave, and the law in the eye;
observing, too, with delight; and remembering
how once on the headland of Bathy at daybreak
you sacrificed a hundred oxen to your godfather, Apollo,
or was it forty or fifty,
and the occasion for it: your vision
of the triangle's godgiven secret, the song of the square
echoing the squares.
            Long ago: far away:
wave-length and trough-length: the little Pan's Pipe
plaintive and sweet on the water at midnight:
yet audible still to the infinitesimal
tambourine of the eardrum. And now you are sixty,
the beard is of sea-moss. At Delphi
you set foot on the salt shingle, climbed
up the path through the rocks to the temple,
where priestesses dreamed with their oakleaves.
What warning or promise from the *tripous?* What cryptic
oracle flung from the sun on the mountain
to bear on the sea-track that beats to the west?
Daybreak it was, with long shadows. Far down,
at the foot of the gorge, you could measure
the toy groves of olives, the hearse-plumes of cypress,
and daisies danced in a ring, and the poppies
in the grass and wild thyme around you
went running, and crackling like fire. Alas!
a few columns, only, still stand there,
and the wild fig roots in the wall. And now,
your galleys hush west on the sea,
as you, old migrant, set sail once again
(like those fins down the stairs to the bay)
with your wife and your sons, and the grandchildren swaddled,
your gear and your goats and your handmaids;

setting forth as aforetime to Thebes.

While we,

secret and silent, sealed off in the west,
sit still and await you. In a different world,
and yet foreseen in your crystal:
the numbers known to your golden abacus,
and the strings that corded your lyre.

II

Six o'clock, here, in the western world, a west
unknown to sailor Kolaios, or the porters of Tartessus.
Stony Brook ferries its fins to the sea. Four bells
sing now in the fisherman's lighted cabin
above the brass binnacle and the floating compass.
Six o'clock in the cone of the equinox, the bells
echo over mud-flats, sift through the nets
where mackerel flap and flash in the pools,
and over the oyster-beds, the shells of the razor-fish,
borne inland, to be echoed again
by the austere bell in the puritan steeple.
At seven, in the ancient farmhouse,
cocktails sparkle on the tray, the careful answer
succeeds the casual question, a reasoned dishevelment
ruffling quietly the day's or the hour's issue.
Our names, those we were born with,
or those we were not born with, since all are born nameless,
become the material, or the figment, if we wish,
of which to weave, and then unweave, ourselves.
Our lives, those we inherited, of which
none can claim ownership in fee simple, but only
a tenant's lease, of unpredictable duration,
rented houses from which have already departed perhaps
those others, our other selves, the children:
ourselves in these on our way beyond death
to become the undying succession of inheritors:
these and other aspects of the immortal moment

glow into consciousness for laughter or tears,
an instant of sympathy or misunderstanding, an exchange
of human touch or tact, or agreement, soon silent.
And here, as in the silence, too, that follows,
like the peacock's eye of shadow round the lifted candle,
is the tacit acceptance of death. We invoke,
and what is life but an invocation,
the shore beyond the vortex, the light beyond the dark,
the number beneath the name. We shall not be here
to pour the bright cocktails, while we listen
to the throb of migrant wings in the night air,
the chorus of departing voices, the bells from the bay;
and yet, brother Pythagoras, like you,
who still set your sail this night to the west,
we too shall be held so. After our deaths
we too shall be held so. And thus, brought together.

III

And yet, if this were so, but in another sense:
the immortality, perhaps, of a different sort:
or death somehow of a different kind: and if it were true,
as in the myth of All Hallows at this season,
when frost beards the pumpkin, and the last apple
thuds to bare earth; and if, from our graves,
whether at Metapontum by the fields of corn,
or by the muddy river at Isle of Hope,
or under the Acropolis on the hill of rocks,
with the moon's shield brazen above us: yes, if, called by name,
you there, I here, we could arise,
and make our way in the dark to the road's edge
for a day or a night of the familiar habits;
what time would it be, brother Pythagoras,
for what custom, and what place?
                                        All life
is ritual, or becomes so: the elusive pattern
unfolds its arcanum of observances,

measured in time, and measured by time, as the heartbeat
measures the blood. Each action, no matter how simple,
is precious in itself, as part of the devotion,
our devotion to life. And what part of this ritual
would we choose for re-enactment? What rite
single out to return for? After the long silence,
and the long sleep, wherein has been never
configuration of dream; no light, no shape;
not the geometer's triangle, flashing in sun,
to be resolved in reason, no, nor the poet's mirage of landscape,
brilliant as the image in the finder of a camera,
nor the gem-carver's little emerald, with lyre and cupido,
or the sculptor's bronze, the *cire-perdue*,
an art fetched from Egypt: no, no sound, no color:
what then would we choose? Carver of gems, lover of crystal,
savior-god of Croton! can you yet soothsay?

Easy enough, it would be, to find in the darkness
the familiar roadside, the shape of a known tree,
and then, how naturally, alas, the faded signpost
stuck in the sand: and on it to make out with joy
the names that point homeward. And easy enough
to fly then as the bee flies, to home as to hive.
And arrived there, to find the door open,
the fire on the hearth, the pot on the trivet,
the dish on the table — with a red rim — for grapes,
and the ripe blue cluster; to feel with one's foot
the slope of the floorboard, and on it the scars
ridged by the adze; the shelves bright with bowls,
and the floor bright with mats, and the walls
bright with pictures. And then, to lift gently
the one thing most loved: as if in this thing
one could best hold them all. And thus, it might be
a spoon from one's childhood: a shell of thin silver,
a handle shaped like a tiny brick chimney,
atop of it, perching, a dwarf with a horn,
a curled horn tilted to heaven.

                                In this,
to achieve the resumption, the chained implication,
backward, then forward, of the whole of one's life.

Too simple perhaps? Or an example, only.
For, to which house, of the many houses,
and all of them loved, would one fare first?
To which altar of the many altars, the changing
gods, with their changing attributes? Which city
of the many dear cities? Samos, with its wall,
and the port, and the Hera Temple, and the tunnel
carved through the rock by Eupalinos, to bring water
for the three brave fountains, praised by Herodotus?
Or Croton, of the Brotherhood? Who can say?
Perhaps for none of these, but, more simply,
for the pronunciation, softly, of a single name:
the observation, precisely, of a single flower:
white crocus, white hyacinth. Or perhaps
we would return if only once more to remember
something secret and precious, but forgotten: something in-
           tended,
but never performed: begun, but not finished.
Or else, to notice, but now with a more careful love,
the little hooked claws, bent down, of the clover:
the white geometry, in clearest numbers,
of those little asters, or asterisks, the snow.
                                Samples, examples!
And perhaps too concrete. The heart might so choose,
but what of the mind? All very well
the sight or the sound, the taste or the feeling, the touch
or the texture. And, as in a dream,
to combine them — delicious! Thus, a ring of your father's,
Mnesarchos, the gem-carver: you watch him at work,
yourself still a boy, and both silent:
the emerald held in a vice, then the green
ice of the clear stone gives up its goddess,
the tiny wave bears up its Venus, green foam

on the brow and the shoulder. The image?
Of course! But beneath or behind it
the knowledge, the craft: and the art, above all.
Would it not be for this, for ruler and compass,
brother Pythagoras, that we would return?

For both: the one is the other. In each lies the other.
Design shines implicit in the blind moment
of self-forgetful perception: belief is steadfast
in the putting forth of a hand, as in the first
wingbeat, or extension of a claw; the law
unfolding and infolding forever.
                              It would be for this
Apollonian fountain of the forever unfolding;
the forever-together, ourselves but a leaf
on the fountain of tree, that we would return:
the crystal self-shaping, the godhead designing the god.
For this moment of vision, we would return.

IV

The admirations come early, crowd through
the lenses of light and the lenses of the eye,
such sudden and inimitable shapes, such colors
confusing and confused, the vast but orderly
outpouring and downpouring and inpouring — who but
a god could distribute so many and so various,
but what god and where? Not Aladdin
in the dark cave walking on jewels and precious stones,
on diamonds and rubies, brushing the walls
of topaz and opal, ever went among such wonders
or was ever so dazzled. The wind's serpent
sibilant and silver in a field of barley
insinuates a pattern, the concentric
ripples in a fountain perpetuate another
the quartz crystal offers a pyramid, and two together,
joined, a cube! Where burns not or shines not

purity of line? The veins of the myrtle
are alive with it, the carpenter's board
diagrams it in a cross-section of history, life
empanelled golden in a design. What does not your hand
turn up or over, living or inanimate,
large or small, that does not signal
the miracle of interconnectedness
the beams meeting and crossing in the eye and the mind
as also in the sun? How can you set end to it
where is no ending and no beginning
save in the one that becomes the many, the many
that compose the one? How shall we praise the forms?
Algebra shines, the rose-tree perfects with precision
its love the rose, the rose perfects with precision
its love the seed, the seed perfects with precision
its love the tree. How shall we praise the numbers?
Geometry measures an arc of orchard an arc of sky
the inward march and arch of the mind. Things
are numbers. Numbers are the shape
given to things, immanent in things past and present
as in the things to come. Not water nor fire
nor Anaximander's cloud nor only
the inexhaustible and unknowable flux which Heraclitus
in vain exhorted to be still, but number
that buds and breaks from number, unfolds in number,
blossoms in number, is born and dies in number.
And the sounds too, your loves the sounds:
in these to find the final of harmonies, the seven
unequal strings of the lyre, the seven notes to be
intertwined or countered, doubled or trebled or wreathed;
seven strings for the seven sages, to each
the *tripous* awarded, as to Pherekydes your teacher:
but not to yourself, except in
the little tripod of silver you minted
for the coins of Croton. And then, ringing all,
encircling the worlds and the god's central fire,
the revolving spheres and the music they chorus

too perfect for hearing.
                    The admirations
come early, stay long, multiply marvelously,
as if of their own volition. In such confusion
what answer for order? The odd and the even,
the prime and the solid, the plane and the oblong:
numbers, shapes, sounds, measurements, all these
to be studied and observed with joy, with passion,
the wind's serpent to be followed where it
vanishes in a spiral of silver through the wheatfield
the ripples to be pursued as they ply outward
over the fountain-face of cloud-flattering water
plangency and pitch of the lyre's note
to be judged exactly by the length of the tight string
notched in the edge of the tortoise-shell:
crystal and asphodel and snowflake
alike melting in the palm of the mind, and the mind
admiring its own admirations, in these too
uncovering the miracle of number: all, at last,
transparent, inward and outward, the one
everlasting of experience, a pure delight.

                              V

What is the voyage and who is the voyager?
Who is it now hoisting the sail
casting off the rope and running out the oars
the helmsman with his hand on the tiller
and his eyes turned to windward? What time is it now
in the westward pour of the worlds and the westward
pour of the mind? Like a centipede on a mirror
the galley stands still in a blaze of light
and yet swims forward: on the mirror of eternity
glitters like a golden scarab: and the ranked oars
strike down in harmony beat down in unison
churn up the water to phosphor and foam
and yet like the galley are still.

So you
still stand there, your hand on the tiller,
at the center of your thought, which is timeless,
yourself become crystal. While we,
still locked in the west, yet are present before you,
and wait and are silent.

In the ancient farmhouse
which has now become your temple
we listen again to the caucus of robins
the whistle of migrant voices and wings
the turn of the great glass of season.
You taught the migration of souls: all things
must continue, since numbers are deathless:
the mind, like these migrants, crosses all seasons,
and thought, like these cries, is immortal.
The cocktails sparkle, are an oblation.
We pour for the gods, and will always,
you there, we here, and the others who follow,
pour thus in communion. Separate in time,
and yet not separate. Making oblation
in a single moment of consciousness
to the endless forever-together.

This night
we all set sail for the west.

The Cicada

Views the phenomenal world as a congeries
of shells, casts, and cast-offs, the envelopes
of dead letters, addressees long since lost,
but still of ghostly substance, flung off
and left behind by that which lived and died,
but now, transmuted, leaves in immutable series
the visual equations of essence. It is illusion?
So be it, but it is our veritable speech, our inimitable
shape. Who goes now to the heart

for certainty, the assayable grain of truth?
Fluid and momentary as the auricle's bloodstream.
But in the fossil's curve, limpid in dark rock,
or in the oak's ring, or the king-crab's carapace,
horned for combat long after his wars are done,
yes, and in the mortmain of the printer's page,
still set as the love-song of an antique May,
of which the weather is unrecorded, or, again,
scrolled in the astronomer's sines and symbols, the algebrist's
diminishing abstractions — in these, in these,
o dearest of ephemerids! — in these
how much more permanent is our exchange
whether of love or friendship, the light eye
sounding the unsoundable in the treacherous instant,
than in the summer song, which seems so long, so long,
of the cicada, that brazen jongleur of the trees,
shaking his iridescent rapture! — the subsiding song
spills from the rusted chestnut leaves, is downward lost,
but under the bough still clings, with hooked and feathered
      claws,
and staring eyes that do not see,
and the split back from which the psyche flew to death,
the crystal chrysalis that will outlast the fall.

What language, this? — The painter's, which is the lover's,
which is the poet's: whose black numbers note
the infinitesimal tick, the monstrous cry.
Grammar and syntax must alike belong
not to the song
but to morphology, the shape that cannot die.

Aubade

Six o'clock in the crystal instant the crystal second
the crystal pause between systole and diastole
the six glass birds fly one from another

eastward to sunrise out of the sleeping tower
O sleeping man, wake, it is the hour
of crystal meditation, you must compose your death

the six glass birds are flown to the six far corners
where the six columns of crystal uphold the sunrise
but the tower sleeps and the man sleeps
while the wave of sunrise unfolds its volute of prism
O sleeping man, wake, your angel weeps
she who in your slumber dreams to compose your death

six songs it might have been or six devotions
or the six words but not the seventh on the cross
six leaves loosening one and then another
from the praying-tree that waits alone in sunrise
O sleeping man, wake, the hour of loss
opens its crystal heart, you must compose your death

compose your death, O sleeping man, while the six heartbeats
distinct as sandgrains in the hourglass fall
the crystal heartbeats loosening one from another
while the long wave of sunrise unfolds its clouds
O sleeping man, wake, and compose of all
these crystal intricacies of nescience death

of the six words and the six leaves and the six bells
eastward bearing like glass birds the sleeping heart
to the altar of sunrise which the columns uphold
the six crystal columns lucent in sunrise
O sleeping man, wake, it is time to depart,
open your crystal zero, compose your death.

Maya

We are not seen here before, nor shall be seen
hereafter, nor our garlands of oak-leaves, either;

time was unnoticed, unnumbered, by our empty hands and eyes,
and will be again:

the rain at seven, who had foreseen its elusive silver,
this minuet from dark eaves falling:
or the snow, with its bland deceit over moss and lichen,
or the algebra on the pane:

and the god, too, fallen dejected from his cross, with
    what surprise
to himself and those who loved him:
and all those other gods, of beast and bird and flower,
who died in vain.

Come, let us seek in ourselves, while time includes us,
the illusion's whorled and whirling center;
and praise the imperishable metal of that flower
whose seed was barren grain.

The Accomplices

A love I love whose lips I love
but conscience she has none
nor can I rest upon her breast
for faith's to her unknown
light-hearted to my bed she comes
but she is early gone.

This lady in the sunlight is
as magic as the sun
and in my arms and all night long
she seems and is my own
yet but a Monday love is she
and Tuesday she is gone.

Rare as charity is her hand
that rests my heart upon
but charity to so many kind

stays for a day with none
a spendthrift love she spends her love
and all will soon be gone.

Yet though my trust has been betrayed
reproaches have I none
no heart but is of treason made
or has not mischief done
and we could be together false
if she would but stay on.

The Meeting Place

The way to meet the unmeetable — ? It is this —
to step into the calyx of the sun
at daybreak or a shade before
(for such is the privilege of imagination)
and it will come to you, the event, in some such form
as history requires, though that is not
for immediate consideration. The history
is indeed another and inalterable matter.
For the moment, to meet the moment, you must step forth
fearlessly or with awareness of fear:
and that is perhaps better, for fear
is that by which you live, with which you die,
the edge of death, as it was the edge of birth.
What, pray, does the ailanthus do with its seeds
shaken at three o'clock by the alien southeast
to a shower of snow or is it sleet or a feathery
rainfall of blossom to the unreceptive
stones of a human path? Out of such
and into such unhuman paths we sow
without hope of fruit, maybe, our deeds or deaths
or seeds of hope. But what then
when the ailanthus in the penultimate April
or ultimate and desired May gives up

bloom for leaves, for the last time leaves
bloom for leaves?
        For then it is, dear tree, dear heart,
dear earth, dear god, and all we love and owned,
when the deciduous becomes tired, that history
begins and speaks. When we no longer dream
forward, but only backward, in the desired May,
and death no longer in the fruit is in the root
then it is that history speaks
and the last sunset is the first, the first
sunrise becomes the last, the tree becomes again the seed,
and in a twinkling is again the tree,
and we are seed and tree, and we
like gods can both remember and forget,
and the unmeetable is met.

The Fluteplayer

Excellent o excellent in morning sunlight
that slides in planes of water through this tree
o chinaberry tree dedicated to daybreak
as daybreak the unfolding rose is dedicated to thee
but who was in this garden what god was in this garden
breathed here upon his flute before we came
who was here of whom we do not know the name

light slides its crystal over silent leaves
crystal delight for thee blest chinaberry tree
but who was he who in this garden
blew on his flute the two-voiced myth
before we came
sounding in changing shapes and guises
his two-voiced name

for there was someone here someone unknown
of whom these shapes and colors speak

someone o chinaberry tree who speaks in thee
on the path this side of night
speaks still in shade or substance the lost name
he left behind, the absent-minded god
who blew his two-voiced flute before we came.

Herman Melville

'My towers at last!' —

                What meant the word
from what acknowledged circuit sprung
and in the heart and on the tongue
at sight of few familiar birds
when seaward his last sail unfurled
to leeward from the wheel once more
bloomed the pale crags of haunted shore
that once-more-visited notch of world:
and straight he knew as known before
the Logos in Leviathan's roar
he deepest sounding with his lead
who all had fathomed all had said.

Much-loving hero — towers indeed
were those that overhung your log
with entries of typhoon and fog
and thunderstone for Adam's breed:
man's warm Sargasso Sea of faith
dislimned in light by luck or fate
you for mankind set sail by hate
and weathered it, and with it death.
And now at world's end coasting late
in dolphined calms beyond the gate
which Hercules flung down, you come
to the grim rocks that nod you home.
Depth below depth this love of man:
among unnumbered and unknown

to mark and make his cryptic own
one landfall of all time began:
of all life's hurts to treasure one
and hug it to the wounded breast,
in this to dedicate the rest,
all injuries received or done.
Your towers again but towers now blest
your haven in a shoreless west
o mariner of the human soul
who in the landmark notched the Pole
and in the Item loved the Whole.

When You Are Not Surprised

When you are not surprised, not surprised,
nor leap in imagination from sunlight into shadow
or from shadow into sunlight
suiting the color of fright or delight
to the bewildering circumstance
when you are no longer surprised
by the quiet or fury of daybreak
the stormy uprush of the sun's rage
over the edges of torn trees
torrents of living and dying flung
upward and outward inward and downward to space
or else
peace peace peace peace
the wood-thrush speaking his holy holy
far hidden in the forest of the mind
while slowly
the limbs of light unwind
and the world's surface dreams again of night
as the center dreams of light
when you are not surprised
by breath and breath and breath
the first unconscious morning breath .
the tap of the bird's beak on the pane

and do not cry out come again
blest blest that you are come again
o light o sound o voice of bird o light
and memory too o memory blest
and curst with the debts of yesterday
that would not stay, or stay

when you are not surprised
by death and death and death
death of the bee in the daffodil
death of color in the child's cheek
on the young mother's breast
death of sense of touch of sight
death of delight
and the inward death the inward turning night
when the heart hardens itself with hate and indifference
for hated self and beloved not-self
when you are not surprised
by wheel's turn or turn of season
the winged and orbèd chariot tilt of time
the halcyon pause, the blue caesura of spring
and solar rhyme
woven into the divinely remembered nest
by the dark-eyed love in the oriole's breast
and the tides of space that ring the heart
while still, while still, the wave of the invisible world
breaks into consciousness in the mind of god
then welcome death and be by death benignly welcomed
and join again in the ceaseless know-nothing
from which you awoke to the first surprise.

Portrait

Seven-starred eyes beneath the seven-starred mind
young Helen's eyes with flaming Troy behind

and in the labyrinths of fatal hair
the dying Minotaur and Theseus on the stair

and as I drink the thieving Argonauts
sail from this table with our ravished thoughts
to trade our love the honey of Hybla bees
beyond the sunset rocks the knees of Hercules.

Arcane immortal shameless is that face
rich with the present timelessness of race
the ageless smile for me but also still
the secret smile of triumph for Samson at the mill —

dead kings dead heroes nailed like stars above
in the cold constellations of her love
none there forgotten none who desired escape
and we, we too, alas, must in that myth take shape.

The Fountain

In the evening we heard the dead leaves
skittering away over asphalt
in the morning saw a sequin of sunlight
slotted through a crack in the wall
bright gold on the woodshed floor
but no it did not tremble it was only
the pale yellow leaf of the locust.

And look now the golden-eyed tree-toad
flips through a thicket of shadow
to breathe by the sodden bird's nest
the goldfinch caught in a ring of light
taps at the eaves and Sheepfold Hill
once more wears its Joseph's coat colors
while wild geese honk at the tideline.

Voices of death voices of creation
for the blonde rondure of the full moon
and the bat's dizzy sky-skatings
we light now the first candle
sheltered between tender-bright palms
for a secret instant of self.
Now phrase be praise and praise be phrase
for the brook with a stone in its path
the man with no thought in his mind
the girl with no love in her heart
the shooting star lost in a vapor
and the wind stilled at sunset.

Caught with these in a moment of silence
we become one instant of the forever-together
the fountain of god-speech motionless in falling
action spellbound in the moment of meaning
words and worlds still enough at last to be counted
if only there was someone to count them.

The Cyclads

They have been no longer than usual in arriving at this place.
Terror of time, they murmur, equals the terror of space.
All cancels out in the end, they say, and the end is nothing.
And all between a nothing in borrowed clothing.
Here we have stars — even of the first magnitude —
how flattering these human terms! — doomed to decrepitude,
all things, even the little atom, in it slow dying, arrive here,
and then slip silently x-ward to a predestined year.
Who would plant trees here? Is it an honest man?
As if to shade coming chaos in his wistful plan?
God knows, not we. At least, we plant no tree.
We only wait in the Absolute and see.

Yes, Old Repetition, they have been no longer than usual:
only to itself, perhaps, does time's cycle seem casual:
and space, this horrid cloaca which we must share,
finds no mirror in which to face its face in when or where.
Not in us surely? But perhaps in these, who seem
the endless repetition of our dream:
cold algebra brought round once more in a concentric hell:
convolute whirlwind in an invisible shell.
How vast, how still, how slow! We sleep, and wake, and then,
cloud-walking, watch our dream pour past again.
They have been no longer than usual, this time, in coming.
Behold the shadows of spokes, the wheels are humming,
street-lights and neon monsters glare on the cloud,
from violet dynamos, an endless belt, spills out the crowd.
And all at once. Dim past, dim future, all at once:
the moral histories, the cracked applause, the festered battle-
    fronts:
the corner drug-store where the lyric cash-tray sings:
and the amateur astronomer peering at Saturn's rings.
But this is not all, by no means, no! This is not all.
No, choose your own show, midway or sideshow: from Adam's
    Fall
to ill-starred Lucifer, and the blind poet's dictated dream:
o purblind doomed panhandler of the siltage in time's stream.

THE MORNING SONG OF LORD ZERO

The Morning Song of Lord Zero

i

Gambler and spendthrift by nature
chameleon soul whose name is Zero
anonymous in headlines
nameless in breadlines
nevertheless I am your hero.
Today an upstart millionaire from Mozambique
polyglot but sans Latin and sans Greek
très debonair très chic
I am inscrutably someone else tomorrow
when I speak
all languages at will:
the cashier's till
spills me a quicksilver word
the gilded shill
coos me another
I am your jack-and-jill
of all trades dubious brother
panhandler father Cassandra mother
and yet in the end insidiously
o indispensably and invidiously
something more.
Watch me sneak from door to door:
with tongue in cheek
but ready with the o so adaptable speech
I knock on each:
listen to my sales-talk: love, and honor,
courage, cowardice, virtue, vice,
belief and disbelief!

Down the immortal and dreadful street
where man your image extends himself forever
I your Greek-gift-bearing donor
I, but believe me! your Cassandra
knock and knock
(do not call me *vox et praeterea nihil*)
and if no answer
stoop and try the lock
hoping still to find
somewhere some day
the sacred and vulgar key
to you or me.

                       Azrael pass thou not by
                       shade not today this tree.

I am he
and this I share with you
in this perhaps alone am true
who cannot infringe upon cannot conceive
the arcane process by which he might believe
or not believe or learn or know
begin or not begin choose or not choose: who came
without a name
as also without intention: knows no measure
save only that with which the umbilical cord
provided him *tout court* of pain or pleasure:
rising not with the sun
but the day well begun
to brush his teeth and defaecate and eat
innocently sans knowledge of their meanings
or of his own:
and thus goes forth to face the preposterous unknown.
Can you remember what I remember?
Are we of one substance? Are we flesh or stone?
Yet brought by solar synthesis together
comedians of the soul's capricious weather
obedient to who-knows-what

we seek to chart
disturbances of the heart
goblin manifestations of All Souls' November
the golden monstrances of May.
I your hero take apart
in layered laminae the infinite platitude
figure degrees of magnitude
in man's imagination
of which the application remains obscure
pick up with tweezers some idiot surd of meaning
so summoning the morning stars to shout together
and thus with gradual decimals construct
the glass-topped hearse
that it our universe.

Belly to belly and skin to skin
o lift the latch and come right in
will you have me now or will you hesitate?
We played pinochle and we stayed out late
ate fish and chips at the Golden Gate
then crumpled the morning papers.
Know what the well-primed critics say
of pseudo-Shakspere's latest play
tragedy or farce or melodrama
witness the sad strip-tease
of Lesbian lads and Panic lasses
forgotten as soon as seen.
Take the express to Bowling Green
and watch the rosy-fingered dawn
practicing her matutinal flattery
above the Battery
then tip out one by one the firefly lights
and change to a golden crab the Staten Island ferry.
Brief is our measure, let us be merry.

ii

Look love the miracle is with us it is the body
the holy dwelling the acceptable machine
our own divine composing room
provided for us from the womb
alive and with its own precipitate and unpredictable aliveness
prismatic vision of the world no less
so brilliant that unless we blink
or do not stop to think
eyes and mind
are both struck blind.
How in this whole magnificence to find
our own self-seeking and self-shaping phrase
and so ordain our days?
Lord how the streets now shine
as the Great Opiate's eastern conduits run with wine
and pour into the sea. Dull would we be
if we withheld the attribute divine
from brick and stone and flesh
and from the awakening and self-breathing tree
the tree of heaven
spellbound in its epiphany
as the proud clocks strike seven.

And the intricacies begin:
without, within,
holy observed and holy observing
leaf adoring tree and tree admiring leaf
shape loving shapelessness and shapelessness shape
as unbelief worships belief!
See how the light shines through
the vascular leaf
green veins with gold shot through:
how we are of star's light made
and now distinct in sun and shade

of bloodstream made
and sunstream made.
Look through your hand and see
the blood against the sun
look into the sea
o mother mother
where with our fanlike fins
mind begins
and intricacy begins:
with what sacred and secret separations
and with what love
we are made to move!
Lightly now softly now
inward now outward now
frowardness and towardness now
dance and chance, as
intricacy begins
and again begins!
Song is our study
this is our body
see how the leaf comes
as out of death come
fresh the belief comes
and time begins!
Here on this hill
we number the possible
resume the acceptable
and intricacies begin!
Sunshape and earthshape
manshape and deathshape
wormshape in sunflower
godshape in dream.

Smith is early today and Jones is late
the box-trees by the Funeral Home have been watered
the newspaper truck throbs by the news-stand at the corner
the Shamrock Grill is open turnstiles are clacking

the cobbler in the window of Shoes Rebuilt
peers down at the heel he is tacking
the green light says Walk the red light says Stop
take me quick to the apothecary shop
we dial Meridian for the split jewel of time
and Weather for the windsong of weather.
Who needs a change of scene
walks with the green
into the unfolding world
himself too unfolding
the stage is struck the lights change
the street grows strange
it leads without hesitation forever
into our own involuntary invention
among the whispers and rainbows
of the unexpected
the fairyland
that waits to be named
between life and death.

> Azrael Azrael
> winged with thunder
> pass thou not by this day
> let no thing die
> the farmer sun is hastening
> the western hill is glistening
> the eastern honeycombs are filled
> with crocus light
> it is farewell to night
> see that this day no thing be killed.

> But if thy daily dead
> old thunder head
> thou yet must have then take instead
> the bee's faint shadow on the hill
> but the bee spare and daffodil
> leave all else living still

under the opening eyelid of the sky
swoop thou not hawklike by.

iii

Who are you? Who?
Fatigue this might be, or repetition
as the shutter dips sunshine in a known pattern,
bright drops falling
in a water-chain of light. The dream
hangs from the morning ceiling like a canopy,
illusory mosquito-net in whose folds
our old terror again insinuates itself to hide:

but no: it is not repetition nor fatigue
nor the prospect of sameness nor apprehension of change:
the footstep shifts to left or right
among crossed grassblades by the broken spout
to the galaxy of pebbles you call a path:
nor is it only the differing heartbeat
which hums in your heart as you go forth to discover:

the hum of the heartbeat linking past and future
as sun binds with gold the leaves in the tree
for the moment of sharing in which you partake
as Socrates lifts his cruse of hemlock:
acceptance and question in a single libation
celebration and farewell in a final gesture
the first and last taking of the breast:

at every instant of the perpetual intersection
of one with another in bloodstream and firmament
you are again born and again die
only o Phoenix to arise again in flame
immutable mutable of sunlight
again dripping from the shutter
and humming in the heart for another morning:
Jesus still walking down the galaxy of pebbles

to divide order from disorder
Blake sucking the wound in Achilles' heel
while the thorn-scratch festers on your ankle
and squirrel kisses squirrel on the bough of balsam:
as moment indivisibly and invisibly creates moment
and you walk from yourself into yourself.

The landscape why is it not as we had foreseen it
there are hills before us but no mountains
and a river winding behind the hills
and see on the hills the blessed creatures
lions composed and unrampant under a flight of birds
in a ladder of light
and there in one corner a last pocket of night
ravelling away to the sun.
The waterfalls are not exactly those of the mind
dropping their blue against the green
it is all familiar but also unfamiliar
known and unknown true and untrue
benign but also perilous
and as we step into the meadow
we feel the shadow that is not precisely a shadow
the breath that is not precisely a breath. Death
surely has not preceded our footsteps here
surely does not follow us? The landscape
opens unhesitatingly before us
hills from rivers roll back
pathways open to left and right
our feet are now in the morning brook
and its clear parable of time
the tree is under our hands and over our heads
and as we move to what we do not know
and can never rightly imagine
all these become the ambiguous language
by which we come to pass
and learn to see
and mean
and be.

The Phoenix in the Garden

The Garden
Silence. The hour of the Phoenix.
And who is waiting, if not ourselves,
for another of the bland sequences of twilight,
that most ambiguous of transformations. We observe
the subtle succession, so innocent, so seemingly unprepared,
from one color to another, from shade to lesser shade,
and thus by degrees to the absolute. But it is not
ourselves alone who are involved: no such thing.
No, not projected by those who dream, far less
by us, who have no meaning, the lawn
(forgive me) is not emerald, nor orient jade, and lately tarnished
by the seasonal trades. Heavy July
has emptied the birds' nests. The frogs
sulk in the pool, diminuendo.
And the ancient trees, our sad acacias,
those dirty trees, the gardener calls them,
forever littering, scattering —

The Streetlamp
Speak for yourself, old garden,
but not for me. Only at nightfall
I light that secret stage of yours:
am but a candle-holder, who, after dark,
will serve to trace, for a serpent's-tongue flicker of time
the broken curve of an arch
or empty an urn of shadow
or expose the brute flank, lichened marble,
of goat-god Pan. Understanding nothing,
remembering nothing. But you
and all your perjured altars —

The Garden
So you might say: and that crude light of yours

a vulgar penetration. Turn away
the indifferent and infertile eye,
that once more I might wonder
why you are you and I am I
and why
together forked in such conjunction,
base gerundive of nature. As if — as if —
But now the clock strikes. Now begin —
Phoenix! — and welcome in
the unwelcome strangers.

> The Phoenix
>   I cry I cry
> human shape not human
> trees not arboreal the terrestrial earth
> not plausible earth and my wings not wings
> but flames that flake and fall and as they fall
> consume us all
> I cry I cry.

> The Garden
> And so it comes again, winter and summer
> sun or rain it comes again.
> The rake is not as cruel with the leaf
> as between new-met lovers disbelief.
> And sod, upturned, discloses,
> the agonizing roots of roses.
>   And here they come.

> The Man
> Perfection, it may be — or imperfection it may be —

> The Woman
> Or confection perhaps. What a delicious garden. The leaves
> are not of the fig, nor figment, one believes
> in neither. And with what grief conceives
> of that pained love, suffocating and insufferable,

the eyes lowered, blinded, the tranquil house
where dwells the spirit
blown in, blown out, by the wind of desire, diswindowed
of time and place!
                              Yet one can wind one's hair
— look now — upon this broken stair
or round a pinchbeck pin
o god as if it were a world
and not have back a word.
                              Garden, garden,
why do we walk here, stand here? And poor man
why flown together?

          The Phoenix
I cry I cry
not flown not flown disown
that word of wings how can you own
human shape not human
embodiment of air and mind together
and so sail off like me in any weather
flame I come and flame I go —

          The Man
I know. And I know more. I know
what the leaf thinks in the pregnant garden, green inscription
decipherable only to the tree and root
and the eventual seed and the inevitable fruit
and yes poor woman
in all that here compels us.

          The Woman
Ophidian and recondite comes the demon.

          The Garden
Look — they have been petrified in the very act
the extreme act
of prayer.

     The Streetlamp
Hair twined with hair beneath my Gorgon stare.

     The Phoenix
I cry and shall cry again
human shape not human
man not man woman not woman
man not woman nor woman man since time began
the ashes sing beneath my wing.

     The Streetlamp
I am a candle-holder, I am patient.
And who knows which most matters, that which happens
or what's in darkness or in light — this garden
and the two strangers and the stranger Phoenix
and all these shuttlings through the shutter of light.
Let them be blest, if blest they can be, by my light.

The Old Man and the Shadow

     The Old Man
Perils of daybreak and the sharp shutters of light,
and you here once again my ancient familiar,
old chameleon, protean ghost:
you down there in the corner of my heart
or abroad in the wilderness of morning
but as always without dimension:
                  Tiny as a caraway seed
or sudden as a tree of lightning
or ingenuous as a cloud in summer.
                  I have watched you sliding
down the black windowpane in a make-believe of rain:
in the hollow of midnight I have heard you
whining like the wind through a crack in the door.

                          Old hieroglyph!
Your name is written indelibly in the innocence of light:
innumerable and ingenious have been your disguises:
but in the end I always unmask you:
and in the end I am always afraid.

        The Shadow
It is yourself of whom you are afraid, Old Man,
it is not I.

        The Old Man
Once I found you hiding in the palm of my hand.
And once at high noon in my own mirrored eye,
a pinpoint of something unknown and invidious
opening subtly as a little shutter into darkness,
to divulge, at the far end of an interior corridor,
that shape which you will never quite confess to.
                              I have felt you hurrying
close behind me in the golden folds of the sunlight
inaudible and invisible footsteps
mischievously following and mocking my own.
Perhaps we were born together, are inseparable?
But no matter what your name is, I am afraid.

        The Shadow
I am the accompaniment, Old Man, you the tune.
But am I not also your invention?
You are the object, I the shadow.
How then can you be afraid?

        The Old Man
Many and diverse have been my studies: of the far and near,
the simple, the recondite, the fabulous, the remote in time,
of abstract theorem and sober particular practice,
of assumed divine and presumed profane.
I have tested like the intrepid and intelligent spider

the webs and calligraphies of the geometer
and those no less diaphanous
of vertebrate and invertebrate verse.
I have considered the intense anatomies of man and mind
and their solubility in the mortal but godlike body
as at last in the understanding of understanding
and the dissolution of the word.
But always inevitably step by step with my study
pari passu pari passu
I have been aware of an accompanying footfall
and an interior purpose and an interior voice.
It is you who introduce the metrical pauses
that give meaning to the far, slow, almost silent song
of the wood thrush hidden in the pinewood
like love concealed in the heart.
                              It is you
who set an end to the song an end to the love
and bring the theorem no matter how perfect
to a silent conclusion. And I am afraid.

    The Shadow
Dismiss me as merely an echo, Old Man,
as perhaps only the slight sound of your own time
your own little machine running down in time.
                              Embrace me
as you would yourself. How then can you be afraid?

    The Old Man
Measure is of no avail in this ulterior kingdom.
Not the pure rondures of simplicity
nor the all-seining nets of subtlety
no nor the arcane notations of the wizard bloodstream
no more than the clear modes of the mountain brook
can here be valid. Flux cannot measure flux.
The partitions and precisions of the caliper
no more endure than the scansions of the verse

as the verse no more endures than the voice.
The intrusion is yours. And I am afraid.

   The Shadow
Perhaps we are functions, one of the other? A conceit of light?

   The Old Man
Yes, it is true, you were always the intruder.
But nevertheless how can we speak of intrusion?
For which comes first, the light or the shadow?
And who am I to pretend to be light?
Together conceived, together created in synthesis,
shadow conspiring with light and light with shadow,
the rose a promise in the invisible
and the invisible a premise of the rose:
must we accept this duplicity? Is this our conclusion?
If so, I am afraid.

   The Shadow
If you are afraid, Old Man, then fear is inborn:
initial: a part of yourself: as I am you.
Change, I change with you: move, I move:
vanish, I vanish. But there is nothing, no, no, nothing,
that I can add or subtract. Not now, not ever.

   The Old Man
The decimals betray it! and the mortal clocks
that appraise and applaud the sun! the moons of the fingernail
declare it and the frost on the sweetfern
and the tide that recedes and the tide that returns
and the galaxies in flight with their seasons.
        The wildflowers
danced on a wave of light to make time and place for man
and will again be gone with the dark.
        Here in my hand
like an ignorant palmist I read

the salt histories of hunger and love
recorded in a whisper of dust that drew breath
to become myself. Let us at last admit it.
Death is born with us. And I am afraid.

Landscape with Figures

Lizard under leaf and the eye gold
the moment motionless the morning silent
spider motionless in spangled web
while the fly buzzes and considers

and then twig falls on silent moss
o as the moment loosens in a dream
image of tree from image of love
or an old hatred from a known face

see how the landscape recedes outward and inward
and is peopled like an old painting with desires
the morning-glory opening its purple sex to the bee
who hums off to the geometric hive

while near at hand the cow crops while bull couples
and children in the swing tell tales
of lewd fathers and aunts in an attic
and pussy drowned in a well

the sun is upended by the turning earth
old lechers that they are in time and turning
plough slants athwart the light and oakleaf too
and the raw furrow shines
and song and song from the woods
o song o song from what does it come
is it there outside from the birds on the hill
or from the inner landscape which is I

birds landscape trees and bees and I
and the cows coupling and the morning-glory
seducing the mind's bee for the mind's crystal hive
all's bloomed and blessed at once

even to the shadow pencilled from the burning bush
which surely points to nightfall
where bee like heart sleeps in the image of death
and landscape inner and outer are again still.

Incipit Finis Finis Incipit

Morning comes, and with renewed devotion.
The dragons and angels of sleep
whirl up our dreams about them and dislimn,
fade far away into the daybreak ocean,
lost in the music of the waking mind,
sans signature. And now the blind
pathway unwinds from inward to outward,
while from the outer world roars sunrise in.

The bird sings sings sings sings
but who can tell
whether from the heart rings that slow bell
or in the eye or on the tongue
outside or inside outdoors or in
still in the dream we hear it begin
telling of break of day or break of heart.

What did we sleep for and why wake?
Who was it made us, and why make?
And who began this lordly give-and-take?
Look, children, rise,
and stroke the cobwebs from your eyes,
the innocence and violence pour in
as day begins

and we begin —
— just where we started from. But where
where where where did we start,
what god invented heart
or the sure stream from heart to hand
from wild sea to wild land
where the bird sings sings sings
into our haunted waking
and thought begins its taking?

This we shall never know,
old ocean-flow from long ago.
Evening, and we shall reach
our ending on that beach
starfish stranded on sand
waiting for morning and renewed devotion
and from the ocean
another dream reaching its curious hand.

A Letter from the Grass

Indeed, child, the little pimpernel, most modest
and obscure of flowers, which here you see
between the tree-roots, the tiny star
of dusty red, or is it vermilion, each petal
with a most delicate point, and the clouded center,
and, yes, like something one might discover
coming through the far eye of a telescope
on a blue night in summer — indeed this little flower
will speak to us if we will listen.
                    It will say

something of the noiseless unfolding of the shutters of daybreak
in the great silence of morning, something too
of the manifold infoldings of nightfall: it will praise
with its own voice, its own small voice, but no less clear

or dear for that, the infinitesimal
tickling and tinklings of its beginnings,
when the pale root-foot breaks the seed
to adventure downward into darkness, while the pale stalk,
longing to be green, to be green, yearns itself upward
to salute with its new hands the sun.
                              It will say

that life is whole, although it be but for a day
of one's own circling with the circling world
until the shut-eye planets bid us to sleep.
One day, and we have learned it all,
from the first feathered shadow's fall,
whether from tree or garden wall,
until once more the invisible ladder
of sunlight climbs to noon. And so revolving,
and so returning with our praise, until that time
when again shadows with the dead moon climb.
Now its eye opens, then it will close.
And this is what it knows.

Count the Summer

Count the summer with your fingers, the minutes fly
from foxglove bell to resinous cone, and it may be
the last of all to come. The song-sparrow
forgets his song, sings only half of it,
and that half-heartedly. Who fears to die,
dies with the fearing
who cares to live
lives in the caring.

Mention the names and with the mention
foxglove and sticky cone and wide-eyed brier
and the seconds of the fountain bright
as falling light
these will become the unsure pulse in the wrist

your love-in-the-mist
the spider's one and only web-caught amethyst
your own invention.

Old heart of self regard your secret weather
in the interstices of leaf and southwest wind
hold up your hand
to see the blood in it against the sun
where now you run
as runs your own self-measuring time.
Caught in this self-wrought and unfinished rhyme
you and the world perish together.

Morning Dialogue

The Young Man
That way the moonflower and the sunflower this
and the garden path that winds between
how can I know what they may mean
in the confusions of my delight?
Old mother oak
whose ferrule is on my forehead
whose mast is on my tongue
tell me, for I am young,
what language I should speak?

The Oak
Speak with the language of the leaf
when what you mean is brief
and with the language of the bough
when what you mean is more than now
but also learn while you are young
speech is not only of the tongue.

The Young Man
This calyx of cerulean blue
now magnified by one clear drop of dew

becomes tremendous in the sun
and every one
of these small dots of cinnamon
seems like a world about to run
into the fiery histories of space
how can I face
these miracles and have no speech?

The Oak
                              I reach
from earth to sky, from one to other,
have no sister and no brother
from the dark underworld
crammed with richness and with death
seek out my way to leaf and breath.

The Young Man
What love is this
that can dispense with words
or all but such as bud and fade and fall
heedless of the song of birds
once more to earth that buries?

The Oak
North wind begins his autumn flurries
a solitary leaf descends
and something ends.
You too must die
and so must I
yet each with different speech can say —

The Young Man
                              — What can we say?

The Oak
I have forgotten. Something simple — ?
That night is night, and day is day.

Or that the languages of sap and blood
are only wood and word
and therefore good.

Three Voices at the Meridian

The Cat

Noon, and its excellent sun, and you, old tree,
and here squat I, heraldic and sejant in sequined shadow,
and the same question taunts us as before,
which is the older? cat or tree? you or me?
The houses with their hands before their eyes
the shuttered houses they are younger surely?
And the pale nuns who pace demurely
under the purple Judas bloom?
But which is the older, you or me?
                              And you, old tomb!
freezing in the shadow, sweating in the sun!
tell us again which is the oldest of us three?
I walk and talk I walk and sleep
my own concerns and seasons keep,
then, twilight come,
put on that evil which is second nature
to every living creature.

The Tree

Nothing is older nothing is evil
thus to question is to invite the devil
by man called conscience or else consciousness
in his unenviable and self-created doom
invented out of time and out of mind
that he might call himself mankind
and who knows why.
                              Better the acorn
dropped for the dark-eyed squirrel to carry and bury
better the bitter berry

for the quail's green crop.
                                    Better the drop
of wild honey or innocent rain
than this all-man-invented pain.

            The Man
Latecomer that I am, old cat, old tree, old tomb,
yet grant me room. Ungainly I
the body awkward and unshod and shoddy
what mind indeed would choose such body
dropped from the bloody womb
the spirit shy?
                                    Yet I
count time and make it rhyme
and know the reasons
for your seasons.

Snapped String, Broken Tree

Never gainsay death
you who visibly die
who shrink from the wind
or the shadow of a wing
and know in the beat of the heart
the shape of things to come
yourself the bare oak
when the north wind whistles
yourself the snapped string
when the music stops.

Stay yourself with icicles
lie down in the new grave
and shroud yourself with rose-petals
or warm yourself with an *ignis ossium*
to dance the rites of spring
you are still the bare oak

motionless in snow
still the snapped string
when the music stops.
And who would ever wish
to gainsay goodfellow death
whose embrace is Judas blossom
whose eye is apple blossom
whose footfall is the sure silence
between tick and tock
who would wish to gainsay
night after day
end after beginning?

The shadow of the oak
becomes a map in the mind
and moves in the mind
on the winds of the mind
and every movement of it
becomes a new word
and every word becomes a new leaf
yourself the bare oak
listening to spring
yourself the tuned string
touched to sing.

Oneiromachia

We are the necromancers who once more
magically make visible the night
recapture that obscure obscene delight
fathom its undertow and in one net
fish up foul fables we must not forget
have them alive and slippery in our hands:
what are we but divided selves that move
to find in all that glittering thrash our love?

We'll summon in one dream all motives forth
and you shall be the south and I the north
and we will speak that language of the brain
that's half of Portugal or all of Spain
or of those yet unsounded seas
that westward spawn beneath the menstrual moon:
what are we but divided souls that live
or strive to in the sundered self of love?

Splinter the light and it will dream a rainbow
loosen the rainbow and it will stream in light
divide the brightness and you'll build a wall.
But we'll a twilight be, a go-between
of midnight and of daybreak, and beget
marvels and monsters we must not forget:
these are the language that love dared not speak
without which we can neither make nor break.

Waking in the Morning

And so, with the ear pressed hard to the pillow,
and the heart held downward, and downward its beating,
the light teasing now at the closed eyes of shutters
as the wild dreams tease at the doors of the mind,
we arrive, old body, old heart, and old mind,
at yet, yet another ambiguous answer,
but perhaps just sufficient with which to begin.

The cat's-cradle wheatstalks become a cloud castle
and the castle a ghost-laden hawsehole of ship
wherefrom come the unknown unknowable voices
crying their who and their when and their where,
and then are withdrawn, as if they were silent,
or only to speak with the sound of the air:
and yet with a meaning, there seems to be meaning.

The light moves a trace to the right, and the heartbeat
shifts as in sympathy too with the light
the ear is now turned to a new pitch of night
and begins all alone by itself to consider
something far off and absurd, a delight
but if so like a light with a cloud at its center,
and the cloud growing greater, the light growing less.

The fabric is bloodstream and bloodstream through measure
and measure through sense-ends and then shuttled back
for the heart and its courage to say yes to, or no to,
and the mind to twist into or out of a shape,
and the fancy, o fancy, what help from the fancy
that meddles and muddles and give itself airs
making riddles of loves and charades of despairs.

Step softly from here to the threshold of birth
the clock's tune and cock's crow and snare for the hare
the dew-betrayed footprint and the breath heard by fox
for death waits outside from the very beginning
our shadow precedes us and gives us our shape
and only in this shall we find out our dancing
and only in dancing find out our escape.

Love's Grammarians

He
Periwinkle — bluet — Quaker Lady —
hear how the history of our love
echoes in these nicknames
as now from the poetry book
we filch a phrase
to say all's over. The gods abandon
those who abandon the gods. There was no truth
in that fine vision we saw
under our Canaletto sunrise

nor at our sunset either
waiting by *traghetto* stairs
for the evening star's first footfall on water.
The fireflies are gone and the lanterns
from under the bridge. And we must run
for our very lives from those two fiends
so like ourselves
who even in the incredulous noon
would drag us back by the hair.
Once more permit them
and we are lost.

She

Presto — a melodrama — lost.
Do I guess what you mean by lost?
Is it an understatement? Do you mean
adulterated? But time and the rain
wash all away.

He

Lost in a repetitive nightmare
of our own invention. The deadly habit
obedient to the clock, and the clock
wound by an indifferent hand. Morning coffee
tiptoed to the bedroom, sherry among the orange trees,
dinner in the air-conditioned rock-garden.
And then the cigarette on the terrace
the whispering and withdrawing hour
while none keep guard at head of stair.
Time and place undid us.
Time's imperceptible sleight of hand
touching with curious frost
the simple heart. Use and satiety
dulling the sense until
nothing is left or only
an event which was over-prepared
for a body which was no longer concerned.

Love's grammarians were we ever?
But we no longer conjugate the tenses
or with each other
so let us part.

      She
Time and place, time and place,
how dull you make them sound:
I'll take a happier ground.
A history and a mystery
of absurd but bewitching secrets
in the May sky tra la in the bloodstream too
in the gay heart and the merry mind
in the dream that sings on the borders of sleep
of worlds lost and worlds to come
all of it woven with needles of light
blossoming and vanishing
flashing and gone. Time and place
but with a difference. Everything
to be touched and loved at once
each fiery item intrinsic and tangible
as the round red moon of the calendar
or the seconds jumping like crickets
on the stupid face of the clock.
The senses are mischievous but also
there's magic in them, and love
lives through the senses only.
Isn't it there that the soul lies?
O yes and lies and lies if you like
for the soul too is a chameleon
where and for how long can it stand still?
Over the steeple and under the hill.
Yet volatile and incorporeal howsoever
— see where it flies! —
it too feeds only through the senses
summoning thus the very quiver of light
to be by this translated

and quickened to an ecstasy.
Now that is gone
and love undone.

             He
So be it. For the last time I invoke
a particular moment. The clock strikes one.
A single snowflake floats against a pebble
clings to it with wings like a moth
and is gone. Our eyes
fill with a light till now unknown:
far recognitions, premonitions,
ethereal divinations
of all that's past and to come.
Those histories and mysteries you speak of
the tangents of sense thrust against sense
but only the more to illumine:
the I and You become a phrase of music
obedient to a counterpoint
of earth air water and fire
which willy-nilly joins them.
Of this angelic confusion
what can we remember?
Only the snowflake falling.
While I for the first time
because it will be for the last time
observe with care the clear shape
of your closed eyelid.

             She
Yes. Remember that. I too
have something to remember. I still see
under the umbrella's singing tent
how that rose-tinted shadow
changed a familiar face.
These shall be time and place.

The Island

Sly catbird it was you who first sang it
with your scrannel song
you among the small leaves
at the tip of the tree
singing it three times over
above the clover
> Do not go to that island
> no do not go to that far island
> it is morning, there is nothing to fear,
> stay here stay here.

Green spurge golden spurge you sang it again
from the top of the stone stair
in a wave of fragrance
sweeter than honey on the tongue of the bee
the wave of gold chiming it three times over
above the clover
> Do not go to that island
> never set sail for that inhospitable island
> there is nothing in the morning to fear
> stay here stay here.

Old heart it was you who then sang it
you with your ancient hourglass song
the song you brought with you from the sea
like a shell that sings of the sea in a green garden
whispering it three times over
above the clover
> Do not go to that unimaginable island
> never cast off to sail to that island
> morning is with us again
> stay here stay here.

THE TINSEL CIRCUIT

Williams & Williams

Curtains at last! The best of acts
goes stale. And then you dream
of dance and turn, and slide and turn,
until you'd like to scream.

Out there, a storm of violins,
while miles of footlights glare,
and we, we're only mannequins,
that step, and stop, and stare.

What fiend it is that pulls the strings,
and what it's for, god knows;
but we could strangle in the wings
whoever it is, that shows

no moment's mercy to the likes
of us who tread his measure,
and break our hearts, four times a day,
to give a moment's pleasure.

Come: we'll invent a change of scene:
the spotlight fizzing blue:
for a novelty called Hallowe'en,
with skulls for me and you.

Sharpe, Moss and Lewis

Heavenly the scene was: how could she wait
for the magical moment when Moss made his exit —

'exiting right with a sneer and a gesture' — ?
Rapture, sheer rapture! For now they could turn
and stare at each other, unashamed and unfeigning,
while slowly, so slowly, they moved to their meeting,
and at last touched hands!

Under her eyelids the footlights were swarming,
out in the dark was a murmur of faces,
but all she could see was the man she loved
(o and she did, for always and ever)
and all that he saw — he said — was a vision,
her hands lifted up in the light.
                              The music, crescendo,
came like a full-moon tide underneath them,
sweet-sweet-sweet! cried Harry Frank's fiddles,
and the bull-frog double-bass throbbed. But then —
the whistle of terror came shrill at the door
and a bullet shattered the mirror behind them
and somebody screamed.

. . . Lovely, o lovely! Alone on the beach
she watched how the slow waves crested and crumbled,
and the seagull shadows flew over the foam,
and thought she never no never had loved him
never o never had ever loved anyone
as now she could love him in this silly scene.

Exit

Yes, there he came, purple as an eggplant,
staggering out to the stage with a blue hand lifted,
and began reciting, for the fourth time that day,
The Face on the Bar-room Floor.
She stood in the wings to listen, but not with pity.
Watched the knees shaking, and the old adam's-apple,
and the fingernails white in the hard light. Noticed again

the red streaks under the ear, where fingernails
had scratched at eczema. The Face on the Bar-room Floor,
etched in sawdust, among cuspidors — old fraud,
he had come singing down the streets, all right,
while the gin lasted, and the voice lasted,
but now that adam's-apple would come to an end.
Brick — stone — dust — were all he had ever touched:
what valentines for him, who had no heart?
And now, and soon, over a windowsill,
in a dark room, on a bed by a speckled mirror,
the indifferent sun would find him dead.

Music must end, she thought, but after the ending,
when it is still, the wonder begins to be heard.
Why, why, it would seem to cry, why must we die?
The first-love rapture in moonlight,
who ever finds it again — ? It is gone with its summer.
But to die like this, at the end of nothing,
in the wall-papered gloom of a furnished room,
to the sound of a cheap tin clock,
was it for this she hurried forever
down narrowing corridors to an unknown door?

The Two Sterretts

You say men flirt with me, and you no longer like me,
because, you say, I let them. Maybe I do.
But if I do, whose fault is it, I wonder?
Right after we first teamed up,
who was it complained because I wasn't sexy?
You said I was tame, and put no life in the act,
that I was prudish and proper as a schoolgirl.
Well, I did as you told me. I put more life in the act,
and wore as little as a girl can get away with.
And what's the result? Surprise. They like it.
And now you complain because I'm not as proper
as the innocent kid you married.

I should have seen it coming. It's the old story —
pull a girl down to your own level, then kick her out,
sick of a thing too like yourselves. And then, why not,
comes somebody else — this doll in Vyo-Lyn!

No, chum, let's get this straight — I understand it.
You're tired of me, just as I'm tired of you.
I'm sorry, too, for at first I loved you —
I think I really did!
But there it is, and it might as well be faced.
Though, gosh, I almost wish we were starting over,
with the sense to see things right!
— She stirred her coffee,
and touched one eyelid to keep a tear from falling.
But he, absorbed in the smoke of a cigarette,
smiling a thin, self-conscious, ironic smile,
did not look up. Thinking that in two weeks
they'd come once more in the bill with Vyo-Lyn.

Professor Lorraine

What worried him was, that he hadn't been drinking:
so how to explain it — ? Those two middle fingers —
was that the trouble — were they getting stiff — ?
He'd flipped the coins, and riffled the cards,
and flopped the rabbits out of the hat,
but then — the goldfish. Just as he started
to slip the bowl from the velvet cloth,
Christ! — And suddenly there they were
flapping all over the floor.

Eighteen years — count them, Professor.
The plain truth was, he was getting old.
Where had it gone? Marie was dead,
and the German girl, whose name he'd forgotten,
had flown the coop to be married.

And now, Felice, who stole his money,
laughed, when he dropped that goldfish bowl.

He put one hand out over the basin,
switched on the light with the other, stared
unhating unloving unknown unseeing
(but why he did it he couldn't have said)
at failure's face and a guilty hand
and turned on the taps and cried.

March Midnight

Who cares where a man is buried, who cares, who cares?
Some like the country, some like the city,
there are trees in one and streets in the other,
but you don't get breakfast at seven in either,
and you don't get bills, and the mail is late.
As for my act, it wasn't too good, and it wasn't too bad,
but then, it was all that I had, and it's over.
                              Just the same,
I'll admit that I had one fault — I was vain.
Vanity, vanity, said the preacher —
but not to me, for I wasn't there.
                              Just the same,
do me a favor. Get out that suit
that I always wore, I wore it out —
purple, you know, with the eyes on the knees.
I'd like to see it again. I'd like to wear it
on my last ride to the not-so-golden gates.
Thanks. That's it. That's the one.

Violet and Leopards

Green eyes, and an emerald flicker behind them,
and when she cracked that blacksnake whip

you'd swear her eyes had done it.
Who was the watcher, who the watched?
Watching, whipping, prodding, cajoling,
cleaning up after them, trying to give them
the love they never accepted—

                       Out, now! — she'd cry —
Out, now! Out, now! — to snarl on pedestals
or leap through diamond hoops.

                       In, now! In, now!
Back to the cages! Live with animals,
become an animal. She was a leopard.

Sidelong she eyed you, sidelong she moved,
her eyes when they met you
gleamed and lost focus. Not strange
when the lights went down and the yellow cats
lapped round her in silence they seemed
as if summoned by magic out of herself
were only a dream and would vanish
back to the dark when the act was over.

Over. Not always. One night
one of the leopards went berserk. The spotlight man
shot down the light, where she stood,
safe as Brunnhilde in a circle of fire.
Now when she dreams she sees
her own heart torn, and hears bones cracking,
and eyes stare up unabashed from blood.

Lissome Lesters

Says Pierrot: You! Columbine!
Come down! The moon is hugely creeping,
and the stars begin to shine.

Says Pierrot: I'll take your hand
and guide you through the chattering dew
where ghosts flit over the sand.

Says Pierrot: I'll kiss your eyes
to such a sleep as that in which
the enchanted princess lies.

I'll play such a wicked melody
on the silver cobwebs of your hair
you'll give your heart to me.

Say no more, says Columbine:
I gave my paper rose to you,
and the stars begin to shine.

I gave my paper rose to you,
but if you seek my heart, who knows,
that may be paper too!

Two shadows dance, then pause to listen,
watching the music rise and glisten,
two shadows meet, and fade away,
hearing the moonlight play.

Curtain

When Vyo-Lyn have come and gone
and Queen Zudora's act is over
and Violet's leopard turn is done
and Felice runs to meet her lover

when cards and wands are laid away
and music stops and people hurry
and the dying man for one more day
postpones the fever and the worry

then, when the birds in hooded cage
are perched in silent rows and sleeping,
the redfaced stage-hand takes the stage,
and noisily goes across it, sweeping

the dust of golden-slippered feet,
spangles, and scraps of rainbow paper,
where Rose or Lily sang so sweet,
and Frost or Coffin cut a caper,

and having swept, turns out the lights,
and knocks his pipe, and leaves the curtain
hung high and dark for other nights,
and other vain things just as certain.

1916–1961

THEE

How to condemn THEE
yet also hymn THEE
how to praise THEE
yet also paraphrase THEE
how to proclaim THEE
yet also shame THEE

Wind blows
and mind blows with it
water flows
and mind flows with it
where shall I abide
cries the spirit
mind changes
and body changes with it
body changes
and mind changes with it

where shall I abide
cries the spirit
but also
says the spirit
north
south
east
west
at every compass point
I am still
I am at rest
I had and have no name
without it came
perhaps the wet
and still-by-night-dew-tightly-twisted
morning-glory
tiger at evening drinking
by moonlit water
and the all-thinking
skin of the earth
in which we move
and are a part
are single and same
all one hate
all one love.

Wind blows
but over what shall it blow
dead men encased in ice
men dying in snow
children lying in stretchers
their faces under the rain
the wounded animal
seeking out a hole
in which to lick his pain
and the bird
that symbol of the soul
coasting on the wind

for the last time
under the balsam
to hide his
death.
Cry death cry death
we come into the world
kicking and screaming
we go out of the world
kicking and screaming
and all between
is but
scheming
and
dreaming
and
seeming.

The spirit says
I am I
the spirit says
somewhere my cry
inarticulate and ignorant
though it be
may be heard
by the ultimate
unimaginable
THEE.
Who is that pitiless THEE
whom only in ourselves we see
or in the lightning-stroke
and stricken oak
and our young darlings doomed too soon to bed
without sin
and from within
by THEE and THINE?

Who is that hateful THEE
who makes a music of the sea

and of the clouds a harmony
or spreads a meadow broad and bright
with colors of delight
or brings the young with joy together
as birds of a feather
makes all the visible world a wedding feast
with love in every eye
and every breast
so that we think too long
that life is only song?
Unfaithful THEE
for suddenly the sea
rises and breaks the ship
blues every lip
cry death cry death
and we
and all the world we brought with us
thanks to THEE
go out of the world
or back to the world
to rejoin
unwillingly
and unconsciously
THEE.

Who is that splendid THEE
who makes a symphony
of the one word
be
admitting us to see
all things but THEE?
In the microcosm
in the macrocosm
it is THEE that we seek out
seeking to find
the workings of our mind
and THINE.

Wild columbine
admits THEE
wild rose
permits THEE
the seasons obey
THY reasons
yet further in our explorations do we go
the less we know.
Visible to the child
as butterfly
as lion
as mother
as father
moving under the microscope
or telescope
as smallest item or utmost star
yet THEE is still invisible
still indivisible.
How explain the morning that we wake to
the opening of the eye
the toothbrush
the toilet
the basket for soiled clothes
the fly's wing so designed
that it might be
a cathedral window
meant
for THEE?
Unkind THEE
did THEE have the fly in mind
and in THY warp and woof enwind
him and all his kind
to live his glorious dunghill day
then swept like snot away?

Who is that glorious THEE
sleeping and waking

the slow hushed life of tree
barely knowing
THINE own growing
then breaking and weeping
from THINE own sleeping?
We break and bud with THEE
put arms out like THY tree
and sing
inaudibly
in spring
as cold bark buds and breaks
and THEE awakes
and south wind shakes
the leaves that are THINE eyes
also THY breath
and
when THY calendar names it
death.

Nameless and shameless we
take THINE identity
to be
then
not to be
sharing with THEE
and daring
and o caring
for what is delicious
and what precious
learning how slowly what to choose
and what refuse
what use
and what abuse.
Laboriously the spirit learns
THY shadow upon us like the cloud's
shadow upon the meadow
as if perhaps in our slow growing

and the beginnings of our knowing
as if perhaps
o could this be
that we
be
THEE?
THEE still learning
or first learning
through us
to be
THY THEE?

Self-praise were then our praise of THEE
unless we say divinity
cries in us both as we draw breath
cry death cry death
and all our hate
we must abate
and THEE must with us meet and mate
give birth give suck be sick and die
and close the All-God-Giving-Eye
for the last time to sky.

Weather changes
and the spirit changes with it
climate changes
and the spirit changes with it
where shall I abide
cries the spirit
north
south
east
west
yet at no compass-point
is final rest
what fatal quest
is this

that we and THEE
in every THING
and every breast
must still pursue
and do?

Magnificent THEE
the syllables I speak
and which are THINE
and mine
still cannot equal THEE
who art becoming and have yet to be
and learn to speak
as we
with THEE.

The Voyagers

What to make
of human sake?
how take care
of man's despair?
or how, how, heaven help us cope
with that inexplicable hope?
Twain unshapely
man and woman
forty or thirty
clean or dirty
by what miracle did they invent
that word human?

Let us start running
from this low cunning
look elsewhere
for solution of their hope
and despair

who somehow from darkness came
and now must darkness blame
or else admit 'of origin unknown.'
And this hand on
to generations born
of love and lust in-torn.
Pitiful creature!
with intolerable feature!
Yet in the mirror he admires,
and sires!

Now mythic gods all gone
new gods come on
those proliferated by the brain
and fingertips
see how we evolute
compute
commute
        even to the moon.
Soon
the man-god comes. What then?
Will these be men?
Winged we are
but winged to fly how far?
Were it not better done
or say undone
beneath the skin
with scalpel and mind
to find
what hides within?
unravel
there
our travail?
And by whose compass shall we steer
right hand courage
left hand fear?
or was this endless voyage, this godlike journey,

dreamed of only
by those who would be lonely — ?

Then said the chinaberry tree
ah yes and what of me
and in the evening's winking golden shadow
the rose
also.

Obituary in Bitcherel

In eighteen hundred and eighty nine
Conrad Aiken crossed the line
in nineteen hundred and question-mark
Aiken's windowpane was dark.
But in between o in between
the things he did the things he'd seen!
Born in beautiful Savannah
to which he lifelong sang hosanna
yet not of southern blood was he
he was in fact a damned Yan-kee:
two Mayflower buds
were in his bloods
and one of them was not so blue—
Allerton, the crook of the crew.
And six generations of Delanos
had sharpened his senses and his nose.
His pa a doctor, painter, writer,
his ma a beauty, but which the brighter?
They brought him up to read *and* write
then turned him loose, to his delight.
Knew every alley and stinking lane
played tricks like tappy-on-the-window-pane
cut elderberry wood to make him a pluffer
with twin chinaberries plugged in as a stuffer
but also learned from the nigger next door

names of snakes and wildflowers galore.
Then all went sour: all went mad:
the kitchen was sullen: the house was bad:
beaten he was: barebacked: crossed hands
on bedstead knobs: trunk-straps, three bands:
for something nobody yet understands.
And the morning quarrel, and shots, and then
four orphaned children taken north again.
To uncles, and cousins, great-aunts and aunts:
this, I suppose, was his second chance.
But, brothers adopted by a cousin named Taylor,
and then his sister, who became the first 'failer,'
where now was left our Quinbad the Quailer?
Out in the cold, where he soon grew old,
Middlesex School became home and fold,
but o dear Jesus was it cruel and cold.
No mind: those years of school and college
baseball and tennis and dear friends and knowledge
o what a delicious delight were these:
the late nights over the piano keys:
resigned from Harvard and gone to Rome
to die in Keats' tomb and live in his home:
and thus by the hard way to wisdom come.
And the poems by god all the while outpouring
by daybreak poring by midnight soaring
gay friends his teachers gay teachers his friends
euphoria: lightning: and life never ends.
But it does and it did and with marriage began
when he found of a sudden that he had to be man:
though he never quite could. And three wives had he
and three blest children by the first of the three.
Those children! Those nuggets! Who promised us this?
And how comprehend or accept such a bliss?
But marriages fade, as has often been said,
whether by bored, or whether by bed,
and at fifty and paunchy he came to a third
and found him that 'angel, half woman, half bird.'

Meanwhile he'd been sinking and rising and drinking
and THINKING, and writing, well, *ad infinitum:*
there were critics to bite and he had to bite 'em
novels to write and he had to write 'em
short stories too and he had to indite 'em.
Consultant in Poetry at Lib. Cong., two years,
where his war with bureaucracy drove him to tears —
tears of blood, too, for he damned near died,
for life MUST have its comical side.
And Awards and Prizes of various sizes
among them a few quite delightful surprises.
Slowing down, slowly: and old age then:
he turned him back to an earlier yen:
to Wall Street returned, became a fast bull
and brought back home his fifty bags full
wife and grandchildren and children and all
would now be secure, for he made quite a haul.
And now waits for death by heart or by head,
or dying piecemeal and daily instead,
of whom at his grave it can truly be said
he cyant do no harm now for now he is dead.
Separate we come, separate go.
And this be it known is all that we know.

Notes

*

The Divine Pilgrim

PREFACE

THE FIRST FIVE of the symphonies that compose *The Divine Pilgrim* were written between 1915 and 1920: 'The Charnel Rose' in 1915, 'The Jig of Forslin' in 1915 and 1916, 'The House of Dust' in 1916 and 1917, 'Senlin: A Biography' in 1918, and 'The Pilgrimage of Festus' in 1919 and 1920. With the completion of 'The Charnel Rose,' the general project was already pretty clear to me, as well as much of the method — for a discussion of the latter the reader can turn if he wishes to the Appendix, where he will find an article-review which I wrote of three of these poems for *Poetry* in 1919. But through a long series of accidents, the projected volume never came out. Partly for reasons of space, and partly because there was insufficient time for the necessary revision, 'The Charnel Rose' was omitted from *Selected Poems* in 1928, and has never since been in print. Similarly the prefaces to 'The Jig of Forslin' and 'The Pilgrimage of Festus,' both of them of considerable importance to the understanding of the poems, were allowed to disappear. Now, therefore, if somewhat belatedly, that young man's book at last comes out as he planned it, or almost as he planned it: for one later poem, 'Changing Mind,' 1925, has been added, and the four earlier poems have been cut and revised, in some cases drastically. 'The Charnel Rose' in particular needed, and received, severe treatment. An almost indispensable part of the general scheme of the poem, and therefore to be salvaged if at all possible, its youthful exuberance and rhetoric, its Blue Flower romanticism and Kraft-Ebing decadence (although admittedly for a purpose) presented after thirty-three years an almost insoluble problem in surgery.

Fortunately, the major cuts had already been made, and a begin-
ning of the revision itself, as early as 1923, so that the problems of
tearing and tissue-mending, especially in a texture so obviously
tender, were worries that had been with me for a quarter of a cen-
tury. I cannot pretend to know whether now it has been improved
— all I can hope is that it has been brought into line with the por-
tions of the poem that succeed it. Tastes change with every literary
generation, literary generations nowadays consist of just about a
decade (perhaps they always did) and it is entirely possible that a
later judgment will prefer 'The Charnel Rose' as it originally was
— half again as long, and in what Poe liked to call an advanced
stage of echolalia. But at all events it is now more of a piece with
'The Jig of Forslin' and 'The House of Dust,' and I merely beg the
reader to be patient with it, and, if he can, to take even a mild inter-
est in it as the earliest specimen in a young poet's endeavors to in-
vent a method, if not a theory. Of the later poems, 'The House of
Dust' has now been much revised also, although not much cut, and
the lost preface restored as well as memory can restore it. 'The Jig
of Forslin' has been little altered. 'Senlin,' considerably revised for
the Hogarth Press edition in 1925, has now been revised again, in
some instances back to the original. 'The Pilgrimage of Festus' is
to all intents unchanged. And 'Changing Mind,' the one later poem
added, as it imports into the cycle the specific 'I' of the artist, or
writer, and his predicament both private and social as the articu-
lator of man's evolving consciousness, is also reprinted as written.

                                                    Brewster, Massachusetts

                                                                           1949

I

THE CHARNEL ROSE

PREFACE

'THE CHARNEL ROSE' needs, perhaps, some explanation. Like pro-
gram music, it is helped by a program: though concrete in its im-
agery, it avoids sharp statement of ideas; implying the theme,

rather than stating it. This theme might be called nympholepsy —
nympholepsy in a broad sense as that impulse which sends man
from one dream, or ideal, to another, always disillusioned, always
creating for adoration some new and subtler fiction.

To exhaust such a theme would of course be impossible. One can
only single out certain aspects of it, indicate with a gesture. In the
present instance it has been my intention merely to use this idea
as a theme upon which one might build wilfully a kind of absolute
music. I have restricted myself to what was relatively a small por-
tion of this idea. Thus, beginning with the lowest order of love,
the merely carnal, the theme leads irregularly, with returns and
anticipations as in music, through various phases of romantic or
idealistic love, to several variants of erotic mysticism; finally end-
ing in a mysticism apparently pure.

It scarcely needs to be said that the protagonist of the poem is
not a specific man, but man in general. Man is seen seeking in many
ways to satisfy his instinct to love, worshipping one idol after an-
other, disenchanted with each in turn; and at last taking pleasure
not so much in anticipation as in memory.

'The Charnel Rose' is called a symphony, and in some ways the
analogy to a musical symphony is close. Symbols recur throughout
like themes, sometimes unchanged, sometimes modified, but al-
ways referring to a definite idea. The attempt has been made to
divest the successive emotions dealt with of all save the most typical
or appropriate physical conditions, suggesting physical and tem-
poral environment only so far as the mood naturally predicates it.
Emotions, perceptions, — the image-stream in the mind which we
call consciousness, — these hold the stage.

1918

II

THE JIG OF FORSLIN

NOTE: The vampire narrative in Part IV is a free adaptation of the story of Gautier — *La Morte Amoureuse.*

PREFACE

IT HAS OFTEN been said that a book which needs an explanatory preface is a book which has not entirely succeeded. In the present instance, however, whether that is true or not, there are other complications: and for that reason I am glad to run the risk of being told that the book is a failure.

These complications arise from the fact that 'The Jig of Forslin' is somewhat new both in method and in structure. It does not conveniently fit in any category, and is therefore liable, like all such works, to be condemned for not being something it was never intended to be. The critics who like to say 'this man is a realist,' or 'this man is a romanticist,' or in some such way to tag an author once and for all, will here find it difficult. For my intention has been to employ all methods, attitudes, slants, each in its proper place, as a necessary and vital part of any such study as this. Consequently, it is possible to pick out portions of this poem to exemplify almost any poetic method or tone. This eclecticism, or passage from one part to another of the poetic gamut, has not been random or for the sake of a mere tour de force: it has been guided entirely by the central theme. This theme is the process of vicarious wish fulfillment by which civilized man enriches his circumscribed life and obtains emotional balance. It is an exploration of his emotional and mental hinterland, his fairyland of impossible illusions and dreams: ranging, on the one extreme, from the desire for a complete tyranny of body over mind, to the desire, on the other extreme, for a complete tyranny of mind over body; by successive natural steps . . . in either direction.

As far as possible, the attempt has been made to relate these typical dreams, or vicarious adventures, not discretely, but in flux. Certain breaks, as between the five main parts of the poem, have been necessary, however, for both artistic and psychological reasons. To break up a single poem of the length of the present one is almost compulsory: the angle of approach must be changed every so often if the reader's attention is to be held at all. On the psychological side, it is obvious enough that the range of vicarious experience, here of necessity only hinted at, or symbolized by certain concrete and selected pictures, is suggested on a completer and more comprehensive plan than will be found in any specific individual: a good many types have been welded, to give the widest possible range. Forslin is not a man, but man. Consequently, opposite types of experience are here often found side by side, and it would be obviously false to force a connection.

As far as the technique of the verse is concerned, — the harmony and counterpoint, if I may use the terms in a general sense, — it has been governed as much, always, by consideration of the whole as of the part.

Cacophonies and irregularities have often been deliberately employed as contrast. Free rhythms, and rhymeless verse, have been used, also, to introduce variety of movement. Mood and movement, in general, have been permitted to fluctuate together, as they would seem to do automatically if not violated by too arbitrary choice of pattern . . . This does not mean, however, that there has been no choice of pattern whatever.

1916

PROGRAM

THE JIG OF FORSLIN is roughly in symphonic form. A program of the more narrative movements may be given as follows:

PART I

PROLOGUE OF FORSLIN
THE JUGGLER
ESCAPING GAS
MERETRIX: IRONIC

PART II

PATRICIAN MURDER
DEATH IN A PEG-HOUSE
THE DIVE OF DEATH

PART III

MERMAIDS AND LAMIAS
LA BELLE MORTE

PART IV

THE MIRACLES
SALOME
THE MONK IS JUDAS

PART V

THE PLAYHOUSE
A DREAM OF HEROIC LOVE
A BLUE-EYED GIRL IN VIRGO
THE CONCERT: HARMONICS
MERETRIX: SENTIMENTAL
CITY NIGHT
EPILOGUE OF FORSLIN

III

THE HOUSE OF DUST

NOTE: I am indebted to Lafcadio Hearn for the episode called 'The Screen Maiden' in Part II.

PREFACE

OUTWARDLY, 'The House of Dust' is a symphonic poem about the city — ancient or modern, it makes no difference — and the crowd-man that inhabits it. It is entered by us at twilight, say, we mingle with its casual or ordered currents, and by degrees come to feel something of its anonymous and multicellular identity, an identity which seems to be in effect the fusion or coalescing of the innumerable living particles that compose it. These particles, too, at first seem to us to be anonymous and amorphous, — particles and nothing more. But gradually, as we explore and participate further, or empathize more willingly, we begin to see that the particles too have identity, or individuality, that in fact they are more and more perceptible as individuals.

Thus, the poem may be said to move from the general to the particular, and again, on a different level, from the external to the internal. But perhaps it would be as well to point out also that its theme is essentially contrapuntal: for the entire poem is really an elaborate progressive analogy between the city, seen as a multicellular living organism, and the multicellular or multineural nature of human consciousness. Progressive, because as I say the movement is intermittently but steadily from simple to complex, from physiological to psychological; and, in the end, from the relatively simpler levels of consciousness to those in which it attempts to see and understand the world, or macrocosm, on the one hand, and the consciousness, or microcosm, that *sees* the world, on the other. Implicit in it, therefore, is the theory that was to underlie much of the later work — namely, that in the evolution of man's consciousness, ever widening and deepening and subtilizing his awareness, and in his dedication of himself to this supreme task, man possesses all that he could possibly require in the way of a religious credo: when the half-gods go, the gods arrive: he can, if he only will, become divine.

The original preface to 'The House of Dust' was lost many years ago. The present one however is a fairly accurate summary of it.

1948

IV

SENLIN: A BIOGRAPHY

WHEN IT WAS first written — and published — in 1918, 'Senlin: A Biography,' which came out in the same volume with 'The Charnel Rose,' had no preface: it was thought that the introduction to the latter poem, with its elucidation of the author's aims at a sort of 'absolute music,' might be sufficient. And perhaps it still needs none. Yet, as it was pretty widely misunderstood, perhaps owing to the then somewhat novel elements in its technique, a very brief note may not be amiss. Senlin — the name was an invented one, like Forslin — means literally the 'little old man' that each of us must become: just as Forslin, a portmanteau of the Latin words *forsan* and *fors,* is a squinting word which means either chanceling or weakling. And the poem is simply an extension and analysis of that perennially fascinating problem of personal identity which perplexes each of us all his life: the basic and possibly unanswerable question, *who and what am I,* how is it that I am I, Senlin, and not someone else? Unanswerable except perhaps in a kind of serial dishevelment of answers, or partial answers: for Senlin discovers not only that he is a whole gallery of people or personalities, rather than one, but also that this discovery is as incommunicable as it is elusive. Is the answer really nothing but a kind of shimmering series? and is there a shape under series, a numerical signature, that gives it meaning? Thus Senlin may be taken as the generic 'I' of the series of poems that compose *The Divine Pilgrim,* the unit of human reference upon which it rests.

1949

V

THE PILGRIMAGE OF FESTUS

A R G U M E N T

Festus is not a Roman emperor, nor the Bishop of Antioch: he is anybody or nobody. His pilgrimage is not real: it is imaginary. It is a cerebral adventure, of which the motive is a desire for knowledge.

Festus conceives himself, to begin with, as a conqueror with nothing more to conquer. But there remains yet to be conquered, after all, the world of himself; and into this world he resolves to set forth anew. . . Will he, perhaps, be content with a pastoral life of seclusion and meditation? He will plant beans, and grow with them out of the darkness. But he is teased by the thought that there may be other things in the world which it would be a pity to have missed. His alter ego, in the shape of an old man, lays the prospect of further experience and understanding pleasingly before him, and Festus finds himself, like his beans, growing upward into a universe of dimensions unexpectedly vast.

His first prepossession is with the possibility of mere power, power of the temporal sort. Halfway measures do not satisfy him, and it is not long before he is conceiving himself to be a Roman emperor of the most imperial hue. To his surprise, power of this kind does not provide him with the little key which unlocks the secret of the universe. Mortality seems to be inconsiderate of empires, and Festus begins to wonder whether spiritual power will offer a solution.

He converses, therefore, in imagination, with Confucius and Buddha and Christ, even with Mephistopheles, in an effort to reach a more perfect understanding of the world of personality with which he finds himself so astonishingly provided. But the remarks of these sages throw little light into the darkness which is himself. His interest in gods and in the eternal feminine seem, distressingly, to be almost identical. It occurs to him that the possibility of knowledge is itself limited: that knowledge is perhaps so conditioned by the conditions of the knower that it can have little but a relative value.

He tries to escape these harrowing implications. For a moment, he almost persuades himself that he is free, that he could himself, had he had the chance, have shaped a more beautiful universe. This satisfaction proves fleeting, however, and at the end, discussing the problem with his alter ego, he comes, not unhappily, to the conclusion that knowledge is inconclusive. To what, precisely, in the world can one devote one's instinct-to-adore? Beauty is inseparably bound up with ugliness. Does one, perhaps, in one's regret for this, hold the key? . . . No answer is provided, but Festus finds himself, at the end as at the beginning, charmed by the prospect of self exploration.

1921

VI

CHANGING MIND

PREFACE

IF 'SENLIN: A BIOGRAPHY' may be said to provide the generic 'I' that underlies *The Divine Pilgrim,* the block unit of human reference, and to illustrate, within prescribed limits, the apparent disintegration of the soul, or ego, with which modern psychology has confronted us, 'Changing Mind' carries the analysis a step farther. For this might be called the specific 'I,' and at a specific moment in its experience, in a specific predicament: the predicament, both private and social, of the writer or artist. Senlin is the purely racial exemplar — the basic stock reacting to basic situations. He is the inheritor of racial memories, and through these of even deeper instinctual responses, but beyond this he is not particularized, and was not meant to be. The wholly anonymous hero of 'Changing Mind,' on the other hand, and perhaps anonymous with reason, is not only particularized, he is also shown to be the willing participant, and perhaps to some extent even the instigator, in the process of seeing himself resolved into his constituent particles: and this with a purpose, that his increased awareness may be put at the service of mankind. Not only does he inherit the ordinary basic unconscious memory of Senlin — he also inherits the complete private situation of a highly complex and self-conscious contemporary individual whose neuroses have made it necessary or desirable that he should be an artist. He must make his experience articulate for the benefit of others, he must be, in the evolving consciousness of man, the servant-example, and in fact he has little choice in the matter. He is himself simply a part of that evolution.

1949

THE DIVINE PILGRIM

APPENDIX

Counterpoint and Implication

The Charnel Rose, by Conrad Aiken. Four Seas Co.

By inviting me to review my own book for POETRY, Miss Monroe puts me in an awkward position. I suspect that a part of her reason for doing this is that she fancies the author can be severer with himself — or shall I say, more accurately severe? — than anyone else can be. She puts me, in a sense, on my honor to defeat myself. But one tires of shadow-boxing: there is no joy in it, for one's antagonist cannot retaliate. So I am going to be, for once, my own apologist. I do not mean by this that I am going to praise myself; any more, at least, than the artist who paints a self-portrait praises himself — which he does, in some degree, by the serious act of self-portraiture. What I do mean is that since, apart from any question of accomplishment, my aims in the writing of poetry interest me extraordinarily, and since I would like (naturally!) to see them more generally espoused, I shall discuss them naïvely and with candor.

Suppose I begin with one statement with which everyone will agree: that it is the aim of every work of art to evoke, or to suggest. There is no quarrel here. What artists will disagree on is as to how this shall be done. Some think it should be accomplished by methods mainly denotative — or realistic: they argue that the best way to imply is (in the correct degree) to state. Others believe the method should be mainly connotative: they argue that the best way to state is (in the correct degree) to imply. Both elements, of course, enter into every work of art, and the only real difference at the bottom is quantitative; yet it is sufficient to account for such wide areas as lie between the work of Masters, let us say, on the one hand, and that of Bodenheim on the other. The one is solid, the other diaphanous; and the difference in tactile quality may be followed even into the choice of language itself; for we see Masters preferring the precise, and as it were the square, and Bodenheim preferring the tenuous and the abstract; Masters employing the object or thing, and Bodenheim the quality of the thing. This is simple enough. But the affair becomes more complex when we observe that any individual artist is not to be confined to one region in this regard, but continually wanders up and down this gamut, striking now at the denotative and now at the connotative chords, never perfectly certain, in fact, which method is the more truly effective; and, of course, obeying not merely a theory but, quite as often, the dictates of compulsions more unconscious. It is going only a step further to note that the larger the medium in which a poet works, the wider and more frequent will be his rangings of this gamut.

It was to make more possible this delicious (and somewhat irresponsible?) ranging of the gamut that I evolved the symphonic form used in *The Jig of Forslin, The Charnel Rose,* and *Senlin.* I will not pretend that this was at the outset entirely conscious or clear. Theory always comes second in these cases. It was partly a natural enough ambition for more room, partly the working of some complex which has always given me a strong bias towards an architectural structure in poetry analogous to that of music. In the three parts of *Earth Triumphant,* anyone who cares to wade through fifteen hundred more or less impeccable octosyllabic couplets will find already a groping towards symphonic arrangement, though it is exceedingly rudimentary. In *Disenchantment,* which was given the subtitle *A Tone Poem,* the idea of variation of form was developed, though not far. In *The Charnel Rose* it was first consciously elaborated, though with errors in proportion. And finally in *Forslin* and *Senlin* it achieved something like a logical outcome.

What I had from the outset been somewhat doubtfully hankering for was some way of getting contrapuntal effects in poetry — the effects of contrasting and conflicting tones and themes, a kind of underlying simultaneity in dissimilarity. It seemed to me that by using a large medium, dividing it into several main parts, and subdividing these parts into short movements in various veins and forms, this was rendered possible. I do not wish to press the musical analogies too closely. I am aware that the word symphony, as a musical term, has a very definite meaning, and I am aware that it is only with considerable license that I use the term for such poems as *Senlin* or *Forslin,* which have three and five parts respectively, and do not in any orthodox way develop their themes. But the effect obtained is, very roughly speaking, that of the symphony, or symphonic poem. Granted that one has chosen a theme — or been chosen by a theme! — which will permit rapid changes of tone, which will not insist on a tone too static, it will be seen that there is no limit to the variety of effects obtainable: for not only can one use all the simpler poetic tones (let us for convenience represent any five such simple poetic tones, each composing one separate movement to be used in a symphony, as *a, b, c, d, e*); but, since one is using them as parts of a larger design, one can also obtain novel effects by placing them in juxtaposition as consecutive movements: such as *ab, ac, cae.* For *a,* it is clear, if it is preceded by *c* and followed by *e,* is not quite the same as *a* standing alone. Something has happened to it. A peculiar light has been cast across it, which throws certain parts of it into stronger relief than others; and *a* itself reacts on *c* (retrospectively) and, a moment later, on *e.* In a sense, therefore, we have created a new poetic unit, *cae,* a unit of which the characteristic pleasure it affords us is really contrapuntal, since it works upon us through our sense of contrast. Each added movement further complicates the tone-effect, adds color to the hover of reverberations, creates a new composite unit. And we get finally a whole major section of the symphony so constructed of contrasts and harmonies; which in turn, if we are careful, will differ clearly in general tone from the next major part. And here the same principles apply. *Part II,* for example, following *Part I,* and preceding *Part III,* is by no means the same affair from the point of view of tone-effect, as *Part II* transferred so as to be *Part IV.* Thus *Part IV* of *The Jig of Forslin* (which deals with Forslin's religious debauch) owes much of its effect to its position following *Part III,* which deals with his caprices among lamias and vampires: an effect which originally, as *Part II,* it did not obtain. It was transferred for that reason.

All this, I must emphasize, is no less a matter of emotional tone than of form; the two things cannot well be separated. For such symphonic effects one employs what one might term emotion-mass with just as deliberate a regard for its position in the total design as one would employ a variation of form. One should regard this or that emotional theme as a musical unit having such-and-such a tone-quality, and use it only when that particular tone-quality is wanted. Here I flatly give myself away as being in reality in quest of a sort of absolute poetry, a poetry in which the intention is not so much to arouse an emotion merely, or to persuade of a reality, as to employ such emotion or sense of reality (tangentially struck) with the same cool detachment with which a composer employs notes or chords. Not content to present emotions or things or sensations for their own sakes — as is the case with most poetry — this method takes only the most delicately evocative aspects of them, makes of them a keyboard, and plays upon them a music of which the chief characteristic is its elusiveness, its fleetingness, and its richness in the shimmering overtones of hint and suggestion. Such a poetry, in other words, will not so much present an idea as use its resonance. It is the apotheosis of the poetic method which we have called implication. It is a prestidigitation in which the juggler's bottles or balls are a little too apt, unfortunately, to be altogether invisible.

I have left myself little space for comment on *The Charnel Rose,* of which this paper is supposed to be a review. In the title poem the reader may observe, if he wishes, this method in process of ghostly evolution: it is, for example, working much more efficiently and consistently in the third and fourth parts than in the first and second, which seem indeed, by contrast, a trifle mawkish and archaic.

Even so, the variation of tone has not been carried far enough: a little more statement and a little less implication would have been a good thing, for it verges on the invertebrate. If the poem is objected to for its decadence, however, it should be recalled that the decadence is, as it happens, implied in the conception, and that the conception has merely been permitted, and in my opinion rightly, to divulge itself. I should object to being called a decadent (as one or two have already called me) merely because of this poem, or because of a few passages in *Forslin,* equally compelled by the thesis. In *Senlin,* the other long poem in the volume, the conception is not decadent, and neither, therefore, is the treatment. The tone is acid, humorous, ironic. In general, too, I think the artistic problem has been a good deal better solved. It lacks here and there the opulence and gleam of parts of *The Charnel Rose,* but it makes up for it in precision, sharpness, and economy. (One always praises economy when one is running out of funds.) The theme is the problem of personal identity, the struggle of the individual for an awareness of what it is that constitutes his consciousness; an attempt to place himself, to relate himself to the world of which he feels himself to be at once an observer and an integral part. Reports that Senlin is — or was — a real person are erroneous. *Variations,* the remaining series of lyrics, was an experiment in modulation of emotion-tone. I do not feel that it was particularly successful. A theory should not be practiced in cold blood, and I am afraid that in this case the compulsion was not for all items sufficiently strong.

It remains, finally, to point out the profound danger of the method I have been outlining: the danger, I mean, that one's use of implication will go too far, and that one will cheat the natural human appetite for something solid and palpable. One cannot, truly, dine — at least every evening — on, as Eliot would remark, 'smells of steaks in passageways.' One must provide for one's symphony a sufficiently powerful and pervasive underlying idea — and, above all, make it sufficiently apparent. Whether the time will come when we shall be satisfied with implication for its own sake, no one, of course, can guess. In the meantime, one must compromise to the extent that one hopes for success. By which I'm not sure that I mean I compromise.

JUNE 1919

The Coming Forth by Day of Osiris Jones

NOTE

FOR SEVERAL PASSAGES in this poem I am greatly indebted to the translations of the 'Coming Forth by Day' by E. A. Wallis Budge, as published by the British Museum in a pamphlet entitled 'The Book of the Dead.' In some cases I have used passages almost verbatim, merely letting them fall — as they seemed to do almost without change — into the form of blank verse.

I am also indebted to my father, William Ford Aiken, for the material in section twelve of this book, which I have taken from a medical report made by him at the Boston City Hospital in 1886, while he was a student at Harvard Medical School.

As regards my title, I can do no better than quote 'The Book of the Dead,' page 29: 'In all the copies of "The Book of the Dead" the deceased is always called "Osiris," and as it was always assumed that those for whom they were written would be found innocent when weighed in the Great Balance, the words "true of voice," which were equivalent in meaning to "innocent and acquitted," were always written after their names.'

It may also be of assistance to the reader to know that in the last section but one ('Speeches Made By Books Stars Things and People') the 'Books' are to be assumed as speaking on behalf of Jones; in other words, they are his memory or consciousness.

The Soldier

NOTES

WIDSITH, THE FAR-TRAVELLER. The reference is to the Old English poem of that title, in which Widsith, or the far-traveller, reports on his travels as a wandering minstrel through many lands and wars. He is here, to begin with, identified with the wind, and then with the principle itself of change and exchange, whether in trade, travel, migration, or even finally in war, which of course must be accepted in the history of man as a true culture-bearer. Cf. Select Translations from Old English Poetry, by Albert S. Cook and Chauncey B. Tinker, Ginn and Co.

'Dark is our past': this passage is a paraphrase of a part of the set of 'Gnomic Verses' on page 67 of the volume mentioned above.

'the harmony warlike' etc. From the discussion of music in Plato's Republic, Book III, p. 104 in Jowett's translation. I have altered the passage somewhat.

'Dark is our past' etc. Cf. 'Gnomic Verses' as mentioned above, pages 67, 68, 69.

'some leaders in battle sectors,' 'carelessness in dress,' etc., from an editorial in The Infantry Journal, June 1943, as reprinted in Yank.

'the Great Wall of China': the four lines at the end of this passage are a very free paraphrase of an anonymous Chinese poem of about 124 B.C., as translated by Arthur Waley. Its title is 'Fighting South of the Castle,' and it can be found in Translations from the Chinese by Arthur Waley, A. A. Knopf.

Thapsacus. Cf. Cenophon, Anabasis, Book I, Chapter 4.

Ctesias the surgeon: Anabasis, Book I, Chapter 8.

'As once by the wall': Cf. Iliad, Book XX, in the Lang, Leaf and Myers version.

Caligula: Cf. Suetonius, Lives of the Twelve Caesars.

Caesar 'the bald-headed lecher': cf. Suetonius, as above.

'Rome sacked': etc., from the letter of St. Jerome, written to a friend at the time of the sack of Rome by Alaric. Cf. A Treasury of the World's Great Letters, edited by M. Lincoln Schuster, Simon & Schuster, page 33.

Bath: cf. 'The Ruined City,' in Translations of Old English Poetry, the version of Chauncey B. Tinker. It seems probable that the city described is Bath. I quote Prof. Tinker's passage almost verbatim.

Leonardo, and the Corsican corporal: cf. 'World's Great Letters,' as above, for the letters of Leonardo and Napoleon.

'the infantry always that does all the dying': I quote from 'The

Strategic Slant,' a daily column about the war by Henry W. Harris in the Boston Daily Globe.

'other arms of the service,' from 'The Strategic Slant,' as above.

Zabatus: cf. Xenophon, Anabasis, Book III, Chapter 3.

'Wet, pain, squalor' etc., the reference is to famous passage on a moral equivalent for war in Varieties of Religious Experience, by William James. Page 357 in the 'Modern Library' edition.

'This is our virtue' etc. The three lines following are taken almost exactly from Hallam Tennyson's prose version of the Song of Brunanburh. Cf. Translations from Old English Poetry, page 178.

'How strange, men of Athens': based on two passages in the speech of Socrates in 'The Apology of Plato.'

'a soldier marching against a battery': from one of the last letters of John Keats.

'One standing beside me': from a letter of Beethoven to his brothers when he first became aware of his approaching deafness. Cf. World's Great Letters.

The Kid

AUTHOR'S NOTE

WHEN THE FIRST SETTLERS of Boston arrived there in 1630, they were not unnaturally astonished to find that someone had been before them. In possession of what is now Boston Common, and the greater part of what was to become the 'old' section of the city, all of which he had bought from the local Indians, was a young man named William Blaxton, or Blackstone. He was a graduate of Cambridge University, or at any rate he had studied there: he had voyaged to America for his own good reasons, on one of the many smaller expeditions in the decade between 1620, the landing at Plymouth, and 1630, that at Boston: quite possibly he had come to Wessagussett, now Weymouth, a little to the south. But apparently preferring his own company to that of his fellow men, this 'solitary bookish recluse,' as the earlier historians describe him, moved to the north, and to Beacon Hill, on the site of Boston, in 1622 or 1623, and when the colonists found him had been the sole resident there for seven years. He had a house, he had books, and if legend can be believed he had a garden. Legend further suggests, too, that he was writing a book of his own. But if he was courteous and helpful to his new neighbors, allowing them the use of his spring and subsequently selling them much of his excellent land, it was evident that the coming of the 'lords brethren' was not much to his liking; and with the later arrival of the 'lords bishop,' and the first ominous shadows of the New England theocracy, he was again up and away. This time he went south, into the wilderness of Rhode Island. He reappeared in Boston a few years later, for just long enough to take a wife and to sell his house, and then went away to settle permanently near what was to become Providence, where he died in 1675 — though, according to another but unsupported legend, he moved yet again, westward, to the region of Hartford, in Connecticut. His book, if completed, or if indeed it really existed, is supposed to have been lost in a fire, and his 'library' also.

He is a tantalizing figure, in many respects the true prototypical American: ancestor alike of those pioneers who sought freedom and privacy in the 'wide open spaces,' or the physical conquest of an untamed continent, and those others, early and late, who were to struggle for it in the darker kingdoms of the soul. Daniel Boone and Johnny Appleseed were his grandchildren. But so too were Thoreau and Melville and Henry Adams. And the outlaws, the lone wolves, the lost souls, — yes, these as well.

C. A.

NOTES

1. *lacrym flood* — The phrase is taken from 'The Flesh and the Spirit,' a poem by New England's first poet, Anne Bradstreet. Her book, *The Tenth Muse,* was published in London in 1650, reprinted in Boston with additional poems in 1678. She was the wife of Simon Bradstreet, a governor of Massachusetts who was not wholly without blame in the persecution of the Quakers.

2. *Southwick* — For an account of the persecution and martyrdom of the entire Southwick family, who were a few only of the

many Quakers so savagely treated by our pious forefathers, I must refer the reader to *The Emancipation of Massachusetts,* by Brooks Adams. In the chapter entitled 'The Quakers,' he will find a dreadful and wholesome reminder of this hideous social crime, which for some reason has been almost totally ignored or forgotten in the teaching of American history.

The Southwicks were an aged couple, with a grown-up son and two small children, a girl and a boy. For being Quakers, for harboring Quakers, for wearing the Quaker hat, and for preferring to worship by themselves and in their own way, they were brutally and repeatedly whipped and imprisoned, and this in the bitterest of New England winter weather. At last, reduced to poverty by the confiscation of their property and utterly exhausted by this merciless treatment, they were banished to Shelter Island, where they perished within a few days of each other.' Josiah, the son, was condemned 'to be flogged through Boston, Roxbury, and Dedham.' As for the children, 'they were fined; and on the day on which they lost their parents forever, the sale as slaves of this helpless boy and girl was authorized to satisfy the debt.'

Adams quotes in full a quite heartbreakingly beautiful letter which the three elder Southwicks, together with two other Quakers, addressed to the magistrates from prison, and of course in vain. But the Southwicks were not alone: other Quakers suffered even more cruelly. As Adams observes: 'Thus were freeborn English subjects and citizens of Massachusetts dealt with by the priesthood that ruled the Puritan Commonwealth. . . It was the mortal struggle between conservatism and liberality, between repression and free thought. The elders felt it in the marrow of their bones, and so declared it in their laws, denouncing banishment under pain of death against those "adhering to or approoving of any knoune Quaker, or the tenetts and practices of Quakers." . . . Dennison spoke with unerring instinct when he said they could not live together, for the faith of the Quakers was subversive of a theocracy.' And at the end of his chapter Adams adds: 'We owe to their heroic devotion the most priceless of our treasures, our perfect liberty of thought and speech; and all who love our country's freedom may well reverence the memory of those martyred Quakers by whose death and agony the battle in New England has been won.'

3. *Hector St. John de Crèvecoeur* — The French agriculturist and writer who emigrated to America in 1754 and settled on a farm in New York. His *Letters From An American Farmer* is of course an early American classic, and it is from this that the references to 'hummingbird fury' and the snakes in combat are taken.

4. *John Chapman* — More familiarly known as Johnny Apple-seed, the half-legendary figure who is supposed to have carried west with him, and sowed in the forests, the first seeds for fruit orchards: also supposed to have lived with the Indians.

5. *Greylock* — The mountain near Pittsfield in western Massachusetts so often affectionately mentioned by Melville. *Moby Dick* was written in his farmhouse here.

Hallowe'en

For the poem 'Hallowe'en' in this volume, I am very greatly indebted to Dr. Richard Sterba, from whose beautiful article on the ritual origins and psychoanalytical implications of Hallowe'en, in *The American Imago* for November 1948, I have drawn not only part of my theme but images and phrases as well. And I should add that my *dramatis persona* is my grandfather, William James Potter, who was nearly all his life minister of the First Congregational Society at New Bedford, and whose religious liberalism was eventually to make him Secretary, and later President, of the Free Religious Association. The passages in quotation marks are drawn from his journal while he was a student abroad, after his graduation from Harvard College. A friend of Emerson, he was in these matters very much ahead of his time.

A Letter from Li Po

In 'A Letter from Li Po,' as anyone familiar with the poetry of Li Po will soon perceive, I have quoted or paraphrased a few passages from the work of that great Chinese poet of the eighth century, as I have drawn on some of the circumstances of his life. Of particular use to me in this have been the beautiful translations of Li Po by Shigeyoshi Obata, *The Works of Li Po,* with his illuminating preface, and *The Poetry and Career of Li Po,* by Arthur Waley. Of use to me also was Herbert A. Giles's *Chinese Literature.* I must also acknowledge indebtedness to a review of Jean Tardieu by Marcel Arland in *La Nouvelle Revue Française* (April, 1953) for other notes and notions. And further, not only in the Li Po poem but in one or two others I have found very suggestive Peter Goffin's brilliant book, *The Realm of Art.*

The Crystal

For the poem called 'The Crystal,' I must acknowledge my very great indebtedness to Charles Seltman, formerly Fellow of Queen's College, Cambridge, whose two articles on Pythagoras in *History Today,* August and September, 1956, provided the poem with just the frame for which it had been waiting. Both poem and title had been in my mind for several years, but it was only when I found these admirable essays on the life and thought of the great Greek philosopher and statesman that the elements of the poem began to fall into place. For this, and for many details as well, of which I would not otherwise have been aware, I offer my grateful thanks.

Index of First Lines

*

A love I love whose lips I love, 957
Absolute zero: the locust sings:, 875
Address him how you will, this golden fly, 510
After the movie, when the lights come up, 3
After the yes and no, the light denial, 539
Ah but all meaning, and all delight in meaning, 698
Ah poor fellow, he has been hurt, he remembers, 671
Alas, if among these volcanic ruins, moonchild, 736
All lovely things will have an ending, 20
All my shortcomings, in this year of grace, 811
All Saints', All Hallows', 892
All this is nothing: all that we said is nothing, 507
And at last, having sacked in imagination many cities, 222
And how begin, when there is no beginning?, 512
And how dismember or dishevel this, 768
And if the child goes out at evening, stands, 562
And if this heart go back again to earth, 523
And if we kiss, remember too how time, 764
And in the darkness touched a face, and knew, 529
And in the hanging gardens there is rain, 447
And in the river the nameless body sifts, 802
And in the wide world full of sounds and nothings, 752
And it is you: toward the light you move, 755
And look and remember well, as with an actor, 748
And search the senses — ah, but not too well!, 761

And so, with the ear pressed hard to the pillow, 990
And so you poise yourself, magnificent angel, 527
And that grin, the grin of the unfaithful, 735
And the child said to me in a dream, 713
And there I saw the seed upon the mountain, 665
And this digester, this digester of food, 692
And this, the life-line, means — why, you are brief, 544
And this, your hand, is but an easy measure, 759
And thus Narcissus, cunning with a hand-glass, 518
And time comes in that is a ball of crystal, 695
And you who love, you who attach yourselves, 684
As I walked through the lamplit gardens, 293
As if god were a gypsy in a tent, 676
As if you were a child again; you smooth, 741
As leaf from wood, the dream will glow from being, 774
As on a stage the backdrop makes the scene, 760
As salvage is too slow, and dives too deep, 758
As this: that I shall speak, being first to die, 766
Ask the wind in, the night too, and the stars, 708
Assurance can come from nothing, or almost nothing, 740
At noon, Tithonus, withered by his singing, 449
At the first stepping-stone, the past of water, 679
Be still, while the music rises about us; the deep enchantment, 480
Begotten by the meeting of rock with rock, 457
Behold me, in my chiffon, gauze, and tinsel, 17
Beloved, let us once more praise the rain, 505
Bend as the bow bends, and let fly the shaft, 758
Best come in, the morning's bitter, 882
Between the curbstone and the brownstone stair, 788
Bird's eye or snake's eye, bright through leaves; the leaf, 777
Blue, blue, and blue again, and blue once more, 763
Blue sky, blue moon, and the secret line is flung, 787